S0-EHD-574

A CLASS-BOOK OF

NEW TESTAMENT HISTORY

A CLASS-BOOK

OF

NEW TESTAMENT HISTORY

BY

THE REV. G. F. MACLEAR, D.D.

WM. B. EERDMANS PUBLISHING COMPANY
GRAND RAPIDS 1952 MICHIGAN

First printed 1866.
Reprinted 1867, 1869, 1871, 1873, 1875, 1877, 1879, 1880, 1882, 1885, 1888, 1890, 1894, 1897, 1902, 1906, 1908, 1909, 1910, 1915, 1920, 1922, 1925, 1932.

Reprinted 1952
by special arrangement with
The Macmillan Company

PHOTOLITHOPRINTED BY CUSHING - MALLOY, INC.
ANN ARBOR, MICHIGAN, UNITED STATES OF AMERICA
1952

NOTICE

THE present Volume forms a sequel to the Author's Class-Book of Old Testament History, continuing the Narrative from the point at which it there ends, and carrying it on to the close of St Paul's second imprisonment at Rome.

In its preparation, as in that of the former Volume, the most recent and trustworthy Authorities* have been consulted, notes subjoined, and references to larger Works added. It is thus hoped that it may prove at once a useful Class-Book and a convenient Companion to the study of the Greek Testament.

* The Edition of the *Synopsis Evangelica* of Tischendorf referred to is the First Edition, 1854; that of Wieseler's *Synopsis of the Four Gospels* is the English Translation by Venables, 1864; that of Conybeare and Howson's *Life and Travels of St Paul* is the People's Edition, 2 Vols. 1864; that of Dean Stanley's *Sinai and Palestine*, the 3rd, 1856.

All questions relating to the Canonicity of the several Books of the New Testament have been considered in another Volume of the *Cambridge School Class-Books*, viz. *The Bible in the Church*, by the Rev. B. F. Westcott.

SYNOPSIS OF CONTENTS

BOOK I

The connection between the Old and New Testaments.

PART I

The Jews under the Persians, and the Kings of Egypt.

PART II

The Jews under the Kings of Syria.

PART III

Rise of the Asmonean Dynasty.

PART IV

Decline of the Asmonean Dynasty; Interference of the Romans, and rise of the Herodian family.

PART V

Retrospect and Reflections.

BOOK II

The Gospel History.

PART I

The Birth and Childhood of Christ.

PART II

From the beginning of the Ministry of the Baptist to the First Passover.

PART III

From the first Passover to the Election of the Apostles.

PART IV

From the Election of the Apostles to the death of John the Baptist.

PART V

From the Death of John the Baptist to the visit of the Saviour to Jerusalem at the Feast of Tabernacles.

PART VI

From the Feast of Tabernacles to the Triumphal Entry into Jerusalem.

PART VII

From the Arrival at Bethany to the Ascension.

BOOK III

The Apostolic History.

PART I

The Church of Jerusalem.

PART II

The Church of Palestine.

PART III

The Church of the Gentiles.

SECTION I

First Missionary Tour of Paul and Barnabas.

SECTION II

St Paul's Second Missionary Journey.

SECTION III

St Paul's Third Missionary Journey and Imprisonment at Cæsarea.

SECTION IV

St Paul's Imprisonment at Rome.

MAPS

MAPS

BOOK I

THE CONNECTION BETWEEN THE OLD AND NEW TESTAMENTS.

PART I

THE JEWS UNDER THE PERSIANS, AND THE KINGS OF EGYPT.

CHAPTER I

HIGH-PRIESTHOOD OF JADDUA—ALEXANDER AT JERUSALEM.

B.C. 413—332.

"AFTER the death of Nehemiah, about B.C. 413, a thick curtain falls on the history of the Jews till the accession of Antiochus Epiphanes, B.C. 175[1]." During upwards of 230 years, a period as long, to compare it with modern history, as from the death of Queen Elizabeth to the accession of Queen Victoria, the record of events is of the scantiest description. It appears certain, however, that Nehemiah was the last of the governors sent from the court of Persia. Judæa itself was annexed to the satrapy of Cœlesyria, and the administration of affairs was entrusted to the high-priest subject to the control of the Syrian Governor. Thus the civil and spiritual functions were united in one person, and the pontifical office became an object of competition to the different members of the family of Aaron, and the cause of many violent and disgraceful contests.

As subjects, however, of the Persian kings, the Jews were pre-eminent for their loyalty and good faith. While Egypt, Phœnicia, Cyprus, and other dependencies of the

[1] Milman's *History of the Jews*, I. 443.

Persian crown, were frequently the scenes of rebellions, which were with difficulty suppressed, the Jews remained steadfast in their allegiance to the "Great King," and increased rapidly alike in wealth and population.

A single incident distinguishes the uneventful annals of this period. During the lifetime of Ezra and Nehemiah, the high-priest was Eliashib. His successor, Joiada, had two sons, the one Jonathan or Johanan (Neh. xii. 11, 22), the other Joshua. Joshua stood high in the favour of Bagoses, the general of the Persian army, and obtained from him the promise of the high-priesthood. Relying on this assurance, he ventured to quarrel openly with his brother in the Temple, and fell slain by his hand within the precincts of the sanctuary itself. So flagrant a crime roused the indignation of Bagoses. Advancing to Jerusalem he demanded admittance into the Temple, and when the Jews would have prevented his entrance, declared he was less unclean than the body of the murdered man, and not only polluted the sanctuary by entering it, but also levied a fine of 50 shekels on every lamb offered in sacrifice during the next seven years.

Like his father, Johanan also had two sons, Jaddua (Neh. xii. 11) and Manasseh. Jaddua succeeded to the high-priesthood, B.C. 341, and distinguished himself by zealously maintaining the Mosaic institutions as restored by Ezra and Nehemiah. Manasseh, on the other hand, married the daughter of Sanballat the Horonite[1], thus contracting one of those alliances, against which the Princes of the Captivity had so energetically protested. This roused the indignation of the elders in Jerusalem, and of Jaddua himself, who declared that Manasseh must put away his wife, or be no longer associated in the priesthood. This the other declined to do, and

[1] Jos. *Ant.* XI. 8. 2. Comp. Article *Jerusalem* in Smith's *Bibl. Dict.* I. 998, and note.

repaired to his father-in-law in Samaria, who suggested the building of a temple on Mount Gerizim, where Manasseh might continue to exercise his priestly functions. With the permission of the Persian court, this was accordingly done, and Manasseh became the first priest of the Samaritans at their rival sanctuary, being joined from time to time by those Jews who had been guilty of criminal offences in their own country, or had any cause for dissatisfaction[1].

Though by these immigrations the Samaritans were more and more recalled from idolatry, the building of this temple tended in no small degree to stimulate the animosity between the two nations. The Jews affirmed that sacrifice could only be offered at Jerusalem; the Samaritans replied that on Gerizim Joshua had built his first altar, and that it was the true place of sacrifice. The controversy thus generated gradually extended, and produced that intense degree of illwill between the two peoples, to which there are several allusions in the New Testament (Lk. ix. 51—56; Jn. iv. 9, viii. 48).

During the high-priesthood of Jaddua, the Persian empire, to which the Jews had so long been faithful, crumbled to pieces before the armies of Alexander the Great. Victorious over the Persian forces at the Granicus, B.C. 334, and again at Issus in the following year, the conqueror captured Damascus, and having taken Sidon, laid siege to Tyre, B.C. 332. Thence he sent a message to the high-priest at Jerusalem, demanding the transference of his allegiance, and auxiliaries and supplies for his army. This Jaddua declared was impossible, on the ground of his oath of fidelity to the Persian monarch. Though incensed at this reply, Alexander delayed to execute his vengeance, till after the reduction of Tyre, and then set out for the Holy City. Jad-

[1] Jos. *Ant.* XI. 8. 7.

dua and his people were in the utmost consternation. Sacrifices were offered, prayers were put up to God, and the Divine aid sought to appease the wrath of the invader. At length the high-priest is said to have been warned in a dream how to act. He hung the city with garlands, threw open the gates, and as soon as he was informed that Alexander drew near, clad in his pontifical robes, and followed by the priests in their ceremonial attire and the people in white garments, he went forth to meet him at Sapha, probably Mizpeh, *the watch-tower*, on the high ridge to the north of the city.

As soon as the Grecian conqueror beheld the venerable form of the high-priest, he fell prostrate, and adored the holy Name inscribed in golden letters on the frontal of his tiara. The Phœnicians and Chaldæans in his retinue, ancient enemies of the Jewish people, were only awaiting the signal to pillage the city and put the high-priest to the torture. They could not, therefore, conceal their astonishment, while the Syrian chiefs concluded that the great conqueror had lost his senses, and Parmenio addressing him enquired why he, whom all the world worshipped, should kneel before the high-priest. "It is not the high-priest," replied the other, "whom I worship, but his God, who has honoured him with the priesthood. In a vision at Dios in Macedonia, I saw him arrayed precisely as he now stands, and when I was debating how I might obtain the dominion of Asia, he exhorted me to make no delay, but boldly cross over the sea, for he would conduct my army, and give me victory over the Persians."

Then taking Jaddua by the right hand, he entered the city, and repairing to the Temple, offered sacrifice to God, and paid high honours to the whole priestly body. The prophecies of Daniel[1] were now read in his hear-

[1] Probably Dan. vii. 6; viii. 3—8, 20, 21, 22; xi. 3.

ing, and overjoyed at the prediction there recorded that a Greek would overthrow the Persian Empire, he offered the Jews whatever privilege they might select. Thereupon they requested that the free enjoyment of their lives and liberties might be secured to them, as also to their brethren in Media and Babylonia, and that they might be exempted from tribute during the Sabbatical years. These privileges the conqueror willingly conceded.

This famous visit is recorded only by Josephus, and has been discredited on the ground that it is not mentioned by Arrian or Plutarch, Diodorus or Curtius. But it has been observed that, though probably incorrect in some of the details, there are several points which confirm the truth of the main facts. Thus Curtius himself relates that, after the capture of Tyre, Alexander visited some of the cities which refused to submit to him, and that he personally executed vengeance on the Samaritans[1]. The Jews, moreover, certainly served in the army of Alexander, and were located by him in great numbers in his new city of Alexandria; while the privileges he is said to have conferred upon them undoubtedly existed in later times, and imply some such relation between them and the great conqueror. Moreover, from policy or conviction, Alexander delighted to represent himself as chosen by destiny for the great acts which he achieved, and his visit to Gordium before the battle of Issus, and his pilgrimage to the shrine of Jupiter Ammon alike illustrate the force of religious feelings in connection with his campaigns[2].

[1] Curtius, IV. 5. 13; IV. 8. 10.

[2] See Thirlwall's *Greece*, VI. 265; Raphall's *History of the Jews*, I. 42—50.

CHAPTER II

PTOLEMY SOTER AND PTOLEMY PHILADELPHUS.

B. C. 323—247.

ON the death of Alexander, B.C. 323, the vast empire, which he had won by his arms, was divided amongst his generals, and Palestine, as a province of Syria, passed into the possession of Laomedon, while Egypt was assigned to Ptolemy Soter. Between these two war soon broke out, and Ptolemy having conquered Cyrene, cast longing eyes on the kingdom of Syria, the harbours of Phœnicia, and the iron and timber, which abounded in Palestine and amongst the lofty ridges of Libanus and Anti-Libanus. Accordingly he invaded the realms of Laomedon, defeated him in a great battle, and gained possession of all Syria and Phœnicia.

The Jews on this occasion manifested such unwillingness to violate their engagements to the Syrian king, that Ptolemy advanced against Jerusalem, and besieged it with a large army. Entering the city B.C. 320, under pretence of offering sacrifice on the Sabbath-day, when the scruples of the inhabitants forbade their offering any defence, he easily succeeded in capturing it. Instead, however, of following up his victory by an indiscriminate massacre, he contented himself with transporting a great number of the inhabitants to Egypt, where he distributed them as garrisons in different places, but especially in Alexandria, and conceded to them equal privileges with the Macedonians themselves. Eight years afterwards he transported another large body of them to Libya and Cyrene, and thus by successive deportations and voluntary immigrations on the part of the people themselves, Egypt became an important centre of Jewish influence.

The king of Egypt, however, was not allowed to remain long in undisturbed possession of his prize, and found it disputed with him by Antigonus, one of the most turbulent of the successors of Alexander. Twice the coveted province fell into the hands of his rival, twice Ptolemy managed to recover it, and it was finally adjudged to his share after the decisive battle of Ipsus in Phrygia, B.C. 301.

Meanwhile Jaddua had been succeeded in the high-priesthood at Jerusalem by his son Onias I., and he again by Simon the Just, the last of the men of the "Great Synagogue[1]," as he was called by the Jews. He superintended the repair of the sanctuary of the Temple, surrounded with brass the cistern or "sea" of the principal court, fortified the city-walls, and maintained the sacred ritual with much pomp and ceremony (Eccles. l. 1—22). He is also said to have completed the Canon of the Old Testament, by adding to it the books of Ezra and Nehemiah, of Chronicles and Esther, as also the prophecies of Malachi[2]. He died B.C. 291.

The battle of Ipsus, besides securing to Ptolemy Soter the dominion of Palestine, Phœnicia, and Cœle-syria, elevated Seleucus to the command of an Empire greater than any other held by the successors of Alexander. He assumed the title of "king of Syria," and his

[1] "The *Great Assembly* or *Synagogue*, whose existence has been called in question on insufficient grounds, was the great council of the nation during the Persian period, in which the last substantive changes were made in the constitution of Judaism. It was organized by Ezra, and, as commonly happens, the work of the whole body was transferred to its representative member. Ezra probably formed a collection of the prophetic writings; and the Assembly gathered together afterwards (as the Christian Church at a later period in corresponding circumstances) such books as were still left without the Canon, though proved to bear the stamp of the Spirit of God." Westcott's *Bible in the Church*, Appendix A.

[2] Prideaux's *Connection*, I. 545.

dominion, in the words of the prophet Daniel (Dan. xi. 5), was *a great dominion*, extending from the Euxine to the confines of Arabia, and from the Hindokush to the Mediterranean. His Eastern capital he founded on the banks of the Tigris, and called *Seleucia*, after his own name. For his western metropolis he selected a spot admirably situated both for military and commercial purposes[1], on the left bank of the river Orontes, just where "the chain of Lebanon running northwards, and the chain of Taurus running eastwards, are brought to an abrupt meeting[2]." Here he founded a city with much display in the year B.C. 300, and called it *Antioch*, after the name of his father Antiochus. Convinced, like the Egyptian monarchs, of the loyalty of the Jews, he began to invite many of them to his new capital and other cities in Asia Minor, assuring them of the same privileges which they enjoyed under Ptolemy in Alexandria. This invitation was readily embraced by many of the Jews, who settled down in Antioch, were governed by their own ethnarch, and were admitted to the same advantages as the Greeks[3].

Ptolemy Philadelphus succeeded his father Ptolemy

[1] "By its harbour of Seleucia it was in communication with all the trade of the Mediterranean; and through the open country behind the Lebanon it was conveniently approached by the caravans from Mesopotamia and Arabia. It united the inland advantages of Aleppo with the maritime opportunities of Smyrna." Conybeare and Howson, *Life and Epistles of St Paul*, I. 118; Smith's *Dict. Geog.* Art. *Antiochia*.

[2] "Few princes have ever lived with so great a passion for the building of cities as Seleucus. He is said to have built in all 9 Seleucias, 16 Antiochs, and 6 Laodiceas. This love of commemorating the members of his family was conspicuous in his works by the Orontes. Besides Seleucia and Antioch, he built, in the immediate neighbourhood, a Laodicea in honour of his mother, and an Apamea in honour of his wife. Conybeare and Howson, I. 119; Merivale, III. 368.

[3] Jos. *Ant.* XII. 3. 1; *Contr. Apion.* II. 4.

Soter, B.C. 283. In pursuance of the policy of the previous reign, he distinguished himself by uniform kindness to the Jewish nation, ransoming many who had been sold as slaves, and inviting many to settle in Egypt. A liberal patron of literature and science, he established a famous library at Alexandria, and spared no pains in procuring books to be deposited therein. He is also represented to have caused the Hebrew Scriptures to be translated into Greek, and thus to have originated the celebrated Version called the *Septuagint*, from the tradition that 72 persons were engaged in the translation, which obtained a wide circulation, and was extensively read. The same monarch conferred costly presents on the Temple at Jerusalem, consisting of a table for the shewbread of marvellous workmanship, cisterns of gold, bowls, and other vessels for the public and private use of the priests[1].

CHAPTER III

PTOLEMY EUERGETES AND PTOLEMY PHILOPATOR.

B.C. 247–222.

ON the death of Philadelphus, Ptolemy Euergetes succeeded to the Egyptian throne. The new king considerably extended the privileges of the Jews, and bestowed many presents upon their Temple. During his reign an incident occurred, which illustrates in a striking manner at once the condition of Judæa at this time, and the influence of individual members of the chosen nation.

On the death of Simon "the Just," his brother Eleazar became high-priest B.C. 291. He was succeeded in

[1] Jos. *Ant.* XII. 2. 10.

B.C. 276, not by his own son Onias, but his uncle Manasseh, the son of Jaddua. At his death, B.C. 250, the son of Simon, Onias II., became high-priest, but inherited none of his father's virtues, being distinguished for nothing but meanness, and an inordinate love of money. The older he grew, the more avaricious he became, and neglected from year to year to remit to Ptolemy Euergetes the customary tribute of 20 talents of silver. At length, about B.C. 226, that king sent his commissioner Athenion to Jerusalem to demand the arrears, and threatened violence, if his claims were not satisfied. The Jews were filled with dismay at the too probable consequences of continued disobedience, but Onias still persisted in his refusal.

At length his nephew Joseph took upon him the task of appeasing the royal anger, and having ingratiated himself with Athenion persuaded him to return to Alexandria, and promised that he himself would speedily follow, and satisfy every demand. Shortly afterwards he himself set out, and on his way fell in with several men of distinction belonging to Phœnicia and Cœlesyria who were going up to the Egyptian capital to compete for the farming of the revenues, which were annually sold to the highest bidder. Not suspecting a competitor in the Jew, whose slender equipage contrasted unfavourably with their splendid cavalcade, they unwittingly revealed the amount at which the revenues had been farmed.

Thereupon Joseph resolved to outbid them, and in an audience with the king contrived by his cleverness and ready address completely to win the royal favour. When the day for the auction came, the nobles of Phœnicia and Cœlesyria bid 8000 talents for the farming of the revenues. But Joseph came forward and engaged to pay twice that sum, in addition to all the goods which should be confiscated for neglect of payment. Thereupon Ptolemy granted his request, and he became collector of the revenues from Judæa, Samaria, Cœlesyria, and Phœnicia, and was furnished with a guard of 2000 soldiers to extort payment from the refractory.

Having liquidated the arrears due from his uncle, Joseph returned to Palestine to carry out his instructions. Excited by the disappointed collectors, Askelon at first refused payment, and treated his demands with insult. But Joseph was not to be trifled with. He slew 20 of the chief inhabitants, and sent 1000 talents of their confiscated property to the king, who highly commended his determination. A similar instance of severity at Scythopolis[1] put down all further opposition, and Joseph was at length universally acknowledged as the collector for the Egyptian king, and held the office upwards of 22 years. He now became the founder of a family, which vied with that of the high-priest in power and influence, and became the occasion of many serious quarrels between them.

The reign of Ptolemy Euergetes came to a sudden and tragical close. In the year B.C. 222 he was assassinated by his own son Ptolemy IV., who in irony was called *Philopator*, *the lover of his father*. As soon as he ascended the throne, he murdered his mother Berenice, and his brother Magas, and gave himself up to luxury and dissipation. Taking advantage of his well-known effeminacy, Antiochus the Great welcomed the offer of Theodotus, governor of Cœlesyria, to surrender that province, and after a brief campaign became master of Phœnicia, Tyre, Ptolemais, Damascus, and the greater part of Cœlesyria. Roused at length from his lethargy, the Egyptian monarch confronted his rival at Raphia,

[1] The Beth-shan of the Old Testament; see *Class-Book of Old Testament History*, p. 316, and 445 note, 2nd ed.

between Rhinocorura and Gaza, and defeated him with enormous loss, B.C. 217, the same year that Hannibal was victorious at Thrasymene.

Meanwhile the Jews had remained steadfast in their allegiance to Ptolemy, and the conqueror visited Jerusalem, offered sacrifices according to the Jewish law, and presented rich gifts to the Temple. Attracted by the beauty of the building, and the solemnity of the service, he desired to penetrate into the Holy of Holies. Simon II., who had succeeded Onias, together with the priests, entreated him to desist from his purpose, but this only increased his determination to view the interior, and he pressed forward, amidst the dismay of the pontiff and the lamentation of the people, towards the sanctuary. Here, however, he was seized with a sudden and supernatural terror, and was carried forth half-dead. Enraged at this repulse, he retired to Alexandria, and wreaked his vengeance on the numerous Jews who had settled there. Some he is said to have put to death, others he degraded from their high positions and consigned to slavery, or reduced to the lowest class of citizens. Thirteen years afterwards, B.C. 204, he died a victim to his sensual habits, and was succeeded by his son Ptolemy Epiphanes, then only five years old.

Meanwhile, since his disastrous defeat at Raphia, Antiochus had been gradually strengthening his position in Upper Asia, where he had won his title of "the Great" by his successes against the Parthians and Bactrians, as also on the banks of the Indus. Having thus re-established the supremacy of the Seleucidæ he returned to Western Asia, to find his old rival dead, and the Egyptian throne in the possession of a child. He instantly embraced the opportunity of attacking the Egyptian dominions, and in concert with Philip III. of Macedon resolved to avenge the defeat at Raphia. In the campaigns that ensued the Jews suffered severely, and became in turn the prey of each of the contending parties[1]. In B.C. 203, Antiochus succeeded in taking Jerusalem. In B.C. 199 it was retaken by Scopas, the general of the Egyptian forces. Next year Antiochus reappeared in the field, and at the foot of Mount Panium[2], near the sources of the Jordan, gained a decisive victory over Scopas, capturing that general himself and the remnant of his forces, which had fled for refuge to Sidon.

Wearied of the struggle, and remembering the indignities offered to their sanctuary by Philopator, the Jews now threw off their subjection to Egypt, welcomed the conqueror as their deliverer, and furnished supplies for his army. Antiochus in his turn treated his new subjects with liberality and kindness. He not only guaranteed to them perfect freedom and protection in the exercise of their religion, but promised to restore their city to its ancient splendour, forbade the intrusion of strangers in their Temple, and contributed largely towards the regular celebration of its services. At the same time, imitating the examples of Alexander and Seleucus, he issued orders to Zeuxis, the general of his forces, to remove 2000 Jewish families from Babylon into Lydia and Phrygia, where they were to be permitted to use their own laws, to have lands assigned them, and to be exempted from all tribute for ten years[3].

[1] Jos. *Ant.* XII. 3. 3.

[2] One of the branches of the Lebanon, containing a cave sacred to Pan, whence it derived its name. See below, p. 218, n.

[3] Jos. *Ant.* XII. 3. 3.

PART II

THE JEWS UNDER THE KINGS OF SYRIA.

CHAPTER I

ANTIOCHUS THE GREAT—SELEUCUS PHILOPATOR.

B.C. 198—175.

THE battle of Mount Panium marks an era in the history of the Jews. For a century since the battle of Ipsus they had been steadfast in their allegiance to the Egyptian throne. They now transferred it from the descendants of the Ptolemies to those of Seleucus Nicator, and their connection with the Syrian kings begins.

Antiochus, who had bestowed upon them so many privileges, did not long enjoy the fruits of his victory. His chief ally in the late campaign had been Philip of Macedon, who, at the conclusion of the third war against Carthage, found himself attacked by the forces of the great Republic of the West now commencing its conquest of the world. Deserted by his friend Antiochus, whose aid he might reasonably have expected, he was forced after three campaigns to sue for peace, and the Romans became supreme in Macedonia and Greece, B.C. 197.

Five years afterwards Antiochus found *his* turn was come to feel the weight of the same all-conquering arms. In the year B.C. 192 he crossed over into Greece on the invitation of the Ætolians, and under the expectation of a general rising of the Greeks ventured on a campaign with Rome, entrenching himself at Thermopylæ[1]. But in the following year the consul M. Acilius Glabrio attacked him in his entrenchments, and speedily put his whole army to flight. Thereupon the Syrian king hastened back to Asia, and employed himself in collecting a vast host from all parts of his dominions, wherewith to prosecute the campaign, which his friend Hannibal truly warned him was close at hand. In B. C. 190 the Romans, under Scipio Africanus and his brother Scipio Asiaticus, crossed the Hellespont, and Antiochus confronted them in the neighbourhood of Magnesia[2], at the foot of Mount Sipylus. His motley hosts, though aided by numerous elephants and the Macedonian phalanx, were utterly unable to resist the terrible Roman legions. Defeated with a loss of 50,000 men, the haughty Syrian was constrained to sue for peace. The conditions exacted by the conquerors were the death-blow of the Syrian empire. Antiochus was forced to cede all his dominions in Asia Minor west of Mount Taurus; to surrender all his ships of war, and retain no more than 10 merchant vessels; to keep no elephants; to raise no mercenaries in any of the countries allied with Rome; to pay down 2500 Euboic talents at once, and 12,000 more by instalments of 1000 a year; and to deliver up Hannibal and other enemies of Rome who had taken refuge in his dominions.

Beaten, baffled, and disgraced, the Syrian monarch returned to his capital. The hard conditions of peace were approved by the senate B. C. 188, and to raise the heavy tribute, which threatened to exhaust all the resources of his empire, he resolved to plunder the temples throughout his dominions. The first attack it was agreed should be made on that of Elymais, situated at the

[1] See Mommsen's *History of Rome*, II. 264.

[2] In the valley of the Hermus, not far from Smyrna. See Livy, XXXVII. 37, foll.; Tac. *Ann.* II. 47.

meeting-point of the caravan routes which connected Media with Persia and Susiana. But the guards of the temple, aided by the hardy mountaineers of the district, made a vigorous defence of their shrine, and Antiochus was slain, B.C. 187[1] (Dan. xi. 19).

On the news of his death, his son Seleucus ascended the throne, and assumed the title of *Philopator*. During the early period of his reign, the new king carefully abstained from giving any offence to the Jewish nation, guaranteed to them the free exercise of their religion, and even contributed to the expenses of the Temple services (2 Macc. iii. 2, 3).

Before long, however, his attention was directed to the riches deposited in the sanctuary at Jerusalem. At this time that city presented an appearance of much external prosperity. The high-priest Onias III, who succeeded Simon B.C. 195, was held in high respect, and ruled the people with firmness and vigour (2 Macc. iii. 1). But an untoward cause of intestine dissension soon arose, and led to the interference of the Syrian king.

Joseph, the collector of the revenues of Phœnicia and Cœlesyria, had left behind him an illegitimate son, named Hyrcanus. Between this son and his legitimate brothers a serious quarrel arose respecting their father's property. Onias espoused the cause of Hyrcanus, and on his death secured his property in the treasury of the Temple, the custody of which was now held by one Simon, who is supposed by some to have been a son of Joseph (2 Macc. iii. 4). Filled with spite against the high-priest he gave information to Apollonius the governor of Phœnicia and Cœlesyria respecting the amount of treasure contained in the Temple, and represented that it might without difficulty be applied to the king's use (2 Macc. iii. 4—6).

[1] Strabo, XVI. 744; Justin, XXXII. 2. 1.

The governor reported this to Seleucus, and the Syrian king, straitened for means to pay the Roman tribute, directed his treasurer Heliodorus not only to penetrate into the Temple, but plunder it of its funds.

Heliodorus arrived at Jerusalem, communicated his instructions, and demanded the surrender of the money. In vain the high-priest expostulated on the insult which would be offered to the national sanctuary, and declared that one half the treasures belonged to God, and the other to widows and orphans, who had placed it there for security. Heliodorus declared that his orders must be carried out, demolished the outer gates, and was on the point of entering the sanctuary, when, like Ptolemy Philopator, he too was struck with a panic terror, which prostrated him speechless on the ground, so that he had to be carried away insensible by his retinue (2 Macc. iii. 26—30). Restored, however, by the prayers of Onias, he gradually recovered, and returning to Antioch related all that had occurred, and declared to his Syrian lord that nothing would induce him to venture again on such an errand.

On the death of Antiochus the Great, it had been agreed between the senate of Rome and Seleucus that he should send his son Demetrius to take the place, as a hostage, of his brother Antiochus, who was to be allowed to come back to Syria. Shortly after his return from Jerusalem, Demetrius departed for this purpose, and Heliodorus, in the absence of the two persons nearest in succession to the throne, poisoned his master and usurped the crown. News of this reached Antiochus as he was visiting Athens on his way to the Syrian capital. He instantly invoked the aid of Eumenes king of Pergamus, at this time master of the greater part of the territories in Asia Minor wrested by the Romans from his father, and having quickly crushed the usurper, ascended the Syrian throne, and assumed the title of Epiphanes, or *the Illustrious*, while his nephew Demetrius remained a hostage at Rome[1], B.C. 175.

CHAPTER II

REIGN OF ANTIOCHUS EPIPHANES.

B. C. 175—170.

THE long-continued subjection of the Jews to Grecian monarchs had by this time exerted a very considerable influence on their habits and mode of life. Familiar not only with the language but the literature and philosophy of Greece, many had acquired a strong taste for Grecian studies, preferred the Grecian religion to their own, adopted Grecian manners, and practised Grecian arts. Amongst this Hellenizing party none was more active than Joshua the brother of the high-priest, who even assumed the Grecian name of Jason.

On the accession of Epiphanes he made his appearance among the princes who flocked to Antioch to assure the new monarch of their allegiance, and by his insinuating manners rapidly rose into high favour. Knowing the depressed condition of the Syrian exchequer, in consequence of the annual tribute to Rome, he offered the king the tempting bribe of 440 talents of silver to secure the deposition of his elder brother, and his own appointment to the high-priesthood. Successful in this he caused Onias to be summoned to Antioch, and kept there as a prisoner at large, and then returning to Jerusalem devoted himself to the work of introducing Grecian customs among the people.

By a second bribe of 150 talents he obtained permission from his patron to establish at Jerusalem a gymnasium for athletic exercises, and with such success that even the priests *despised the Temple* and *neglected the sacrifices* to take part in the games (2 Macc. iv. 14).

[1] Livy, XLI. 19, 20.

He next procured a license to establish an academy in which the Jewish youth might be brought up in the Grecian fashion, and was empowered to confer the citizenship of Antioch on many of his fellow-countrymen, who eagerly coveted the empty honour (2 Macc. iv. 9). Not content with this, in the year B.C. 174 he went so far as to send a deputation with 300 drachmas of silver to Tyre, towards the celebration of the games in honour of the tutelary deity, Hercules. But even his own partizans shrunk from such open idolatry, and in place of bestowing the money on the games, preferred to offer it towards the building of a fleet (2 Macc. iv. 20).

For three years the high-priest continued his work of corrupting the manners of his people, and then found the means he had used to acquire his ill-gotten dignity turned against himself. Having occasion to send his brother Onias IV., who had assumed the name of Menelaus, to the Syrian court, his envoy embraced the opportunity of offering Antiochus 300 talents a year more than his brother had paid for the office of high-priest, and succeeded in supplanting him in the royal favour (2 Macc. iv. 24). Escorted by a body of Syrian troops, he then expelled Jason, who fled into the country of the Ammonites, and assuming the position and title of high-priest, proved even more wicked than his predecessor.

For some time, however, he delayed to make the stipulated payment to Antiochus, and when Sostratus, the commander of the Acra, had made several ineffectual demands for it, they were both summoned to the Syrian capital. At the time of their arrival Epiphanes was absent in Cilicia, and had left Andronicus in charge of affairs. Finding that in some way the money must be procured, Menelaus sent instructions to his brother Lysimachus to abstract some of the golden vessels of the Temple, and having secretly sold them at Tyre, obtained sufficient money to liquidate the debt and bribe over

Andronicus to espouse his cause. The sacrilegious sale, however, transpired, and came to the ears of the venerable Onias III., the legitimate high-priest, who severely reproved the usurper for his conduct. Enraged at this reproof, Menelaus prevailed on the king's deputy to seize the aged priest and put him to death (2 Macc. iv. 27—35). This atrocious deed roused the utmost indignation amongst the Jews at Antioch, and the Syrian king stripped Andronicus of the purple, and ordered him to be executed on the very spot, where the venerable priest, whose *sober and modest behaviour* (2 Macc. iv. 37) he always respected, had been murdered.

At this time the thoughts of Antiochus were fixed on the reduction of Egypt. In B.C. 171 he led his forces through Palestine and defeated the Egyptians before Pelusium. In the following year he led a second expedition, and taking advantage of the occupation of the Romans with the war against Perseus, the last king of Macedonia, evaded the condition of the late treaty[1], which restricted his fleet to 10 ships, and attacked Egypt by sea and land. Again he was successful, and reduced the whole country with the exception of Alexandria.

While he was before the walls of this city, a report reached Palestine that he was dead. On this Jason, taking advantage of the unpopularity of Menelaus, placed himself at the head of 1000 men, seized Jerusalem, and, while his brother secured himself in the castle of Zion, put great numbers of the Jews to death (2 Macc. v. 5, 6).

The first intelligence of these events received by Antiochus represented that all Judæa was in a state of rebellion, and that the Jews were rejoicing in his supposed death. Enraged at these tidings he instantly made

[1] See above, p. 17.

preparations for marching upon Jerusalem, whence Jason, hearing of his approach, fled into the country of the Ammonites. The city was taken by storm, and the late proceedings being considered as a revolt, it was resolved to inflict a proportionate punishment. Accordingly for three days Antiochus surrendered the capital to the fury and license of his soldiers, and during this period 40,000 of the inhabitants were slain, and an equal number sold into captivity. Under the guidance of the impious Menelaus, he then entered the Sanctuary, seized all the sacred vessels, and searching even the subterranean vaults, carried off treasure to the amount of 1800 talents of gold. He next ordered a great sow to be sacrificed on the brazen altar of burnt-offering, a portion of the flesh to be boiled, and the liquor poured over every part of the Temple; and having thus drained the capital of its treasure, drenched the streets with blood, and profaned its Sanctuary, handed it over once more to the administration of Menelaus, supported by Philip, a Phrygian, and *for manners more barbarous than he that set him there* (2 Macc. v. 15—23; 1 Macc. i. 20—28).

CHAPTER III

PERSECUTION OF THE JEWS UNDER EPIPHANES.

B. C. 169—167.

HIS exchequer recruited by this valuable plunder, Antiochus in the following year, B.C. 169, led a third expedition into Egypt, and once more laid siege to Alexandria. But his late proceedings at Jerusalem had raised against him fiercer enemies even than the Egyptians. The Jews, who formed a full half of the population, stung to the quick by the indignities offered to their fellow-countrymen and the desecration of the national Temple, assisted the Alexandrians with the fiercest zeal in repelling his attacks, and once more forced the king to raise the siege.

Undaunted, however, by this second repulse, he reappeared before the walls the next year, B.C. 168, and having a still larger force at his command, determined to reduce the city to subjection. But he was now confronted with a power it was impossible to resist. Having defeated Perseus at the decisive battle of Pydna, and reduced Macedonia to the condition of a Roman province, the Romans had at length found themselves able to listen to the repeated entreaties of the Ptolemies for assistance.

Accordingly Antiochus, on invading Egypt for the fourth time, found at Eleusis, about 4 miles from Alexandria, Caius Popilius Lænas, Caius Decimius, and Caius Hostilius, ambassadors from Rome, who commanded him to abstain from all hostilities against the Ptolemies, or prepare for war against the haughty republic of the West. During his long residence at Rome[1], Antiochus had made the acquaintance of Popilius, and seeing him at the head of the embassy, stretched forth his arms to embrace him. But the Roman sternly repelled the salute, and handed to him the written orders of his government. The Syrian monarch requested time to refer the matter to his council, but Popilius drew a circle on the sand with his staff round the king, and declared that he should not leave it, till he had given him an answer, which he could report to the senate. Confounded at this determined conduct, Antiochus was obliged to yield, and having, after a brief struggle, consented to bow to the senate's decree, was rewarded with the ambassador's hand[2].

Accordingly the command was given to desist from any attack upon Alexandria, and the Syrian mercenaries prepared to evacuate the land of the Ptolemies. But the rage and disappointment of Antiochus knew no

[1] See above, p. 19. [2] Livy, XLV. 12.

bounds. The imperious commands of the haughty Romans roused him to positive phrenzy. His private life had long since procured for him the title of *Epimanes*, "the madman," instead of *Epiphanes*, "the illustrious[1]." Uniting "the quick and versatile character of a Greek with the splendid voluptuousness of an Asiatic[2]," he thought nothing of debasing the royal dignity by mingling with the revels of his meanest subjects. He would scour the streets, visit the lowest places and the commonest baths, or, like Peter of Russia, converse with the artizans in their shops respecting their various trades. Sometimes he would mingle with some drunken revellers, and amuse them by singing or playing on his flute. At other times he would array himself in a white robe like the candidates for office at Rome, and in this guise go about the streets of Antioch, saluting the citizens, taking them by the hand, and supplicating their votes for some Roman office, of which in all probability they had never heard the name. Having in this way obtained a sufficient number of votes he would, with all the solemnity of a tribune or an ædile, take his seat in the market-place after the Roman fashion, and deliver judgment with all the gravity of a Roman magistrate. Immoderately fond of wine, he became under its influence a madman, and when thwarted in any design his fury knew no bounds. At the same time he was bigoted and intolerant to an extent almost incredible. His favourite deity was Zeus Olympius, and in his honour he was in the habit of celebrating games at Daphne, which exceeded in splendour anything that his predecessors had ever attempted, and erected a magnificent temple, at which he offered the most sumptuous and extravagant sacrifices.

[1] Polyb. XXVI. 10; Livy, XLI. 19, 20.
[2] Milman's *History of the Jews*, I. 457.

Such was the man, now goaded into even more than usual fury by the disappointments of his designs on Egypt, who was forced to bow before the power of Rome. As he returned to his own dominions, Jerusalem unfortunately lay in his way. Accordingly, he detached Apollonius, one of his generals, with a division of 22,000 men, and ordered him to wreak that vengeance on the city which he could not inflict on Egypt. As he was the chief collector of the tribute throughout Judæa, Apollonius found no difficulty in effecting his way into the capital, and no suspicions were entertained of his designs. He then waited till the first sabbath after his arrival, when he knew no resistance was to be dreaded, and suddenly let loose his soldiers on the unresisting multitude, instructing them to slay all the men they met, to make slaves of the women and children, plunder the houses, and throw down the city walls (2 Macc. v. 24—26).

His orders were executed with relentless severity; the streets of the city and the courts of the Temple ran with blood; the houses were pillaged; the dwellings near Mount Zion demolished; and with the materials thus obtained the fortifications of that citadel were strengthened, and occupied with a Syrian garrison (1 Macc. i. 33). This fortress overlooked the Temple, and the Jews could no longer steal into the city, and offer sacrifice in the accustomed place. The daily sacrifice therefore ceased in the month of Sivan, B. C. 167; Jerusalem became deserted; her inhabitants fled; *her sanctuary was laid waste like a wilderness; her feasts were turned into mourning; her sabbaths into reproach; her honour into contempt* (1 Macc. i. 39).

But the persecution did not end here. Like Nebuchadnezzar before him, Antiochus resolved on obtaining a uniformity of worship throughout his dominions. A decree therefore was issued from the Syrian capital enjoining his subjects to worship the gods of the king, and none other. Some of the Jews now fled from the land, or concealed themselves in caves or mountains. Others, long secretly attached to Grecian customs, consented to conform, *sacrificed unto idols, and profaned the Sabbath* (1 Macc. i. 43).

Before long a royal commissioner, named Athenæus, arrived with instructions to enforce a general compliance to the royal edict. He re-consecrated the Temple in honour of Zeus Olympius; erected on the brazen altar of burnt-offering another in honour of that god; offered swine's flesh upon it; and introduced the heathen ritual with all its lascivious accompaniments. Having thus set up *the abomination of desolation upon the altar* (1 Macc. i. 54; comp. Dan. xi. 31), he made the observance of any portion of the law of Moses a capital offence. Circumcision, the keeping of the Sabbath, the reading of the Law, were strictly forbidden. Every copy of the sacred books that could be found was seized and defaced, torn to pieces or burnt. Groves were at the same time consecrated, heathen altars set up in every city, and every month, on the birthday of the king, the people were ordered to offer sacrifice and eat swine's flesh. Moreover, in place of the Feast of Tabernacles, they were compelled to observe the licentious festival of the Bacchanalia, to join in the procession, and to appear crowned with the ivy wreaths sacred to the god of wine (2 Macc. vi. 3—7).

Proceedings equally tyrannical were enacted in other parts of the land. The Samaritans, on the occasion of the visit of Alexander the Great, had claimed relationship with the Jews. They now wrote to Antiochus, stating that they were Zidonians, and offering to dedicate their temple on Mount Gerizim to Zeus Xenios, *the Defender of Strangers.* With this proposal the Syrian monarch complied, and the temple was dedicated accordingly. Meanwhile all who refused to yield to the orders of the persecutor suffered the most fearful tortures. Two women, who had dared to circumcise their children, were led round the streets of Jerusalem with their babes hanging round their necks, and were cast down the battlements into the deep valley below the city-walls. Eleazar, an aged man, and one of the principal of the scribes, for refusing to eat swine's flesh was beaten to death, while a mother and her seven sons for the same offence were executed after enduring the most revolting and horrible tortures (1 Macc. i. 61; 2 Macc. vi. vii.).

PART III

RISE OF THE ASMONEAN DYNASTY.

CHAPTER I

MATTATHIAS AND JUDAS MACCABÆUS.

B. C. 167—165.

NEVER did the fortunes of the Chosen People look so dark and troubled as now; never did the nation itself, never did the religion of Jehovah appear so near to total extermination. But it was at this very time, when the gradual prevalence of Grecian manners, Grecian idolatry, and Grecian corruption threatened to eradicate all real attachment to the Law of Moses, that God interposed in behalf of His people, and through the genius, bravery, and heroic devotion of one noble-minded family, raised them from their prostrate misery to a height of power, which recalled the glory and the splendour even of the reign of David.

At Modin[1], a town situated on an eminence on the road between Jerusalem and Joppa, there lived a priest, named MATTATHIAS, of the line of Joiarib, the first of the 24 courses (1 Chron. xxiv. 7). The son of Jochanon, the son of Simon, the son of Asamonæus or Chasmon, from whom the family took its name, he could boast of noble blood. At this time he was advanced in years, but his sons were in the prime of life, and were five in number, Johanan, Simon, Judas, Eleazar, and Jonathan.

The sad declension of the nation and the ruthless persecution of Antiochus had already roused his keenest indignation, when a royal commissioner, Apelles, arrived at Modin, charged to carry out the edict against the Jewish religion, and to require the people to offer idolatrous sacrifice. Knowing his influence in the place, the commissioner used his utmost efforts to induce Mattathias to conform to heathen customs. But it was in vain. The aged priest not only declared his resolution to live and die in the faith of his fathers, but when an apostate Jew approached the altar which Apelles had erected to offer sacrifice, struck him down, and then, aided by his sons and the men of the town, rushed upon the commissioner himself, slew him and his retinue, and tore down the altar (1 Macc. ii. 15—29). The first blow thus struck, he called upon all such of his fellow-townsmen as were zealous for the Law of Moses to follow him, and, unfurling the banner of the national Faith, fled to the dark and rugged mountains of Judæa, where he was soon joined by many who feared God, and hated idolatry.

Tidings of these events quickly reached the ears of

[1] Identified with the half-ruined village of Latrôn, the *Castellum boni Latronis* of the Mediæval writers, from the tradition that it was the residence of the penitent thief Dysma. Porter's *Handbook*, I. 285.

the Phrygian governor at Jerusalem, and he dispatched a large force, which attacked the patriots on the Sabbath-day, when they were unlikely to offer any resistance, and slew upwards of 1000, with their wives, children, and cattle (1 Macc. ii. 31—38). This untoward incident awoke the little army of Mattathias to the conviction that they would be *rooted out of the earth* (1 Macc. ii. 40), if they persisted in their resolve not to act in self-defence on the Sabbath-day. With the sanction, therefore, of their brave leader, they determined to break through this overscrupulous observance, and though they would not attack, they henceforth considered it lawful to defend themselves on this day.

Before long, they were joined by the "Assideans," the zealots for the Law (1 Macc. ii. 42), and by numbers flying from the persecution still going on throughout the country, and prepared to conduct the war of independence with prudence and discretion. For a time, therefore, they laid hid in their mountain fastnesses, and, as opportunity offered, poured down upon the towns, destroyed the heathen altars, enforced circumcision, punished all apostates who fell into their hands, recovered many copies of the Law from the possession of their enemies, and re-established public worship.

But the hardships of the campaign did not suit the advanced age of Mattathias. Sinking under the weight of years, he called together his followers, exhorted them in noble words to constancy and devotion, and bequeathed the command of his little army to Judas, the third and most valiant of all his sons, associating with him Simon, his second son, as chief counsellor (1 Macc. ii. 49—69). Having given them this prudent advice, he died, and was buried in the sepulchre of his fathers at Modin, amidst the universal lamentations of the people, B.C. 166[1].

[1] Jos. *Ant.* XII. 6. 4.

Though Judas was young in years, he lacked neither energy nor prudence, and succeeding to the designs of his aged father, first unfolded the banner of the MACCABEES. This name is of uncertain meaning. Some derive it from the concluding letters of a sentence in Exod. xv. 11, Mi Camo Car Baalim Jehovah, i. e., *Who is like unto Thee among the gods, O Jehovah?* Others, again, derive it from the banner of the tribe of Dan, which is said to have contained the three last letters of the names of Abraham, Isaac, and Jacob. Others, with more probability, understand it to have been a personal appellation of Judas himself, meaning the *Hammerer*, like Martel, the surname of the famous Carlovingian chief, Charles.

Whatever was the precise meaning of the name, the new leader *girt his warlike harness about him* (1 Macc. iii. 3), rallied his forces, and bent all his energies to the task of uniting in a compact body all who were zealous for the national faith. "By night attacks, by sudden surprises (2 Macc. viii. 6, 7), he taught his people how to fight and conquer. Alert of foot and quick of brain; yesterday in the mountains, to-day in the plain; now marching on a post, now storming a castle; in a few months of service he changed his rabble of zealots into an army of solid troops, capable of meeting and repelling the royal hosts commanded by generals trained in the Macedonian school of arms[1]."

At length Apollonius, who had recently signalized himself by plundering Jerusalem and massacring its inhabitants, deemed it time to interfere. At the head of a large army, mostly composed of Samaritans and apostate Jews, he marched against the patriot chief, but was totally defeated and slain (1 Macc. iii. 10—12). Tidings of this disaster roused Seron, the deputy-governor of

[1] Hepworth Dixon's *Holy Land*, I. 64.

Cœlesyria, and he went forth at the head of a still larger force, determined to have his revenge. Judas did not decline the combat, which took place at Beth-horon, famous as the scene of Joshua's victory over the southern Canaanites [1], and resulted in the complete defeat of the Syrian general, whose troops were driven in confusion down the rocky pass to the western lowlands (1 Macc. iii. 24).

These two disasters moved the indignation of Antiochus beyond measure. He was himself, however, unable to take the field, for his exchequer being exhausted by his prodigal munificence (1 Macc. iii. 29), and his eastern provinces, Armenia and Persia, refusing to pay any further tribute, he deemed it expedient to lead an expedition thither in hopes of recruiting his treasury. Accordingly he entrusted the government of all that portion of his empire, which lay between the Euphrates and the borders of Egypt, to Lysias, one of his nobles and of the blood royal, and gave him the command of half his army, with instructions utterly *to destroy and root out the strength of Israel and the remnant of Jerusalem* (1 Macc. iii. 35).

CHAPTER II

BATTLE OF EMMAUS—RE-DEDICATION OF THE TEMPLE.

B. C. 165.

ON the departure of Antiochus, the regent, who entered zealously into all his plans, began to concert measures with Ptolemy Macron, the governor of Cœlesyria, and diligently collecting his forces, early the next year dispatched 40,000 troops into Judæa, under the

[1] *Class-Book of Old Testament History,* p. 212 and note.

command of Gorgias and Nicanor, two generals of tried ability.

While the Syrian troops, who were shortly joined by 7000 cavalry, encamped at Emmaus, about a mile to the north-east of Modin, Judas had assembled his little army of 6000 devoted followers at Mizpeh, *the Watch-tower*, over against Jerusalem (1 Macc. iii. 46), where Samuel, in one of the darkest periods of his nation's history, had erected the Stone of Eben-ezer, *the rock of help*, after the Lord had given victory to the people[1]. Here the Maccabæan chieftain kept a solemn fast, laid open the book of the Law, *wherein the heathen had sought to paint the likeness of their images* (1 Macc. iii. 48), and made a public confession of the national sins. In strict conformity with the command of Moses (Deut. xx. 5—8), he then bade all, who in the course of the year had built a house, or betrothed a wife, or had planted a vineyard, or were fearful, to return every man to his home. Half of his little army obeyed the invitation, and with barely 3000 men, *who had neither armour nor swords to their minds* (1 Macc. iv. 6), he was left to confront the vast hosts of the enemy.

So certain did the Syrians deem themselves of a victory in the approaching encounter, that Nicanor had proclaimed beforehand in all the cities and seaports round about (1 Macc. iii. 41) a sale of Jewish captives, at the rate of 90 for a talent. This proclamation attracted numbers of slave-merchants to his camp, who with their servants made every preparation to carry off their anticipated booty. Hearing through his scouts of the reduction of the forces of Judas, he now dispatched Gorgias with 5000 infantry and 1000 cavalry, to surprise him by night, and cut off his retreat into the mountains. But equally well served by *his* spies, the Jewish warrior

[1] See *Class-Book of Old Testament History*, p. 275.

was no sooner made aware of his intention, than he instantly conceived the daring design of attacking the camp of Nicanor, in the absence of his brother commander, and sallying forth early in the evening, fell upon it with the utmost fierceness at midnight.

Fully believing in the certain success of Gorgias, Nicanor had made no provision against such an attack, and was roused from sleep only to find his camp in inextricable confusion. The terrible bravery of the Maccabees filled the Syrians with a sudden panic, and they were as little able to resist the fury of their attack as the Midianites to oppose the onset of Gideon's three hundred men. Without striking a blow, they fled precipitately to Gazara[1], the plain of Idumæa[2], Azotus[3], and Jamnia[4],

[1] An important stronghold (comp. 1 Macc. ix. 52; xiii. 53; xvi. 1) in all probability the same as the ancient Gezer or Gazer (Josh. x. 33; xii. 12), between the lower Beth-horon and the sea. Thither we find David pursued the Philistines (2 Sam. v. 25; 1 Chr. xiv. 16), and the place was fortified by Solomon as commanding the communication between Egypt and Jerusalem. See *Class-Book of Old Test. Hist.* p. 361.

[2] During the Captivity the Idumæans advancing westward had occupied the whole territory of the ancient Amalekites (Jos. *Ant.* II. 1. 2), and even took possession of many towns in Southern Palestine, including Hebron (Jos. *Ant.* XII. 8. 6; *B. J.* IV. 9. 7). The name Edom, or rather its Greek form Idumæa, was now given to the country lying between the valley of Arabah and the shores of the Mediterranean; and Roman authors sometimes give the name Idumæa to all Palestine, and even call the Jews Idumæans. Virgil, *Georg.* III. 12; Juvenal, VIII. 160.

[3] The ancient Ashdod. See *Class-Book of Old Testament History*, pp. 259, 263, 272.

[4] The Greek form of the ancient Jabneel (Josh. xv. 11), the modern *Yebna*, 11 miles S. of Jaffa, 4 from Ekron. In the time of the Maccabees it was a strong place. After the fall of Jerusalem it became one of the most populous places in Judæa, was the seat of a famous school, and according to an early Jewish tradition, the burial-place of the great Gamaliel.

and left their camp at the mercy of their foes, with all the wealth which it contained.

Meanwhile Gorgias was wandering in the mountains, vainly searching for the little army of Judas, who having persuaded his men to restrain themselves from rifling the Syrian camp till their victory was complete, calmly awaited his return. The first sight that met the Syrians, when they came back, was the flame of their blazing tents; the first sound, the signal from the Maccabæan trumpets for the onset. Filled with alarm they too fled precipitately, nor attempted to lift a hand against the victorious Hebrews.

After these two routs, in which the Syrians lost upwards of 9000 men, their camp could be plundered with impunity of its gold and silver, provisions, and rich merchandise (1 Macc. iv. 23). The numerous slave-dealers who had followed the Syrians for the purpose of buying up the Jewish captives were themselves sold into bondage, and the spoil was divided partly amongst the conquerors, and partly amongst the numerous widows and orphans of the late persecutions. Nicanor himself escaped from the field in the disguise of a slave, and flying to Antioch, openly acknowledged the power of that God who had so mightily avenged the wrongs of His people, and raised them up from their former prostrate condition.

Thus closed the first campaign of the Maccabees. Furnished from the recent spoils with ample arms and ammunition, and joined by numerous fresh followers, Judas was now in a position to cope with the forces of Timotheus, governor of the country beyond the Jordan, as also of Bacchides, an experienced Syrian general, who next invaded Judæa with a large army. Defeating them in a pitched battle, he captured upwards of 20,000 stand of arms, and ample provisions. Next year he was called to confront Lysias himself, who with 60,000 infantry and 5000 cavalry marched through Idumæa, and encamped before Beth-sura[1], or Beth-zur, a strong fortress in the mountains of Judæa, north-west of Hebron. Though the Maccabæan chief had but 10,000 men, with whom to confront this formidable array, he did not scruple to meet them in the field, and again succeeded in obtaining decisive advantages (1 Macc. iv. 29, 34).

The Syrian regent now returned to Antioch, and Judas, successful on every side, turned his thoughts towards the capital of the recovered province of Judæa. On ascending Mount Moriah, and entering the courts of the Temple, a sad scene of desolation met his eyes. The altar of burnt-offering was surmounted with that dedicated to Zeus Xenios; the gates were in ashes; the priests' chambers were in ruins; *shrubs grew in the courts as in a forest, or on one of the mountains* (1 Macc. iv. 38); while the sanctuary itself was empty and exposed to all eyes. Having taken the precaution to fill the avenues with his choicest troops to be on the watch against the Syrian garrison in the Acra, Judas at once cleared the sacred precincts, took away the polluted altar, constructed a new one, replaced the holy vessels, reinstated the priests, rekindled the sacred flame, and three years after its desecration by Apollonius celebrated the re-dedication of the Temple, on the 25th of the winter month Chisleu, in the year B.C. 165, with a festival which lasted 8 days (1 Macc. iv. 45—59).

[1] Beth-sura, or Beth-zur, *house of rock*, is named between Halhul and Gedor in Josh. xv. 58, and was fortified by Rehoboam for the defence of his new kingdom (2 Chr. xi. 7). It occupied a strong position, and commanded a great road, the road from Beer-sheba and Hebron, which has always been the main approach to Jerusalem from the south.

London: Macmillan & Co. Ltd

CHAPTER III

EXPLOITS AND DEATH OF JUDAS MACCABÆUS.

B. C. 165—161.

THIS recovery of a powerful city by the skill and energy of one man, was regarded with no friendly feelings by the surrounding nations. But Judas, resolving to be beforehand with any opposition they might offer, carried his victorious arms into the territories of the Idumæans and Amorites. Then, having strengthened the outer wall of the Temple, and placed there a garrison to act against the Syrians in the Acra, and fortified the stronghold of Beth-zur, he divided his army into three parts. With 8000 men he himself crossed the Jordan into the land of Gilead; his brother Simon with 3000 was stationed in Galilee; while Joseph and Azariah were posted with the remainder in Judæa, with express orders not to venture on any attack before they were joined by the rest of the patriot forces.

As before, the energy of the brothers was irresistible. Simon fought many battles in Galilee, chased the Syrians to the gates of Ptolemais[1], and restored many Jewish captives to their own land (1 Macc. v. 21—23). Judas with his brother Jonathan captured numerous cities in Gilead, ransomed many captives, and returned in triumph to Jerusalem to find that the captains he had left there, disregarding his instructions, had made an unsuccessful attack upon the sea-ports of Jamnia, and had been driven back with severe loss.

Meanwhile Epiphanes, the terrible oppressor of the Jews, had died. Repulsed in an attempt to capture the

[1] The ancient Accho (Judg. i. 31). During the period that Ptolemy Soter was in possession of Cœlesyria, it received the name of *Ptolemais* from him, by which it was long distinguished.

rich Temple of Nanea, the Moon Goddess, at Elymais, which was hung with the gifts of Alexander the Great (1 Macc. vi. 1, 2; 2 Macc. i. 13—16), he fell back upon Ecbatana, and there received intelligence of the disasters which had befallen his arms in Palestine. Filled with rage and vexation, he urged his troops westward, but, struck with an incurable disorder which preyed upon his vitals, he died, B.C. 164, at the village of Tabæ near Mount Zagros, on the road to Babylon, having appointed his foster-brother Philip regent of Syria, and guardian of his son, Antiochus the Fifth.

On receiving intelligence of his death, Lysias, who was himself of the blood royal (1 Macc. iii. 32), assumed the government as guardian of Antiochus Eupator, another son of the deceased king, who was at this time but nine years old. His first act was to attempt the reconquest of Judæa, to which he was urged at once by the representations of many apostate Jews, and by the Syrian garrison at Jerusalem, which Judas was now besieging with banks and engines (1 Macc. vi. 18—27). Accordingly assembling all his forces to the number of 180,000 infantry, 20,000 cavalry, and 32 elephants, he marched, accompanied by the young king, through Idumæa, and once more laid siege to Beth-zur. The Jewish garrison posted there made a vigorous defence, and succeeded for some time in keeping off the assailants. Resolved to succour them, Judas marched forth from Jerusalem, and encamped at Bethzacharias, an almost impregnable position about nine miles north of Beth-zur. Thither Lysias also marched with all his elephants, each attended by a thousand of his troops, and bearing a strong tower of wood containing 32 men. Several obstinate contests took place, in one of which Eleazar covered himself with glory by rushing under an elephant, and stabbing it in the belly, to be himself crushed to death by its fall (1 Macc. vi. 32—46).

Perceiving the strength of the foe, Judas now fell back upon Jerusalem, and entrenched himself in the Temple-fortress. Thereupon the garrison at Beth-zur, pressed by famine, capitulated on honourable terms, and the Syrians advanced against the capital. But the stronghold of Zion resisted all their efforts, and assault after assault was delivered in vain. Soon however, for it was a Sabbatical year (1 Macc. vi. 53), the garrison began to be hard pressed by famine, and many effected their escape. At this juncture Lysias received information that Philip had been appointed regent by the late king, and had succeeded in taking Antioch. On this he hastily concluded a treaty with the Jews, guaranteeing to them the use of their own laws and religion, and retired to Syria, taking with him the apostate Menelaus, whom he persuaded Antiochus to smother in the Ash-tower at Berœa, as being the cause of all the late reverses. Judas was now recognised as governor of Palestine, and from this year, B.C. 163, his accession to the principality is usually dated.

On reaching Antioch, Lysias defeated Philip, but in the course of a year was himself put to death by another aspirant to the Syrian throne. It has been mentioned, that in the year B.C. 175, Demetrius was sent as a hostage to Rome, in exchange for his uncle Antiochus Epiphanes. Secretly leaving Italy, he now landed with a small force at Tyre, and having given out that the Romans had recognised his claim to the Syrian throne, easily succeeded in putting Antiochus and Lysias to death, and seizing the crown (1 Macc. vii. 1—14).

At the same time that he put Menelaus to death at Berœa, Lysias had conferred the high-priesthood on one Jakim, or Joachin, who, according to the prevailing fashion of adopting Grecian names, was also known by that of *Alcimus*. One of the stock of Aaron, but not of the pontifical family, the new high-priest was a zealous adherent of the Hellenizing party. In him, Demetrius saw a ready instrument for sowing discord among the Maccabæan patriots. Accordingly he confirmed him in the sacerdotal dignity, and sent him to Jerusalem, accompanied by Bacchides, governor of Mesopotamia, and one of his most able generals. With a large force they appeared before Jerusalem, and the zealots for the Law, unwilling to reject a descendant of Aaron, admitted Alcimus within the walls, and acknowledged him as high-priest. So long as the Syrian general remained in the neighbourhood, Alcimus was able to assert his authority, and take a cruel revenge on his enemies. But no sooner had Bacchides withdrawn his troops, than Judas, quickly recovering his old influence, compelled the innovating high-priest to fly to Antioch.

By dint, however, of large bribes, Alcimus again succeeded in persuading Demetrius to assist him in recovering his authority, and crushing the Maccabæan chief. Accordingly a large army was entrusted to Nicanor, with strict injunctions to cut off the partisans of Judas, and reinstate Alcimus in power. Nicanor, taught by past experience on the disastrous field of Emmaus to entertain a wholesomer dread of his enemy's prowess, at first endeavoured to get him into his power by treachery (1 Macc. vii. 27—31). Unsuccessful in this, and urged on by the express orders of Demetrius, he then ventured to attack him at Capharsalama, but was defeated with the loss of 5000 men. Shortly afterwards, with 40,000 men he again attacked him at Adasa, about 30 stadia from Beth-horon, where his whole army sustained a total rout, and he himself fell amongst the slain (1 Macc. vii. 40—47; 2 Macc. xv. 36).

This signal victory restored peace for a short time to Judæa, and was deemed of sufficient importance to justify an annual commemoration on the 13th of the month Adar. Fully aware of the necessity of providing against the ceaseless animosity of Demetrius, Judas resolved to improve this interval by concluding an alliance with the Romans. He had heard much of the fame of this great nation, of their conquests in Gaul, Spain, and Greece, of their victories over Philip and Perseus, and the great Antiochus (1 Macc. viii. 1—16). Accordingly he sent two ambassadors to the metropolis of the West, and the Roman senate, whose settled policy it was to weaken great states by forming alliances with smaller ones, readily passed a decree acknowledging the Jews as their friends and allies, and resolved to send a letter to Demetrius, commanding him, on pain of their heavy displeasure, to desist from any further attacks upon them (1 Macc. viii. 17—32).

Before, however, the ambassadors could return, the Syrian king keenly resenting the disaster which had befallen the army of Nicanor, had sent Alcimus and Bacchides with the entire force of his realm into Palestine. Never were the Maccabæan patriots so ill prepared to meet this fresh invasion. The mass of the people were tired of constant fighting, and the late negociations with Rome had alienated a considerable number of the Jewish zealots from the councils of Judas. In consequence the brave Maccabee was unable to bring more than a very small force into the field, and of these, a large portion deserted him on the eve of battle (1 Macc. ix. 6). With 800 men, however, he ventured to attack the Syrian host at Eleasa, not far from Ashdod, and actually succeeded in routing their right wing with enormous loss. But the odds were far too desperate, and the brave chief fell amongst a number of gallant followers, and was buried amidst universal lamentation in the ancestral tomb at Modin (1 Macc. ix. 19—21).

CHAPTER IV

JONATHAN MACCABÆUS.

B.C. 161—146.

THE death of their great leader was a terrible blow to the hopes of the Jewish patriots, and for a short time their plans were totally disorganized. The Syrians regained their ascendancy everywhere, Alcimus was reinstated in the high-priesthood, and Bacchides wreaked his vengeance on the adherents of Judas with unrelenting cruelty. All the advantages which that brave chieftain had gained during six years of incessant warfare, seemed to have been utterly thrown away, and the national cause to be on the verge of destruction.

At length, however, the Maccabæan party rallied, and offered the command to Jonathan, surnamed Apphus (*the wary*), the youngest son of Mattathias. In view of the present desperate circumstances of the nation, the new leader did not attempt to operate in the open country, but retired to the wilderness of Tekoa, where the Syrian general in vain endeavoured to surprise and capture him. Thence, crossing the Jordan, he carried on a guerilla warfare, while Bacchides resolving to keep the Jews in subjection, employed himself in strengthening the fortifications of Emmaus, Beth-horon, Gazara, and Beth-zur. At the same time he furnished the garrison in the Acra, which commanded the city and temple of Jerusalem, with fresh supplies of arms and provisions, and placed there the children of several of the chief Jewish families as hostages. Meanwhile Alcimus, bent on his plan of fusing Jew and Gentile, gave orders that the wall of the inner court of the sanctuary should be pulled down, and was in the act of seeing them carried out, when he was suddenly struck with paralysis, and died in great misery.

Upon this, Bacchides returned to Antioch, and Jonathan re-appearing from his hiding-place, established himself in Judæa, where, for upwards of two years, he was left unmolested by the Syrians, in accordance with orders from Demetrius, who by this time had received the commands of the Roman senate forbidding all hostilities towards their new allies. This condition, however, of tranquillity by no means fell in with the views of the large Hellenizing party in Judæa, and they invited Bacchides to return once more and crush their enemy. Accordingly the Syrian commander re-entered Judæa at the head of a considerable army, and Jonathan retiring as before into the wilderness, maintained a desultory warfare, while his brother Simon occupied the fortress of Beth-basi, in the Jordan valley, not far from Jericho. Though he attacked it with all his forces, Bacchides was utterly unable to reduce this stronghold, and at length, wearying of a campaign which brought little glory and less profit, he turned against those who had advised the expedition, and sought means to secure an honourable retreat. Informed of the altered feelings of his foe, Jonathan thereupon sent envoys, and succeeded in concluding a peace, agreeing to acknowledge Bacchides as governor under the Syrian king, and obtaining a promise from that general that he would not enter the land again.

On these terms, hostilities were suspended, and the authority of Jonathan as deputy governor of Judæa was publicly recognised. Establishing himself at Michmash (1 Macc. ix. 73), he ruled the people according to the law of Moses, though Jerusalem and many of the stronger towns were still retained by garrisons of Syrians or apostate Jews.

After the lapse, however, of a very few years, a revolution took place in Syria, which produced a surprising change in his fortunes. About the year B.C. 153, Demetrius retired to a new palace he had built at Antioch, and there gave himself up to pleasure, and various luxurious excesses[1]. This, added to other causes, made him extremely unpopular with his subjects, and gave rise to a conspiracy which was fostered by Ariarathes king of Cappadocia, Attalus king of Pergamus, and especially by Ptolemy Philometor king of Egypt, from whom Demetrius had taken the island of Cyprus. By their connivance, a young man named Balas[2] was persuaded to give himself out as the son of Antiochus Epiphanes, and to claim the Syrian throne. Through the intrigues of Heraclides, a former treasurer of Epiphanes, his claim was admitted by the Romans, and on his landing at Ptolemais after a visit to Rome, the place was betrayed by the garrison, and his standard was joined by numerous disaffected subjects of Demetrius, B.C. 152.

Roused at last from his lethargy, that monarch collected an army, and prepared to defend his crown. Both kings had an equal interest in securing the friendship of Jonathan, who could render essential service to whichever side he joined. The promises of Demetrius were lavish even to desperation. He offered to make Jonathan commander-in-chief over Judæa, to allow him to levy soldiers, and also undertook to release the Jewish hostages held by the Syrian garrison in the Acra. Jonathan read the letter containing these offers to the soldiers in the citadel, and they straightway delivered up the hostages, while the garrisons retired from most of the stronger towns, save those of Beth-zur and Jerusalem, which were chiefly composed of apostate Jews (1 Macc. x. 3—9, 12—14), who dreaded to leave their

[1] Jos. *Ant.* XIII. 2. 1.

[2] According to some, he was a natural son of Antiochus Epiphanes (Jos. *Ant.* XIII. 2. 1), but he was more generally looked upon as an impostor who falsely laid claim to the connection. Justin, XXXV. 1; Polyb. XXXIII. 16.

places of refuge. The power of the Maccabæan chief was thus greatly extended; he levied troops, and supplied them with arms; he rebuilt and repaired the walls of Jerusalem, particularly around Mount Zion, which were strongly fortified, and took up his own abode in the capital (1 Macc. x. 10, 11).

It was now the turn of Balas to court the alliance of the Jewish prince, and he resolved to outdo Demetrius in the liberality of his promises. Accordingly, he wrote a letter in which he saluted Jonathan as his "brother" (1 Macc. x. 18), conferred upon him the high-priesthood, which had now been vacant seven years, and sent him the purple robe, and the crown of an *ethnarch*, or independent prince of Judæa. Jonathan accepted all that the other conferred, and without openly espousing the cause of either king, assumed the pontifical robes at the Feast of Tabernacles (1 Macc. x. 21), and with them the purple. Thus the high-priesthood, which had remained in the family of Jozadak ever since the time of Cyrus, was transferred to that of Joiarib, and the reign of the Priest-kings of the Asmonean line commenced, B.C. 153.

As soon as Demetrius was informed of the offers of Balas, he wrote a second time to Jonathan, and made him the most extravagant promises if he would espouse his cause. But the Jews, remembering what they had suffered at his hands, could not be convinced of his sincerity, and threw all the weight of their influence into the cause of his rival. At first the efforts of Balas were unsuccessful, but eventually, B.C. 150, he succeeded in completely routing the army of Demetrius, mounted the Syrian throne, and at Ptolemais was united in marriage with Cleopatra, the daughter of Philometor, king of Egypt. On this occasion Jonathan also repaired to that city, where he was received by Balas with every mark of friendship and regard, raised to the rank of *meridarch*, or ruler of a part of the empire (1 Macc. x. 65), and invested with regal honours.

But the prosperity of the usurper of the Syrian throne was shortlived. So long as the contest with the late king continued, he evinced both energy and courage, but no sooner was his power confirmed, than he gave himself up without restraint to the indulgence of the worst passions, and became only an object of contempt to his subjects. At this time Demetrius, surnamed afterwards *Nicator*, was at Cnidus. Hearing of the feelings with which Balas was regarded, he landed in Cilicia at the head of a considerable force, and rapidly gained over a number of adherents, and amongst them Apollonius, governor of Cœlesyria, who openly revolted and espoused his cause. Jonathan, however, still remained faithful in his allegiance, and attacking Apollonius near Azotus, completely defeated him, laid that city in ashes, and returned to Jerusalem with rich spoils. This complete suppression of the revolt in Cœlesyria excited the warmest gratitude in the heart of Balas, who sent his faithful ally a rich gold chain, such as was worn by none but princes of the highest rank (1 Macc. x. 88, 89), and bestowed upon him the city and territory of Ekron as a free gift.

But though checked in Cœlesyria, the rebellion made such progress in other parts of his dominions, that he shut himself up in the city of Antioch, and appealed for aid to Philometor, the father of his wife Cleopatra.

Accordingly, B.C. 146, that monarch set out attended by a fleet and a numerous army to assist his son-in-law. As he proceeded along the coast of Palestine, every city threw open its gates in token of friendship, and at Joppa he was met by Jonathan, who escorted him as far as the river Eleutherus (1 Macc. xi. 1—7). No sooner, however, had he reached Antioch, than he threw off the mask, and wrote to Demetrius offering to support his claims, and to unite him in marriage with his daughter. Demetrius eagerly accepted his offer, and, though not without some difficulty, was acknowledged as king. Early in the following year Balas made a determined effort to recover his crown, but being defeated in battle, fled to Abæ in Arabia, where five days after he was murdered by a native chief named Zabdiel, who sent his head to Demetrius (1 Macc. xi. 17).

CHAPTER V

EXPLOITS AND DEATH OF JONATHAN.

B.C. 146—144.

THE accession of the new Syrian monarch once more raised the hopes of the faction opposed to Jonathan, who had gathered his forces and laid siege to the Syrian garrison in the Acra (1 Macc. xi. 20). This was eagerly reported to Demetrius, and he instantly sent for the priest-king to meet him at Ptolemais. Great as was the risk, without suspending the siege, Jonathan forthwith set out thither with some of the elders of the Sanhedrim, and pleaded his cause with such effect that he not only succeeded in silencing the clamour of his enemies, but was confirmed in all the dignities he had received from Balas, and even secured for himself still further advantages. Three principalities, hitherto included in the district of Samaria, were added to his dominions, and all previous claims for tribute due from his kingdom were remitted (1 Macc. xi. 23—37).

Successful beyond his utmost expectations, Jonathan returned to Jerusalem, and again pushed forward the siege of the Syrian garrison. But such was the energy of the defenders, and such the strength of the fortress, that all his efforts were frustrated, and he resolved on making an application to Demetrius for an order directing the evacuation of the stronghold, as also of Beth-zur.

At the time when this request reached him, Demetrius himself was in the greatest straits. Young and inexperienced he had entrusted the entire management of his affairs to a Cretan officer, named Lasthenes, who had assisted him in obtaining his crown with a large body of mercenaries (1 Macc. x. 67[1]), and by his advice had disbanded the whole of the national troops. This, added to the ferocious conduct of his general, naturally roused the illwill of the citizens of Antioch, and they broke out into a furious revolt, which all the efforts of the king were unable to quell. At this juncture he received the message of Jonathan, and anxious for assistance from whatever quarter, professed his readiness to grant all his demands, on condition of receiving help in putting down the rebellion of his own subjects. To this Jonathan readily assented. A force of 3000 Jews marched to Antioch, and, aided by the royal mercenaries, slew upwards of 100,000 of the rioters, and quenched the rebellion in blood. But the priest-king soon found reason to regret the step he had taken. Once more secure upon his throne, Demetrius not only refused to order the evacuation of the fortress, but demanded the speedy payment of all the tribute, which he had agreed to remit at Ptolemais[2].

But in a very short time he learned to repent of his perfidy. Attached to the court of the late usurper Balas was a Syrian Greek, named Diodotus, or, as he was afterwards called, Tryphon, *the Luxurious*. Perceiving the growing unpopularity of Demetrius, he repaired to the Arab chief Zabdiel, to whom Balas had entrusted the care of his young son Antiochus, and by dint of much importunity prevailed upon him to surrender the young prince into his charge. Then returning to Antioch he shewed him to the disaffected soldiers, whom Lasthenes

[1] Comp. Jos. *Ant.* XIII. 4. 3.

[2] Comp. 1 Macc. xi. 33; Jos. *Ant.* XIII. 5. 3.

had disbanded, and easily persuaded them to revolt against Demetrius. A battle was fought in which that king was defeated, and the young prince was crowned at Antioch, and assumed the title of Theos, *the God.*

One of the first steps of the new monarch was to secure the co-operation of Jonathan and his people. Accordingly he not only confirmed all former grants made to the Jewish nation, and remitted all arrears of tribute, but sent him a purple robe and gold chain, and invested his brother Simon with the command of all the royal forces between the "ladder of Tyre" and the frontiers of Egypt. Jonathan, who had every reason to resent the ingratitude of Demetrius, readily accepted his proposals, and at tho head of a large army speedily subdued the entire country, as far as Damascus, to the power of Antiochus, while Simon captured the fortress of Beth-zur, and garrisoned it with Jewish soldiers (1 Macc. xi. 65, 66)[1].

Resolved to make the most of the present advantageous turn of events, the Jewish prince now sent ambassadors to Rome, renewed the previous treaty, and at the same time concluded another with the Lacedæmonians (1 Macc. xii. 1, 2)[2]. Meanwhile Demetrius had assembled an army, with which he encamped at Hamath on the extreme north of Palestine. Thither Jonathan quickly went forth to meet him, and gaining information that a night attack on his camp was meditated, made such a disposition of his troops that the enemy gave up their design, and retired beyond the river Eleutherus. Returning thence he fell upon the Nabathæan Arabs, who had espoused the cause of Demetrius, and defeated them, while Simon attacked and succeeded in taking Joppa (1 Macc. xii. 25—35).

Never did the fortunes of the Jewish patriots appear

[1] Jos. *Ant.* XIII. 5. 6. [2] Jos. *Ant.* XIII. 5. 8.

brighter than at this period. Masters of the entire province of Judæa, strong in the confidence of the Syrian monarch, invested with the command of numerous trained warriors, the Maccabæan brothers seemed on the verge of restoring their country to a condition of complete independence. Accordingly they convened an assembly of the elders, and consulted on the present state of affairs. The reduction of the garrison in the Acra was the great object of the national hopes. It was clear that this could never be accomplished so long as the garrison was able to communicate, as had hitherto been the case, with the city and the country, and there buy provisions. While therefore Simon was sent to fortify several of the more important towns, Jonathan himself remained in the city, and superintended in person the erection of new defences. Accordingly the wall of the Temple was repaired, especially on the eastern side, towards the valley of the Kidron, while a new wall was built between Mount Zion and the rest of the city, of such a height and strength as to cut off the hostile garrison from all communication with the city on the west, and the country on the east[1] (1 Macc. xii. 36, 37).

It soon appeared that these precautions had not been unreasonable. Tryphon, though he had placed Antiochus on the throne, now resolved to usurp the royal authority for himself. The only serious obstacle to his design was the faithfulness of Jonathan to the Syrian king. At all risks, therefore, he determined to get the Jewish prince into his power, and for this purpose advanced into Palestine as far as Beth-shan or Scythopolis, with a considerable force. Here Jonathan met him with an army of 40,000 men. Afraid to confront so numerous a force, Tryphon resorted to treachery, and pretended that the sole object of his coming was to mark

[1] Jos. *Ant.* XIII. 5. 11; Smith's *Bibl. Dict.*, Art. *Jerusalem*.

his gratitude for Jonathan's services in the cause of Antiochus, by placing him in possession of Ptolemais[1]. Completely deceived, the Jewish prince disbanded all his forces, excepting 3000 men, and having left 2000 of these in Galilee, set out with the scanty remainder for Ptolemais. No sooner however had he entered the city, than the traitor Tryphon ordered the gates to be shut, butchered Jonathan's retinue to a man, and flung him loaded with chains into a dungeon (1 Macc. xii. 37—52).

CHAPTER VI

SIMON MACCABÆUS.

B. C. 144—135.

NEWS of these occurrences filled the Jews with the deepest sorrow and the utmost consternation. For 17 years their late leader had conducted the affairs of the country with prudence, vigour and success. Now all their fair hopes seemed destined to be crushed, if the perfidious Tryphon should succeed in following up the success he had already gained. In this emergency the eyes of all were turned towards Simon surnamed *Thassi*, the elder and only surviving brother of Jonathan, whom the aged Mattathias on his death-bed had commended for his prudence in council. He therefore assumed the command of the patriot forces, and was acknowledged as their leader.

His first step was to finish the walls and fortifications of Jerusalem and to place the country in a complete posture of defence (1 Macc. xiii. 10, 11). He then went forth to meet Tryphon, who taking Jonathan with him, had moved up from Ptolemais with a large force, and encamped at Adida or Adithaim (Joshua xv. 36), a town on an eminence overlooking the low country

[1] Jos. *Ant.* XIII. 6. 1.

of Judæa. No sooner however did he find a Jewish army ready to oppose him, than he once more had recourse to treachery, and representing that Jonathan was merely held in custody on account of a debt of 100 talents, offered to deliver him up on condition of receiving the money and two of his children as hostages. Though he was certain this was nothing more than an artifice, Simon determined that it never should be said he had left any means untried for the release of his brother (1 Macc. xiii. 17—19), and accordingly sent the money and the hostages. But, as he had expected, Tryphon failed to fulfil his word, and began to ravage the neighbouring country.

Meanwhile the Syrian garrison in Jerusalem, suffering severely from the long-continued blockade, sent messengers begging Tryphon to come to their aid. Thereupon the other ordered his cavalry to press forward instantly to their relief, but a heavy fall of snow rendered the roads impassable, and Tryphon finding it impossible to render the required assistance, retired across the Jordan into the land of Gilead. Here he put the heroic Jonathan to death at the city of Bascama, and hurrying into Syria, murdered the young king Antiochus, and seized the supreme power, which he exercised with cruelty and violence (1 Macc. xiii. 23). As soon as he retired Simon sent to Bascama, and brought thence the body of his brother to Modin, where he laid it with great pomp in the ancestral tomb, and erected over it a magnificent monument, consisting of seven pillars, and adorned with the beaks of ships, a conspicuous sea-mark for all the vessels which sailed along the coast (1 Macc. xiii. 27—30).

The continued tyranny of Tryphon once more raised the hopes of Demetrius, and the Jews resolved to espouse his cause in preference to that of his treacherous enemy. Accordingly Simon sent an embassy offering to acknowledge his supremacy, and to aid him against the usurper. Demetrius received the proposition with alacrity, and in a royal edict formally drawn up and ratified, agreed to recognize Simon as the high-priest and prince of Judæa, to renounce all claims on the Jewish nation for tribute, customs, and taxes, and to grant an amnesty for all past offences against himself. This amounted to a virtual recognition of the complete independence of the country, and the year B.C. 143, in which it was granted, was regarded as the first year of the "freedom of Jerusalem" (1 Macc. xiii. 42).

Secure from all immediate danger of foreign interference, Simon now devoted his energies to provide for the internal security of his kingdom. He began by reducing the fortresses that still held out, and garrisoned Gaza, Jamnia, and Joppa. He then turned his attention to the Syrian garrison in the Acra, and reduced it to such straits that the troops composing it were in imminent danger of perishing by famine, and finally agreed to evacuate the fortress on condition that their lives were spared. These terms were accepted, and, to his inexpressible satisfaction, Simon entered the place on the 23rd day of the second month of the year B.C. 142, *with thanksgivings, and branches of palm-trees, and with harps and cymbals, and with viols and hymns and songs* (1 Macc. xiii. 51). The fortress was then entirely demolished, and the eminence on which it had stood was lowered, until it was reduced below the height of the Temple-hill beside it. This operation cost incredible labour, and occupied upwards of 3 years[1]. The fortifications of the hill, on which the Temple stood, were next strengthened, and a fortress, called Baris[2], was

[1] Jos. *Ant.* XIII. 6. 7; Smith's *Bibl. Dict.*, Art. *Jerusalem.*

[2] "Nehemiah mentions a palace, or rather fortress, which appertained to the Temple (Neh. ii. 8); and in the Hebrew Birah we have probably the origin of the Greek Baris, which

erected to command the site of the Acra, and here Simon and his immediate adherents took up their abode.

The dominion of the priest-king was now confirmed on every side, and the land enjoyed profound quiet. His subjects *tilled their ground in peace, and the earth gave her increase, and the trees of the field their fruit. The ancient men sat all in the streets, communing together of good things, and the young men put on glorious and warlike apparel...every man sat under his vine and his fig-tree, and there was none to fray them* (1 Macc. xiv. 4—13). Taking advantage of these circumstances Simon sent an ambassador to Rome bearing a golden shield weighing upwards of 1000 pounds. His present was accepted, and Lucius the consul (1 Macc. xv. 16) sent letters recognizing his authority, and claiming protection for the Jews from the kings of Syria, Pergamus, Cappadocia, and Pontus, from the inhabitants of Sparta, Delos, Sicyon, Gortyna in Crete, Samos, Cos, Rhodes, Myndus, Halicarnassus, Cnidus, Aradus, Cyprus, and Cyrene (1 Macc. xv. 22, 23); "a singular illustration," it has been remarked, "of the widespread dispersion of the Jews, and of the all-commanding policy of Rome[1]." In the same year, B.C. 141, an assembly of the elders met at Jerusalem, and out of gratitude for the services rendered to the nation by the house of Mattathias, it was resolved that the high-priesthood and the dignity of regent should be henceforth hereditary in the family of Simon. This resolution was then engraven upon tables of brass, and set up in a conspicuous place in the Temple, and copies of it were deposited in the treasury (1 Macc. xiv. 41—49).

Josephus tells us was the name of the fortress subsequently called *Antonia*. It was the fortress of the Temple, as the Temple was of the city." Porter's *Handbk.* I. 128, 129.

[1] Milman's *History of the Jews,* II. 21.

During this period, taking advantage of the disturbed condition of Syria, Arsaces VI., king of Parthia, who was also called Mithridates, had extended his authority from the Euphrates to the confines of India. Wishing to collect forces, or in some way to strengthen his position against the usurper Tryphon (1 Macc. xiv. 1), Demetrius penetrated into the Parthian territory, and after several engagements was taken prisoner B.C. 139. The conqueror, however, treated his captive honourably, gave him his daughter Rodoguna in marriage, and permitted him to reside in Hyrcania, with every indulgence due to his rank (1 Macc. xiv. 3).

News of this marriage, and of the improbability of her husband ever returning no sooner reached his wife Cleopatra, whom he had left regent, than she sent to his younger brother, who was then residing at Rhodes, and offered him her hand and kingdom. Antiochus entered into the project with all the eagerness of youthful ambition, levied an army, and assuming the title of king of Syria, wrote to Simon begging his aid in recovering his father's dominions from the usurper Tryphon, and in turn confirming all his former privileges, and further conceding that of the right to coin money of his own. Then sailing to Syria, he married Cleopatra, and joining her forces to his own, commenced hostilities against Tryphon, who fled to Dora, on the coast of Samaria, where he straitly besieged him (1 Macc. xv. 11—14)[1]. Thence, however, he managed to effect his escape to Apamea in Syria, and there was put to death, or, according to some authorities, committed suicide.

Antiochus Sidetes[2] had no sooner become undis-

[1] Comp. Jos. *Ant.* XIII. 7. 2.

[2] By this king the privilege of a national coinage was granted to Simon, 1 Macc. xv. 6. "Numerous examples of them are extant, bearing the dates of the first, second, third and fourth years of the 'liberation of Jerusalem;' and it is a

turbed master of the Syrian kingdom, than, forgetting the promises already made to Simon, he sent Athenobius to Jerusalem to demand the surrender of Gazara and Joppa, of the fortress on Mount Zion, and other strongholds, or in lieu of these 500 talents of silver, and an additional 500 as a compensation for the injuries done to the Syrian dominions. Simon replied that he was willing to give 500 talents for Gazara and Joppa, but the other places were the inheritance of his fathers, and could not be given up or bartered. This answer greatly irritated Antiochus, and as soon as he had reduced Dora, he sent Cendebeus, the governor of Phœnicia, to invade Judæa with a portion of his forces, and enforce the payment of his demands.

Accordingly the Syrian general entered upon the expedition with a powerful army of horse and foot, and capturing Cedron near Azotus and Jamnia, fortified it in order to command the road of Judæa (1 Macc. xv. 39; xvi. 9), and ravaged the neighbouring country. Simon was at this time far too advanced in age to bear the fatigues of a campaign, and therefore entrusted the command of the Jewish forces to his two sons John Hyrcanus and Judas. The brothers forthwith set out, and bivouacking for the night at Modin, descended on the following day into the lower ground, and after a sharp engagement succeeded in defeating the Syrian general, and carried a portion of his forces into Cedron,

remarkable fact confirming their genuineness, that in the first year the name Zion does not occur, as the citadel was not recovered till the second year of Simon's supremacy, while after the second year Zion alone is found. The emblem which the coins bear have generally a connexion with Jewish history—a vine-leaf, a cluster of grapes, a vase (of manna?), a trifid flowering rod, a palm-branch, surrounded by a wreath of laurel, a lyre, a bunch of branches symbolical of the feast of Tabernacles." Smith's *Bibl. Dict.*, Art. *Maccabees*.

and the remainder into Azotus, the tower of which they laid in ashes (1 Macc. xvi. 1—10).

This invasion repulsed, the Jews enjoyed during three years a season of peace, and the priest-king, though far advanced in age, devoted himself assiduously to the superintendence of the internal affairs of his people, while his three sons guarded the frontier. In the prosecution of his design of inspecting in person the national defences, he now visited Jericho where his son-in-law Ptolemy held the supreme command. A prominent leader of the Hellenizing faction, and a man of great wealth, Ptolemy bore no good-will towards the priest-king, and, in concert, it is probable, with Antiochus Sidetes, had resolved to assassinate his father-in-law, and raise himself to supreme power. The visit of Simon, with his two younger sons Judas and Mattathias, presented a favourable opportunity for carrying out his designs, and he treacherously murdered the three at a banquet, B.C. 137. Then sending messengers to John Hyrcanus at Gazara he instructed them to stab him also, and would have succeeded, had not the latter received speedy tidings of what had occurred at Jericho. He therefore put the intended assassins to death, and hurrying to Jerusalem, was acknowledged as his father's successor, and afterwards besieged Ptolemy in his stronghold of Dôk, whence he effected his escape to the court of the prince of Philadelphia, to be heard of afterwards no more (1 Macc. xvi. 15—21)[1].

CHAPTER VII

JOHN HYRCANUS, AND ALEXANDER JANNÆUS.

B C. 135—79.

THOUGH the confederacy between Ptolemy and Antiochus was thus disconcerted by the rapid move-

[1] Jos. *Ant.* XIII. 8. 1.

ments of Hyrcanus, the Syrian monarch nevertheless led his forces into Palestine, overran the whole country, and laying siege to Jerusalem, reduced Hyrcanus to the greatest extremities. So close, in fact, was the siege, that for fear of famine Hyrcanus was constrained to expel from the city all such as were, from age or infirmity, unable to bear arms. As the Syrians refused them a passage through their ranks, the fugitives presented a miserable spectacle, wandering about between the two armies, and perishing in extreme wretchedness amidst the outworks[1].

At length the Feast of Tabernacles drew near, and Hyrcanus requested a week's respite to celebrate that time-honoured festival. With rare generosity, his adversary not only granted his request, but supplied the besieged with victims for the sacrifices, and gold and silver vessels for the Temple service. Such kindness induced Hyrcanus to send an embassy, and endeavour to obtain a suspension of hostilities. In this he succeeded, and peace was concluded on far better terms than he had any right to expect. A portion of the fortifications of the city was dismantled, tribute was exacted for the fortresses held out of Judæa, but the conqueror was induced, by a present of 500 talents, to forego the rebuilding of the fortress on the Acra, and the introduction of a Syrian garrison[2].

The unexpected forbearance of Antiochus on this occasion won for him not only the admiration, but the friendship of Hyrcanus, and when the Syrian king led an expedition against the Parthians, who were now extending their dominions on every side, the Jewish prince resolved to accompany him. For this purpose he took into his pay a body of foreign mercenaries, and with these and a detachment of his Jewish forces followed

[1] Jos. *Ant.* XIII. 8. 2. [2] Jos. *Ant.* XIII. 8. 3.

him across the Tigris. At first Antiochus was successful, but his army giving themselves up to luxury and dissipation, he was unexpectedly attacked, and lost his life, B.C. 128.

Disorders of every kind, civil wars, murders, and mutinies of troops, now rapidly succeeded one another in the Syrian kingdom, and Hyrcanus, who had fortunately returned to Jerusalem before the overthrow of his late ally, now threw off the Syrian yoke altogether, and employed himself in extending his own kingdom. After reducing, therefore, various fortresses on the further side of the Jordan, he invaded Samaria, captured Sychem, and levelled with the ground the temple on Mount Gerizim, which for 200 years had been a constant offence to his subjects. Then, B.C. 129, turning his arms against the Idumæans, who had made themselves masters of the southern part of Judæa, he vanquished them in battle, and offered them the choice of leaving the country, or adopting the Jewish religion. They chose the latter alternative, submitted to circumcision, and became so completely identified with their conquerors, that their name as an independent power henceforth disappears.

During the next 20 years Judæa enjoyed profound peace under the energetic government of Hyrcanus, who renewed the treaties with Rome, and secured his subjects from foreign aggression. At length, B.C. 110, he resolved to overpower the province of Samaria, and entrusted the command of the expedition to his two sons, Aristobulus and Antigonus. Twice the Samaritans applied for aid to Antiochus Cyzicenus, prince of Damascus, who was twice defeated by the Jewish forces, and at length, after an obstinate defence which lasted an entire year, their capital fell, and with Scythopolis and other towns, passed into the hands of the conqueror [1].

[1] Samaria itself was now razed to the ground, the hill on

During his long and prosperous reign, Hyrcanus had raised his nation to a height of greater power and dignity than it had ever enjoyed since the return from the Captivity. But while triumphant abroad, his domestic peace began to be troubled by serious dissensions between two rival parties, now rapidly growing in power, the *Pharisees* and *Sadducees*. An examination of their respective tenets may be reserved for another place. For the present it will be sufficient to say that Hyrcanus was an adherent of the Pharisaic party, till a characteristic incident induced him to espouse the cause of their rivals. Towards the close of his administration he invited the chiefs of the Pharisees to a banquet, and requested them to inform him if he had been guilty of any dereliction of duty towards God or man. All the guests with one accord testified to his blameless integrity, and praised his government, save one, Eleazar, who affirmed that he ought to resign the high-priesthood, because his mother had once been a captive, and it was doubtful whether he was descended from Aaron, or from a heathen. Indignant at this calumnious charge, Hyrcanus demanded the trial of Eleazar for aspersions upon his character. By the influence of the Pharisees the sentence was limited to scourging and imprisonment, and the priest-king, considering this a proof of hostility to himself, listened to the representations of Jonathan, a Sadducee, that the rival faction was bent on lowering his sovereign power, and henceforth alienated himself entirely from the Pharisaic party, and deposed from their high offices many who had been the firmest supporters of his dynasty[1].

Escaping the fate of the older members of the Mac-

which it had stood being full of springs, was pierced with trenches, and the site of the city flooded and converted into a pool of water. Jos. *Ant.* XIII. 10. 3.

[1] Jos. *Ant.* XIII. 10. 6.

cabæan family, Hyrcanus died in peace, B.C. 106, bequeathing the sovereignty to his wife. And now the decline of the Asmonean dynasty rapidly set in. Aristobulus, the son of the deceased king, seized the supreme power, flung his mother into prison, and starved her to death. He also imprisoned three of his four brothers, sparing but one, Antigonus, the next in age to himself. Assuming the diadem and the royal title, he hastened to take advantage of the distracted state of affairs in Syria, and turning his arms against Ituræa, a district south of Anti-Libanus, forced the inhabitants, like the Idumæans, to conform to the Jewish religion, on pain of being expelled from their country. During this expedition he was seized with a dangerous illness, which compelled him to return to Jerusalem, and leave his brother Antigonus to complete the subjugation of the country. As he had no children, his queen Salome, according to the Jewish law, would, in the event of his death, be expected to marry Antigonus; but such was her aversion to him, that she resolved to compass his death rather than be united with him in marriage[1].

An opportunity soon presented itself for carrying out her design. Successful in subjugating Ituræa, Antigonus returned to Jerusalem, and at the Feast of Tabernacles hastened to the Temple, with his body-guard, to offer up his petitions for his brother's recovery. This act was represented to Aristobulus as covering a seditious design against his own life. Scarcely able to credit such a calumny, the king, who still lay sick in his chamber in the tower of Baris, desired that his brother should appear before him, but without arms. A dark underground passage led from the Temple to the tower, and here, by the queen's connivance, a company of soldiers

[1] Raphall's *History of the Jews*, II. 103.

was stationed with instructions to put Antigonus to death if he appeared clad in armour. She then caused it to be represented to the unfortunate prince that it was the royal will he should appear in a suit of splendid armour, which his brother wished to see. Thus deceived he entered the underground passage, and was instantly assassinated. What had occurred was reported to Aristobulus, and brought on a sudden paroxysm of his malady followed by an excessive hæmorrhage. A slave bore away the vessel into which the blood had flowed, and stumbling on the very spot where Antigonus had been murdered, caused the blood of the two brothers to mingle on the floor. A cry of horror ran through the palace, and reaching the ears of the king, roused a wish to know the cause. For some time his attendants refused to tell the truth, but at length he forced them to declare what had occurred, and had no sooner heard it than he was seized with such an agony of remorse that he instantly expired.

After this tragical event, Alexander Jannæus, the eldest of the imprisoned brothers, was placed upon the throne, B.C. 104. Taking advantage of the disordered condition of the Syrian kingdom, he turned his arms against Moab, Gilead, Ammon, and Arabia Petræa, and after several successes laid siege to the port of Ptolemais. The inhabitants called in the aid of Ptolemy Lathyrus, who came to their aid with an army of 30,000 men. But no sooner did he appear before the gates, than the very party which had invoked his aid refused to admit him. On this he turned his arms against Gaza, and Jannæus, while pretending to negotiate with him for a friendly surrender of the place, secretly corresponded with his mother Cleopatra, the queen of Egypt, and besought her aid in expelling him from the country. Discovering this, Ptolemy marched into Judæa, defeated Alexander with enormous loss, and to spread the terror of his name, fell upon some villages, murdered the women and children, and cutting their bodies in pieces boiled their flesh.

The kingdom of Judæa would now have been totally lost, had it not been for the intervention of an Egyptian army led by two Jews of Alexandria. They drove Lathyrus into Cœlesyria, and once more restored to Jannæus the sovereignty of the country, who now embarked on fresh expeditions east and west of the Jordan, captured Gadara, Raphia, and Anthedon, and at length succeeded in reducing Gaza.

But the domestic discords, which had distracted the reign of Hyrcanus, broke out with tenfold violence in that of his son. The Pharisees had by this time gained an extraordinary degree of influence over the people. Detesting their turbulence and lofty pretensions, Alexander attached himself to the Sadducaic faction, and thus brought down upon himself the concentrated hatred of the Pharisees, who lost no opportunity of aspersing his name and character. At length their opposition took a more violent turn, and at the Feast of Tabernacles, when the priest-king, clad in his gorgeous robes, was officiating before the altar, they excited the people to fling at him the citrons, which it was the custom of the Jews to carry in their hands at this feast, and to deny his right to the high-priesthood. A fearful outbreak ensued, in the midst of which Alexander ordered his body-guard to fall on the unarmed multitude, and slew upwards of 6000.

To obviate a recurrence of such insults, he next caused a wooden partition to be erected between the court of the priests and that of the people, and surrounded himself with Pisidian and Cilician mercenaries. But a defeat he sustained, while carrying on an expedition in the country east of the Jordan, was the signal for a general rising, which resulted in civil war carried on for upwards of six years, and marked by the most shocking barbarities on both sides.

At first Jannæus met with much success, but on endeavouring to come to terms with his subjects, they declared that nothing would satisfy them short of his death, and even invoked the aid of Demetrius Euchærus, king of Syria, and in a battle near Shechem utterly routed the priest-king, with the loss of all his mercenaries. Thereupon he fled to the mountains, rallied fresh troops, drove Demetrius from the country, and took the majority of his rebellious subjects prisoners in the fortress of Bethone. Returning to Jerusalem he crucified 800 of them in one day, and seated at a banquet surrounded by his concubines, caused their wives and children to be slain before their eyes, and glutted his vengeance with the spectacle of their dying agonies.

This shocking act, which won for him the title of "the Thracian," shews how terribly the Asmonean princes were degenerating. Externally, indeed, the country appeared to be prosperous, for the realm of Jannæus extended over Samaria and Idumæa, the entire western seaboard from *Strato's Tower* to Rhinocorura, and a considerable district beyond the Jordan, but the temper neither of prince nor people was the same as in the times of Mattathias and Judas, and evil days were at hand.

Four years after his triumph over his rebellious subjects, Alexander Jannæus died, B.C. 79, having on his death-bed advised his queen Alexandra to ally herself closely with the Pharisaic faction, as being alone able to control the people. Acting on this advice, she convened the most eminent of that faction, and entrusted to them the entire management of affairs. Upon this their conduct underwent an instant change; the highest honours were paid to the memory of the late king, and the priesthood was conferred on his eldest son Hyrcanus II.

PART IV

DECLINE OF THE ASMONEAN DYNASTY; INTERFERENCE OF THE ROMANS, AND RISE OF THE HERODIAN FAMILY.

CHAPTER I

HYRCANUS II. AND ARISTOBULUS; POMPEIUS AND CRASSUS.

B. C. 79—53.

BESIDES the new high-priest, Alexander had left another son named Aristobulus, a man of an ardent and impetuous temper, who took no pains to conceal his dislike of his mother's proceedings. Placing himself at the head of the now offended and persecuted Sadducees, he encouraged them in their opposition to the triumphant Pharisees, and so far prevailed with the queen, that the leaders of the Sadducaic faction were allowed to retire to the frontier fortresses of the kingdom. Shortly afterwards he himself was sent on an expedition to Damascus, to check the depredations of Ptolemy, who governed a small independent kingdom at Chalcis[1]. The young prince did not lose the opportunity thus afforded him of ingratiating himself with the soldiers, and began to form designs of usurping the kingdom.

After a successful reign of 9 years, queen Alexandra died, B. C. 69, and the Pharisaic party immediately placed Hyrcanus II. on the throne. This was regarded as the signal for definite action by Aristobulus. Quickly summoning his adherents from the frontier cities, he marched towards Jerusalem, where the partisans of Hyrcanus seizing his wife and children, placed them as hostages in the Tower of Baris, and then prepared to meet the invader at Jericho[2]. But so strongly did the feeling of

[1] Jos. *Ant.* XIII. 16. 3. [2] Jos. *Ant.* XIV. 1. 2.

the army declare itself in favour of Aristobulus, and so many were the desertions to his side, including even not a few members of the Sanhedrin, that Hyrcanus fell back upon Jerusalem, and with such of his adherents as still remained faithful took refuge in the fortifications of the Temple. But provisions failing them, they were unable to stand a lengthened siege, and were soon compelled to yield to Aristobulus, who thus obtained possession of the entire kingdom, while his brother, who was of a feeble and indolent disposition, retired into private life after a brief reign of three months.

But now a different actor appeared upon the scene, destined to prove a far more fatal enemy to the Asmonean dynasty, and to raise his own house upon its ruins. This was Antipater, the son of an officer who had been high in the confidence of Alexander Jannæus, and had been appointed governor of Idumæa. A man of great courage, astuteness, and decision, he had acquired a complete mastery over the feeble Hyrcanus, and in concert with the Pharisees repeatedly urged him to attempt the recovery of his throne, but for a long time the indolent prince absolutely refused to listen to his suggestions. At length, by representing that his life was in danger, he succeeded in persuading him to fly with himself to the court of Aretas, king of Arabia, whom he induced, by promising to restore twelve frontier cities which Jannæus had taken and united to Judæa, to espouse his cause. At the head of 50,000 men Aretas marched into the country, and being joined by the partisans of Hyrcanus, defeated Aristobulus, and closely besieged him in the Temple-fortress at Jerusalem[1]. The feast of the Passover drew near, during which even heathen generals had been wont to allow the sacrificial victims to be introduced into the city. But such was the fury of the

[1] Jos. *Ant.* XIV. 2. I.

rival claimants for the supreme power that even this indulgence was refused to the besieged. When Aristobulus let down baskets from the top of the wall with 1000 drachmas of silver for each victim, the besiegers took the money, but returned the baskets empty, or, as some say, even laden with swine[1].

At this juncture news reached Jerusalem that a Roman army had seized Damascus, and was advancing towards the country. Bent on their plan of establishing a universal empire, the great republic of the West was now busily engaged in those wars, which gradually placed at her feet the old Asiatic monarchies. The Syrian kingdom, since B.C. 83, had passed into the power of Tigranes, king of Armenia. This monarch, as well as Mithridates, king of Pontus, was utterly defeated by Pompeius, B.C. 66, and the ancient realm of the Seleucidæ was now reduced to a Roman province. Retiring himself into lesser Armenia, the conqueror placed his lieutenants Scaurus and Gabinius at Antioch and Damascus, the two great capitals of the Syrian Empire.

This intelligence determined both brothers to try and secure the aid of these powerful arbitrators, and their emissaries soon appeared before Scaurus at Damascus, with 400 talents. The Roman general at first hesitated which side to espouse, but at length reflecting that Aristobulus was in possession of the Temple-fortress, and therefore of the treasures, he ordered Aretas to withdraw, and break up the siege[2]. The Arabian chief was forced to comply, and taking with him Hyrcanus and Antipater marched away with his army, but not before Aristobulus had sallied forth and inflicted upon it a considerable loss.

His triumph, however, was shortlived. Before long

[1] Milman, *History of the Jews*, II. 42.
[2] Jos. *Ant.* XIV. 2. 3; *B. J.* I. 6. 3.

Pompeius arrived in person at Damascus, and twelve kings crowded together to pay him homage. The king of Egypt brought him a crown worth 4000 pieces of gold. Aristobulus sent him a golden vine upon a square mount, the leaves and branches most skilfully wrought, beneath which were lions, deer, and other animals in lifelike attitude[1]. His present was accepted, but instead of his own name, that of his father was inscribed upon it, and after hearing the ambassadors of each brother, the conqueror declared that they must attend and plead their cause before him in person early in the following year B.C. 63.

At the time appointed the brothers appeared, attended by numerous witnesses in support of their respective claims, as also by representatives of the Jewish people. Pompeius listened with attention to their arguments, and then closed the conference by announcing his purpose of settling the question in person at Jerusalem, intending first to subjugate Aretas and to conquer Petra. The impetuous Aristobulus, divining that the decision would be adverse to his interests, prepared for resistance by flinging himself into the fortress of Alexandrium, on the road between Jericho and Jerusalem, a position well adapted for resisting an approach to his capital.

Professing the greatest indignation at this conduct, and relieved from the necessity of invading Arabia by the timely submission of Aretas, Pompeius marched through the country east of the Jordan, and besieged the impetuous Asmonean in his stronghold. After three fruitless interviews, Aristobulus was forced to sign written orders for the surrender of all his strongholds, and on promise of obedience was liberated. Fleeing to Jerusalem, he now betook himself to the Temple-fort-

[1] Jos. *Ant.* XIV. 3. 1.

ress, and prepared for a siege. Pompeius advanced to Jericho[1], where his soldiers were struck with admiration by the beautiful palm-groves and balsam-trees of that tropic region, and then pressed on to Jerusalem. The partisans of Hyrcanus, who were the most numerous, threw open the gates, those of Aristobulus remained within their stronghold, and resolutely refused the summons of the Roman general to surrender.

On this Pompeius sent to Tyre[2] for his military engines, and prosecuted the siege with the utmost vigour for three months[3]. It might have been protracted still longer, but for the suspension of hostilities by the Jews on the Sabbath-day. At length the largest of the towers was thrown down by one of the battering engines, and Cornelius Faustus, a son of Sylla, mounted the breach, and the day was gained B.C. 63. A terrible carnage now ensued, during which the priests remained unmoved at the altar, and continued their solemn services, pouring their drink-offerings, and burning their incense, till they were themselves stricken down. The conqueror entered the Temple, and, amidst the horror of the Jews, explored the total darkness of the Holy of Holies, and found, to his great amazement, neither symbols, nor statues, nor representation of any deity[4]. He surveyed with interest the sacred vessels, the golden altar of incense, the golden candlestick, and the Temple treasures, but with politic generosity left them untouched. He then ordered the sacred enclosure to be cleansed from the profanation of his soldiers, nominated Hyrcanus to the high-priesthood, though without the royal diadem, and confined the limits of his jurisdiction to Judæa. The walls of the city having been demolished, he then set out for Rome, taking with him the captive Aristobulus,

[1] Jos. *B. J.* I. 6. 6. [2] Jos. *B. J.* I. 7. 3.
[3] Liv. *Epit.* 102.
[4] Comp. Cic. *pro Flacco*, c. xxviii; Tac. *Hist.* v. 5.

as also his two sons and two daughters to grace his splendid triumph.

On the way, however, Alexander, the eldest son of the captive king, managed to effect his escape, and returned to Judæa, where, rallying round him the partisans of his father, he seized the fortresses of Alexandrium, Hyrcania, and Machærus, and began to attack the adherents of Hyrcanus. Alarmed at the progress of the invader, and unable to make head against him themselves, the ethnarch and Antipater called in the aid of the Romans, and Gabinius, who had been appointed prefect of Syria, B.C. 57, deputed Marcus Antonius, his master of the horse, to render the required assistance. Antonius, having defeated the invader in a short engagement, shut him up in the stronghold of Alexandrium, and on the arrival of Gabinius forced him, after a somewhat protracted siege, to purchase his life by the surrender of the three fortresses, which were now demolished[1].

Gabinius now employed himself in completely reorganizing the government of the country. Hitherto the nominal power had centred in Hyrcanus. Now he was deprived of even this semblance of authority, which was placed in the hands of the aristocracy, five independent senates or Sanhedrins being established, the first sitting at Jerusalem, the second at Jericho, the third at Gadara, the fourth at Amathus, the fifth at Sepphoris[1]. These arrangements made for destroying the influence of the capital as a centre of union, Gabinius returned to Syria. But scarcely had he done so, when Aristobulus himself reappeared, having escaped from Rome with his younger son, Antigonus. He was, however, more quickly disposed of even than Alexander had been, for the prefect of Syria instantly dispatched a force against him, and

[1] Jos. *B. J.* I. 8. 5; *Ant.* XIV. 5. 2—4.

having overpowered his adherents, sent him back as a prisoner to Rome with his son, who was afterwards, however, released.

Gabinius now proceeded with Antonius to Egypt to place Ptolemy Auletes upon the throne, and both generals were strenuously assisted by Hyrcanus and Antipater, who sent supplies for their armies, and urged the Jews at Leontopolis to befriend them in like manner. Taking advantage of the absence of the legions, Alexander made a second attempt to recover the supreme power, but only to be a second time defeated near Mount Tabor by the Roman commanders on their return from Egypt, with a loss of 10,000 men.

The next year, B. C. 54, the prefect was recalled to Rome, where numerous charges of rapacity and extortion were preferred against him, and though defended by Cicero he was ignominiously banished[1]. The celebrated triumvir Marcus Crassus now succeeded to the prefecture of Syria, a man of mean abilities, but enormous wealth, and unbounded avarice. Armed like Pompeius with proconsular authority for five years, and empowered to maintain as large a force as he might see fit, and to carry on wars without consulting the senate and people of Rome, Crassus resolved on entering upon a war with Parthia. Hurrying to his province, with some of the troops he had already collected, he entered Jerusalem, attracted by the well-known fact that the treasury of its Temple contained 2,000 talents, equivalent to nearly £2,000,000 sterling, besides vessels of gold and silver to an almost equal amount. The Jews were powerless to resist his intentions, but Eleazar, the guardian of the Temple, offered him a solid bar of gold weighing nearly 1000 pounds, concealed in a beam of wood, on condition that he left the rest of the trea-

1 Merivale's *Romans under the Empire*, I. 381, 382.

sures untouched. Crassus solemnly promised to be satisfied with this huge ingot, took it, and then, in defiance of his plighted faith, robbed the Temple of all the treasures he could lay his hands on, not sparing even the sacred vessels. The total amount he carried off is said to have been worth upwards of 10,000 Attic talents, and consisted of the gifts and offerings which during a hundred years the annual contributions of Jews from well-nigh every quarter of the world had amassed[1]. He then set out against the Parthians, crossed the Euphrates, and plunged into the sandy deserts of Mesopotamia, to be defeated with the loss of nearly his entire army at the disastrous battle of Carrhæ, B.C. 53.

CHAPTER II.

ANTIPATER AND HEROD; JULIUS CÆSAR AND ANTONIUS.

B. C. 53—41.

MISFORTUNE seemed to follow in the footsteps of every Roman general that interfered in the affairs of Judæa. Gabinius was ignominiously exiled, Crassus perished miserably in a foreign land, and now the disastrous issue of the battle of Pharsalia, B.C. 48, drove Pompeius to the shores of Egypt, there to perish by the blow of an assassin.

A new actor now appeared upon the stage. Master of Rome, nominated dictator for the second time, Julius Cæsar repaired to Egypt in pursuit of his rival, and a few days after his death arrived at Alexandria. For the purpose of effecting a diversion in his favour, he had liberated Aristobulus, and sent him to Palestine with two legions to overawe Syria. But the partisans of Pompeius managed to poison him on the way, and Scipio,

[1] Jos. *Ant.* XIV. 7. 2; *B. J.* I. 8. 8, 9; Milman, II. 51.

who held the command in Syria, seized his son Alexander, and caused him to be beheaded after a mock trial at Antioch[1].

The supremacy was thus left in the hands of Hyrcanus, or rather of his minister Antipater, who really ruled in his name. With prudent alacrity the wily Idumæan completely changed his tactics, and did everything in his power to promote the cause of Cæsar. Resolved to settle the disputes concerning the succession to the throne of Egypt, and determined to uphold the claims of Cleopatra, who had completely won his heart, this general embarked in a war, in which for some time he was exposed to great danger on account of the small number of his troops. Antipater seized the opportunity of displaying a prudent activity on his behalf. He assisted his ally, Mithridates, king of Pontus, in marching to his relief, he contributed to the reduction of Pelusium, he conciliated the Jews in Egypt, who had espoused the cause of the opposite party, and received wounds in almost every part of his body[2], while fighting on his behalf.

Cæsar was not slow to declare his gratitude. Having brought the Egyptian war to a close B.C. 47, he conferred upon his friend the privileges of Roman citizenship, and at the same time at his request confirmed Hyrcanus in the high-priesthood[3]. But Antigonus, son of Aristobulus, now appeared before him, and breaking forth into the fiercest accusations against Antipater, charged him with cruelty towards himself, oppression of the Jews, and an insincere friendship for his patron. The Idumæan was equal to the occasion. Throwing open his vest, he exposed the numerous wounds he had received in Cæsar's cause, and protested his innocence and fide-

[1] Jos. *Ant.* XIV. 7. 4. [2] Jos. *Ant.* XIV. 8. 1; *B. J.* I. 9. 5.
[3] Jos. *Ant.* XIV. 8. 3; *B. J.* I. 9. 5.

lity. The Dictator could not resist such an appeal, appointed him procurator of Judæa, and granted him permission to restore the ruined fortifications of Jerusalem[1].

Having made these arrangements Cæsar marched through Syria towards Pontus, to attack Pharnaces, the son of Mithridates the Great, who had defeated one of his lieutenants. Antipater conducted him beyond the Syrian frontiers, and returning to Jerusalem, commenced rebuilding the walls which had been overthrown by Pompey. He then set out on a tour through the country, suppressing tumults, and exhorting all to submit to the rule of Hyrcanus; soon waxing bolder, and taking advantage of the indolence of his nominal sovereign, he appointed his eldest son Phasael military governor of Judæa, and conferred the tetrarchy of Galilee on his younger son Herod, afterwards Herod the Great.

Though but a youth of 15, according to Josephus[2], but more probably of 25[3], the new governor of Galilee soon began to give signs of that decision of character which subsequently distinguished him. Turning his energies against numerous robber bands, who infested his province as also the confines of Syria, he put to death Hezekias, one of their notorious chiefs, with nearly all his associates. Such energy and determination won the delighted approval of the Syrians, who sang his praises in their villages and cities[4], and not less of Sextus Cæsar, the new president of that province.

But the news of these successes of the young man filled Hyrcanus and many of the national party at Jerusalem with indignation. The priest-king felt that the family of Antipater was everything, while he himself was nothing. Herod was, therefore, summoned before

[1] Jos. *B. J.* I. 10. 2, 3; *Ant.* XIV. 8. 5.

[2] Jos. *Ant.* XIV. 9. 2.

[3] Merivale, III. 377.

[4] Jos. *Ant.* XIV. 9. 2; *B. J.* I. 10. 5.

the Sanhedrin to answer for his conduct in putting so many to death without a trial. He came, not in the garb of a suppliant, but clothed in purple, accompanied by a strong escort, and bore with him a letter from Sextus Cæsar, ordering his acquittal of the capital charge[1]. The great council was terrified. Not a man dared to lift his voice to accuse him, backed as he was by the terrible power of the Roman governor, save Sameas, or Shammai, one of the most learned Rabbis and a man of unblemished character. He sternly rebuked the accused for the haughty independence he had evinced, and the others, emboldened by his conduct, were ready to pronounce the sentence of death[2]. Hyrcanus now interposed, and secretly advised Herod to fly from the city. He took the advice and hurried to Damascus, where he threw himself at the feet of Sextus Cæsar, and in consideration of a heavy bribe, was appointed governor of Cœlesyria and Samaria. Burning with rage, he now gathered an army, marched against Jerusalem, and would have taken summary vengeance on his opponents, had it not been for the intervention of his father and brother, who advised him to be satisfied with his acquittal and draw off his troops.

Two years afterwards, B.C. 44, Cæsar was assassinated on the Ides of March, in the senate-house at Rome. Cassius, the chief conspirator, betook himself to Syria, to secure the troops stationed at Apamea[3], and began to impose heavy tribute on the various cities of Asia Minor, and the Syrian provinces. Palestine was assessed to pay the enormous sum of 700 talents of silver[4], and Antipater commissioned his son Herod to collect the contribution from Galilee, while Malichus, a powerful Jew, and principal adherent of Hyrcanus, col-

[1] See Merivale, III. 375.
[2] Jos. *Ant.* XIV. 9. 4.
[3] Jos. *B. J.* I. 11. 1.
[4] Jos. *Ant.* XIV. 11. 2.

lected the rest. With characteristic tact, Herod employed himself diligently in raising his quota, and repairing to Cassius with 100 talents gained his hearty good will, while Malichus so incensed him by his dilatoriness, that he would have put him to death, had not Hyrcanus soothed the Roman's anger by the present of another 100 talents[1].

The influence of Antipater on this occasion Malichus deemed unendurable. He saw that his patron Hyrcanus was rapidly losing even the semblance of power, and he resolved to compass the Idumæan's death. Suspecting his designs, Antipater fled beyond the Jordan, and collected a body of men to defend himself. But persuaded that his suspicions were groundless, he returned to Jerusalem, where he was shortly afterwards poisoned with a glass of wine at an entertainment in the high-priest s palace, B.C. 43. Herod would have instantly avenged his father's murder, but Phasael persuaded him to bide his time, and the brothers celebrated their father's obsequies with the greatest splendour, pretending to believe the assassin's assertion of innocence. Before long, an opportunity of revenge presented itself. On the capture of Laodicea by Cassius, the kings and nobles of the surrounding provinces assembled, bearing gifts and crowns. Amongst the rest came Hyrcanus and Malichus, and on the way stayed at Tyre, where Herod, who had joined them, invited them to a banquet, and sending secret instructions to the Roman soldiers, caused Malichus to be dispatched on the seashore. The feeble Hyrcanus witnessed the bloody deed, and immediately fainted away, but no sooner heard that it had been done by command of Cassius, than he acquiesced, and denounced Malichus as the enemy of his country.

It was now clear that the virtual supremacy lay in

[1] Jos. *B. J.* I. 11. 3; *Ant.* XIV. 11. 2.

the hands of the sons of Antipater, and that the party of Hyrcanus could but struggle in vain against their influence. It was not, however, their interest to come to an open rupture with the high-priest, and Herod for the sake of conciliating the people, who still clung with unabated devotion to that noble race, resolved to ally himself with a princess of the Asmonean family. He had already married Doris, a native of Judæa, and by her had become the father of a son Antipater. He now was betrothed to the beautiful and accomplished grand-daughter of Hyrcanus, the famous Mariamne, who was as yet a child.

Meanwhile, B. C. 42, the forces of Brutus and Cassius had met their opponents Antonius and Octavius on the bloody field of Philippi, and had sustained a disastrous defeat. The conquerors separated; Octavius departed for Italy, Antonius for Asia. On his arrival in Bithynia, a number of influential Jews waited upon Antonius with bitter complaints against Phasael and Herod[1], but Herod plied him with such heavy bribes, that the deputation withdrew unable to effect anything. Shortly afterwards another deputation met him at Daphne near Antioch, and with them came Hyrcanus. The Roman listened to their complaints, and then turning to the high-priest, asked whom he deemed best fitted to rule the country? Influenced probably by the projected alliance between Herod and his grand-daughter, he named the brothers. Antonius, who had been hospitably entertained by their father Antipater, when he accompanied Gabinius to Egypt[2], readily assented, and named them tetrarchs of Judæa, nor could a subsequent deputation of 1000 Jews, who waited upon him at Tyre, avail to alter his decision[3].

[1] Jos. *B. J.* I. 12. 4; *Ant.* XIV. 12. 2.

[2] See above, p. 71.

[3] Jos. *B. J.* I. 12. 6; *Ant.* XIV. 13. 1, 2.

A single obstacle to the complete success of the brothers still remained in the person of Antigonus. He had already made an ineffectual attempt to recover the throne, and now assistance appeared in an utterly unexpected quarter. While Antonius was wasting his time in the society of Cleopatra, queen of Egypt, the Parthians, under Pacorus, entered Syria, overran the whole country, and made themselves masters of Sidon and Ptolemais. Antigonus resolved to court the assistance of these unexpected allies, and by a bribe of 1000 talents and 500 Jewish women, persuaded Pacorus to espouse his cause. With a division of the Parthian army he now marched against Jerusalem, and an obstinate struggle commenced. At length the Parthian general with a few horsemen was admitted into the city, and offered to act as umpire between the rival claimants. Phasael assented, and in an evil hour for himself, accompanied by Hyrcanus repaired to the court of Barzapharnes, the new Parthian governor of Syria, who threw them into chains[1]. Meanwhile Herod, suspecting treachery, and warned by Mariamne, secretly escaped with a picked body of troops from Jerusalem[2], and made his way to Masada[3], a strong fortress on the south-

[1] Jos. *B. J.* I. 13. 4—6.

[2] Jos. *B. J.* I. 13. 6; *Ant.* XIV. 13. 7—9.

[3] Masada, now called *Sebbeh*, was situated at the S.W. end of the Dead Sea, on a rock from 1200 to 1500 ft. in height, separated from the adjoining range of mountains by deep ravines on the N. and S., and only attached to them on the W. by a narrow neck about two-thirds of its height. The fortress was first built by Jonathan Maccabæus, but Herod the Great added to it and made it an impregnable place of refuge for himself in case of danger. The rock on which it was built overhung the Dead Sea, and was only accessible by two rock-hewn paths, one on the W., the other on the E. side, carried up from the shore by a zigzag cut in the precipice, and called "the Serpent." The summit of the rock was not pointed, but a plain of 7 stadia in circumference, surrounded by a wall of

western side of the Dead Sea. So desperate were his circumstances, that he was with difficulty restrained from making away with himself[1], and finally, leaving Mariamne and his family at Masada, in charge of 800 men, he fled to Petra, to try to obtain help from the successor of Aretas. This being denied, he dismissed the remainder of his forces, and made his way to Pelusium, and so to Alexandria, whence declining the command of an expedition offered him by Cleopatra, he took ship, although it was the depth of winter, and sailed for Rome[2], B.C. 40.

CHAPTER III

HEROD, KING OF JUDÆA.

B. C. 40—33.

MEANWHILE the Parthians had made themselves masters of Jerusalem, reinstated Antigonus in the supreme power, and delivered into his hands the captives Hyrcanus and Phasael. The new ruler, unwilling to put his aged uncle to death, but determined that he should never be able to hold the office of high-priest again, caused his ears to be cropped off[3], and then sent him to Seleucia in Babylonia to be retained as a prisoner of the Parthians. Phasael, knowing his death was certain, anticipated the executioner by beating out his brains against the walls of his prison.

In the mean time Herod had reached Rome, where he

white stone, 12 cubits high and 8 thick, fortified with 37 towers of 50 cubits in height, and adorned with a palace and baths. The interior being left free for cultivation, so that the garrison might partially raise their own food. Traill's *Josephus*, II. 109—115; Porter's *Handbk. of Syria and Palestine*, p. 239.

[1] Jos. *Ant.* XIV. 13. 8.

[2] Jos. *B. J.* I. 14. 2; *Ant.* XIV. 14. 2, 3.

[3] Jos. *B. J.* I. 13. 9; *Ant.* XIV. 13. 10.

found Antonius at the very summit of power. The Roman received him with much kindness, and introduced him to Octavius, who calling to mind the aid which the great Julius had received from Antipater during his Egyptian war[1], was no less ready to befriend him. Herod protested he wished for nothing more than that Aristobulus, the brother of his betrothed Mariamne, should be placed on the throne of Judæa. But the triumvirs would not entertain the proposition for a moment. Who was more fit to receive the title of king than Herod himself? Who was more likely to cope effectually with Antigonus, and to render aid in the projected war with Parthia? Accordingly with the assent of the senate he was formally nominated King of Judæa, and preceded by the consuls and other magistrates, walked in procession between Antonius and Octavius to the Capitol, where the usual sacrifices were offered, and the decree formally laid up in the archives[2].

A week only had elapsed since the arrival of Herod in Italy. But without losing a moment he hurried to Brundusium, and thence took ship for Ptolemais, where he presented himself after an absence of barely three months. Meanwhile Antigonus had been unsuccessfully besieging the fortress of Masada, with the design of obtaining possession of Mariamne and Aristobulus. The first object of the newly-arrived king was to relieve this stronghold, and the recollection of his energy as a governor in Galilee quickly attracted many to his standard. He also invoked the aid of Ventidius the Roman general, who had been sent to check the advance of the Parthians and had encamped before Jerusalem, and partly through his aid but still more by his own energy succeeded in raising the siege of Masada, liberated his

[1] Jos. *B. J.* I. 14. 4. See above, p. 73.
[2] Jos. *B. J.* I. 14. 4; *Ant.* XIV. 14. 5.

relatives, and recovered the treasures he had deposited there.

His next step was to march upon Jerusalem, and having united with the Roman forces, encamped on the west side of the city B.C. 38. Finding, however, that he could not reduce it with the forces then at his command, he repaired to Samaria, and there was formally united in marriage with the beautiful Mariamne. Early in the following spring, B.C. 37, he again set out for Jerusalem, supported on this occasion by Sosius, the lieutenant of Antonius, with 11 legions and 6000 cavalry. Now for the first time the Romans found how desperate an enemy they had to encounter in the Jews, who defended Antigonus with all the constancy of their race. Upwards of 40 days elapsed before the first wall was taken, 15 before the second was reduced. Fighting with reckless courage, the besieged were driven successively from the outer court of the Temple and the lower city into the interior of the Sanctuary, nor was it till after five long months of combat that the signal could be given for an assault. No sooner had this been given than a dreadful massacre ensued. Exasperated by the obstinacy of the foe, the Romans struck down all whom they met, without distinction of age or sex. Multitudes were butchered in the narrow streets, many crowded together in their homes, many flying for refuge to the Sanctuary. Herod used every effort to mollify the wrath of the legions, and even threatened to cut down any who attempted to penetrate into the Holy of Holies. Finding all was lost, Antigonus descended from the Baris, where he had taken refuge, and flung himself at the feet of Sosius. The Roman treated him with contempt and scorn, called him in derision *Antigona*, and put him in chains. Then laden with munificent presents from the new ruler of Jerusalem, he retired to Antioch with his captive, to await the pleasure of Antonius himself. The latter, at the request of his favourite now installed in power, had the unfortunate prince tried and condemned, and after he had first been scourged by the Roman lictors, struck off his head[1]. Thus ignominiously perished the last priest-king of the Asmonean dynasty, 126 years[2] after Judas Maccabæus obtained the government of Judæa.

Herod had now attained the highest object of his ambition. In the prime of his vigour and great abilities he had become ruler of Palestine, being lifted into his high position by the Roman legions, and by uniting himself with one of the Asmonean line he had conciliated somewhat the popular favour. But though successful, he clearly foresaw the difficulty and danger of his position, for the partisans of Antigonus still retained much influence, and the people were strong in their attachment to the Asmonean dynasty. But the Idumæan had profited in the school of the Roman proscriptions, and selecting 45 of the most prominent partisans of Antigonus, he put them all to death, and confiscated their estates to liquidate the heavy debt he had contracted with Antigonus. He next wreaked his vengeance on the Sanhedrin, every member of which was executed save two only, Sameas and Pollio, who alone during the late siege had urged their countrymen to capitulate and receive him as king.

The question of the appointment to the high-priesthood next required to be disposed of. Hyrcanus was in captivity at Seleucia, where the Parthian Phraates treated him with every consideration, and allowed him to live at full liberty among many of his own nation, who had settled in that region[3]. Herod sent an embassy requesting that his former patron might be per-

[1] Jos. *B. J.* I. 18. 3. "Antonius was the first of the Romans who consented to smite a king with the axe." Merivale. III. 382.

[2] Jos. *Ant.* XIV. 16. 4.

[3] Jos. *Ant.* XV. 2. 2.

mitted to return, and pretended a wish to recompense him for old kindnesses. The Jews in Seleucia easily divined his insidious designs. But the weak old man heeded not their council, and returned to Jerusalem. The mutilation of his ears by Antigonus rendered it impossible for him to hold the office of high-priest, and Herod, while treating him with much apparent respect, conferred the coveted post on Ananel, an obscure priest of the line of Aaron, whom he had summoned from Babylon.

But this selection was regarded with feelings of detestation by Aristobulus, his youthful brother-in-law, his wife Mariamne, and her mother-in-law, Alexandra. Well acquainted with Cleopatra, queen of Egypt, at whose court Antonius was now living in luxury and indolence, Alexandra began to address her complaints to her, and succeeded in awakening an interest in her favour. The secret correspondence coming to the ears of Herod, he forthwith deposed Ananel, and with great pomp installed Aristobulus in his stead. The people were delighted at his elevation, and when the handsome youth the descendant of their ancient princes appeared before them at the feast of Tabernacles B.C. 35, clad in the gorgeous robes of his office, they could not restrain the expression of their admiration, and their shouts of acclamation rent the air.

This sealed the doom of the unfortunate young man. Seeing in him a possible rival, and suspecting the designs of Alexandra, Herod resolved to compass his destruction, and an opportunity soon presented itself. At the close of the solemnities he repaired with the youthful high-priest to Jericho, where Alexandra had invited them to an entertainment. The day was close—sultry, even for that tropical region—and the two, with many of their retinue, betook themselves to the fish-ponds, for the purpose of bathing. At first the attendants alone plunged into the water, and Herod and the high-priest merely looked on. But as it grew dark, the king proposed that his companion should join the rest in the water, where several of the attendants, suborned for the purpose, plunged him under the water, and held him down till life was extinct[1]. Next day it was announced at Jerusalem that Aristobulus had been accidentally drowned, and the spectacle of the dead body excited the wildest sorrow. Herod himself pretended the utmost grief. But neither the tears he shed, nor the magnificent funeral with which he honoured the young man's remains, could divert the popular suspicion and indignation. Least of all could he deceive the bereaved mother. The grief of Alexandra was intense, and more than once she was on the point of laying violent hands upon herself. At length she resolved to appeal for the second time to the friendship of Cleopatra, and wrote her a full account of the treacherous deed. The Egyptian queen, herself a woman and a mother, moved by her touching story, would not let Antonius have any rest till he had promised that the matter should be investigated.

On his arrival, therefore, at the Syrian Laodicea[2]
B.C. 34, the triumvir sent to Herod, and demanded an explanation of the death of Aristobulus. Though Herod was well aware of the ill-will of Cleopatra towards himself, and of the risk he ran, he dared not disobey this summons, and resolved to go in person and plead his cause. Before setting out he entrusted to his uncle Joseph not only the government of Jerusalem, but the care also of the beautiful Mariamne, strictly enjoining him, in the event of his own death, to slay her rather than let her fall into the hands of Antonius. Having thus provided for the worst he departed, and, on his arrival at Laodicea, presented himself before the Roman and his

[1] Jos. *Ant.* xv. 3. 4. [2] Jos. *Ant.* xv. 3. 5.

Egyptian enchantress. Cleopatra, eager to add Judæa to her dominions, exhausted every expedient to ensure his ruin. But by his confidence, and still more by his lavish bribes, Herod succeeded in defeating her designs, and in clearing himself in the opinion of her paramour, so that Antonius not merely dismissed the charges against his favourite, but placed him by his side on his judicial throne, invited him to his luxurious banquets, and heaped upon him every mark of distinction.

Meanwhile very different events had occurred at Jerusalem. In an evil hour Joseph had revealed his secret instructions respecting Mariamne, and while she and Alexandra were indulging in transports of rage, a sudden rumour reached the city that Herod had failed in his mission, and been put to death. Instantly both mother and daughter took measures for seizing the supreme power, and Alexandra indulged the hope that the glorious beauty of her daughter might win the affections even of the paramour of Cleopatra. But in a moment all these schemes were dashed to the ground. Letters arrived announcing Herod's complete success, and soon he himself appeared. His sister Salome, jealous of the charms of Mariamne, filled his mind with suspicions against her, which at first he refused to credit. But unhappily one day, as he was protesting his undying love, she chanced to inquire how, if he really loved her, he could have given the order for her execution. Furious at the discovery of his secret compact, he rushed from her arms, and was on the point of putting her to death with his own hand. Her loveliness, however, induced him to spare her, and he contented himself with ordering the instant execution of his uncle Joseph, and flinging Alexandra into prison with every mark of insult.

CHAPTER IV

HEROD, KING OF JUDÆA.

B. C. 34—24.

MEANWHILE the friendship between Octavius and Antonius had at length been broken, and the whole East rang with preparations for the coming contest between the triumvirs for the supremacy of the world. Herod raised a body of troops to assist Antonius, but the latter declined his aid, and being thus excused taking any prominent part in a doubtful struggle, he turned his arms against Malchus, king of Arabia. The artful designs of Cleopatra had involved him in this war. Already mistress of Cœlesyria, and of the palm-groves around Jericho by the concessions of her Roman lover, she cast longing eyes upon Judæa also. The Arabian king, emboldened by the rupture between the Roman triumvirs, had withheld the payment to her of his annual tribute, an insult which Antonius directed Herod to avenge. Seeing her opportunity, she urged Herod to embark in the war, hoping if he was successful to become mistress of Arabia, if unsuccessful, of Judæa.

But the Jews were exceedingly unwilling to undertake a war against a nation with whom they had no quarrel, and Herod was defeated in the first campaign with great loss. His troops were still more unwilling to engage a second time, but fortune came to his aid. A sudden earthquake convulsed the cities of southern Palestine, and destroyed in one day upwards of 30,000 of the inhabitants. Taking advantage of the consternation thus caused, the Arabs slew the Jewish ambassadors who had come to treat of peace. News of this treachery roused once more the martial spirit of the nation, and enabled Herod to win a signal triumph over his foes, and to reduce the country to subjection.

On his return from this expedition he received intelligence that his patron Antonius had been defeated in the decisive battle of Actium, B.C. 31, and had left the supremacy of the world to his rival Octavius. His first impulse was to urge the triumvir to seize Egypt, and put to death Cleopatra, the faithless cause of his misfortunes. But the infatuated Roman, rejecting this advice, followed his enchantress to Alexandria. There twelve months afterwards, deserted by his troops, and unable to come to any terms with Octavius, he fell upon his sword, and Cleopatra, rather than grace a Roman triumph, applied the fatal asp to her breast.

Herod's fate once more seemed to tremble in the balance. But, equal to the emergency, he provided with characteristic energy and boldness an escape from his embarrassments. He first resolved to put Hyrcanus out of the way, as the last remnant of the Asmonean dynasty, and on a charge of a treasonable correspondence with the king of Arabia, dragged him before the Sanhedrin, and caused him to be executed. He next resolved to make a personal appeal to Octavius, and before he left sent his mother, sister, and children to Masada, and placed Mariamne in the fortress of Alexandrium, under the custody of faithful adherents, Soemus the Ituræan, and Joseph his steward, again enjoining that, in the event of his death, Mariamne should be instantly dispatched.

Then setting out for Rhodes he appeared before Octavius without the diadem, but with all the spirit and dignity of a king, and addressed him in a speech of the utmost freedom[1]. He did not in the least disguise his friendship for the late triumvir. He had given him, he said, the best advice in urging him to put Cleopatra to death, and prosecute the war with vigour. But Antonius had rejected his counsels, and pursued a course ruinous to himself and beneficial only to his rival. If Octavius, seeing the steadiness of the speaker's friendship towards

[1] Jos. *Ant.* XV. 6. 6; *B J.* I. 20. I.

his late foe, would honour him with his confidence, he might count on being served with the same steadiness and the same fidelity. His frankness completely won over the arbiter of the world, who restored to him the diadem, treated him with the greatest distinction, and assured him of his friendship and confidence[1].

Thus successful beyond his utmost expectations, Herod returned to Jerusalem. But the secret orders entrusted to the guardian of Mariamne had been again disclosed, and she met his greeting with coldness and aversion, and reproached him bitterly with the murder of her grandfather Hyrcanus. Herod's anger was deeply roused, but for the present other and more public duties demanded his attention. Bent on the invasion and conquest of Egypt, Octavius passed through Syria and arrived at Ptolemais. Thither Herod went to meet him, presented him with 800 talents, and supplied provisions in great abundance for his troops. This still further conciliated the Roman's favour, and on his return from Egypt, where the suicide of Antony and Cleopatra removed all obstructions to the reduction of the country to a Roman province, he not only conferred upon him the territory around Jericho, which had been ceded to the late Egyptian queen, but reannexed to his dominions the cities of Gadara, Hippo, and Samaria, together with the maritime towns Gaza, Joppa, and Strato's Tower[2], B.C. 30.

But these successes did little towards compensating the Jewish king for the loss of the affections of Mariamne, who persisted in rejecting his caresses, and reproaching him with his cruelty towards her family. At this juncture the envious Salome suborned the royal cupbearer to accuse the queen of having bribed him to poison his master. This new accusation filled Herod

[1] Jos. *B. J.* I. 20; Merivale, III. 356.

[2] He at the same time bestowed upon him the 400 Gauls, who had formed the bodyguard of Cleopatra. Jos. *Ant.* XV. 7. 3; *B. J.* I. 20. 3.

with such rage that he ordered Mariamne's favourite eunuch to be put to the rack. The wretched man denied all knowledge of the plot, but confessed that the secret orders given to Soemus had excited the queen's hatred and disgust. Furious at what he deemed a second proof of her infidelity, Herod directed that Soemus should be instantly executed, and arraigned Mariamne before a tribunal of judges on a charge of adultery. The judges, too terrified to do any thing but obey his bidding, pronounced her guilty, and sentenced her to death. But though he had procured her condemnation, the tyrant shrunk from proceeding to her execution. His mother and sister, however, suffered him to have no rest, and so worked upon his feelings that at length he signed the fatal order for her execution, and Mariamne was led forth to die, B.C. 29.

But now a reaction set in. The terrible reality of the deed, combined with a sense of his own loss, so wrought upon his feelings, that he became the victim of the most violent remorse. "Everywhere, day and night, he was haunted by the image of the murdered queen; he called upon her by name; he perpetually burst into passionate tears; he ordered his servants to bring Mariamne to him, as though she were yet alive. In vain he tried every diversion,—banquets, revels, the excitements of society. A sudden pestilence breaking out, to which many of the noblest of his court and of his own personal friends fell a sacrifice, he recognised and trembled beneath the hand of the avenging Deity. On pretence of hunting he sought out the most melancholy solitude, till the disorder of his mind brought on a disorder of body, and he was seized with violent inflammation and pains in the back of his head, which led to temporary derangement[1]."

[1] Milman's *Hist. of the Jews*, II. 70; Jos. *Ant.* XV. 7. 7; Merivale, III. 386.

After lying in this state for some time in his palace at Samaria, he was at length partially restored to health, and came forth gloomy, stern, revengeful, more ready than ever to resort to cruelty and bloodshed. Alexandra was his first victim. Taking advantage of his malady she had again renewed her intrigues, and tried to gain possession of Jerusalem. She was now executed, together with Costobaras, governor of Idumæa and Gaza and husband of Salome, who was accused of harbouring some of the Asmonean dynasty, with many others of rank and influence[1].

Meanwhile, B.C. 27[2], the senate of Rome had conferred upon Octavius the title of *Augustus*, the *august*, the *divine*, and soon in every part of the empire temples began to rise in honour of the divinity of the Emperor. Herod resolved not to be behindhand in adulation towards his patron, and, all being now dead who had any claims to the crown, he devoted himself to the introduction of foreign customs into the country. Though fully aware of the intensely national feelings of his subjects, he resolved to lose no opportunity of breaking down the wall of partition between them and the surrounding nations.

He introduced, therefore, public exhibitions and spectacles of all kinds; erected a theatre within, an amphitheatre without, the walls of Jerusalem; instituted quinquennial games, which were celebrated on a scale of the most lavish magnificence; invited to his capital the professors of every kind of gymnastic exercises, and did not even shrink from exhibiting in the city of David shows of gladiators and combats with wild beasts.

The stricter Jews regarded with horror those inno-

[1] Jos. *Ant.* XV. 7. 9. 10.

[2] Jan. 13, A.U.C. 727, B.C. 27. Dion LIII. 16; Liv. *Epit.* 134; Merivale's *Romans under the Empire*, III. 417.

vations, but their indignation knew no bounds when, for the purpose of celebrating the victories of Octavius, he set up in his theatre complete suits of armour captured during the imperial wars. Nothing could persuade them to believe that these trophies did not conceal heathen images, and it was only when they had been taken to pieces, and the bare peg of wood exposed underneath, that their suspicions were removed. This raised a laugh, but the deepfelt exasperation of the majority was not removed. At length ten men formed a conspiracy to assassinate the king as he entered the theatre. The plot was betrayed, and they were put to death with the most cruel tortures. The people, sympathising with their sufferings, seized the informer who had betrayed the secret to Herod, tore him to pieces, and flung his flesh to the dogs. This roused the king in his turn to retaliate, and seizing the ringleaders he put them to death, together with their families, B.C. 25.

These risings, however, convinced him that his life was insecure, and he had recourse to various measures of precaution. He erected a palace on the impregnable hill of Sion; restored and enlarged the Baris, and named it Antonia, after his former patron. At the same time he rebuilt and founded various cities to serve as military ports and retreats on occasions of danger, such as Gaba in Galilee, and Heshbon in Peræa. Samaria also, which had been destroyed by John Hyrcanus, once more rose from its ruins, was surrounded with a wall, strongly fortified, and peopled with 6000 veterans devoted to the king's interests. A temple also was erected within it, dedicated to the occupant of the imperial throne, in whose honour the city also was now called Sebaste, *the August*[1].

But Herod[2] further resolved that his kingdom should

[1] Jos. *Ant.* XV. 8. 5; *B. J.* I. 21. 2.

[2] In B.C. 22 he contracted another marriage, and united

have a naval harbour and a maritime city, whereby he might communicate more securely with the western world. A convenient point along the inhospitable coast-line of Palestine offered itself at a spot called Strato's Tower, situated about 30 miles south of Mount Carmel, and 70 miles north-west of Jerusalem, on the line of the great road from Tyre to Egypt. To protect the shipping from the violent south-west winds, which blew along the coast, it was first necessary that a breakwater should be constructed. Accordingly enormous stones were sunk in deep water to form a mole 2000 feet in length. This supported a pier, 200 feet wide, defended by a wall and towers, and formed a sort of double harbour equal in size to the Piræus at Athens, and surrounded with broad landing wharves. The entrance was from the north, so that a vast fleet could ride at anchor with perfect safety. Above the harbour rose the city, built on the Greek model with a forum and amphitheatre, and called, in honour of the king's friend on the imperial throne, Cæsarea. Upwards of 12 years were spent in the erection of this important maritime city[1].

himself with a second Mariamne, the daughter of one Simon, an obscure priest of Jerusalem, whom he raised to the dignity of high-priest, after deposing Joshua, the son of Phaneus. thus again throwing discredit on an office which he persisted in depriving of all political weight and influence.

[1] The full name was Cæsarea Sebaste, Jos. *Ant.* XVI. 5. 1, but it was sometimes called Cæsarea Stratonis, or Cæsarea Palestinæ, or the "City by the Sea," Jos. *B. J.* III. 9; VII. 1. 3. Its modern name is *Kaisariyeh.* It became the official residence of the Herodian kings, as also of Festus, Felix, and other Roman procurators. Tacitus calls it "the head of Judæa," *Hist.* II. 79. In the centre of the city rose a vast temple, conspicuous from the sea, dedicated to Octavius, and adorned with two colossal statues, one of the Emperor, the other of the Imperial city. The foundations were laid in B.C. 21, and the work was completed in B.C. 10. Jos. *Ant.* XV. 9. 6; Lewin's *Fasti Sacri*, p. 89.

CHAPTER V

HEROD, KING OF JUDÆA.

B.C. 24–14.

THUS Judæa seemed to be sinking more and more into the form of a Roman province, while Herod rivalled the other vassal kings of Rome in subservience to the master of the world. It was a saying that Cæsar assigned to him the next place in his favour to Agrippa, while Agrippa esteemed Herod higher than all his friends, except Augustus[1]. The three vied with one another in mutual courtesies, and whenever either Cæsar or Agrippa visited the Eastern provinces, the Jewish king was sure to be first to pay his homage, and to assist with his personal support and advice.

In return for these attentions the Roman emperor was profuse in his concessions. When Herod sent his two elder sons by Mariamne, Alexander and Aristobulus, to Rome for their education, he received them into his palace and treated them with the utmost care and distinction[2]. Moreover, besides the large addition he had already made to Herod's territories, he now conceded to him the district east of the Lake of Gennesaret, known as Trachonitis, with Batanæa and Auranitis, and afterwards appointed him procurator of the province of Syria, and with such authority, that his colleagues in command could take no step without his concurrence[3]. At the same time a tetrarchy was conferred on his brother Pheroras, and in memory of these concessions, Herod

[1] Jos. *B. J.* I. 20. 4. [2] Jos. *Ant.* XV. 10. 1.
[3] Jos. *Ant.* XV. 10. 3; *B. J.* I. 20. 4.

erected a splendid temple of white marble at Paneas, near the sources of the Jordan, and dedicated it to his benefactor[1].

But while the Jewish king was on terms of such intimate friendship with his imperial patron, his relations with his own subjects were far from satisfactory. In spite of the profuse liberality with which he had poured forth the contents of his treasury, and even parted with the silver plate of his table to satisfy their wants during a severe famine, B.C. 25, in spite also of his munificence in diminishing a third of the annual taxation, the murmurs of the populace against his rule could not be restrained.

Strong as was the party which favoured his designs and approved his policy, the majority of the nation regarded with undissembled suspicion and mistrust his numerous innovations, and the introduction of foreign rites and customs. In vain he forbade any assemblages of the citizens for feasting or deliberation; in vain he kept himself informed through his spies of all who disapproved of his government, threw them into prison, and sometimes punished them with death; in vain he tried to compel all his subjects to take an oath of fidelity towards himself and his dynasty; he could not control the opposition of the powerful Pharisaic faction[2], or check the general feeling of disaffection.

At length, B.C. 20, he determined on a measure which he trusted might have the effect at once of giving employment to large numbers, and winning the favour of the nation. He resolved to rebuild the Temple.

Since the construction of the second Temple by Zorobabel that structure had suffered much from dilapidation, and bore unmistakeable traces of the assaults of various armies. The evident need, therefore, of renewal,

[1] Jos. *B. J.* I. 21. 3. [2] Jos. *Ant.* XV. 10. 4.

induced the king to hope that no obstacle would be put in the way of his design. But on laying his project before the assembled people, he found that it was regarded with little favour and greater suspicion[1]. Under pretence of rebuilding, many believed he really intended to destroy their national sanctuary.

Great caution was therefore needed, and everything was done that could be devised to allay the popular mistrust. Vast preparations were made before a single stone of the old building was removed, and two years were spent in bringing together all the materials; 1000 waggons were constructed for the purpose of bearing stones for the building, and upwards of 10,000 of the most skilful workmen, superintended by 1000 Levites, who had been taught the arts of carpentry and stone-cutting, were employed on the works[2].

In the 20th year of Herod's reign, or B.C. 18, the erection of the new structure began. The foundations of the Temple of Zorobabel were removed, and on those laid by Solomon the new pile arose, built of hard white stones of enormous size. The Porch, Holy Place, and Holy of Holies, were completed in a year and a half[3]; the rest of the pile, with the courts and cloisters, in eight years more, so as to be fit for the actual services of religion, but the whole structure was not finally completed[4] till A.D. 65[5].

On the highest level of the rocky platform stood the

[1] Jos. *Ant.* XV. 11. 2.
[2] Jos. *Ant.* XV. 11. 2.
[3] Jos. *Ant.* XV. 11. 6.
[4] Jos. *Ant.* XX. 9. 7.
[5] For the maintenance of the service the half-shekel claimed by the Law (Ex. xxx. 13) from every male Israelite above twenty years old was religiously executed. This is the tribute-money mentioned Matt. xvii. 24, under the name *τὰ δίδραχμα*, and according to Josephus, was collected from all Jews even in foreign countries, their foreign coins being exchanged by the *κολλυβισταί* for the half-shekels of the temple-money (Matt. xxi. 12; Mk. xi. 15; Jn. ii. 15).

Temple itself, divided as in the days of Solomon, and covered with plates of gold, which shone like a meteor under the rays of the sun, so that the eye could hardly bear to rest upon them. Twelve steps below was a second level, occupied by the *Court of the Priests*, with the Great Laver, and the Altar of Burnt-offering. Three flights of steps below this was the *Court of the Israelites*, with the houses of the priests, the various offices, and hall of the Sanhedrin. Fourteen steps more led down to the *Court of the Gentiles*, which was hardly regarded as a part of the Temple, and was open to men of all nations and became a kind of exchange and market-place.

While the Sanctuary had been left to the care of the priests, Herod exhausted all his taste on this Court of the Gentiles. "Cloisters ran round the wall on the inner side, sustained on rows of columns exquisitely wrought, the capitals being ornamented with the acanthus and waterleaf, as in the famous Tower of the Winds. West, north, and east these columns were in three rows; on the south they were in four. The floor made a shaded walk, like the colonnade in Venice, and the roof an open walk like the gallery of Genoa. The pavement was inlaid with marbles of many colours. Leading into this Court from the city and the country were many noble gates; one of these on the Eastern side, facing the Mount of Olives, was called *Solomon's Porch*, and a second near by it was called the *Beautiful Gate*[1]."

Immediately after the completion of the Sanctuary, which was commemorated with lavish sacrifices and splendid feasts[2], Herod set out for Rome, to bring back his sons Alexander and Aristobulus. On his arrival

[1] Dixon's *Holy Land*, II. 47, 48; Raphall's *History of the Jews*, II. 335—337; Milman, II. 77.

[2] Jos. *Ant.* xv. 11. 6.

in the imperial city[1], he was received by Augustus with every mark of regard, and returned with his two sons apparently in the spring of the year B.C. 15. During the autumn his friend Agrippa visited Judæa[2], and Herod shewed him his new cities, Sebaste and Cæsarea, and the fortresses of Alexandrium, Herodium, and Hyrcania. Then conducting him to Jerusalem, he entertained him at a sumptuous banquet, while the people welcomed the great minister of Augustus with acclamations, and Agrippa offered a sacrifice of 100 oxen in the Temple, and feasted the subjects of the Jewish king at a splendid entertainment.

CHAPTER VI

HEROD, KING OF JUDÆA.

B. C. 15—4.

BUT the return of the young princes, Alexander and Aristobulus, from Rome was the signal for a scene of bloodshed, still more awful than that which had darkened the beginning of Herod's reign.

The monarch married them, Alexander to Glaphyra, daughter of Archelaus, king of Cappadocia; Aristobulus to Berenice, the daughter of his sister Salome[3]. The grace and beauty of the young men, added to their descent through their mother from the great Asmonean house, made them objects of the utmost interest to the people, and they were regarded as the future rulers of Palestine.

The popular favour, however, which they thus at-

[1] On the way he gave proof of his ardent zeal for Grecian customs, stopping at Elis to witness the Olympic games, and settling an annual revenue on the inhabitants. Jos. *B. J.* I. 21. 12.

[2] Jos. *Ant.* XVI. 2. 1.

[3] Jos. *Ant.* XVI. 1. 2.

tracted, aroused the keenest hatred of Salome and Pheroras. Conscious of the part they had played in the execution of Mariamne, they looked with dismay at the future elevation of the young princes. Taking advantage, therefore, of some incautious expressions they chanced to let fall respecting the execution of their mother, they began by circulating rumours that the young men were bent on avenging their mother's death, and bore no goodwill towards the king. For some time Herod refused even to listen to these rumours. But before long they acquired fresh strength and consistency, and to check their pride, he sent for Antipater, the son of his first wife Doris, and set him up as a foil to the aspirations and popularity of Alexander and Aristobulus[1].

Salome had thus a ready tool for prosecuting her cunning designs, and as Herod had permission from Augustus to appoint whom he pleased as his successor, the two together bent all their efforts towards alienating him from the sons of Mariamne.

In the beginning of B.C. 13, the king went to join Agrippa at Sinope, and attended him through Paphlagonia, Cappadocia, Phrygia, and Ionia, to Ephesus. On this occasion he introduced Antipater to his powerful friend, and sent him in his train on a visit to Rome, with many costly presents and an introduction to Augustus. Even at Rome the crafty Idumæan did not remit his machinations against his rivals, but in every letter to his father dropped something to the discredit of the sons of Mariamne, veiling his real designs under pretence of great anxiety for Herod's security.

By these artful means the suspicions of the king were at length raised to such a pitch, that he resolved on formally accusing his sons before the tribunal of Augustus. Accordingly, B.C. 11, he conducted them to

[1] Jos. *Ant.* XVI. 3. 3; *B. J.* I. 23. 1.

Rome, and in the presence of the emperor charged them with designs upon his life. Augustus perceived that the accusation rested only on hearsay and suspicion, and after hearing the case succeeded in reconciling the young men to their father, and the three, accompanied by Antipater, returned to Jerusalem apparently on terms of amity and goodwill.

On regaining his capital, Herod convened an assembly of the people, introduced to them his three sons, and formally announced his design that they should succeed him in the order of their birth, first Antipater, then Alexander, and lastly Aristobulus[1]. But this arrangement was satisfactory to no one. The sons of Mariamne were indignant that the right of primogeniture should have been confined to Antipater, while Antipater was indignant that they should obtain honours even second to his own[2].

While the jealousies in the royal household were thus for a short time hushed, the building of the new and magnificent city of Cæsarea was completed, B.C. 10. This event was celebrated with an imposing ceremonial, with shows, games, exhibitions of gladiators, and sumptuous entertainments, to which the wife of Cæsar herself contributed largely[3]. Other cities now arose in honour of different members of Herod's family. Antipatris[4], between Cæsarea and Lydda, preserved the name of his father *Antipater;* Cypron, near Jericho, of his mother *Cyprus;* Phasaelis, in the plain near the same city, of his brother *Phasael.*

But soon the quarrels in the royal household broke

[1] Jos. *Ant.* XVI. 4. 6; Comp. *Ant.* XV. 9. 6.
[2] Jos. *B. J.* I. 24. 1.
[3] Jos. *Ant.* XVI. 5. 1.
[4] Built on the site of the more ancient town of *Caphar Saba,* sixteen Roman miles from Joppa, and twenty-six from Cæsarea. The old name lingers under the modern form *Kefr-Saba.*

out afresh. With a strange lack of caution, the sons of Mariamne again indulged their dissatisfaction by the use of intemperate language, which the artful Antipater managed to report to Herod, exaggerated or distorted, as best suited his purpose. Knowing not whom to trust, the king had no rest night or day. At length he ordered some of the confidential slaves of the young princes to be put to the torture, and they, to obtain relief from their agony, made false declarations respecting Alexander, who was immediately flung into prison and loaded with chains.

There the wretched young man had recourse to a strange expedient. He sent four papers to his father, in which he accused himself of all kinds of treasonable practices, but added that Pheroras, Salome, and several of the king's most intimate friends, were his accomplices. The whole court was now a scene of suspicion and distrust. Herod knew not which way to look or whom to believe. In a state of phrenzy he day after day caused persons of all grades to be apprehended; some of these he executed; others he tortured to compel them to confess, and with such severity that several of them died under the hands of their tormentors. In the midst of these troubles, Archelaus, king of Cappadocia, and father-in-law of Alexander, arrived at Jerusalem, and succeeded in obtaining his release, and restoration to Herod's favour.

But the lull was only temporary. A few months had barely elapsed before Salome and Pheroras, regaining all their old ascendancy, poisoned the king's mind with suspicions. Unable to trust any one around him, Herod once more had recourse to Augustus, and poured forth the bitterest complaints against the sons of Mariamne. In reply, the emperor advised him to summon a council of sovereigns at Berytus[1], with Volumnius and Saturninus

[1] Jos. *Ant.* XVI. 11. 1—6. Berytus was a town of Phœnicia,

the prefects of Syria, and formally arraign the young men before them.

Acting on this advice, Herod thereupon summoned a council of princes. Upwards of 150 met together, and before them he pleaded his own cause, examined witnesses, read documents, and accused his sons with the utmost vehemence. After hearing the charge, Saturninus expressed himself in favour of mercy; Volumnius and the majority for condemnation. For a short time Herod appeared to hesitate, but the malice of Salome eventually had its reward, and the young men were strangled at Sebaste[1], B.C. 6.

But they had scarcely perished before Herod found himself exposed to a far more terrible danger. Pheroras had married a slave, who attached herself to the powerful Pharisaic party. For the second time the king ordered the members of this influential sect to take the oath of allegiance to Augustus and himself. Upwards of 600 positively refused, and were sentenced to pay heavy fines. These the wife of Pheroras instantly liquidated out of her own property, and the Pharisees, grateful for such kindness, began to whisper that God intended the kingdom for her and her husband[2].

Salome announced these signs of dissaffection to Herod, who instantly executed the ringleaders of the Pharisees, and ordered Pheroras to put away his wife. This his brother absolutely declined to do, and retired to his own tetrarchy in Peræa, while the wily Antipater contrived to get himself summoned to Rome.

identified by some with the Berotha, or Berothai of Scripture (2 Sam. viii. 8; Ezek. xlvii. 16). After its destruction by Tryphon B.C. 140, it was reduced by Agrippa, and colonised by the veterans of the V. Macedonica Legio, and VIII. Augusta, and became a Roman colony under the name of *Colonia Julia Augusta Felix Berytus*. See Smith's *Dict. Geog.*, Art. *Berytus*.

[1] Jos. *Ant.* XVI. 11. 7.

[2] Jos. *Ant.* XVII. 2. 4.

Shortly afterwards Pheroras sickening, Herod came to visit him, and on his death gave him a magnificent funeral. He was scarcely buried before rumours of foul play were bruited about. To ascertain their truth, Herod ordered a strict examination of the female slaves of his brother's wife, and under the agonies of torture a horrible secret came to light.

Antipater, for whom Herod had strangled the sons of Mariamne, whom he had designed as his successor, had been associated with Pheroras in a plot against his life, and his brother's widow was in possession of a subtle poison, with which it had been intended to take him off on the first opportunity. Thereupon she was examined, acknowledged her guilt, and immediately after flung herself from the roof of the house. The fall, however, was not fatal, and being brought before Herod, she recounted the whole history of the plot, adding that his kindness to her husband on his deathbed had caused him to relent, and he had bidden her fling the poison into the fire. This she had done, and had reserved only a small portion, which was now produced[1].

Just at this juncture, a freedman of Antipater's arrived from Rome, with letters for the king, accusing Archelaus and Philip of disaffection towards their father. The man was instantly placed upon the rack, and confessed that he had brought another phial of poison, which he was to entrust to Pheroras, in the event of the first not proving successful. The proofs of this dark treachery being thus complete, Herod wrote to Antipater requesting his instant return, and at the same time gave orders that the roads should be strictly guarded, and that not a word should be allowed to drop respecting what had transpired at Jerusalem.

[1] Jos. *Ant.* XVII. 4. 2.

Triumphing in the success of his base intrigues, and confident of his succession to the throne, Antipater had already set out, and arrived at Celenderis in Pamphylia. News of the death of Pheroras had reached him at Tarentum, and excited some misgivings, but, contrary to the advice of many of his friends, he continued his journey and entered the port of Cæsarea.

Here his fears were still more excited. The crowded harbour appeared like a solitude. Not a soul approached to salute or congratulate him on his return. The few who did meet him turned aside, or looked on, as if they now dared to shew the hatred they had long borne towards him. Every one seemed in possession of some dark secret, of which he alone was ignorant[1].

Dissembling, however, his fears, he pressed on, for it was too late to fly, and reaching Jerusalem, hurried to his father's palace. At the gates his retinue was denied entrance, and with Herod he found Quintilius Varus the prefect. Advancing to salute the king, he was angrily repelled, informed of the charge against him, and told that his trial would take place on the morrow before the prefect.

Accordingly, on the next day the accusers appeared. The evidence of his guilt was conclusive. The cup of poison was brought in, and a criminal under sentence of death being ordered to drink it, expired on the spot. Antipater was condemned and placed in bonds, but Herod delayed the execution of the sentence, till the will of Augustus could be ascertained.

By this time the king was 70 years of age, and being seized with a severe illness, removed for the sake of change of air to Jericho, and resolved to make the final alterations in his will. Passing over Archelaus and Philip, whom Antipater had accused of disaffection, he nominated Antipas as his successor in the

[1] Jos. *Ant.* XVII. 5. 1; *B. J.* I. 31. 4.

kingdom, and bestowed rich donations of money and lands upon Salome, and other members of his own family.

But during his absence fresh symptoms of disaffection appeared amongst his subjects. Of all his numerous innovations, none had irritated the Jews more than the placing of a large golden eagle, the emblem of Roman power, over the principal gate of the Temple. Two of the most learned rabbis, Judas and Matthias, resolved to have it removed. Accordingly they instigated some daring and fanatical youths to take down the offensive symbol. Emboldened by a sudden rumour of the death of Herod, the young men lowered themselves by ropes from the roof, and cut away the eagle with hatchets. They could never have hoped to execute so daring a deed with impunity, and being apprehended and brought before Herod, boldly avowed their guilt, and gloried in the success of the feat. Dissembling his auger, the king assembled the chiefs of the nation at Jericho, and reproaching them bitterly for their ingratitude after all the favours he had bestowed upon them, ordered the instigators of the deed to be burned alive[1].

In the meantime his disorder had made rapid progress. A slow fire seemed to consume his vital parts. His appetite became ravenous, but he dared not gratify it on account of dreadful pains and internal ulcers, which preyed on the lower parts of his body. Moreover his breathing became difficult, and violent spasms convulsed his frame, and imparted supernatural strength to his limbs[2]. But in spite of these accumulated sufferings he still clung to life, and cherishing hopes of recovery caused himself to be conveyed across the Jordan to Callirrhoë[3], hoping to obtain relief from its warm bitumin-

[1] Jos. *Ant.* XVII. 6. 2. 3.

[2] Jos. *Ant.* XVII. 6. 5; *B. J.* I. 33. 5.

[3] On the eastern side of the Jordan, and not far from the Dead Sea. Jos. *Ant.* XVII. 6. 5.

ous baths. Arrived there, the physicians advised that he should be fomented with warm oil. For this purpose, he was lowered into a vessel filled with that fluid, when his eyes relaxed, and he suddenly fell back as if dead. Roused, however, by the cries of his physicians, he revived, and was conveyed back to Jericho, where, as if defying death, he devised a new atrocity. Knowing the joy his death would cause, he gave instructions that the men of distinction from every town in Judæa should be assembled in the hippodrome, and secretly confided to Salome his pleasure that they should be butchered immediately upon his decease, that thus his funeral might at least be signalized by a real mourning.

He had scarcely given these orders, when his messengers returned from Rome, and announced the ratification of the sentence against Antipater. Instantly the tyrant's desire for life revived, but being as quickly followed by a sudden racking pain, he called for an apple and a knife, and in an unguarded moment tried to stab himself. He might have succeeded had not an attendant seized his hand. The clamour that followed reached the ears of Antipater, who was in bonds in a neighbouring apartment. Thinking his father was dead, he made a desperate effort to escape by bribing his guards. Informed of this Herod instantly ordered a spearman to dispatch him on the spot. Antipater having thus paid the penalty of his life of treachery, the king once more amended his will, nominated his eldest son Archelaus as his successor to the throne, and appointed Antipas tetrarch of Galilee and Peræa, Herod Philip tetrarch of Auranitis, Trachonitis, and Batanæa, and Salome mistress of Jamnia and some other towns. Five days more of excruciating agony remained to the tyrant, and then he expired[1], after a reign of 34 years.

[1] Probably some day between the 13th March and 4th April A.U.C. 750 = B.C. 4. See Wieseler's *Synopsis*, p. 51.

PART V

RETROSPECT AND REFLECTIONS.

CHAPTER I

DISPERSION OF THE JEWS—RISE OF SYNAGOGUES.

ARRIVED at the threshold of the Gospel History, it may not be amiss to survey some of the more prominent features of the period we have traversed, and to notice some of the changes which it had produced on the Jewish nation.

The influences, under which the Jews had been brought since the Captivity were, as we have seen, of a very varied character. For two centuries after that event, they were subject to the dominion of Persia; for nearly a century and a half they were under Greek rulers; for a century they enjoyed independence under their native Asmonean princes; and for more than half a century, while nominally ruled by the family of Herod, were really in subjection to the power of Rome[1].

In the present Chapter we shall notice,

(a) *The Wide Dispersion of the Jews*, (b) *The Change in their Vernacular Language*, and (c) *The rise of Synagogues.*

(a) *The Wide Dispersion of the Jews.*

About the time of the building of Rome the ten tribes were carried away by the Assyrian monarchs, and

[1] Westcott's *Introduction to the Gospel History*, pp. 47, 48.

130 years after, this event was followed by the removal of their brethren of Judah and Benjamin to Babylon. The influential results of this earliest migration, it has been observed, "may be inferred from the fact, that about the time of the battles of Marathon (B.C. 490) and Salamis (B.C. 480), a Jew was the minister, another Jew the cupbearer, and a Jewess the consort, of a Persian monarch[1]." Once settled under the shadow of the Babylonian and Persian kings, the Jews were very loth to quit the country of their adoption, and comparatively few availed themselves of the permission of Cyrus to return to their native land. The important colony in Babylonia which afterwards exerted a very remarkable influence, threw off shoots which extended to the borders of the Caspian Sea and the confines of China.

Important, however, as were the results of this earliest dispersion, they were exceeded by those which attended the policy of Alexander and his successors. That great conqueror, as we have seen, removed a great number of Jews to his new city of Alexandria[2], and there conferred upon them many and important privileges, setting an example, which Ptolemy Soter and Philadelphus were alike not slow to follow[3]. To such an extent did the Egyptian Jews increase, that Philo estimates them in his time at little less than 1,000,000, and declares that two of the five districts of Alexandria derived their names from them. From Egypt they quickly spread along the coast of Africa to Cyrene (Acts ii. 10), and the towns of the Pentapolis, and inland to the realms of Candace, queen of Ethiopia (Acts viii. 27).

The Seleucidæ, in their turn, were equally anxious to locate colonies of Jews in the cities which they founded. Seleucus Nicator invited them to his new capital at An-

[1] Conybeare and Howson, *Life and Travels of St Paul*, I. 16; Merivale, III. 358.

[2] See above, p. 7.

[3] See above, pp. 8, 9.

tioch[1]; Antiochus the Great removed 2000 Jewish families from Babylon to Lydia and Phrygia[2]. Led on by that love of trade which now began to distinguish them, they soon became numerous in the commercial cities of Western Asia, Ephesus and Pergamus, Miletus and Sardis. The Archipelago furnished a natural bridge whereby to cross over into the countries of Europe and to settle at Philippi (Acts xvi. 12), Berœa (Acts xvii. 10), and Thessalonica (Acts xvii. 1); Athens (Acts xvii. 17); and Corinth (Acts xviii. 4); and the decree of Lucius[3], the consul during the reign of Simon Maccabæus, gives us a vivid idea of the extent to which they spread themselves in every direction, and no less of the power of the Sanhedrin[4] at Jerusalem, to which all Jews, wherever located, were amenable.

[1] See above, p. 10. [2] See above, p. 15.

[3] See above, p. 54. This was probably Lucius Calpurnius Piso, consul in B.C. 139.

[4] The *Sanhedrin*, or supreme court of judicature amongst the Jews, in things spiritual and temporal, consisted of seventy, seventy-one, or seventy-two members, chosen from the chief priests, scribes, elders, and some of the inferior members of the priestly order. Its President, generally but not always the high-priest, was called *Nasi;* the vice-president, *Ab Beth Din*, its place of meeting (βουλή, βουλευτήριον) was the chamber *Gazith* in the temple, where the members sat in a half-moon.

The Jews traced back its origin to the time of Moses (Deut. xvii. 8), but it is only after the return from the Captivity, and especially during the Asmonean era, that we find it first mentioned.

Its decrees were of binding force not only in Palestine, but amongst the extensive colonies of Jews in Egypt, Babylonia, and Asia Minor, and related to the worship of the temple, offences against the state, the levying of war, claims to the prophetical office, and questions appertaining to the high-priest's functions. Ordinary cases came before the *Lesser Sanhedrin*, of which courts there were two at Jerusalem, and one in every town containing more than 120 inhabitants.

The jurisdiction and authority of the Sanhedrin were

At Rome itself they first appeared in the train of captives led up by Pompeius to the Capitol, but their captivity was of no long duration, and under the protection of Julius Cæsar, who reproduced in the West the privileges they had enjoyed under the Ptolemies and Seleucidæ in the East, they quickly multiplied, and not only appropriated a whole quarter in the capital[1], but spread into other towns of Italy. Thus the Nation, whose native land had for centuries been in the centre of the world's power, civilization, and commerce, now, under the superintending Hand of Providence, was scattered everywhere, East and West, North and South, bearing about with them their peculiar customs and institutions, and diffusing a knowledge of the Law and the Prophets.

(b) Corresponding to this wide diffusion of the Elect Nation was the *change which gradually grew up in their vernacular language.*

i. The earliest dispersion in Babylonia produced a change in the older Hebrew of Judæa. The language spoken in the days of David and Solomon was gradually exchanged for the Chaldee or "Syrian tongue." (Comp. 2 K. xviii. 26; Isai. xxxvi. 11; Dan. ii. 4.) And those who returned from the Captivity and settled in Palestine and Syria, used Chaldee Targums or paraphrases for the interpretation of the Old Hebrew Scriptures, and spake kindred Aramæan dialects, and hence were known as the Aramæan Jews.

ii. After the conquests of Alexander, Greek became the language almost of the whole world[2]. It was a Greek

much curtailed, first by Herod, see above, p. 82, and afterwards by the Romans (Comp. Jn. xviii. 31; xix. 6; Jos. *Ant.* XX. 9. 1).

[1] Comp. Hor. *Sat.* I. ix. 69 sq.; Juvenal, III. 296; XIV. 96; Cic. *pro Flacco,* ch. XXVIII.

[2] Merivale's *Romans under the Empire,* III. 369. "We find

speech that Pompeius was reading, preparatory to delivery, when he received his deathblow off the port of Alexandria. It was in Greek that Brutus conversed with his friends on the evening of the battle of Philippi. The mass of the poorer population at Rome were Greek either in descent or speech. The Jews, therefore, dispersed by the Ptolemies and the Seleucidæ over the shores of the Mediterranean, were forced to adopt the Grecian language, and to use the Septuagint translation made at Alexandria, hence their name of *Hellenists*[1], or "Jews of the Grecian speech," which we shall find recurring so often in the Acts of the Apostles.

(c) *The Rise of Synagogues.*

During the captivity, when of course the Temple ritual was suspended, we gather that the devouter Jews were wont to assemble round the prophet Ezekiel and listen to his words and counsel[2] (Ezek. viii. 1; xiv. 1; xxiii. 31). Such meetings Ezra reproduced in Palestine

that at Tyre, at Sidon, and at Ascalon, the Romans published their decrees in the Latin and the Greek idioms; in the Latin, in token of their own supremacy; in the Greek, as the language most generally understood by the conquered people. Ascalon became famous for its Greek writers in philosophy, history, and grammar. Gadara, a city of Greek foundation, is celebrated by Strabo for its contributions to Hellenic science."

[1] The three words for the elect nation used in the New Testament are

i. Ἰουδαῖος = a Jew as regards his nation, in opposition to Ἕλλην, a Gentile;
ii. Ἑβραῖος = a Jew in respect to his language and education, in opposition to Ἑλληνιστής, a Jew of the Grecian speech;
iii. Ἰσραηλίτης = a Jew in respect to his religious privileges, the sacred name. Trench, *N. T. Synonyms.*

[2] Compare with this the assemblies for prayer and worship held by the prophets or their scholars in the kingdom of the Ten Tribes, 2 K. iv. 33.

amongst those who returned from Babylon (Ezra viii. 15; Neh. viii. 2; ix. 1, &c.), and after the Maccabæan period they spread through every town and village, and in course of time gave rise to buildings called *Synagogues*, in which they might be held.

i. These Houses of Meeting varied in size according to the town or village in which they were built[1]. They were usually erected on the highest ground available, and so constructed, that a worshipper, when entering, or kneeling in prayer, might have his face towards Jerusalem. Like the ancient Tabernacle, they were divided into two parts by a hanging veil, behind which, at the upper end or that facing Jerusalem, was the ark containing the Book of the Law. Before this veil were the "chief seats," for which the Pharisees strove so eagerly (Matt. xxiii. 6); a silver lamp always kept burning; and an eight-branched candlestick, only lighted on the greater festivals. About the centre of the building was a raised platform, on which was a desk, where the reader *stood* to read the lesson or *sat down* to teach (Acts xiii. 16; Lk. iv. 20). All round were seats, where the men sat on one side, and the women on the other, separated by a low partition[2].

ii. The chief officers of each synagogue were (*a*) a kind of Chapter or college of elders, presided over by the *ruler of the Synagogue* (Lk. viii. 41, 49; Acts xviii. 8, 17), who superintended the services, and had the power of excommunication[3]; (*b*) the *Sheliach*, or officiating minister, who read the prayers and the Law;

[1] Generally they were erected and maintained by the congregation, but sometimes were built by private individuals: Comp. Lk. vii. 5.

[2] Godwyn's *Moses and Aaron*, p. 71.

[3] The officers of the synagogue exercised a judicial power. And in the building itself could (i) bring an offender to trial (Lk. xii. 11; xxi. 12); and (ii) scourge (Matt. x. 17; Mark xiii. 9; Acts ix. 2).

(*c*) the *Chazzan*, ὑπηρέτης (Lk. iv. 20), a sort of deacon, whose office it was to open the doors, prepare the room for service, maintain order, scourge the condemned; (*d*) ten men called *Batlanim* (men of leisure), who attended the week-day as well as sabbath services, and were at once representatives of the congregation, and collectors of alms[1].

iii. The worship of the Synagogues was on the model of the Temple Services, and at the same hours, the third, sixth, and ninth[2] (Acts iii. 1; x. 3, 9). On entering, the people bowed towards the ark, and took their places in the body of the building; the elders ranged themselves on the raised platform; the rich went up to the "chief seats" near the ark. A prayer was said, and a psalm was sung. Then the *Chazzan* walked towards the veil, drew it aside with reverence, took out the Book of the Law from the ark; and as he carried it to the platform, on which the *Sheliach* stood, every one pressed forward to kiss or touch it with his hand.

Taking the roll, the *Sheliach* rose, and commenced reading a portion according to a fixed cycle, the interpreter rendering the sacred verses from the Hebrew into the vulgar tongue[3]. The writings of the Prophets formed a second lesson, and were also read according to a fixed order. Then followed the delivery by one of the Elders sitting, of the *word of exhortation* (Lk. iv.; Acts xiii. 15), at the close of which the roll of the Law was carried back towards the ark, while as before, men and women stretched out their hands and tried to touch or kiss it. The Law replaced in the ark, the

[1] Smith's *Bibl. Dict.*, Art. *Synagogue*.

[2] The service was held on Sabbaths and feast-days, later on the Mondays and Thursdays also.

[3] This would be the case at least in the Palestine synagogues.

Prayers began and were carried on till the close of the service.

Such were the Synagogues, one of which was at this time to be found in every town, and almost in every village throughout Palestine, as also in every city in Syria, Asia Minor, and Greece, where was a Jewish settlement. In Jerusalem itself there are said to have been upwards of 480[1], some of which were built specially for the use of the foreign Jews of Cilicia, Alexandria, and other countries, resident in or visiting the capital. Comp. Acts vi. 9. Where the Jews did not exist in sufficient numbers to found or fill a synagogue, a Proseucha[2] or 'Place of Prayer' was built, sometimes open, sometimes covered in, usually outside towns and near running water, for the ablutions before prayer (Acts xvi. 13).

It is easy to see how the synagogues thus scattered through wellnigh every town or city in the countries bordering on the Mediterranean, and in which not "Moses" only but "the Prophets" *were read every sabbath-day* (Acts xv. 21), tended to keep alive Israel's hopes of the Advent of the Messiah, and to diffuse the expectation of the kingdom of Heaven.

CHAPTER II

THE JEWISH SECTS.

HAVING considered in the previous Chapter the wide dispersion of the Jewish nation, the change in their language, and the general adoption of synagogue worship, we shall now proceed to notice the rise of various sects among the Jews themselves.

(i) Of these sects the most important were (*a*) THE SADDUCEES, (*b*) THE PHARISEES, (*c*) THE ESSENES, (*d*) THE HERODIANS.

[1] Godwyn's *Moses and Aaron*, pp. 69—73; Conybeare and Howson, I. 59.

[2] Comp. Juv. III. 296, *in quâ te quæro proseuchâ?*

(*a*) *The Sadducees.*

It has been already observed that the long-continued subjection of the Jews to Grecian monarchs exerted a very marked influence on their habits and modes of life. Familiar not only with the language but the literature and philosophy of Greece, many acquired a strong taste for Grecian studies, preferred the Grecian religion to their own, adopted Grecian manners, and practised Grecian arts[1]. We have seen from time to time how it became the fashion even for many amongst the highest families to adopt Grecian names, and to recommend themselves in every conceivable way to Grecian rulers in the courts of Alexandria and Antioch. The Law, with its restraints and strict requirements, was regarded by them as a heavy yoke, and they affected the gymnasia, the theatres, and all the worldly pleasures of Grecian life.

To such aspirants after freedom the principles of the Epicurean philosophy would naturally recommend themselves, the more so as they found special acceptance in the Syrian courts. Amongst the scholars of Simon the Just[2] was Antigonus of Socho, the first of the Jewish doctors who bears a Greek name. Antigonus was the master of one Sadoc[3] (B.C. 291—260), the essence of whose teaching was that virtue is its own reward, that men ought not to serve the Lord for the sake of gain, but to do good because it is right.

True as this doctrine was in itself, it was perverted by the disciples of Sadoc, who first attract our attention under the name of *Sadducees*[4], in the time of Jonathan the Asmonean[5]. While on the one hand

[1] See above, p. 20. Comp. Merivale, III. 370.

[2] See above, p. 9.

[3] See Raphall's *History of the Jews*, Vol. I. pp. 160, 162.

[4] Others, however, derive their name from Tsadikim, 'the righteous,' but its origin appears uncertain.

[5] See above, p. 60.

especially after the Maccabæan period, they were far removed from any actual adoption of Grecian customs, or apostasy from the national faith, yet on the other, they betrayed evident marks of the influence on their opinions of Grecian philosophy.

Hence they denied the doctrine of the Resurrection[1] (Mtt. xxii. 23; Lk. xx. 27), any rewards or punishments after death, and the existence of angels or spirits (Acts xxiii. 8). Holding that the actions of men depended entirely on their own free will, they denied that there was such a thing as destiny, and while they admitted the creation, they removed the Deity as far as possible from any actual administration of the world. It has been thought that they recognised as Scripture only the five books of Moses, but the truth appears to be that while holding the Law in higher estimation than the prophetical and other books of Scripture, they acknowledged the authority of the Old Testament like the rest of the Jews, but refused to hold the authority of tradition.

Aiming as they did at a philosophic elevation of sentiment they found little favour with the common people, and caring little about making proselytes numbered their followers chiefly among the rich and powerful[2], and especially the young men of Judæa, and those who were in a position to live a life of ease and worldly enjoyment[3].

(b) *The Pharisees.*

The tendency to adopt Grecian customs and modes of thought above alluded to was not, of course, shared by the entire nation. When Mattathias unfurled the

[1] Jos. *Ant.* XVIII. I. 4.

[2] Jos. *Ant.* XIII. 10. 6; XVIII. I. 4.

[3] The later sect of the Karaites, or *Karæans*, 'Scripturists,' succeeded to the Sadducees, but chiefly in respect of the rejection of tradition. and their strict adherence to the letter of the law.

banner of revolt against the heathenizing policy of Antiochus Epiphanes, it will be remembered that he was joined before long by a class calling themselves *Assideans*[1] (1 Macc. ii. 42), who seem to have been already in existence as a distinct party, and bound by a vow to the strict observance of the Law. The name they assumed sufficiently indicates their views. Living in times when their countrymen were becoming more and more infected with heathen customs, they protested against such declension from the spirit of the law, and in opposition to *the impious* (1 Macc. iii. 8; vi. 21; vii. 5), *the lawless* (1 Macc. iii. 6; ix. 23), *the transgressors* (1 Macc. i. 11), as they called the Hellenizing faction, adopted for themselves the title of the Assideans, *the pious*, and in these days of *mixing* (2 Macc. xiv. 3, 38) maintained the strictest observance of the Law[2].

Amongst a nation, which prided itself on its distinction from all other people on the earth, such a party would naturally have great influence, and when the Maccabees triumphed over their Syrian tyrants, the tenets of the Assideans rapidly gained ground, and received their complete development in those of the *Pharisees*, from *Perashin*, to separate, *the Separatists*, who are also first distinctly mentioned during the time of the high-priest Jonathan, B.C. 145[3].

Like their earlier prototypes, the Pharisees were distinguished by great zeal for the Mosaic Law and the whole Canon of Scripture. But in their rigorous

[1] See above, p. 30.

[2] The *Scribes* (γραμματεῖς) are often mentioned in the Gospels in connection with the Pharisees and elders. Originally they appear to have been employed in transcribing the Jewish Scriptures, but subsequently became interpreters of the Law and teachers of the people. The majority of them probably belonged to the sect of the Pharisees, but not all, see Acts xxiii. 9.

[3] Jos. *Ant.* XIII. 5. 9, and see above, p. 60.

interpretation of its precepts and doctrines, they were mainly guided by Oral Tradition, *the traditions of the Elders* (Mtt. xv. 2; Mk. vii. 3). This Oral Tradition, which was regarded as supplementary to the written Law, was said to have been received by Moses on Sinai, to have been delivered by him to Joshua, by Joshua to the elders, by the elders to the prophets, by the prophets to the men of the Great Synagogue.

Of this Law the Pharisees were regarded as the highest interpreters, and presided over various schools, the principal of which in the time of the New Testament, were those of Hillel and Shammai, the former a moderate, the latter the strictest sect.

They held, (i) the existence of angels and spirits, good and bad; (ii) the immortality of the soul; (iii) a state of rewards and punishments after death; (iv) a resurrection of the just and unjust[1] (Comp. Acts xxiii. 8). As exponents of the Law, (i) they attached an undue importance to the outward act as compared with the inward spirit and motive; (ii) they were rigorous in exacting every external ceremonial, especially in reference to washings, fastings, tithes and alms; and (iii) were noted for pride and austerity.

Their political influence we have already seen was very great[2]. Holding strongly that the nation ought to be independent of foreign rule, standing high in favour with the people, and especially with the women[3], pervading the entire country and forming the majority in the Sanhedrin, they wielded a very considerable power in the state, against which we have seen Hyrcanus, and Jannæus, vainly struggling[4], and which Herod, with all his energy, was unable to control.

[1] Jos. *Ant.* XVIII. I. 3.
[2] Jos. *Ant.* XIII. 10. 5; *B. J.* I. 5. 2, 3.
[3] Comp. above, p. 63, and Luke xi. 43.
[4] See above, pp. 60, 62.

The writings of the New Testament illustrate, amongst many others, the following features of their character as a sect: *their high repute*, Jn. vii. 48; Acts xxii. 3; *their regard for externals*, while they disregarded the weightier matters of the Law, Mtt. xxiii. 24; xii. 2, 7; Mk. vii. 1; Lk. vi. 7; Jn. ix. 16, &c.; *their regard to tradition*, Mtt. xv. 2; Mk. vii. 3; *their scrupulous exactness of washings, tithes, alms*, &c., Mtt. ix. 14; xxiii. 15, 23; Lk. xi. 39 sq.; xviii. 12; *their excessive zeal in making proselytes*[1], Mtt. xxiii. 15; *their lax morality*, Mtt. v. 20; xv. 4, 8; xxiii. 3, 14, 23, 25; Jn. viii. 7.

(*c*) *The Essenes.*

Though nowhere mentioned in the New Testament, the *Essenes* were a numerous body, amounting, according to Philo, to upwards of 4000. Dating, like the other sects already mentioned, from about the middle of the second century B.C., they formed a purely ascetic order, and dwelt far from the distractions of their age in the villages along the western shore of the

[1] The Jews of later times were very zealous in making *proselytes* (Comp. Horace, *Sat.* I. iv. 143), and succeeded to a great extent, especially among the women. They are said, though it does not appear absolutely certain, to have been divided into two classes; (i) *Proselytes of righteousness,* who were admitted to all the privileges of Judaism after submitting to circumcision, and baptism, and offering sacrifice: (ii) *Proselytes of the gate,* who were not circumcised, but simply bound themselves to observe what were called 'the seven precepts of Noah,' i. e. (1) to renounce idolatry, (2) to worship the one true God, (3) to abstain from bloodshed, (4) incest, (5) robbery, (6) to be obedient to the magistrates, (7) to abstain from eating flesh with the blood. Josephus calls such Proselytes οἱ σεβόμενοι, *the worshippers,* and they are supposed to be meant by the same word, rendered in our Version *devout men* in such passages as Acts xiii. 50; xvi. 14; xvii. 4, 17; xviii. 7.

Dead Sea, where they led a life of labour, abstinence, and meditation[1].

They were divided into four orders, but permitted marriage only in one of them, maintained a community of goods, and inculcated a hatred of all riches and all luxury. Sacrifice they did not allow, and though they sent gifts to the Temple, never resorted to it, but held religious assemblies on the Sabbath, where they read the Scriptures, and listened to the expositions of their elders.

Even in their intercourse with one another they observed the greatest secrecy, dreaded contact with all who were not circumcised, and would rather die than eat food which had not been prepared by themselves or those of their own order.

(*d*) *The Herodians.*

This sect, which is twice mentioned in the Gospels (Mtt. xxii. 16; Mk. iii. 6; xii. 13), was rather a political than a religious body. Taking alike their names and their views from the family of Herod, the Herodians held that the hopes of the Jewish nation rested on the Herods as a bulwark against Roman ambition, and almost looked to them for a fulfilment of the prophecies of the Messiah[2]. Hence many amongst them would not regard with dissatisfaction that fusion of the national faith and heathen civilisation, which it was the great object of Herod the Great and his successors to bring about.

It is not improbable that the Herodians in some respects approached very nearly to the Sadducees in their opinions (Comp. Mk. viii. 15 with Mtt. xvi. 6), for both

[1] Analogous to the Essenes were the *Therapeutæ*, who lived in Egypt, were bound by even stricter rules, and spent their time in still greater seclusion, Godwyn's *Moses and Aaron*, I. 12.

[2] Conybeare and Howson, I. 33; Godwyn, Lib. I. 13.

would hold the duty of submission to the Romans, and join in supporting the throne of Herod. The hostility of the Pharisees to the teaching of our blessed Lord may be estimated by the fact that they joined their enemies the Herodians in attempting to ensnare Him (Mtt. xxii. 16).

(ii) Before concluding this Chapter, this seems the appropriate place for noticing *the Samaritans*, who are frequently mentioned in the New Testament.

In the year B.C. 721 Sargon captured Samaria, and removed into captivity the remains of the ten tribes, already decimated by Tiglath-Pileser[1], and located them partly in Gozan or Mygdonia, and partly in cities recently captured from the Medes. This was not a partial but a complete evacuation of the country, which was wiped clean of its inhabitants as *a man wipeth a dish* (2 K. xxi. 13), in accordance with a not unusual custom of Oriental conquerors actually to exhaust a land of its inhabitants[2].

In this desolate condition the country remained till about the year B.C. 677, when Esarhaddon during the invasion of Judah perceived the impolicy of leaving it thus exposed, and resolved to garrison it with foreigners. Accordingly he gathered men *from Babylon*, and *from Cuthah*, and *from Ava*, and *from Hamath*, and *from Sepharvaim* (2 K. xvii. 24; comp. Ezra iv. 2, 9, 10), and entrusting them to an officer of high rank, *the great and noble Asnapper*, had them conveyed to the country formerly occupied by the Ten Tribes, and there settled them.

These *strangers* (comp. Lk. xvii. 18) from the further East[3] were of course idolaters, and worshipped

[1] *Class-Book of O. T. History*, p. 434.

[2] Compare for a notice of such a process, Herod. III. 149; VI. 21, quoted in Trench, *Miracles*, p. 311, note.

[3] Comp. Jos. *Ant.* X. 9. 7; IX. 14. 3.

various deities, and knowing not the God of the land provoked Him by their heathenish rites to send lions among them, *which slew some of them* (2 K. xvii. 25). In their distress they applied to the king of Assyria, who sent one of the captive priests to instruct them *how they should fear the Lord.* Under his teaching they added the acknowledgment of Jehovah as the God of the land, to their ancient idolatries, and in course of time detached themselves more and more from heathen customs, and adopted a sort of worship of Jehovah.

Refused permission, on the return from the Captivity, to participate in the rebuilding of the Temple, they became the open enemies of the Jews, and erected a rival temple on Mount Gerizim[1], where they continued to worship till it was destroyed by John Hyrcanus, B.C. 130. After this they built another temple at Shechem, and there, under its modern name of *Nablûs*, they have a settlement, consisting of about 200 persons, at the present hour.

Gradually detaching themselves from their ancient idolatries, the Samaritans adopted the Mosaic religion, but received as Scripture only the Pentateuch, rejecting every other book in the Jewish Canon. They celebrated the Passover (and celebrate it even now), on Mount Gerizim, and even after their temple had fallen, directed their worship towards that mountain. Holding the doctrine of the coming of the Messiah (Jn. iv. 25), whom they called *Hashah*, "the Converter[2]," their conceptions

[1] See above, p. 5.

[2] 'The Samaritans have a firm belief in the coming of Messiah. They found this upon the words of Moses (Deut. xviii. 15). They differ, however, with regard to the character of the Messiah, as well from Jews as from Christians. They ridicule the Jewish idea of his being a king and a great conqueror. His mission, they say, is not to shed blood, but to heal the nations; not to make war, but to bring peace. He is to be, according to Moses' promise, a great

of His functions and character were derived chiefly from the original promise of a Saviour (Gen. iii. 15), the Shiloh or Peace-maker predicted by Jacob (Gen. xlix. 10), and the Prophet promised to the Israelites like unto Moses (Num. xxiv. 17; Deut. xviii. 15), and they mainly expected that He would *teach all things* (Jn. iv. 25), and restore the glory of the holy Law on Mount Gerizim[1].

The feud between the Jews and Samaritans, engendered by the refusal of the former to permit their participation in the rebuilding of the Temple, ripened into a mutual hostility of the most bitter description.

The Jews were perpetually reminding the Samaritans that they were "Cuthites," mere "strangers from Assyria." They loved to call them "proselytes of the lions" (2 K. xvii. 25), and to accuse them of worshipping the idol-gods buried long ago under the oak of Shechem (Gen. xxxv. 4). To such an extent did they carry their dislike, that they cursed them publicly in their synagogues; declared their testimony was naught, and could not be received; affirmed that any who entertained a Samaritan in his house was laying up judgments for his children; that to eat a morsel of his fare was to eat swine's flesh[2]; refused to receive him as a proselyte, and declared that he could have no part in the resurrection of the dead. Moreover they would have no

Teacher, a Restorer of the Law, one that will bring all the nations, by the illumination of his teaching, to unite in one service to one God. Therefore his common name with them is *Taebah* (תהבה), though the better known name is *Hatah* or *Hashah*, the Restorer, or the Arabic equivalent, Al Mudy, because it is he whose mission it is to turn the ungodly and unbelieving unto the Lord.' Mill's *Modern Samaritans*, 215, 216.

[1] Westcott's *Introduction to the Study of the Gospels*, 148, 9.

[2] Godwyn's *Moses and Aaron*, Lib. I. p. 48; Trench, *Miracles*, p. 311.

dealings with them that they could possibly avoid, and in travelling from the South to the North preferred to take the long circuit through Peræa rather than pass through their hated country.

On the other hand, the Samaritans were not behindhand in recriminations. They would refuse hospitality to the pilgrim companies going up to the feasts at Jerusalem (Comp. Lk. ix. 53), and sometimes even waylay and murder them[1]. On one occasion certain of them are said to have entered the Temple at Jerusalem, and defiled it by scattering on the pavement human bones[2]. One special mode of annoyance was frequently practised. The Jews were in the habit of communicating to their numerous brethren in Babylon, the exact day and hour of the rising of the Paschal moon, by means of a system of beacon fires, which telegraphed the welcome news from the Mount of Olives, through Auranitis, to those who *sat by the waters of the Babylon.* The Samaritans would, therefore, annoy the watchers on the mountain-tops by kindling a rival flame on the wrong day, and thus perplex them, and introduce confusion.

[1] Jos. *Ant.* XX. 6. 1; *B. J.* II. 12. 3.
[2] Jos. *Ant.* XVIII. 2. 2.

NOTE

The Expectation of the Messiah.

From the earliest period of their national history the Jews had been pre-eminently "the people of the future," and at the period we have now reached they were filled with the expectation that an extraordinary Being would appear, and prove Himself the Messiah or Deliverer. But though in the Temple of Prophecy * there had from the beginning ever been heard two Voices mysteriously blended, one jubilant

* See *Class-Book of Old Testament History*, p. 483.

and glad, telling of victory and of triumph, the other subdued and mournful, whispering of shame and suffering, yet to one of these Voices only had attention been really paid.

The characteristics attributed by the nation to the Messiah were (i) *regal*, and (ii) *prophetic*.

i. Many looked for a great Conqueror, whom God would send, investing Him with the attributes of majesty and humanity, describing Him as the "Elect One," the "Anointed," the "Son of Man," who should "execute a terrible vengeance on the enemies of His people," "cleanse Jerusalem," and exalt the Jews above all other nations*. These attributes, ascribed to the Messiah in early Jewish literature, receive illustration from the Gospel Narrative. It was the opinion of the national teachers that His coming would be heralded by Elias, and the belief was shared by the common people (Mtt. xvii. 10 and the parallels; Comp. also xvi. 14).

There was considerable uncertainty, indeed, as to the precise *manner* of His appearance (Jn. vii. 27), but it was fully expected that He would be born *at Bethlehem, the city of David* (Mtt. ii. 5; Comp. Jn. vii. 41, 42); that He would be *David's Son*, and should *sit on David's throne* (Mtt. xxii. 42; xii. 23; ix. 27; xx. 30; xv. 22); that He would *abide for ever* and *set up a kingdom* in which He would dispense honours *on His right hand and on His left* (Mtt. xx. 21; Mk. x. 37).

ii. With these regal attributes others combined prophetic functions, and looked for *the Prophet* that should come into the world (Comp. Jn. vi. 14; i. 21, 46; vii. 40; 1 Macc. xiv. 41), expecting that He would show "signs" not unlike the giving of the manna in the wilderness, and instruct the people *in all things* (Jn. iv. 25), and instead of altering or abolishing any of the Mosaic ordinances, would enhance them to a greater glory, making the sacrifices, purifications, Sabbaths, festivals, and all other usages, far more resplendent and glorious than they had ever been before. That the Messiah would ever *suffer* or *die* was an idea, from which, to the last, even the Apostles shrank with horror and amazement (Mtt. xvi. 22, 23; Lk. xxiv. 21; Jn. xx. 9).

* Ebrard's *Gospel History*, p. 487; Westcott's *Introduction to the New Testament*, pp. 92, 95.

BOOK II

THE GOSPEL HISTORY.

PART I

THE BIRTH AND CHILDHOOD OF CHRIST.

CHAPTER I

THE BIRTH OF JOHN THE BAPTIST.

A. U. C. 749, B. C. 5.

ABOUT the year B.C. 5, when the bloodstained reign of Herod was approaching its close, there lived in Judæa, either at the little village of Juttah, or the time-honoured city of Hebron[1], an aged priest named ZACHARIAS. His wife ELISABETH was also of the priestly family (Lk. i. 5), and both enjoyed a high reputation for piety and uprightness of life, being alike *righteous before God, walking in all the commandments and ordinances of the Lord blameless* (Lk. i. 6). One great sorrow, however, cast a deep shadow over their daily life. They were now old and well-stricken in age, but no child had ever gladdened their humble home.

In the time of Solomon the priests were divided into twenty-four "courses," each of which served at the Temple in weekly rotation (1 Chr. xxiv. 1—19). Of these, four only returned from the captivity, but they were

[1] So Grotius, Lightfoot and others. Reland and Robinson identify it with Juttah in the mountain-region of Judah, near Maon and Carmel (Josh. xv. 55), allotted to the priests (Josh. xxi. 16), now *Yŭtta.* The traditions of the Greek and Latin Churches point on the other hand to *Ain Karim,* a village near Jerusalem. Thomson's *L. and B.* 664.

again divided into twenty-four, and received the same names as the original courses. The course, to which Zacharias belonged, was the eighth, known as that of Abiah or Abijah (1 Chr. xxiv. 10), and in process of time, in accordance with the prescribed arrangement, it devolved on him to go up to the Holy City. Of all the services at the Temple (which to avoid contention were uniformly decided by lot), none was deemed more honourable than that of entering into the Holy Place and offering incense on the Golden Altar[1]. This was done twice every day, before the morning and evening sacrifice, *i.e.* at 9 in the morning and 3 in the afternoon. The sound of a small bell announced the priests' entrance for this purpose, and on hearing it the Priests and Levites took up their position before the Altar of Burnt-offering, the space between the Porch and the Altar was cleared, and the people in the different courts stood and prayed in solemn silence (Rev. viii. 1) so long as he remained within the Holy Place. As soon, however, as he re-appeared, they laid the sacrifice on the altar, and the Levites, amidst the full burst of the Temple music, commenced the sacred Psalmody[2].

Such was the august office which now fell to the lot of Zacharias. Bearing the incense in a large vessel of gold, he entered into the Holy Place, and was kindling it on the Golden Altar, when he was accosted by an Angel standing at the right side of the Altar. This sudden apparition startled and affrighted him. But the Angel calmed his fears, and announced that the prayers he had offered to God in secret were heard. Though Elisabeth was stricken in years, she should yet become the mother of a son, who was to be named John[3],

[1] See *Class-Book of O. T. History*, p. 123. For the composition of the Incense, *Ibid.* p. 135.

[2] See Smith's *Bibl. Dict.*, Art. *Incense.*

[3] Hebrew Jochanan = *God is gracious.*

From the first hour of his existence this child should be filled with the Holy Ghost, and drinking neither wine nor strong drink, in accordance with the Nazarite's vow, *should be great in the sight of the Lord.* As the second Elijah, to whom the finger of prophecy had pointed (Isai. xl. 3; Mal. iii. 1), he should be the immediate forerunner of the long-expected Messiah, and *make ready a people prepared for him* (Lk. i. 12—17).

Astounded by so sudden an announcement, the aged priest sought some assurance of the promised blessing. On this the Angel, who announced himself as no other than he that had appeared many years before to the prophet Daniel under the name of GABRIEL (Dan. viii. 16; ix. 21), replied, that such an assurance would be vouchsafed, but, because of his unbelief, it should be in the shape of a judgment. *He should be dumb, and not able to speak, till the day that these things should be performed* (Lk. i. 20).

While Zacharias was receiving this mysterious intimation within the Sanctuary, the people[1], who crowded the Temple-courts, were anxiously expecting his return, and marvelled at his unusual delay. At length he reappeared. But his strange aspect shewed that something had occurred. When questioned he could not return any answer, and intimated by signs that he had seen a vision in the Sacred Place. Then at the close of his week of ministration he returned to his own house, where, in accordance with the announcement of the Angel, Elisabeth *conceived, and hid herself for five months* in quiet and peaceful retirement (Lk. i. 24).

Six months after his appearance in the Temple, the same Angel was sent from God to NAZARETH[2], a

[1] The number present appears to indicate that it was the Sabbath-day.

[2] It is one peculiarity of the Galilæan hills, as distinct from those of Ephraim or Judah, that they contain or sus-

secluded village unknown and unnamed in the Old Testament, hidden away amongst the hills of Galilee, and within the limits of the ancient tribe of Zebulun. At this village there lived a lowly Virgin named Mary, or Miriam. She belonged to the royal tribe of Judah, and the lineage of David (Lk. i. 32; Rom. i. 3), and was connected by marriage with Elisabeth (Lk. i. 27), who belonged to the tribe of Levi. Moreover, she was at this time betrothed to Joseph, who occupied a humble position as a carpenter at Nazareth, but like herself was *of the lineage of David* (Lk. i. 27; ii. 4).

To this lowly Virgin the Angel Gabriel now appeared, and announced that by virtue of the operation of the Holy Ghost, she should become the mother of a Son, whom she was to call Jesus[1] (*God the Saviour*). He

tain green basins of table-land just below their topmost ridges; forming marked features in any view from the summit of Tabor, or further north from the slopes of Hermon..... Such above all is Nazareth. Fifteen gently rounded hills "seem as if they had met to form an enclosure" for this peaceful basin—"they rise round it like the edge of a shell to guard it from intrusion. It is a rich and beautiful field in the midst of these green hills—abounding in gay flowers, in fig-trees, small gardens, hedges of the prickly pear; and the dense rich grass affords an abundant pasture. The expression of the old topographer, Quaresmius, was as happy as it is poetical: 'Nazareth is a rose, and, like a rose, has the same rounded form, enclosed by mountains as the flower by its leaves.'" Stanley's *Sinai and Palestine*, p. 365.

[1] As the first leader of the hosts of Israel was called first Hoshea, a *Saviour*, and afterwards Jehoshua or Joshua, *God the Saviour* or *God's Salvation*, in Greek, ΙΗΣΟΥΣ, Jesus, and saved the Israelites from their enemies the Canaanites, so the second Joshua was to save His people from enemies no less real—even *their sins* (Matt. i. 21). Compare the title of Conqueror so often applied to our blessed Lord in the Book of Revelation, as ii. 7, 11; iii. 5, 12, 21; v. 5; vi. 2, &c., as also in St John's Gospel, xvi. 33, and in 1 Jn. ii. 13, 14; iv. 4. See Pearson *On the Creed*, Art. ii.; *Class-Book of O. T. History*, pp. 173, 223.

should be great, and should be called the Son of the Highest, should *sit on the throne of His father David, and reign over the house of Jacob for ever* (Lk. i. 30—33). Though at first startled at the sudden address of an angelic visitant (Lk. i. 29), the Virgin received his announcement with implicit faith, and prayed that it *might be with her according to his word* (Lk. i. 38), and being informed of what had occurred to her relative Elisabeth, arose with haste to seek out her home amidst the Judæan hills. The journey of four or five days[1] accomplished, she reached the humble abode, and had no sooner crossed the threshold, and saluted the aged wife of Zacharias, than the other addressed her as *the mother of her Lord*, and fully confirmed the words of the angel. Thus assured of the certainty of the mighty event about to happen, the lowly virgin, like Hannah at the birth of Samuel, burst forth into words of holy praise and exultation, and gave utterance to the inspired hymn, which under the name of the *Magnificat*, remains one of the most precious treasures of the Church, and the most familiar of her hymns (Lk. i. 46—56).

After a sojourn of about three months with Elisabeth, Mary returned to Nazareth, and Joseph perceived that she was with child. Being a just man, he resolved on privately giving her a bill of divorcement, instead of

[1] The distance from Nazareth to Jerusalem is about 80 miles, and if Zacharias lived at Hebron 17 miles south of Jerusalem, the whole journey would occupy four or five days. (i) The most direct route was by Nain and Endor, and through Samaria and southward by Bethel. (ii) If for any cause Samaria was to be avoided, the Jordan would be crossed near Scythopolis, and the way followed through Peræa along its eastern bank. This was the common route with the Jews in their journeyings to the feasts, if they wished specially to avoid Samaria. (iii) Still a third way was by Dor on the sea-coast, passing through Lydda, and thence over the mountains of Ephraim. Andrews, p. 64.

making her a *public example* (Mtt. i. 19). But as in deep perplexity he pondered on these things, he too was visited by an Angel in a dream, and bidden not to be afraid to take to him Mary as his wife. That which was conceived in her was *not of blood, nor of the will of the flesh, nor of the will of man*, but of the Holy Ghost, and the Son, to whom she would give birth, he was to name Jesus, for *He should save His people from their sins* (Mtt. i. 21).

Meanwhile the event announced in the Temple to the aged Zacharias had taken place, and Elisabeth brought forth a son. Such an event in the East is always an occasion of unbounded joy. In the present instance it would be still more so, and the relatives and neighbours of Elisabeth came together with no ordinary feelings to rejoice with her. On the eighth day, the child was brought to the priest for circumcision, and the relatives proposed that it should be named after his father, but Elisabeth demurred, and declared that it should be called John (*the grace of God*). Marvelling at her wishing for a name, which had no precedent in the family, they appealed by signs to the speechless Zacharias. The aged priest called for a writing tablet, and wrote *His name is John*, and then, while all were lost in astonishment, his mouth, which had been closed for nine months, was opened, and he too burst forth into an inspired Psalm of exultant thanksgiving, in which he acknowledged the faithfulness of God in the birth of his son, and foretold his future greatness as the forerunner of the Messiah (Lk. i. 61—79).

Born as *one out of due time* the child grew, *waxed strong in spirit* (Lk. i. 80), and, in accordance with the words of the Angel, adhered steadfastly to the Nazarite vow[1]. Like Samson, like Samuel, no razor was suffered

[1] See *Class-Book of O. T. History*, p. 158.

to come near his head. Drinking *neither wine nor strong drink*, he systematically denied himself all the pleasures and indulgences of ordinary life. The son of a priest, he doubtless received a strict religious education, and at some period, though when we are not told, retired to the dreary deserts west of the Dead Sea. Here, like Moses in Midian, he prepared himself by solitary communion with God for his high emprise, assumed the garb of one of the old prophets, the robe of camel's hair fastened round the body by a leathern girdle (2 K. i. 8), and subsisted on such fare as the desert afforded, eating *locusts*[1] *and wild honey* (Mtt. iii. 4).

CHAPTER II

THE NATIVITY OF CHRIST.

A.U.C. 750, B.C. 4.

THE voice of Prophecy (Mic. v. 2) had declared that the Messiah should be born at Bethlehem of Judæa, a spot endeared to every Jew as the birth-place of the son of Jesse. Though Mary was now living at Nazareth, a circumstance apparently fortuitous, under the superintending hand of Divine Providence, brought about a fulfilment of the prediction.

At this particular period there was peace throughout the dominions of the Roman empire. The Temple of Janus was shut[2]. The fierce contests, which for so many

[1] Locusts were frequently used as an article of food (comp. Levit. xi. 21, 22), being sometimes ground and pounded and then mixed with flour and water and made into cakes, sometimes salted and then eaten, or prepared in many other ways. See Kitto's *Bible Illustrations*, VII. 191, 2; Kirby and Spence's *Entomology;* Thomson's *Land and the Book*, pp. 419, 20.

[2] Merivale's *Romans under the Empire*, III. 401, smaller edition.

years had been carried on with such relentless persistence, which had drenched with blood the fairest fields in the dominions of Augustus, had ceased, and the din of battles was hushed. As that monarch revolved in his mind the most suitable means for the administration of his numerous dependencies, it occurred to him that it would be well to carry out a general registration[1] of all his subjects, with a view to some fixed scale of taxation. He issued, therefore, a decree that *all the world,* which owned his sway, should *be taxed*[2] (Lk. ii. 1). Judæa was

[1] From Suetonius (*Aug.* Chap. XXVII.) we learn that Augustus three times held a census for Italy, A.U.C. 726, 746, and 767; and Strabo speaks of one in Gaul and another in Spain. Tacitus (*Ann.* I. 11) tells us that he had a little book written out in his own hand treating of the numbers of his soldiers, the taxes, imposts, &c., of his empire, which is also alluded to by Suetonius and Dion Cassius, and must have been based on surveys of all parts of the empire. It is also well established that he commenced, if he did not carry out, a complete geometrical survey of the empire (see Merivale's *Romans,* III. 404). Though these facts do not absolutely *prove* the holding of a general census, they go far to *confirm* the Evangelist's statement.

[2] St Luke relates that *this taxing or enrolment took place as a first one, when Cyrenius was governor of Syria* (Lk. ii. 1). But Josephus states that Cyrenius was sent as governor of Syria after the deposition of Archelaus and the annexation of Judæa as a Roman province to Syria, and that he then instituted a census. This could not be earlier than A.U.C. 758 or 760; but the Saviour was born before Herod's death in A.U.C. 750. Various explanations have been offered of the Evangelist's words:

i. Some would throw the emphasis on the ἐγένετο, and translate, "This enrolment first *took effect* when Cyrenius was governor of Syria," i.e. the enrolment, enumeration of persons, *descriptio capitum,* was made at the time of our Lord's birth, but its actual execution was deferred some nine or ten years, till Judæa was made a Roman province, when (Acts v. 37) the rebellion took place against the actual levying of the taxes.

ii. Others would render πρώτη *before,* as in the some-not indeed at this time a Roman "province," but its reduction to that condition sooner or later was already determined[1]. The imperial edict, therefore, declaring the will of his master was placed in the hands of the Idumæan Herod as in those of other rulers, and he would naturally ordain that while the Roman orders were obeyed, the customs and traditions of the country should not be entirely overridden[2].

Toilsome, therefore, as was the journey, and not altogether free from danger, the Virgin left the place of her usual abode, and set out for the village of Bethlehem

what parallel passages in Jn. i. 15, 30, where it is used as=πρότερος, and translate, "This enrolment took place *before Cyrenius was governor of Syria.*"

iii. It appears, however, almost certain, Merivale says *demonstrated*, that Publius Sulpicius Quirinus (Cyrenius) was *twice* governor of Syria, *first* from A.U.C. 750—753, or B.C. 4—1, and *secondly* from A.U.C. 760—765, or A.D. 6—11. It is true that Cyrenius does not appear to have been governor till the autumn of A.U.C. 750, but the enumeration may have begun or been appointed under Varus the preceding governor, and being suspended in consequence of Herod's death and the disturbances that followed it, was reserved for execution to Cyrenius, with whose name it was connected. Merivale, IV. 457; Ellicott, p. 58 n.; Andrews, 5—8; and see the results of Zumpt's dissertation *De Syriâ Romanorum provinciâ* in Wieseler's Synopsis, 129—135.

[1] On Herod's completely tributary relation to Rome, see Wieseler, *Chronol. Synop.* pp. 84, 85.

[2] "In the kingdoms of their allies the Romans adopted at first a milder, and even when circumstances dictated it, an exceedingly lenient form of census. This we may be sure would have been the case in the census of Palestine under Herod, who reigned over the entire nation of the Jews, a people so much inclined to revolt. It is probable that the forms for holding the census, issued by Rome, were adapted as closely as possible to the conditions of the country, while the execution of it was, as far as practicable, entrusted to the sole management of Herod and his officers." Wieseler, p. 82.

accompanied by Joseph. This he would have done as her natural protector, but the Jewish law required his presence in the town of his forefathers, *because he,* like Mary, *was of the house and lineage of David* (Lk. ii. 4)[1]. Accordingly, in the society, probably, of others bound on the same errand as themselves, they proceeded on their southward journey, either through Samaria or across the Jordan through Peræa[2], and after probably visiting and passing through Jerusalem, surmounted the long ascent leading to the village of Bethlehem, and sought shelter in the inn or *khan*, which the inhabitants had provided for the reception of strangers.

But they had reached it too late. Every guest-chamber was already full, and crowded with strangers, who, like themselves, had come up to be taxed. They were constrained, therefore, to seek shelter amongst the cattle and beasts of burden of the wayfarers, and so it was, that while they were there, the days were accomplished that the lowly Virgin should be delivered, and *she brought forth her firstborn Son*, and *wrapped him in swaddling clothes*, and laid Him in one of the mangers by her side (Lk. ii. 6, 7).

Such was the first Advent of the Saviour "in great humility." Thus did He who was with the Father before all worlds, *by whom all things were made, and without whom was not any thing made that was made* (Jn. i. 1—3), deign to take upon Him our nature. Unimportant, however, as appeared the event that had just taken place in that crowded inn, unknown to the Idumæan

[1] Under purely Roman law "Joseph might *perhaps* have been enrolled at Nazareth," but the fact that he is described by the Evangelist as journeying to Bethlehem to be enrolled at the town of his forefathers, is in remarkable accordance with "the perplexed political relations of the intensely national yet all but subject Judæa." Ellicott's *Lectures*, p. 60.

[2] On the reasons why this journey was often taken by the Jews, see above, pp. 122, 123.

Herod, unknown to his imperial master in the City of the Cæsars, signs were not wanting that it had moved all heaven to its centre, and was there hailed with rapturous acclaim. On the bleak downs of Bethlehem shepherds were that night keeping watch over their flocks, when suddenly there came upon them a light brighter than the brightest of the countless stars that spangled the midnight sky, and *the glory of the Lord shone round about them* (Lk. ii. 9). Sore afraid, they would have fled in dismay. But a Voice came to them which calmed their fears. An Angel addressed them, and announced the Glad Tidings that in the city of David had that day been born to them *a Saviour, even Christ the Lord*, whom they would find *wrapped in swaddling clothes and lying in a manger* (Lk. ii. 11, 12). He ceased, and then a multitude of the heavenly host brake the silence of the night, and sang *Glory to God in the highest, and on earth Peace, Goodwill towards men.* Such an announcement roused all the wonder of the simple, humble men who heard it. Hastily leaving their flocks they repaired to Bethlehem, where they *found Mary and Joseph, and the Babe lying in the manger*, and recounted all that they had heard from the heavenly visitants concerning the Child. Great was the astonishment of those who listened to their tale, but the holy Virgin treasured their words in her heart, and the shepherds returned to their lowly occupation, glorifying and praising God for all they had seen and heard (Lk. ii. 16—20).

Born *under the Law* (Gal. iv. 4) the Saviour was to submit to all its ordinances. Accordingly on the eighth day after His birth He was circumcised, like any other Jewish child, and received the name of JESUS. Moreover on the fortieth day after His birth, the Virgin repaired to the Temple, and presented her humble offering of a *pair of turtle doves or two young pigeons* (Lev. xii.

2, 6, 8), according to the law of her purification. Without pomp or earthly circumstance, the infant Saviour, the Messenger of the Covenant, came to His temple (Mal. iii. 1), and might have left it equally unnoticed. But two humble worshippers, who had long been *waiting for the consolation of Israel* (Lk. ii. 25), recognized "in helpless infancy and clad in mortal flesh" the long-expected Messiah.

There was living at Jerusalem a *just and devout man* named Symeon. Though far advanced in years, he had received divine intimation that he *should not see death* till his eyes had rested on the Lord's Christ. He was now present at the national sanctuary, when His parents brought in the Child *to do for Him after the custom of the Law* (Lk. ii. 27), and no sooner did he behold the Child, than he saw that the long-promised hour was come. He *took Him up in his arms*, and blessed God that at length his eyes had been permitted to *see His Salvation, the Light to lighten the Gentiles, and the Glory of His people Israel* (Lk. ii. 32). Then while Joseph and Mary were marvelling at his words, the aged seer, already on the verge of the eternal world, blessed them also, and addressing the Virgin Mother declared that her Child was *appointed for the fall and rising again of many in Israel*, and that *a sword should* in days to come *pierce through her own heart*. At the same time there came forward an aged woman, a prophetess, Anna, the daughter of Phanuel. Seven years had she lived with her husband after quitting her maiden state, and since his death had remained in widowhood upwards of 84 years. Though the territories of the tribe of Asher, to which she belonged (Lk. ii. 36), were at a great distance from the Holy City, yet there she had taken up her abode, and was constant in every act of worship and in her attendance at every sacred service. She too drew near while the Holy Child was being brought into His Father's house, and, like the aged Symeon, *gave thanks to God*, and *spake of Him to all those that were looking for redemption in Jerusalem* (Lk. ii. 38).

But as she was thus proclaiming to the faithful in the Holy City the Advent of their King, pilgrims and worshippers were drawing near from far different and far distant lands. A short time after Joseph and Mary had returned to Bethlehem, there appeared certain travel-stained pilgrims, whose arrival stirred Jerusalem to its very centre. In their native home in Arabia or Persia, their attention had been directed to a luminous body in the sky, which had guided them to Palestine, and they now enquired where was He that was *born King of the Jews*[1], and declared that they had seen His star in the East, and had come to worship Him. The arrival of these Magi[2], as they were called in their own land, was quickly announced to Herod, and the enquiry respecting an hereditary *King of the Jews* roused the alarm and suspicion of one so jealous for the integrity of his own dynasty[3]. Hastily convening a formal assembly of the Chief Priests and Scribes, he enquired where, according

[1] It is not impossible that these Magi were acquainted with Balaam's prophecy respecting a star to rise out of Jacob (Num. xxiv. 17; *Class-Book of O. T. History*, 191, 192), and very probable that they were not ignorant of the Prophecies of Daniel. The general expectation in the East at this time that a king should arise in Judæa to rule the world, is mentioned in Suetonius, *Vesp.* c. IV., Tac. *Hist.* v. 13.

[2] The Magi were a tribe of the Medes, like that of Levi among the Jews, to whom were entrusted all the priestly functions connected with the practice of their religion, the chief feature of which was a worship of the elements, as also the study of astrology, and the interpretation of dreams.

[3] Though the terrible disorder which carried him off was already afflicting him, and it wanted probably but a few days of the period when he sought relief in the baths of Callirhoe; see above, p. 104, Ellicott's *Lectures*, p. 75, n.

to the prophetical books, the long-expected Messiah was to be born. Without the least hesitation they pointed to the words of the prophet Micah (v. 2), which declared *Bethlehem in Judœa* to be the favoured place. On this the monarch sought a private interview with the Magi (Mtt. ii. 7), and made diligent enquiries respecting the time of the appearance of the Star, and then bade them repair to Bethlehem and seek diligently for the young Child, declaring his intention, if they found Him, to come himself and lay his honours at the feet of the heir of David's throne.

Thus advised the Magi set out, when lo! the Star, which they had seen in their far-off eastern home appeared before them, and guided their feet to the lowly abode where lay the object of their search. With great joy (Mtt. ii. 10) they entered the house, and seeing the young child and Mary His mother fell down and worshipped Him, and opening their treasures brought forth costly gifts of *gold*, *frankincense*, *and myrrh*[1]. Then warned in a dream not to return to the perfidious tyrant, they made their way to their own land by another route. Thus He, who had been "manifested" to the shepherds, to the faithful Symeon and Anna, was manifested also to these His first Gentile worshippers from the distant East.

But that same night Joseph was also warned in a dream, of peril awaiting the young Child. Herod was watching his opportunity to put Him to death, and it was necessary that he should fly. So Joseph arose, and taking the Infant and His mother, went down into Egypt, where He and they were to remain till they received further intimations respecting their course.

Their departure had not been too soon. Perceiving

[1] The customary gifts of subject nations, see Gen. xliii. 11; Ps. lxxii. 15; 1 Kings x. 2, 10; 2 Chron. ix. 24; Cant. iii. 6; iv. 14.

that the strange visitors to his capital had not returned, and that his design against the young Child's life had been frustrated, with a reckless ferocity, which, we have seen, he too often displayed, Herod sent and slew every male child in Bethlehem *from two years old and under*, to make sure that he had included the Object of his terrible vengeance. His cruel edict was carried out, and filled many a home in Bethlehem with sorrow and mourning[1]. The voice of lamentation and weeping arose in Ramah, of which an inspired Prophet (Jer. xxxi. 15) had spoken 400 years before, and which the Jewish historian Josephus does not record, even if he knew of it, as though it was a matter of little moment compared with other atrocities[2] of the same monarch, who could butcher on one occasion well-nigh every member of the Sanhedrin[3], and on the very eve of his death meditate the wholesale slaughter of the chiefs of the Jews in the Hippodrome[4] at Jericho.

[1] Under any circumstances the number of children thus ruthlessly murdered could not have been large. "In peaceful times such an act as this, even if executed, as this probably was, in secresy, would have excited general indignation when it became known; but now the Jewish people had so long 'supped with horrors,' and were so engrossed in the many perils that threatened their national existence, that this passed by comparatively unnoticed. Such a deed, from a man of whom Josephus says that 'he was brutish and a stranger to all humanity,'... could have awakened no surprise. It was wholly in keeping with his reckless and savage character, but one, and by no means the greatest of his crimes. It is therefore possible that it may never have come to the knowledge of the Jewish historian, writing so many years after the event." Andrews, p. 89, Rawlinson's *Bampton Lectures*, pp. 352, 3 and note.

[2] Compare the execution of the zealots for pulling down the Golden Eagle, above, p. 104.

[3] See above, p. 82. [4] See above, p. 105.

CHAPTER III

THE SAVIOUR'S EARLY LIFE AT NAZARETH.

B.C. 4—A.D. 27.

THIS ferocious action was one of the last crimes in the bloodthirsty career of this guilty monarch. Very shortly afterwards he died under circumstances already related[1] at Jericho A.U.C. 750. This event was made known to Joseph by an Angel in a dream (Mtt. ii. 19), and he was bidden to arise and return with the young Child and His mother into the land of Israel. Accordingly he set out, but hearing that the tyrant's son Archelaus[2], who enjoyed a reputation worthy of his father, was reigning in his stead, he was afraid to continue his journey, and was only encouraged to proceed by another supernatural intimation. The place whither he was to go had not before been distinctly specified, and he might have supposed that Bethlehem, the city of David, was the proper place to rear the Son of David, so near to Jerusalem, the most religious, the most sacred part of Palestine[3]. But now he was directed to repair to the safer obscurity of his former residence in Galilee, and accordingly went down from the highlands of Judæa to Nazareth, and there the Holy Child *grew and waxed strong in spirit, filled with wisdom, and the grace of God was upon Him* (Lk. ii. 40).

From this time till the commencement of His public

[1] See above, p. 105.

[2] He was the son of Herod by his Samaritan wife Malthace (Jos. *Ant.* XVII. 8. 1; *B. J.* I. 28. 4). He was guilty of great cruelty and oppression. Not long after his accession he put to death in the Temple 3000 of the Jews, letting loose upon them his entire army during the Paschal Festival (Jos. *Ant.* XVII. 9. 3; *B. J.* II. 1. 3). The Samaritans also suffered terribly from his cruelties (*B. J.* II. 7. 3).

[3] Andrews' *Life of our Lord on Earth*, p. 91; Ellicott, p. 81.

ministry a thick veil conceals from us all details of the Saviour's life. The Evangelists pass this period by with a solemn reserve. One event, and one only, emerges from the obscurity that enshrouds it.

It was the custom of Joseph, and even of Mary[1], to go up year after year to attend the celebration of the great festival of the Passover at Jerusalem (Lk. ii. 41). When He had attained the age of twelve years, A.U.C. 762, the Holy Child accompanied them, having attained to that period of life when Jewish children were required to attend the feasts and began to be instructed in the Law. At the close of the Festival, and probably on the eighth day, His parents, in company with other pilgrims (Lk. ii. 44), set out on their return to Galilee. On reaching, however, their resting-place on the first evening[2], they found their Son was missing, and, full of trouble and anxiety, returned a day's journey, and *sought Him amongst their kinsfolk and acquaintance*, and the travelling companies hastening homewards from the Holy City. But they found Him not. Still another day was spent in searching for Him in the city itself, but with the same result. At length on the third day[3] they found Him in the precincts of the Temple, probably in one of the chambers where the Rabbis were

[1] The attendance of women at the great feasts was not *required* by the Law. Ellicott, p. 89.

[2] "As is well known, the first day's journey of a company of eastern travellers is always short. On that day it is not customary to go more than six or eight miles, and the tents are pitched, for the first night's encampment, almost within sight of the place from which the journey commences." Hackett, *Script. Ill.* 12, quoted in Andrews, p. 96.

[3] This we may compute in two ways; either (i) the *first*, that of their departure from Jerusalem; *second*, the day of their return; *third*, the day when He was found; or (ii) excluding the day of departure; *first*, the day of their return; *second*, the day of search in Jerusalem; *third*, the day when He was found. *Ibid.*

wont to give instruction during the festivals[1], sitting in the midst of learned Masters of Israel, not only listening to their words, but *asking them questions.* While all present were marvelling at the understanding He displayed, His parents drew near, and were amazed to find their Son in the midst of so august an assemblage, and the holy Mother expostulated with Him on the anxiety His absence had caused. To this He replied in artless but mysterious words, *How is it that ye sought Me? Wist ye not that I must be about My Father's business?* proving that even already He was aware of His heavenly origin. Then, while they understood not the saying, which nevertheless His Mother kept and treasured in her heart, He went down with them to the lowly home in despised Galilee. There in meek subjection He abode beneath their humble roof, and probably shared[2] in His reputed father's earthly labours, *growing in wisdom and stature, and in favour with God and man* (Lk. ii. 52; Mk. vi. 3).

While thus in silence and seclusion the Holy One was advancing towards man's estate, great changes were taking place in the fortunes of the Jewish nation, which now demand our attention.

After the death of Herod some considerable delay took place before the confirmation of his will by Augustus arrived from Rome, and Jerusalem was the scene of tumult and violence. At length that emperor was pleased to announce his approval, and Archelaus was appointed to the government of Judæa[3], Idumæa, and

[1] See above, p. 96; comp. Lightfoot *Hor. Heb.* on Lk. ii. 46.

[2] This was the general opinion of the early Fathers; is in accordance with the settled custom of the Jews to bring up their sons to some trade; and is implied in the question of the inhabitants of Nazareth, "*Is not this the carpenter?*" (Mtt. xiii. 55, Mk. vi. 3).

[3] The *Roman province of Judæa* extended from the plain of Esdraelon southwards to the desert, and in our Lord's

Samaria, with the title of ethnarch; Herod Antipas obtained Galilee[1] and Peræa[2]; Herod Philip, Auranitis[3], Gaulanitis[4], Trachonitis[5], Batanæa[6] and Ituræa[7]; while

time *included Samaria*, which had now no separate political existence. On Idumæa, see above, p. 32 and note.

[1] Galilee, from the Hebrew form *Galil* or *Galilah* (comp. Jos. xx. 7; 1 Kings ix. 11; Is. ix. 1), denoting "a circle" or "region," and "implying the separation of the district from the more regularly organized tribes or kingdoms of Samaria and Judæa," extended from the region of Lebanon to the southern border of the plain of Esdraelon. It thus comprised the district formerly occupied by the tribes of Asher, Naphtali, Zebulun, Issachar, and part of Manasseh, and was divided into two sections: (i) *Lower Galilee*, which included the rich plain of Esdraelon and the whole region from the plain of Akka to the shores of the Lake of Gennesaret. (For the fertility of this region, see *Class-Book of O. T. History*, pp. 219, 220.) (ii) *Upper Galilee*, which "embraced the whole mountain-range lying between the Upper Jordan and Phœnicia," and was also called *Galilee of the Gentiles* (Matt. iv. 15; 1 Macc. v. 15), for twenty of its towns were given by Solomon to Hiram king of Tyre (1 K. ix. 11), and were then or afterwards colonised by strangers (Is. ix. 1), who increased in number during the Captivity and the times of the Maccabees (1 Macc. v. 20—23), and chiefly consisted of Syrians, Phœnicians, Arabs, and Greeks. It was probably from contact with this large body of foreigners that the pronunciation of the Jews residing in Galilee became peculiar (Mtt. xxvi. 73; Mk. xiv. 70).

[2] A region extending from the Arnon to the Hieromax.

[3] *Auranitis* was the Greek form of the old name Hauran (Ezek. xlvii. 16), and was the name of the district in the upper valley of the Hieromax.

[4] *Gaulanitis* derived its name from the ancient Levitical city of refuge (Jos. xx. 8; xxi. 27), Golan, in the territory of Manasseh (Deut. iv. 43), and included the district immediately east of the lake of Gennesaret, and the Upper Jordan. Its principal cities were Golan, Hippos, Gamala, Bethsaida-Julias (Mark viii. 22) and Seleucia.

[5] *Trachonitis* was the Greek form of the Hebrew Argob =*stony*. See *Class-Book of O. T. History*, p. 185.

[6] *Batanæa*, the Græcized form of the Hebrew Bashan, included, probably, the mountain-district east of Auranitis.

[7] *Ituræa* was a little province lying between Gaulanitis

Salome was declared mistress of Jamnia, Azotus, and Phasaëlis, with a palace at Askelon and a revenue of 60 talents[1]. The emperor promised to Archelaus the title of king, if he proved worthy of it. But his government was marked by such gross cruelty and injustice both towards the Jews and Samaritans that complaints were lodged against him before the emperor. After a reign, therefore, of nine years he was summoned to Rome, and his cause having been formally heard, sentenced to be banished to Vienne in Gaul[2], and to forfeit his estates[3], A.D. 6.

And now in truth the *sceptre departed from Judah* (Gen. xlix. 10), and the kingdom of David and Solomon, of the famous Asmonean house and of Herod, sank into the form of a Roman province[4], and was annexed to the

on the south, Trachonitis on the east, Hermon on the west, and the plain of Damascus on the north. It derived its name from *Jetur*, a son of Ishmael, who colonised it (Gen. xxv. 15, 16). His descendants were conquered by the half-tribe of Manasseh (1 Chr. v. 19—23) but not annihilated, for, as we have seen, above, p. 61, Aristobulus re-conquered their colony, then called Ituræa, and gave them their choice between Judaism or banishment (Jos. *Ant.* XIII. 11. 3). Remnants, however, still survived, and retiring to the neighbouring rocky fastnesses "became known as skilful archers and daring plunderers" (Virgil, *Georg.* II. 448; Cic. *Phil.* II. 24; VIII. 19; XLIV. 112; V. 18). When Pompeius came into Syria it was ceded to the Romans, and was heavily taxed by M. Antonius; it then fell into the hands of a chief called Zenodorus, but about B.C. 20 was bestowed by Augustus on Herod the Great (see above, p. 93), who bequeathed it to his son Philip. Jos. *Ant.* XVII. 8. 1; Smith's *Bibl. Dict.* and *Dict. Geog.*

1 Jos. *B. J.* II. 6. 3.

2 According to Dion Cassius he was banished by Augustus to Vienne in Gaul, in the consulship of Marcus Æmilius Lepidus and L. Arruntius, after reigning from A.U.C. 750 to A.U.C. 759, Wieseler, *Chronol. Synop.* p. 50.

3 Jos. *B. J.* II. 7. 3; Lewin's *Fasti Sacri*, p. 146.

4 From the time of Augustus (B.C. 27) the provinces

prefecture of Syria. This office was now conferred on P. Sulpicius Quirinus, but the immediate government of Judæa and Samaria was given to a procurator, Coponius[1], a man of equestrian rank, who had a body[2] ot

subject to the Roman sway were divided into two classes, (i) *Senatorial*, and (ii) *Imperial*.

(i) *Senatorial* provinces were governed by a *Proconsul*, called in Greek Ἀνθύπατος (Acts xiii. 7; xviii. 12; xix. 38), who was appointed by lot, held his authority for a year, carried with him the lictors and fasces, the insignia of a consul, but had no military power.

(ii) *Imperial* provinces were governed by a *Proprætor*, in Greek Ἀντιστράτηγος, or as he was sometimes termed "Legatus," or Πρεσβευτής, the representative or "Commissioner" of the emperor. He was appointed by the emperor himself, held his authority as long as the latter wished, and went from Italy with all the pomp of a military commander.

Syria was an *imperial* province, and therefore was governed by a Legatus, or "Commissioner" of the emperor, and Judæa, partly on account of its remoteness from Antioch, partly from the peculiar character of its inhabitants, was ruled by a special procurator, subject to the governor of Syria, but vested within his own province with the power of a Legatus. Hence we never find the title Proconsul applied to Quirinus, Pilate, Festus, or Felix, but Ἡγεμών, a general term = the Latin *præses* (Comp. Lk. ii. 2; iii. 1; Acts xxiii. 24). The procurator of Judæa (*a*) had his head-quarters at Cæsarea (Acts xxiii. 23); (*b*) was assisted by a council consisting of assessors (Acts xxv. 12); (*c*) was attended by six lictors, wore the military dress, and had a cohort as a body-guard (Matt. xxvii. 27); (*d*) came up to Jerusalem at the time of the great festivals, when, according to Josephus, he resided in the palace of Herod (*B. J.* II. 14. 3); (*e*) had an audience-chamber (Acts xxv. 23), and a judgment-seat (Acts xxv. 6); (*f*) had the power of life and death (Matt. xxvii. 26), and sent appeals to the emperor (Acts xxv. 12).

[1] During his procuratorship occurred the pollution of the temple by the Samaritans, related above, p. 123. Up to this time they had been admitted to the temple, but were now excluded.

[2] "Sebaste and Jerusalem being far from Antioch, the

troops at his command, and was entrusted in certain cases with the power of life and death[1].

Quirinus, as we have seen above[2], had in all probability been already governor of Syria, and in this capacity had conducted the preliminary enrolment of names preparatory to a general census. This census he was now entrusted to carry out[3], and with it a levying of imposts and rates in money. This was regarded by the Jews as the last and most degrading mark of their subjection to a foreign power. The whole country was in a ferment, and though the energy of the high-priest Joazar[4] repressed any actual outbreak at Jerusalem, the popular feeling could not be restrained in the provinces. At the head of the disaffected appeared one Judas of Gamala[5] in Gaulanitis.

A man of energy, eloquence, and undaunted courage, he quickly gathered around him a body of adventurers, and aided by a confederate Sadoc, of the Pharisaic faction, unfurled the banner of resistance to foreign dominion, and especially to foreign tribute. For a time the country was at the mercy of the fierce and lawless throng, which flocked to his standard, but the effort was utterly fruitless. Nothing could withstand the terrible Roman legions; Judas himself was slain (Acts v. 37), and his followers were dispersed, but his work lived after him, and the Zealots and Sicarii or *Assassins*, who drank deeply of his fierce and independent spirit, long kept alive the popular discontent under a foreign sway.

mountains difficult and the people turbulent, Quirinus was allowed to treat these new districts of the empire as a sub-province, placing them under a procurator of their own, with a provincial capital at Cæsarea on the sea-coast." H. Dixon's *Holy Land*, I. 236.

[1] Jos. *B. J.* II. 8. I.

[2] See above, p. 135, note.

[3] Jos. *Ant.* XVI. 13. 5.

[4] *Ib.* XVII. I. I.

[5] Jos. *Ant.* XVIII. I. I; *B. J.* II. 8. I.

Having completed the confiscation of the property of Archelaus, Quirinus deposed Joazar from the high-priesthood, and substituted in his place Annas, the son of Seth[1], the ablest friend of Rome. He then returned to Syria, and Coponius having planted a small garrison on Zion and a guard at the Temple-gate, took up his abode at Cæsarea on the sea.

So long as Augustus filled the imperial throne the procurators in Judæa held their commands for a very limited number of years, and were rapidly changed. Thus Coponius, whose supremacy began in A. D. 6, was succeeded after four years, in A.D. 10, by Marcus Ambivius[2]. In three years Marcus Ambivius handed over the reins of power to Annius Rufus, who in the following year made way for Valerius Gratus. But in A. D. 14 Augustus died, and Tiberius resolved that such rapid changes should be discontinued[3]. Gratus, therefore, held his command till A.D. 26. He deposed the high-priest Annas, and set up Ishmael, son of Phabi, but a furious uproar ensuing he deposed Ishmael, and elevated Eleazar, a son of Annas, to the pontificate, permitting the latter, under the name of Sagan, or *deputy*, to discharge the spiritual functions of his office and conduct the ceremonial rites. But this appointment was of no long duration. Deeming Annas to possess too much influence the procurator deposed Eleazar, and set up Simon, son of Kamith, who held the office for less than a year, and then made way for Joseph Caiaphas, the Sagan's son-in law[4]. These rapid changes shew how

[1] Jos. *Ant.* XVII. 2. 1.

[2] Jos. *Ant.* XVIII. 2. 2; Lewin's *Fasti Sacri*, p. 160, 1.

[3] Seeing that a rapid succession of governors only increased the oppressions and exactions of the provinces; the governor, who anticipated but a short harvest, making the most of his time, and extorting as much as he was able in the shortest possible period. Jos. *Ant.* XVII. 7. 5; Merivale, V, 281.

[4] Jos. *Ant.* XVIII. 2. 2. Some think that Annas was now

entirely the high-priesthood was at this time at the mercy of the Roman governors.

Valerius Gratus was succeeded in A.D. 26[1] by Pontius Pilate[2]. He brought with him his wife, and a Roman household, established himself at Cæsarea, but repaired oftener than any of his predecessors to Jerusalem. Resolved to keep on good terms with the noble families, and to unite with himself as many as possible who were likely to help him to preserve the public peace, he suffered the Jewish priests to manage their own affairs. So Annas remained Sagan, and Caiaphas high-priest.

But one of his first acts roused the furious animosity of his new subjects. He resolved to transport the head-quarters of the army from Cæsarea to Jerusalem. With the soldiers, followed, as a matter of course, the standards, bearing the image of Cæsar; but as they were introduced in the night-time they did not at first attract attention[3]. No sooner, however, was the fact observed, than there were no bounds to the rage of the people. They resorted in crowds to his residence at Cæsarea, and besought him to remove the obnoxious emblems. For five days they beset his palace, and at length he gave the signal to his troops to put them to death, unless they desisted from troubling him. Thereupon the petitioners flung themselves upon the ground, and declared their willingness to meet death in any shape,

Nasi or President of the Sanhedrin, an office not always held by the high-priest. Ellicott, 333, n.

[1] The *gens* of the Pontii, with whom he may have been connected either by descent or adoption, is first conspicuous in Roman history in the person of C. Pontius Telesinus, the great Samnite general. Smith's *Bibl. Dict.*

[2] By some (i) deemed to denote "armed with the *pilum*, or javelin;" by others (ii) considered an abbreviation of pileatus, from *pileus*, "the cap or badge of manumitted slaves," indicating that he was either a *libertus*, i. e. "freedman," or descended from one. Smith's *Bibl. Dict.*

[3] Jos. *Ant.* XVIII. 3. 1.

rather than see their city polluted with heathen symbols. Their undaunted bearing had its effect. The procurator deemed it best to concede the point, and the standards were brought back to Cæsarea.

In spite, however, of this warning, he on another occasion had a clear proof of the refractory spirit of the people. Anxious to signalise his reign in Judæa by erecting a noble aqueduct, which was to bring a supply of water to the city from a distance of twenty-five miles, and wanting funds, he appropriated the Corban[1], or the money laid up in the Temple and dedicated to God. This act roused the Jews to madness. They gathered in thousands and tens of thousands before his palace-gates, obstructed the works, and demanded that the sacred treasures should be restored[2]. Resolved not to be thwarted, Pilate ordered a company of the legionaries, carrying daggers under their garments, to surround and disperse them. The soldiers carried out his orders with greater cruelty than he had intended, charged the rioters, chased them into the Temple-courts, slew great numbers, and wounded many more, so that their blood was mingled with the blood of the victims on the altar.

Such was the man who now presided over the province of Judæa. Under his rule, and that of his predecessors, the Roman yoke cut more and more deeply into the heart of the nation. Finding no hope from their own chiefs, who all sided with the Romans, the people prayed with increased earnestness that the Messiah, the Deliverer, would come. The Galilæans in the North, the Separatists in the South waxed hotter and hotter in their hatred of their heathen rulers[3]. Many

[1] Comp. Mark vii. 11.

[2] Jos. *Ant.* XVIII. 3. 2.

[3] "With the Roman legions came the Roman fiscal system; harbour-dues, post-dues, town-dues, customs, excise; in the streets a house-tax, in the markets a fruit-tax,

claiming the title of Messiah appeared, and gathered numbers of excited followers. But their careers were soon cut short, and they were swept away before the Roman legions.

But before Pilate had been many months in power, all Jerusalem and Judæa was roused by the appearance of a strange Preacher on the banks of the Jordan[1], announcing the advent of a very different Messiah from that expected by the nation, and the speedy establishment of a kingdom not of earth but of heaven.

everywhere a poll-tax. The Jews began to groan under the weight, and sicken under the names of these Roman imposts...their nationality was gone, they were denied the grain of comfort which an Oriental finds in seeing and kissing the foot that grinds him into dust. For many years after Archelaus left Jerusalem, the Jews rarely saw the faces of their lords. Augustus dwelt at Rome, Quirinus at Antioch, Coponius at Cæsarea. Jerusalem was garrisoned by a subaltern, governed by a priest." H. Dixon's *Holy Land*, I. 238.

[1] The 15th year of Tiberius mentioned by St Luke iii. 1. either (i) includes the two years during which Tiberius appears to have been associated with Augustus, or (ii) coincides not with the first appearance, but the captivity of John the Baptist, "the epoch, from which, in accordance with ancient tradition, the narrative of the first three Gospels appears to date." Ellicott's *Lectures*, 104, n.; Wieseler's *Chronol. Synop.*

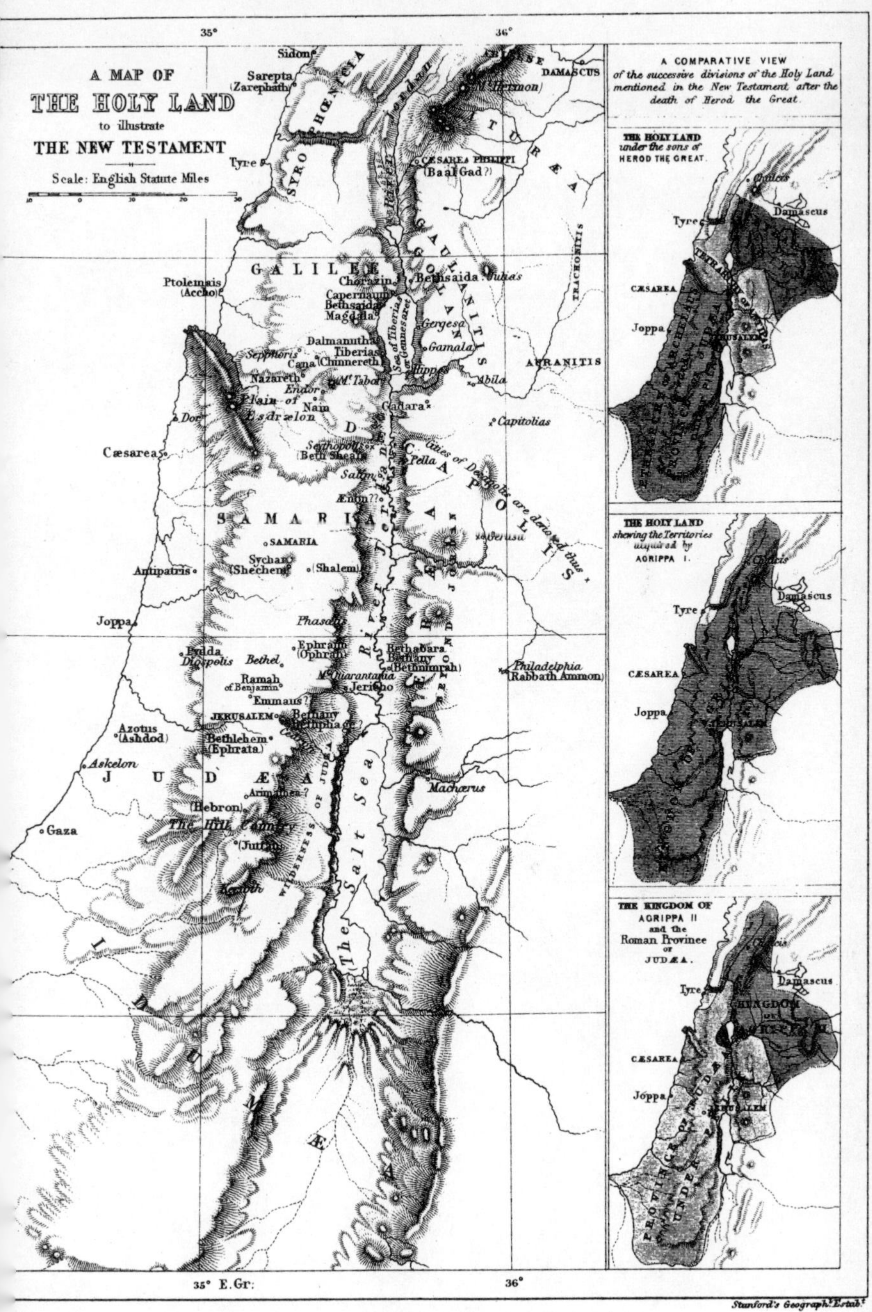

A MAP OF
THE HOLY LAND
to illustrate
THE NEW TESTAMENT
Scale: English Statute Miles
35°
36°
Sidon
Sarepta
(Zarephath)
Tyre
SYRO PHOENICIA
DAMASCUS
(Mt Hermon)
ITUREA
CÆSAREA PHILIPPI
(Baal Gad?)
GAULANITIS
TRACHONITIS
GALILEE
Ptolemais
(Accho)
Chorazin
Bethsaida Julias
Capernaum
Bethsaida
Magdala
Gergesa
Gamala
Dalmanutha
Tiberias
(Chinnereth)
Sea of Tiberias or Gennesaret
Sepphoris
Cana
Nazareth
Mt Tabor
Hippos
Abila
AURANITIS
Endor
Nain
Plain of Esdrælon
Gadara
Capitolias
Dor
Cæsarea
Scythopolis
(Beth Shean)
Pella
Cities of Decapolis are denoted thus
DECAPOLIS
Salim
Ænon??
SAMARIA
Gerasa
Sychar
(Shechem)
(Shalem)
Antipatris
Joppa
Phasaelis
River Jordan
Lydda
Diospolis
Bethel
Ephraim
(Ophrah)
Bethabara
Bethany
(Bethnimrah)
Philadelphia
(Rabbath Ammon)
Ramah
of Benjamin
Mt Quarantania
Jericho
Emmaus?
JERUSALEM
Bethany
Bethphage
Azotus
(Ashdod)
Bethlehem
(Ephrata)
Askelon
JUDÆA
Arimathea?
(Hebron)
The Hill Country
(Juttah)
Gaza
WILDERNESS OF JUDEA
The Salt Sea
Machærus
IDUMÆA
35° E.Gr:
36°
A COMPARATIVE VIEW
of the successive divisions of the Holy Land mentioned in the New Testament after the death of Herod the Great.
THE HOLY LAND
under the sons of
HEROD THE GREAT.
Chalcis
Damascus
Tyre
CÆSAREA
Joppa
JERUSALEM
THE HOLY LAND
shewing the Territories acquired by
AGRIPPA I.
THE KINGDOM OF
AGRIPPA II
and the
Roman Province
of
JUDÆA.
KINGDOM
PROVINCE
Stanford's Geograph. Estab.
London: Macmillan & Co. Ltd.

PART II

FROM THE BEGINNING OF THE MINISTRY OF THE BAPTIST TO THE FIRST PASSOVER.

CHAPTER I

THE PREACHING OF JOHN—THE BAPTISM OF CHRIST.

A.U.C. 780, A.C. 27.

THE strange Preacher was none other than John, the son of Zacharias. Recalling in his garb and appearance one of the Prophets of the Old Testament, he now came forth from his retirement, and straightway commenced his task of preparing the way for the Messiah. The wilderness of Judæa (Mtt. iii. 1), that is the dry and unpeopled region extending from the gates of Hebron and Jerusalem to the shores of the Dead Sea, was the first scene of his ministration. Thence he moved northwards towards the Jordan, and at Bethabara, or rather Bethany[1], administered the rite of baptism in its rushing waters to all who were willing to receive it.

The news of his appearance quickly spread throughout the length and breadth of the land. From Jerusalem, the towns of Judæa, and the Jordan valley, multi-

[1] Situated either thirty miles north of Jericho, near Succoth, the northern ford, or nearly east of that city, the ordinary point of passage across the river. Ellicott's *Lectures*, 106, n.

tudes flocked forth to hear him (Mtt. iii. 5; Mk. i. 5). The river's banks became like the streets of a crowded city. Pharisees and Sadducees (Mtt. iii. 7), tax-gatherers (Lk. iii. 12), and soldiers (Lk. iii. 14), rich and poor, gathered around him and listened to his burning words. No temporal Messiah did he proclaim, no king higher than the Cæsars, no rising against the Roman yoke. Personal repentance, personal reformation, this was his message. To all alike his language was bold, severe, uncompromising. The chiefs of the great religious parties approached him, and were bidden to abjure all trust in mere descent from Abraham (Mtt. iii. 9), to bring forth fruits worthy of the repentance they professed, and to flee *from the wrath to come*. The multitudes groaning under the Roman dominion drew near, and enquired what they should do in view of the great crisis he proclaimed to be at hand, and were bidden to cultivate mutual charity (Lk. iii. 11). The tax-gatherers offered themselves for baptism, and were told that there was room for them, if they would practise justice (Lk. iii. 12). Rough, and too often brutal, soldiers enquired what they should do, and they too were not rejected, but exhorted to abstain from violence and pillage, and to be content with their wages (Lk. iii. 14).

With a boldness hitherto unparalleled, save in the teaching of the sternest of the prophets of the Old Covenant, the son of Zacharias declared *the whole nation* to be spiritually unclean. The baptism, which the Jewish teachers required of all who would be admitted as proselytes from heathenism[1], he demanded of the elect nation itself, of high and low, rich and poor, learned and unlearned, if they would be prepared for the coming of the Messiah. *The axe*, he cried, *lay at the root of the trees*, and EVERY *tree which brought not forth good*

[1] See above, p. 118, note.

fruit would be hewn down and cast into the fire (Mtt. iii. 10).

Great were the searchings of heart caused by the appearance of this strange Preacher, and the utterances of this *Voice crying in the wilderness* (Lk. iii. 15). Some thought he was the Messiah, the hope of Israel; others Elias; others the Prophet of whom Moses had spoken. John replied he was none of these. He was only preparing the way for Another. He, indeed, baptized with water unto repentance, but One was at hand far *mightier than himself, the latchet of whose shoes he was not worthy to bear*[1], *He should baptize with the Holy Ghost and with fire. His winnowing fan was in His hand, and He would throughly purge His floor, gathering the wheat into His garner, but burning up the chaff with unquenchable fire* (Lk. iii. 16—18).

The impression thus made upon the people was profound. How long the Baptist continued his work of preparation we are not told[2]. But at length, even as he declared, the MESSIAH appeared, and commenced His public ministry. Leaving the home of His childhood in retired Nazareth (Mtt. iii. 13; Mk. i. 9), probably about the close of the year A.D. 27, JESUS advanced southward towards the Jordan Valley. Either at the northern ford of Succoth or the more southern one east of Jericho, He found His great Forerunner, and desired to be baptized by him. The Baptist, who had hitherto rebuked without distinction the sins of all classes and all grades, was deeply moved by the request. With an instinctive conviction of the immaculate purity of Him, whose ad-

[1] "Lightfoot shews that it was the token of a slave having become his master's property, to *loose* his shoe, to *tie* the same, or to *carry* the necessary articles for him to the bath." Alford on Matt. iii. 11.

[2] Probably about six months after his ministry had begun. Ellicott's *Lectures*, 102, n.

vent he had announced, he sought to prevent[1] Him, saying, *I have need to be baptized of Thee, and comest Thou to me?* (Mtt. iii. 14). But his objection was overruled. *Suffer it to be so now*, replied the Holy One; *for thus it becometh us to fulfil all righteousness* (Mtt. iii. 15). Then at length the Baptist consented, and when all the people had been baptized (Lk. iii. 21), descended with Him into the river, and administered the initiatory rite, after which the Redeemer ascended from the water, and was engaged in solemn prayer (Lk. iii. 21), when the heavens were opened, and in an embodied form, like unto a Dove, the Holy Spirit descended, and *abode upon Him.* But this was not all, for at the same time there came a Voice from heaven, saying, *Thou art My beloved Son, in whom I am well pleased* (Mtt. iii. 16, 17; Lk. iii. 22; Mk. i. 11).

Thus in the presence of His Forerunner, the Divine nature of the Messiah was attested, and His work of Redemption inaugurated. He had come to *destroy the works of the devil* (1 Jn. iii. 8), His very first work, therefore, was to enter on a conflict with the great Enemy of mankind. *Full of the Holy Ghost*, He was *led up* by the motions of that Spirit (Mtt. iv. 1), either into the wilderness of Judæa, or the lonely desert mountains east of the Jordan[2], to *be tempted by the devil* (Mtt.

[1] Διεκώλυεν, Mtt. iii. 14, a much stronger word than the simple ἐκώλυεν, and denoting earnestness and an active endeavour to prevent him.

[2] Ellicott, p. 109. The traditional site is the mountain Quarantania, "a high and precipitous wall of rock 12 or 1500 feet above the plain west of the Jordan near Jericho." The side facing the plain is as perpendicular and apparently as high as the rock of Gibraltar, and upon the summit are still visible the ruins of an ancient convent. Midway below are caverns hewn in the perpendicular rock, where hermits formerly retired to fast and pray in imitation of the "Forty Days." Robinson's *Palestine*, I. 567; Thomson's *L. and B.* 617; Tristram, pp. 208, 209.

iv. 1; Mk. i. 12). For forty days and forty nights He remained amidst the thickets and caverns of that dreary region, abounding in fierce and savage beasts (Mk. i. 13), and during all this period He had nothing to eat.

At length, when hunger had weakened the energies of the body, the Tempter approached, and suggested that if He was in truth the Son of God, He should command the stones that lay around to become bread. But the Holy One detected at once the subtle insinuation to mistrust His heavenly Father's power, and in the words of Scripture (Deut. viii. 3) replied, *It is written, Man shall not live by bread alone, but by every word that proceedeth out of the mouth of God* (Mtt. iv. 4; Lk. iv. 4).

Foiled in his attempt to induce the Redeemer by a selfish display of power to satisfy the wants of the body, the Tempter now sought by another avenue to achieve a victory over Him. Taking Him up to an exceeding high mountain, he displayed before His eyes in a moment of time all *the kingdoms of the world and the glories of them*, promising to place all in His power, if He would only fall down and worship him. But this temptation also the Holy One repelled. Falling back a second time on the revealed Word, and the same portion of it (Deut. vi. 13), He replied, *It is written, Thou shalt worship the Lord thy God, and Him only shalt thou serve.*

But yet again the Evil One renewed his attack. Taking the Redeemer into the Holy City, he placed Him on the lofty pinnacle, the topmost ridge of the South side of the Temple, and bade Him, if He were the Son of God, vindicate His eternal nature, cast Himself down, and thus display by one dazzling exhibition of power His relation to the Supreme, and confirm His Messianic claims. But he was no more successful than before. The Redeemer saw through his wiles, and the sophistry wherewith he sought to support his demand by quoting the language of the Psalmist (Ps. xci. 11), *He shall give His angels charge concerning Thee, and in their hands they shall bear Thee up, lest at any time Thou dash Thy foot against a stone.* For the third time He had recourse to the written Word, and for the third time referring to the same portion of it (Deut. vi. 16), made answer, *Thou shalt not tempt the Lord thy God.*

With this last assault the Temptation was ended. Where the first Adam had fallen, the second Adam had triumphed, nor swerved for a moment from the path of strictest obedience to the will of His Father in Heaven. The Devil now left Him *for a season* (Lk. iv. 13), or rather till a more convenient occasion for renewing his attempt, *and angels came and ministered unto Him*, who had already proved Himself "more than conqueror" over the crafts and assaults of the Wicked One.

CHAPTER II

CALL OF THE FIRST DISCIPLES—THE MARRIAGE AT CANA.

A. D. 27.

SUSTAINED by the ministries of these blessed spirits the Saviour returned towards the Jordan Valley, and drew near the ford of Bethabara or Bethany (Jn. i. 28). Here again He met the Baptist, who was still prosecuting his work, and baptizing the multitudes who flocked around him. Such was the effect produced by his preaching, that the rulers at Jerusalem determined to interpose, and the day before a formal deputation had waited upon him to enquire whether he was the Messiah, or Elias, or the prophet predicted by Moses (Jn. i. 21). Again he declared that he had no pretensions to such a dignity, that he was but the *Voice of one crying in the wilderness*, and preparing the way of the Messiah, of One infinitely mightier than himself, *the very latchet of whose shoe he was unworthy to unloose.*

But now, lifting up his eyes, he beheld Him to whom he had borne such faithful testimony (Jn. i. 29), and addressing Him as *the Lamb of God, who taketh away the sin of the world*, repeated his solemn and assured conviction of His Divine nature (Jn. i. 30—34). Again, the day following, as he was standing in the company of two of His disciples, he beheld the Redeemer, and in their hearing pointed Him out under the same impressive title. On this occasion his words were not without their effect. The two disciples, one of whom was Andrew, a native of Bethsaida (Jn. i. 41), and the other, in all probability, the Evangelist St John, were so powerfully affected by them, that, drawn as it were by a powerful magnet, they left the Baptist and *followed Jesus* (Jn. i. 37).

The Redeemer perceived them following Him, and enquired what they sought? *Rabbi, where dwellest Thou?* was their reply. He mercifully bade them *come and see*, and they went and abode with Him for the rest of that day (Jn. i. 39), and resolved to follow Him. Others soon followed their example. Andrew went in quest of his own brother Simon, and declaring that the true Messiah had been found brought him to Jesus, who named him Cephas or Peter, *the Rock-man.* The day following, the Saviour set out in the direction of Galilee, and finding Philip, a native, like Andrew and Peter, of Bethsaida, bade him join their company. Philip obeyed, and falling in with Nathanael[1], the son of Tolmai, a

[1] The identity of Nathanael and Bartholomew appears highly probable.

a. St John twice (i. 45; xxi. 2) mentions Nathanael, never Bartholomew.

b. The other Evangelists (Mtt. x. 3; Mk. iii. 18; Lk. vi. 14) all speak of Bartholomew, never of Nathanael.

c. Philip first brought Nathanael to Jesus, and Bartho-

native of Cana in Galilee (Jn. xxi. 2), announced that He, of whom Moses and the Prophets had written, had been discovered in the person of Jesus of Nazareth, the Son of Joseph. Though a native of Galilee, Nathanael could not at first believe that any good could come out of a town which enjoyed so low a reputation as Nazareth. But his friend bade him come and judge for himself. He obeyed, and was drawing near the Holy One, when he heard His declaration that he was *an Israelite indeed in whom was no guile* (Jn. i. 48). So little was Nathanael prepared for such words of praise, that he could not refrain from enquiring how he had become known to Jesus. *Before that Philip called thee, when thou wast under the fig-tree*[1], answered the Holy One. The reply convinced the other that One from whom no secrets were hid could be no ordinary Being. *Rabbi*, said he, *Thou art the Son of God, Thou art the King of Israel*, and was enrolled in the number of his new Master's followers.

On the third day after His departure towards Galilee, the Saviour with His five disciples reached the little village of Cana[2], situated no great distance from Naza-

lomew is mentioned by each of the first three Evangelists immediately after Philip.

d. St Luke couples Philip with Bartholomew precisely in the same way as Simon with his brother Andrew, and Joses with his brother John.

[1] Perhaps for the purpose of prayer and meditation. "The foliage of the fig-tree produces a thick shade, and the Jewish Rabbis were accustomed to rise early and study beneath it." Wordsworth's *Notes*.

[2] Identified either with (i) *Kefr Kenna*, a small village about 4½ miles N.E. of Nazareth, which "now contains only the ruins of a church, said to stand over the house in which the miracle was performed;" or (ii) *Kana el Jelil*, about 5 miles north of Sepphoris, and 9 from Nazareth, near Jotapata, the name of which is considered by some completely to represent the Hebrew original. Robinson, II. 346—349; Thomson, *Land and Book*, p. 425; Stanley, *S. and P.* 367.

reth. Here a marriage-feast was about to be celebrated, at which the Virgin was present, and the Holy One with His new found followers was invited as well. Their presence appears to have increased beyond expectation the number of the guests, and to have rendered the provision made for their entertainment insufficient. When, therefore, they wanted wine, the mother of the Saviour directed His attention to the fact. Whatever was the precise meaning she herself attached to her words, they drew down upon her a slight rebuke. *Woman*, was His reply, *what have I to do with thee? Mine hour is not yet come.* But as though these words concealed a real granting of her request, she bade the servants execute any command He might give, and the issue justified her expectations (Jn. ii. 2—5).

In the apartment, where the feast was proceeding, were placed, for the sake of the frequent lustrations of the Jews, six large waterpots of water, containing as much as two or three firkins a-piece. These the Saviour commanded the servants to fill with water. And on their filling them up to the brim, bade them draw out and bear to the master of the feast, *i.e.* either one of the guests set over the banquet by general consent of the guests, or a chief attendant who ordered the course of the feast, and superintended the ministrations of the inferior servants. He tasted the water now converted into wine, and knowing not whence it was, remarked that men usually set forth good wine at the beginning of the feast, and afterwards that which was worse, but *He had kept the good wine* until then (Jn. ii. 10).

Unobtrusively, however, as it had been wrought, the reality of this first miracle could not escape the notice of the guests. The *glory* of the Saviour hitherto hidden was now *manifested*, and the faith of the disciples in their new-found Master was confirmed. The marriage festivities of the Jews usually lasted six or seven days, and at the close of this period with His mother, His brethren, and His five disciples (Jn. ii. 12), the Saviour went down to Capernaum[1] on the shore of the lake of Gennesaret. The Passover was now nigh at hand, and Capernaum would afford a convenient point for joining the pilgrim companies going up to Jerusalem[2], and there He abode a few days (Jn. ii. 12), engaging, probably, in private intercourse with His disciples, rather than any public ministrations in the city.

CHAPTER III

THE FIRST PASSOVER, AND CLEANSING OF THE TEMPLE.

A. D. 28.

AFTER a stay of not many days at Capernaum (Jn. ii. 12) the Redeemer and His five disciples turned their steps southward towards Jerusalem, to celebrate the first Passover of His public ministry (Jn. ii. 13).

Strange and full of deep significance was the scene which the Holy City presented at this season. The streets were filled with multitudes of Jews and proselytes, who had come up from all quarters of the world to celebrate the Feast. The hills around were whiten-

[1] It is a striking confirmation of our Lord's words (Mtt. xi. 23) that the very site of Capernaum, then a flourishing and populous place, is now one of the most hotly-contested points connected with the geography of Palestine: (i) some would place it at *Khân Minyeh*, at the N.E. end of the Plain of Gennesaret: (ii) others place the Fountain of Capernaum, mentioned by Josephus (*B. J.* III. 10. 8) at *Et-Tabiga*, a little to the north of *Khân Minyeh*, and the town itself at *Tell Hum*, where there are the remains of a place of considerable extent, "consisting chiefly of the fallen walls of dwellings and other buildings, all of unhewn stone." Robinson, I. 540; Thomson, *L. and B.*

[2] Lange's *Life of Christ*, II. 298.

ed with countless flocks of lambs[1] and kids. The gates, especially the Sheep-gate, were choked with moving masses of helpless victims ready to be examined by the priests, and on being pronounced free from blemish, to be selected by each Paschal company for their Paschal meal.

In the midst of a moving scene like this He, who had been already pointed out as the *Lamb of God*, entered the city. Repairing to the Temple, He was confronted, probably in the Court of the Gentiles, with a scene of desecration, which called forth the first[2] display of holy zeal for the dwelling-place of Him, whom He had already declared to be His Father (Lk. ii. 49). For the convenience of Jews and proselytes residing at a distance from the Holy City, a kind of market had been established in the outer court, and here sacrificial victims, incense, oil, wine, and other things necessary for the service and the sacrifices, were to be obtained. The common money, moreover, circulated in foreign countries not being receivable within the Temple, the money-changers had set up their tables in the same locality, to exchange all common and foreign coins for the sacred shekel, alone current in the Temple precincts. But together with the money-changing other business had gradually crept in, and in place of the order and decorum that ought to have reigned there, the noisy huckstering of merchants and traders disturbed the devotions of the worshippers, and converted the Sanctuary of the most High into the likeness of a wrangling mart.

Such was the scene that presented itself to the Saviour in the courts of His Father's House. As soon as

[1] Josephus (*B. J.* VI. 9. 3) estimates the number of lambs sacrificed at the Passover in the time of Nero at 256,500.

[2] This cleansing of the Temple recorded by St John is clearly distinct from the later one mentioned by Mtt. xxi. 12, &c.; Mk. xi. 15, &c.; Lk. xix. 15, &c.

His eye had rested upon it, He made *a scourge of small cords* (Jn. ii. 15), and with this simple weapon, singly and alone, drove forth the sheep and oxen. Then overthrowing the tables of the money-changers, He poured out their unholy gains, and with a voice of conscious authority bade even those who sold doves, to take those things thence, nor make *His Father's house a house of merchandise.* Awed by His words and His calm majesty, the desecrators left the scene of their unholy traffic, while others wondering at an act, which legally could only be performed by one of the Sanhedrin or a prophet, approached Him and requested a sign, the performance of some miracle or prodigy, in attestation of His right to do these things[1] (Jn. ii. 18).

Thus challenged the Holy One did not withhold a "sign." With that majestic calmness, which ever distinguished Him, but without a single word of comment or explanation, He said, *Destroy this Temple, and in three days I will raise it up.* Perplexed and confounded the Jews replied, *Forty and six years was this Temple in building, and wilt Thou raise it up in three days?* But to their enquiry no answer was vouchsafed. They had asked for a "sign," and a "sign" had been given, but in the shape of a "parable," a "dark saying," which they never forgot[2], and which, though not understood by the disciples at the time, was after-

[1] "Any Jew might come forward as a zealot against illegal abuses in the national life (Num. xxv. 7), but the greatest zealots generally justified their proceedings as prophets and workers of miracles (1 K. xviii. 23, 24). By His act the Lord had rebuked the whole nation, and the Sanhedrin itself; they demanded, therefore, a sign to legitimate His proceeding." Lange, II. 300; Milman, I. 159 n.

[2] How widely this mysterious saying, though misunderstood, was circulated, and how deep was the impression it made, is clear from several subsequent incidents. See Mtt. xxvi. 61; Mk. xiv. 58; Mtt. xxvii. 39, 40; Mk. xv. 29.

wards revealed to them in all its deep meaning (Jn. ii. 21, 22).

But another incident was to render this Passover for ever memorable. During His stay at Jerusalem (Jn. ii. 23) the Saviour wrought signs and wonders, which stirred the hearts of those who witnessed them, and caused many to *believe on His Name.* But their faith sprang from imperfect motives, and He, who knew what was in man, would not entrust Himself to them, or unveil the mysteries of His kingdom. Still even thus early there was one to whom He could more nearly reveal Himself.

One of the members of the Sanhedrin[1] at this time was a Pharisee, named Nicodemus, who had probably heard of the marvellous incident, which had so lately occurred in the Temple-courts, and had witnessed one or more of the mighty works, which the Stranger from Nazareth had wrought. Convinced that He could be no ordinary person, that unassisted by Divine Power He could not perform such signs and wonders, he had resolved, in spite of his position, in spite of the risk he ran, in spite of the natural prejudice against so obscure a teacher, to go himself and ascertain who and what He was.

Under cover of night, therefore, he sought out the Saviour, who not only graciously received him, but unfolded to him the mystery of a birth, *not of the will of man, nor of the will of the flesh*, but of water and of the Holy Spirit (Jn. iii. 5—8). And when the wondering ruler enquired *how could these things be*, He went on to hint at a still deeper mystery, and to intimate the true purport of the coming of the Son of Man, the Messiah, whom he and the nation expected. *As Moses*, that Moses whose writings he studied and expounded,

[1] Comp. Jn. iii. 1; vii. 26, 50; Lk. xxiv. 20.

lifted up the serpent in the wilderness[1], *even so must the Son of Man be lifted up, that whosoever believeth in Him should not perish, but have everlasting life* (Jn. iii. 12—16). How far the Jewish ruler entered into the meaning of this mysterious intimation, so entirely opposed to all that was expected by his nation of their Messiah, and how far it served to stimulate him to still deeper enquiries into the Law and the Prophets, we are not told. Certain, however, it is that he was not entirely alienated from the new Teacher, and we shall find at a later period that he, who thus came to Jesus by night, lived to plead for Him in open day before the council of the nation (Jn. vii. 50, 51), and to do honour to His crucified body, when all the Apostles had forsaken Him and fled (Jn. xix. 39).

PART III

FROM THE FIRST PASSOVER TO THE ELECTION OF THE APOSTLES.

CHAPTER I.

IMPRISONMENT OF THE BAPTIST—THE WOMAN OF SAMARIA.

A. D. 28.

THE private interview with Nicodemus just related appears to have closed the occurrences at this first eventful Passover. When the pilgrim-companies broke up each for their own homes, the Saviour repaired with His more immediate followers to the north-eastern parts

[1] For the circumstances here alluded to see *Class-Book of O. T. History*, pp. 182, 183.

of Judæa near the Jordan. Here He too administered the rite of baptism by the hands of His disciples (Jn. iii. 22; iv. 2), and quickly drew around Him so great a number of followers, that the adherents of the Baptist began to find a sensible decrease in the multitude that flocked around their master.

Repairing, therefore, to him at Ænon[1] near Salim[2], where he was baptizing, they drew his attention to the fact that HE, to whom he had borne witness, was also baptizing, and all men were flocking to Him. But John knew nothing of the mortification of his followers. With a true greatness of soul far exalted above their wounded feelings, he asserted in the most emphatic manner that his position was only secondary with that of the Prophet of Nazareth. He *must decrease*, but the Other would *increase*, for He was the Bridegroom and had the Bride. He himself was but the *friend of the Bridegroom*, and rejoiced to *hear His voice*, and was satisfied with that measure of joy (Jn. iii. 29—32).

This was the last public testimony of the Baptist to the exalted nature of the Saviour's person and work. His own career was rapidly drawing to a close. The place where he was baptizing was close to the dominions of Herod-Antipas, the ruler of Galilee and Peræa. This monarch had been married by his father to the daughter of Aretas, king of Arabia Petræa, but becoming acquainted at Rome with Herodias, the wife of his

[1] Ænon means *place of fountains*, a Greek form of the Chaldee word denoting the same.

[2] According to Eusebius and Jerome, Salim existed in their day near the Jordan, eight Roman miles south of Scythopolis. In exact accordance with this position the name *Salûm* has been lately discovered six English miles south of Beisan, and two miles west of the Jordan. Beside it there gushes out a splendid fountain, and rivulets wind about in all directions, so that of few places in Palestine could it be said so truly *there was much water there*. Van de Velde, II. 356.

half-brother Herod-Philip, he made overtures of marriage to her, which were accepted, on condition that he divorced the daughter of Aretas[1]. But the facts becoming known to the latter, she fled to her father's court, who forthwith assembled an army to avenge her wrongs, and punish her guilty husband. The contest waxed hot on the frontier of Herod's dominions, and it was, not improbably, on his way to confront his father-in-law, when he first encountered the Baptist. If he had hoped to escape the censure of one, whose influence with all classes was unbounded, he was utterly deceived. The Baptist was no *reed shaken by the wind* (Lk. vii. 24). Boldly, straight-forwardly, he not only rebuked the king for his notorious offences (Lk. iii. 19), but denounced the royal incest, and declared the marriage unlawful (Mtt. xiv. 4; Mk. vi. 18). Such an outspoken reproof from one, whom all reverenced as a prophet, the monarch could not forgive, and therefore flung the bold preacher into prison, probably in the gloomy castle of Machærus, which his father had built on the eastern shore of the Dead Sea to overawe the wild Arab tribes[2].

The imprisonment of His great forerunner was announced to the Saviour at a time when He was also aware that the results of His ministry had roused the jealousy of the Pharisees (Jn. iv. 1). Accordingly, He left Judæa, and prepared to return by the shortest route through Samaria to the hills of Galilee (Jn. iv. 3, 4). It was now late in December, four months from the harvest[3] (Jn. iv. 35), when He thus set out with His disciples, and reaching the well near Shechem[4], which Jacob had built in the parcel of ground he gave to his son

[1] Jos. *Ant.* XVIII. 5. 1.　[2] Jos. *Ant.* XVIII. 5. 2.

[3] See the Calendar in *Class-Book of O. T. History*, p. 155.

[4] At this time called Sychar by the Jews of the south, in studied contempt, as denoting either *falsehood*, i.e. *idol-worship* (Hab. ii. 18), or *drunkard*.

Joseph, He sat upon it, weary with travel, for it was the sixth hour, the sultry hour of noon[1].

As He sat there alone, for His disciples had gone to the neighbouring town to purchase provisions, a woman of Samaria approached with her pitcher on her head, and the Saviour requested of her water to quench His thirst. Astounded that such a request should be made to her by a Jew, she enquired how He could thus address a Samaritan, with whom it was not lawful to have any dealings[2]? On this, drawing, as was ever His wont, similitudes from present circumstances, He excited her wonder by telling her of *living waters* at His command *springing up unto everlasting life* (Jn. iv. 10, 14), and increased it by revealing His acquaintance with the secret of her life, for she was living in adultery (Jn. iv. 18). Roused by this proof of superhuman knowledge to the fact that she was in the presence of no ordinary Being, she instantly sought to change the subject, and pointing to the slopes of Gerizim[3] near at hand, remarked that her fathers worshipped on that mountain, while the Jews affirmed that in Jerusalem was the place where

[1] Jacob's well is a spot the identity of which has never been seriously questioned; Jews and Samaritans, Christians and Mahommedans, unite in attesting it. It is situated "on the end of a low spur or swell, running out from the north-eastern base of Gerizim," the mouth being encumbered by the ruins of a Christian church once built over it. "The width of the bore is about nine feet, the upper portion built in with neatly dressed and squared stones like the masonry of the wells of Beersheba, the lower portion hewn, to all appearance, out of the solid rock." The well is still deep, about seventy-five or eighty feet, though evidently choked with many feet of rubbish, and oftentimes filled with much water. Robinson, III. 132; Tristram, 146; Stanley's *S. and P.* pp. 240, 241.

[2] On the feeling of the Samaritans towards the Jews, see above, p. 122.

[3] For the building and destruction of the temple there, see above, pp. 3, and 57.

men ought to worship. Thereupon the Saviour assured her that *an hour was at hand, when neither on Gerizim nor yet at Jerusalem would men worship the Father; the Samaritans worshipped they knew not what; the Jews worshipped that which they knew, for of them was salvation; but a time was coming when the true worshippers would worship the Father in spirit and in truth.* The astonished woman replied that this might be, when Messiah came, for He could *teach them all things* (Jn. iv. 25), and then heard from the Speaker's own lips the first clear and distinct announcement that He was the long-expected Messiah (Jn. iv. 26)[1].

At this juncture the disciples returned with the provisions they had bought, and marvelled that their Master talked with one of the hateful race, but ventured on no open expostulation. Meanwhile the woman herself had returned to the town, and bade the inhabitants come and see One, who had *told her all that ever she did,* and could be no other than the Messiah (Jn. iv. 28, 29). Accordingly the townsfolk came forth to see the Saviour, and requested Him to abide with them, which He did, staying amongst them two days, during which period, the number, which had learned to believe on Him on account of the woman's testimony to His Omniscience, was increased by many others, who, listening to His own gracious words, were convinced that He was indeed *the Saviour of the world*[1] (Jn. iv. 42).

Thus to a woman of Samaria He, whose *meat it was to do the will of Him that sent Him and to finish His work* (Jn. iv. 34), revealed Himself as the true Messiah, and she became the first herald of the Gospel, the first-fruits of a harvest now sown and to be afterwards reaped by Philip the Deacon (Jn. iv. 38; Acts viii. 5; &c.).

[1] On the Samaritan expectation of the Messiah, see above, pp. 121, 122.

CHAPTER II.

SECOND VISIT TO CANA AND JERUSALEM.

A. D. 29.

AFTER this stay in Samaria the Saviour returned to Galilee. Thither had gone before Him the fame of the miracles He had wrought at Jerusalem, reported by those Galilæans who had returned from the Passover (Jn. iv. 45), and this was now confirmed by a second miracle wrought at Cana.

While staying in this little village, He was visited by a nobleman, or officer of state[1], not improbably in the service of Herod-Antipas, who besought him to go down to Capernaum, and heal his son who was lying at the point of death. Though he was clearly unable to conceive of any cure, save through the Lord's bodily presence, and was urgent that He should come down to Capernaum, the Holy One sent him away with the assurance that his son was alive. Contented with this word, the father returned, and on the morrow was met by his servants, who announced his son's recovery, and in answer to his enquiries when the youth had begun to amend, informed him that the day before, at the seventh hour[2], the fever not only began to abate, but *left* or suddenly forsook him. This the other remembered was the very hour when the Lord had assured him of his son's recovery, and he became a believer with all his family (Jn. iv. 53).

[1] Τις βασιλικός (Jn. iv. 46). Some have supposed him to have been Chuza, Herod's steward, whose wife was among the holy women that *ministered unto the Lord of their substance* (Lk. viii. 3). "This is not wholly improbable," writes Archbishop Trench, "for it would seem as if only some mighty and marvellous work of this kind would have drawn a steward of Herod's with his family into the net of the Gospel," *On the Miracles*, p. 119.

[2] One hour after noon.

After a brief stay in Galilee, the season approached for the celebration of the Feast of Purim[1], and the Redeemer went up to Jerusalem (Jn. v. 1). At this time there was near the Sheep-gate, through which the victims intended for sacrifice were usually brought into the city, a pool called in the Hebrew language Bethesda[2], or *the House of Mercy*, which at certain seasons possessed remarkable healing properties, heralded it would seem by a violent commotion or bubbling of the waters. Around the pool, sheltered by five porticoes (Jn. v. 2), there was wont to assemble a multitude of diseased persons, *lame, blind, withered, waiting for the troubling of the waters* (Jn. v. 3).

Amongst these was one who for upwards of 38 years had been a helpless paralytic, and had long watched in vain for an opportunity to descend into the healing stream. As often as with slow and painful motion he crawled towards the waters, another was certain to step in before him, and anticipate him in acquiring the welcome cure. Seeing this miserable sufferer, and knowing how long he had been thus afflicted, the Saviour drew near, and enquired whether he wished to be made whole. Deeming, probably, that he was only listening to words of casual sympathy, and little expecting a cure, the man contented himself with relating the sad story of his constant disappointments (Jn. v. 7). Great, then, must have been his astonishment, when the Saviour not

[1] The true reading in Jn. v. 1 appears to be ἑορτὴ without the article, and the feast spoken of is identified by Wieseler, Tischendorf, Ellicott and others, with that of Purim; for the institution of which see *Class-Book of O. T. History,* p. 475.

[2] By some identified with a large reservoir called the *Birket Israil* within the walls of the city and close to St Stephen's Gate, under the N.E. wall of the haram area. Robinson, however, identifies it with the "Fountain of the Virgin," in the Kedron valley, a little above the pool of Siloam. Smith's *Bibl. Dict.*

only bade him rise and take up the bed or pallet on which he had lain so long, but with the word gave him also the power to obey, so that he was instantly made whole, and taking up his bed bore it away with healthy tread.

It was a Sabbath-day on which this marvellous cure was wrought, and the carrying of any burden was regarded by the Pharisaic interpreters of the Law as a heinous violation of the sanctity of the day. The sight, therefore, of a man whose case must have been well known, thus openly and publicly violating a received rule, could not but excite much attention. Accordingly "the Jews," a term by which St John generally denotes the adherents of the Sanhedrin, summoned him before them, and questioned them closely concerning his conduct. With artless simplicity, the man replied that he was only acting up to the command of his Healer, but when further questioned who He was, could not say, for Jesus had vanished from the crowd when the cure was wrought (Jn. v. 13).

Shortly afterwards, however, he met his Healer in the Temple, and then returning informed the authorities that Jesus was the author of his cure. On this the Saviour Himself was called to account for His conduct (Jn. v. 16, 17), and proceeded to avow before His astonished and indignant auditors His union in dignity and honour with the eternal Father. This avowal, added to the fact that He had shewn dishonour to the Sabbath, roused the first symptoms of hostility on the part of the authorities at Jerusalem, and they even sought to kill Him (Jn. v. 18). But, undeterred by their opposition, the Holy One went on to claim plainly and unreservedly, the character and functions of the Messiah, to reiterate the fact of His Divine Original, and to declare that He was invested with power as the future Judge of mankind (Jn. v. 22—30). In support of these claims,

He appealed to the testimony which the Baptist had publicly borne to His exalted nature (Jn. v. 33—35), to the miracles which He had wrought (Jn. v. 36), to the authority of the sacred writings which testified of Him (Jn. v. 39), and to the great Lawgiver Moses, who, He declared, had written of Him (Jn. v. 46).

This incident forms an important epoch in the Gospel history[1]. The degree of toleration, and even of acceptance, with which the preaching of the Saviour had been received in Judæa, was exchanged for hostility, which, though as yet it led to no attempt to seize His Person, manifested itself with increasing distinctness. Accordingly, He left Judæa, which had shewn itself unwilling to receive Him, and retired to Galilee, and there taught in the synagogues (Lk. iv. 15).

CHAPTER III

MIRACLES AT NAZARETH AND CAPERNAUM.

A.D. 28.

AMONGST the places He now visited, the Redeemer repaired to Nazareth, where *He had been brought up* (Lk. iv. 16), and where many, if not all His kindred were residing. The Sabbath came round, and, as was His wont, He entered the Synagogue, and for the first time stood up to read in His native village. The worship, which began with prayer, was followed by the reading of the Law and the Prophets, and the portion of the latter either appointed for the day, or selected by His own Divine wisdom and foreknowledge, was taken from the 61st chapter of the prophet Isaiah. This portion was by universal consent applied to the Messiah, and

[1] Ellicott's *Lectures*, pp. 141, 142.

spoke of Him as anointed *to preach the Gospel to the poor*, as sent *to heal the broken-hearted*, *to preach deliverance to the captives and recovery of sight to the blind*, *to set at liberty them that were bound* (Lk. iv. 18, 19). Accordingly the Saviour read the words in the ears of those assembled, and then folding up the scroll, returned it to the *chazzan* or minister, and sat down[1].

This last act was a sign that He intended to take upon Himself the office of interpreter, and *the eyes of all were fastened upon Him* (Lk. iv. 20). *This day*, He began to say, *is this Scripture fulfilled in your ears*, and proceeded to pour forth the long-hidden treasures of wisdom and grace. The first effect upon His audience was one of signal approval. They all marvelled at the *gracious words which proceeded out of His lips* (Lk. iv. 22). But other and very different feelings soon arose in their minds. They began to recall the fact of His lowly origin (Lk. iv. 22), and when the Holy One went on to intimate that no prophet was accepted in his own country, that, as was illustrated, even in Old Testament times, by the cases of the widow of Zarephath and Naaman the Syrian, the mercies of God were not restricted to the Jews only (Lk. iv. 24—28), they were wrought up to such a pitch of fury, that they not only arose and thrust the Speaker out of their synagogue, but leading Him to *the brow of the hill on which their city was built*[2], would have cast Him down headlong, had He not, probably by an exercise of Di-

[1] For the service of the Synagogue see above, pp. 111—113.

[2] "They arose," it is said of the infuriated inhabitants, "and cast Him out of the city, and brought Him to *a brow of the mountain* (ἕως ὀφρύος τοῦ ὄρους) on which the city was built, so as to *cast Him down the cliff* (ὥστε κατακρημνίσαι αὐτόν). Most readers probably from these words imagine a town built on the summit of a mountain, from which summit the intended precipitation was to take place. This is

vine power, escaped from their hands, and disappeared (Lk. iv. 30).

Thus rejected at Nazareth as He had been at Jerusalem, the Saviour turned His steps towards the busy neighbourhood of the lake of Gennesaret, and took up His abode at Capernaum[1] (Mtt. iv. 13; Lk. iv. 31), whence He could easily communicate, as well by land as by lake, with many important towns, and in the event of

not the situation of Nazareth. Yet its position is still in accordance with the narrative. It is built 'upon,' that is, on the side of 'a mountain,' but the 'brow' is not beneath but over the town, and such a cliff (κρημνός), as is here implied, is to be found, as all modern travellers describe, in the abrupt face of the limestone rock, about thirty or forty feet high, overhanging the Maronite convent at the south-western corner of the town." Stanley's *S. and P.* p. 367; Robinson, II. 335; Tristram's *Land of Israel*, p. 121.

[1] "The Saviour *came down* (Lk. iv. 31; Jn. iv. 47, 51) from the high country of Galilee, where He had hitherto dwelt, and from henceforth made His permanent home in the deep retreat of the sea of Galilee...It was no retired mountain-lake by whose shore He took up His abode, such as might have attracted the eastern sage or western hermit. It was to the Roman Palestine almost what the manufacturing districts are to England. Nowhere, except in the capital itself, could He have found such a sphere for His works and words of mercy; from no other centre could *His fame* have so gone throughout all Syria (Mtt. iv. 24)...Far removed from the capital, mingled with the Gentile races of Lebanon and Arabia, the dwellers by the sea of Galilee were free from most of the strong prejudices which in the south of Palestine raised a bar to His reception. *The people in the land of Zabulon and Nephthalim, by the way of the sea, beyond Jordan, Galilee of the Gentiles,* had *sat in darkness;* but from that very cause *they saw* more clearly *the great Light* when it came: *to them which sat in the region and the shadow of death,* for that very reason *light sprang* up the more readily. He came to *preach the Gospel to the poor,* to *the weary and heavy laden; to seek and to save that which was lost.* Where could He find work so readily as in the ceaseless toil and turmoil of these teeming villages and busy waters? The heathen or half-heathen *publicans* or tax-

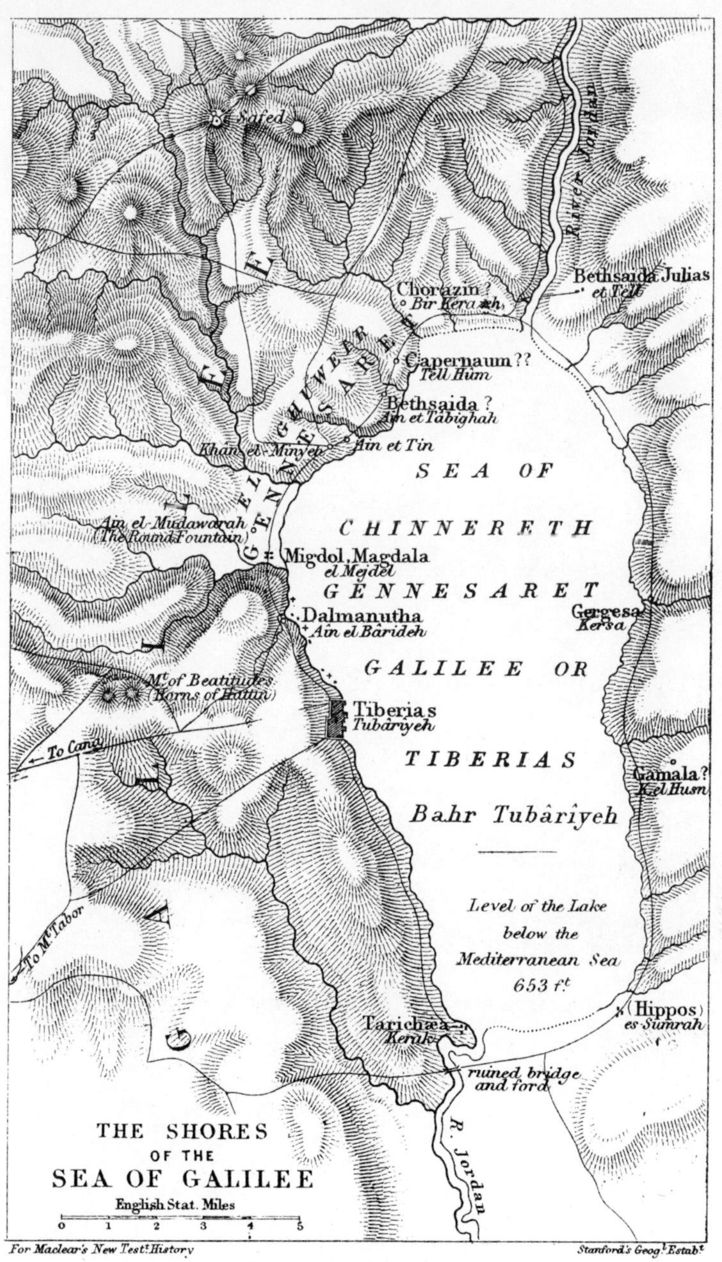

THE SHORES
OF THE
SEA OF GALILEE

London: Macmillan & Co. Ltd

any threatened persecution retire into a more secure region[1].

The recent cure of the son of the officer in Herod's court was not forgotten at Capernaum, and *many pressing* upon the Saviour *to hear the word of God* (Lk. v. 1), it became clear that an opportunity was now afforded for an active and systematic ministry among a people *sitting in darkness and in the shadow of death* (Mtt. iv. 16). The first act, therefore, of the Redeemer was permanently to attach to His Person, and invest with the authority of teachers, four of the number afterwards known as the "twelve Apostles." As He walked by the lake, He saw Simon and Andrew employed in fishing, and the sons of Zebedee[2], James and John, in a vessel mending their nets (Mk. i. 16, 19; Mtt. iv. 18, 21; Lk. v. 2—6). They had already known Him for above a year, and now He would formally call them to leave their earthly occupations, and become *fishers of men*[3].

As the people, therefore, pressed upon Him, He

gatherers would be there, sitting by the lake side *at the receipt of custom.* The *women who were sinners* would there have come, either from the neighbouring Gentile cities, or corrupted by the license of Gentile manners. The Roman soldiers would there be found quartered with their slaves (Luke vii. 2), to be near the palaces of the Herodian princes, or to repress the turbulence of the Galilæan peasantry. And the hardy boatmen, filled with the faithful and grateful spirit by which that peasantry was always distinguished, would supply the energy and docility which He needed for His followers." Stanley's *S. and P.* 375—377; comp. Jos. *B. J.* III. 3. 2.

[1] Milman, I. 177; Andrews, p. 179.

[2] The notice of *the hired servants* (Mark i. 20), the *two vessels* employed (Luke v. 7), and the subsequent mention of St John's acquaintance with one in so high a position as the high priest (John xviii. 15), seem to indicate that Zebedee, if not a wealthy man, was at any rate of no mean position in Capernaum. See Ellicott, 169 n.

[3] Trench, *Miracles*, 127, 128.

requested Simon to push off his boat a little way from the shore, that He might teach the multitude, and at the close of His discourse, bade him thrust out into the deeper waters, and let down his net for a draught. The ill success that had attended his efforts the previous night, made Simon at first hesitate, but he had no sooner made the trial, than the net enclosed such a multitude of fishes, that it began to break (Lk. v. 6). On this he and Andrew beckoned to James and John, and their companions in the other boat, who had doubtless watched all that had occurred, and they immediately came to their help, and filled both the boats so that they began to sink (Lk. v. 7). So deep was the impression made by this unlooked-for success upon the mind of Peter, that yielding as always to the impulse of the moment, he cried, *Depart from me, for I am a sinful man, O Lord*[1]. But the emblem of their future destinies, and the pledge of future success, having thus been given them, the Saviour bade him and the others leave their ships and become *fishers of men.* And thus Peter and Andrew, James and John, quitting their earthly occupations, henceforth became His regular attendants and disciples.

The report of this miracle, and of the determination of the four to follow the Prophet of Nazareth, would soon be noised abroad among the populous villages along the lake. It is no wonder, then, that on the following Sabbath the words of the Saviour were eagerly listened to in the synagogue of Capernaum (Mk. i. 22; Lk. iv. 32), confirmed as they also were by a remarkable occurrence that now took place. A man was present in the synagogue possessed with an evil spirit, which, in the hearing of all, cried out, *What have I to do with*

[1] Comp. Exod. xx. 18, 19; Judg. xiii. 22; Dan. x. 17; Isai. vi. 5.

Thee, Jesus of Nazareth? art Thou come to destroy us? I know Thee who Thou art, the Holy One of God. Thereupon the Redeemer rebuking him, and bidding him hold his peace, commanded the Evil Spirit to leave the sufferer he was tormenting, and the demon having thrown the man into strong convulsions (Mk. i. 26), and "uttering an inarticulate cry of rage and pain[1]" left him, amidst the awe and wonder of those assembled.

This miracle—the first of the kind—over unclean spirits was speedily noised abroad throughout the whole region of Galilee, and excited a strong enthusiasm in favour of the *Prophet of Nazareth.* Leaving the synagogue, the Saviour repaired to the abode of Peter, whose wife's mother lay struck with a violent fever[2], and taking her by the hand lifted her up. Immediately the malady yielding before that Divine rebuke (Lk. iv. 39), left her, and in place of the exhausted energy and prostration usually following it, she found herself able not only to rise, but even to minister to the Healer and His disciples (Mk. i. 31).

When, however, the sun began to set, the effect of the miracle in the synagogue became still more apparent. The whole city seemed to have collected about the abode of the humble fisherman, bringing with them all who were sick, or afflicted with demons, and placed them before his Master. Nor did they come in vain, for laying His hands upon each of them, He, who *Himself took our infirmities and bare our sicknesses* (Is. liii. 4; Mtt. viii. 17), restored to them the blessing of health.

[1] Trench, 232.

[2] Or "great fever," one of the expressions often cited as illustrating St Luke's professional acquaintance with disease. The Greek medical writers recognised a marked distinction between "great" and "small" fevers.

CHAPTER IV

CALL OF MATTHEW—HOSTILITY OF THE PHARISEES.

A. D. 28.

EARLY on the following morning Peter and his companions found that their Master had left the city, and retired to a solitary place for the purpose of engaging in secret prayer. Having discovered the place of His retreat, they announced that the excitement of the previous evening was not subsided, that *all were seeking Him* (Mk. i. 37); and soon their words were confirmed by the coming of a crowd, who besought Him not to leave them. But this could not be. The Divine Purpose required that He should proclaim the Glad Tidings of His kingdom in otner places also; and He commenced a tour throughout Galilee, teaching in the synagogues, casting forth demons, and healing all manner of sickness and disease (Mtt. iv. 23; Mk. i. 39).

Among other recipients of His gracious bounty, was one afflicted with the awful malady of leprosy, which none ever hoped could be cured. Bearing about him all the emblems of his sad condition, his clothes rent, his head bare (Comp. Num. vi. 9; Ezek. xxiv. 17), his lip covered (Ezek. xxiv. 17), he drew near the Saviour, and flinging himself on the ground before His feet, besought Him, if it was His will, to cleanse him. Though the Law forbade all contact with one, afflicted with a disease, to which the Jews gave the significant name of *the Stroke*, the Holy One put forth His hand, and touched Him, saying, *I will, be thou clean.* Instantly his flesh returned to him as the flesh of a little child, and he was clean, and, at the command of his Healer, repaired to the priests at Jerusalem to present the offering required of one so cleansed[1], and thus in his own person bear witness against them[2], and their unbelief.

Obedient to this injunction of his Healer, the cleansed leper found it more difficult to remember His other command, and abstain from saying anything to any one of the way in which he had been healed (Mk. i. 44; Lk. v. 14). In the fulness of his exulting thankfulness he could not contain himself, but, wherever he went, began *to blaze abroad the matter*, so that crowds gathered round the Saviour, and, unable to enter Capernaum (Mk. i. 45), He was fain to remain in secluded places, where He continued in prayer (Lk. v. 16) and ministered unto such as sought Him (Mk. i. 45).

After the subsidence, however, of the first excitement, He returned to Capernaum (Mk. ii. 1), and either in His own abode (Mk. ii. 1), or possibly that of Peter, preached the word to the multitudes, who flocked thither. During His absence there had arrived not only from Galilee, but even from Judæa and Jerusalem (Lk. v. 17), Pharisees and lawyers, who insidiously watched all that He did. As, then, He was proclaiming the doctrines of the kingdom in their presence, an incident occurred, which roused in no small degree the ill-will of these doctors of the law. Four men approached the chamber where the Saviour was, bearing upon a litter a helpless paralytic, and finding an entrance in the usual way impracticable, they bore the man up the outside staircase, and let him down through the roof into His presence.

Perceiving their faith, the Saviour was ready to bestow upon the object of so much solicitude the boon they craved. But, instead of assuring him of the cure

[1] See *Class-Book of Old Testament History*, p. 150.

[2] Comp. Mk. vi. 11, *for a testimony unto them*, with Luke ix. 5, *for a testimony against them.*

of his malady, He addressed the paralytic with the words *Son, thy sins be forgiven thee.* This expression, more startling than anything He had yet said, inasmuch as it implied a distinct equality with God in respect to one of His most incommunicable attributes, roused much disputing among the watchful emissaries from Jerusalem. Was not this a blasphemous utterance, for who could forgive sins, save God only? But, unmoved by their dark suspicions, and knowing the secret thoughts of their hearts, the Holy One bade the man rise, take up his bed, and walk, which he straightway did, and so revealed the completeness of his restored powers to the astonishment of all the spectators, who confessed that they had *seen strange things that day*, and *glorified God, who had given such power unto men* (Lk. v. 26; Mtt. ix. 8).

Overpowered by their wonder at this signal miracle, the Pharisees and Scribes did not give further vent to their indignation at this claim to exercise the awful power of forgiving sins. But their national prejudices were soon to receive a still greater shock. As He walked by the side of the lake of Gennesaret, the Saviour beheld *sitting at the receipt of custom*, probably at the port of Capernaum, a tax-gatherer named Levi or Matthew[1], the son of Alphæus. Though he belonged to a

[1] The identity of Matthew and Levi seems to follow from

(i) The perfect agreement in the narratives of the calling of the one (Matt. ix. 10), and of the other (Mark ii. 15; Luke v. 29);

(ii) The absence from the lists of the Apostles of any trace of the name *Levi*, while that of *Matthew* occurs in all.

It is not improbable that the grateful "publican" changed his name after and in memory of his call, so that he, who was before called Levi, was now known as Matthew, or Matthias, which is equivalent to *Theodore*, the "gift of God." See Ellicott's *Lectures*, 172 n.

class above all others hated and despised by Jews of all orders, the Lord did not hesitate to invite him to become one of His immediate followers. The tax-gatherer, who may have had some prior acquaintance with the Prophet of Nazareth, straightway gave up his usual calling, and in honour of his new Master made *a great feast* (Lk. v. 29; Mk ii. 15), to which he invited many of his old associates.

When the Scribes and Pharisees beheld Him thus openly associating with a degraded caste, they could not restrain themselves, and openly protested against such an infraction of custom and right behaviour. But they were speedily silenced by His wise reply. If those, amongst whom He sat, were sinners, then to them was it specially meet that He should vouchsafe His presence, for, as the Physician of souls, He had specially come to call *not the righteous but sinners to repentance* (Mtt. ix. 13; Mk. ii. 17; Lk. v. 31, 32). Nor were they more successful in contrasting His apparent laxity and freedom with the strictness and austerity of the Baptist. The very garments worn by those around, the very wine they were drinking, suggested similes that conveyed the true answer to their objections[1]. To *sew a piece of new cloth on an old* and ragged garment, to *pour new wine into old bottles* of skin, was not more foolish than to attempt to unite with the Dispensation He was inaugurating the dead formalities of one which was rapidly passing away for ever (Mtt. ix. 14—17; Mk. ii. 18—22; Lk. v. 33—39).

The day following was a Sabbath, *the second-first Sabbath*[2], as St Luke calls it (Lk. vi. 1), and the Saviour

[1] Ellicott's *Lectures*, p. 173.

[2] By some explained as

(i) The Sabbath that succeeded the second day of the Passover;

walked through the corn-fields with His disciples, who began to pluck the ears of ripening grain, and to eat them, rubbing them in their hands. Such an act, though not forbidden by the Mosaic code, was declared unlawful by the traditional expounders[1]. The Pharisees, therefore, already scandalized by His assumption of power to forgive sins, and His associating with publicans, now urged a third complaint against His allowing His disciples to do what was unlawful on the Sabbath. But in full and explicit vindication of what they had done, the Saviour not only referred His accusers to the well-known incident in the life of David, when flying from Saul, he ate the shewbread, forbidden to all except the priests (1 Sam. xxi. 6), and to the words of the Prophet, who had declared that God would *have mercy, and not sacrifice* (Hos. vi. 6), but openly declared that He, as the Son of Man, was *Lord also of the Sabbath*, which had been *ordained for man, and not man for the sabbath* (Mtt. xii. 8).

A week afterwards He entered the Synagogue, and descried a man having his right hand withered, occupying, it would seem, a prominent position, and surrounded by Scribes and Pharisees, who were maliciously on the watch to see what He would do, and to obtain matter for accusation (Mtt. xii. 10; Mk. iii. 2; Lk. vi. 7). They now propounded the distinct question whether it was lawful to heal on the Sabbath-day. In reply the Saviour reminded them that the Law allowed a man, whose sheep had fallen into a pit, to lift it out on the Sabbath,

(ii) The 15th of Nisan, the 14th being, it is asserted, always coincident with the Sabbath;
(iii) The first Sabbath of a year that stood second in a Sabbatical cycle.

[1] "He that reapeth corn on the Sabbath, to the quantity of a fig, is guilty; and plucking corn is as reaping." Lightfoot, quoting the Mishna.

and enquired whether they deemed it more consistent with the holiness of the day to do good or to do evil, to save life or to slay. Silenced and abashed they had not a word to urge in their own defence, and were obliged to stand by, while He, *looking round about on them with anger, being grieved for the hardness of their hearts* (Mk. iii. 5), bade the man stretch forth his hand, which was instantly restored whole as the other.

Such an exhibition of Divine power, such a calm and unanswerable protest against their narrow bigotry, was more than they could bear. Filled with *madness* (Lk. vi. 11), the Scribes and Pharisees went forth and called a council (Mtt. xii. 14), and not ashamed to unite with their political opponents, the followers of Herod Antipas (Mk. iii. 6), began to form plans for compassing His death (Mk. iii. 6; Lk. vi. 11).

PART IV

FROM THE ELECTION OF THE APOSTLES TO THE DEATH OF JOHN THE BAPTIST.

CHAPTER I

CALL OF THE APOSTLES—SERMON ON THE MOUNT.

A.D. 28.

WE have now reached a very important turning-point in the Gospel History. While the fame of the Saviour had spread abroad in every direction throughout the land, the animosity of the ruling powers had clearly displayed itself alike in Judæa and in Galilee, and there was already an active correspondence between the Scribes and Pharisees in both districts respecting His claims and pretensions. As yet, while the current of popular feeling ran in His favour, their hostility confined itself to secretly plotting against Him, and devising means for hindering Him in His work, with the hope that some imprudence or sudden change in the feeling of the multitude might put him in their power.

It was at this juncture, then, that He took a more decided step towards the establishment of His Divine work. Hitherto He had seemed to stand almost alone. Though a few had been gathered around Him as His disciples they did not present the appearance of a regular and organized community, of which He was the Head, nor had they received a distinct and solemn commission to disseminate His doctrines.

Such a commission was now to be given.

Attracted by His miracles of healing, crowds gathered about Him not only from Judæa, Jerusalem and Galilee, but even from Peræa, Idumæa, and the country around Tyre and Sidon (Mk. iii. 7, 8; Lk. vi. 17), bringing such as were afflicted with any diseases, and beseeching his aid. While, therefore, He did not withhold that Divine assistance which they so eagerly craved (Lk. vi. 9), but graciously healed them, He now retired from the constant interruption, to which their coming exposed Him, and sought a retreat in the lonely mountain-range west of the sea of Tiberias. There he spent a night in solemn meditation and prayer (Lk. vi. 12), and on the following morning called to Him His disciples, and made selection amongst them of Twelve, who should be in continual personal attendance upon Him (Mk. iii. 14), and whom He might send forth to preach in His name, and to exercise power over evil spirits (Mk. iii. 15).

The Twelve thus selected and denominated Apostles were :—

1. Symeon or Simon, the son of Jonas (Jn. i. 42; xxi. 16), called also Cephas[1] or Peter (a *stone* or *rock*).
2. Andrew, his brother (Mtt. iv. 18), a native of Bethsaida, and a former disciple of the Baptist[2].
3. James, the son of Zebedee (Mtt. iv. 21) and Salome (Mk. xv. 40), also of Bethsaida, and
4. John, his brother, afterwards known as "the friend of Jesus," the "disciples whom Jesus loved" (Jn. xiii. 23), and in the ancient Church as ὁ ἐπιστήθιος, he who "leaned on His breast[3]."
5. Philip, a native of Bethsaida, and one of the earliest disciples (Jn. i. 43)[4].
6. Bartholomew = Bar-Tolmai, "the son of Tolmai," most probably identical with Nathanael[5].
7. Matthew or Levi, a collector of customs at Capernaum[6].
8. Thomas or Didymus (*a twin*), (Jn. xi. 16; xx. 24).
9. James, the son of Alphæus, or "James the Less."
10. Judas, a brother or, possibly, a son of James (Acts i. 13), and surnamed Thaddæus and Lebbæus (Mtt. x. 3; Mk. iii. 18).
11. Simon the *Cananite* (Mk. iii. 18) or *Cananæan* (Mtt. x. 24), in Greek *Zelotes* (Lk. vi. 15; Acts i. 13), one, probably, who before his call had belonged to the sect of the zealots[7].

[1] See above, p. 159. [2] See above, p. 159.

[3] It was probably now that the Saviour called these brothers Boanerges, "*Sons of Thunder*," from their burning and impetuous spirit, of which we trace indications in Lk. ix. 54, Mk. ix. 38.

[4] See above, p. 159. [5] See above, p. 159, n.

[6] See above, p. 182. [7] See above, p. 148.

12. Judas, sometimes called the *son of Simon* (Jn. vi. 71; xiii. 2, 26), more generally *Iscariot, i.e.* probably a native of Kerioth (Josh. xv. 25), a little village in the tribe of Judah.

After this formal selection and ordination of the Twelve Apostles, the Saviour descended from the mountain-peak[1], where He had spent the night, to a more level spot (Lk. vi. 17), and sitting down in the formal attitude of a Teacher in the presence of His disciples and the multitude, which had gathered around Him, proceeded to deliver that wondrous summary of Christian doctrine and practice known as the "Sermon on the Mount"[2] (Mtt. v.—vii.; Lk. vi. 20—49).

At its conclusion, He repaired again to Capernaum (Lk. vii. 1), where He was met by certain elders of the synagogue bearing a message from a centurion belonging to the Roman garrison quartered in the place, one of

[1] Tradition places the scene of the Sermon on the Mount on a hill known as the "Horns of Hattin," a ridge no great distance from *Tell Hûm*, running east and west for about a quarter of a mile, and called by the Latins the Mount of Beatitudes. Stanley thinks "the situation so strikingly coincides with the intimations of the Gospel narrative as almost to force the inference, that in this instance the eye of those who selected the spot was for once rightly guided," *S. and P.* p. 360. On the peculiar acoustic properties of the neighbourhood, see Tristram's *Land of Israel*, p. 433.

[2] In reference to the Sermon on the Mount as related by St Matthew and St Luke, it may be observed that the differences are on the whole few when compared with the resemblances: Thus (i) both have the same beginning and ending; (ii) the order is generally similar; (iii) the expressions are often identical; (iv) the audience (Mtt. iv. 25; Lk. vi. 17; Mk. iii. 7, 8) was the same, and included crowds from every part of the land; (v) probably St Matthew relates it *substantially* as it was delivered, and writing for Jews retains those portions which relate to the Jewish sects and customs, while St Luke has modified it to meet the wants of those for whom he more especially wrote. Ellicott's *Lectures*, p. 180, n. and Andrews, p. 223.

whose slaves lay stricken with paralysis. Though an officer of imperial Rome, he had not regarded with contempt the religion of the people amongst whom He was placed, but had aided them in building their synagogue, and evinced much kindness towards them. At their request, therefore, the Saviour proceeded towards his house, but on the way was met by certain of the centurion's friends, who bade Him not trouble Himself to enter his abode, but speak the word, and he was assured his slave would recover. Such faith, the faith of a true soldier[1], who could believe that the Holy One was as well able to command the unseen agencies producing sickness, as he was himself to rule his own soldiers, moved the wonder even of the Lord, and was quickly rewarded by the healing of apparently the first Gentile sufferer[2].

On the following day (Lk. vii. 11), leaving Capernaum, accompanied by His disciples and a large multitude, the Saviour proceeded in the direction of Nain, then a place of considerable extent in the Esdraelon plain, now little more than a cluster of ruins[3]. As he drew near, a sad and mournful spectacle met his eyes. A young man, *the only son of his mother*, and *she a widow* (Lk. vii. 12), was being carried on a bier towards his last resting-place, probably in one of the sepulchral caves which perforated the rock on the western side of the town. Beholding the forlorn and desolate mother, the Holy One was filled with the deepest compassion, and bidding her not weep, advanced towards the bier and touched it. Thereupon the bearers stood still,

[1] Trench *On the Miracles*, pp. 225, 226.

[2] Ellicott's *Lectures*, p. 181.

[3] Now called *Neïn*. It was near the source of the brook Kishon, not far from Endor, and 2½ leagues from Nazareth. The name means "the lovely," and was perhaps given on account of its pleasant situation in the plain of Esdraelon.

while addressing the corpse He said, *Young man, I say unto thee, Arise*, at which word of power the dead man instantly sat up and began to speak, and was restored to his wondering and rejoicing mother (Lk. vii. 15).

This first signal victory over death filled all those, who witnessed it, with awe and astonishment, and they thankfully glorified God who had raised up a prophet among them and truly *visited His people* (Lk. vii. 16). No such miracle had been wrought since the days of Elisha, and the fame of it *went forth throughout all Judæa, and throughout all the region round about.* (Lk. vii. 17). Amongst those to whom it was related, together with the mighty works of the Saviour, was the Baptist, still detained in prison in the gloomy castle of Machærus[1] (Mtt. xi. 2; Lk. vii. 18). Thereupon he sent two of his disciples[2] to Jesus with the question, *Art Thou He that should come, or do we look for another?* Whatever was his precise motive in making this formal enquiry, whether it was for the sake of fully convincing his own disciples, or from a desire for the comfort of a definite assurance from the Saviour's own lips, or from impatience at the slow establishment of the kingdom of the Messiah, it was fully answered. At the hour when the messengers arrived, the Saviour was actively engaged in His daily labours of love, healing diseases, casting out demons, and restoring sight to the blind (Lk. vii. 21); He therefore bade the two disciples return and tell their master what things they had seen and heard, *how the lame walked, the lepers were cleansed, the dead were raised, the poor had the Gospel preached to them* (Mtt. xi. 5). But besides these proofs of His Messiah-

[1] Jos. *B. J.* VII. 6. 1—3.

[2] Like Socrates, the Baptist, though in confinement, was allowed to hold intercourse with his disciples. Comp. Mtt. xxv. 36; Acts xxiv. 23. Lange, III. 116, n.

ship, which, as the Baptist could hardly fail to remember, had been distinctly indicated by the Prophets (comp. Isai. xxxv. 5, 6; lxi. 1), the Holy One added a special word for John's weary prison-hours and the doubts of his disciples, saying, *Blessed is he, whosoever shall not be offended in Me* (Mtt. xi. 6; Lk. vii. 23), "at My calm and unassuming course of mercy and love to mankind, at My total disregard of worldly honours, at My refusal to place Myself at the head of the people as a temporal Messiah[1]."

No sooner, however, had the messengers departed than the Saviour took the opportunity of vindicating before the bystanders[2], who, perhaps, from the enquiry he had put, might receive an unfavourable impression respecting the Baptist, the true greatness of his character. *No reed shaken by the wind* was he, whom, a little more than a year ago, all Judæa and Jerusalem had flocked forth *into the wilderness to see;* no effeminate prince clad in luxurious apparel; no prophet merely, such as those of the Old Testament dispensation. Himself the subject of prophecy (Mtt. xi. 10), he was greater than all the prophets that had preceded him, being no other than the long-expected Forerunner of the Messiah (Mtt. xi. 10; Lk. vii. 27), the true Elias of whom Malachi had spoken, as destined *to prepare His way before Him.*

CHAPTER II

TEACHING IN GALILEE.

A.D. 28—9.

APPARENTLY while He was in the neighbourhood of Nain[3], the Saviour received an invitation from a

[1] Milman, I. 215. [2] Lange, III. 108.
[3] Ellicott, p. 182.

Pharisee, named Simon, to enter his house, and sit at meat with him (Lk. vii. 36). Among the guests there pressed in a woman of unchaste life[1], which had brought her into bad repute amongst her neighbours. Standing behind Him weeping, she kissed His feet, and anointed them, as He reclined at meat, with a costly unguent from an alabaster box[2], and wiped away with her hair the copious tears that fell from her eyes. Shrinking from any moral or physical uncleanness, Simon marvelled that the Holy One suffered such a woman to approach Him, and could only attribute it to His ignorance of her real character. But the Saviour addressing His entertainer in the touching parable of the "Two Debtors[3]" (Lk. vii. 40—43), pointed out that there was hope and mercy even for the lowest and most degraded, and turning to the woman bade her go in peace, for her faith had saved her, and *her sins, though many, were forgiven* (Lk. vii. 10, 47).

Almost immediately after this striking incident, accompanied not only by the Twelve, but by pious women, amongst whom were Mary of Magdala, Joanna the wife of Chuza, Herod's steward[4], Susanna, and many others (Lk. viii. 3), He proceeded on a somewhat lengthened tour through the cities and villages of Galilee, preaching the kingdom of God. Returning, as it seems most probable, to Capernaum, the multitude quickly gathered around Him, thronged Him in such numbers, and

[1] There is no real ground for identifying this woman with Mary Magdalene. It is true that she was a victim of Satanic influence (Lk. viii. 2), but it does not follow that she had been guilty of sins of impurity.

[2] This anointing is not to be confounded with that recorded in Mtt. xxvi. 6, &c., Mk. xiv, 3, &c., Jn. xii. 1, &c. The two anointings differ in time, and place, as well as the chief actors. Trench *On the Parables*, p. 290.

[3] Trench *On the Parables,* pp. 289—293.

[4] See above, p. 171.

importuned Him with such persistent craving for His merciful aid, that neither He nor His disciples had sufficient leisure *even to eat bread* (Mk. iii. 20.) The enthusiastic zeal of Him, whose *meat it was to do the will of Him that sent Him and to finish His work* (Jn. iv. 34) inspired His mother and brethren with the desire to interpose, and to protest against such exhausting labours[1] (Mk. iii. 21). But the intelligence that they were without the circle of the crowd seeking Him, did not induce Him to suspend His loving toil. Stretching forth His hands towards His disciples (Mtt. xii. 49), He declared that they and all who heard and *did the will of His Father in heaven* were as dear to Him as *brother*, *or sister*, *or mother* (Mtt. xii. 49, 50; Mk. iii. 34, 35; Lk. viii. 21).

While, however, the feelings of the multitude were thus openly enlisted on the side of the Redeemer, those of the Scribes and Pharisees from Jerusalem were tinged with the intensest virulence and hostility. The miraculous cure of a deaf and dumb demoniac (Mtt. xii. 22) caused the greatest astonishment amongst the multitudes, and roused the enquiry whether this was not the Messiah, the son of David (Mtt. xii. 23). Resolved to check their enthusiasm, the Pharisaic faction openly declared that the Saviour owed His authority over the inferior demons to a secret compact with Beelzebub, the prince of the powers of darkness (Mk. iii. 22). Such a fearful charge, which ascribed to the influence of the Author of Evil works of beneficence and divine power, brought down upon those who urged it a terrible reply. The Saviour's acts, they were reminded, were those of purest beneficence, while evil spirits took a malignant pleasure in the miseries of men. Could it be believed that Satan would allow his kingdom thus to be divided,

[1] See Ellicott, p. 184, and note.

that he would cast out those who were only accomplishing his will? Such an ascription of works of purest mercy to the energy of the Prince of Darkness, was an outward expression of an inward hatred of all that was good and Divine, and bordered closely on a terrible climax of sin, incapable of forgiveness either in this world or the world to come, even sin against the Holy Ghost (Mtt. xii. 24—37; Mk. iii. 22—30; Lk. xi. 17—23).

In the afternoon or evening of the day on which these solemn warnings were uttered, the Lord went down to the shores of the Lake (Mtt. xiii. 1; Mk. iv. 1), followed by a great multitude from all the towns round about. So numerous, indeed, were the crowds which gathered around Him, that, for the sake of more conveniently addressing them, He entered into one of the fishing-vessels, and sitting there a little distance from the water's edge, addressed them in a series of parables[1]

[1] On the scenery around the lake which would suggest the majority of the Parables now delivered, see a striking passage in Stanley's *Sinai and Palestine*, pp. 425—427. "A slight recess in the hill-side, close upon the Plain of Gennesaret, disclosed at once, in detail, and with a conjunction I remember nowhere else in Palestine, every feature of the great parable of the Sower;" there was

i. The undulating *corn-field* descending close to the water's edge, over which hovered countless *birds* of various kinds. Comp. also Tristram, p. 431;

ii. The *trodden pathway* running through the midst of it, with no fence or hedge to prevent the seed from falling here and there on either side of it or upon it; itself hard with the constant tramp of horse and mule and human feet;

iii. The *rocky ground* of the hill side protruding here and there through the corn-fields, as elsewhere through the grassy slopes;

iv. The large *bushes of thorn*, the "Nabk," springing up like the fruit-trees of the more inland parts, in the very midst of the waving wheat;

v. The *good rich soil*, which distinguishes the whole of the Plain of Gennesaret and its neighbourhood from

illustrative of the growth and extension of His kingdom —*the Sower* (Mtt. xiii. 3—9; Mk. iv. 3—9; Lk. viii. 4—15); *the Wheat and the Tares* (Mtt. xiii. 24—30); *the Seed growing secretly* (Mk. iv. 26—29); *the grain of Mustard-seed* (Mtt. xiii. 31—33; Mk. iv. 30—32; Lk. xiii. 18—21); *the Hid Treasure* (Mtt. xiii. 44); *the Merchant and the Pearl* (Mtt. xiii. 45, 46); *the Draw-net* (Mtt. xiii. 47—50).

Later in the evening He requested of His disciples

the bare hills elsewhere descending into the lake, and which, where there is no interruption, produces one vast mass of corn;

vi. The women and children picking out from the wheat the tall green stalks, called by the Arabs *Zurwân*, = the Greek *Zizania*, = the *Lollia* of the Vulgate, = the *tares* of our version, which if sown designedly throughout the fields would be inseparable from the wheat, from which, even when growing naturally and by chance, these are at first sight hardly distinguishable;

vii. The *mustard-tree* (in Arabic *Khadel*, in Hebrew *Chardal*, in N.W. India *Khardel*), growing especially on the shores of the Lake, [as also near Damascus, Jerusalem, and the Dead Sea], rising from *a small seed* into a *large shrub or tree*, 25 ft. high, and producing numerous branches and leaves, among which *the birds take shelter*.

viii. The great *fisheries*, which once made the fame of Gennesaret, with

(1) the busy fishermen plying

(*a*) the *drag-net*, or *hawling-net*, σαγήνη (Mtt. xiii. 47, 48), the Latin *tragum* or *tragula*, the English *seine* or *sean*, sometimes half a mile in length (Trench, *Parables*, 134, n.);

(*b*) the *casting-net*, ἀμφίβληστρον (Mtt. iv. 18; Mk. i. 16), the Latin *funda* or *jaculum*, circular in shape, "like the top of a tent" (Thomson, *L. and B.* 402);

(*c*) the *bag-net and basket-net*, so constructed and worked as to enclose the fish out in deep water (Lk. v. 4—9), Thomson, p. 402.

(2) "The marvellous shoals of fish of various kinds, the most striking phenomenon of the lake" (Tristram, p. 432).

that they would push across the lake towards the Eastern shore; on which, they took Him *as He was* (Mk. iv. 36), *i.e.* without any preparations for the voyage, and made for the opposite coast. Wearied with the toils of that long and exhausting day He fell asleep on a cushion in the stern, when suddenly from one of the deep clefts in the surrounding hills a violent storm of wind[1] (Mk. iv. 37; Lk. viii. 23) burst upon the surface of the lake, lashed it into waves (Mk. iv. 37), which almost hid the little vessel (Mtt. viii. 24), and threatened to sink it to the bottom. Terror-stricken at the sudden tempest, the Apostles hastily awoke Him, and implored His aid, lest they should perish, whereupon He arose, *rebuked the wind* and the surging waters, and instantly *there was a great calm* (Mtt. viii. 26; Mk. iv. 39), amidst which they reached next morning the other side, deeply wondering at the power of their Master, which could reduce even the winds and the sea to obedience to His word.

In the country of the Gadarenes[2], where they now

[1] With reference to the sudden and violent tempests, to which the lake is exposed, "we must remember," writes Thomson, "that it lies low, 600 feet lower than the ocean; that the vast and naked plateaus of the Jaulan rise to a great height, spreading backwards to the wilds of the Hauran, and upward to snowy Hermon; that the water-courses have cut out profound ravines, and wild gorges converging to the head of the lake, and that these act like gigantic funnels to draw down the cold winds from the mountains. And moreover, these winds are not only violent, but they come down suddenly, and often when the sky is perfectly clear," *The Land and the Book*, p. 374; Tristram, p. 430.

[2] The MSS. in all three Evangelists vary in their readings between Γαδαρηνῶν, Γερασηνῶν, and Γεργεσηνῶν. Gadara, the capital of Peræa, lay S. E. of the southern extremity of Gennesaret, at a distance of about sixty stadia from Tiberias, its country being called Gadaritis. Gerasa lay on the extreme E. limit of Peræa, and was too far from the lake to give its name to any district on its borders. It is

arrived, a fearful spectacle awaited them. Amongst the tombs, which existed, and can even now be traced in more than one of the ravines on the Eastern side of the lake, dwelt two demoniacs. The more notable or fiercer of the two was possessed of such extraordinary muscular strength that all efforts to bind and restrain him had proved ineffectual, and the chains and fetters, with which he had at times been secured, had been broken and crushed, nor had any been able to tame him (Mk. v. 4). Fleeing from the fellowship of his kind (Lk. viii. 27), he had for a long time taken up his dwelling in the tombs, and there in the paroxysms of his misery he often cried out and cut himself with stones (Mk. v. 5), and so terrified all travellers, that they dared not *pass by that way* (Mtt. viii. 28).

Such was the miserable being, who now in company with his companion, without any garment to cover him (Lk. viii. 27), issued from his lonely abode, and seeing the Saviour afar off (Mk. v. 6) ran and fell down before Him crying out *What have I to do with Thee, Jesus, Thou Son of the most high God? I adjure Thee by God that Thou torment me not* (Mk. v. 7; Lk. viii. 28).

Resolved in His infinite mercy to rid him of the terrible spirit that possessed him, the Great Physician enquired his name. Thereupon he replied, *My name is Legion, for we are many,* comparing the cruel and inexorable powers that mastered him to the "thick and serried ranks of a Roman legion, that fearful instrument

the opinion of Dr Thomson that St Matthew, "writing for those intimately acquainted with the topography of the country in detail, names the obscure and exact locality *Gergesa,* while SS. Mark and Luke, writing for those at a distance, simply name the country *Gadara,* as a place of importance, and acknowledged as the capital of the district." Directly opposite Gennesaret this traveller visited some ruins called by his guide *Kerza* or *Gersa,* which he identifies with the Gergesa of St Matthew, *Land and Book*, p. 375.

of oppression, that sign of terror and fear to the conquered nations[1]."

Sensible that they were in the presence of the Lord of the spirit-world, the demons possessing him besought the Holy One that He would not drive them out of the country (Mk. v. 10), or send them into the Abyss of Hell[2], the abode of the lost (Lk. viii. 31), but suffer them to enter into a herd of swine (Mk. v. 12; Mtt. viii. 31), which numbering nearly 2000 was feeding close at hand (Mk. v. 13). The Saviour gave the required permission, and the whole herd rushing wildly down the cliff[3] into the lake were choked and destroyed.

Such a remarkable incident paralysed the keepers of the herd with fear, and straightway flying to the city, they recounted all that had occurred, as also the marvellous change, which had come over the terrible demoniac. Their report brought out wellnigh all the inhabitants (Mtt. viii. 34), and though in the man, probably a fellow-citizen[4], who *sat at the feet of Jesus, clothed, and in his right mind* (Mk. v. 15), they saw a proof of the superhuman power of his Deliverer, they yet besought Him to depart from their neighbourhood.

Thereupon the Saviour, taking them at their word,

[1] Trench, *Miracles*, p. 170.

[2] Εἰς τὴν ἄβυσσον (Lk. viii. 31), translated in the English version *the deep*, which leads to a confusion of ideas. The word occurs here and in Rom. x. 7, where also *Hell* would be the better translation, and several times in Revelation, as ix. 1, 2, 11; xi. 7; xvii. 8; xx. 1, 3; in which places it corresponds to τάρταρος Tartarus, and γέεννα Gehenna (2 Pet. ii. 4), Trench, *Miracles*, p. 171, n.

[3] At *Kerza* or *Gersa*, "while there is no precipice running sheer to the sea, but a narrow belt of beach, the bluff behind is so steep, and the shore so narrow, that a herd of swine, rushing frantically down, must certainly have been overwhelmed in the lake before they could recover themselves," Tristram, p. 462.

[4] Trench, *Miracles*, p. 176.

turned towards the lake, and was in the act of stepping into the boat (Mk. v. 18), when the healed man prayed that he might be allowed to accompany Him. But this the Holy One did not see fit to concede, and bade the man return to his friends, and recount to them what great things the Lord had done to him. On which the other went his way, proclaiming throughout the region of Decapolis[1] the story of his wonderful deliverance, himself a witness and a standing monument of the Saviour's grace and power.

CHAPTER III

MIRACLES AT CAPERNAUM—DEATH OF THE BAPTIST.

A. D. 29.

IMMEDIATELY after this miracle the Lord crossed over to the western shore of the lake (Mk. v. 21), where a great multitude was awaiting Him, and amongst them one of the prefects of the synagogue, probably of Capernaum, whose name was Jairus. Falling down before His feet, he earnestly besought Him to come to his house, and lay His hands upon *his little daughter*, who was at the point of death. Thereupon the ever compassionate Redeemer arose and followed him, ac-

[1] Decapolis, "the ten cities" (Mtt. iv. 25; Mk. v. 20; vii. 31), all lay, with the exception of Scythopolis, East of the Jordan, and to the E. and S. E. of the sea of Galilee. They were, 1. Scythopolis, 2. Hippos, 3. Gadara, 4. Pella, 5. Philadelphia, 6. Gerasa, 7. Dion, 8. Canatha, 9. Abila, 10. Capitolias. They were rebuilt, partially colonized, and endowed with peculiar privileges immediately after the conquest of Syria by the Romans, B.C. 65. The limits of the territory of Decapolis were not very clearly defined, and the word was sometimes used to designate a large district extending along both sides of the Jordan: see Smith's *Bibl. Dict.*

companied by His disciples, and a curious and eager crowd.

Amongst the rest, who thus followed and pressed upon Him, was a woman, that had laboured for upwards of twelve years under an issue of blood, which all the efforts of many physicians had proved powerless to assuage. Believing that, if she could but touch His clothes, she would be made whole, she now came behind, and touched the hem or blue fringe on the border of His garment. No sooner had she done so, than she felt within herself that the long wished-for cure had at length been accomplished. The fountain of her blood was stanched, and she was healed. But she was not to bear away the boon thus totally unobserved. Perceiving that power had gone out of Him, and turning round amidst the crowd, the Saviour enquired who had touched Him? The Apostles, with Peter at their head, would have put the enquiry aside, but the Saviour repeated it, and then the woman, trembling and alarmed, came and fell down before Him, confessed all that she had done, and was gladdened by the cheering words, *Daughter, be of good cheer, thy faith hath saved thee, go in peace* (Mk. v. 34; Lk. viii. 48).

Meanwhile, though the delay must have been a sore trial to Jairus, "now when every moment was precious, when death was shaking the last few sands in the hour-glass of his daughter's life[1]," he betrayed no signs of impatience at a boon so readily bestowed upon another. But at this juncture his faith was still more put to the proof. Messengers arrived informing him that the worst was over, and that his daughter was already dead, and suggesting that he should no further trouble the Master. Overhearing the announcement (Mk. v. 36), the Holy One bade him not be afraid, but only believe, and hast-

[1] Trench, *Miracles*, p. 181.

ened towards his house. Entering it, accompanied only by Peter, James, and John, and the father and mother of the maiden, He advanced into the chamber of death, where He found a number of hired mourners weeping and wailing with all the boisterous and turbulent symbols of Oriental grief. Putting them forth, while they laughed to scorn His announcement that the damsel was not dead but only asleep, He went forward to the bed, and said, *Talitha Cumi*, "Maid, arise." Instantly His word was obeyed. The spirit of the maiden came to her again, and she arose straightway, and began to walk, while "at once to strengthen that life which was come back to her, and to prove that she was indeed no ghost, but had returned to the realities of a mortal existence, *He commanded to give her meat*[1] (Mk. v. 43)."

Soon afterwards, accompanied by His disciples, He left Capernaum, and for the second time appeared on a Sabbath in the synagogue of His own town of Nazareth (Mk. vi. 2; Mtt. xiii. 54). The conduct of His hearers on this occasion did not betray the frantic violence they exhibited during His previous visit. The miraculous works wrought by His hands, of which they must have heard, could not be gainsaid, and the wondrous wisdom with which He spake filled them with astonishment (Mtt. xiii. 54; Mk. vi. 2). But again their minds recurred to the thought of His lowly origin, to the fact that He was the son of a carpenter, that his family connections were well known to them, and living in their midst (Mk. vi. 3; Mtt. xiii. 55). Stumbling at this rock of offence (Mtt. xiii. 57) they still refused to believe in Him, and the Lord Himself *marvelling at their unbelief* (Mk. vi. 6), confined His designs of mercy to laying His hands on *a few sick folk* (Mk. vi. 5), who felt the influence of that Divine touch and were healed.

[1] Trench, *Miracles*, p. 186.

On the morrow He and His disciples set out on another circuit amongst the towns and villages of Galilee (Mtt. ix. 35—38; Mk. vi. 6), preaching the glad tidings of the Kingdom, and healing the sick. Great multitudes from that thickly-peopled district followed Him, and deeply moved to see them scattered *like sheep without a shepherd* (Mtt. ix. 36), He said to His disciples that *the harvest truly was plenteous, while the labourers were few*, and calling the Apostles to Him (Mtt. x. 1; Mk. vi. 7; Lk. ix. 1), formally bestowed on them power over unclean spirits, and the ability to heal diseases, and sent them forth two and two with instructions not to enter into any heathen or Samaritan city (Mtt. x. 5), but to proclaim to the *lost sheep of the house of Israel* the near approach of the Kingdom of Heaven. Accordingly they went forth and preached in the various towns and villages the message of repentance, casting out demons, and healing the sick, and at the conclusion of this trial of their powers, returned to their Master, probably at Capernaum (Mk. vi. 30; Lk. ix. 10).

Meanwhile important events occurred in the gloomy prison, where John the Baptist was confined. The anger he had excited in the breast of Herodias by his outspoken denunciation of her sin, never slumbered or slept. She constantly kept her eye upon him, and would have put him out of the way without scruple, but Herod, though there was little from which he would shrink, dared not lay hands on one so venerated by the people, and whose exhortations he himself was not above listening to and in some respects obeying (Mk. vi. 20).

At length an opportunity for gratifying her revenge presented itself, which she instantly embraced. Herod's birthday [1] came round, which, like a true Herod, con-

[1] Such is the usual explanation of γενέσια. Wieseler, however, and others, consider it refers to a feast kept in

forming in this as in other things to Roman customs, he kept probably at Machærus, with feasting and revelry, surrounded by the petty chiefs and grandees of Galilee, the lords of his court, and the officers of his camp (Mk. vi. 21). During the feast the youthful Salome, the daughter of Herodias, entered the banqueting hall, and danced before the riotous company. So delighted were the guests, and especially Herod, with the brilliancy of her movements, that in the delirium of his admiration, he promised her anything, everything *even to the half of his kingdom*, and ratified his word with the royal oath.

The maiden departed, and consulted with her mother. Herodias saw that at last her hour was come, that at length the long-desired vengeance was within her grasp. No jewelled trinket, no royal palace, or splendid robe should be the reward of her daughter's feat; *Ask*, said she, *for John Baptist's head in a charger* (Mtt. xiv. 8; Mk. vi. 24), *i. e.* on one of the dishes on which the fruits and viands of the table had been served. Forthwith (Mk. vi. 25), as though not a moment was to be lost, Salome returned, and named her price to the assembled company.

Herod's brow instantly fell. Even amidst the delirium of that riotous hour he was *exceeding sorry* (Mk. vi. 26) for the brave preacher, whose words he had so often listened to, and for whom he entertained much reverence. But he had promised, and ratified the promise with an oath. The captains and great lords, who had heard him swear, sat round the festive board, and none in that riotous company would say a word for the friendless prophet. So the word was given, and an officer was bidden to seek out the Baptist's dungeon and

honour of his accession to the throne, and so make the date of the Baptist's execution April 11, A. U. C. 782, since Herod the Great died a few days before the Passover, A. U. C. 750. Wieseler's *Synopsis*, p. 265; Andrews, p. 254.

bring the reward which the maiden claimed. He went, and executed his command, and Salome bore the bleeding head to her mother (Mk. vi. 28).

Before long the news of their master's death became known to the disciples of the Baptist, and having consigned his headless body to the grave (Mtt. xiv. 12; Mk. vi. 29), they went and recounted all that had occurred to the Saviour (Mtt. xiv. 12), whom they appear to have found in or near Capernaum (Mtt. xiv. 13; Mk. vi. 30; Lk. ix. 10). On receiving these sad tidings respecting His Forerunner, the Lord left the place with His Apostles, who had just returned from their tentative mission, and crossing the lake of Gennesaret (Mtt. xiv. 13), sought the neighbourhood of Bethsaida-Julias[1] (Lk. ix. 10).

Meanwhile the news of the Baptist's death excited much consternation amongst the Jews[2], who all regarded him as a prophet (Mtt. xiv. 5), and Herod's conscience allowed him little rest after the cruel murder. Returning to Galilee[3], he received intelligence, probably from those who had witnessed the mission of the Twelve, of the wonderful works of the Prophet of Nazareth (Mtt. xiv. 1; Mk. vi. 14; Lk. ix. 7). Perplexed at the appear-

[1] Bethsaida-Julias was at the N. E. extremity of the lake of Gennesaret. It had been a village, but was rebuilt and adorned by Herod Philip, who raised it to the dignity of a town, and called it Julias after the daughter of Augustus (Jos. *Ant.* XVIII. 2. 1; *B. J.* II. 9. 1; III. 10. 7).

[2] Jos. *Ant.* XVIII. 5. 2.

[3] Greswell, *Harm.* III. 428, thinks that during the earlier period of the Saviour's ministry Herod had either been engaged in hostilities with Aretas, or had been on a visit to Rome, whither he went about this time, and so had remained ignorant of what had already taken place. The late mission of the Twelve would be very likely to rouse attention, indicating, as it apparently did, a purpose to disseminate His doctrine more widely, and to make disciples in larger numbers, Andrews, p. 256.

ance of a new Teacher he enquired who this could be, and received different answers. Some said He was the awful Elias, whose coming had been so often predicted; others that He was *a prophet, or as one of the prophets* (Mk. vi. 15). But the uneasy and superstitious king could not be satisfied with these replies, and declared Him to be none other than *the Baptist risen from the dead* (Mk. vi. 16), come back to haunt his footsteps, and reproach him with his crimes. All that he heard awakened in him a desire to see the new Teacher, and destined he was to see Him, but not now (Lk. ix. 9).

PART V

FROM THE DEATH OF JOHN THE BAPTIST TO THE VISIT OF THE SAVIOUR TO JERUSALEM AT THE FEAST OF TABERNACLES.

CHAPTER I

THE FEEDING OF THE FIVE THOUSAND, AND THE WALKING ON THE LAKE.

A.D. 29.

AT this time the Passover, the second Passover, as seems most probable, during the Saviour's public ministry, drew nigh (Jn. vi. 4), but on this occasion He does not appear to have gone up to Jerusalem, where the determined hostility of the ruling powers rendered any further activity dangerous, at least for the present.

It was, probably, to commune in retirement with the

Twelve, and to afford them a season of comparative rest after their late labours, that the Lord now sought the neighbourhood of Bethsaida-Julias (Mk. vi. 31). But the numbers moving about the country in consequence of the near approach of the great Festival, who came on foot from all the towns round about to see and hear Him (Mtt. xiv. 13; Mk. vi. 32; Lk. ix. 11), rendered the desired solitude impossible. The sight, moreover, of these multitudes *scattered as sheep without a shepherd* (Mk. vi. 34), again roused His deepest compassion, and He not only *taught them many things concerning the Kingdom* of God, and healed those amongst them that were afflicted with various diseases (Mtt. xiv. 14), but was moved on this occasion to minister still further to their temporal necessities.

Accordingly at a somewhat early period, as it would seem, in the afternoon[1], He enquired of the Apostle Philip where bread might be bought to satisfy the hunger of the multitudes (Jn. vi. 5). Though *He Himself knew what He would do*, He put this question to prove the trust of the Apostle. But Philip, thinking of no other supplies save such as natural means could procure, replied that *two hundred pence* (or rather *denarii*) would not be sufficient to procure sustenance for such a number (Jn. vi. 7). Having thus obtained from his own mouth a confession of the inability of all human power to satisfy the present need, the Holy One left "the difficulty and perplexity to work in his mind and the minds of the Apostles[2]," and thus prepare them for what He was about to do.

As the evening, however, drew on (Mtt. xiv. 15; Lk. ix. 12) the disciples approached Him, and drawing His attention to the desert[3] character of the locality, pro-

[1] Trench, *Miracles*, p. 262. [2] Trench, p. 262.

[3] "There is now, and probably always was, one characteristic feature of the Eastern side of the Lake—its *desert cha-*

posed that He should send away the multitudes, in order that they might seek refreshment in the neighbouring towns and villages. To this He replied that *they need not depart* (Mtt. xiv. 16), and bade *them* supply their needs, and when, reiterating the assertion[1] of Philip, they declared how impossible it was to do such a thing, He sent them to see what supplies they had. Returning they informed Him that from a lad in their company they had been enabled to procure *five barley loaves and two small fishes* (Jn. vi. 9), and were thereupon bidden to marshal the multitudes *in companies*[2] amid the green grass of the rich plain around. This done, He took the loaves and the two fishes and *looking up to heaven He blessed*, and brake, and gave of the food to the Apostles, who in their turn distributed to the different groups, till *they did all eat and were filled.* When the wondrous meal was over, the Holy

racter. Partly this arises from its near exposure to the Bedouin tribes, partly from its less abundance of springs and streams. There is no recess in the Eastern hills; no towns along its banks corresponding to those in the Plain of Gennesaret. Thus the wilder regions became a natural refuge from the active life of the Western shores." Stanley's *S. and P.* 379.

[1] Compare Trench, *Miracles*, p. 264.

[2] Consisting some of 50, some of 100, and, in the graphic words of St Mark, showing like so many *garden plots* (*πρασιαὶ πρασιαί*), on the green turf. "Our English '*in ranks,*' does not reproduce the picture to the eye, giving rather the notion of continuous lines. Wiclif's was better, '*by parties.*' Perhaps '*in groups*' would be as near as we could get to it in English," Trench, *Miracles*, p. 265. "In the parts of the plain not cultivated by the hand of man would be found *the much green grass* (Mk. vi. 39; Jn. vi. 10) still fresh in the spring of the year, before it had faded away in the summer sun—the tall grass which, broken down by the feet of the thousands there gathered together, would make as it were couches (Mk. vi. 39, 40) for them to recline upon." Stanley's *S. and P.* 381.

One, who, as the Lord of nature, ever "makes the most prodigal bounty go hand in hand with the nicest and truest economy," bade the disciples *gather up the fragments that remained, that nothing might be lost,* and though 5000 men *besides women and children* (Mtt. xiv. 21) had eaten and been satisfied, yet they took up twelve baskets full of fragments that still remained over and above (Mtt. xiv. 20; Mk. vi. 43; Jn. vi. 13).

The impression made upon the people by this miracle was profound. It was the popular expectation that the Messiah would repeat the miracles of Moses[1], and this "bread of wonder," of which they had partaken, vividly recalled to the minds of the multitude their great Lawgiver, who had given their fathers manna in the wilderness. They were convinced, therefore, that the Holy One was none other than the Prophet, of whom Moses had spoken (Deut. xviii. 15), and in this conviction would have taken *Him by force and made Him a king* (Jn. vi. 14, 15).

To defeat this their intention, the Saviour bade His Apostles take ship and cross over to Bethsaida[2] (Mk. vi. 45), on the other side of the lake, while He dismissed the multitudes. Having done so, He ascended to a point in the neighbouring mountain-range, and there continued in solitary communion with His Heavenly Father till near the fourth watch[3] of the night (Mtt. xiv. 23—25; Mk. vi. 46).

[1] Trench, *Miracles,* p. 271, and note.

[2] The Western Bethsaida, the city of Philip, and Andrew, and Peter, is placed by Robinson at the modern *Et-Tabighah,* by Ritter at *Khân Minyeh.* Ellicott, 207, note.

[3] The proper Jewish reckoning recognised only *three* such watches, entitled (i) *the first or beginning of the watches* (Lam. ii. 19), lasting from sunset to 10 P.M.; (ii) *the middle watch* (Judg. vii. 19), from 10 P.M. to 2 A.M.; (iii) *the morning watch* (Ex. xiv. 24; 1 Sam. xi. 11), from 2 A.M. to sunrise. After the Roman supremacy the number of watches

Meanwhile the Apostles had rowed about 25 or 30 furlongs[1] (Jn. vi. 19), when one of those sudden storms of wind to which the lake is subject, rushed down from the western mountains, and lashing the usually placid surface into waves (Mtt. xiv. 24) prevented them making their way towards Capernaum, and exposed them to imminent peril. At this moment, to add to their fears, they discerned amidst the darkness (Mk. vi. 50) a Figure walking on the water and approaching their vessel. Thinking it could be nothing but a Phantom, they cried out in their terror, when a well-known Voice was heard saying *It is I, be not afraid.* Thereupon the ardent, impetuous Peter replied, *Lord, if it be Thou, bid me come unto Thee on the water.* The rejoinder was *Come;* and so descending from the vessel (Mtt. xiv. 29) amidst the darkness and howling wind the Apostle made some little way towards his Lord. But soon the wind roared (Mtt. xiv. 30 and the waters raged, and his heart failed him, and beginning to sink he cried, *Lord, save me.* Thereupon Jesus *stretched forth His hand and caught him,* and gently rebuking him for his want of faith took him with Him into the ship, which amidst the calm that now stilled the waves, quickly reached the harbour of Capernaum, while the Apostles, *amazed beyond measure* (Mk. vi. 51), worshipped Him, saying, *Truly Thou art the Son of God* (Mtt. xiv. 33).

was increased to *four*, sometimes described by their numerical order (as Mtt. xiv. 25), sometimes by the terms "*even,*" closing at 9 P.M.; "*midnight;*" "*cock-crowing*" at 3 A.M.; "*morning*" at 6 A.M.; See Smith's *Bibl. Dict.*

[1] Scarcely, therefore, more than half the way, the lake being 40 or 45 furlongs in breadth.

CHAPTER II

THE DISCOURSE IN THE SYNAGOGUE OF CAPERNAUM.

A.D. 29.

THE fact of the Saviour's presence on the western side of the lake was soon spread abroad amongst the people (Mk. vi. 54), and, as so often before, they brought their sick, who experienced the effects of the healing word (Mtt. xiv. 36). Meanwhile many of the five thousand, who on the previous evening had witnessed the marvellous multiplication of the loaves, not finding the Lord on the eastern side of the lake, had taken ship[1] and crossed over to Capernaum *seeking Him* (Jn. vi. 24). Knowing that He had not embarked with His disciples after the miracle, they wondered how He had crossed over, and finding Him in the Synagogue of Capernaum (Jn. vi. 59) eagerly questioned Him on the subject.

But, as in the case of Nicodemus, the Holy One was not pleased to vouchsafe a direct answer to their question. He knew the superficial character of their enthusiasm, and the merely temporal objects that had brought them to Him; *Verily, verily, I say unto you*, He replied, *ye seek Me, not because ye saw the miracles, but because ye did eat of the loaves and were filled. Labour not for the meat which perisheth, but for the*

[1] "The contrary wind, which, blowing up the lake from the south-west would prevent the boat of the Apostles from returning to Capernaum, would also bring *other boats* (Jn. vi. 16—24) from Tiberias, the chief city on the south, to Julias, the chief city on the north, and so enable the multitudes, when the storm had subsided, to cross at once, without the long journey on foot which they had made the day before." Stanley's *S. and P.*, p. 382.

meat which endureth unto everlasting life, which the Son of Man shall give unto you, for Him hath God the Father sealed. Apparently understanding the Bread He spoke of in a literal sense, they replied by asking *how they might work the works of God*, whereupon the Holy One declared that the work acceptable to God was *to believe on Him whom He had sent* (Jn. vi. 29). To this they rejoined, with their usual craving for miracle after miracle, by asking for some sign to confirm their belief in Him, and then proceeded to suggest "a sign from heaven" such as they desired. The miracle of the preceding evening had convinced many of them that the Speaker was indeed the Prophet *that should come into the world*, and whose Advent had been predicted by Moses. That Lawgiver had given them bread from heaven not once only, but during a space of forty years; could He give them such a sign from heaven?

In condescension to the associations they had themselves recalled, the Saviour replied that Moses had not given them the bread from heaven, but His Father was giving them the true Bread, even HIM *who cometh down from heaven, and giveth life unto the world* (Jn. vi. 33). Still understanding Him to speak of some miraculous life-sustaining food, the Jews begged that He would *evermore give them that Bread*, whereupon, passing from indirect to direct assertions, He replied in the ever-memorable words,

I am the Bread of Life;

and in language majestic in its very simplicity proceeded to vindicate His Divine nature and His descent from heaven.

This last assertion gave great offence to His hearers; they called to mind the earthly parentage of the Speaker (Jn. vi. 42), and marvelled how He could claim a Divine origin. But, unmoved, unruffled by their increasing discontent, whether "they would hear or whether they would forbear," He went on to repeat that He was the Bread from heaven, that the Bread He would give was *His flesh*, which He was about *to give for the life of the world* (Jn. vi. 47—51).

These mysterious words provoked still greater opposition on the part of the Jews; they *strove with one another, saying, How can this man give us His flesh to eat?* But their opposition and questionings moved not His calm majesty. With the same formula of solemnity, which He had already thrice used[1] (Jn. vi. 53), He resumed in language still more emphatic His assertion, that unless they *ate the flesh of the Son of Man, and drank His blood, they could have no life in them—that His Flesh was meat indeed, and His Blood drink indeed—that whoso ate His Flesh and drank His Blood had eternal life, and He would raise him up at the last day* (Jn. vi. 53—58).

These solemn words, so entirely in keeping with the associations of the Passover, now on the point of being[2] celebrated at Jerusalem, exerted a great influence on those who heard them. The Jews, as we have seen, were deeply offended. But many even of His disciples regarded what they had heard as *a hard saying* (Jn. vi. 60), and walked no more with Him (Jn. vi. 66). Turning to the Twelve, the Saviour enquired whether they too were about to join the general defection, whereupon Peter replied, in the name of the rest, that there was no other Teacher to whom they could go, for He had the words of eternal life, and they believed and

[1] *Verily, verily, I say unto you,* Jn. vi. 26; vi. 32; vi. 47; vi. 53.

[2] If it was not actually being celebrated. Many hold that the day on which this momentous discourse was delivered in the synagogue of Capernaum was the 15th of Nisan, the second day of the Paschal Feast. See Wieseler, p. 281; Tischendorf, *Synop. Evang.* XXXIV.; Ellicott's *Hulsean Lectures,* p. 210 and note.

were assured that He was the *Holy One*[1] *of God* (Jn. vi. 69). This declaration of faithful adherence their Omnipotent Master accepted, but with the sad remark that even now there was a traitor in their midst (Jn. vi. 70, 71).

After this memorable day in the synagogue of Capernaum, the Holy One appears to have continued a short time in the Plain of Gennesaret, during which period the excitement caused by His first landing was not diminished, His popularity was great in spite of the mysteriousness of His doctrines, and His mighty power continued to be marvellously displayed[2].

But soon His labours of love were interrupted. Having kept the Feast at Jerusalem the Scribes and Pharisees returned (Mk. vii. 1), and soon found matter for accusation against Him. In the social gatherings of the Saviour and His Apostles they noticed that He did not observe the strict and minute traditions of the elders, but ate bread with unwashen hands (Mtt. xv. 2; Mk. vii. 5). In reply the Holy One told them that by those *commandments of men* which they so studiously observed they were making of none effect the commandments of God, whom, in the words of the prophet Isaiah, *they honoured only with their lips, while their hearts were far from Him* (Isai. xxix. 13). The external defilement they were so careful to avoid was, He declared in the hearing of the people (Mk. vii. 14), nothing compared with the defilement of the heart, out of which proceeded all manner of evil thoughts, which ripened into the worst crimes—these truly defiled a man (Mtt. xv. 13—22).

[1] Ὁ ἅγιος τοῦ Θεοῦ (Jn. vi. 69): such appears to be the preferable reading. See Scrivener's Greek Testament.

[2] It is not necessary to regard the statements in Mk. vi. 54, 55 as descriptive of an activity confined to that one day. Andrews, p. 269.

The severity with which He thus, in the presence of the people, rebuked the rulers of the nation for a hypocritical observance of vain traditions, roused to a still greater height the animosity of the Pharisaic faction (Mtt. xv. 12). Knowing that He could not now shew Himself openly without being exposed to their machinations[1], the Lord passed north-west through the mountains of upper Galilee, and thence into the border-land of Tyre and Sidon (Mtt. xv. 21; Mk. vii. 24). Here He *entered into a house, and would have no man know it* (Mk. vii. 24). But the rest and seclusion He sought were not to be found. A Syrophœnician[2] woman crossed the frontier (Mk. vii. 25), and earnestly besought His aid in behalf of her daughter, who was grievously afflicted with a demon. At first it seemed as though she had come in vain. But in spite of silence (Mtt. xv. 23), refusal (Mtt. xv. 24), and seeming reproach (Mtt. xv. 26), she persevered in her petition, and at length, when the trial of her faith was ended, she obtained that which she had sought so earnestly, and with the encouraging assurance that though a descendant of ancient idolaters, her faith was great (Mtt. xv. 28), and that her daughter was made whole, returned to the place whence she came forth.

After a short stay in this region, the Saviour pro-

[1] Lange on Mtt. xv. 21.

[2] A *woman of Canaan* according to St Matthew (xv. 22), *a Greek* or *Syrophœnician* according to St Mark (vii. 26). The first term describes her religion, that it was not Jewish, but heathen; the second, the stock of which she came, "which was even that accursed stock once doomed of God to a total excision, but of which some branches had been spared by those first generations of Israel that should have extirpated them root and branch. (See *Class-Book of Old Testament History*, pp. 225—227.) Everything, therefore, was against this woman, yet she was not hindered by that everything from drawing nigh, and craving the boon that her soul longed after," Trench, *Parables*, p. 339.

ceeded northwards, still nearer, as it would seem, to pagan Sidon[1], and thence passing round the sources of the Jordan and in a south-easterly circuit through Decapolis (Mk. vii. 31), to the further shore of the sea of Gennesaret. In this region His merciful aid was besought in behalf of a deaf and dumb[2] man (Mk. vii. 32), whom He withdrew from the throng of bystanders (Mk. vii. 33), and after using special outward signs[3] gradually restored to the full possession of his faculties, charging the multitudes to preserve a strict silence respecting the miracle (Mk. vii. 36). This injunction, however, was not obeyed, for the spectators spread abroad the news far and wide (Mk. vii. 36), and the effect was that many who were *lame, blind, dumb, maimed* (Mtt. xv. 30), were brought to Him, and experienced the beneficent results of the healing word.

CHAPTER III

THE FOUR THOUSAND FED—THE CONFESSION OF ST PETER.

A. D. 29.

THE effect of these miraculous cures on the inhabitants of the half-pagan district of Decapolis was

[1] If not *through Sidon*, according to a reading, διὰ Σιδῶνος, in Mk. vii. 31, found in several MSS., in several ancient Versions, and adopted by Tischendorf, Alford, Tregelles and others, and "which certainly appears to deserve the preference thus almost unanimously given to it." Ellicott, 218, n. What part of the Decapolis the Lord visited is not mentioned.

[2] Not, indeed, absolutely dumb, but unable to utter intelligible sounds, having, as our Version renders the word, an impediment in his speech; Greek μογιλάλος = βραδύγλωσσος.

[3] *He put His fingers into His ears, and spat, and touched His tongue, and looking up to heaven He sighed, and saith unto him, Ephphatha, that is, Be opened* (Mk. vii. 34).

very great, and they confessed that the God who had chosen Israel was indeed above all gods[1] (Mtt. xv. 31). Before long, therefore, a great multitude, amounting to upwards of four thousand besides women and children (Mtt. xv. 38), were collected from the neighbouring region, and continued with the Lord three days (Mtt. xv. 32), beholding His works and listening to His words.

They had not, like the multitude earlier in the year, assembled for the purpose of going up to Jerusalem to keep the Passover, and their scanty provisions failing them, could only retire to their mountain-homes through the passes by which they had followed the Lord[2]. The compassionate Redeemer had no wish that they should return only *to faint by the way* (Mk. viii. 3), and enquired of the disciples how many loaves they had with them. To this they replied, *Seven, and a few small fishes* (Mtt. xv. 34), and were thereupon commanded to make the men sit down[3], when their scanty supply in the hands of Him, who was the true Bread from heaven, proved sufficient for the hungry multitude: they did eat and were filled, *and took up of the broken meat that was left seven baskets*[4] *full* (Mtt. xv. 37).

Having dismissed the recipients of His bounty, the Lord immediately entered with His disciples into a

[1] Trench, *Miracles*, p. 353.

[2] Lange on Mtt. xv. 32.

[3] *Where* is not very distinctly specified. All we can certainly gather is that it was on the Eastern side of the lake, and in a *desert spot* (Mtt. xv. 33), possibly about the middle or southern end of the Lake.

[4] The baskets on this occasion are called σπυρίδες (comp. Acts ix. 25), on the occasion of the feeding of the Five Thousand, κόφινος (Mtt. xiv. 20 and the parallels). When alluding to the two miracles subsequently (Matt. xvi. 9, 10; Mk. viii. 19, 20), the Saviour preserves the distinction. For the word κόφινος, compare Juvenal, III. 13,

Judæis, quorum cophinus fœnumque supellex.

ship[1], and crossed over, according to St Matthew, *into the coasts of Magdala*[2] (xv. 39), according to St Mark, *into the parts of Dalmanutha*[3] (viii. 10), a village close by. Here, however, His stay was of no long duration, for certain Pharisees, now for the first time combined with the Sadducees, approached (Mtt. xvi. 1) with a demand that He would shew them *a sign from heaven.* This request, already twice preferred[4], and now urged in explicit terms, He, who knew the hearts of those who claimed it, would not gratify. *Sighing deeply in His spirit* (Mk. viii. 12), and grieved at their continued unbelief, He denounced them as hypocrites, who could *discern the face of the sky*, but not *discern the signs of the times* (Mtt. xvi. 3), and refusing to give them any other sign than that of *the prophet Jonah* (Mtt. xvi. 4), straightway entered the vessel, in which He had come (Mk. viii. 13), and made for the other side.

Warning His disciples during the voyage against the

[1] Possibly the ship kept specially for His own use.

[2] Now unanimously identified with a miserable collection of hovels (Stanley's *S. and P.*, p. 382) known as *el-Mejdel,* on the western side of the lake, and at the S. E. corner of the Plain of Gennesaret. Its name "is hardly altered from the ancient Magdala or Migdol, so called, probably, from an ancient watch-tower that guarded the entrance of the plain." Stanley, *l. c.*; compare Tristram, p. 425; Thomson, *L. and B.*

[3] "Just before reaching Mejdel we crossed a little open valley, the *Ain-el-Baridah,* with a few rich corn-fields and gardens straggling among the ruins of a village, and some large and more ancient foundations by several copious fountains, and probably identified with the Dalmanutha of the New Testament." Tristram, *l. c.* "We conjecture that the Lord touched the shore somewhere between these two villages." Lange on Mtt. xv. 39.

[4] Comp. Jn. ii. 18, above, p. 164; Jn. vi. 30, above, p. 211. A sign from heaven denoted either (i) some visible manifestation of the *Shechinah,* or (ii) some change in the sun or moon, some meteor, or thunder and lightning. Comp. Lange on Mtt. xvi. 1.

leaven of the Pharisees and the Sadducees (Mtt. xvi. 5—12; Mk. viii. 14—21), he reached the eastern shore of the lake and the neighbourhood of Bethsaida-Julias (Mk. viii. 22). Here a blind man was brought to Him, with a petition that He would touch him. Taking him, like the deaf and dumb man spoken of above, outside the village, the Lord anointed his eyes with the moisture from His own mouth, and laying His hands upon him enquired whether he saw aught? To this the sufferer looking up replied that he *saw men, as trees, walking* (Mk. viii. 24). Thereupon the Redeemer laid His hands again upon his eyes, and his sight was completely restored.

From Bethsaida, accompanied by His Apostles, He now set out in a northerly direction, and travelling along the eastern banks of the Jordan and beyond the waters of Merom, reached the confines or *the villages* (Mk. viii. 27) of Cæsarea Philippi[1]. In this neighbourhood, on one occasion, the Apostles found their Master

[1] A town, not Canaanite but Roman, "in its situation, in its exuberance of water, its olive-groves, and its view over the distant plain, almost a Syrian Tivoli." Stanley's *S. and P.*, p. 398. (i) Its ancient name was *Panium* or *Paneas* (Jos. *Ant.* xv. 10. 3, and see above, p. 13), so called from a cavern near the town, "abrupt, prodigiously deep, and full of still water," adopted by the Greeks of the Macedonian kingdom of Antioch as "the nearest likeness that Syria affords of the beautiful limestone grottos which in their own country were inseparably associated with the worship of the sylvan Pan," and dedicated to that deity. Hence its modern appellation, *Banias.* (ii) The town retained its old name under Herod the Great, who built here a splendid temple, of the whitest marble, which he dedicated to Augustus Cæsar (see above, p. 94). But Herod Philip made great additions to the town (Jos. *Ant.* XVIII. 2. 1; *B. J.* II. 9. 1), and called it Cæsarea Philippi, partly after his own name, and partly after that of the Emperor. Agrippa II. afterwards called it Neronias (Jos. *Ant.* XX. 9. 4), and here Titus exhibited gladiatorial shows at the close of the Jewish war (Jos. *B. J.* VII. 2. 1).

engaged in solitary prayer (Lk. ix. 18), a solemn and significant action, the precursor of not a few important events[1], as now of a deeply momentous revelation. For as they resumed their journey, He addressed to them the formal enquiry, *Whom do men say that I am?*

This was not an ordinary question. He was speaking to those who had now for some time been His constant companions, hearers of His words, and spectators of the signs which accompanied them. He seems to have wished to ascertain from their own lips the results of those labours, which now, in one sense, were drawing to a close, and thence to pass on to other and more painful truths, which He had to communicate to them[2]. To this enquiry, then, the Apostles replied in words that reflected the various opinions then held amongst the people; *Some say John the Baptist, others Elias, others Jeremias, or one of the prophets* (Mtt. xvi. 14; Mk. viii. 28; Lk. ix. 19). *But*, continued the Holy One, *whom say ye that I am?* To this the Apostle Peter, speaking in the name of the rest, made the ever-memorable reply, *Thou art the Christ, the Son of the living God* (Mtt. xvi. 16).

The object for which the question had been put was now partly achieved. By the mouth of one of their number the Apostles had expressed the conclusion, to which they had come after so long enjoying the society of their Master, that He was no other than the Messiah, the Son of God. This their testimony He accepted; acknowledged the truth of the Apostle's confession; declared that it had not been revealed to him *by flesh and blood, but by His Father in heaven;* and bestowed

[1] i. The *Baptism* (Lk. iii. 21); ii. The *Election of the Twelve* (Lk. vi. 12, 13); iii. The *Discourse in the Synagogue* of Capernaum (Mtt. xiv. 23); iv. Now *the Transfiguration* (Lk. ix. 28); v. The *Agony* (Lk. xxii. 44).

[2] Stier, II. 329; Lange's *Life of Christ*, III. 229.

upon him the promise of peculiar dignity in the Church He was about to establish (Mtt. xvi. 18, 19).

But now, having, as three Evangelists distinctly tell us (Mtt. xvi. 20; Mk. viii. 30; Lk. ix. 21), charged them strictly not to divulge the fact of His Messiahship to the world at large, He began to reveal to them strange and mournful tidings respecting Himself. *The Son of Man*, He declared, *must go up to Jerusalem, and there suffer many things from the elders, chief priests, and scribes, and be put to death, and after three days rise again.* This was the first announcement, clear, distinct, peremptory of what lay before Him (Mk. viii. 32), revealing not only that He should suffer, but the agents in His sufferings, the form they would take, the place where He would undergo them, and their issue, a mysterious resurrection after three days. To the Apostles the announcement sounded utterly strange and inconceivable. The selfsame Peter, who, a moment before, had witnessed so noble and outspoken a confession to his Lord's Divinity, was utterly unable even to endure the thought of His suffering. *That be far from Thee, Lord,* was his indignant reply. But with a solemn rebuke the Holy One checked his untimely expostulations, which savoured of the weakness of flesh and blood, not of holy obedience to a heavenly Father's will. Nay more, as if to seal the words He had uttered in the presence of many witnesses, He called to Him some of the people that were standing near (Mk. viii. 34), and in their hearing, as well as that of the Apostles, bade any who would come after Him, *take up his Cross* and follow Him, for through the gate of suffering lay the road to Glory, not only for Himself, but for all His followers (Mtt. xvi. 24; Mk. viii. 34; Lk. ix. 23).

CHAPTER IV

THE TRANSFIGURATION—THE LUNATIC CHILD.

A. D. 29.

AFTER the announcement we have just considered, the teaching of the Lord as addressed to His disciples assumed a new character. The mysterious close of His life had been already[1] more than once hinted at in figures or parables, but now He began gradually, as they were able to bear it, to speak clearly and openly of His death and rejection by the Jews. So far from establishing any earthly kingdom such as they expected, in which they might occupy distinguished places, He proceeded from this time to intimate in precise and distinct language how very different was the end that really awaited Him.

To the Apostles, who indulged to the close in dreams of a reign like that of earthly kings, these intimations of their Master sounded strange and unaccountable. To cheer, therefore, their wounded spirits, to enable them in some measure to comprehend the supernatural character of His kingdom, the Holy One was pleased to assure them that there were *some standing there*, who

[1] Already by His very name the deepest purport of His mission had been declared to be the *delivery of His people from their sin* (Mtt. i. 21); already the aged Symeon had foreseen *heart-piercing anguish* in store for His mother (Lk. ii. 35); already the Baptist had twice pointed Him out as the *Lamb of God* destined *to take away the sin of the world* (Jn. i. 29); already at the first Passover He had spoken to the Jews of a *Temple to be destroyed and rebuilt in three days* (Jn. ii. 19); and to Nicodemus of *a lifting up of the Son of Man* even as Moses had *lifted up the serpent in the wilderness* (Jn. iii. 12—16); already at the second Passover He had declared that He was about to give His flesh *for the life of the world*, that His flesh was *meat indeed*, and His blood *drink indeed* (Jn. vi. 47—51).

should not *taste of death till they had seen*, in spite of the sad announcement He had just made, *the Son of Man coming in His kingdom* (Mtt. xvi. 28; comp. Mk. ix. 1; Lk. ix. 27).

Accordingly six days afterwards, with three of the most privileged of their number, who had already in the chamber of Jairus witnessed their Master's power over death[1], He retired to one of the numerous mountain-ranges in the neighbourhood, not improbably one of the summits of Hermon[2]. From St Luke's intimation that one object of His own withdrawal was that He might engage in solitary prayer (Lk. ix. 28), and that the three Apostles were wearied and oppressed by sleep (Lk. ix. 32), we infer that evening was the time of this retirement of the Holy One, the close, it may be, of a long day spent in going about doing good. While, then, they slept and He continued engaged in prayer, a marvellous change came over His person (Lk. ix. 29). His raiment suddenly became shining, *exceeding white as snow, the fashion* also *of His countenance* was altered, *and shone like the sun* (Mtt. xvii. 2; Mk. ix. 3; Lk. ix. 29).

Roused at length by the supernatural brightness around them, the Chosen Three awoke[3], and shaking off their slumbers, perceived not only the mysterious change that had come over their Master, but also that He was no longer alone! He was accompanied by *two men*, in whom they were enabled to recognize no others than the great pillars and representatives of the Old Testament

[1] See above, p. 201.

[2] Stanley, *S. and P.*, 399; Lightfoot on Mk. ix. 2.

[3] It is clear that the occurrence was no waking vision or "dream." Peter and they that were with him *had been weighed by sleep* (ἦσαν βεβαρημένοι ὕπνῳ), *but they thoroughly roused themselves* (διαγρηγορήσαντες δέ), *and saw* His glory and the two men standing with Him. Lk. ix. 32. See Alford *in loc.*

dispensation, *Moses and Elias.* Nor did they only see their transfigured Lord attended by these strange visitants from the world of spirits, but they were privileged to overhear the subject of their mutual converse. *They spake of*, or described[1], *the decease He was about to accomplish at Jerusalem* (Lk. ix. 31).

Upon the ardent, impulsive Peter it was the scene itself, and not the topic of mysterious converse he over heard, that made the most impression. To him it seemed as though the kingdom of heaven was indeed "revealed in power." In the excitement of the moment he would have made three tabernacles, one for his Lord, one for Moses, and one for Elias, in order that from thence the laws of the kingdom might be promulgated, and all men might recognise the true Messiah attended by the Pillars of the old Economy. But it was not to be. While he was yet speaking there came a cloud overshadowing them, and out of it there came a Voice, saying, *This is My Beloved Son, hear ye Him.* And then all was over. While the Apostles lay panic-stricken on their faces, their Master once more joined them, and bade them *rise and not be afraid*, and, as they descended from the Mount, He charged them to reveal to no man what they had seen, *till* (again the mysterious words recurred) *He should have risen from the dead* (Mtt. xvii. 9; Mk. ix. 9).

Rejoining the rest of their fellow-Apostles, the Chosen Three found them surrounded by a great crowd, amongst which were certain of the Lord's old adversaries, the Scribes, not unwilling witnesses of a defeat which His

[1] Ἔλεγον τὴν ἔξοδον αὐτοῦ, Lk. ix. 31. "An unusual construction of λέγειν," it has been remarked, "though it occurs again in Rom. iv. 6, and in the earliest ecclesiastical writers, in the sense of *recounting, relating the details of, describing.*" Westcott's *Introd. to the Study of the Gospels*, p. 298, n. For the word Ἔξοδος here used compare Wisdom vii. 6; 2 Pet. i. 5.

disciples had sustained. During their Master's absence a man had besought their aid in behalf of his son, who was possessed with an evil spirit of peculiar malignity. But he had besought their aid in vain. The Nine had been unable to expel the demon, and the Scribes, making the most of their discomfiture, were eagerly disputing with them (Mk. ix. 14), and doubtless "arguing from the impotence of the servants to the impotence of the Master[1]," when He suddenly appeared, bearing, it would seem, on His face and person traces of the celestial glory of the past night. *Greatly amazed* (Mk. ix. 15) at His appearance, the multitude no sooner saw Him, than they *ran to Him and saluted Him* (Mk. ix. 15), and as He was asking of the Scribes the reason of their dispute with His disciples, the father drew near, related what had occurred, and the terrible condition of his only son (Lk. ix. 38). Possessed he had been for a long time with a dumb spirit (Mk. ix. 17), but at times it seized him with such violence, that he *foamed and gnashed with his teeth* (Mk. ix. 18), or was driven with almost irresistible impulse into the water and into the fire (Mtt. xvii. 15).

With a sad rebuke of the faithlessness of the generation in which He lived, the Lord commanded the boy to be brought into His presence. He was brought, but no sooner did he see the Saviour (Mk. ix. 20), than he was seized with one of those sudden paroxysms, which the father had described, and falling on the ground, he *wallowed foaming* at the mouth (Mk. ix. 20). On beholding the miserable sufferer, the Lord enquired of his father how long he had been in this case. To this the other replied that it dated from his childhood (Mk. ix. 21), and described the terrible nature of the fits which came upon him, ending with a touching request, that if

[1] Trench, *Miracles*, p. 361.

He could do anything, He would have compassion on him, and help him. *All things are possible*, said the Holy One, *to him that believeth. Lord, I believe*, replied the agonized father, *help Thou mine unbelief* (Mk. ix. 23, 24), and his faith, though but a little spark, was rewarded. Addressing the demon in words of solemn and conscious authority the Holy One commanded him to leave the child and *enter him no more* (Mk. ix. 25), and the foul spirit, unable to resist the word of power, uttering a piercing cry and rending the sufferer with one last convulsive paroxysm (Mk. ix. 26), left him lying on the ground, to all appearance dead. But his merciful Healer took him by the hand, and, invigorated by that touch, he rose up, and was restored to his rejoicing father (Lk. ix. 42).

CHAPTER V

THE COIN IN THE FISH'S MOUTH—TOUR THROUGH SAMARIA.

A.D. 29.

AFTER the incidents just related, the Redeemer appears to have again turned His steps southward through the northern parts of Galilee and in the direction of Capernaum (Mtt. xvii. 22; Mk. ix. 30). This journey He wished should be as private as possible (Mk. ix. 30), undisturbed by the presence of the large crowds that usually gathered about Him. For now that He had so plainly and unreservedly spoken to His Apostles of His approaching death and resurrection, He desired that these His words should *sink deep into their ears* (Lk. ix. 44), and that they should be more fully instructed respecting their reality and certainty. Once more, therefore, He began to tell them of His coming rejection by the rulers of the nation, of His death, and resurrection. But His words took no root in the minds of His hearers. His "thoughts were not their thoughts," nor His "ways their ways;" they could not understand that whereof He spake, or how One, whom they believed to be the Messiah, could be called upon to suffer, and were afraid to ask Him personally what He meant (Mk. ix. 32; Lk. ix. 45).

On their arrival at Capernaum, the collection of the half-shekel[1] due from every male Israelite, who had attained the age of 20 years, for the service of the sanctuary at Jerusalem, was going on. Approaching the Apostle Peter, the collectors enquired whether his Master did not pay this sum (Mtt. xvii. 24), to which he replied in the affirmative. Shortly afterwards on reaching the house where they were about to lodge (Mtt. xvii. 25), the Lord, aware of the incident, enquired of the Apostle whether earthly monarchs levied custom and tribute[2] of their own children or of strangers. *Of strangers*, was the instant reply. *Then*, said the Holy One, alluding to His own relation to His heavenly Father, *are the children free*, and He as the Son of God was exempt from a payment which went to the support of His Father's house. Lest, however, it should be said that He and His Apostles despised the Temple, and so men should be offended, He bade him go down to the lake, cast in a hook, and take the first fish that came up, assuring him that, when he had opened its mouth, he

[1] The *Didrachma* (Matt. xvii. 24) was exactly the sum mentioned in Ex. xxx. 11—16, due for the current expenses of the tabernacle, and afterwards of the Temple. The shekels, half-shekels, and quarter-shekels, which the Jews were permitted in the time of the Maccabees to coin (see above, pp. 55, 56), becoming scarce, and not being coined any more, "it became the custom to estimate the Temple-dues as two drachmas (the δίδραχμον here required)," Trench, *Miracles*, p. 373.

[2] Κῆνσος = the capitation-tax; τέλη = customs or tolls on goods, Trench, *Miracles*, p. 380.

would find sufficient[1] to pay both for the Apostle and his Master (Mtt. xvii. 27).

In spite of His repeated intimations respecting His own coming sufferings, the thoughts of the Apostles were still running on the high places they believed in store for them in their Master's kingdom, and the late selection of three of their number to behold the glory of His transfiguration, added to the prominence of Simon in the miraculous payment of the tribute-money, excited their jealousy and carnal aspirations. While their Master was contemplating the cross, their imaginations were apportioning crowns, and the question which was the greatest amongst them excited much discussion (Mk. iv. 33; Lk. ix. 46, 47). Knowing their thoughts He replied to their question respecting the disputed point (Mtt. xviii. 1) by a touching symbolical action. Taking a little child in His arms (Mk. ix. 36) He placed him in their midst, and solemnly (Mk. ix. 35) declared that unless they laid aside all their thoughts of dignity and place and power, and became like little children (Mtt. xviii. 3), they could not hope to enter into His Kingdom at all; for in that Kingdom he was greatest who could humble himself like the little child before them, and whoso received even one such little child in His Name, received Him.

These last words reminded the Apostle John of a fault which he now confessed. On one occasion he and the rest of the Apostles had seen a man trying to cast out demons by pronouncing over the possessed the name of Jesus (Comp. Acts xix. 13), and they had forbidden him, on the ground that he was not one of their Master's avowed followers (Mk. ix. 38; Lk. ix 49). On being informed of this, the Holy One gently rebuked the spirit

[1] The coin he was told he would find in the fish's mouth was a *Stater* (στατήρ, Matt. xvii. 27) = a whole shekel, which amounted to about 3 shillings and 3 pence, or just the sum required.

which had prompted the Apostle thus to act. *No man*, He declared, *who could work a miracle in His name, could lightly speak evil of Him; he that was not against them was for them; and even a cup of cold water given to a disciple in His name should not lose its reward* (Mk. ix. 41). Having thus urged upon them the duty of child-like humility, He proceeded to enforce that of avoiding offences (Mtt xviii. 10), and of cultivating a spirit of love towards their Lord's little ones. Then by the Parable of the *Lost Sheep* He taught them the joy that pervaded heaven at the repentance of a single sinner (Mtt. xviii. 10, &c.; Lk. xv. 3—7), and by that of the *Debtor who owed ten thousand talents* (Mtt. xviii. 23—35), how they were bound to forgive every one his brother their trespasses.

While the Apostles were being thus gradually trained for the reception of other ideas than those of earthly glory, in respect to the establishment of their Master's Kingdom, the season for the celebration of the feast of Tabernacles drew near (Jn. vii. 2). The harvest being over, and the grapes trodden in the winepress, numerous caravans of Jewish pilgrims would be gathering together to go up to the Holy City and keep the Feast. At this juncture, then, the Lord's brethren[1] (Jn. vii. 3) who, though they did not believe in His Divinity (Jn. vii. 5), were yet not above cherishing feelings of pride and exultation at the mighty works which He wrought[2], bade Him leave Galilee, and display proofs of His wonder-working power, no longer in obscure northern towns, but in the streets of Jerusalem itself (Jn. viii. 3—6).

[1] From Mtt. xiii. 56 we learn that their names were *James, Joses, Judas,* and *Simon.* By some they are regarded as the actual brethren of our Lord; by others as his first cousins, being the sons of Alphæus or Clopas and Mary the sister of the Virgin.

[2] Ellicott, 246 n.

Though He intended to keep the feast, the Redeemer could not go up to it for such a manifestation of Himself to the world as they desired (Jn. vii. 4). His Hour, the Hour for a very different exaltation, was not yet come (Jn. vii. 6), nor for the present could He take part in festal solemnities. They accordingly went their way to Jerusalem, and on their departure, amidst no open, avowed procession of a mere wonder-worker, but privately and unobtrusively as became a lowly Redeemer (Jn. vii. 10), accompanied by His Apostles, He set His face to go up to the Holy City (Lk. ix. 51).

Instead of taking the longer and more frequented route through Peræa, for the sake, probably, of greater seclusion, the Saviour chose that through Samaria (Lk. ix. 52), and sent messengers before Him to prepare for His coming. Entering a certain village of the Samaritans, the Apostles sought to do as He had bidden them. But the churlish inhabitants, perceiving the reason why He was passing through their land, usually so studiously avoided, refused to receive Him[1] (Lk. ix. 53). Indignant at this rebuff, the impetuous "Sons of Thunder," James and John, would have had their Master act in the spirit of Elijah[2], and call down fire from heaven on the inhospitable and churlish villagers. But the Holy One rebuked their intemperate zeal, and the forgetfulness they evinced of the true spirit that became them as His followers, and sought shelter in another village (Lk. ix. 56).

[1] Ellicott, 249.
[2] See *Class-Book of Old Testament History*, p. 403.

PART VI

FROM THE FEAST OF TABERNACLES TO THE TRIUMPHAL ENTRY INTO JERUSALEM.

CHAPTER I

THE FEAST OF TABERNACLES—HOSTILITY OF THE SANHEDRIN.

A. D. 29.

MEANWHILE the excitement at Jerusalem respecting the Saviour was very great. The Festivals of Passover and Pentecost had alike passed away, and He had not assumed publicly the title or functions of the Messiah. The question whether He would present Himself at the Feast of Tabernacles was eagerly discussed (Jn. vii. 11), and many were the opinions advanced concerning Him; some affirming Him to be *a good man;* others, a *deceiver of the people;* while fear of the ruling powers in the city prevented any open declaration in His favour (Jn. vii. 12).

When, however, the Feast had reached its midst, He suddenly appeared in the Temple, and began to teach openly in its crowded courts. Such a step at a time when the Sanhedrin had pronounced Him guilty of a capital offence[1], when they were even seeking to kill Him (Jn. vii. 25), excited the greatest astonishment. That One, who had been brought up at the feet of none of the recognised and celebrated teachers (Jn. vii. 15), should venture thus openly to instruct the people, should claim for His doctrines a mysterious and exalted origin (Jn. vii. 16, 17), should justify His violation of the Sab-

[1] Comp. Jn. v. 16—18, and see above, p. 173.

bath by His works of mercy (Jn. vii. 21),—this, added to the hesitation and inactivity of the ruling powers[1], caused much perplexity. While, therefore, some could not recognise His claims to be regarded as the Messiah with His well-known Galilæan origin, and the uncertainty which was popularly ascribed to the quarter whence the Messiah was to come (Jn. vii. 27), many could not resist the impression His wondrous works made upon their minds, and refused to believe that the long-expected Deliverer would perform any greater miracles than those they now witnessed (Jn. vii. 31).

These murmurs of the multitude at length reached the ears of the Sanhedrin, and they resolved to take steps for securing His person (Jn. vii. 32). For this purpose they sent their officers to seize Him on the first favourable opportunity. But their hostility, though now clearly avowed, did not stay the Lord from continuing His teaching; He knew He was to be but a little while longer with the multitude, who listened to Him gladly, before He returned to Him that had sent Him, and now for the first time publicly, though darkly, hinted at His speedy removal (Jn. vii. 33—36), and on the last, *the great day of the Feast* (Jn. vii. 37), taking up His parable from the water brought in a golden vessel from the Pool of Siloam and poured before the Brazen Altar[2], preached with peculiar appropriateness on *the living waters* of the Spirit, which should flow forth when He was glorified (Jn. vii. 39).

This boldness, added to the solemnity of His words, exerted a still greater influence on the multitudes. Some declared He must be *the Prophet* (Jn. vii. 40); others that He was the Messiah (Jn. vii. 41); others would have thought so too had He not risen out of Ga-

[1] Milman, I. 244.
[2] See *Class-Book of O. T. History*, p. 154, and note.

lilee instead of Bethlehem of Judæa, as Prophecy had indicated (Jn. vii. 42; Mic. v. 2), while a fourth, but clearly a smaller party, wished to apprehend Him, but dared not from fear of the people.

Accordingly the Sanhedrin met a second time, and the officers they had deputed to effect His apprehension appeared before them (Jn. vii. 45), and in reply to the enquiry why they had not brought Him, declared it was impossible—*never man spake like Him*—and they felt powerless to carry out their instructions. Such an avowal was received with undisguised contempt (Jn. vii. 47, 48), but the Sanhedrin found that the influence of the mysterious Teacher had penetrated within their own council. While they were, apparently, proceeding to discuss some plan for His condemnation, Nicodemus interposed with the enquiry whether the Law did not demand an open examination of a man's claims before they pronounced judgment? This candid and generous suggestion drew down upon the speaker the uttermost derision. He was asked whether he too was from Galilee, and bidden to search and see whether any prophet had risen out of that despised and half-heathen region[1]? (Jn. vii. 52).

On the following day the Pharisees, finding open hostility ineffectual, made a crafty and insidious effort to undermine the growing popularity of the Saviour[2]. When He returned from the Mount of Olives (Jn. viii. 1), and reappeared in the Temple surrounded by the multitude, they brought to Him a woman who had been taken in the act of adultery, and placing her in the midst requested His decision respecting her. The Law

1 "This was not historically true; for two prophets at least had arisen from Galilee: Jonah of Gath-hepher, and the greatest of the prophets, Elijah of Thisbe; and perhaps also Nahum and Hosea. Their contempt for Galilee made them lose sight of historical accuracy." Alford *in loc.*

2 Milman, *Hist. of Christianity*, I. 246.

of Moses certainly denounced death as the penalty of her crime (Lev. xx. 10), but, owing to the corrupt morals of the times, such a sin seldom incurred any other penalty than divorce. If, then, He decided *for* the punishment of death, He would, they expected, lose ground with the people by rigidly adhering to an enactment which they themselves were wont to mitigate[1]; if, on the other hand, He pronounced her acquittal, they could denounce Him as One who set at nought the Law of Moses, and lowered its time-honoured authority (Jn. viii. 6).

While, however, they were eagerly claiming His decision, the Holy One, as if indifferent to their request, continued seated (Jn. viii. 2), and stooping down appeared to be tracing characters with His fingers in the dust. At length He looked up (Jn. viii. 7), and said, *He that is without sin amongst you, let him first cast a stone at her*, and then again bending downwards resumed the writing on the floor. Such was the solemnity of His words, and such the authority with which they appealed to the consciences of all present, that they dared not persist in advancing their charge, and stole out one by one. When, therefore, He looked up again, He found Himself alone with the woman, and enquired whether none was present to convict her. To this she replied, *No man, Lord*, and He, declining to assume the functions of the judge, or to pronounce her condemnation, bade her *go and sin no more* (Jn. viii. 11).

[1] Milman, I. 246.

CHAPTER II

THE OPENING OF THE EYES OF ONE BORN BLIND.

A. D. 29.

AFTER this signal discomfiture of His enemies, the Redeemer would seem to have been permitted to resume His discourses to the people in one of the temple corridors, known as the Treasury, where stood the numerous treasure-chests[1] to receive the contributions of the worshippers (Jn. viii. 20). Resuming, then, His teaching on the first Sabbath, probably, after the late festival, He reiterated with increasing boldness and authority His claims to be the Messiah, and drew attention to the testimonies whereby they had been confirmed (Jn. viii. 12, 20). Again, too, He hinted at His approaching removal, and declared with unruffled composure that, when He should have been lifted up upon the Cross, then men would truly know who He was, and recognise the authority with which He spake (Jn. viii. 28, 29).

The effect of these solemn declarations was again apparent, and *many believed on Him* (Jn. viii. 30). But His advice to those, who thus professed their belief in Him, *to abide in His word*, and His assurance that thus they would *know the truth*, and the truth *would make them free* (Jn. viii. 32, 33), excited much discussion amongst the Jews. How could they, the descendants of Abraham, who had never been slaves to any one, be made free? Though, as the Roman garrison in the tower of Antonia all too plainly attested, they were nationally in a condition of vassalage to a foreign power, they protested against the idea of their being in a state

[1] Lightfoot (Wks. I. 325) says they were 13 in number, and stood in the Court of the Women.

of bondage, and urged their descent from the great patriarch Abraham. The children of Abraham, the Holy One replied, they were not, for they were seeking to kill Him, Whose *day Abraham had desired to see*, and *had rejoiced to behold.* This assertion roused the utmost fury of their wrath; they heaped upon Him the most bitter taunts, declared Him a Samaritan, and possessed with a demon, and taking up some of the stones lying about ready for some repair of the temple, were on the point of inflicting upon Him the punishment of a blasphemer, when He passed through the midst of them, and withdrew beyond the present reach of their malice (Jn. viii. 33—59).

The Sabbath, however, was not to close without another manifestation of His divine and merciful power even in the midst of those who sought His life. As He passed by, accompanied by His disciples, he encountered a man, who, it was well known, had been blind from his birth (Jn. ix. 1). His sad affliction suggested to the Apostles the enquiry whether it was to be ascribed to sins of his own or to those of His parents; to which the Lord replied that it was due to neither of the causes they suggested; that his privations were intended to subserve higher objects of God's love; and making clay with the moisture from His mouth, He anointed the sufferer's eyes, and sent him to the Pool of Siloam, with the injunction to wash therein. The man went, and returned perfectly restored to sight (Jn. ix. 7).

Such a recovery of such a man, in such a manner, excited no small stir amongst his kinsfolk and acquaintance, and some actually doubted whether he could be the same as the man they had so long remembered sitting in pitiable plight at the corner of the street and begging alms of every passer by. He, however, persisted that he was really the same, and related in simple and artless language the particulars of his cure.

A miracle like this could not fail to arouse much attention, and the Sanhedrin determined, if possible, to invalidate its effect on the public mind, and summoning the man before them, began to investigate the circumstances of the cure. Their questions he answered with the same simplicity as those of his kinsfolk—whereas he was blind, now through the power of One, who had put clay upon his eyes, he saw. But it was a Sabbath-day when the cure had been effected, and some of the council wished to decide at once that one, who had flagrantly violated the law, could not be acting under the sanction of God (Jn. ix. 16). Others, however, were too much impressed by the evidence of the miracle, to acquiesce in such an off-hand decision, and there was a division in the council (Jn. ix. 16).

The man himself, therefore, was again examined, but he could add nothing to the information he had already given, and expressed his conviction that his Healer must be a Prophet (Jn. ix. 17). Hoping next in some way to throw discredit on the reality of his malady and its cure, they sent for his parents, who allowed that he was their son, and that he had been born blind, but, fearful of the terrible sentence of excommunication, with which the Council had threatened all the followers of Jesus, referred the judges to their son for any further information they might require.

Turning therefore, once more, to the healed man, they bade him give praise for the blessing he had received to God alone (Jn. ix. 24), and take no thought about Jesus of Nazareth, whom they authoritatively pronounced to be *a sinner*. But their dicta had no effect upon his resolute and honest temper; whether his Healer was a sinner or not he would not discuss before such an assembly; of the reality of his cure he was certain, and that was enough for him; it was useless to question him further, unless, perchance, they desired to become the disciples of Jesus.

This opened a door for the more violent party in the council. They began to revile the man, and to declare their conviction that he was a secret adherent of Jesus, while they were the followers of Moses. God had spoken to that great Lawgiver, but of the origin of Jesus they avowed themselves utterly ignorant. With increasing boldness the man commented on the extraordinary fact that One, of whose origin such a learned body was in such complete ignorance, could perform so great a miracle, utterly unheard of before, and inexplicable save on the supposition of Divine power (Jn. ix. 33). This outspoken language excited the utmost indignation, and after taunting the poor man with his blindness in which he had been born, and which marked him out as accursed of God, the Council proceeded to pass upon him the terrible sentence of excommunication (Jn. ix. 34).

Informed of the step they had taken, the Lord sought out the late recipient of His bounty, and enquired whether he believed on the Son of God? To this question the other replied, *Who is He, Lord, that I may believe on Him?* (Jn. ix. 35, 36); *I that speak unto thee*, rejoined the Holy One, *am He*, and accepted his act of instant adoration and avowal of belief (Jn. ix. 37).

But the present visit to Jerusalem was to be marked by yet another protest against the assumptions and errors of the ruling party in the city. The Holy One affirmed that they were guilty of misleading the people; that, whereas they pretended to see, they saw not; that they were hireling shepherds, caring not for the lives and souls of the people; that He, and He alone, was the true, the genuine Shepherd, the purport of whose coming into the world was *to lay down His life for the sheep* (Jn. x. 1—17). With this sublime discourse respecting the *Good Shepherd*, the occurrences of this visit to Jerusalem appear to have come to a close. On no occasion does such an effect appear to have been made on the minds of the people. We are told indeed of few works of mercy and redeeming power; but the gracious words that fell from His lips appear to have sufficed to produce a great influence on many and divers classes. "The mixed multitude, the dwellers at Jerusalem (Jn. vii. 25), the officials of the Temple (Jn. vii. 46), and to some extent even the hostile Jewish party (Jn. viii. 30), bore witness to the more than mortal power of the teaching of Jesus of Nazareth[1]."

CHAPTER III

MISSION OF THE SEVENTY—DISCOURSES AND MIRACLES.

A. D. 29.

FROM this point the exact movements of our blessed Lord are enwrapped in some obscurity, and the region whither he now retired is a matter of conjecture. It seems probable, however, that He did not leave Judæa, but continued His ministrations within its frontier, and about this period sent forth the Seventy Disciples[2] (Lk. x. 1—6), two and two before His face, to preach the word, and to visit various towns whither He Himself also intended to come (Lk. x. 1). After receiv-

[1] Ellicott, p. 256.

[2] From the fact that the Jews divided the heathen world into 70 nations, it has been supposed that this mission of "the Seventy" hinted at the future destination of the Gospel for the whole world, just as the mission of "the Twelve" Apostles typified its first offer to the twelve tribes of Israel. Lightfoot, *Hor. Heb. in Joann.* VII. 37. Lange's *Life of Christ*, III. 403 n. E. T.

ing specific instructions respecting their mission, the Seventy set out probably in the direction of Peræa, and after some short time returned to recount with much joy (Lk. x. 17) the success of their ministrations, and their discovery that even the evil spirits were subject to their Master's Name.

One of the places visited by the Saviour during the present sojourn in Judæa, was the village of Bethany[1] (Lk. x. 38), situated about 15 stadia from Jerusalem (Jn. xi. 18). Here the abode of two sisters, Martha and Mary[2], and their brother Lazarus, was gladly thrown open to welcome Him, and each member of the little family enjoyed a share of His peculiar affection (Jn. xi. 5), and from time to time the sunshine of His presence.

Scanty as are the indications of the places the Holy One now visited, it seems clear that the effect of His ministry was not inconsiderable: multitudes gathered about Him to hear the Word of Life[3] (Lk. xi. 16), and

[1] This village, now called *el'Azarîyeh,* from the name of Lazarus, is situated on the E. slope of the Mount of Olives, "not very far from the point at which the road to Jericho begins its more sudden descent towards the Jordan valley." Bethany is usually taken to mean *House of Dates,* just as Bethphage close by denotes *House of Figs.* Another explanation is *House of Misery, Poor-House,* see Deutsch's Note in Hepworth Dixon's *Holy Land,* II. 214—219.

[2] Several circumstances appear to indicate that the family at Bethany were not amongst the poorest of their people: *e.g.* (i) They possess a family vault (Jn. xi. 38), which was a privilege of the wealthier orders; (ii) The number of Jews (Jn. xi. 19) who assembled from Jerusalem to condole with them were of the higher class (comp. St John's use of the term οἱ Ἰουδαῖοι in i. 19; vii. 13; viii. 22; ix. 22, &c.); (iii) the costly box of spikenard with which Mary anointed the Saviour's feet (Jn. xii. 3). Trench *On the Miracles,* 410.

[3] "To this period we may assign that instructive series of discourses which extend from the middle of the xth to the middle of the xiiith chapter of St Luke." Ellicott, p. 257.

behold His works of power[1]. But the enmity of the Pharisees and the ruling body of the nation increased rather than lessened in intensity (Lk. xi. 53, 54). They still persisted in ascribing His power over unclean spirits to a secret collusion with the Evil One (Lk. xi. 14, 15; Mtt. ix. 32—34); reiterated their demand for *a sign from heaven* (Lk. xi. 29—36); carped at His refusal to conform to their superstitious observances in respect to *divers washings* (Lk. xi. 37—42); and stung to the quick by His denunciations of their hypocritical and bloodthirsty spirit[2], bent all their efforts to entangle Him in His talk, and find some matter for accusation against Him (Lk. xi. 54).

Undeterred, however, by their ceaseless hostility, He persevered in His ministrations, warned His disciples in the presence of the multitudes, who crowded around Him in such numbers *as to tread upon one another* (Lk. xii. 1), against the *leaven of the Pharisees, which is hypocrisy* (Lk. xii. 1—4); reiterated His solemn words respecting blasphemy against the Holy Ghost (Lk. xii. 10); and, refusing to accede to a request to divide an inheritance amongst two brothers, took occasion to warn His hearers against covetousness, and delivered the striking parable of the *Rich Fool* (Lk. xii. 13—21). Not merely, however, would He warn them against this common sin, but "knowing how often it springs from a distrust in God's providential care[3]," He proceeded to teach them where they might find a preservative against over-anxiety[4] about the future, in

[1] Such as the cure of a deaf and dumb demoniac (Lk. xi. 14, 15).

[2] On the blood of Zacharias the son of Barachias, who perished between the sanctuary (ναός) and the altar of burnt-offering, see *Class-Book of O. T. History*, p. 425, and note.

[3] Trench *On the Parables*, p. 341.

[4] Distracting anxiety. Such is the full force of μέριμνα, from μερίζειν *to divide, cleave asunder.*

the assurance of the loving care of a Father in heaven, who feeds the fowls of the heaven, though they *neither sow nor reap*, and have *neither storehouse nor barn* (Lk. xii. 22—24), and clothes the *lilies*[1] *of the field* with a beauty, such as *Solomon in all his glory* never approached (Lk. xii. 27).

It was probably about this time that certain persons informed the Lord of a fresh outrage amongst the many that Pilate had committed[2]. On the occasion of the visit of a body of Galilæans, whose turbulent character has been already noted[3], to Jerusalem, the governor for some unrecorded reason had slain them, and mingled their blood with the blood of the slain beasts they were offering on the Altar at the Temple[4]. If men "might have been supposed to be safe anywhere, or at any time, it would have been at the altar of God, and while in the act of offering sacrifices unto Him[5];" their terrible death, therefore, appears to have been urged by the narrators of this outrage as a peculiar evidence of God's anger against them, and of some unknown awful guilt[6]

[1] On the "Lily" of Palestine, see Stanley, *S. and P.* pp. 139, 429. "The lilies of the field are all out, a few tulips cover the rocks, but the scarlet anemone (*Anemone coronaria*, L.) now dominates everywhere, and a small blue bulbous iris, almost rivalling it in abundance and brilliancy of colour. There have been many claimants for the distinctive honour of *the lilies of the field;* but while it seems most natural to view the term as a generic expression (comp. Stanley, *S. and P.*, p. 429), yet if one special flower was more likely than another to catch the eye of the Lord as He spoke, no one familiar with the flora of Palestine in spring-time can hesitate in assigning the place to the anemone," Tristram's *Land of Israel*, p. 433.

[2] See above, p. 151. [3] See above, p. 148.

[4] This outrage very probably was, if not the cause, at least one of the causes of the quarrel between Herod and Pilate, alluded to in Lk. xxiii. 12.

[5] Trench *On the Parables*, p. 343.

[6] Compare the same argument as addressed to the patriarch Job, *Class-Book of O. T. History*, p. 24.

on their part (Lk. xiii. 1, 2). But such hasty and cruel judgments the Lord instantly rebuked, and declared that the terrible ends of these sufferers no more marked them out as *sinners above all other* of their fellow-countrymen than certain eighteen persons on whom a tower of Siloam[1] had recently fallen and crushed them beneath its ruins (Lk. xiii. 4). In such swift calamities they were not to trace the evidence of a pre-eminence of guilt on the part of the sufferers[2], but a call to remember their own uncertain tenure of life, and to repentance[3] while as yet the day of grace lasted, which solemn considerations He still further enforced by the appropriate parable of the *Barren Fig-Tree* (Lk. xiii. 6—9).

On a subsequent occasion the Lord entered a synagogue on the Sabbath-day (Lk. xiii. 10), where there was a woman inwardly afflicted in her spirit[4] (Lk. xiii. 16), and outwardly with a permanent and unnatural contraction of her body (Lk. xiii. 11). Without waiting till His aid was sought, He forthwith called her to Him, and laying His hands upon her, said, *Woman, thou art loosed from thy infirmity*, whereupon the affliction of eighteen long years (Lk. xiii. 11) instantly left her, *she*

[1] Probably close to the fountain of Siloam: see above, p. 235.

[2] Trench *On the Parables*, p. 346.

[3] *Except ye repent, ye shall all likewise perish.* "As the tower of Siloam fell and crushed 18 of the dwellers at Jerusalem, exactly so multitudes of its inhabitants were crushed beneath the ruins of their temple and their city; and during the last siege and assault of that city, there were numbers also who were pierced through by the Roman darts, or more miserably yet by those of their own frantic factions (Jos. *B. J.* v. 1. 3), in the courts of the temple, in the very act of preparing their sacrifices, so that literally their blood, like that of these Galilæans, was mingled with their sacrifices, one blood with another." Trench *On the Parables*, p. 346.

[4] Trench *On the Parables*, p. 323.

was made straight, and glorified God. Such a cure, which excited the wonder of all present, was more than the ruler of the synagogue could bear, and he openly expressed his indignation at this violation of the Sabbath, remarking that there were six days in the week when such servile working as healing might be done, and bidding those who needed help come then, and not degrade the sanctity of the Sabbath-day (Lk. xiii. 14). Such hypocritical strictness on the part of one who sat in Moses' seat and was regarded as a teacher of the Law, moved the Saviour's righteous indignation. In words, the force of which was irresistible (Lk. xiii. 17), He justified that He had done by the "very relaxations of the Sabbath strictness[1]," which the ruler of the synagogue himself allowed. Would he not *loose his ox or his ass from the stall and lead him away to water* on the Sabbath-day, and should he be blamed for merely speaking a word and releasing a daughter of Abraham from a bond with which Satan had enthralled her for so many years? The question admitted of no reply; even His adversaries were ashamed, while the multitude rejoiced for all the glorious things that had been done by Him (Lk. xiii. 17).

CHAPTER IV

THE FEAST OF DEDICATION—TOUR IN PERÆA.

A.D. 29.

BY the time the incident recorded in the last Chapter took place, the season of winter had returned (Jn. x. 22), and the snow lay upon the mountains[2]. With the return of winter came also the celebration of the Feast

[1] Trench *On the Parables*, p. 326.
[2] See the Calendar in *Class-Book of O. T. History*, p. 155.

of Dedication[1], on the 25th of the month Chisleu, which lasted eight days. On this occasion the Lord once more visited Jerusalem, and presented Himself in the Temple, and probably on account of the wintry state of the weather sought shelter in "Solomon's Porch[2]," where He was speedily encircled by the Jews (Jn. x. 24), who began with eager impetuosity to enquire how long He intended to keep them in suspense, and to ask that if He was the Messiah He would tell them so plainly and distinctly (Jn. x. 24).

The question appears to have been put neither in a hostile nor unfriendly tone, and indicates a wish on the part of the ruling powers to discover whether He might not be induced to set Himself forth as the Messiah they expected, and, like a second Judas Maccabæus, whose exploits they were commemorating, deliver them from the hated yoke of the foreigner[3].

In reply, however, to their question, the Holy One contented Himself with pointing to the wonderful works He had already wrought in their midst. This testimony they had refused to receive, for neither in their aims nor desires were they of His sheep (Jn. x. 26). *His sheep heard His voice, and He knew them, and He would give them eternal life, nor should any ever snatch them out of His hand* (Jn. x. 27, 28); *for the Eternal Father in heaven had given them to Him, and He and the Father were one* (Jn. x. 29).

This solemn and mysterious language, this claim to

[1] For its institution, see above, p. 36, and *Class-Book of O. T. History*, p. 154.

[2] See above, p. 96. "This cloister had its name from the circumstance that, according to the Jewish tradition, it was a relic of Solomon's temple, left standing when the Babylonians destroyed the rest of the sacred edifice." Lange's *Life of Christ*, III. 432, n. E. T.

[3] Lange's *Life of Christ*, III. 432, E. T.

essential unity with the eternal Father, again[1] provoked the anger of His hearers. Their earthly and carnal hopes centered on some great earthly conqueror. The words of the Holy One sounded in their ears like blasphemy, and taking up some of the stones lying around for the repairs[2] of the Temple which were almost always going on, they were on the point of stoning Him as He stood.

But He calmed their fury by enquiring for which of His many works, that proved by their moral goodness no less than the power they displayed, His union with the Father, they wished to stone Him. In reply the Jews declared that it was His blasphemous words which made them act as they now did, for though a man, He claimed a union with God (Jn. x. 32, 33). This charge the Holy One repelled by reference to their own sacred books[3]. Was not the title of God sometimes applied there to the judges and rulers of the nation (Ps. lxxxii. 6)[4], and was it with less justice applicable to One, whose wondrous works proved His intercommunion with the Father and His Divine mission to the world? (Jn. x. 34—38). This reply only excited a fresh burst of fury, and though the Jews gave up their design of stoning Him, they tried to apprehend Him and bring Him before their courts (Jn. x. 29).

But His "hour" was not yet come, and retiring from the capital, He crossed the Jordan, and sought the fords of Bethabara or Bethany, where His forerunner *at first*

[1] See above, p. 235.

[2] For illustrations of this, see Josephus, *Ant.* XX. 9. 7; XVII. 10. 2; XVII. 9. 3.

[3] The *Law* here alluded to is used in its widest acceptation for the whole Old Testament, as in Jn. xii. 34; xv. 25.

[4] This Psalm is directed against the tyranny and injustice of judges in Israel, and the argument is, if in any sense they could be called *gods* (as in Ex. xxi. 6; xxii. 9, 28), how much more He, "the only One, sealed and hallowed by the Father, and the Son of God," Alford on Jn. x. 36.

baptized (Jn. x. 40). In this region, where that eminent servant of God had closed his course[1], it was proved that "though dead he yet spake." Many remembered his burning words and faithful testimony to the Messiah, whom the Jews at Jerusalem had rejected, and acknowledging the truth of His words, gathered round the Saviour (Jn. x. 41), and avowed their belief in Him.

Still even here He had to encounter hostile opposition. His indefatigable enemies, the Pharisees, penetrated His seclusion and represented that Herod Antipas, within whose dominions He now was, sought opportunity to kill Him (Lk. xiii. 31). But He saw through their cunning and hypocrisy, no less than the fox-like (Lk. xiii. 32) craft of the Tetrarch, by whom they had been probably suborned[2]. He, doubtless, would be glad to get out of his territory[3] One, whose fame caused him so much perplexity, and they would be no less anxious to drive Him from a quarter, where He was comparatively safe, to the hostile neighbourhood of Jerusalem[4]. But though it was impossible that a prophet could perish elsewhere than in a capital, which had slain so many who had been sent to it[5], yet there was still time for the performance of works of mercy (Lk. xiii. 32, 33), for the healing of the sick, and the expulsion of demons, before He went up to Jerusalem, whose children He would so often have gathered together *as a hen gathereth her chickens under her wing*[6], *but they*

[1] See above, p. 153.

[2] Lange's *Life of Christ*, III. 374, E.T.; Alford on Lk. xiii. 31; Bengel *in loc.*

[3] Ellicott, 263, and note.

[4] Milman's *History of Christianity*, I. 262.

[5] "Every murder of a prophet, perpetrated by the Jews, proceeded either mediately or immediately from the rulers of the people, whose residence was at Jerusalem," Oosterze on Lk. xiii. 31.

[6] It seems not unreasonable to suppose that these words

would not, and whose house was now left unto them desolate (Lk. xiii. 34, 35).

Of the works of mercy here mentioned, apparently but one is actually recorded by the Evangelist. At the house of one of the leaders of the Pharisees, to which He had been invited (Lk. xiv. 1) on the Sabbath-day, for a hostile purpose[1], the Holy One healed a man afflicted with dropsy (Lk. xiv. 2—6), and taking occasion from the associations of the time and place, not only rebuked the haughty selfishness with which the Pharisees claimed the chief seats at feasts (Lk. xiv. 7—14), but also uttered the appropriate parable of the *Great Supper* (Lk. xiv. 15—24).

In the same neighbourhood also, finding Himself surrounded by great crowds, amongst which some indicated a wish to follow Him, He addressed them solemnly on the self-denial required of all who would be His real disciples (Lk. xiv. 25—35), and the necessity for first counting the cost, and taking up the cross if they would truly follow Him. On another occasion a great number of tax-gatherers, who were very numerous near Jericho and the Jordan fords[2], gathered round Him, together with many regarded as profligate sinners. Their eagerness to listen to His teaching, and His willingness to receive and eat with them (Lk. xv. 1), roused again the hostility of the Pharisees and Scribes, and provoked them to open murmuring. But, undeterred by their opposition, the Good Shepherd, with striking appropriateness now, gave utterance to the parables of the *Lost*

were uttered on two different occasions, now and afterwards, as recorded in Mtt. xxiii. 37 sq. See Ellicott, 264, n.: Alford on Lk. xiii. 34.

[1] Ἦσαν παρατηρούμενοι, Lk. xiv. 1. Comp. vi. 7; xx. 20; Mk. iii. 2. See Trench *On the Miracles*, p. 328, n.

[2] Where our Lord now probably was. See Lange's *Life of Christ*, III. 388.

Sheep (Lk. xv. 1), the *Lost Coin* (Lk. xv. 8—10), and the *Prodigal Son* (Lk. xv. 11—32), and afterwards addressed to His disciples, though in the hearing of the Pharisees, those of the *Unjust Steward* (Lk. xvi. 1—13), and of *Lazarus and the Rich Man* (Lk. xvi. 19—31).

CHAPTER V

THE RAISING OF LAZARUS.

A.D. 30.

WHILE the Lord was in Peræa, and apparently in the neighbourhood of Bethabara, a messenger reached Him from the sisters Martha and Mary[1], announcing that their brother Lazarus was sick (Jn. xi. 13). On receiving this intelligence, He replied in the hearing of His Apostles, but chiefly to the messenger, and for him to bring back to those that had sent him[2], *This sickness is not unto death* (Jn. xi. 4), *but for the glory of God, that the Son of God might be glorified thereby.*

Whatever amount of hope this announcement may have raised in the minds of the sisters was for the present at least dashed to the ground. For He, to whom they had sent their simple message, and who had so often healed others at a distance by simply uttering a word, now neither spoke the word of power, nor came to them, but *remained still two days in the same place where He was* (Jn. xi. 6), and in the meantime Lazarus died, and was laid in a rock-hewn sepulchre.

At the close, however, of the two days, the Holy One proposed to His disciples that they should go into Judæa again. But the trembling Apostles, recollecting the extreme danger He had so lately incurred at Jerusalem,

[1] See above, p. 239, and note.
[2] Trench *On the Miracles*, p. 391.

ventured to expostulate: a short time back the Jews were seeking to stone Him (Jn. xi. 8), and for the sake of safety He had been constrained to seek the seclusion of the region where He now was, would He venture then, so soon to incur afresh the malice of His foes?

Thereupon He calmed their apprehensions, and announced that their friend Lazarus *was asleep*, but He intended to *wake him out of sleep* (Jn. xi. 12). This announcement perplexed the Apostles still more. If Lazarus slept, it indicated a favourable crisis of his illness, and the perilous journey was unnecessary. Perceiving that they understood His words literally, He now told them plainly that *Lazarus was dead*, but still declared His intention of going to Bethany (Jn. xi. 15), on which the Apostle Thomas, betraying the tendency to misgiving and despondency which distinguished him[1], and convinced that his Master would fall into the hands of His deadly enemies, proposed to the rest that at least they should accompany Him, and share His end (Jn. xi. 16).

With these sad forebodings the Apostles accompanied their Lord, and on reaching Bethany found that Lazarus had been already dead four days[2], and as the village lay only three quarters of an hour's journey from

[1] For other indications of the character of St Thomas, see Jn. xiv. 5; xx. 25. We gather that he was (i) deeply attached to his Master, (ii) prepared to die with Him, but (iii) ever ready to take the darker view of things, and (iv) unable to believe other and more than he saw.

[2] "He had most likely died on the same day that the messenger announcing his illness had reached the Lord...the day of his arrival would be one day; two our Lord abode in Peræa after He had dismissed him, and one more He would have employed in the journey from thence to Bethany...dying upon that day, he had, according to the custom of the Jews, which made the burial immediately to follow on the death, been buried upon the same day" (cf. Acts v. 6—10). Trench *On the Miracles*, p. 397.

Jerusalem, many Jews (Jn. xi. 19) had come thither over the Mount of Olives, to pay the customary visit of condolence to the two sisters[1].

Tarrying Himself outside the village (Jn. xi. 30), the Lord suffered the tidings of His arrival to go before Him, and no sooner did Martha become aware of it, than she hurried forth to meet Him, while Mary remained in the house. In few and touching words Martha revealed the anguish of her heart. *Lord*, said she, *if Thou hadst been here, my brother had not died*, but added, shewing that even now she had not abandoned every hope, *I know that even now, whatsoever Thou wilt ask of God, God will give it Thee* (Jn. xi. 22). In reply the Holy One assured her that her brother would rise again, and when she answered that she knew he would *rise again at the last day* (Jn. xi. 24), proceeded to declare Himself to be the *Resurrection and the life*, in whom whosoever believed should live though he died, and whosoever lived and believed should never die (Jn. xi. 25, 26).

Having spoken of Himself in these solemn and momentous words, He enquired whether Martha herself believed He was what He thus claimed to be. *Yea, Lord*, was her reply: *I believe that Thou art the Christ, the Son of God, which should come into the world* (Jn. xi. 27), and with this assurance hastened away, and secretly called her sister. Informed of her Lord's arrival Mary also hurried to meet Him, and was quickly followed by a large number of the Jews, who took for granted that, according to the usual custom[2], she was proceeding to the grave to weep there. Arrived at the spot where Jesus was, Mary could only fall down before His feet (Jn. xi. 32), and falter out the words her sister had already uttered, and then gave way to passionate

[1] Compare Thomson's *Land and the Book*, pp. 102, 103.

[2] See *Ibid.* pp. 101, 2.

grief. The spectacle of her deep sorrow deeply affected many of the Jews also, and they mingled their tears with hers, while the Lord Himself *groaned in spirit and was troubled*, and enquired where they had laid the dead (Jn. xi. 33).

With the words *come and see*, they conducted Him to the sepulchre, and on the road[1] He Himself, borne away by the "great tide of sorrow[2]" around, joined His tears with theirs (Jn. xi. 35).

On reaching the sepulchre, which, like the family vaults of the Jews, was a cave[3], with recesses in the sides, in which the bodies were laid, He commanded the stone, which closed the entrance, to be removed. On this Martha, shrinking from the exposure to the eyes of strangers of the body of one so dear, and already partially decomposed (Jn. xi. 39), ventured to expostulate; but Jesus reminded her of His promise that, if she believed, she should *see the glory of God*, and calmed her feelings. Accordingly the stone was removed, and then the Holy One, after a brief pause, during which He thanked the Eternal Father for having heard Him (Jn. xi. 41, 42, cried with a loud voice, *Lazarus, come forth.* Instantly the word of Power was

[1] The question of some of the spectators, *Could not this Man, which opened the eyes of the blind, have caused that even this man should not have died?* (Jn. xi. 47) is characteristic of the exact truth of the narrative...dwellers in Jerusalem, they refer to a miracle so well known amongst themselves, rather than to the former raisings of the dead, of which, occurring at an earlier period and in the remote Galilee, they had probably heard by rumour only. Trench, p. 408; Lange's *Life of Christ*, III. 473, n.

[2] Trench *On the Miracles*, p. 407.

[3] "Sometimes natural (Gen. xxiii. 9), sometimes artificial, and hollowed out by man's labour from the rock (Isai. xxii. 16; Mtt. xxvii. 60), in a garden (Jn. xix. 41), or in some field, the possession of the family (Gen. xxiii. 9, 17—20; xxxv. 18; 2 K. xxi. 18)." Trench *On the Miracles*, p. 409.

obeyed. There was a stir in the sepulchre. The dead man rose, and came forth, *bound hand and foot with grave clothes, and his face covered with a napkin*, while the Lord, who was never calmer than when during His greatest works, simply bade the bystanders *loose him and let him go* (Jn. xi. 44).

CHAPTER VI

RESOLVE OF THE SANHEDRIN—JESUS RETIRES TO EPHRAIM.

A.D. 30.

THE remarkable miracle recorded at length in the preceding Chapter marks an important epoch in the life of our Lord.

The effect it exerted upon those who witnessed it was twofold. Many of those, who had come to mourn with the sisters of Bethany, avowed their belief in the Saviour's claims (Jn. xi. 45), but others, with no friendly intentions, hurried to the Pharisees and recounted to them all that had taken place. Their report led to instant measures.

The ruling powers, hitherto comparatively calm, became very uneasy. A meeting of the Sanhedrin was convened, at which Caiaphas presided, and the course to be followed was keenly debated. It was clear that the sentence of excommunication (Jn. ix. 22), lately passed upon the followers of the Saviour, had not counteracted the impression made by His ministry on the minds of the people[1]. The notable miracle He had just wrought could not be gainsaid, and its effect upon the multitude was profound. If he was suffered to continue His ministry, all, it was argued, would believe on Him, and in all probability proclaim Him as their

[1] Neander's *Life of Christ*, p. 378.

King. Such a proclamation would inevitably lead to a riot, a riot to a visit from Pilate, the ruthlessness of whose character had been again and again experienced[1], and this would be followed by a massacre, and the total deprivation of what remained of their national existence.

Many measures were, probably, advocated by various members of the Council, but found no general acceptance. At length Caiaphas arose, and with unconcealed contempt declared that his weak and vacillating colleagues *knew nothing at all* (Jn. xi. 49). The life and teaching of One Man threatened to imperil the whole nation, and to bring them into collision with their Roman masters. One effectual remedy alone existed. *It was expedient* that He should be put to death rather than the whole nation should be swept away. As a Sadducee[2] (Acts v. 17) Caiaphas believed in the might of the Roman legions, though he denied the doctrine of the resurrection and the existence of spiritual powers, and rather than embroil the nation in fresh troubles with their unscrupulous masters, he advocated the death of the Holy One, all unconscious[3] of the momentous results of the step he advised.

Though there were some dissentients (Lk. xxiii. 50, 51), his words expressed the feelings of the majority of

[1] See above, pp. 150, 151.

[2] "Having much to risk, and nothing to gain by change, the Sadducees, or aristocratic party, were anxious to keep things safe, so as to prevent any action on the side of Rome." H. Dixon's *Holy Land*, II. 221. Josephus says of the Sadducees, εἰσὶ περὶ τὰς κρίσεις ὠμοὶ παρὰ πάντας τοὺς Ἰουδαίους, *Ant.* XX. 9. 1, and the spirit of the family of Annas, whose son-in-law Caiaphas was, was haughty, bold, and cruel. See Jos. *Ib.*; *Bell. Jud.* II. 8. 14.

[3] "Caiaphas was only consciously stating what he deemed politically advisable, but he was nevertheless, as the inspired Evangelist distinctly tells us (Jn. xi. 51), at the time actually prophesying." Ellicott's *Lectures*, 269, n. Alford on Jn. xi. 51.

the Council. The more decided and violent party triumphed. It was deliberately determined that Jesus should be put to death, and from that day forward continual councils were held to decide how this should be brought about (Jn. xi. 53).

But the Holy One, knowing that His "hour" was not yet come, retired with His disciples to Ephraim, a town situated[1] in the wide desert country north-east of Jerusalem, not far from Bethel, and on the confines of Samaria.

Here in quiet and seclusion He remained till the approach of the Passover, and then commenced a farewell-journey along the border-line of Samaria and Galilee, in the direction of the Jordan (Lk. xvii. 11; Mtt. xix. 1), and so to Peræa (Mk. x. 1).

It was probably while yet on the confines of Samaria, that at the entrance of a village, the name and position of which are not recorded, He encountered Ten Lepers, one of whom was a Samaritan[2] (Lk. xvii. 16). Standing *afar off* (Lk. xvii. 12), they all *lifted up their voices*, and implored His aid, on which, filled with compassion for their miserable condition, He bade them go and *shew themselves to the priests* at Jerusalem. Though they must have been aware that they could not expect healing from the priest, whose only office it was either to pronounce the sufferer affected with this fearful malady, or to restore him with ceremonial washings to the society of his fellow-men[3], the Lepers nevertheless

[1] Robinson identifies Ophrah with Ephraim (comp. 2 Chr. xiii. 19), and with a village on a conspicuous conical hill, 4 or 5 miles east of Bethel, and 16 from Jerusalem. *Bib. Res.* I. 447.

[2] "In this border-land it was more natural than elsewhere that they should find themselves in one company, and thus a Samaritan had found admission into this forlorn assembly." Trench *On the Miracles*, p. 332; Alford on Lk. xvii. 11.

[3] See *Class-Book of O. T. History*, p. 157.

set out, and lo! as they went (Lk. xvii. 14), their flesh came back to them *like unto the flesh of a little child* (2 K. v. 14), and they were cleansed. But though they all experienced His unlooked-for blessing, one only, and he a Samaritan, returned to give thanks to His Healer, who, accustomed as he was to man's ingratitude, yet marvelled at this striking proof of it (Lk. xvii. 17, 18), and dismissed the grateful man with a higher and a peculiar blessing[1], saying, *Go thy way, thy faith hath made thee whole* (Lk. xvii. 19).

Continuing His journey towards the Jordan, the Saviour at some place, the name of which is not mentioned, encountered certain Pharisees, who professed, probably in treachery or mockery, a question respecting the coming of the kingdom of God, to which He replied, that it would be with no such visible establishment as they expected (Lk. xvii. 20, 21), and proceeded to found upon the question a warning to His own disciples on the same subject (Lk. xvii. 22—37). It was now also, in all probability, either before or just after He crossed into Peræa[2], that He delivered the parables of the *Unjust Judge* and the *Pharisee and Publican* (Lk. xvii. 1—14), and replied to a question respecting the lawfulness of divorce (Mtt. xix. 3—12; Mk. x. 2—12), on which the rival schools of Hillel and Shammai[3] held opposite opinions.

In striking contrast to the malice which prompted these questionings, certain parents, who probably ho-

[1] Trench *On the Miracles*, p. 336.

[2] Probably at Scythopolis, where there was a bridge. See Lightfoot, *Hor. Heb. et Talm.* on Lk. xvii. 11.

[3] The former adopting the more lax, the latter the stricter view. Lightfoot, *Hor. Heb. et Talm.* on Mtt. xix. 3. The object of the question may also in some degree have been "to involve Him with the adulterous tetrarch in whose territory He then was." Ellicott, p. 272.

noured Him, and valued His benediction, brought their children to Him, and begged that He would lay His hands upon them and offer up a prayer in their behalf (Mtt. xix. 13). To the disciples such an act appeared unfitting, and they would have kept back those that brought them (Mk. x. 13; Lk. xviii. 15), but with touching condescension He not only rebuked their interference (Mk. x. 14), and said, *Suffer the little children to come unto Me, and forbid them not, for of such is the kingdom of heaven*, but called them to Him (Lk. xviii. 16), *took them up in His arms, laid His hands upon them, and blessed them* (Mk. x. 16; Mtt. xix. 15).

It was in this region also that a rich young ruler approached Him, desiring to know what he should do to inherit eternal life (Mtt. xix. 16; Mk. x. 17). The Holy One referred him to the commandments. These the other declared he had kept from his youth (Mk. x. 20), on which the Lord looked upon him with a glance of deep affection, informed him that he lacked *yet one thing* (Lk. xviii. 22), and bade him *go and sell all that he had, and give to the poor*, and take up his cross (Mk. x. 21) and follow Him. Such a demand, so totally opposed to the popular notions of the kingdom of the Messiah, in which the Jews expected every form of temporal blessing, was too severe a test for the ruler's sincerity; he *had great possessions* (Mtt. xix. 22; Mk. x. 22), which he could not part with, and in sorrow he left the Saviour and went his way.

But the same ideas of temporal blessings were still held by the Apostles themselves. They had left everything to follow their Master, might they not look for some great reward? To Peter, who put the question (Mk. x. 28; Mtt. xix. 23) the Holy One replied, by assuring him and the rest that a reward they should have, though very different from what they expected, and taking them apart (Mtt. xx. 17; Mk. x. 32) began for the third time[1], and with greater particularity than before, to speak of the future that awaited Himself; how at Jerusalem He should *be delivered into the hands of the Gentiles, and be mocked, and scourged, and crucified* (Mtt. xx. 18—24; Mk. x. 33—40; Lk. xviii. 32—34). But though awed by the unusual solemnity of His manner (Mk. x. 32), and the dauntless resolution with which He pressed on towards Jerusalem (Mk. x. 33), they could not enter into the meaning of His words. His predictions of suffering and death clashed with all their deeply-rooted ideas of the nature of the Messianic kingdom, and it was now that two of their number, James and John, encouraged by their mother, preferred the request[2] that in His kingdom they might *sit the one on His right hand, and the other on His left.* Even His reply that they should indeed *drink of His cup, and be baptized with His baptism,* sounded to the rest like the concession of some mysterious dignity, and provoked a jealousy on their part, which the Holy One strove to check by reminding them once more of the true nature of His kingdom, that therein He is truly *first who is the servant of all; even as the Son of Man came not to be ministered unto, but to minister, and to give His life a ransom for many.*

With this final proof of the utter inability even of His own chosen Twelve to lighten by their sympathy a particle of what lay before Himself, the Holy One, having recrossed the Jordan, continued His way amidst the crowd of pilgrims setting forth towards Jerusalem

[1] The two other occasions being (i) in the neighbourhood of Cæsarea Philippi just after St Peter's confession (see above, p. 219); (ii) shortly afterwards, during the return to Capernaum (see above, p. 225).

[2] Or perhaps the mother was the actual speaker, while the two Apostles were the instigators. Ellicott, p. 374, note.

Approaching Jericho He healed two blind men[1], who sat by the wayside begging and implored His aid; He accepted in the City of Palm Trees itself the hospitality of Zacchæus[2], a superintendent of customs or tribute there (Lk. xix. 1—10); corrected, by delivering the Parable of *the Pounds*[3], the idea that the Kingdom of Heaven was *about immediately to appear*, and at length, six days before the Passover, reached the safe seclusion of the mountain hamlet of Bethany (Mtt. xxvi. 6—13; Mk. xiv. 3—9; Jn. xii. 1—11).

[1] Perhaps, as in the case of the Gadarene demoniacs, the one, whom St Mark (x. 46) names as Bartimæus, was better known, and hence his case is more particularly recorded; and "the one who is mentioned at our Lord's entry into Jericho as having learnt from the crowd who it was that was coming into the city (Lk. xviii. 37), was not healed *then*, but in company with another sufferer, when the Saviour was leaving the city." Ellicott, p. 274, n.; Trench *On the Miracles*, p. 428.

[2] St Luke (xix. 2) calls him ἀρχιτελώνης, an unusual term, which probably denotes an administrator of taxes, who was entrusted with the superintendence of other publicans, and perhaps was the agent of one of the Roman knights, who often filled the office of *publicanus*. "The collection of customs at Jericho, which at this time produced and exported a considerable quantity of balsam, was undoubtedly an important post, and would account for Zacchæus being a rich man, Lk. xix. 2." On the palm-groves of Jericho and its balsam-trade, see above, p. 86.

[3] See Trench *On the Parables*, p. 512.

JERUSALEM in the time of OUR LORD

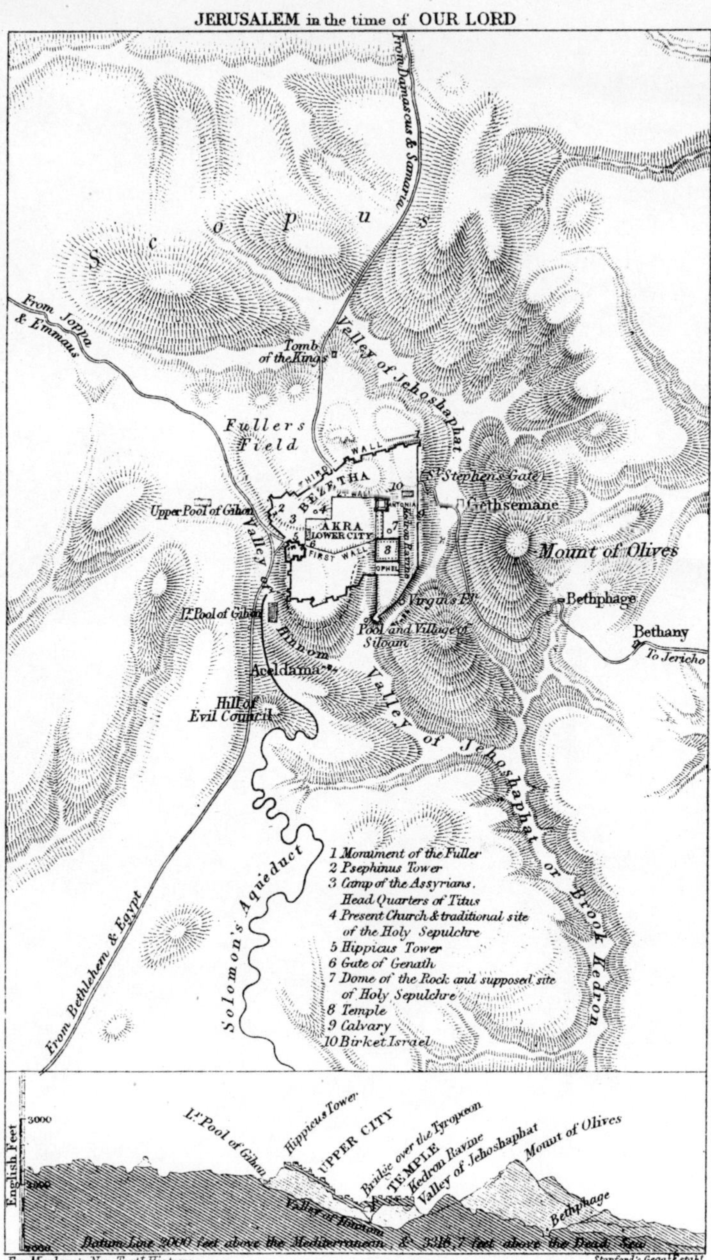

London : Macmillan & Co. Ltd.

PART VII

FROM THE ARRIVAL AT BETHANY TO THE ASCENSION.

CHAPTER I

THE ANOINTING AT BETHANY—THE TRIUMPHAL ENTRY.

A. D. 30.

IT was apparently on a Friday evening when the Saviour reached the hamlet of Bethany, where in quiet retirement He could spend His last earthly Sabbath. At Bethany resided one Simon (Mtt. xxvi. 6; Mk. xiv. 3), who had been a leper[1], and possibly had been restored by the Lord Himself, and at his house the sisters of Lazarus provided a festal repast[2], to welcome Him who had in so signal a manner restored happiness to their little circle (Jn. xii. 2).

In keeping with her character Martha on this occasion busied herself in ministering to the Lord (Jn. xii. 2), while Lazarus reclined at the table as one of the guests. As the feast proceeded, Mary approached with an alabaster casket in her hand, containing a pound of pre-

[1] It is the opinion of some that he was a connection of the family of Lazarus.

[2] For another feast upon a Sabbath, comp. Lk. xiv. 1. "The Sabbath is still among the Jews preferred for the enjoyment of feasts; but the food was prepared previously, and even the tables must have been arranged in order before the Sabbath began," Hengstenberg on St John xii. 2.

cious spikenard[1] (Jn. xii. 3), and breaking off the closed top (Mk. xiv. 3), poured a portion on the head of the Saviour. Then kneeling down she anointed His feet also (Jn. xii. 3), while the sweet odour diffused itself through the whole room.

But her act of beautiful affection did not win the approval of all the guests at the table. Judas Iscariot enquired why a casket of such precious unguent, which might have been sold for more than 300 denarii[2] and given to the poor, should be wasted in such a useless piece of extravagance[3] (Jn. xii. 5), and even others of the Apostles sympathised with his views, and had indignation and murmured against her (Mtt. xxvi. 8). He, however, for whom she had thus manifested her affectionate adoration, suffered scarcely a moment to elapse before He signified *His* opinion of that she had done. Not only did He bid the murmurers desist from troubling her, but declared that she had wrought a beautiful and worthy deed. The poor, for whom they pretended so much anxiety, they *had always with them*, but Himself they would not *have always* (Mk. xiv. 7), thus reminding them again of that speedy removal He had so

[1] Of the costliness of a casket of spikenard some idea may be formed from the fact that it was among the gifts sent by Cambyses to the Ethiopians (Herod. III. 20); compare also Horace's words, *Carm.* IV. xii. 16, 17:

Nardo vina merebere.
Nardi parvus onyx eliciet cadum.

[2] Τριακοσίων δηναρίων (Jn. xii. 5). On the denarius, see below, p. 269, note.

[3] St John remarks that he said this, not *because he cared for the poor, but because he was a thief, and had the bag, and bare what was put therein* (Jn. xii. 6). From which observation we gather (i) that the brotherhood of the Twelve had a common treasury, and received contributions for the poor; (ii) that Judas was their steward or almoner; (iii) that he had already proved unfaithful, and been guilty of embezzlement. See Lange's *Life of Christ*, IV. 29.

often predicted. Moreover, He proceeded to declare that what she had done had a special significance. In reference to the mysterious event so soon about to befall Him, wherein He should receive so little assistance or comfort from any human being, she at least *had done what she could* (Mk. xiv. 8), *she had come beforehand to anoint His Body for the burying*, and wherever the Gospel should be preached throughout the whole world, there should also the deed which had moved their unworthy indignation be *told for a memorial of her* (Mtt. xxvi. 13; Mk. xiv. 9). Thus by a prophetic word He elevated and interpreted her act of affectionate adoration.

Thus the eventful evening wore on. Meanwhile the news of the Saviour's presence at Bethany had reached Jerusalem, and great crowds (Jn. xii. 9) resorted thither not only to see Him but Lazarus also, whose resurrection from the dead caused many to avow their belief in the Lord of life (Jn. xii. 11). This fact was well known to the chief-priests, and a council was convened to consider the propriety of putting him also to death (Jn. xii. 10).

The next day dawned, the first day of the Holy week. Leaving Bethany, the Saviour proceeded towards Bethphage[1], and sending two of His disciples, desired them to bring an ass, and her colt with her, which they would find tied at the entrance of the village (Mtt. xxi. 2, 3; Lk. xix. 30; Mk. xi. 2). The disciples went, and in answer to the question of the owners (Lk. xix. 33), why they

[1] Bethphage (*house of unripe figs*), a place on the Mount of Olives, on the road between Jericho and Jerusalem. "It was apparently close to Bethany, and from its being named first of the two in the narrative of a journey from East to West, it may be presumed that it lay, if anything, to the eastward of Bethany." No remains answering to this position, according to Robinson, have been found, but see Barclay's *City of the Great King*, p. 65.

thus loosed them, replied, as bidden, that *the Lord had need of them*, and returned to their master.

The voice of ancient prophecy (Zech. ix. 9) had declared that her King would come to Zion *meek, and sitting on an ass, and a colt the foal of an ass;* and the hour for its fulfilment had now come. The road from Bethany to Jerusalem wound through rich plantations of palm-trees, and fruit- and olive-gardens[1], and was now crowded with pilgrims making their way towards the Holy City, or the encampments on the declivity of the Mount of Olives[2]. Amongst these would naturally be many who had witnessed the Saviour's miracles in Galilee, and their enthusiasm would be much increased by the news of the wondrous event at Bethany. The heart of the people, therefore, was deeply stirred, and the disciples, filled with the general excitement, spread their garments on the animals they had brought to their Master (Mtt. xxi. 7), and placed Him thereon. Soon the crowds began to express their joy in a more lively manner. Some strewed their garments[3] on the rough mountain-path, others cut down branches[4] from the neighbouring gardens, and threw them on the road before Him.

[1] Lange, IV. 39; Stanley, *S. and P.* 191. In Mk. xi. 8 the Vatican and Cambridge MSS. read ἐκ τῶν ἀγρῶν, "having cut the branches from the gardens." Eastern gardens are not flower-gardens, nor private gardens, but the orchards, vineyards, and fig-enclosures round a town.

[2] Lange's *Life of Christ*, IV. 41, n.

[3] Τὰ ἱμάτια, the "abba" or "hyke," the loose blanket or cloak worn over the tunic or shirt (χιτών). A striking instance of the practice is mentioned by Robinson, II. 162, when the inhabitants of Bethlehem threw their garments under the feet of the horses of the English consul of Damascus, whose aid they were imploring. Stanley, *S. and P.* p. 191, n.

[4] "The *branches* (κλάδοι) cut from the trees as they went (Mtt. xxi. 8) are different from the mattings στοιβάδες (Mk. xi. 8), which they had twisted out of the palm-branches as they came," *S. and P.* 191, n.

Meanwhile a second stream issuing from the Holy City (Jn. xii. 12) came forth to meet the Conqueror of Death, and meeting the others coming from Bethany, turned round, and swelled the long procession towards Jerusalem. As they approached the descent of the Mount of Olives (Lk. xix. 37), their feelings found expression in the prophetic language of the Psalms, and with loud Hosannas they glorified God (Lk. xix. 37), and proclaimed the approach of the *Son of David* to receive the kingdom of His Father, and to establish His Messianic kingdom (Mtt. xxi. 9; Mk. xi. 9). Certain of the Pharisees alone were found to murmur. They would have had the Saviour rebuke the zeal of the multitude, but pointing to the stones beneath their feet, He declared that *they would immediately cry out if these were to hold their peace.*

Thus amidst loud Hosannas the procession swept along, till on a nearer approach, the whole of the magnificent City, as if rising from an abyss, burst into view, "with its back-ground of gardens and suburbs[1]," and its glorious Temple-tower. The procession paused, and the hour of triumph became the hour of deepest sorrow. In strange contrast with the excited emotions of the crowds around Him, the Holy One wept over the devoted city, foresaw the Roman legions gathered round its fated walls, its proud towers laid low in the dust, and its children within it, because they knew not *the day of their visitation* (Lk. xix. 41—44).

Such things were hidden from the eyes of the eager throngs who were shouting "Hosanna," and believed

1 "Again the procession advanced. The road descends a slight declivity, and the glimpse of the city is again withdrawn behind the intervening ridge of Olivet. A few moments, and the path mounts it again, it climbs a rugged ascent, it reaches a ledge of smooth rock, and in an instant the whole city bursts into view." *S. and P.* 193; Tristram's *Land of Israel*, p. 196.

that now at length the Messiah, welcomed and accepted, would claim the sceptre and ascend the throne. Passing through the City the Holy One advanced towards the Temple. Jerusalem was stirred to its very centre. *Who is this?* enquired many. *This is the Prophet, Jesus, of Nazareth of Galilee* (Mtt. xxi. 10, 11), was the eager reply of His believing followers, expecting, doubtless, that some unmistakeable sign would be given of His real character.

They were doomed to disappointment. Entering the Courts of the Temple, He surveyed with a clear and searching glance (Mk. xi. 11) the scene of disorder and mercenary desecration which they again presented, and in the evening returned with the Twelve (Mk. xi. 11) to the seclusion of Bethany, and the great Palm-Sunday was over.

CHAPTER II

THE SECOND CLEANSING OF THE TEMPLE.

A. D. 30.

THE country between Bethany and Jerusalem, as has been observed in the previous Chapter, abounded in gardens of fig-trees, from which fact indeed Bethphage, or the "House of Figs," derived its name.

Early in the morning after the Triumphal Entry the Saviour set out once more for the Holy City, where, as the inspection of the previous evening had too clearly testified, a second vindication of the sanctity of His Father's house was needed. Being a hungred, probably after a night of fasting, and perceiving *afar of* (Mtt. xi. 13) a fig-tree standing alone *by the way side* (Mtt. xxi. 19), which presented an unusual show of leaves for the season, He went up to it to see *if haply*[1] *He might find*

[1] Εἰ ἄρα, if, as was reasonable to expect under such circumstances, fruit was to be found. Ellicott, 294, n.; Lange on Mk. xi. 4.

fruit thereon (Mk. xi. 13), but on reaching it found nothing but leaves. Though at this early period of the year neither leaves nor fruit were to be *expected* on a fig-tree, this tree by its ample foliage appeared to give promise of the fruit, which ordinarily appears before the leaves[1]. But a nearer approach proved that this promise it fulfilled only in appearance, and in the hearing of His disciples the Holy One laid upon it the doom of utter barrenness, saying, *Let no man eat fruit of thee hereafter for ever*, and straightway it was dried up (Mtt. xxi. 19), and withered.

Passing onwards to Jerusalem, He entered the Temple. The nefarious scene He had rebuked at the first Passover of His public ministry was still enacted. The evil practices which had called forth that first display of holy zeal for the honour of His Father's house had by degrees returned. The fruit, the reality of righteousness, which He had come seeking then and sought in vain, He found not now. As before, therefore, so on this occasion, He drove forth the intruders, the buyers, the sellers, and the money-changers, upset their tables, and poured forth their unholy gains, and declared in words of conscious authority that His House was not for thievish traffic, but for prayer and praise (Mk. xi. 17; Mtt. xxi. 13).

Having thus once more vindicated the sanctity of

1 "This tree, so to speak, vaunted itself to be in advance of all the other trees, challenged the passer by that he should come and refresh himself with its fruit. Yet when the Lord accepted its challenge, and drew near, it proved to be but *as* the others, without fruit as they; for indeed, as the Evangelist observes, the time of figs had not yet arrived,—its fault, if one may use the word, lying in its pretension, in its making a show to run before the rest, when it did not so indeed." Trench *On the Miracles*, p. 440; Lange on Mtt. xxi. 18. Thomson, *The Land and the Book*, p. 349, states that in sheltered spots figs of an early kind may occasionally be found ripe as soon as the beginning of April.

the Temple, He commenced teaching in its courts, and speedily gathered around Him many eager to listen, and astonished at His doctrine (Mk. xi. 18). But works of mercy were now to follow words of power. Those who needed His help sought Him in the Temple itself. The blind and the lame (Mtt. xxi. 14) came to Him, and experienced the effects of the healing word. The marvels that He wrought (Mtt. xxi. 15) moved the youngest pilgrims at the festival, and children's voices cried *Hosanna to the Son of David.* This was more than the chief priests and scribes could endure. Eager as they were to put Him to death, they dared not lift a hand or show open violence, for the whole multitude *hung upon Him* to hear His words (Lk. xix. 48). In a tone of expostulation, however, they ventured to enquire whether He heard what these children were saying, to which He replied by asking whether they had never read the words of the Psalmist, *Out of the mouth of babes and sucklings Thou hast perfected praise* (Ps. viii. 2); with which rebuke He left them, and when even was come returned to Bethany (Mk. xi. 19; Mtt. xxi. 17).

As He proceeded towards Jerusalem on the following day, the Apostles observed with surprise how rapidly the tree doomed the day before had withered away. The late hour at which they left the City the preceding evening had probably prevented their noticing it before, and now the Saviour took occasion by it to teach them a lesson respecting the nature and power of Faith (Mtt. xxi. 20—22; Mk. xi. 20—25).

On entering the Temple and recommencing His gracious work of teaching those assembled there, He was interrupted by the arrival of a formal deputation from the Sanhedrin, which had resolved to discredit Him if possible with the people (Mtt. xxi. 23; Lk. xx. 1).

They began by enquiring by what authority He acted as He was doing, and from whom He had received it

(Mk. xi. 28). This question the Holy One met by another. Two years before[1] they had sent a deputation to the Baptist (Jn. i. 26), and he had borne a public and emphatic testimony to His Messianic claims. The prophetic character of John was generally admitted (Mtt. xxi. 26), and his bold rebuke of Herod had endeared him to the hearts of many—*Whence, then, was his baptism, from heaven or from men?* The question filled his hearers with embarrassment. If they replied that his was a divine commission, they exposed themselves to the obvious rejoinder, why had they not received his testimony respecting the Messiah? If they said of men, they would expose themselves to popular indignation (Mk. xi. 31, 32). Accordingly they preferred to own that they could not tell, whereupon He also declined to answer the question they had put to Him respecting His mission (Mtt. xxi. 27; Lk. xx. 8).

Though thus repulsed, His enemies do not appear to have left the Temple-courts, and were condemned to listen to still more humiliating language. In the parables of the *Two Sons* (Mtt. xxi. 28—32), and the *Wicked Husbandmen* (Mtt. xxi. 33—44; Mk. xii. 1—11; Lk. xx. 9—18), the Redeemer set forth with the utmost distinctness their neglect of their high vocation, the guilt of that outrage which they already meditated against Him in their hearts, their speedy rejection, and the bestowal of the privileges they had abused on other nations.

The drift of these parables the Pharisees and chief priests clearly discerned, and sought earnestly to lay hands upon Him (Mk. xii. 12; Lk. xx. 19), but feared to do so openly because of the multitude, who all regarded Him as a Prophet (Mtt. xxi. 46). Undeterred, however, by these manifestations of intended violence He warned them solemnly, for the last time, in the Parable of the

[1] See above, p. 158.

Marriage of the King's Son (Mtt. xxii. 1—14), that a day was at hand when the kingdom of God would be taken away from the Jewish people who had despised its privileges, and be bestowed upon the Gentiles[1].

CHAPTER III

THE DAY OF QUESTIONS—THE ENQUIRING GREEKS.

A. D. 30.

THUS far the efforts of the ruling powers had been of no avail. The authority of the Lord with the people remained unshaken, His career was unchecked, and they themselves had been humiliated in the very midst of the Temple-courts[2]. A formal council was therefore held (Mtt. xxii. 15), and it was resolved to organize some plan for *ensnaring* Him in His speech (Mtt. xxii. 15; Mk. xii. 13), and beguiling Him into statements which might afford a pretext for delivering Him up to the Roman procurator (Lk. xx. 20). United, therefore, in one formidable conspiracy, the Pharisees[3], Sadducees[3], and Herodians[3], suborned (Lk. xx. 20) men, to all appearance right-minded and thoroughly in earnest, to propose various cases of conscience to Him as the Lord and Judge in the land[4].

i. First, then, approached the Herodians with certain of the Pharisees (Mtt. xxii. 16) enquiring whether it was *lawful to give tribute to Cæsar, or not?* How keenly this question was debated in Palestine, and what disturbances it had caused, especially in Galilee, the province of Herod, has been already noticed[5]. To answer

[1] Trench *On the Miracles*, 211, 212.

[2] Lange's *Life of Christ*, IV. 69; Milman, I. 287.

[3] For their distinctive tenets, see above, pp. 114—119.

[4] Lange, IV. 69; Ellicott, 302.

[5] See above, p. 148.

it now, and to avoid on the one hand giving offence to the excited crowds in the Temple-courts, and on the other supplying matter for accusation before the Roman governor in the Tower of Antonia, so close at hand, appeared impossible. No patriotic Jew would admit that tribute was due to Cæsar. No one claiming to be the Messiah could allow it for a moment, unless he would forfeit all his popularity with the people. And yet if the Redeemer denied this, a charge of treason, which the Romans were always quick to hear, was clearly made out. But the Holy One, thrown off His guard neither by the affected courtesy nor adulation of their address (Mtt. xxii. 18; Lk. xx. 23), saw through their hypocrisy and the snare they had laid. With infinite wisdom He called for the tribute-money. They brought Him a *denarius*[1]. *Whose image and superscription is this ?* He enquired. They answered, *Cæsar's. Render, therefore,* He replied, *to Cæsar the things that are Cæsar's, and to God the things that are God's.* The snare they had laid so cunningly was broken. A single word had rent the whole "web of craft and hypocrisy." The enquirers themselves acknowledged the wisdom of His answer. There was nothing they could *take hold of* (Lk. xx. 26). *They were silent, and went their way* (Lk. xx. 26).

ii. The Herodians thus repulsed, the Sadducees approached. With their wonted[2] philosophic pride they usually kept aloof from all popular religious movements.

[1] "The little silver coin (in value about 7½*d.*), bearing on its surface the head encircled with a wreath of laurel, and bound round with the sacred fillet—the well known features, the most beautiful and the most wicked, even in outward expression, of all the Roman Emperors—with the superscription running round, in the stately language of imperial Rome, *Tiberius Cæsar, Divi Augusti filius Augustus, Imperator.*" Stanley's *Canterbury Sermons*, p. 108.

[2] See above, p. 115.

Now, however, they advanced to the encounter with a religious difficulty respecting the position in another world of a woman who had had seven husbands in this[1]. But their coarse question was met with Divine wisdom. Had they known the Scriptures, or the power of God, they could never have asked it (Mtt. xxii. 29). Such corporeal and earthly relationships ceased with this life, and in the next man would be exalted to a higher order of beings by the almighty power of Him, who even in the Law[2], which they professed to receive, had declared Himself *the God of Abraham, the God of Isaac, the God of Jacob, the God of the living, and not of the dead* (Ex. iii. 6).

iii. Struck with the singular wisdom, with which He had *put the Sadducees to silence* (Mtt. xxii. 34), a scribe belonging to the Pharisaic sect (Mk. xii. 28) now drew near, requesting information as to the relative greatness of the commandments of the Law (Mtt. xxii. 36). The point was probably one much debated in the Rabbinical schools, though it is not clear in what way it was calculated to ensnare the Saviour. But the sublime, though simple response it received, comprising the whole of religion, under the precepts of Love to God and Love to Man, struck even the questioner with admiration (Mk. xii. 32); he frankly owned that such love was better than all *burnt-offerings and sacrifice*[3], and obtained the gracious declaration from the Redeemer that he was *not far from the kingdom of God* (Mk. xii. 34).

[1] The Sadducees appear to have held that the soul perishes with the body: as "the cloud faileth and passeth away," they said, "so he that goeth down to the grave doth not return." Lightfoot on Mtt. xxii. 23; Comp. Jos. *Ant.* XVIII. I. 4; *B. J.* II. 8. 14.

[2] See above, p. 115.

[3] Which seems to confirm Lightfoot's opinion that the enquiry turned on the importance of the ceremonial as compared with the moral law. Lightfoot on Marc. xii. 28.

After such successive proofs of Divine wisdom the Pharisees did not venture[1] to put any more questions to the Redeemer, and He Himself, taking advantage of the opportunity, now assumed the character of a questioner, and interrogated them (Mtt. xxii. 41) respecting the descent of the Messiah. Speaking under the influence of the Spirit, David in the Psalms (Ps. cx. 1) had called Him Lord, saying, *The Lord said unto My Lord, Sit Thou on my right hand, till I have made Thy foes a footstool for Thy feet.* If the Messiah was to be David's *son*, how could He be at the same time his *Lord*, thus mysteriously uniting a Divine and a human nature?

To this profound question those addressed did not even venture to make a reply, and were in their turn constrained to listen, while in words of awful and righteous judgment He denounced the hypocrisy (Mtt. xxiii. 1—12) and tyranny (Mtt. xxiii. 13—18) of the Pharisees, their bigoted attachment to the most minute observances, and their blindness to the spirit of true religion (Mtt. xxiii. 18—36), which had led them to pour out the blood of Jehovah's prophets, even as they now thirsted for His own. For them and for their city the hour of desolation was at hand. The times of mercy, when He would have gathered the children of Jerusalem *as a hen gathereth her chickens under her wing*[2] (Mtt. xxiii. 37—39), had passed away, never to return.

After this stern denunciation of the ruling powers, who veiling their malice and wickedness under the pretence of righteousness had so pertinaciously sought to

[1] Some, however, would refer to this occasion the question respecting the woman taken in adultery (Jn. viii. 1—11). See Ellicott's *Lectures*, 310, and notes.

[2] It is not improbable that the solemn apostrophe to Jerusalem, uttered on the occasion of the triumphal entry, was now in part repeated. See Ellicott's *Lectures*, 314, and note.

entrap Him, the Redeemer sat down opposite the Treasury, in the Court of the Women[1], and looking up beheld the multitude casting in their voluntary[2] gifts and contributions. Amongst the rest His eye rested on a certain poor widow, one of the helpless class which He had just described as devoured by the extortion of the Scribes and Pharisees (Mk. xii. 40; Lk. xx. 47). All her possessions consisted of *two mites*[3], which together made *a farthing*, both of which she now cast into the Treasury, and knew not that One had called to Him His disciples (Mk. xii. 43), and declared that she had cast in *more than all the rest*, and that her gift should be known and remembered till the end of time.

It was apparently while the Redeemer was still in the Court of the Women that two of the Apostles, Andrew and Philip, approached Him with what they deemed a strange announcement. Amongst the thousands that crowded the Holy City were certain Greeks, not Grecian Jews[4], but Gentiles, proselytes of the gate, who were in the habit of coming up to the Feast. In common with many others they had heard of the famed

[1] So called, not because "women only entered in there, but because women might not go further," just as the court of the Gentiles was so called, "not because heathens only might enter there, but because they might not go further." Lightfoot *in loc.*

[2] "Before the Passover, free-will offerings, in addition to the temple-tax, were generally presented." Lange on Mk. xii. 41.

[3] Λεπτὰ δύο, ὅ ἐστιν κοδράντης, Mk. xii. 42. The λεπτόν was the very smallest copper coin. Two made one Roman *quadrans*, which was ¼th of an *as*. The *as* in Cicero's time = nearly a halfpenny, and the *quadrans* = one tenth of a penny. Lange on Mk. xii. 41.

[4] The regular word for which is Ἑλληνισταί, but Ἕλληνες, Gentile Greeks. Lange, IV. 53. See above, p. 110. For the attendance of proselytes of the gate at the feasts at Jerusalem, comp. Acts viii. 27, Jos. *B. J.* VI. 9. 3, and Lightfoot on Jn. xii. 20.

Teacher of Nazareth, of His mighty works, and His wondrous words, and they wished with their own eyes to behold Him (Jn. xii. 21). Shrinking, however, from approaching Him directly, they had applied to the Apostle Philip, possibly on account of his Græcised name[1], saying, *Sir, we would see Jesus.* Philip, apparently perplexed, consulted his brother Apostle Andrew, and together the two went and told their Lord.

No sooner did the Saviour hear their announcement, and perhaps behold these enquirers from the West, than He instantly broke forth into words of mysterious joy: *The Hour*, He declared, as if in a transport of holy rapture, *The Hour is come that the Son of Man should be glorified. Verily, verily I say unto you, Except a corn of wheat fall into the ground and die, it abideth alone; but if it die, it bringeth forth much fruit. He that loveth his life shall lose it; and he that hateth his life shall keep it unto life eternal. If any man serve Me, let him follow Me; and where I am, there will also My servant be; if any man serve Me, him will My Father honour* (Jn. xii. 24—26).

But with the thought of the seed-corn cast into the ground and dying, and the spectacle of these pledges[2] of the vast multitude He should draw unto Him if He was lifted up, came the thought of all that He must first undergo. There fell upon Him the shadow of the dreadful hour so close at hand, and He exclaimed, *Now is My*

[1] Or they may have come from some of the Greek towns of Galilee—Galilee of the Gentiles. See Lightfoot on Jn. xii. 20, and above, p. 145, n.

[2] *Prœludium regni Dei a Judæis ad gentes transituri.* Bengel. "These men from the West represent at the end of Christ's life that which the wise men from the East represented at its beginning; but those came to the cross of the King, even as these came to His manger, and receive presently more full intelligence," Stier, VI. 78.

soul troubled, and what shall I say? Father, save Me from this hour; and then, as though a cloud had rolled away, the perfectly willing spirit spoke again, *For this cause came I unto this hour*[1]*: Father, glorify Thy Name* (Jn. xii. 27, 28).

But these words, expressive of such deep, such infinite resignation, were not to pass unheeded; they called forth the last of the Three[2] Heavenly Voices, which, during His life on earth, attested the Divinity of His mission. The Voice, which had been heard on the banks of Jordan and on the Mount of Transfiguration, was now heard in the courts of the Temple itself, saying in response to the Redeemer's significant utterance, *Father, glorify Thy Name; I have both glorified it, and will glorify it again.*

Various[3] were the interpretations of this mysterious Voice by the surrounding crowd. Some thought that *it thundered,* others that *an angel had spoken to Him* (Jn. xii. 29). But the Redeemer set all doubts at rest, saying, *This Voice came not because of Me, but for your sakes;* and then He exclaimed in the same strain of triumph, which the announcement of two Apostles respecting the enquiring Greeks had called forth, *Now is the judgment of this world; now shall the Prince of this world be cast out; and I, if I be lifted up, will*

[1] Concurrebat horror mortis, et ardor obedientiæ: Veni in hanc horam, ut venirem in hanc horam, eamque exemplarem. Bengel.

[2] See above (i) p. 156 and (ii) p. 223.

[3] Compare Acts ix. 4, 7, with Acts xxii. 9, and xxvi. 14. (i) "The more dull-hearted heard the *sound,* recognized from whence it came, but mistook it for thunder; (ii) the more susceptible hearers perceived it to be a *voice,* but were unable to distinguish what was uttered; (iii) the smaller circle, of which the Apostle who relates the occurrence was one, both heard the voice, knew whence it came, and were enabled to understand the *words* that were spoken," Ellicott, 318, n.

draw all men unto Me, signifying, adds the Evangelist, *by what death He should die*[1].

This striking incident was the appropriate close of this great day in the Temple. The public work of the Holy One was now over. He had given His last counsels and His final warnings to the ruling powers; He now departed and *hid Himself from them* (Jn. xii. 36). In spite of the mighty works He had wrought (Jn. xii. 37), the Jewish nation did not believe on Him. Many, indeed, of the rulers could not resist the evidence of His life and works, but they dared not openly avow their faith for fear of the Pharisees and the terrible ban of excommunication (Jn. xii. 42).

As thus, however, He quitted the Temple, which as a Teacher He was never to enter again, a striking incident took place. His disciples began to invite His attention to the magnificence and solidity of the structure, the enormous size of the stones (Mk. xiii. 1), the glistering of its marble blocks, and the gorgeous gifts with which it was endowed[2] (Mtt. xxiv. 1; Lk. xxi. 5). But their words of admiration could not mislead Him. The imposing building might seem to them to be founded for eternity. But He told them that a day was coming, when not one of these enormous masses of stone should be left standing upon the other.

With this mysterious announcement of a dreadful doom awaiting their national sanctuary ringing in their ears, the Apostles accompanied their Lord along the well-known road towards Bethany. But when they reached the Mount of Olives, He sat down (Mtt. xxiv. 3; Mk. xiii. 3), as if to take one last look at the glorious

[1] Compare the intimation made to Nicodemus two Passovers before, above, p. 165.

[2] Their remarks were possibly called forth by His own words, Mtt. xxiii. 38. On the nature of the buildings, see Jos. *Ant.* XI. 5; *B. J.* v. 5. 6; and above, pp. 95, 96.

city and its still more glorious Temple. And as He sat there directly opposite to it in the evening twilight[1], four of the Apostles, Peter, James, John, and Andrew (Mk. xiii. 3), disquieted by the announcement of the coming destruction of their City, approached with an earnest enquiry *when all these things should come to pass, and what should be the sign of His coming, and of the end of the world* (Mtt. xxiv. 3 ; Lk. xxi. 7).

In reply to their enquiries the Holy One, with the utmost conceivable solemnity, proceeded to set forth the judgments destined to befall Jerusalem, and from these to lead up their thoughts to the contemplation of His own second coming to judge the world (Mtt. xxiv. 5—42), to describe the events that should precede it, and to enforce the necessity on their part of watchfulness and preparation by the striking parables of the *Ten Virgins*

[1] "It is impossible to conceive a spectacle of greater natural or moral sublimity than the Saviour seated on the slope of the Mount of Olives, and thus looking down, almost for the last time, on the Temple and City of Jerusalem, crowded as it then was with near three millions of worshippers. It was evening, and the whole irregular outline of the city, rising from the deep glens, which encircled it on all sides, might be distinctly traced. The sun, the significant emblem of the great Fountain of moral light, to which Jesus and His faith had been perpetually compared, may be imagined sinking behind the western hills, whilst its last rays might linger on the broad and many fortifications on Mount Zion, on the stately palace of Herod, on the square tower, the Antonia, at the corner of the Temple, and on the roof of the Temple, fretted all over with golden spikes, which glittered like fire; while below, the colonnades and lofty gates would cast their broad shadows over the courts, and afford that striking contrast between vast masses of gloom and gleams of the richest light which only an evening scene, like the present, can display... The effect may have been heightened by the rising of the slow volumes of smoke from the evening sacrifices, while even at the distance of the slope of Mount Olivet the silence may have been faintly broken by the hymns of the worshippers." Milman's *History of Christianity*, I. 294, 295.

(Mtt. xxv. 1—13) and *the Talents* (Mtt. xxv. 14—30), closing His solemn revelations with a distinct declaration of the circumstances of the Awful Day, when the Son of Man should come in His glory to judge both the quick and dead (Mtt. xxv. 31—46).

CHAPTER IV

THE COMPACT OF JUDAS—THE LAST SUPPER.

A.D. 30.

AT the close of these solemn prophecies the Redeemer reminded the Apostles that after two days the Passover would be celebrated, and the Son of Man would be betrayed to be crucified (Mtt. xxvi. 1, 2). Having thus indicated the precise time, when the Hour so often spoken of before should come, He retired in all probability to Bethany[1], and there, hidden in holy seclusion (Jn. xii. 36), spent the last day preceding His sufferings.

Meanwhile the rulers of the nation were holding a formal and deliberate consultation as to the best means for putting Him to death. Humbled as they had been that day in the Temple in the eyes of the people, and disappointed in all their projects of ensnaring Him in a capital charge, they saw that their influence was lost unless they were willing to take extreme measures[2]. The chief priests, therefore, the scribes, and the elders (Comp. Mtt. xxvi. 3; Mk. xiv. 1) assembled not in their usual place of conclave, the hall Gazith[3] on the Temple Mount, but in the court of the palace of Caiaphas, the high-priest (Mtt. xxvi. 3). He, as we have seen, had already advised that the Holy One should be put to death[4], and doubtless many of those present would have

[1] Wieseler, *Chronol. Synop.* p. 363.
[2] Lange's *Life of Christ*, IV. 151.
[3] See above, pp. 96, 108, n. [4] See above, p. 253.

gladly resolved on seizing Him by force. But by degrees they became alive to the difficulties of the case.

The recent events on the day of the Triumphal Entry convinced them of the great influence which the Redeemer wielded over many of the nation, and especially the bold and hardy mountaineers of Galilee. The only place where He appeared in public after the nights had been spent at Bethany was the Temple. But to seize Him there in the present excited state of popular feeling would certainly lead to a tumult (Mtt. xxvi. 5; Mk. xiv. 2; Lk. xxii. 2), and this to the interposition of the procurator in the fortress of Antonia. Forcible and hasty measures were therefore to be avoided, and it was formally resolved to take Him by craft, and therefore secretly, and for this purpose to await a favourable opportunity[1].

While, however, they were thus debating, a mode of apprehending Him suddenly presented itself which they had never anticipated[2]. Judas Iscariot, whose chagrin at the discovery of His real character[3] and the rebuke

[1] Lange's *Life of Christ*, IV. 151; Milman, I. 301.

[2] Neander's *Life of Christ*, 419 and note; Milman, I. 303.

[3] Amongst the motives which led him to the betrayal of his Master we may perhaps give prominence to three. (i) Avarice; (ii) Disappointment of his carnal hopes; (iii) A gradual growth of hostility to his Master.

(i) *Avarice.* This feature in his character has been already noticed above, p. 260, note. The germs of this vice probably unfolded themselves gradually (Stier, VII. 40—67), and in spite of many warnings which he must have heard from his Lord, as Mtt. vi. 19—34; xiii. 22, 23; Lk. xvi. 11; Mk. x. 25 (Article *Judas* in Smith's *Bibl. Dict.*); but gathered strength and developed into unfaithfulness and embezzlement as he became entrusted with larger sums. Hence when he presented himself before the Sanhedrin, *he probably expected more, but was not unwilling to take what they offered.*

(ii) *Disappointment of his carnal hopes.* What were the Messianic expectations of the Apostles we have seen again and again—a visible kingdom, an earthly throne, high places,

of His Master on the evening of the Anointing at Bethany has been already described, approached with an enquiry as to the sum they were willing to give him in the event of his betraying the Holy One into their hands (Mtt. xxvi. 14). Thereupon with a joyous alacrity (Mk. xiv. 11; Lk. xxii. 5) they covenanted to give him *thirty pieces of silver*[1], and he on his part began to watch for a seasonable occasion of delivering Him into their hands, without rousing the feelings of the multitude (Lk. xxii. 6).

Thus, then, the day of seclusion at Bethany, the Thursday of the Holy Week, passed away. Meanwhile the hour for the celebration of the Passover drew near. The Saviour had already reminded His disciples of its approach, and connected it with His own death. Accordingly the Apostles now enquired of Him where He intended to celebrate it, and in reply He bade two of their number, Peter and John, go into the city (Lk. xxii. 8), and informed them that on entering it

and temporal blessings; these they looked forward to in common with their nation. To one like Judas, then, the issue of the Triumphal Entry must have been a deep disappointment.

(iii) *A gradual growth of hostility towards his Master.* His practical and administrative talents which caused him to be made treasurer were closely allied with carnal selfishness (Neander's *Life of Christ*, 424) which was early rebuked (Jn. vi. 70), see above, p. 213, but still more sharply during the supper at Bethany (see above, p. 260). As he became aware that his real character was known to the Lord, and found his earthly hopes more and more disappointed, his "attachment to his Master would turn more and more into aversion; when the manifestation of Christ ceased to be *attractive* it became *repulsive*, and more and more so every day." (Neander, p. 424, and comp. Smith's *Bibl. Dict.* I. 1066.)

[1] "Thirty shekels = 120 denarii, and one denarius was at that time the ordinary wages for a day's labour (Mtt. xx. 2); so that the whole sum amounted to about 4 months' wages of a day-labourer. Thirty shekels, it is to be noticed, was the value set upon a single slave, according to Exod. xxi. 32." Neander's *Life of Christ*, 421, n.

they would meet a man bearing a pitcher of water, whom they were to follow to whatever house he should enter. On reaching it they were to address to the owner[1] of this house the significant words, *The Master saith, My time is at hand; where is the guest-chamber where I may eat the Passover with My disciples?* and he would shew them a large upper-room *furnished and prepared;* there they were *to make ready*[2] (Mtt. xxvi. 18; Mk. xiv. 14; Lk. xxii. 11).

[1] Probably a believing follower: *Discipulus, sed non ex duodecim.* Bengel. See also Stier, vii. 77; Ellicott's *Lectures*, 321, n.

[2] At this point it may be well to try and realize the manner in which the Paschal Feast was at this time celebrated by the Jews.

The company at the Table, which might not be less than 10 persons, usually included from 10 to 20, according to the family, or the number of strangers that might be present. They met in the evening and reclined on couches, this being the usual posture then, as standing had been originally.

The rites of the Feast were regulated according to the succession of 4, sometimes 5, cups of red wine mixed with water, which were placed before the head of the house, or the most eminent guest, who was called the Celebrant, the President, or *Proclaimer of the Feast.*

i. When they had reclined, he began by taking one of the four cups of wine in his right hand, and pronounced the benediction over the wine and the feast, saying, *Blessed be Thou, O Lord our God, the King of the universe,* who hast *created the fruit of the Vine.* He then drank the first cup, and the remainder of the household followed his example.

ii. Water was then brought in, and he blessed for the washing of hands, and washed, followed by the rest.

iii. The table was next set out with the unleavened bread, the sauce called Charoseth, the Paschal Lamb, and the flesh of the *Chagigah* or feast-offerings.

iv. The Proclaimer of the Feast then blessed God for the fruits of the earth, and taking a portion of the bitter herbs dipped it in the sop, and ate it with all who reclined at the table.

v. The *Haggadah* or *showing forth* now commenced, and the Celebrant declared the circumstances of the delivery from

Thus directed, the two Apostles went their way, and found everything as their Lord had described with such striking minuteness. The large upper-room is represented as already *furnished and prepared* (Mk. xiv. 15; Lk. xxii. 12). Hence we may perhaps infer that the searching for and putting away of every particle of leaven (1 Cor. v. 7), so important a preliminary to the Passover, had already been carried out, and that the preparation made by the Apostles included the provision of the unleavened cakes, of the bitter herbs, and the cups of wine; of everything, in short, that could be

Egypt, as commanded in the law (Ex. xii. 27; xiii. 8). Then the second cup of wine was filled, and a child or proselyte enquired, *What mean ye by this service?* (Ex. xii. 26), to which reply was made according to a prescribed formula or liturgy, and the wondrous events of the Exodus were related, after which Psalms cxiii, cxiv. were repeated, followed by a solemn blessing and drinking of the second cup.

vi. Then, after a second washing of hands, taking two of the unleavened cakes, the Celebrant broke one of them, pronouncing the consecration in these words; *Blessed be Thou, O Lord our God, King of the Universe, who bringest forth fruit out of the earth,* and distributed a piece to each person around him, saying, *This is the Bread of Affliction which our fathers did eat in the land of Egypt.* All present then dipped their portions with the bitter herbs into the Charoseth and ate them.

vii. The flesh of the Lamb was now eaten, and the Celebrant, lifting up his hands, blessed the third cup of wine, specially known as the *Cup of Blessing,* and handed it round to each person.

viii. After thanksgiving for the food of which they had partaken, for the delivery from Egypt, the covenant of circumcision, and the Law, a fourth cup was filled and drunk, known as the *Cup of Joy,* for the remainder of the Hallel, Ps. cxv—cxviii. was now sung.

ix. Occasionally a fifth cup was drunk, while Psalms cxx—cxxviii. were chanted, but no more. See Buxtorf, *de Cœnâ Domini;* Lightfoot's *Temple Service;* Pedahzur's *Book of Jewish Ceremonies,* 51—56; Freeman's *Principles of Divine Service,* II. 29—39.

prepared on the day before the sacrifice of the Paschal Lamb[1].

This done, they probably returned to their Lord, who later in the evening, when *the hour was come* (Lk. xxii. 14), left the little village of Bethany, crossed the Mount of Olives, and entering the city repaired with the Twelve to the upper-room. There they sat down, or reclined, according to the usual custom, and the Redeemer, taking the place of Celebrant or Proclaimer of the Feast, said, *With desire have I desired to eat this Passover with you before I suffer; for I say unto you, I will no more eat thereof until it be fulfilled in the Kingdom of God.* With these words He took a Cup, the first Cup we may believe, usually devoted to the "announcement" of the Feast, and gave thanks, and said, *Take ye this, and divide it amongst you; for I say unto you, I will not drink of the fruit of the Vine, till the Kingdom of God shall come* (Lk. xxii. 17, 18).

But even now, even in this solemn hour, the old contention touching priority again broke out among the Apostles (Lk. xxii. 24). Thereupon the Holy One spake a few gentle but solemn words to repress so unseemly a dispute (Lk. xxii. 25—30); and to teach them in the most striking manner possible a lesson of humility, took upon Him the form of a servant, and girding Himself with a towel washed His disciples' feet (Jn. xiii. 1—6). Simon Peter, with his wonted impetuosity, would have checked the loving designs of His Master, and when the Redeemer told him that, unless He washed his feet he had no part with Him (Jn. xiii. 9), with that quick re-

[1] The view here taken, then, is that (i) the Supper, to which our Lord sat down, was, as the first three Evangelists (Mtt. xxvi. 17; Mk. xiv. 12; Lk. xxii. 7) clearly intimate, a *Paschal* Supper; (ii) that He ate it on the eve with which Nisan 14 commenced; (iii) and thus twenty-four hours earlier than the time when it was eaten by the chief priests and rest of the nation. See Ellicott, 322, and notes.

vulsion so natural to him, he begged that He would wash not only his feet, but his hands and his head. *He that hath bathed*, replied his Master, *needeth not save to wash his feet, but is clean every whit; and ye are clean, but not all* (Jn. xiii. 10, 11).

With this sad intimation of treachery in their midst the Feast was resumed[1], and probably the second Cup of Wine was drunk. But soon the consciousness of the Traitor's presence so wrought upon the Saviour, that His inmost soul was deeply moved and troubled, and He testified and said, *Verily, verily, I say unto you, that one of you will betray Me* (Jn. xiii. 21). This announcement excited great surprise and deep sorrow among the Apostles, and many were the earnest questionings, *Lord, is it I?* At length He gave a special and private indication to the disciple that reclined upon His bosom. He was the Traitor to whom *He should give the sop*[2], *when He had dipped it* (Jn. xiii. 26). At this point Judas Iscariot, though he had already made his compact with the chief priests, dared to enquire, *Lord, is it I?* (Mtt. xxvi. 25). *Thou hast said*, replied the Redeemer, and gave him the sop, adding shortly afterwards, *That thou doest do quickly* (Jn. xiii. 27). The real import of these words remained unknown to the rest of the Apostles, and they imagined that they related only to the provision of something needed for the feast, or the bestowal of some charity on the poor. As soon, then, as he had received the sop, Judas arose and went forth to execute his awful purpose, *and it was night* (Jn. xiii. 30).

[1] Even if δείπνου γενομένου be the right reading in Jn. xiii. 2, the meaning must be *when supper was begun*. A preferable reading is γινομένου.

[2] The portion of bread dipped into the sauce *charoseth*, and consisting according to some of vinegar and water, according to others of a "mixture of vinegar, figs, dates, almonds, and spice." Smith's *Bibl. Dict.* II. 716.

On his departure the Saviour was no more troubled in spirit, but brake forth into the same triumphant language which fell from His lips when He heard of the request of the Greeks in the Temple Courts: *Now*, said He, *is the Son of Man glorified, and God is glorified in Him; if God is glorified in Him, God will also glorify Him in Himself, and will straightway glorify Him* (Jn. xiii. 31, 32).

Again the Meal proceeded, and soon taking one of the unleavened cakes that had been placed before Him, and giving thanks, probably in the usual words, He brake it, and gave it to His Apostles, saying,

Take, eat: this is My Body, which is given for you: do this in remembrance of Me[1].

Afterwards He took a Cup of wine, in all probability the third Cup, and known as the "Cup of blessing," and having offered thanks, gave it unto them saying,

Drink ye all of this; for this Cup is My Blood of the New Covenant, which is shed for you and for many, for the remission of sins: this do ye, as oft as ye shall drink it, in remembrance of Me[2].

The Holy Eucharist thus instituted, He conversed with the Apostles concerning the events that were soon to happen to Himself and them, how they would desert Him in His most critical and trying hour, how their faith would fail, how they would be dispersed each unto his own. These announcements of coming failure sounded unbearable to the Apostle Peter. *Lord*, said he, *I*

[1] Τοῦτό ἐστι τὸ σῶμά μου (Mtt., Mk., Lk., 1 Cor. xi. 24), τὸ ὑπὲρ ὑμῶν διδόμενον (Lk.), τὸ ὑπὲρ ὑμῶν [κλώμενον], (1 Cor. xi. 24), τοῦτο ποιεῖτε εἰς τὴν ἐμὴν ἀνάμνησιν (1 Cor. xi. 24).

[2] Πίετε ἐξ αὐτοῦ πάντες (Mtt.), τοῦτο γάρ ἐστι τὸ αἷμά μου τῆς διαθήκης (Mtt., Mk.), ἡ καινὴ διαθήκη ἐν τῷ αἵματί μου (Lk., 1 Cor. xi. 25), τὸ περὶ πολλῶν ἐκχυνόμενον (Mtt.), τὸ ἐκχυνόμενον ὑπὲρ πολλῶν (Mk.), τὸ ὑπὲρ ὑμῶν ἐκχυνόμενον (Lk.), εἰς ἄφεσιν ἁμαρτιῶν (Mtt.), τοῦτο ποιεῖτε, ὁσάκις ἂν πίνητε εἰς τὴν ἐμὴν ἀνάμνησιν (1 Cor. xi. 25).

am ready to go with Thee unto prison and to death—I am ready to lay down my life for Thee (Mtt. xxvi. 33; Jn. xiii. 37). *Verily, verily, I say unto thee*, replied the Master, in solemn words, *This night, before the cock crow twice, thou shalt deny Me thrice* (Mtt. xxvi. 34; Mk. xiv. 30; Jn. xiii. 38). But this sad announcement, so far from solemnising the Apostle's feelings, provoked him to fresh protestations of fidelity (Mk. xiv. 31). With still greater vehemence he declared, *If I should die with Thee, I will not deny Thee;* and in these well-meant but short-sighted declarations the rest of the Apostles joined also (Mtt. xxvi. 35; Mk. xiv. 31).

And now, whereas at the usual Paschal Feast it had been customary to continue long in religious conversation respecting the great events of the Exodus, and the national deliverance from Egypt, so on this occasion did the Saviour continue long in earnest conversation with His chosen ones. But He spake to them of other and still more exalted themes; of His own departure to the Father and the coming of the Comforter (Jn. xiv. 1—31); of Himself as the true Vine and His disciples as the branches (Jn. xv. 1—6); of the hatred of the world and its sin against Him (Jn. xv. 18—25); of the trials which the Apostles must expect, and the assured aid of the Comforter (Jn. xvi. 1—16); of offering up prayer in His name (Jn. xvi. 23—27). And at the close of these solemn and affecting discourses, lifting up His eyes to heaven in rapt and solemn devotion, He committed the Apostles to the guardian care of the Eternal Father, and dedicated to Him His own completed work, contemplating it once more in its issues not only on these then present, but on all that should believe on His Name (Jn. xvii.).

The night was now far advanced. A hymn, probably the Hallel, was sung, and the Apostles went forth with their Lord through the quiet streets of the city towards the Mount of Olives (Mtt. xxvi. 30; Mk. xiv. 26).

CHAPTER V

THE AGONY AND BETRAYAL—PETER'S DENIAL.

A.D. 30.

THE road, which the Redeemer and His Apostles now traversed, led across the Kidron, and thence to a garden at the foot of the Mount of Olives, which from the produce of the adjacent hills was called Gethsemane[1], or *the oil-press*[2], and was a spot to which He often resorted with His disciples (Jn. xviii. 2).

On reaching this garden, the Holy One left the greater number of His Apostles at the outskirts (Mtt. xxvi. 36), while with three chosen witnesses[3], Peter and the two sons of Zebedee, He Himself advanced further into the shadow of the overhanging olives. Here He began to be *sore amazed* (Mk. xiv. 33) and *very heavy* (Mtt. xxvi. 37; Mk. xiv. 33), and His *soul exceeding sorrowful even unto death*, and as a last request He begged them to watch, while He proceeded about a *stone's throw further* (Lk. xxii. 41) and engaged in solitary prayer. And now had come the hour for the last and most terrible assault of the Prince of Darkness

[1] The site of the modern Gethsemane lies somewhat to the East of the valley of Kedron, at a point where two paths meet, each leading over the Mount of Olives. Descending from St Stephen's gate and crossing a bridge it is easily reached. Within the enclosure are 8 venerable olive-trees, their trunks much decayed, but their branches flourishing. "The most venerable of their race on the face of the earth, their gnarled trunks and scanty foliage will always be regarded as the most affecting of the sacred memorials in or about Jerusalem." Stanley, *S. and P.*, p. 455.

[2] See Ellicott, p. 327, and note.

[3] Witnesses before (i) of the resurrection of the daughter of Jairus, see above, p. 201, and (ii) of the Transfiguration, see above, p. 222.

(Comp. Lk. iv. 13). Kneeling down (Lk. xxii. 41), and falling forward on the earth (Mk. xiv. 35), He twice prayed that, *if it were possible*, the cup of suffering might pass from Him, and as often with infinite resignation added, *Not as I will, but as Thou wilt* (Mtt. xxvi. 39). Soon the conflict deepened in intensity, and being in an "agony" He prayed *yet more earnestly*, while drops of bloody sweat fell from Him, and testified to the terrible nature of His sufferings (Lk. xxii. 44). Twice, as if to assure Himself of their sympathy and watchfulness, He came to the three Apostles, who had promised so eagerly even to die with Him, and twice He found them sleeping (Mtt. xxvi. 40, 43). The first time He awoke them, saying to Simon, *Simon, sleepest thou? couldest not thou watch with Me one hour? Watch and pray, lest ye enter into temptation* (Mk. xiv. 37, 38). But on the second occasion He uttered not a word. Alone He retired to renew once more the conflict, and to offer for the third time the prayer of mingled entreaty and resignation to His Father in heaven; and then, having been strengthened by an angelic being, He for the third time revisited the Apostles to find them still sleeping. On this occasion, however, He awoke them, and with words of sorrowful expostulation told them that the golden opportunity for watching and prayer was over: *Rise*, said He, *let us be going; behold he that betrayeth Me is at hand* (Mtt. xxvi. 46; Mk. xiv. 42).

He had scarcely spoken, when the Garden was filled with armed men, and flashed with the light of numerous lanterns and torches[1]. At the head of a portion of the

[1] Though the Paschal moon was at the full. On the rocky valley of the Kedron "there fell great deep shadows from the declivity of the mountain and projecting rocks; there were there caverns and grottoes, into which a fugitive might retreat; finally, there was probably a garden-house and towers, into whose gloom it might be necessary for a searcher to throw light around," Lange, IV. 292.

Roman cohort[1] with its captain (Jn. xviii. 12) in attendance on the procurator (Jn. xviii. 3), and of the Levitical guards of the Temple, attendants and apparitors of the Sanhedrin, the traitor[2] approached. Advancing he saluted his Master with a kiss, the signal which had been agreed upon, and received the reproachful reply, *Friend, wherefore art thou come? betrayest thou the Son of man with a kiss?* (Mtt. xxvi. 50; Lk. xxii. 48). Having thus rebuked the traitor, the Lord proceeded towards the entrance of the garden[3] (Jn. xviii. 4), and meeting the soldiers and officers enquired whom they sought. They replied, *Jesus of Nazareth. I am He,* answered the Holy One, and immediately, awed by His calm majesty and the sudden appearance of One whose name had so long had for them a mysterious significance, they recoiled backwards and *fell to the ground* (Jn. xviii. 6)[4]. *Whom seek ye?* the Redeemer again

[1] Stationed during the Feast at the Tower of Antonia.

[2] Of the movements of Judas, after he left the Supper, none of the Evangelists give us an account. It seems, however, most probable that going immediately to Caiaphas, or some other leading members of the Sanhedrin, he informed them where Jesus was likely to be found (Jn. xviii. 2), and announced that he was ready to fulfil his agreement, and at once make the arrest. "It was not the intention to arrest Him during the Feast, lest there should be a popular tumult (Mtt. xxvi. 5), but now that an opportunity offered of seizing Him secretly at dead of night, and therefore without danger of interference or uproar, His enemies could not hesitate. Once in their hands, the rest was easy. A hasty trial, a prejudged condemnation, an immediate execution, and the hated prophet of Galilee might be for ever removed out of their way." Andrews, p. 414.

[3] Lange, iv. 293.

[4] "At this moment Judas was already back among the people. He must have hastened back quickly upon the sharp rebuke of Christ. Probably by this hasty retreat he threw the first element of sympathetic terror into the mass, which now fully developed itself at the saying of Christ." Lange, iv. 294.

enquired, and when they answered as before, again declared that He was the object of their search, and covenanting only for the safe dismissal of His followers, freely surrendered Himself into their hands (Jn. xviii. 7—9).

But one of His followers was not minded to yield thus willingly. Drawing his sword the impetuous son of Jonas cut off the ear of Malchus, a servant of the high-priest. The soldiers were just on the point of laying hands on the Holy One, and taking Him into custody, but seeing what His Apostle had done, He said to them, *Suffer ye thus far*, and touching the ear of the wounded man restored it whole as before (Lk. xxii. 51); then rebuking the disciple for his over-hasty zeal, and protesting[1] meekly against the mode in which He had been arrested by His captors, He allowed Himself to be bound and led towards the city; for it was their *hour and the power of darkness* (Lk. xxii. 53).

On the part of the Apostles all was now terror and confusion. Though they had all promised to die with Him, they now forsook their Master and fled (Mtt. xxvi. 56; Mk. xiv. 50). Their last hope of a temporal kingdom of the Messiah had crumbled to pieces[2].

Meanwhile the Roman guard and the officers (Jn. xviii. 12) led the Saviour over the Kidron, and up the road leading into the city, and either at the suggestion of some of the ruling powers, or in accordance with previous concert, conducted Him to the palace of Annas[3], who as the father-in-law of Caiaphas, and as an able

[1] From St Luke's account, xxii. 52, it is clear that not only the officers of the Temple, but some of the Sanhedrin had now joined the crowd.

[2] Lange, IV. 301.

[3] On the history of Annas, see above, p. 149, and notes. He obtained the high-priesthood not only for Caiaphas his son-in-law, but subsequently for four other sons. Jos. XX. 9. 1.

and experienced counsellor, had great influence with the nation.

It is not improbable that both Annas and his son-in-law occupied[1] a common official residence, and that before it or within the outer porch was a large square open court, in which public business was transacted. Into this court[2] or hall the Redeemer was led, and thither two of the Apostles, John and Peter (Jn. xviii. 15), recovering from their first alarm, ventured to follow. The former, as being acquainted with the high-priest[3], easily obtained admittance into the hall, but Peter appears to have been at first rejected by the porteress. After a while John missed his companion, and going back spake to the porteress, who thereupon immediately allowed him to enter (Jn. xviii. 16).

The night was chilly, and the servants having made a fire of charcoal in the centre of the court, were warming themselves before it (Jn. xviii. 18; Mk. xiv. 54), and thither Peter pressed forwards, anxious to *see the end* (Mtt. xxvi. 58). As he sat there, the porteress, whose suspicions appear to have been aroused, approached the group, and fixing her eye steadfastly upon him (Lk. xxii.

[1] Milman, I. 309.

[2] "An Oriental house is usually built around a quadrangular interior court, into which there is a passage (sometimes arched) through the front part of the house, closed next the street by a heavy folding-gate with a smaller wicket for single persons, kept by a porter. In the text, the interior court, often paved and flagged, and open to the sky, is the αὐλή (translated *palace, hall,* and *court*), where the attendants made a fire; and the passage beneath the front of the house, from the street to this court, is the προαύλιον or πύλων (both translated *porch*). The place where Jesus stood before the high-priest may have been an open room or place of audience on the ground-floor, in the rear or on one side of the court; such rooms open in front being customary." Robinson's *Harmony*, p. 225.

[3] See above, p. 177, n.

56) said, *Surely thou art one of this Man's disciples.* Thrown off his guard, and perhaps disconcerted by the searching glances of the bystanders, the Apostle replied at first evasively[1], *I know not what thou sayest* (Mtt. xxvi. 70; Mk. xiv. 68), and then more strongly, *I know Him not* (Lk. xxii. 57; Jn. xviii. 17).

Thus silenced the maid withdrew, and after a brief delay the Apostle, anxious probably for a favourable opportunity of retiring, went back towards the porch (Mtt. xxvi. 71; Mk. xiv. 68). But here another maid approached and said to the bystanders, *This fellow was also with Jesus of Nazareth* (Mtt. xxvi. 71). Thus a second time assailed, and not knowing what might happen, his faith again failed him, and with an oath he declared *I know not the Man* (Mtt. xxvi. 72); *and the cock crew.*

While this sad scene of moral cowardice was going on, Annas began to put several questions to the Saviour respecting His disciples and His doctrine (Jn. xviii. 19). Thus interrogated, the Redeemer appealed to the publicity of His teaching, and referred His enquirer to His hearers, whom he had so often addressed in the wonted places of resort, the synagogue and the Temple (Jn. xvii. 20, 21): He had no secret doctrines, and no secret society of dependants[2] for purposes either of tumult or sedition. This reply was the signal for the first beginning of a dreadful scene of insult and violence. An officer of the high-priest struck Him on the mouth, saying, *Answerest thou the high-priest so? If I have spoken ill, bear witness of the ill,* meekly replied the Holy One, *but if well, why smitest thou me?* (Jn. xviii. 22—24).

The day was now rapidly dawning, and the Sanhedrin, which had been hastily summoned, had begun to

[1] Lange, IV. 316. [2] *Ibid.* IV. 305.

assemble. Annas therefore sent the Saviour, who was still in bonds, to the official judgment-hall of Caiaphas (Jn. xviii. 24), and it was not improbably as He was crossing the court[1], that He *turned and looked upon* the Apostle, who now for the third time denied that he had ever known Him. Recognised at the porch, Peter, it would seem, had returned again to the fire, and there mingling with the group of soldiers and servants (Jn. xviii. 25), conversed with them freely in his rough uncouth Galilæan dialect[2]. This excited suspicion, and an hour had scarcely elapsed (Lk. xxii. 59) before certain of the bystanders began to express their opinions. *Surely*, said one, *this fellow was one of them. Thou art a Galilæan*, said another (Mk. xiv. 70). *Thy speech bewrayeth thee*, added a third (Mtt. xxvi. 73). *Did I not see thee in the garden with Him?* broke in a fourth, a kinsman of the servant whose ear the Apostle had cut off (Jn. xviii. 26). Thus attacked on all sides he fell deeper still. With oaths and curses (Mtt. xxvi. 74; Mk. xiv. 71) he declared, *I know not the Man*, and for the second time the cock crew (Mk. xiv. 72). It was this base denial that the Holy One now overheard. *Turning round He looked upon Peter* (Lk. xxii. 61). The remembrance of all that He had said rushed to the Apostle's recollection. He could not linger a moment in that Presence. His faith indeed had not *utterly*[3] *failed*, but Satan had *sifted him as wheat. He went forth and wept bitterly* (Mtt. xxvi. 75; Lk. xxii. 62)[4].

[1] Lange, IV. 313; Ellicott's *Lectures*, 334.

[2] See above, p. 145, n.; Lange, IV. 317.

[3] Such is the full force of ἐκλείπῃ in Lk. xxii. 32: "I have prayed for thee that thy faith may not *utterly fail*," or be *totally extinguished*. Comp. Heb. i. 12.

[4] The order of the denials of the Apostle here given mainly coincides with that suggested in Lange's *Life of Christ*, IV. 314—319; Ellicott's *Lectures*, 334, n.; Andrews, pp. 426, 427.

CHAPTER VI

THE JEWISH TRIAL—REMORSE AND SUICIDE OF JUDAS.

A.D. 30.

BY this time the entire body of the Sanhedrin had assembled in the palace of Caiaphas, and the Redeemer was placed before them.

The first object was to secure the agreement of two witnesses on some specific charge (Mtt. xxvi. 59; Mk. xiv. 55). But this was found to be a matter of the utmost difficulty. Many indeed were at hand suborned to utter any falsehood, but their testimony was so confused and contradictory (Mk. xiv. 56), that the council could not receive it. At length two were found who could testify to the words the Holy One had uttered on the occasion of His first visit to the Temple[1]. *This fellow said*, was their charge, *I will destroy this Temple made with hands, and in three days I will raise up another made without hands* (Mk. xiv. 58). But besides the fact that their allegations were exaggerated, they themselves did not agree in their statements (Mk. xiv. 59), and though eager to pronounce the capital sentence, the council felt themselves unable with any decency to do so on such evidence.

Meanwhile the Redeemer preserved a solemn and impressive silence, neither interrupting, nor replying to the questions of the high-priest or the statements of His accusers (Mtt. xxvi. 62; Mk. xiv. 60). He condescended not to any defence.

Nothing therefore remained but, if possible, to make Him criminate Himself. Once more, then, the high-

[1] See above, p. 164.

priest *stood up in the midst* (Mk. xiv. 60), and in the most solemn manner adjured Him in the name of Jehovah to declare whether *He was the Messiah, the Son of God* (Comp. Mtt. xxvi. 63; Mk. xiv. 61).

Thus formally addressed, the Holy One at length broke the silence He had hitherto maintained, saying, in reply to the question, *I am; and hereafter ye shall see the Son of Man sitting on the right hand of power, and coming in the clouds of heaven*[1]. He thus in the most solemn and explicit manner asserted that He was not only the Messiah, but the Son of God, and that in the sublimest sense of the words.

All was now uproar and confusion. In token of his horror the high-priest rent his clothes, and pronounced the utterance of the Redeemer to be direct and treasonable blasphemy. *What further need*, he exclaimed, *have we of witnesses? Ye have heard His blasphemy: what think ye?* (Mtt. xxvi. 65; Mk. xiv. 63, 64). Carried away by his vehement gestures and words, and his great influence, the court pronounced their opinion, *He is guilty of death* (Mtt. xxvi. 66). Worse than false prophet, worse than false Messiah, He had declared Himself to be the *Son of God*, and that in the presence of the high-priest and the great council of the nation. He had incurred the capital penalty.

And now ensued a scene of fearful violence. The bystanders were permitted to do their worst to One thus declared guilty of blasphemy. Some *spat upon His face;* others *smote Him with the palms of their hands;* others *blindfolded* Him, and in derision of His Messianic claims bade Him detect the hand that had been raised against Him (Mtt. xxvi. 67, 68; Mk. xiv. 65; Lk. xxii. 63, 64).

[1] Herein probably alluding to the prophecy of Daniel vii. 13, 14, universally admitted to refer to the reign of the Messiah.

But though the great council of the nation had thus passed sentence, there remained a serious obstacle before they could carry it out. Cases punishable with death, such as false claims to prophetic inspiration, or blasphemy, they were fully competent to *try*[1] (Comp. Acts iv. 5—21; v. 17—40; vi. 12—15; xxiii. 1—10), but they could not *execute* the sentence of death, for the right had been taken from them ever since Judæa became a Roman province[2]. Mistrusting, therefore, the people who might attempt to rescue the Holy One from the hands of their own officers, reluctant to incur the odium of profaning so sacred a day with a public execution, anxious to shift the responsibility from their own head upon that of the Romans, yet determined to insure the destruction of their Victim, they again reassembled their court (Mtt. xxvii. 1; Mk. xv. 1), and resolved to send the Redeemer before the tribunal of Pilate, who, they might not unreasonably suppose, "would not hesitate, at once, and on their authority, on the first intimation of a dangerous and growing party, to act without further examination or inquiry, and without scruple add one victim more to the robbers and turbulent insurgents, who, it appears, were kept in prison, in order to be executed, as a terrible example at that period of national concourse[3]." Pilate had, as usual, come up to Jerusalem to preserve order during the Passover, and was now residing either in a palace near the tower of Antonia[4], or in the splendid and luxurious structure which had been erected by Herod the Great[5]. Thither, therefore, the Saviour, after He had

[1] Andrews, p. 428; Alford's note on John xviii. 31.
[2] See Lightfoot on Mtt. xxvi. 3.
[3] Milman, I. 317.
[4] Ewald's *Life of Christ;* Lange, IV. 337, n.
[5] Lange's *Life of Christ*, IV. 338, n.; comp. Jos. *B. J.* II. 14. 8: II. 15. 5; Ellicott, 339, n.

been again placed in bonds (Mtt. xxvii. 2), was led, attended by a deputation of the Sanhedrin to support and explain the charge[1].

Meanwhile the fact of His condemnation had become known[2] to the traitor Judas (Mtt. xxvii. 3), and filled him with the deepest remorse. Hitherto he had been lured on by covetousness, and his eyes had been blinded by the Evil One. Now they were opened, and he saw what he had done. *He had betrayed innocent blood* (Mtt. xxvii. 4). Filled with terror and anguish, he hurried to the chief priests and elders, and openly confessed his awful crime. But they received his confession with gibes and taunts. *What is that to us?* said they; *see thou to that* (Mtt. xxvii. 4). In frantic despair the wretched man resolved to get rid of the reward of his treachery. Rushing into the sanctuary[3] he flung down the thirty pieces of silver before the priests, and went and hanged himself[4] (Mtt. xxvii. 5), but, probably in consequence of the rope breaking, he

[1] Milman, I. 317.

[2] "He might readily learn that Jesus had been condemned. But he also *saw* it, from the procession in which the Pharisees conducted Jesus to Pilate, which could have no other object than to procure His condemnation." Lange on Mtt. xxvii. 3; *Life of Christ*, IV. 335.

[3] Ῥίψας τὰ ἀργύρια ἐν τῷ ναῷ, the inner portion of the Temple, the sanctuary. See Lange on Mtt. xxxvii. 5, and Ellicott, 339, n. If while a deputation of the Sanhedrin attended the Saviour to the *prætorium* of Pilate, the rest retired to their own council-chamber in the Temple, it is easy to understand how he could be near the sanctuary.

[4] It is not improbable that Judas hanged himself over an abyss, perhaps the valley of Hinnom, and the rope giving way, or the branch to which he hung breaking, he fell down headlong (on his face, πρηνής, Acts i. 18), and was crushed and mangled on the rocky pavement below. See the quotation from Hackett's *Ill. Script.* in Andrews, p. 440; Ebrard's *Gospel History*, p. 427; Ellicott, 339; Lange's *Life of Christ*, IV. 334.

fell headlong, and burst asunder in the midst (Acts i. 18), so that, when his body was found, *all his bowels had gushed out.* With the blood-money he had left in the Temple the chief priests were at first perplexed what to do. Though they had not scrupled to pledge it as the reward of the basest treachery, yet they were unwilling to return it to the Temple funds, and at length resolved to apply it to the purchase[1] of a field for the burial of strangers, which was afterwards known as Aceldama[2] (Acts i. 19), or the *Field of Blood* (Mtt. xxvii. 6—10; Zech. xi. 13).

[1] St Matthew (xxvii. 7, 8) states that the chief priests bought with the money the potter's field to bury strangers in, and that therefore that place was called the *Field of Blood*. St Peter (Acts i. 18) says that Judas purchased a field with the reward of iniquity. Perhaps the latter statement may be understood as meaning to say, that whereas Judas had with the rest of the Apostles obtained the glorious lot of the apostolate (Acts i. 17), yet actually he had purchased for himself a mere corner of a field in the valley of Genhinnom, as the reward of unrighteousness. The field was bought not by himself in person, but with his money, the wages of his iniquity, and received the name of the *Field of Blood*, (i) as the spot on which his mangled body fell, and (ii) as purchased by the chief priests with the blood-money. See Lange's *Life of Christ*, IV. 333—336; Ebrard's *Gospel History*, p. 427; Smith's *Bibl. Dict.* Art. *Judas*.

[2] "*The Field of Blood* is now shewn on the steep southern face of the valley or ravine of Hinnom, near its eastern end on a narrow plateau, more than halfway up the hill-side." Smith's *Bibl. Dict.*

CHAPTER VII

THE TRIAL BEFORE PILATE—THE CONDEMNATION.

A. D. 30.

WHAT amount of knowledge Pilate already possessed of the Saviour's person and character is not known. But he could not fail to have been surprised, on this occasion, at the earnest request so early in the morning to decide the question respecting the Teacher from Galilee. The deputation from the Sanhedrin would not enter his prætorium, lest they should incur pollution, and be unable to keep the Passover (Jn. xviii. 28). Yielding, therefore, to the popular custom[1], with political tact he came forth from his palace (Jn. xviii. 29), and enquired the nature of the accusation against the Redeemer.

At first they replied evasively, and as if they felt hurt at the question, *If this fellow were not a malefactor we would not have delivered Him unto thee* (Jn. xviii. 30). But this would not satisfy Pilate, and he replied ironically[2], *Then take ye Him, and judge Him according to your law*, as if anxious to refer the whole matter back to themselves. To this the Jews replied that it was not lawful for them to put any one to death (Jn. xviii. 31), and having thus intimated that the Redeemer had committed a crime, for which the punishment of death was due, artfully put forward a charge, which, as a Roman procurator, Pilate could not overlook. *We found this fellow*, said they, *perverting*

[1] Stier, VII. 339.
[2] Stier, VII. 340; Lange, IV. 339.

our nation, and forbidding to give tribute to Cæsar, saying that He is Christ a King (Lk. xxiii. 2).

Though Pilate must have known the Jews too well to imagine that the Sanhedrin would really hate and persecute One, whose sole crime was an anxiety to free them from the Roman power[1], he saw that the case could not be hastily put aside, involving as it did three grave charges; (i) seditious agitation, (ii) attempted prohibition of the payment of the tribute-money, and (iii) the assumption of the suspicious title of "King of the Jews."

It was clearly necessary that he should at least examine the Accused, and, as a *procurator*[2], he was bound to conduct the examination himself.

Withdrawing, accordingly, with the Redeemer into the interior of the prætorium (Jn. xviii. 33), he began by enquiring, *Art thou the King of the Jews?* (Jn. xviii. 33; Mtt. xxvii. 11). To this the Holy One replied by asking the governor whether he put this question of himself, or at the suggestion of others (Jn. xviii. 34). Apparently offended at such a rejoinder, and disclaiming all communion with the prejudices of the Jews[3], Pilate responded that he was not a Jew; His own countrymen, and the ruling powers of the nation, had brought Him before his tribunal, *what had He done?*

Thus interrogated the Saviour replied by an assertion of the real nature of His kingdom: *My kingdom*, said He, *is not of this world; had my kingdom been of this world, then would my servants have con-*

[1] Stier, VII. 343.

[2] "Pilate being only a Procurator, though a *Procurator cum potestate*, had no quæstor to conduct the examination, and thus, as the Gospels most accurately record, performs that office himself." Ellicott, 342, n.; Smith's *Classical Dictionary*, Art. *Provincia*.

[3] Milman, I. 322.

tended that I should not be delivered to the Jews: My kingdom is not from hence. Art Thou[1], *then, a king?* enquired the wondering governor. *Thou sayest it*, answered the Redeemer; *for I am a King. For this purpose was I born, and for this purpose came I into the world, that I might bear witness unto the truth. Every one that is of the truth heareth My Voice* (Jn. xviii. 37, 38). These mysterious words from the lips of One, whose life seemed to be entirely at his mercy; this denial that He was a king in a worldly sense, and the implication that in another sense He was[2]; this declaration that the object of His birth and of His life was to bear witness to *the truth*, increased the procurator's perplexity. *What is truth?* he asked, partly in sadness, partly in irony, partly from a real inability to discern the connection of such an abstract matter with "the present question, with a question of life and death, with a capital charge brought by the national council before the supreme tribunal[3]." He could connect a kingdom with *power*, but not with *truth.*

The only sect Pilate could have ever heard of that believed in such a kingdom was the Stoics[4], and their opinions he would naturally regard as those of visionary enthusiasts. The Accused might be a dreamer, but certainly He was not one who had done anything deserving of the sword of the civil power, and going out to the Jewish deputation standing before the gate (Jn.

[1] Σύ is emphatic in Jn. xviii. 37.

[2] Neander's *Life of Christ*, p. 460.

[3] Milman, I. 323; Stier, VII. 370; Ellicott, 342, n.

[4] Compare Horace, *Epist.* II. i. 106:

Ad summum sapiens uno minor est Jove, dives,
Liber, honoratus, pulcher, Rex denique regum.

and *Sat.* I. iii. 125, and *Epist.* I. i. 59:

At pueri ludentes, rex eris, inquit,
Si recte facias...

quoted in Milman, I. 332.

xviii. 38), he declared his conviction of His innocence; *he found no fault in Him* (Lk. xxiii. 4).

But this was the signal for a furious clamour on the part of the chief priests and the members of the Sanhedrin. *He stirreth up the people*, they cried, *teaching throughout all Judæa, beginning from Galilee even unto this place* (Lk. xxiii. 5). Pilate thereupon turned once more to the Accused, and enquired what answer He had to give to these charges (Mtt. xxvii. 13). But the Holy One continued silent, and answered not a word. This increased still further the astonishment of the procurator (Mtt. xxvii. 14; Mk. xv. 5), but he fancied he had discovered an escape from the dilemma. The word *Galilee* had not escaped his ears (Lk. xxiii. 6). Galilee was in the jurisdiction of Herod-Antipas, who was now present in the city as a worshipper at the Feast (Lk. xxiii. 7), and by sending the case before him[1], he might at once rid himself of a troublesome responsibility[2], and conciliate one, with whom he had hitherto been on no friendly terms[3] (Lk. xxiii. 12). Having assured himself, therefore, that the Accused was a Galilæan (Lk. xxiii. 6), he sent Him before Herod's tribunal.

The tetrarch of Galilee[4], as we have seen before, had often heard of the Saviour, and had long desired to see Him[5] (Lk. xxiii. 8). He was highly pleased, therefore,

[1] It was not an unusual practice to refer the case of a criminal from the *forum apprehensionis* to the *forum originis*. Comp. Acts xxvi. 3. Lange, IV. 347.

[2] Stier, VII. 378; Milman, I. 324.

[3] The cause is not known. Some think it was the recent slaughter of the Galilæans (Lk. xiii. 1).

[4] Where Herod was now residing is not known: some think he occupied his father's palace with Pilate; others, that while the Procurator resided in the fortress Antonia, Herod occupied his father's palace; others would make his abode the old palace of the Maccabees. Jos. *Ant.* XX. 8. 11.

[5] See above, p. 205.

when informed who was awaiting an audience with him, and hoped his curiosity to see some sign of supernatural magical power might be gratified. With this view he *put many questions* to Him, but the Redeemer maintained an imperturbable silence. Meanwhile the chief priests and scribes, who had followed into the presence of Herod, persisted in their furious accusations. But neither their charges nor the questions of the tetrarch could induce the Holy One to utter a word. Provoked at being thus disappointed of the object of his hopes, Herod's superstitious curiosity was exchanged for scorn. He did not venture indeed to condemn the Accused to death, and saw that there was nothing He had done which rendered Him liable to punishment, but he did not scruple to insult Him, and therefore handed Him over to his soldiers, amongst whom probably, as in his father's body-guard[1], were Gaulish and Thracian barbarians, who treated the Holy One with every kind of indignity (Lk. xxiii. 11). This done, he sent Him back to the Roman procurator, clad in a purple robe, and the ill-feeling between the two was from that day exchanged for friendship (Lk. xxiii. 12).

Perplexed, as Pilate probably was, at finding the case thus thrown back upon his hands, he was more than ever convinced that the Holy One was entirely innocent of such grave charges as had been made against Him. He therefore summoned the chief priests and rulers of the people (Lk. xxiii. 13) together, and once more declared his conviction that their accusations could not be sustained, and added that in this he was fortified by the judgment of Herod also. He offered, however, to scourge Him before letting Him go (Lk. xxiii. 16).

This first symptom of weakness and irresolution was not lost upon the Jewish rulers, and their followers

[1] See above, p. 88, n.; Milman, I. 325.

assembled before the *prætorium*, and the proposition merely to scourge the meek Sufferer found little favour with them. Pilate therefore resolved to try another method of making the proposed acquittal more acceptable[1].

It appears to have been a custom, the origin of which is wholly unknown[2], to release at the season of the Passover any prisoner whom the people might select. There was at this time in confinement a celebrated (Mtt. xxvii. 16) bandit, named Barabbas[3], who with others had committed murder in an insurrectionary tumult (Mk. xv. 7) in the city (Lk. xxiii. 18). The procurator therefore, in accordance with this custom, proposed to the Jews that they should select for release one of the two, either Barabbas, a condemned murderer and insurgent, or the Prophet of Nazareth. He saw clearly that it was envy of His fame and popularity (Mk. xv. 10) which had induced the ruling powers to accuse the Holy One, and he hoped by this appeal to the people to procure His release. Indeed so certain does he appear to have been that they would select for release One, whom thousands had so lately welcomed with loud Hosannas as their Messiah, that he ascended and sat down upon the judgment-seat[4] as if to ratify and formally accept their decision (Mtt. xxvii. 19).

1 Lange, IV. 353.

2 Possibly it was of Jewish origin, adopted and continued by the Roman governors from motives of policy. According to Lk. xxiii. 18 the request respecting Barabbas came first from the people; according to Mtt. xxvii. 17, from Pilate; Mark, however (ch. xv. 8), seems "to represent the people as making the request in general terms, while Pilate availed himself of it in the present emergency of this particular case." Ellicott, 345, n.

3 A patronymic denoting *Son of Abba*. Many of the later MSS. of Mtt. xxvii. 16 give his name as Ἰησοῦς Βαραββᾶς.

4 The βῆμα was a portable tribunal (see above, p. 147, n.) and stood, St John tells us (Jn. xix. 13), on a tesselated pave

But at this moment, as if to increase his perplexity, an attendant approached bearing a message from his wife[1] imploring him to have nothing to do with the *just person* (Mtt. xxvii. 19) standing before his tribunal. During the night she had probably been roused by the messengers[2] of the high-priest requesting a Roman guard, and a fearful and harrowing morning (Mtt. xxvii. 19) dream concerning the righteous Prophet of Nazareth had induced her thus to appeal to her husband in His behalf.

Pilate's feelings of awe and amazement were now intensified, and his determination to release his Prisoner increased. But the chief priests and the Sanhedrists had improved their opportunity while he was listening to his wife's message, and when he composed himself afresh to receive their decision, he saw that malice and bitter, determined hatred had done their work. Persuaded by their teachers, the multitude cried out, *Not this Man, but Barabbas.* In vain the procurator tried to stem the torrent, in vain he expostulated (Mk. xv. 9), in vain he re-asserted his conviction of the innocence of the Accused. Loud clamour, and furious faces, and uplifted hands, told him that the feelings of the throng

ment, called in Greek *Λιθόστρωτον*, in Hebrew *Gabbatha*, which "perhaps formed the front of the Procurator's residence," Ellicott, 346, n. So necessary was the tesselated pavement and the tribunal deemed to the forms of justice, that Cæsar carried about with him, on his expeditions, pieces of marble ready fitted and a tribunal. Suet. *Jul.* c. 46.

[1] In early times the Roman magistrates had not been permitted to take their wives with them into the provinces. This rule, however, had gradually been relaxed, and lately a proposition of Cæcina to enforce it had been rejected, Tac. *Ann.* III. 33, 34. According to tradition, the name of Pilate's wife was Procula, or Claudia Procula, and she is said to have belonged to the class of proselytes of the gate. Lange's *Life of Christ*, IV. 351.

[2] Lange, IV. 351.

were excited beyond such efforts. Equally powerless was a solemn and significant action, by which he strove to represent in the most striking manner possible, how strongly he was convinced of the perfect innocence of the Holy One. Calling for water, he washed his hands publickly (Mtt. xxvii. 24) before the whole multitude, saying, *I am guiltless of the blood of this Just Person: see ye to it. His blood be upon us and upon our children*, was the frantic reply, and Pilate saw that further opposition would only increase the tumult (Mtt. xxvii. 25).

One hope, however, he still seems to have retained[1]. Perhaps that tossing clamorous throng would be satisfied with the infliction of a punishment only less terrible than death. Perhaps the inhuman scourge of the Roman soldiers would be enough[2], without the penalty of crucifixion, for which so many were already clamorous. He gave the order, therefore, that He should be scourged, and appears to have again sat down on the judgment-seat while the command was carried into effect.

The soldiers executed his orders with their wonted severity, and then flung around the bleeding body of the Divine Sufferer a purple[3] robe (Mtt. xxvii. 28; Jn. xix.

[1] Lange, IV. 355. Hengstenberg on Jn. xix. 1.

[2] "Generally the scourging before crucifixion (Jos. *B. J.* II. 14. 9; V. 11. 1; VII. 6. 4; Livy, XXXIII. 56) was inflicted by lictors. But Pilate, as sub-governor, had no lictors at his disposal, and therefore had it inflicted by soldiers." Lange, IV. 356, n. The Roman scourging was so painful and horrible, nails and pieces of bone being stuck into the scourges, that the sufferer not unfrequently died under it. Compare the *horribile* flagellum of Hor. *Sat.* I. iii. 119; Smith's *Dict. of Antiquities*, Art. *Flagellum.*

[3] Χλαμύδα κοκκίνην, Mtt. xxvii. 28; πορφύραν, Mk. xv. 17; ἱμάτιον πορφυροῦν, Jn. xix. 2. "A war-cloak, such as princes, generals, and soldiers wore, dyed with purple; probably therefore, a cast-off robe of state out of the prætorian wardrobe," Lange, IV. 357; Ellicott, 348, n.

2), and placing a reed in His right hand (Mtt. xxvii. 29), and a crown of thorns[1] upon His head, bowed the knee before Him, and in cruel mockery saluted Him, saying, *Hail, King of the Jews* (Mtt. xxvii. 29; Mk. xv. 18). Not satisfied with this outrage, they took the reed and struck Him with it on the head, and spat in His face (Mtt. xxvii. 30; Mk. xv. 19), and heaped upon Him every kind of indignity.

The scourging appears to have been inflicted within the *prætorium* (Mtt. xxvii. 27), and when it had been carried out, Pilate himself went and led forth the Sufferer wearing the crown of thorns and the purple robe (Jn. xix. 4, 5), and presented Him to the people, saying, *Behold the Man*[2]. Would not this spectacle of terrible suffering suffice? Could cruelty demand yet more? *Crucify Him* was the cry of the chief priests and their attendants (Jn. xix. 6). The sight of so much suffering so meekly borne drew forth no pity, and no relenting. *Take ye Him, and crucify Him*, replied the procurator; *for I find no fault in Him. We have a law*, rejoined the Jews, *and by our law*[3] *He ought to die, because He made Himself the Son of God.*

These last words roused afresh all Pilate's fears (Jn. xix. 8). Taking his bleeding, lacerated Prisoner once more within the prætorium he enquired anxiously, *Whence art Thou*[4]*?* But the Holy One made him no

[1] What exact species is unknown. "As *mockery* seems to have been the primary object, the choice of the plant was not suggested by the sharpness of its thorns: the soldiers took what first came to hand, utterly careless whether it was likely to inflict pain or no." Ellicott, 348, n.

[2] Comp. Isai. liii. 3; Ps. xxii. 7.

[3] Comp. Lev. xxiv. 16.

[4] The mysterious title υἱὸς Θεοῦ suggested to Pilate that He might be one of his own heroes or demi-gods. Fearing he might be braving the wrath of some unknown deity, he enquired whether His descent was indeed such as the title

reply. Startled by this continued silence the procurator asked whether He did not know that he had power to release Him, and power to crucify Him. *Thou couldest have had no power at all against Me,* was the mysterious reply, *unless it had been given thee from above; therefore he*[1] *that delivered Me unto thee hath the greater sin* (Jn. xix. 11). This answer, so calm, so gentle, so full of mystery, made a deep impression on Pilate, already awed by the message of his wife, and still more by the infinite patience of the accused, and he resolved to make one last effort to release Him (Jn. xix. 12). But it was too late. A cry, far more formidable to himself than any he had yet heard, struck upon his ears: *If thou let this Man go,* cried the Jews, *thou art not Cæsar's friend: whosoever maketh himself a king speaketh against Cæsar* (Jn. xix. 12). It was a crafty, well-chosen cry. Pilate knew that the Jews already had matter for accusation against him[2], and could well divine the consequences, if they accused him before the gloomy suspicious Tiberius of sparing a prisoner who had been accused of treason[3]. Loss of place, degradation, banishment, perhaps a death by torture, stared him in the face. His fears for his own personal safety turned the scale. He must save *himself*[4], even though he sacrificed One

seemed to imply, Lange's *Life of Christ,* IV. 361; Hengstenberg on Jn. xix. 8.

[1] Probably the reference is to Caiaphas, who "formally gave over our Lord to the Roman governor (Mtt. xxvii. 2; Mk. xv. 1)," Ellicott, 349, n.

[2] See above, p. 150.

[3] Addito majestatis (treason) crimine, quod tum omnium accusationum complementum erat, Tacitus, *Ann.* III. 38. Atrocissimè exercebat leges majestatis, Sueton. *Vit. Tib.* c. 58. The release of a criminal from punishment came under the head of majestas; see Merivale's *History of the Romans,* V. 251.

[4] All that he feared, however, came upon him. On the complaint of the Samaritans of Pilate's cruelty, Vitellius,

whom he had confessed to be innocent. Once more, therefore, he took his seat upon the tribunal (Jn. xix. 13), but even now he could not resist the impulse to bid the Jews bethink themselves before it was too late. *Behold your King*, said he. His words were the signal for uproarious cries of *Away with Him! Away with Him! Crucify Him! Shall I crucify your King?* asked the procurator. *We have no king but Cæsar*, replied the chief priests (Jn. xix. 15), thus renouncing altogether the hope of the Messiah in order to satisfy their thirst for the Redeemer's blood, and Pilate seeing it was useless to prolong the controversy, pronounced the word, the irrevocable word, *Let Him be crucified* (Joh. xix. 16).

CHAPTER VIII

THE CRUCIFIXION.

A.D. 30.

THUS the Holy One was formally delivered into the hands of the soldiers[1], who instantly made their preparations for His crucifixion. The place of execution was a spot of slightly rising ground without the gates of

the prefect of Syria, in A.D. 36, sent his friend Marcellus to administer the affairs of Judæa, and ordered Pilate to repair to Rome, to answer the accusation before the emperor (Jos. *Ant.* XVIII. 4. 2). Tiberius, however, died before he reached the capital, and Pilate is said to have laid violent hands upon himself about A.D. 40. See Euseb. *Hist. Eccl.* II. 7. "From the confidence with which Tiberius was appealed to on a matter of such remote concern, it would seem that the vigilance of his control was not generally relaxed even in the last moments of his life," Merivale's *History of the Romans*, V. 420.

[1] Pilate not having lictors, to whom this duty specially belonged, soldiers would be naturally employed on this occasion.

the city, called, probably from the shape of its rounded summit[1], Golgotha[2], *the place of a skull* (Mtt. xxvii. 33; Jn. xix. 17). Thither, therefore, after stripping Him of the purple robe, and putting on Him His own garments (Mtt. xxvii. 31; Mk. xv. 20), the soldiers led Him forth bearing[3], as was customary, the Cross on which He was to suffer (Jn. xix. 17), attended by a centurion[4], and two malefactors who were to be crucified with Him[5] (Lk. xxiii. 32).

As they proceeded from the city, the Redeemer, exhausted by the grievous sufferings He had already undergone, sank under the heavy weight of the Cross,

[1] Not from being, as some think, strewn with the remains of condemned malefactors, for the Jews always buried them.

[2] St Luke, according to his usual practice, omits the Hebrew word Golgotha, and gives (xxiii. 33) only the Greek equivalent *κρανίον*, *the place called a Skull*. From the Vulgate rendering of this verse *et postquam venerunt in locum, qui vocatur Calvariæ* (=*a bare skull*), the word *Calvary* has been introduced into the English Version, obscuring the Evangelist's meaning. It was (a) apparently a well-known spot, (b) outside the gate (comp. Heb. xiii. 12), but (c) near the city (Jn. xix. 20), and (d) on a thoroughfare leading into the country (Lk. xxiii. 26), and (e) contained a garden or orchard, *κῆπος* (Jn. xix. 41). See Robinson's *Bib. Res.* I. 376, n.

[3] Patibulum ferat per urbem, deinde affigatur cruci, Plaut. *Carbonar.* Hence the term *furcifer* = cross-bearer. This was typified by Isaac bearing the wood of the burnt-offering, Gen. xxii. 6. Pearson *On the Creed*, Art. IV.

[4] Exactor mortis, Tac. *Ann.* III. 14; XI. 37. Centurio supplicio præpositus, Seneca. Lange, *Life of Christ*, IV. 373.

[5] The cause of execution was generally inscribed on a white tablet, called *σανίς*, *λεύκωμα*, titulus, *αἰτία*, (*Titulus, qui causam pœnæ indicaret*, Sueton. *Calig.* 32) and borne either suspended from the neck, or carried before the sufferer, *precedente titulo*, Sueton. The latter was probably the mode in our Lord's case. Lange, IV. 373. Pearson *On the Creed*, Art. IV.

and the soldiers meeting one Simon[1] of Cyrene in Northern Africa, coming from the country[2], laid hold upon him, and compelled[3] him to assist in bearing it (Mtt. xxvii. 32; Mk. xv. 21; Lk. xxiii. 26). And so the mournful procession was resumed, followed by a great multitude, amongst which many women began to utter loud laments at the sad spectacle. Turning to these *daughters of Jerusalem* the exalted Sufferer with superhuman composure bade them *weep not for Him, but for themselves;* for nameless sorrows awaited them, days when they would *bless the wombs which had never borne*, and *the paps that had never given suck*, when they would *cry to the mountains to fall upon them, and to the hills to cover them*[4] (Lk. xxiii. 28—31).

On reaching the appointed place, the hole for the Cross was dug in the ground, and the customary stupefying potion[5] of wine mingled with myrrh was offered to the Holy One. He touched it with his lips (Mtt. xxvii. 34), but would not drink it, being resolved to pre-

[1] He was a Hellenistic Jew, the father of Alexander and Rufus (Mk. xv. 21), the latter of whom is probably the one mentioned in Rom. xvi. 13.

[2] Ἐρχόμενον ἀπ' ἀγροῦ, Lk. xxiii. 26; Mk. xv. 21.

[3] Ἀγγαρεύουσι, Mk. xv. 21, Mtt. xxvii. 32. It only occurs again in Mtt. v. 41, and denotes military compulsion. Comp. Herod. VIII. 98.

[4] For the fulfilment of these words, see Jos. *B. J.* VI. 8. 5; 9. 4.

[5] This was a Jewish not a Roman custom, though probably permitted by the Romans. See Lightfoot on Mtt. xxvii. 34. "It was likely that only a bad sort of wine (ὀξίνης a medium between οἶνος and ὄξος) would be given to those who were led away to capital punishment, especially if the wine was to be changed by the addition of bitter spices into a compound draught... And it was natural that the bitters infused as a soporific into this poor vinegar wine would be as strong as possible, whence such an ingredient might be called gall (Mtt. xxvii. 34)." Lange, IV. 383.

serve His senses clear, and to endure all the coming agony in the full possession of His consciousness. Then the soldiers stripped Him of His garments, nailed His hands and feet to the Cross[1], placed over His head the title[2] which Pilate had written in three languages, Hebrew, Greek, and Latin,

This is Jesus the Nazarene, the King of the Jews, and between the two malefactors, one on His right hand and the other on His left (Isai. liii. 12), the Redeemer hung suspended between heaven and earth, breathing forth even under the hands of His murderers words of infinite love, *Father, forgive them, for they know not what they do* (Lk. xxiii. 34).

It was now about the *third hour*[3] (Mk. xv. 25), and the quaternion or party of four soldiers[4] (Jn. xix. 23), with their centurion (Mtt. xxvii. 54), whose special duty

[1] There were four kinds of crosses: (i) the *crux simplex*, a single stake driven through the chest or longitudinally through the body; (ii) the *crux decussata* (X); (iii) the *crux immissa* (†); and (iv) the *crux commissa* (T). See the Notes on Pearson *On the Creed*, Art. IV. Article *Cross* in Smith's *Bibl. Dict.* From the mention of the Title placed over the Saviour's head it is probable that His cross was of the third kind. The upright post was by no means so lofty as is often represented in pictures, but generally only so high as to raise the sufferer (who sat on a little projection, *sedile*, lest the arms should be torn from the nails), a foot or two above the earth. The feet were not always, nor generally, though certainly not seldom nailed, but whether with one or two nails is disputed. The nailing of the Lord's feet is apparent from Lk. xxiv. 39, 40.

[2] See above, p. 309, note.

[3] "The difference between Jn. xix. 14 (ἕκτη) and this statement of St Mark seems clearly to point to a different mode of reckoning." Westcott's *Introduction to the Gospels*, p. 305, n.

[4] Four soldiers were required, according to the Roman appointment of military service, *ad excubias*. See Petr. *Sat.* III. 6.

it was to see that the bodies of those who suffered by crucifixion were not taken away, sat down and watched (Mtt. xxvii. 36). According to custom, the clothes of the Redeemer had become their perquisite. Of the outer garment they made four parts, probably loosening the seams[1]. But the inner garment[2] *was without seam, woven from the top throughout* (Jn. xix. 23 . That they might not rend this garment, therefore, they drew lots for it whose it should be, and thus unconsciously fulfilled the words of the Psalmist, *They parted My raiment among them, and for My vesture they did cast lots* (Ps. xxii. 18; Jn. xix. 24).

While, however, the soldiers were thus employed, and the high-priests were busy wrangling with Pilate respecting the title he had placed upon the Cross, a few faithful ones had ventured to draw near the suffering Redeemer. Near His Cross stood His mother, His mother's sister, Mary the wife of Clopas[3], and Mary Magdalene (Jn. xix. 25), and with them the Apostle John. Looking upon His mother, and seeing standing by her the disciple whom He loved, He said to her, *Woman, behold thy son*, and to the disciple, *Behold*

[1] Lange, IV. 390.

[2] Ὁ χιτὼν (Jn. xix. 23), was a closely-fitting garment, worn next the body (Hom. *Od.* xv. 60), usually made in two pieces, sewn together at the sides. "This, however, was the so-called *toga ocellata*, or *byssina*, and was fastened round the throat with a clasp. It was properly a priest's garment (Jos. *Ant.* III. 7. 4), and was woven of linen, or perhaps of wool." Alford *in loc.* Over the χιτὼν was worn a wide cloak called φᾶρος, χλαῖνα, or ἱμάτιον. The ἱμάτια the soldiers divided (Jn. xix. 23), with the rest of His habiliments; for the χίτων they cast lots.

[3] From a comparison of Jn. xix. 25 with Mtt. xxvii. 56, and Mk. xv. 40, it appears that Mary the wife of Clopas was the same as Mary the mother of James the Less and of Joses.

thy mother, and from that hour the Apostle *took her to his own home*[1] (Jn. xix. 27).

But soon others than these faithful ones drew near. The passers-by began to vent their mockery and bitter gibes upon The Redeemer. Some reminded Him in derision of His deep saying at the first Passover of His public ministry, and bade Him who could *destroy the Temple and build it in three days, save Himself* (Mtt. xxvii. 39, 40; Mk. xv. 29). Others, and especially the chief priests, bade Him if He was in truth the Son of God, the Messiah, and King of Israel (Mtt. xxvii. 42; Mk. xv. 32), *come down from the Cross.* The soldiers also took up their words, and drawing near offered Him in mockery their sour wine[2] (Lk. xxiii. 36), and required Him, if, as His title portended, He was the King of the Jews, to deliver Himself, and soon even the crucified malefactors followed their example, and cast the same in His teeth (Mtt. xxvii. 44; Mk. xv. 32).

But as the weary time wore on, the feelings of one of the two, won over by the heroic bearing of the Saviour and His infinite patience, underwent a striking change. He began to reprove the other for his revilings (Lk. xxiii. 40). They indeed were suffering justly, and *receiving the reward of their misdeeds,* but the Holy One in their midst *had done nothing amiss.* This avowal, made amidst all His present agony and degradation, was a great step, but soon it led to another. The more

[1] Probably for the present to his lodging during the feast. It seems likely that St John immediately led her away, and then returned and witnessed what he has recorded in Jn. xix. 31—37.

[2] The wine or strong drink turned sour, drunk by the Jews, was acid even to a proverb (comp. Prov. x. 26; Ps. lxix. 21). "The acetum of the Romans was a thin, sour wine consumed by soldiers, either in a pure state, or, more usually, mixed with water, when it was termed *posca.*" Smith's *Bibl. Dict.*

the penitent malefactor reflected on the sinlessness of Him who hung beside him, the more he contrasted it with his own shortcomings, the more the light streamed into his soul, and at length the eye of faith opening to discern the invisible, and the conviction dawning upon him that this was his Lord, the true King of the Jews, he turned and said, *Lord, remember me when Thou comest in Thy kingdom*, and received the comforting reply, *This day shalt thou be with Me in paradise* (Lk. xxii. 43).

But now the greatest and most mysterious period of the Passion drew near. Already nature herself had begun to evince her sympathy with the awful scene that was being enacted. At the sixth hour, the hour of noon, the clearness of day began to be obscured. A fearful darkness[1] gradually spread over the whole land (Mtt. xxvii. 45; Mk. xv. 33; Lk. xxiii. 44)[2], and deepened in intensity till nearly the ninth hour, the hour of the evening sacrifice. Meanwhile the Holy One began to be sensible of the burning thirst, which is the most painful aggravation of a death by crucifixion, and gave expression to it in words (Jn. xix. 28). Close at hand stood a vessel full of vinegar, and one of the soldiers took a sponge, and filling it with the fluid put it on a hyssop-reed, and raised it to His lips. At this moment the Redeemer gave utterance to the prophetic words of the xxiind Psalm, in which, in the bitterness of his heart, David had complained of the desertion of his God, and said, *Eloi, Eloi, lama sabachthani? My God, My God, why hast Thou forsaken me?* (Mk. xv. 34).

On hearing this exclamation, some of those standing

[1] Not proceeding from an eclipse of the sun, for such a phenomenon could not occur at the time of the full moon, but probably due to some special and peculiar derangement of the terrestrial atmosphere.

[2] Lange, IV. 404; Milman, I. 335.

near, either misapprehending His words, or in wilful mockery, declared that He called not on Eli, God, but on Elias, whose appearance was universally expected as the sign of the Messiah's kingdom. They would, therefore, have waited to see whether the great prophet would really come (Mk. xv. 36), and would have arrested the compassionate hand that was raising the vinegar. But the moment of release was near. As soon as He had tasted the vinegar (Jn. xix. 30), the dying Redeemer cried with a loud voice, *It is finished; Father, into Thy hands I commend My spirit, and gave up the ghost.*

These last words had hardly been uttered before a wondrous event took place in the Temple. The veil, the beautiful veil, inwrought with figures of Cherubim, which separated the Holy Place from the Most Holy, was suddenly *rent in twain from the top to the bottom*[1] (Mtt. xxvii. 51; Mk. xv. 38; Lk. xxiii. 45), and at the same moment the earth trembled with the convulsion of an earthquake, and the rocks were rent, laying open many of the sepulchres with which they were perforated on all sides of the city[2] (Mtt. xxvii. 52).

These marvellous incidents made a deep impression, not only on the centurion and his soldiers who had been stationed to watch the cross, but on the multitudes who had been spectators of all that had occurred, and the women and kinsmen of the Holy Sufferer who *stood*

[1] For the full symbolism of this, see Heb. ix. 3; x. 19. In reference to the record of the fact itself, we must remember, (i) the almost certain spread of the rumour, and (ii) that subsequently a great number *of the priests became obedient unto the faith* (Acts vi. 7). Alford *in loc.*

[2] The resurrection of many *bodies of the saints that slept* (Mtt. xxvii. 52) was *the result*, not *the immediate accompaniment*, of the opening of the tombs (Alford *in loc.*). It was μετὰ τὴν ἔγερσιν αὐτοῦ that they appeared unto many in the Holy City.

gazing afar off (Mtt. xxvii. 55; Mk. xv. 40). The people beating their breasts in deep but unavailing sorrow (Lk. xxiii. 48) began to pour back with fearful forebodings into the city, while the Roman officer, who though he had often looked upon death and its victims in various forms, had never witnessed such a death as this[1], under the influence of deep emotion testified that He, who had been condemned as a blasphemer, was indeed a *righteous man* (Lk. xxiii. 47), nay more, that He was in truth the *Son of God*[2] (Mtt. xxvii. 54; Mk. xv. 39).

CHAPTER IX

THE BURIAL AND RESURRECTION.

A. D. 30.

THE day was now far advanced. Unconscious that the true Paschal Lamb, the antitype of all previous sacrifices, had offered up Himself upon the altar of His Cross for the sins of the whole world, numerous bands of householders were gathering towards the Temple to slay their victims and make ready for the Feast[3]. The morrow *being a high day*, at once the Sabbath and the solemn fifteenth of Nisan[4] (Jn. xix. 31), the Jewish rulers would be more than usually anxious that the bodies of the Saviour and the two malefactors should not remain upon the cross, profaning the sanctity of their great national festival, and violating one of the strict injunctions of their law[5].

[1] Lange, IV. 422.

[2] "Thus this believing heathen became the first representative of the heathen world, which in after times bowed the knee before the might of Christ's Cross." Lange, IV. 423.

[3] Ellicott, p. 360.

[4] Comp. Ex. xii. 16; Lev. xxiii. 7.

[5] Comp. Deut. xxi. 22, 23; Jos. *B. J.* IV. 5. 2.

It was not indeed the Roman custom to remove the crucified from the cross. Instead of shortening their agonies the Roman law had left them to die by a lingering[1] death, and suffered their bodies to moulder under the action of the sun and rain[2], or to be devoured by wild beasts[3]. The more merciful Jewish custom, however, did not allow such barbarities, and their Roman masters had made an express exception in their favour. The Jewish rulers therefore repaired to Pilate, and requested that the legs[4] of those on Golgotha might be broken and their bodies removed (Jn. xix. 31). The Procurator gave his consent, and the soldiers entrusted with the task repaired thither, and broke the legs of one malefactor and then of the other. When however, they came to the Body of Jesus, they found that He was dead already (Jn. xix. 33). Unconsciously fulfilling, therefore, the typical language of Scripture respecting the Paschal Lamb, which declared that *not a bone of it should be broken* (Ex. xii. 46; Ps. xxxiv. 20), and a

[1] Death after crucifixion did not generally supervene even for three days, and "was at last the result of gradual benumbing and starvation." Sometimes the crucified were despatched by a fire kindled below them, or by lions or bears sent to devour them. Lange, V. 2, n.

[2] Comp. Cic. *Tusc. Q.* I. 43: *Theodori nihil interest, humine, an sublime putrescat.* Pearson *On the Creed,* Art. IV. note.

[3] See Pearson *On the Creed,* Art. IV., who quotes Hor. *Epist.* XVI. 48: *Non hominem occidi: non pasces in cruce corvos;* Juvenal, *Sat.* XIV. 77: *Vultur, jumento et canibus crucibusque relictis, Ad fœtus properat, partemque cadaveris affert.* The very object of setting the guard was *cruces servare, ne quis ad sepulturam corpora detraheret,* Petron. III.

[4] "Sometimes fractures of the legs, *crucifragium* (Plaut. *Pœn.* IV. 2. 64) was especially adopted by the Jews to hasten death, and it was a mitigation of the punishment, as observed by Origen." Smith's *Bibl. Dict.* The *coup de grace* was, as a rule, combined with it. Lange, V. 2, n.; Neander's *Life of Christ,* 473, n.

prediction that men should look upon *Him whom they pierced* (Zech. xii. 10), they abstained from breaking His legs, but one of them, as if resolved to give a stroke of itself sufficient to cause death, thrust his spear[1] into His side, whence immediately there flowed forth Blood and Water, a wondrous incident, of which the Evangelist St John was himself a spectator (Jn. xix. 35).

Meanwhile, before the tidings of the Saviour's death could reach the ears of Pilate, Joseph of Arimathæa[2], a man of wealth (Mtt. xxvii. 57), a member of the Sanhedrin (Lk. xxiii. 50), and a secret disciple of Jesus (Jn. xix. 38), who had not consented to the cruel resolution of the rest to put Him to death (Lk. xxiii. 51), boldly went in to the Procurator, and requested that the Body of the Redeemer might be given up to him (Mk. xv. 43). Filled with astonishment that death had so speedily taken place, Pilate called in the centurion who had kept watch on Golgotha, and enquired whether this was really the case (Mk. xv. 44). Assured that it was so, he freely granted the request, and Joseph having purchased fine linen (Mk. xv. 46) repaired to Golgotha, to take down the Holy Body. Here he was joined by Nicodemus (Jn. xix. 39), who, probably informed of his successful petition to the procurator, had brought *a mixture of myrrh and aloes, about a hundred pound*[3]

[1] Λόγχη, Jn. xix. 34, the only place where it occurs in the New Testament. This was the ordinary Roman *hasta*, "a lighter weapon than the *pilum*, consisting of a long wooden shaft with an iron head, which was the width of a handbreadth and pointed at the end, and so was egg-shaped." Lange, v. 3, n.

[2] Probably the same as Ramah, the birthplace of the prophet Samuel (1 Sam. i. 19), called in the LXX. Armathaim ('Αρμαθαίμ), and by Josephus (*Ant.* v. 10. 2), Armathia.

[3] The Attic *Litra* of 12 ounces is here spoken of. Both the myrrh and aloes appear to have been pulverized and strewn in the folds of the linen in which the body was wrapped, Lange, v. 13; Pearson *On the Creed*, Art. IV. note.

weight (Jn. xix. 39). Together, then, they took down the Body, wrapped it in the linen clothes, sprinkled the myrrh and aloes amongst them, and conveyed the Holy One to a tomb which was close at hand. It was a new tomb, wherein no man had ever yet been laid (Lk. xxiii. 53), and had been hewn by Joseph himself out of a rock in a garden, which he possessed hard by Golgotha (Jn. xix. 41). Hither they bore the Body, and in the presence of Mary Magdalene, Mary the Mother of Joses, and other women who had followed the Saviour during His lifetime from Galilee (Mtt. xxvii. 61; Mk. xv. 47; Lk. xxiii. 55), laid it in the receptacle[1], and with the utmost despatch, *for the Sabbath was drawing on* (Lk. xxiii. 54), rolled a great stone to the entrance, and departed.

Thus He, who all His life long had been the poorest of the poor, made *His grave with the rich* (Is. liii. 9), and received the anointing of the great ones of the earth. But though the outward temple of His body had been *destroyed*, the Pharisees and chief-priests could not forget the mysterious saying of His that in *three days He would raise it up*, and probably were not altogether unaware of the more direct assertions He had made to His Apostles respecting the same subject[2]. These words now recurred to them with such alarming force that on the morning after the Crucifixion, though it was their great Paschal Sabbath, they met together, and repairing to the residence of Pilate, informed him of what *that Deceiver* had said, and requested that the sepulchre might be made secure till the third day, lest His disciples should come and steal

[1] The Jewish tombs had then probably, as these have now, steps and a descent in a perpendicular direction, or an entry in a sloping or horizontal position.

[2] Comp. Jn. ii. 19 with Mtt. xii. 40.

Him away, and give out that He had risen (Mtt. xxvii. 63, 64).

With the curtness of one, who felt himself fatigued and wearied out, the Procurator replied, *Ye have*, or rather, *Take*[1] *a watch, and make it secure as ye know how.* Accordingly with the guard thus deputed they went their way, sealed[2] the stone at the entrance of the sepulchre with their official seal in the presence of the soldiers, and then consigned to them the duty of watching the tomb of the Holy One.

Though both Joseph of Arimathæa and Nicodemus had assisted in embalming the Body of the Saviour, it had necessarily been done in haste, and the women who had witnessed the entombment resolved to complete it, and on the evening of the Crucifixion had prepared spices and ointments for that purpose (Lk. xxiii. 56). With these, then, early in the morning of the first day of the week, while it was yet dark (Jn. xx. 1), Mary Magdalene[3], Mary the Mother of James, and Salome (Mk. xvi. 1), set out for the sepulchre, their thoughts occupied on the way with the natural question *who would roll away the great stone*[4] they had seen fitted into its appointed place (Mk. xvi. 3).

[1] The only κουστωδία at the actual disposal of the Sanhedrin would be, as Bp. Ellicott remarks, the temple-guards, but the watchers were Roman soldiers; it seems more natural therefore to take ἔχετε as an imperative in Mtt. xxvii. 65, though λάβετε might have been rather expected. See Alford *in loc.*

[2] A string or cord was probably stretched across the stone and sealed at either end with sealing-clay. For the custom of using sealing-clay on tombs, see Smith's *Bibl. Dict.* Art. *Seal.*

[3] Or Mary of Magdala (now called *el-Mejdel*), a town near the lake of Tiberias. On the erroneousness of the idea of her character generally entertained, see Article in Smith's *Bibl. Dict.*

[4] They did not know of the sealing of the stone, and the

While they were thus musing, and, as it would seem, were as yet some distance from the sepulchre, the earth quaked beneath their feet with a mighty convulsion (Mtt. xxviii. 2), and an angel descended and rolled away the stone and sat upon it; his countenance was like lightning and his raiment white as snow, and before him the Roman sentinels fell prostrate for fear, *and became as dead men* (Mtt. xxviii. 3, 4).

Bewildered by the sudden earthquake, the women advanced nearer, and beheld the stone rolled away from the tomb (Mk. xvi. 4; Lk. xxiv. 2). Summoning courage two of them thereupon entered in (Lk. xxiv. 3), and became assured of the fact that the tomb was empty, that the Holy Body they had seen securely placed therein, was there no longer.

While, however, they were standing bewildered at this unexpected discovery, one of their number, Mary Magdalene, had already hurried back to Jerusalem. The sight of the stone rolled away had roused her worst apprehensions, and she could think of nothing but that the Body of her Lord had been taken away and the tomb violated. Resolved, therefore, to seek more effectual aid than such as weak women could afford, she ran with all speed to Simon Peter[1], and announced to him and the Apostle John, who was apparently with him, that the tomb was empty, and she and her companions[2] of the morning knew not whither the Body of their Lord had been conveyed (Jn. xx. 2). On receiving this startling intelligence the two apostles forthwith set out

setting of the watch, which took place on the eve of the Sabbath.

[1] It seems not impossible that St Peter, who must by this time have won back the respect of the rest by his deep repentance (Lange, v. 46), was in the same abode, to which the Apostle John had conveyed the mother of the Redeemer.

[2] Οὐκ οἴδαμεν, Jn. xx. 2, an incidental notice that she had not been the sole visitant of the tomb. Ellicott, 381.

towards the tomb (Jn. xx. 3), followed by Mary Magdalene herself (Jn. xx. 11).

Before, however, they reached the spot, the women who had remained behind, and who had ventured into the open sepulchre, had received other and still more startling tidings. As they were standing irresolute and bewildered by the sight of the empty tomb, there appeared to them *two* (Lk. xxiv. 4), or, as it seemed to others of their number, *one* of the heavenly host (Mk. xvi. 5) in mortal guise indeed but clad in glistering apparel, who announced to them, while ready to fall prostrate in alarm and terror, that their *Lord was risen:* there was no need for them *to seek the living amongst the dead* (Lk. xxiv. 5); He had told them that on the third day He should rise again (Lk. xxiv. 7), and thus His words were fulfilled; the spot, where they had seen Him laid, did not contain Him now (Mk. xvi. 6); let them, therefore, go to His Apostles, and announce the joyful tidings that their risen Lord was going before them into Galilee, and there they should see Him (Mtt. xxviii. 7).

Without losing a moment (Mtt. xxviii. 8), agitated at once by mingled fear and joy (Mk. xvi. 8), which sealed their lips to any whom they chanced to meet upon the road (Mk. xvi. 8)[1], the women hurried with all speed to the Apostles, and recounted their cheering tidings (Lk. xxiv. 9). But in their deep sorrow (Mk. xvi. 10) they regarded the words of the women as no better than an *idle tale* (Lk. xxiv. 11), and could not credit their announcement, on which the latter, saddened it may be by their refusal to believe, returned once more to the sepulchre.

Meanwhile the two Apostles, Peter and John, had

[1] Οὐδενὶ οὐδὲν εἶπον· ἐφοβοῦντο γάρ, and see Ellicott, 381, n.

been running thither with all speed, to ascertain the truth of what they had heard from Mary Magdalene. Outrunning his fellow Apostle, John first reached the tomb, and *stooping down saw*[1] *the linen clothes lying* there, but probably from feelings of awe entered not in. The characteristic energy of Peter overcame such feelings, and entering in he steadily contemplated the state of the sepulchre and the position of the grave-clothes; there lay the swathing-bands in one place (Jn. xx. 6); there was the napkin which had been about His head, not lying with the rest of the clothes, but folded up in another spot by itself. There was nothing to indicate disorder or confusion, or any violation of the tomb. Encouraged by the other's boldness, the Apostle John also now ventured to enter in, and surveyed the condition of the sepulchre, and though as yet neither of them understood the announcements of the resurrection contained in the Scripture (Jn. xx. 9), yet he could not resist the evidence of his senses[2]. The position of the grave-clothes precluded the idea that the Holy Body had been removed by enemies: he believed that his Lord had risen, and turned back towards Jerusalem[3] with his fellow Apostle, who marvelled at what had taken place (Lk. xxiv. 12).

But these signs did not carry conviction to the mind of Mary, who had followed them, but more slowly. Unable to tear herself away from the sepulchre, she stood

[1] Such appears to be the force of θεωρεῖ in Jn. xx. 6. "Ipsius animi intentionem denotat quâ quis intuetur quidquam." Tittman, *Synon. N. T.* cited by Ellicott, 283, n.

[2] Such appears to be the force of the word ἐπίστευσεν in Jn. xx. 8. See Lange, v. 46; Ellicott, 384, n.

[3] The ἀπῆλθον πάλιν πρὸς αὑτοὺς (Jn. xx. 10) appears, as Bp. Ellicott remarks, to denote that they returned to the places, or perhaps rather place, where they were abiding, to meditate on the amazing miracle (Lk. xxiv. 12).

outside weeping (Jn. xx. 11), and stooping down beheld two angels in white standing, the one at the head, the other at the feet, where the body of her Lord had lain, who said to her, *Woman, why weepest thou?* She replied, *They have taken away my Lord, and I know not where they have laid Him;* and turning away even from their sympathy, beheld One standing near, in whom she did not recognise her Lord, but who repeated the angels' question why she wept? Thinking it was the keeper of the garden, and that he could give her further information, she replied, *Sir, if thou hast borne Him hence, tell me where thou hast laid Him, and I will take him away* (Jn. xx. 15). She had hardly spoken, when the Stranger addressing her in well-known intonations, said, *Mary.* Instantly she knew who He was. Prostrating herself before Him, she called Him in the Hebrew dialect *Rabboni* (Jn. xx. 16), and apparently in her bewildered joy sought to clasp the feet of His risen Body. But this might not be. The relations between herself and the mighty Conqueror of death were changed. *Touch Me not*[1], said He, *for I am not yet ascended unto My Father: but go unto My brethren, and tell them, I am about to ascend to My Father, and your Father, to My God, and your God* (Jn. xx. 17). And Mary went, and thus she, out of whom the Lord had cast seven demons, became the first messenger of His resurrection to His disciples[2].

Soon, however, the other women, who had brought the first tidings to the Apostles, and who appear to

1 Or rather, "Do not continue to cling to Me." See Donaldson's *Gk. Gram.* 414. Ἅπτεσθαι denotes the retaining of an object for some time, with perhaps here a reference to clasping the knees as a suppliant or worshipper. The Risen Saviour had not entered into those relations in which He might truly thus be "touched."

2 Lange, v. 57.

have also returned towards the sepulchre, were met by their risen Lord (Mtt. xxviii. 9), who saluted them with the word *Hail*. Thereupon they drew near and worshipped Him, and, like Mary Magdalene, were bidden to announce to His brethren the joyous news that He was going before them into Galilee (Mtt. xxviii. 10).

As they departed to execute His commands, certain of the Roman sentinels entered into the city and recounted to the chief priests all that had occurred (Mtt. xxviii. 11). On the receipt of this startling intelligence, a meeting of the Sanhedrin was convened, and it was resolved that by some means the miraculous disappearance of the Body of the Redeemer must be concealed. Accordingly the soldiers were called in, and by dint of heavy bribes (Mtt. xxviii. 14) persuaded to give out, that, while they were sleeping at their posts, the disciples had come and stolen away the Body of their Master, and this story obtained a very general circulation amongst the Jews.

CHAPTER X

THE GREAT FORTY DAYS AND THE ASCENSION.

A.D. 30.

THUS the morning of the world's first Easter-day passed away, and the risen Saviour had revealed Himself to Mary Magdalene and the other ministering women.

Early in the same afternoon two[1] of the disciples, Cleopas[2] and another, whose name is not recorded, set

[1] Not of the Twelve, nor necessarily of the Seventy, but of the wider circle of the Redeemer's followers now assembled at Jerusalem. Lange on Lk. xxiv. 13.

[2] Cleopas = Κλεοπάτρος, altogether different from Κλωπᾶς, Jn. xix. 25. According to Eusebius he was a native of Em-

out from Jerusalem in the direction of the village of Emmaus[1] (Lk. xxiv. 13). As they went, they conversed earnestly about the events that had so lately occurred in the Holy City, and that with heavy hearts, for every hope was buried in their Master's grave. While they were thus engaged, He of whom they spake drew near, and accompanying them along the road began to enquire the meaning of their sorrowful looks, and of the earnest conversation they were holding with one another. Not recognising Him (Comp. Lk. xxiv. 16; Mk. xvi. 12), and surprised that even a stranger at Jerusalem could be ignorant of the event which filled their hearts, and had stirred their whole capital, they proceeded to give full vent to their disappointed hopes. Jesus of Nazareth, they said, had appeared amongst them, and had proved Himself a Prophet[2], mighty both in word and deed, before God and all the people; they had joined themselves to Him in the full belief that He was the long promised Redeemer of Israel, but their chief priests and rulers had condemned and crucified

maus. Nothing further is known of him, or who the other disciple was: some have conjectured Nathanael; others Simon; others Luke himself.

[1] There were two places of the name of Emmaus; (i) a town, afterwards called Nicopolis, 22 Roman miles from Jerusalem, where Judas Maccabæus defeated Gorgias, see above, p. 33; (ii) another is mentioned by Josephus, *B. J.* IV. 1. 3, before the city Tiberias, and interpreted the "warm baths." St Luke however states that this Emmaus was 60 stadia (A. V. *threescore furlongs*), = about 7½ miles from Jerusalem, and Josephus mentions a village at the same distance, *B. J.* VII. 6. 6. Robinson, because two uncial MSS. and a few cursives insert ἑκατον in Lk. xxiv. 13 and thus make the distance 160 stadia, identifies it with the Emmaus = Nicopolis. But the best critics do not accept this reading, and the site of Emmaus remains yet to be identified, though some would place it at *Kubeibeh*, about 3 miles west of the ancient Mizpeh, and 9 miles from Jerusalem.

[2] Comp. Mtt. xxi. 11, 46.

Him[1], and three days had now passed since His death: some women, indeed, of their company had gone to His tomb early that morning, and had returned with the mysterious tidings that His Body had disappeared, and that they had seen a vision of angels, who declared that He was alive, and on this certain disciples had repaired thither also and found that the Body indeed had disappeared, but they had not *seen* their risen Lord (Lk. xxiv. 19—24).

Such was the touching record of their deep disappointment. But to their surprise it evoked serious reproof instead of sympathy from their companion. *O foolish, and slow of heart to believe all that the Prophets have spoken*, said He: *ought not the Messiah to have suffered these things, and to have entered into His glory?* and then beginning from Moses and all the Prophets He expounded to them in all the Scriptures the things relating to the Messiah's work and person (Lk. xxiv. 26, 27).

Meanwhile the hours had sped quickly, and by the time He had finished speaking, the two disciples found themselves close to Emmaus (Lk. xxiv. 28). Their Companion appeared to be going further, but they could not bear the idea of parting with One, who had opened up such new fields of hope. *Abide with us*, said they earnestly; *the day is far spent, and it is towards evening;* nor did they cease till they had constrained Him to enter their abode (Lk. xxiv. 28, 29).

There they quickly prepared an evening meal, and their Companion, assuming the office of "Master of the House," took bread, and pronouncing probably the grace[2], with which the Jews commenced their meals,

[1] Ἀλλά γε καί, Lk. xxiv. 21 = *beside all this.*

[2] The Jewish rule was *three eating together were bound to give thanks.* The usual words were, *Blessed be Thou, O Lord*

proceeded to distribute it amongst them (Lk. xxiv. 30). But while so doing, the tone of His voice, or some well-known gesture, or, it may be, the marks of the nails in His hands, revealed to them who He was. Their eyes were opened and they recognised Him, and at the same moment *He vanished out of their sight* (Lk. xxiv. 31).

Certain now who it was that on the road had caused *their hearts to burn* within them, as He talked with them and opened up the Scriptures, they instantly hurried back, though it was dark, to Jerusalem, and ascended to the upper-room, where the Apostles and others were assembled with closed doors for fear of the Jews[1] (Lk. xxiv. 33; Jn. xx. 19). They thought they were the bearers of strange and welcome tidings. But their companions had equally joyous news for them. The Lord was risen indeed, and by a special appearance had revealed Himself to the repentant Simon[2] (Lk. xxiv. 34; comp. 1 Cor. xv. 5).

Then they told their tale, and suddenly, while they yet were speaking, and perhaps replying to the others'

our God, King of the Universe, who bringest forth fruit out of the earth.

[1] Is it not possible that on their way through the city they may have met and told some of the *οἱ λοιποί*, not Apostles, but general body of disciples, who refused to credit their intelligence, as related in Mk. xvi. 12?

[2] Of this appearance here incidentally mentioned, and more prominently by St Paul in 1 Cor. xv. 5, we know nothing: all that is certain is that it was after the return from the sepulchre (Lk. xxiv. 12, Jn. xx. 10), but whether (i) *before*, or (ii) *after* the appearance to the two disciples on the road to Emmaus cannot be determined. The effect, however, it produced was clearly very great on the disciples who had given little credence to the accounts of the women. See Ellicott, 398, n. It is observable that on this occasion "he is called by his original name Simon, not Peter; the higher designation was not restored until he had been publicly reinstituted, so to speak, by his Master." Smith's *Bibl. Dict.*, Art. *Peter*.

doubting questions[1], *the Lord stood in their midst* (Lk. xxiv. 36; Jn. xx. 19), and saluted them with the words, *Peace be unto you.* Terrified by so sudden an apparition, they imagined that they beheld a spectre or phantom, and shrunk back. But He calmed their fears. *Why are ye troubled*, He enquired, *and why do thoughts arise in your hearts? Behold My hands and My feet, for a spirit hath not flesh and bones as ye see Me have.* But though He shewed them His hands and His side (Jn. xx. 20), their joy still struggled with unbelief (Lk. xxiv. 41) and bewilderment, on which He enquired whether they had anything to eat, and when they gave Him a piece of a broiled fish and of an honeycomb, the remains probably of their evening meal, He took and ate in their presence (Lk. xxiv. 42, 43). Then with the reiterated salutation, *Peace be unto you* (Jn. xx. 21), He proceeded, *As the Father hath sent Me, even so send I you;* and with these words *He breathed on them* and said, *Receive ye the Holy Ghost: whosesoever sins ye remit, they are remitted; and whosesoever sins ye retain, they are retained* (Jn. xx. 23).

On the evening, however, of this first Easter-day, when the risen Saviour thus manifested Himself to the Apostles, and bestowed upon them the firstfruits[2] of the effusion of the Holy Spirit, one of their number,

1 Even if Mk. xvi. 12 refers to this, there is no real contradiction. The ten believed (i) that the Lord was really risen, and (ii) that He had appeared to Peter (Lk. xxiv. 34), but that One, who had gently rebuked the adoring touch of Mary Magdalene, should have accompanied them as a humble wayfarer to Emmaus, and sat down with them to their evening meal, may have appeared at first incredible: see a note in Ellicott, 400, n. "They would naturally be ignorant of the properties of His Risen Body, and its powers of sudden transition from place to place." Andrews, p. 516.

2 Lange, v. 83.

Thomas[1], was not present. Why he was not has been much debated. Some suppose it was owing to an accident. Others imagine that he had thrown away all hope, that he had concluded it was impossible that his crucified Lord could ever revive. Certain it is that he was not with the rest in their wonted place of meeting. When, therefore, he was informed by the others of the wondrous appearance in the upper-room, he utterly refused to believe it. *Unless*, said he, *I shall see in His hands the print of the nails, and put my finger into the print of the nails, and thrust my hand into His side, I will not believe* (Jn. xx. 25). Slow of faith, subject to despondency, ever ready to take the darker view of things, and to distrust extraordinary good news all the more because it was good, he could not accept the evidence of his fellow Apostles in so weighty a matter as the resurrection of his Lord, he must see and touch Him for himself[2].

Seven days passed away, and no recorded appearance of the risen Saviour was vouchsafed. On the eighth, the first day of the week, the Apostles were again assembled in the upper-room. On this occasion Thomas was not absent. Hope probably had revived, and he expected some removal of his doubts. While, then, the doors were shut as before from fear of the Jews, suddenly the familiar words, *Peace be unto you* (Jn. xx. 26), struck on the astonished ears of the assembled Eleven, and their risen Lord *stood in their midst.* Knowing all things, knowing therefore all the hesitation and doubt of His apostle, with infinite condescension He gave him the required sign. *Thomas*, said He, *reach*

[1] For indications of his character, see above, p. 249, n.

[2] "In the famous statue of him by Thorwaldsen in the Church at Copenhagen, the Apostle stands, thoughtful, meditative, with the rule in his hand for the due measuring of evidence and argument." Smith's *Bibl. Dict.*

hither thy finger, and see My hands, and reach hither thy hand, and thrust it into My side, and be not faithless but believing (Jn. xx. 27).

Whether the Apostle touched his Lord or not is not recorded. The impression is that he did not. But whichever was the case, certain it is that the effect upon him was instantaneous. All his doubts fled away like the morning mist. In the fulness of believing faith, he exclaimed, *My Lord and my God.* Because *thou hast seen Me*, replied the ever-merciful One, *thou hast believed: blessed are they that have not seen Me, and yet have believed* (Jn. xx. 29).

At some period after this last appearance, though when exactly we are not told, obedient to their Lord's repeated commands, the Apostles returned to the region of Galilee[1] and the familiar neighbourhood of the lake of Gennesaret. Here once more amidst old haunts, and quiet scenes of nature, some of them resumed, probably for the sake of their daily sustenance[2], their former occupations as fishermen; and on one occasion, seven of their number, Peter, Thomas, Nathanael Bar-Tolmai, James, John, and two others, whose names are not mentioned, entered into a boat at eventide and plied their craft[3] (Jn. xxi. 1—3). Hour after hour passed

[1] "The feast of the passover was completed on Thursday the 21st of Nisan. The disciples remained over the approaching Sabbath, on the 23rd of Nisan, and also the 24th, as the day which commemorated their Lord's resurrection. After this, there was nothing to prevent their leaving Jerusalem, and therefore they obeyed their Lord's command to go into Galilee." Wieseler, *Chronol. Synop.* p. 395.

[2] Trench *On the Miracles*, p. 453.

[3] Probably from Bethsaida, the fishing-town of Capernaum. Evening was the usual time then for commencing fishing, as it is now. "The fishermen here (lake of Gennesaret), as elsewhere, toil all night." Tristram's *Land of Israel*, p. 428.

away, and still they toiled but took nothing. Just, however, as the morning broke (Jn. xxi. 4), and the sun bursting forth began to reveal distinctly each cleft and broken cliff[1] down the rocky sides of the hills fringing the lake, a Voice was heard through the still morning air, saying, *Children, have ye any meat?* They answered, *No.* Thereupon the Voice spake again, *Cast the net on the right side of the boat, and ye shall find* (Jn. xxi. 6).

Ready after the ill success of the previous night "to take any suggestion by whomsoever offered," they did so, and straightway found themselves unable to drag the net in again by reason of the multitude of the fish they had enclosed. Awakened partly by the incident itself, partly perhaps by the Voice of the Stranger, to the recollection of a former and similar experience (Lk. v. 5)[2], the Apostle John felt sure He knew who was standing on the beach, and said to Simon Peter, *It is the Lord* (Jn. xxi. 7). Instantly the son of Jonas, eager, ardent, impetuous as of old, girding his fisher's coat[3] about him, flung himself into the lake, and by

[1] Stanley's *S. and P.*, p. 378. "It seems natural to think that the friendly voice, 'calling, after the manner of the East, *Children*' (Stanley, *S. and P.*, 374), and inquiring if they had any προσφάγιον, was conceived by the disciples to be that of one who wished to buy of them—ὡς μέλλων τι ὠνεῖσθαι παρ' αὐτῶν, Chrysost. *in loc.*" Ellicott, p. 405, n.

[2] See above, p. 178. For the contrast between the first and second miraculous draughts of fishes, see Trench, *Miracles*, 456—459.

[3] Τὸν ἐπενδύτην διεζώσατο, Jn. xxi. 7: "resuming the dress, which, like Eastern boatmen, he had thrown off whilst struggling with the net." Stanley, *S. and P.*, p. 378; compare however Tristram, p. 438, and see note in Trench, *Miracles*, p. 455. For the various nets and fish, see above, p. 195. "Each of the Apostles comes wonderfully out in his proper character: he of the eagle eye first detects the presence of the Beloved, and then Peter, the foremost ever in act, as John is profoundest in speculation, unable to wait till the ship should be brought to land, throws himself into the

swimming and wading reached the shore, followed by the rest in the boat dragging the net with the fish they had caught.

On landing they not only found themselves in the presence of their risen Lord, but perceived mysterious provision made for their wants after the wearying night. On the smooth margin of the lake[1] was a fire of charcoal[2], and fish laid thereon and bread, and the Redeemer bade them add to these some of the fish they had just brought to land. In obedience to this command Peter drew the net to shore, and brought of the fish, which numbered *a hundred and fifty and three* (Jn. xxi. 11), and then all sat down to the early morning meal as in former days, when dwelling with Him by the shore of that same lake. And now too, as at Emmaus, the risen Saviour as Master of the family took of the bread and fish, and distributed unto them, while they, filled with reverential awe, though certain that it was He, did not venture to question[3] Him with regard to the exact "state of His holy personality[4]."

sea that he may find himself the nearer at his Saviour's feet." Trench, p. 455.

[1] All round the lake (which is about 13 miles long, and in its broadest parts 6 miles wide) runs, "like a white line," "a level beach; at the southern end roughly strewn with the black and white stones peculiar to this district, and also connected with its volcanic structure; but the central or northern part formed of smooth sand, or of a texture of shells and pebbles so minute as to resemble sand, like the substance of the beach on the banks of 'Akaba." Stanley's *S. and P.*, 371.

[2] Ἀνθρακία only occurs elsewhere in Jn. xviii. 18, when St Peter *denied* his Lord.

[3] Ἐξετάσαι, Jn. xxi. 12, is more than *ask*. It denotes *studiose quærere* (Bretschneider), to *question*, to *prove*. The word only occurs in two other places in the New Testament, (i) Mtt. ii. 8, where Herod bids the Magi enquire accurately (ἀκριβῶς ἐξετάσατε) concerning the Child, and (ii) Mtt. x. 11, where accurate enquiry is also hinted at.

[4] Ellicott, *Lectures*, p. 407.

When the meal was over, turning to the Apostle Peter the risen Saviour enquired, *Simon, son of Jonas, lovest*[1] *thou Me more than these? Yea, Lord, Thou knowest that I love Thee*, replied the Apostle, but not as on the sad evening of the Betrayal, exalting himself on his own faithfulness above his fellow-disciples[2] (Jn. xxi. 15). *Feed My lambs*, responded his Lord. A second and yet a third time was the question repeated, till the Apostle touched probably by this reminder of his three denials, and flinging himself on the Omniscience of the Holy One made answer, *Lord, Thou knowest all things; Thou knowest that I love Thee.* Once more the command *Feed My sheep* was given, and thus the Apostle was restored to his old place in the circle of the Twelve (Jn. xxi. 16, 17).

But this was not all. The Apostle was to learn what great things he must suffer for the Master, who had thus reinstated him in his Apostolic office. *When thou wast young*, the Lord continued, *thou girdedst thyself, and walkedst whither thou wouldest: but when thou*

[1] (i) The Saviour enquires ἀγαπᾷς με; to which the Apostle replies, ...φιλῶ σε; (ii) He asks again ἀγαπᾷς με; and the Apostle answers, ...φιλῶ σε; (iii) He asks, φιλεῖς με; and the Apostle replies, σὺ γινώσκεις ὅτι φιλῶ σε. "Ἀγαπᾷν = *diligere* (= *deligere*) has more of judgment and deliberate choice; φιλεῖν = *amare*, has more of attachment and peculiar personal affection. Thus the ἀγαπᾷς on the lips of the Lord seems to Peter at this moment too cold a word; as though his Lord were keeping him at a distance; or at least not inviting him to draw as near as in the passionate yearning of his heart he desired now to do. Therefore he puts by the word and substitutes his own stronger φιλῶ in its room. A second time he does the same. And now he has conquered, for when the Lord demands a third time whether he loves Him, He does it with the word which alone will satisfy Peter, which alone claims from him that personal attachment and affection, with which indeed he knows that his heart is full." Trench, *Miracles*, p. 464, n.; *Synonyms*, I. 48.

[2] Comp. Mtt. xxvi. 33; Trench, *Miracles*, p. 463.

shalt be old, thou shalt stretch forth thy hands, and another shall gird thee, and carry thee whither thou wouldest not (Jn. xxi. 18). And with this intimation of the death that awaited the Apostle, of a day when he should be bound to the cross, and his hands be extended upon it[1], He added, *Follow Me, i. e.* even unto that martyr's death for His name which He had just foretold[2]. Apparently not understanding the meaning of the command, the Apostle interpreted it literally, and while advancing perceived the "loved disciple" also following, and filled with a desire to know what lot awaited him, enquired, *Lord, and what shall this man do?* (Jn. xxi. 21). But the question, whatever was its precise motive, was gently put by: *If I will that he tarry till I come*, replied the Saviour, *what is that to thee? Follow thou Me;* which intimation of long tarrying in store for St John, in contrast to the sharper discipline for which his fellow Apostle was destined, originated the mistaken idea that the "loved disciple" was to leave the world without undergoing the penalty of death (Jn. xxi. 23).

This was the third occasion on which the Saviour appeared to His Apostles after His resurrection, and it was probably now that He gave them specific directions respecting a manifestation to a still larger assembly, which was not long delayed. For apparently a short time after this last appearance, the Eleven repaired to a mountain[3] in Galilee which He Himself had indicated

[1] At Rome, and according to early writers, at or about the same time as St Paul, and in the Neronian persecution. According to Origen (see Euseb. III. 1) he was crucified with his head downwards. For the legend found in St Ambrose touching his death, see Article *Peter* in Smith's *Bibl. Dict.* and the notes.

[2] Ellicott, 408, n.

[3] Possibly Tabor, or the Mount of the Beatitudes, or of the Transfiguration. Lange, V. 109; Ellicott, 409, n.

(Mtt. xxviii. 16), and there He appeared not only to them but in all probability to the *five hundred brethren* of whom St Paul speaks[1] (1 Cor. xv. 6). Even now some *doubted* whether they were really beholding their Lord (Mtt. xxviii. 17), but the Eleven no sooner saw Him than they offered Him their reverent adoration (Mtt. xxviii. 17), which He accepted, and declared that now *all power was given Him in heaven and in earth*, and at the same time gave them His great commission;

Go ye into all the world, and make disciples of all nations, baptizing them into the Name of the Father and of the Son and of the Holy Ghost, teaching them to observe all things whatsoever I have told you, and lo! I am with you alway, even unto the end of the world (Mtt. xxviii. 19, 20; Comp. Mk. xvi. 15—18).

And now the great Forty Days (Acts i. 3) were rapidly drawing to a close[2]. Warned it may be by the Saviour Himself, or attracted by the near approach of

[1] See Wieseler, *Chronol. Synop.* p. 396; Lange, v. 108.

[2] During this period the risen Saviour had *manifested Himself from time to time* (ὀπτανόμενος, Acts i. 3) to certain chosen witnesses, and these appearances according to the order followed in the text were (1) to Mary Magdalene; (2) to the other ministering women; (3) to the two disciples journeying to Emmaus; (4) to St Peter; (5) to the ten Apostles; (6) to the eleven Apostles; (7) to seven Apostles by the lake of Tiberias; (8) to the eleven Apostles, and probably the 500 brethren (1 Cor. xv. 6), on the appointed mountain; (9) to James (1 Cor. xv. 7); (10) to the Apostles in or near Jerusalem just before the Ascension. See Wieseler, *Chronol. Synopsis;* Tischendorf's *Synopsis Evangelica;* Ellicott's *Lectures*, p. 414, n. "Thus," in the words of Paley, "it was not one person but many who saw Him; they saw Him not only separately but together; not by night only but by day; not at a distance but near; not once but several times; they not only saw Him but touched Him, conversed with Him, ate with Him, examined His person to satisfy their doubts." See also Pearson *On the Creed*, Article v.

the festival of Pentecost[1], the Apostles and their companions left Galilee and returned to Jerusalem. There once more amidst the scene of His late sufferings they saw their risen Lord, and for the last time received from His own Divine lips instruction in the things concerning the kingdom of God, and learned to trace in the prophetic Scriptures, in the Law, and in the Psalms, intimations of the sufferings and resurrection of the Messiah (Lk. xxiv. 44—48). There too they received His last command to remain in Jerusalem (Acts i. 4) till the promise of the Eternal Father should receive its accomplishment, and they should be *baptized with the Holy Ghost*, and *endued with power from on high* (Acts i. 5; Lk. xxiv. 49).

At last one day He bade them accompany Him along the road towards Bethany and the Mount of Olives (Lk. xxiv. 50), associated with so many memories of the risen Lazarus, of the Triumphal Entry, and the last sad days in His earthly life.

Convinced that something mysterious was about to happen, and with their carnal hopes still set on the idea that He was about to commence His long-looked for reign, they began to enquire, *Lord, wilt Thou at this time restore the kingdom to Israel* (Acts i. 6)? But their enquiries were solemnly silenced. It was not for them to know *the times or the seasons, which the Father had put in His own power*. A time was at hand when, on the descent of the Holy Spirit, they should receive power, and become witnesses to their Lord in *Jerusalem, and all Judæa, in Samaria, and unto the uttermost parts of the earth* (Acts i. 8).

Thus conversing they followed Him even to the borders of the district of Bethany, to one of the secluded

[1] Ellicott, p. 411. For the Festival, see *Class-Book of Old Testament History*, p. 152.

hills which overhang the village of Bethany on the Eastern slope of Olivet[1]. There they received His last solemn and abiding blessing (Lk. xxiv. 50), and while His hands, bearing the marks of the wounds which man had inflicted, were yet uplifted in benediction (Lk. xxiv. 51), He *began to be parted from them*, and *there came a cloud* (Acts i. 9), in which slowly and gradually He rose from Olivet, till at length He was lost to sight, and ascended up to that highest heaven, where He was in the glory of the Father before the world was.

Long time stood the Eleven looking wistfully upwards, and watching Him as He receded more and more from view (Acts i. 10). At length two angelic beings clad in white apparel addressed them, saying, *Ye men of Galilee, why stand ye gazing up into heaven? This same Jesus, who hath been taken from you into heaven, shall so come in like manner as ye have seen Him go into heaven* (Acts i. 11).

And then all was over. With hearts subdued and solemnized the Apostles returned to the Upper Room at Jerusalem, and *there continued with one accord in prayer and supplication, with the women, and Mary*[2] *the mother of Jesus, and with His brethren* (Acts i. 14).

[1] "A more secluded spot could scarcely have been found so near the stir of a mighty city: the long ridge of Olivet screens the hills, and the hills themselves screen the village beneath from all sound or sight of the city behind." Stanley, *S. and P.*, p. 454. "Not altogether into Bethany, but so far as the point where Bethany came into sight," Stier.

[2] The last occasion on which she is mentioned in the New Testament. From the commencement of the Saviour's ministry she is withdrawn almost altogether from sight. Four times only is the veil removed, (i) at the marriage at Cana (Jn. ii.); (ii) the attempt which she and His brethren made *to speak with Him* (Mtt. xii. 46; Mk. iii. 31; Lk. viii. 19); (iii) the Crucifixion; (iv) the present occasion.

BOOK III

THE APOSTOLIC HISTORY.

PART I

THE CHURCH OF JERUSALEM.

CHAPTER I

THE ELECTION OF MATTHIAS—THE PENTECOSTAL EFFUSION.

A. D. 30.

IN accordance with the command of their lately ascended Lord, the Apostles remained in the Holy City, and there *continued with one accord in prayer and supplication* (Acts i. 14) with the rest of the little company. This now amounted in all to about 120 (Acts i. 15), and consisted of

1. The Eleven,
2. The Virgin, the women, who had accompanied the Saviour from Galilee to Jerusalem, Mary Magdalene, Mary the mother of James, Salome, Joanna, Susanna, and others,
3. The *brethren*[1] of the Lord, who though at an early period they were not for but against Him (Jn. vii. 5), now undoubtedly believed on Him,
4. The other disciples.

[1] See note above, pp. 228, n., 229.

Though the duty enjoined upon them at this time, was that of patient waiting for the bestowal of the promised gift of the Holy Ghost, one thing could be done by way of preparation for the work they were called to perform. They could restore their original number as it was composed by their Lord, and fill up the gap which the treachery of Judas had made in their body.

Accordingly, the Apostle Peter, already beginning to take that lead for which his natural gifts no less than the prophetic words of the Saviour had destined him, stood up in their midst, and called attention to the deserted seat of the traitor. He had fallen, as they all knew, and after a terrible end[1] had gone *to his own place* (Acts i. 25). The language of inspired prophecy had not been silent respecting his shameful treachery, but the same Psalms (Ps. lxix. 25; cix. 8), which had foreshadowed his fall, had spoken also of the election of another to take his charge or office of oversight (Acts i. 20). He advised, therefore, that they should proceed to choose a new Apostle, and suggested, as the conditions of his election, that he should be one who had companied with them from the beginning to the close of their Lord's official ministry, from the Baptism of John to the Ascension, and so be qualified in an especial degree to be a witness of His Resurrection (Acts i. 22).

His suggestion found favour with the assembled body of the brethren, and they nominated two of their number, who eminently possessed their confidence, as also the special qualifications thus laid down. One was Joseph Bar-Sabas, surnamed Justus, and Matthias, of whom, however, nothing further is known in the New Testament[2]. These they put forward, and leaving to

[1] See above, p. 297, and note.

[2] According to Eusebius, *H. E.* I. 12, he, as also Joseph Bar-Sabas, was one of the Seventy, and is said to have preached and suffered martyrdom in Ethiopia.

the Lord the final determination, they prayed that, as the Searcher of hearts, He would indicate whom He had selected for the office, and then *gave forth their lots*[1], *and the lot fell upon Matthias and he was numbered* with the Eleven Apostles (Acts i. 26).

Thus quietly and without observation was the first seed sown of what was destined to grow into a *great tree*[2] (Mtt. xiii. 31—33). Never did it seem more unlikely that the religion of the crucified Redeemer could be revived. The City had been restored to peace, as though nothing extraordinary had taken place. The Roman guard had been bribed to contradict any rumour that might be bruited about of the Resurrection; in the popular estimation the death of Jesus had extinguished all ideas that He was the Messiah; and no leader of any weight appeared likely to rally the little band of His once attached followers[3]. The triumph of the Sanhedrin appeared complete.

But this was the very hour when the new Faith was to achieve its first conquest. Ten days passed away after the Ascension. The Fiftieth, the day of Pentecost[4], the

[1] The use of lots occurs frequently in the Old Testament; compare, among others, that at (i) the division of the land of Canaan (Num. xxxiv. 13), (ii) at the detection of Achan (Josh. vii. 14, 18), (iii) the Election of Saul (1 Sam. x. 20, 21); (iv) over the two goats at the feast of the Atonement (Lev. xvi. 8); (v) the distribution of the priestly offices of the temple-service (1 Ch. xxiv. 3, 5, 19, and comp. Lk. i. 9, above, p. 128). "Tablets, on which the names of Joseph and Matthias were written, were probably placed in a vessel, and that lot which, on the shaking of the vessel, first fell out, gave the decision." Lechler.

[2] See above, p. 195, and note.

[3] Milman, *History of Christianity*, I. 352.

[4] Ἐν τῷ συμπληροῦσθαι τὴν ἡμέραν = "was now fully come, or rather, perhaps, *was on the point*, or *in the act, of being* fulfilled; just dawning, we may suppose, for the day to run its course;" Vaughan *on the Acts*, I. p. 42.

Feast of Weeks, was come[1]. The Holy City, crowded with strangers from every quarter of the then known world, presented a scene of unusual animation. There was scarcely a region but had its representative in its streets. Not only from Palestine[2] itself, but from the lands beyond the Euphrates, whither the Israelites had been carried by the Assyrian and Babylonian captivities[3], Parthia and Media, Elam[4] and Mesopotamia[5]; from the various districts of Asia Minor, Cappadocia and Pontus[6], Phrygia and Pamphylia, as well as those fringing the Western coast-line, Mysia, Lydia, and Caria, and now comprehended under one name, *Roman Asia*[7]; from

[1] See *Class-Book of O. T. History*, p. 152. This festival lasted one day, and was distinguished by the offering of two leavened loaves, made from the new corn of the now completed harvest. That it was likewise a memorial of the giving of the Law from Sinai, is a supposition which rests only on later Jewish traditions. Neander's *Planting*, I. 5, E. V.

[2] The Catalogue (Acts ii. 9—11) proceeds from the North East to the West and South.

[3] On the colonies of Jews in Babylonia, see above pp. 7, 107.

[4] In pure Greek the inhabitants were called Ἐλυμαῖοι, from Elam or Elymais, a Semitic people, see Gen. x. 22. "Elam is mentioned in connection with Babylon (Gen. xiv. 1); with Media (Isai. xxi. 2; Jer. xxv. 25); with Assyria (Ezek. xxxii. 24), as a province of Persia (Ez. iv. 9)." Josephus (*Ant.* I. 6. 4) makes the Elymæans the progenitors of the Persians.

[5] A name apparently not older than the Macedonian conquests for the Hebrew *Aram-Naharaim*, or Syria of the two rivers, Tigris and Euphrates, of which we first hear in Gen. xxiv. 10.

[6] The former kingdom of Mithridates, situated along the southern coast of the Euxine, now divided into petty principalities, subject to Roman protection, but under Nero made a Roman province. It is mentioned again in Acts xviii. 2; 1 Pet. i. 1.

[7] Τὴν Ἀσίαν, Acts ii. 9. This expression, which frequently occurs in the New Testament, denotes the *Roman province of Asia*, which embraced the western part of the peninsula of Asia Minor, and had Ephesus for its capital. It included

the islands of the Mediterranean[1]; from populous Alexandria and the flourishing region of Cyrene[2]; from the capital of the West itself, Jews and Hellenists, "proselytes of righteousness[3]" and "proselytes of the gate," had flocked to take part in the great Festival (Acts ii. 9—11).

All gathered together in one place, the disciples were awaiting any indications of the Divine will, when suddenly there arose out of heaven a sound as of a *rushing mighty wind*, which filled the whole house where they were sitting (Acts ii. 2), and simultaneously tongues as if of fire[4] distributed[5] themselves amongst and settled upon each one of them (Acts ii. 3). The Strengthener, the Comforter, had come, the disciples were all filled with the Holy Ghost, and though poor, illiterate, and obscure men of Galilee, found themselves by the operation of the indwelling Spirit able to speak not only in their own rough unpolished language, but in as many dialects as were represented that day at Jerusalem[6] (Acts ii. 4).

the territory anciently subdivided into Æolis, Ionia, and Doris, and afterwards into Lydia, Mysia, and Caria. Originally bequeathed to the Romans by Attalus, king of Pergamus, (Hor. *Od.* I. 1. 12; II. 18. 5), or king of Asia, (see 1 Macc. xi. 13), B. C. 133, it was, after some rectifications of the frontier, constituted a province, and placed by Augustus amongst those subject to the senate, and therefore governed by a procurator. Comp. Acts xix. 38, and see above, p. 147, n. Within its boundaries were the seven Churches of the Apocalypse; see Con. and Howson, *Life and Ep. of St Paul*, chap. xiv.; Spruner's *Atlas Antiquus*, Ed. 3.

1 On the Islands of the Mediterranean in connection with the dispersion of the Jews, see above, p. 108.

2 For notices of Jews in Egypt and Cyrene see above, pp. 8, 107.

3 On the proselytes, see above, p. 118, n.

4 They were not πυρός but ὡσεὶ πυρός, not burning but luminous, in appearance like fire: see Lechler *in loc.*

5 Διαμεριζόμεναι, in our version rendered *cloven*, but rather = *distributed or parting themselves among them.*

6 See Neander's *Planting*, I. 12—15.

Meanwhile the noise[1], with which the mighty rushing wind had descended from heaven, had been audible all over the city, and attracted a great multitude to the abode of the disciples. Arriving there they were confounded to find natives of the despised region of Galilee speaking *of the wonderful works of God*, not only in the language, but the very dialect of the language, which each recognized as his own (Acts ii. 6). In the minds of most this strange portent excited emotions of serious awe. *What meaneth this?* they exclaimed; *are not all these which speak Galilæans?* There were not wanting, however, some who ascribed the strange sounds they heard to the effects of drunken excess; *these men*, said they, *are full of new wine* (Acts ii. 13).

Thereupon the Apostle Peter stood up with the Eleven, and having in a loud voice indignantly refuted the charge of drunkenness by a reference to the hour of the day, the third only from sunrise[2] (Acts ii. 15), proceeded to explain the meaning of what they heard and saw.

"Eight hundred and fifty years before, as they knew from the Scriptures of the Old Testament, the prophet Joel (ii. 28, 29) had foretold the coming of days, when God would pour out of His Spirit on all flesh, not on one or two only, but upon His people generally without distinction of age or rank or sex, upon *sons and daughters*, upon *young men and old*, upon *servants and handmaidens* (Acts ii. 17, 18). Thus had the prophet spoken, and this day they beheld the fulfilment of his words. Jesus of Nazareth, a Man approved[3] amongst them

[1] Τῆς φωνῆς ταύτης, Acts ii. 6, not this rumour, but the noise of the rushing mighty wind: Vaughan and Alford *in loc.* Neander's *Planting*, I. 17.

[2] The first hour of prayer = 9 A.M., before which, especially on a feast-day, no Israelite ventured to taste anything. Lightfoot *in loc.*

[3] Ἀποδεδειγμένον, demonstratum, attested and demon-

by miracles[1], and wonders, and signs, which God had wrought by Him in their midst, as they themselves knew full well, they had taken and by the wicked hands of Roman soldiers had crucified and slain. But in so doing they had not frustrated the gracious purposes of Him who had sent Him. All things had happened according to His *determinate counsel and foreknowledge* (Acts ii. 23), and He had raised up that same Jesus, and had loosed the pangs of death, because it was not possible that He could be permanently mastered by them. For He, of whom the Psalmist had said that God would not leave His soul in Hades[2] nor suffer Him to see corruption, could not be the patriarch David. He had died and been buried, and his ashes had long reposed in the tomb which was before their eyes. It was not of *himself* that he had thus spoken, but of Another, the fruit

strated, *shewn* to be that which He claimed to be. See Alford *in loc.*

[1] Four names for what we commonly call "a miracle" occur in the New Testament, (1) Τέρας, *a wonder* (never used alone, but always with one of the other names), the effect of astonishment which the work produces upon the beholder being transferred to the work itself; (2) Σημεῖον, or *sign* (an especial favourite with St John), a token and indication of the near presence and working of God, the seals and credentials of a higher power; comp. Exod. vii. 9, 10; (3) Δύναμις, *a power*, or *mighty work*, that is, of God; as in the term *wonder*, the effect is transferred and gives a name to the cause, so here the cause gives its name to the effect; (4) Ἔργα, *works*, a significant term often used by St John, the *works* of Him whose name is Wonderful (Isai. ix. 6), and who therefore does works of wonder (comp. Jn. v. 36; vii. 21; x. 25, 32, 38, &c.). Trench *on the Miracles*, pp. 2—8; *Synonyms of the N. T.*, Pt. II. 177—181.

[2] Εἰς ᾅδου in Hades = the abode of departed spirits, translated in our Version "hell," which from *hælen* to cover, denotes, like the Hebrew *Sheol*, literally "the covered place," the place of departed spirits. On the word Gehenna, the place of torment, ἡ ἄβυσσος, the bottomless pit, see above, p. 198.

of his loins, whom as a prophet he foreknew God would raise up to sit upon his throne; and this King was no other than Jesus (Acts ii. 32). Him God had raised from the dead, and exalted to the right hand of power, and made both Lord and Christ, and He had that day bestowed upon His disciples those wonderful gifts which they saw and heard, the expressions and indications of the presence of the Spirit promised by the Father."

Such was the substance of the Apostle's words, and though they clashed with the strongest prejudices of those who had so short a time before given such fearful evidence of their hatred of that crucified Saviour, they produced a deep impression. Pricked to the heart they addressed him and the rest of the Eleven, saying, *Men and brethren, what shall we do? Repent*[1], was the reply, *and be baptized every one of you in the name of Jesus Christ for the remission of sins, and ye shall receive the gift of the Holy Ghost* (Acts ii. 38); *for the promise is unto you, and to your children, and to all that are afar off*[2], *even as many as the Lord their God shall call.* These and many other similar words of his were not lost; many received them gladly, and were baptized, and the same day there *were added to the Church about three thousand souls*[3] (Acts ii. 41).

[1] Μετανοήσατε, not μετανοεῖτε, as in Mtt. iii. 2, iv. 17. The aorist denotes a definite, sudden act: the present, a habit, more gradual; "The word imports *change of mind*, here a change from thinking Jesus an impostor, and scorning Him as one crucified, to being baptized in His Name, and looking to Him for the remission of sins, and the gift of the Spirit." Alford *in loc.*

[2] Πᾶσι τοῖς εἰς μακρὰν = the Gentiles (comp. Eph. ii. 13), whose conversion the Apostles expected, like all other pious Jews, but not *as Gentiles*, which was not yet revealed to them.

[3] Thus the Apostle, the former fisherman of the lake, now the fisher of men, launched forth, and cast his net into the deep, amongst the multitudes of Jerusalem, and enclosed many of every kind; see above, p. 178.

CHAPTER II

ACTIVITY OF THE APOSTLES PETER AND JOHN.

A. D. 30.

THUS at the Feast which celebrated the ingathering of the natural harvest, a rich harvest of souls was for the first time gathered into the Christian garner, the Church assumed its separate and organised existence, and its members gave themselves up to the full requirements of their new life:

1. *They continued*[1] *steadfastly*, or waited constantly *upon the Apostles' doctrine* (Comp. Mtt. xxviii. 20), by whose hands many wonders and signs were wrought (Acts ii. 43), and who were enlightened to remember and commissioned to teach all that their Lord had said and commanded (Jn. xv. 26; xvi. 13).

2. *They persevered in fellowship and communion with one another*[2], cultivating and fostering a spirit of mutual love, and instead of living each for themselves, *had all things common*, selling their possessions and lands, and parting them to all men, *as every man had need* (Acts ii. 42—45).

3. *They attended constantly on the breaking of the Bread*[3], and thus consecrated their chief daily meal

[1] Ἦσαν προσκαρτεροῦντες τῇ διδαχῇ τῶν ἀποστόλων, Acts ii. 42. Made disciples when they had been baptized into Christ; detailed instruction, and gradual increase in knowledge and holiness must now follow.

[2] Τῇ κοινωνίᾳ, ver. 42, explained by the εἶχον ἅπαντα κοινά of ver. 44.

[3] Τῇ κλάσει του ἄρτου, Acts ii. 42, where the force of the article is observable. "The Eucharist was at first, and for some time, till abuses put an end to the practice, inseparably connected with the ἀγάπαι or Love-Feasts of the Christians, and unknown as a separate ordinance;" Alford *in loc.* "We can scarcely doubt that this implies that the chief actual meal of each day was one at which they met as brothers,

with the celebration of that Feast, which shewed forth (1 Cor. xi. 26) their Lord's death, and the sacrifice He had offered.

4. *They were stedfast* also in their attendance at the public prayers[1] in the Temple, at the stated hours of the national worship (Acts ii. 42, 46), *praising God, and having favour with all the people.*

And in the Temple occurred the next eventful incident in the history of the early Church. Two of the Apostles, Peter and John, were going up thither at the ninth hour[2], the hour of prayer and the offering of the evening sacrifice. At the entrance they encountered a man lame from his birth, who was in the habit of being laid day by day at the Gate known as the "Beautiful Gate[3]," for the purpose of exciting the compassion and appealing to the charity of the passing worshippers. On the present occasion he appealed to the two Apostles, and supplicated their aid. Thus accosted they stopped, and fixing upon him an earnest gaze, bade him *look on them* (Acts iii. 4). Expecting perhaps some charitable offering, he did so[4], when Peter addressing him said, *Silver and gold have I none, but what I have give I thee: In the name of Jesus Christ of Nazareth rise up and walk* (Acts iii. 6, 7), and with the words took him by the right hand and lifted him up, and he, who had been

and which was either preceded or followed by the more solemn commemorative acts of the breaking of the Bread and the drinking of the Cup." Smith's *Bibl. Dict.* Art. *Lord's Supper:* see also Neander's *Planting*, I. 23.

[1] Ταῖς προσευχαῖς, *the* prayers, not of course excluding private prayer among themselves. See Vaughan's *Church of the First Days*, p. 88.

[2] Or 3 in the afternoon. See above, p. 112. Note the imperfect ἀνέβαινον = *were going up*, in Acts iii. 1.

[3] See above, p. 96.

[4] He fixed his attention on them, ἐπεῖχεν (τὸν νοῦν) αὐτοῖς, Acts iii. 5.

lame from his birth, found strength suddenly restored to his crippled feet[1] and ankles, found himself able to spring up, stand, and walk, found himself able to accompany the Apostles into the Temple, and there give thanks to God (Acts iii. 8).

The cure of such a man in such a manner was quickly noised abroad amongst the worshippers crowding the Temple-courts. Filled with wonder and amazement the people ran together with one accord into the porch or colonnade of Solomon[2], and there beheld the two Apostles, and clinging[3] to them in the first transport of grateful attachment, the very man they had so long and so often seen sitting for alms at the Beautiful Gate (Acts iii. 11). It was a meet occasion for addressing the astonished throng, and Peter commenced one of those heart-stirring discourses, whereby in these early days, as his Lord had predicted, he *strengthened his brethren* (Lk. xxii. 32).

"*Why marvel ye*, said he, *at this?* Why look ye so earnestly on us, as though by magical power or holiness of our own we have caused that this man should walk? The God of your fathers, the God of Abraham, Isaac, and Jacob, whom for years ye have owned and worshipped, He and no other has been working by us. Though ye delivered up, and denied in the presence of Pilate His Servant[4] Jesus, and demanded that, in place of the Holy One and the Just, a murderer, Barabbas, should be granted unto you; though ye killed the Prince of life, yet God hath raised Him from the dead, and our faith in His Name hath restored this cripple, as your eyes behold (Acts iii. 16).

[1] Βάσεις = the *soles* of his feet; σφυρὰ = *the ankles.*

[2] See above, p. 244, n.

[3] Κρατοῦντος = *holding fast*, Acts iii. 11.

[4] Τὸν παῖδα αὐτοῦ Ἰησοῦν. Not *Son*, for which υἱός is always used, but *Servant* of God, as the word is used in Isa. xlii. 1; xlix. 3; Zech. iii. 8.

"In ignorance, indeed, ye and your rulers did this. But in so doing ye fulfilled a mysterious purpose of Divine Love, even the counsels of that God, who predicted by the mouth of all His prophets that Christ should suffer. Repent ye, therefore, and be converted, that your sins may be blotted out, and that so[1] seasons of refreshing may come from the presence of the Lord, and He may send unto you Christ Jesus, whom the heavens must retain till the times of the restitution of all things, of which God from the beginning hath spoken by the mouth of His holy prophets. Moses, your great lawgiver, said when your fathers stood before the awful mount of Sinai, *A Prophet shall the Lord your God raise up unto you from among your brethren. Him shall ye hear according to all things whatsoever He shall say unto you, and it shall be, that every soul which shall not hear that Prophet shall be destroyed from among the people* (Deut. xviii. 15, 18). This Prophet hath appeared in the person of Jesus, and to you first[2] hath God sent Him forth, blessing you in turning away each one from your iniquities (Acts iii. 17—26)."

This powerful address had a still greater effect than the previous discourse of the Apostle. Upwards of five thousand avowed themselves believers in the Crucified, and swelled the ranks of the Christian Church (Acts iv. 4). But it had other issues also. The Sanhedrin, which had hitherto stood aloof[3] from all notice of the movements of the Apostles, resolved to act with decision. As the evening of this eventful day closed in, the

[1] Ὅπως ἂν cannot mean *when*, as in our Version, it can only denote *in order that*.

[2] In accordance with the Saviour's command (Mtt. xxviii.). On the nature of the subsequent call of the Gentiles expected by the Apostle, see above, p. 348 and note.

[3] Either from (1) awe, or (2) miscalculating contempt, or, (3) it is possible, internal dissension, Milman, I. 357.

priests, the captain of the Levitical guard[1], and the Sadducees[2], naturally annoyed at the proclamation of the resurrection of the dead through the power of a risen Saviour, laid hands on the two Apostles and the healed cripple[3] (Comp. Acts iv. 14), and committed them to prison, intending on the morrow to institute a formal trial (Acts iv. 3).

Accordingly on the next day the rulers, the elders, and scribes, Annas[4] the high-priest and Caiaphas, John[5] and Alexander[6], and others of the pontiff's family, as-

1 Ὁ *στρατηγὸς τοῦ ἱεροῦ* (Acts iv. 1; comp. Lk. xxii. 4) was not a Roman but a Jewish officer, and corresponded to the *προστάτης τοῦ ἱεροῦ* spoken of in 2 Macc. iii. 4; comp. 2 K. xii. 9. He was the captain of the Levitical guard, spoken of by Josephus, *B. J.* VI. 5. 3; *Ant.* XX. 6. 2, under the name of *στρατηγός*, whose duty it was to visit the sentries in the Temple during the night, and see that they did their duties. See Lightfoot *in loc.*

2 "It does not appear that the Pharisees, though they had taken the lead in the condemnation of Christ, were eager, after that event, to persecute His followers. They looked on the illiterate Galilæans as worthy of no further attention, especially since they observed the ceremonial law, and at first abstained from controverting the peculiar tenets of their party; they allowed them to remain undisturbed, like some other sects by whom their own interests were not affected...But the Sadducees were exasperated with the Apostles for so zealously advocating the doctrine of the resurrection." Neander's *Planting*, I. 41, 45; Milman (I. 359) thinks the Sadducees "had gained a temporary ascendancy in the great council."

3 Neander's *Planting*, I. 43.

4 See above, pp. 150, 253, and note.

5 Identified by Lightfoot with Rabbi Johanan ben Zacchai, who lived 40 years before the destruction of the Temple, and was president of the great synagogue after its removal to Jamnia.

6 Apparently holding some high office, and identified by some with Alexander the Alabarch at Alexandria, the brother of Philo-Judæus, whom Josephus mentions as a friend of the Emperor Claudius. Jos. *Ant.* XVIII. 8. 1; XIX. 5. 1; See Smith's *Bibl. Dict.*

sembled probably in their hall Gazith, and when the Apostles had been placed in the midst of the judicial circle, enquired by what authority and by virtue of what commission they had acted as they had done.

Thereupon Peter, *filled with the Holy Ghost* (Acts iv. 8), again stood forward, and boldly declared that the miracle of the previous day was due entirely to the mighty working of Jesus of Nazareth, whom they had crucified, but whom God had raised from the dead. He was the Stone whom, in the language of the cxviiith Psalm, they the builders of the nation and its appointed teachers had rejected as worthless, but which had become *the head of the corner*, nor was there in any other the Salvation, for which all hoped; for there *was no other Name under heaven given among men, whereby they could be saved* (Acts iv. 8—12).

The boldness, power, and knowledge, which this speech betrayed, astonished the Sanhedrin beyond measure, and the more so when they reflected that the speaker and his fellow Apostle were of the common class, unlearned and ignorant[1], in whom they recognised[2] the obscure followers of Jesus of Nazareth (Acts iv. 13). The miracle, indeed, which they had wrought could not be gainsaid, for the restored cripple, a man more than 40 years of age (Acts iv. 22), stood beside them (Acts iv. 14), ready to support by his testimony the power by which he had been so marvellously healed. It was deemed, therefore, inexpedient to go into the question of evidence, and after a secret conference (Acts iv. 15) it was resolved to prevent, if possible, the spread of the report of the miracle amongst the people, and to forbid for the future any preaching or teaching in the name of Jesus.

[1] That is, who had not been educated in the Jewish schools.

[2] Ἐπεγίνωσκον, Acts iv. 13.

Accordingly the Apostles, who had been ordered to withdraw during the consultation, were recalled and informed of their decision. But they absolutely declined to act upon it. They could not, they said, refrain from proclaiming what their own eyes had seen and their own ears had heard, or hearken to the council rather than to that God, whose commissioned witnesses they were. After further threats, therefore, they were dismissed; for the Sanhedrin saw plainly that they had done nothing deserving punishment, and the popular feeling ran so strongly in their favour, that they dared not resort to violence (Acts iv. 21).

Thus released they returned to the rest of the disciples, and recounted all that had occurred. Their tidings had not the effect of lessening the courage of their hearers. Lifting up their voices with one accord to the Lord and Maker of heaven and earth, they declared their conviction of the vanity of the machinations of their rulers against the Supreme and the Messiah whom He had sent. Herod, and Pontius Pilate, the nations and people of Israel, had gathered themselves together against their Master, but only to do what His hand and counsel had foreordained should come to pass. The threats, therefore, of their foes they regarded not, and only prayed that, while[1] the Lord stretched forth His hand to heal, and caused signs and wonders to be performed through the Name of His holy servant Jesus, they themselves might receive still greater strength to preach His Word (Acts iv. 23—30).

Their petition received an immediate and sensible response. The place where they were assembled was shaken as by an earthquake, and a fresh and special communication of the Holy Ghost filled them with still

[1] Ἐν τῷ τὴν χεῖρά σου ἐκτείνειν σε = *in the stretching forth of Thy hand* (*while Thou stretchest forth Thy hand*) *for healing*, Acts iv. 30.

greater boldness to proclaim their message and deliver their testimony (Acts iv. 31).

CHAPTER III

ANANIAS AND SAPPHIRA—RENEWED HOSTILITY OF THE SADDUCEES.

A. D. 30—34.

THUS terminated the first collision of the Christian community with the ruling powers at Jerusalem. Within that community itself all as yet went well. While the Apostles with increased power gave forth their testimony to the resurrection of their Lord, the disciples proved the sincerity of their convictions by the self-denial of their lives. All being *of one heart and of one soul* (Acts iv. 32), they regarded their possessions as belonging to a common fund, and such as were possessed of lands or houses sold them, and brought the price and laid it at the Apostles' feet, who caused distribution to be made thereof according to the requirements of each (Acts iv. 35).

Of this self-denying goodwill no one afforded a brighter example than a man of the tribe of Levi[1], and a native of Cyprus, whose name was Joseph, or, as he was called by the Apostles, Barnabas[2], the *Son of Con-*

[1] Though originally excluded from the possession of land (see *Class-Book of Old Testament History*, p. 220), this tribe had begun to possess land, as in Jerem. xxxii. 7, and this must have been generally the case after the captivity. See Lechler *in loc.*

[2] Υἱὸς παρακλήσεως = *son of prophecy* or *exhortation.* If a native of Cyprus, he would be a Hellenist, and "the schools of Tarsus, the birth-place of St Paul, may naturally have attracted him, for Cyprus was within a few hours' sail from

solation, or rather of *Exhortation,* on account of the extraordinary gifts of inspired discourse and exhortation by which he was distinguished[1] (Acts iv. 36). His estates, which were probably considerable, he sold, and rejoiced in the distribution of the price amongst his poorer brethren.

Before long, however, a sad incident occurred, which told of evil already at work within the Christian society. A certain man named Ananias, with the privity of his wife Sapphira, sold a possession, and having appropriated a portion of the price, laid the remainder at the Apostles' feet, giving it to be understood that that was the whole sum he had received (Acts v. 1, 2). But his aspiration after high honour amongst his brethren with so little cost to himself did not escape the detection of the Apostle Peter. Fixing his eye upon him as he brought the portion and laid it before him, he enquired how he had permitted Satan to tempt him to deceive the Holy Ghost. *While it remained,* said he, *was it not thine own? and after it was sold, was it not in thine own power? Thou hast not lied unto men, but unto God* (Acts v. 4). At these words, so stern, so solemn, and yet so true, reading his heart to its lowest depths, the wretched man was utterly overwhelmed, and *fell down and gave up the ghost.* When the awe of the assembly at this instant judgment on the sin of hypocrisy had somewhat subsided, the young men[2] who were present rose up, and wrapping the body in the

Cilicia, and there the friendship of the two may have begun." See Con. and Howson, I. 101.

[1] See Lechler and Alford *in loc.*

[2] By some supposed to have been a class in the congregation accustomed to perform such services, but more probably the younger members of the church acting perhaps in accordance with Jewish custom, perhaps on some hint from the apostle. See Alford *in loc.*

usual burial clothes[1] bore it forth to a tomb without the city[2] (Acts v. 6).

Three hours had scarcely elapsed before his wife Sapphira, not knowing what had occurred, entered the place where the disciples were met together, and was straightway asked by Peter whether she and Ananias had really sold the farm for the price which the latter had alleged. To this she replied in the affirmative, and thus made her husband's sin her own, and deliberately confirmed the fraud. The Apostle had not denounced the awful judgment, which had befallen her husband, he had only denounced the offender. But now he not only denounced the sin, but declared its instant penalty, saying, *Behold the feet of them which buried thy husband are at the door, and shall carry thee out.* Thus informed at one and the selfsame moment of her husband's fate and her own, she too dropped down a corpse, and was instantly conveyed to the grave by those who had just returned from burying Ananias (Acts v. 8—10).

The effect of this terrible but just judgment was very great. Fear came upon all who saw and all who heard what had taken place, and the Apostles, by whose hands many *signs and wonders* continued to be wrought, acquired still greater reverence. Those who did not yet believe, forbore to join themselves to the Christian society rashly or from light motives, while the common people, impressed with a sense of the supernatural power possessed by the Apostles, brought forth their sick, and placed them on beds and couches in the streets, that they might have the benefit even of Peter's shadow

[1] Or their own mantles, taken off in preparing to carry him out. Alford *in loc.*

[2] On the shortness of the time after death allowed in the east before burial, see above, p. 249, n. The practice was to bury before sunset of the same day.

passing by[1] (Acts v. 15). Soon the populations of the towns round about Jerusalem imitated their example, and experienced the effects of the healing word as addressed either to the sick or those possessed by unclean spirits (Acts v. 16).

The excitement thus aroused could not escape the notice of the Sanhedrin. Annas and Caiaphas and the Sadducaic faction saw that they must make another effort to suppress the new sect so quickly gaining adherents in their very midst. Accordingly they caused the Apostles to be seized and cast into the common prison, and on the morrow calling together the whole Council, sent their officers to summon them into their presence.

When, however, they reached the prison, the officers found indeed the doors fast closed, but the prisoners had disappeared! On receiving this intelligence the high-priest and the Sanhedrin[2] were in the utmost perplexity, which was still further increased by the entrance of a messenger, announcing that the Apostles were in the Temple, where indeed they had been since daybreak, having been released by an angel during the night (Acts v. 18—25). Thereupon the Captain of the Levitical guard was despatched to fetch them, and even he found himself obliged to act with caution and gentleness, for the feelings of the people were largely on the side of the Apostles, and stones were ever ready at hand in the precincts of the Temple, to furnish weapons for a tumultuous resistance[3].

But the Twelve readily accompanied the officers, and presented themselves before the Sanhedrin, and

[1] Now was fulfilled his Master's promise, Mtt. xvi. 18.

[2] The ἀρχιερεῖς mentioned in Acts v. 24 as members of the Council were the *titular High-priests;* partly those who had served the office, partly the presidents of the 24 courses, partly the kindred of the High-priest. Alford *in loc.*

[3] Milman, I. 361: see above, p. 235.

in reply to the high-priest's complaint that they had not obeyed the injunctions of the council to forbear preaching in the Name of Jesus, evinced even more boldness and resolution than before. Peter, once more their spokesman, declared that obedience was due to God rather than to man, for He had raised up from the dead that same Jesus, whom they had crucified and slain, and exalted Him to be a Prince and a Saviour, *to give repentance to Israel and forgiveness of sins.* To the fact of His resurrection they were witnesses, and their testimony they were bound to deliver (Acts v. 29—32).

These words, breathing such dauntless resolution, roused the Council to the utmost fury, and the majority, especially the Sadducaic party, were eager for the execution of their prisoners. But the rising of one of their number was the signal for calmer measures.

This was the famous Rabbi Gamaliel[1], an illustrious teacher of the Law, who was held in the utmost reverence by the people, and according to Jewish tradition was the president of the Sanhedrin. He advised that the Apostles should withdraw for a while, and then pro-

1 This eminent teacher was the son of Rabbi Simeon, and grandson of the celebrated Hillel, of the sect of the Pharisees, but untrammelled by their narrow bigotry, and distinguished for candour and wisdom. "His learning was so eminent, and his character so revered, that he is one of the seven who alone among Jewish doctors have been honoured with the title of 'Rabban' (= the *Rabboni* of Jn. xx. 16). As Aquinas, among the schoolmen, was called *Doctor Angelicus,* and Bonaventura *Doctor Seraphicus,* so Gamaliel was called the *Beauty of the Law,* and it is a saying of the Talmud, that since *Rabban Gamaliel died, the glory of the Law has ceased.*" He was president of the Sanhedrin under Tiberius, Caligula, and Claudius, and died 18 years before the destruction of Jerusalem, or about the time of St Paul's shipwreck at Malta. Conybeare and Howson, I. 56, and notes.

ceeded to urge his brethren to moderation and calmness. There was no need, he said, for any apprehension from such an obscure band of Galilæans. Could not the Council recall how a few years before one Theudas[1] had arisen, boasting himself to be some great one, and had collected a body of 400 followers? But what

[1] Because a Theudas is mentioned by Josephus (*Ant.* XX. 5. 1) as having been an insurgent in the time of Claudius, or about A. D. 44, and St Luke places this Theudas before the time of Judas of Galilee, he has been accused with the utmost inconsistency of historical inaccuracy. But there are two solutions of the apparent difficulty, either of which meets all the requirements of the case: (i) St Luke represents this Theudas as having appeared before the time of Judas the Galilæan, and therefore he cannot have appeared later than the close of the reign of Herod the Great. Now the year of that monarch's death (as mentioned above, pp. 104, 144) was one of great turbulence, and Palestine was overrun by insurrectionary chiefs and fanatics, of whom Josephus mentions but three by name, Judas the son of the bandit Hezekias, Simon a slave of Herod, and Athronges, and passes over the rest with a mere allusion (comp. *Ant.* XVII. 9. 3; XVII. 10. 4—8). Now of these Theudas might easily have been one, for the name was not uncommon. (ii) Others would identify him with Judas, the son of Hezekias mentioned above, or more probably with the second insurgent, Simon, one of Herod's slaves (*Ant.* XVII. 10. 6), a man of great personal strength and comeliness, who assumed the diadem and the title of king, "deeming himself more worthy of that dignity than any one else" (*Ant. loc. cit.;* comp. Acts iv. 36, *λέγων εἶναί τινα ἑαυτόν*), gained a certain number of followers, chiefly from Peræa, burned and plundered the palace of Jericho, and many other places, and was devastating in all directions till he was attacked by Gratus the procurator (see above, p. 149), who utterly defeated his followers and beheaded Simon himself. Being originally a slave he might easily have assumed the name of Theudas with the diadem, and have been mentioned by Gamaliel under one, by Josephus under the other appellation. See Neander's *Planting,* I. 47, n.; Lightfoot, *Hor. Hebr.* IV. 54; Biscoe's *History of the Acts,* p. 428; Rawlinson's *Bampton Lectures,* 261, and notes.

was the issue? Was he not slain, and as many as followed him dispersed and annihilated? And then again *in the days of the taxing* did there not rise up[1] Judas of Galilee, who also drew away much people after him? But was he a whit more successful? Did he not perish with all his followers? Let these instances, he continued, suffice, and let the assembly *refrain from these men.* If their work or counsel was of men, it would come to nought, but if it was of God, it would be impossible to overthrow it, and they ought to be on their guard lest they should by any chance *be found fighting against God*[2] (Acts v. 34—39).

The weight of the speaker's name and his high reputation prevailed over the bitterness of faction. His prudent advice was adopted. The Apostles were recalled, and after being beaten with rods, were dismissed with strict injunctions to abstain from speaking any more in the name of Jesus (Acts v. 40). But threats and stripes were alike ineffectual to seal their mouths. They went forth from the council *rejoicing that they had been found worthy to suffer for the Name* of their Master, and ceased not publicly in the Temple courts, and privately from house to house, to proclaim Jesus as the Messiah (Acts v. 41, 42).

[1] This rising of Judas is described above, p. 148.

[2] On the probable tone of Gamaliel's feeling towards Christianity see Neander's *Planting*, I. 47.

CHAPTER IV

THE INSTITUTION OF DEACONS—MARTYRDOM OF STEPHEN.

A. D. 34—36.

UP to this time, it will be observed, the attempts to put down the new Faith had come from the Sadducaic party. Separated in no respect from the nation, the members of the Christian society attended the festivals, worshipped in the Temple and the Synagogue, and observed the ordinances of the Law side by side with the "breaking of the Bread" from house to house[1]. Conforming, then, to national rites and usages, and agreeing with the Pharisees in opposition to the Sadducees respecting the resurrection of the dead, their relations with the more moderate portion at least of the former were of an amicable character[2].

But they were now destined to incur the hostility of both sects alike. Their own numbers, so far from suffering any diminution in consequence of the recent persecutions, steadily increased, and were swelled by the adhesion of *multitudes of men and women* (Acts v. 14), both Hebrews or Jews proper, and Hellenists or Jews of the Grecian speech[3]. For some time the same brotherly love which had prevailed before, distinguished all alike, and out of the common fund daily distribution was made according to the requirements of each person and household.

But before long in the midst of this general benevolence arose suspicions that the distribution was not made with perfect fairness. Between the Jews who

[1] See Lightfoot's *Commentary on the Galatians*, pp. 278, 9; Stanley's *Apostolical Age*, p. 92; and above, p. 349.

[2] Neander's *Planting*, I. 48.

[3] See above, pp. 109, 110.

spoke the sacred tongue of Palestine, and those scattered in different lands, who had adopted the Grecian language[1]; between the zealous Aramæan, who read the Scriptures in the Hebrew, and the Hellenists, who read the Septuagint, and whose most learned teachers strove to "accommodate Jewish doctrines to the mind of the Greeks, and to make the Greek language express the mind of the Jews," there had long been a feeling of mutual jealousy and dislike.

This now re-produced itself even within the Christian community. There arose a murmuring between the "Hellenists" and the "Hebrews," on the ground that the widows of the former were overlooked in the daily distribution[2] (Acts vi. 1). Such complaints, if not checked, might lead to disastrous results. Accordingly the Apostles met together, and having assembled the general body of the disciples (Acts vi. 2), urged that it was not meet to expect them to leave the ministry of the word and *serve tables*, and advised that seven men of good report, full of the Holy Ghost and of practical wisdom, should be selected, who might devote themselves to the superintendence of this distribution, while they confined themselves to the more spiritual functions

[1] Conybeare and Howson, I. 85. Alexandria was the metropolis of Hellenistic theology, Philo their great representative. "The Greek learning was not more repugnant to the Roman Cato, than it was to the strict Hebrews. They had a saying, *Cursed is he who teacheth his son the learning of the Greeks.*" For other illustrations, see Con. and Howson, I. 85, n.; Biscoe *On the Acts*, p. 60; Lightfoot, *Hor. Hebr. et Talm.* IV. 60; and compare above, p. 116. The ill-feeling lasted at least down to the time of Justinian.

[2] "The Jews of Palestine were relatively poor, compared with those of 'the dispersion.' We see this exemplified on later occasions, in the contributions which St Paul more than once anxiously promoted; see Acts xi. 29, 30; Rom. xv. 25, 26; Acts xxiv. 17; 1 Cor. xvi. 1—4; 2 Cor. viii. 1—4." C. and H., I. 64.

of their office (Acts vi. 3, 4). The proposal met with universal acceptance, and the general body of the disciples submitted to the Apostles seven men, whose names appear to indicate that they were of Hellenistic, rather than Jewish extraction, Stephen[1], Philip, Prochorus, Nicanor, Timon, Parmenas, and Nicolas[2] *a proselyte of Antioch* (Acts vi. 5). The Twelve approved of the selection, and after offering prayer they laid hands upon them[3], and thus solemnly consecrated them to their office[4].

Thus a danger, which threatened a breach in the Christian community, was happily removed by a wise and liberal concession. The Hellenists were introduced into the actual ministry of the Church, and the admission of a body more free than their Hebrew brethren from local and national prejudices was doubtless divinely ordered to pave the way for still greater results. Meanwhile the Word of God had free course and was glorified, the multitude of the disciples in Jerusalem was largely increased, and a great company even of the priests, whose antecedents and prepossessions would be all strongly against such a step, *became obedient to the faith* (Acts vi. 7).

[1] "His Hebrew (or rather Syriac) name is traditionally said to have been Chelil, or Cheliel (*a crown*) ;" Smith's *Bibl. Dict.*

[2] By some supposed, by others denied, to have been the founder of the sect of the Nicolaitans mentioned in Rev. ii. 6, 15. See Smith's *Bibl. Dict. sub voc.;* Lightfoot *On the Galatians,* 281 n.

[3] An ancient and familiar practice in (i) pronouncing a blessing (Gen. xlviii. 14—20), (ii) appointing to an office (Num. xxvii. 18—21), transferring guilt (Lev. iii. 2).

[4] It will be noticed that the term "deacons" is nowhere applied to them. They are called "the Seven" (Acts xxi. 8), and two of them perform the work of preachers and evangelists. See Article in Smith's *Bibl. Dict.;* Stanley's *Apostolical Age,* p. 62.

One of the "Seven" now admitted into the ministry of the Church was destined to be the proximate cause of its first collision with the Pharisaic party, and to prepare the way for the admission of the Gentiles into the Christian fold. This was Stephen, a man full of faith and power, of irresistible spirit and wisdom. Though appointed to superintend the distribution of secular funds, he soon became eminent for other gifts, and not only wrought great wonders and signs amongst the people (Acts vi. 8), but proved himself able to argue with the Jews of Cyrene and Alexandria, of Cilicia[1] and Roman Asia, as also the Libertini[2] or enfranchised Jews, in their several synagogues in Jerusalem, and that with such wisdom and power that they were unable to confute his arguments, or resist *the spirit by which he spake* (Acts vi. 10).

Freed by the circumstances of his birth and education from mere local and national prejudices, he ap-

[1] Among the conspicuous opponents of the great Hellenist in the synagogue of Cilicia was doubtless *a young man* (Acts vii. 58) a citizen of Tarsus, distinguished already by his zeal and talents among the younger champions of the Pharisaic party; see Gal. i. 13, 14; Acts xxii. 3; xxiii. 7; xxvi. 5; Phil. iii. 5, 6.

[2] Of the various explanations of the Λιβερτίνων in Acts vi. 9, the most probable are (i) that they were the inhabitants of Libertum, a town in the proconsular province of Africa, a bishop of which place is mentioned in the Council of Carthage, A.D. 411; (ii) that they were Jews, who having been taken prisoners by Pompeius and other Roman generals during the Syrian wars (see above, p. 109), were reduced to slavery, and being afterwards emancipated returned, either permanently or for a time, to Palestine, and had a synagogue at Jerusalem. Tacitus states (*Ann.* II. 85) that 4000 of the *libertini generis* (said by Josephus to have been Jews, *Ant.* XVIII. 3. 5) were banished by Tiberius, A.D. 19, to Sardinia, under an edict for the suppression of Egyptian and Jewish mysteries, and they are thought to have found their way to Jerusalem. See Humphry *On the Acts;* Smith's *Bibl. Dict.;* Orellius *in Tac. Annal.* II. 85; Biscoe *On the Acts,* p. 69.

pears to have spoken strongly of the fulfilment of the Mosaic ordinances[1] by the Founder of the Christian Church, and to have proclaimed that a time was at hand when, in the words of the Holy One to the woman of Samaria[2], men should *worship the Father in spirit and in truth*, not in the Temple only, or in Jerusalem only, but everywhere throughout the world. This teaching roused a furious opposition, and unable to oppose the eloquent Hellenist by fair means, those whom he addressed had recourse to artifice. Having privily suborned[3] men, who affirmed that they had heard him utter blasphemous words against the Temple and the Law; that they had heard him say that Jesus of Nazareth would destroy the national sanctuary and change the rites which Moses had ordained; they succeeded in stirring up the people, as also the ruling powers of the nation (Acts vi. 12). Accordingly an assembly of the Sanhedrin was convened, Stephen, who had in the meanwhile been apprehended, was placed before them, and the charges formally preferred against him.

[1] Although the accusations made against Stephen "are represented as the depositions of *false* witnesses, it does not follow that all they said was a fabrication, but only that they had, on many points, distorted his assertions, with an evil intention. Yet he must, by what he said, have given them some ground for their misrepresentations, for before this time nothing similar had been brought against the publishers of the Gospel; hence we may make use of their allegations to find out what Stephen really said." Neander's *Planting*, I. 51; compare Milman, I. 364. "Stephen is the acknowledged forerunner of the Apostle of the Gentiles. He was the first *to look steadfastly to the end of that which is abolished*, to sound the death-knell of the Mosaic ordinances and the temple-worship, and to claim for the Gospel unfettered liberty and universal rights." Lightfoot *On the Galatians*, p. 281.

[2] See above, p. 169.

[3] Comp. above, p. 268.

As he stood in the midst of the council-hall, the members of the Council looked steadfastly upon him and observed his face *as it had been the face of an angel* (Acts vi. 15) lighted up with supernatural radiance and serenity. At length, as in the case of the trial of his Lord[1], the high-priest enquired what he had to say respecting the accusations brought against him, and Stephen commenced his reply, "the framework of which was cast in a summary of the history of the Jewish Church[2]," and treated of all the great epochs of the national existence,—from Abraham to Joseph,—from Joseph to Moses,—from Moses to David and Solomon[3]. Keeping in mind the charges, of which he was accused, he shewed that the Divine blessing had not been confined to the Jews solely as inhabitants of the sacred land of Palestine, or as partakers in the Temple-worship.

The original cradle of their faith was not Palestine but Mesopotamia, and not only had the patriarch

[1] See above, p. 293.

[2] It is remarkable how completely St Stephen is the forerunner of St Paul, both in the form and the matter of his defence. (i) His securing the attention of the Jews by adopting the historical method, is exactly what the Apostle did in the synagogue at Antioch in Pisidia (Acts xiii. 16—22); (ii) His assertion of his attachment to the true principles of the Mosaic religion is exactly what St Paul said to Agrippa (Acts xxvi. 22); (iii) The words used by Stephen of the Temple call to mind those which the Apostle used at Athens (Acts xvii. 24); (iv) When he speaks of the Law as received *by the disposition of angels* he anticipates the language of Gal. iii. 19; (v) When he declares that the Jews had received the Law and had not kept it, he foreshadows the language of the great Apostle himself, Rom. ii. 17—29: Con. and Howson, I. pp. 69, 70: Mr Humphry also in his *Commentary on the Acts* compares (*a*) Acts vii. 44 with Heb. viii. 5; (*b*) Acts vii. 5—8 with Rom. iv. 10—19; (*c*) Acts vii. 60 with 2 Tim. iv. 16.

[3] Con. and Howson, I. 69.

Abraham been called from the far distant *land of the Chaldæans* (Acts vii. 2—5), but whole centuries of the nation's existence had been spent in *a strange country*. In Egypt the Divine blessing had not failed to rest upon the piety of Joseph (Acts vii. 6—10), or upon the descendants of Jacob, when they all went down and sojourned there (Acts vii. 11—16). In Egypt God raised up Moses their great Deliverer, preserved his life from the machinations of Pharaoh, and so ordered events that he became *learned in all the wisdom of the Egyptians, and mighty in words and in deeds*[1] (Acts vii. 17—22). In Midian He revealed Himself to him in the vision of the Burning Bush, and sent him forth to lead the ransomed people towards the Promised Land; but though by his hands their fathers had received the Law, it had not kept them from idolatry[2]; though he had set up the tabernacle of witness, it had not kept them from setting up *the tent of Moloch, and the star of their god Remphan*[3] (Acts vii. 22—44): nay, when, on the subjugation of the Canaanitish nations, that Tabernacle had been brought into Canaan, and was there after a long delay exchanged for the Temple, on which the Jews threw the whole stress of their dependance, neither Solomon himself who built it, nor the prophets[4] had ever regarded it as in the highest sense the dwelling-place of the Most High (Acts vii. 44—50).

Thus far the great Hellenist was heard with patience.

[1] On this period of the life of Moses, see *Class-Book of O. T. History*, pp. 81, 82, and note.

[2] On this period of Israel's history, see *Class-Book of O. T. History*, pp. 178, 179.

[3] Remphan (Acts vii. 43) and Chiun (Amos v. 26) appear to be the names of two idols worshipped by the Israelites in the wilderness, akin probably to *Ken* and *Rempu*, two Egyptian divinities; see Article *Remphan*, in Smith's *Bibl. Dict.*

[4] Comp. Isai. lxvi. 1, 2: Jer. xxiii. 24.

"It was the story of the Chosen People, to which every Jew listened with interest and pride[1]." But now,—perhaps perceiving that his hearers had caught the real drift of this review of their national history,—perhaps carried away by the retrospect of their narrow and persistent opposition to the divine counsels which it suggested,—in a strain of holy indignation he rebuked the unbelieving hypocritical disposition of the Jews, whose conduct in reference to the divine communications had been the same from the time of Moses up to that very moment[2]; who had always resisted the Holy Ghost, persecuted the prophets, and slain those that had predicted the coming of the Just One; who had betrayed and murdered Him, and had not kept the Law which they had received by *the disposition of angels* (Acts vii. 50—53).

This severe though just rebuke was the signal for an outburst of wrath and fury on the part of his judges. They were *sawn asunder*[3] in their hearts, *and gnashed upon him with their teeth.* Perceiving what was coming, and unaffrighted by their tumultuous rage, he looked up to heaven, and exclaimed, *Behold, I see the heavens opened, and the Son of Man*[4] *standing*[5] *on the right hand of God* (Acts vii. 56). This last declaration was more than the Sanhedrin could bear. Breaking

[1] Con. and Howson, I. 69.

[2] Neander's *Planting*, I. 54.

[3] Διεπρίοντο ταῖς καρδίαις αὐτῶν (Acts vii. 54).

[4] One of the only three passages in the N. T. where the title *Son of Man* is applied to the Redeemer by any save Himself; the two others being Rev. i. 13; xiv. 14.

[5] "In other places (Eph. i. 20; Col. iii. 1; Heb. i. 3, viii. 1, x. 12, xii. 2) He is represented as *sitting* at the right hand of the Father—here alone he is said to be standing. It is as if (according to Chrysostom's beautiful thought) He had risen from His throne, to succour His persecuted servant, and to receive Him unto Himself." Con. and Howson, I. 71.

forth into a loud yell (Acts vii. 57), they stopped their ears, as if to close them against any more words of blasphemy, and rushing upon him with one accord led him forth outside the city gate to stone him[1] (Lev. xxiv. 16). The instruments of punishment were collected, the witnesses threw off their loose outer garments (Deut. xvii. 7), laid them at the feet of a young Pharisee, a prominent member of the Cilician synagogue, named Saul, and hurled the first stones. As they fell, the martyr cried to Him whose form he had so lately seen standing at the right hand of God, *Lord Jesus, receive my spirit* (Acts vii. 59). Then falling on his knees, he exclaimed with a loud voice, in the words of his Master on the Cross, *Lord, lay not this sin to their charge*, and—in the touching language of the narrator, "who now uses for the first time the word, since applied to the departure of all Christians, but here the more remarkable from the bloody scenes in the midst of which the death took place—*he fell asleep*[2] (Acts vii. 60)."

1 "It was sentence and execution all at once; an act of violence without regular judicial examination," Neander's *Planting*, I. 55. "It was a savage and disorderly condemnation," Con. and Howson, I. 71.

2 Smith's *Bibl. Dict.*

PART II

THE CHURCH OF PALESTINE.

CHAPTER I

DISPERSION OF THE CHRISTIANS—ACTIVITY OF PHILIP.

A.D. 36.

THE martyrdom of the great Hellenist, who was conveyed to his grave amidst much lamentation *by devout men*[1] (Acts viii. 2), was the signal for a furious persecution of the Christians. The protection with which the prudence of Gamaliel had hitherto shielded them was now withdrawn. Pharisee and Sadducee alike[2], in the absence or with the connivance of the Roman procurator[3], turned against the hated sect, and the young Cilician of Tarsus, who was *consenting to the death* of Stephen (Acts viii. 1), and probably was now or shortly afterwards a member of the Sanhedrin[4], found himself able to give vent to the full fury of his zeal.

[1] Probably the class of Hellenists and proselytes to which he belonged, *οἱ εὐσεβεῖς*. Smith's *Bibl. Dict.*

[2] "This persecution must have been more severe and extensive than the former; for by the manner in which Stephen entered into conflict with Pharisaism, he had roused to hostilities against the teachers of the new doctrine the sect of the Pharisees, who had the most credit with the common people (see above, p. 117), and were powerful and active, and ready to leave no means untried to attain their object whatever it might be," Neander's *Planting*, I. 56.

[3] C. and H., I. 75.

[4] *Ibid.*

Resolved *to make havoc of the Church* (Acts viii. 3), he invaded the dwellings of those who professed adherence to the Christian faith, dragged forth their inmates, whether men or women, and committed them to prison (Acts viii. 3, xxvi. 9, 10, xxii. 3). Some of these persecuted people he scourged, *often, in many synagogues* (Acts xxvi. 11); some he strove to compel to blaspheme the Holy Name whereby they were called (Acts xxvi. 11); others he brought before the Sanhedrin, and when it was decided that they should be put to death, *gave his vote against them*[1] (Acts xxvi. 10), so that his fame as an inquisitor spread beyond the boundaries of Palestine, and reached even the distant city of Damascus (Acts ix. 13).

From a persecution instigated by such a zealous leader the disciples fled in different directions throughout Judæa and Samaria, and even further north still, to Phœnicia, Cyprus, and Antioch (Acts xi. 19), but the Apostles remained firm at their posts, and for the present did not leave Jerusalem (Acts viii. 1).

Amongst those, who were thus dispersed abroad, was one of the "Seven" who had been elected with Stephen to superintend the distribution of the funds of the Christian society. Between Judæa and Galilee lay the district of Samaria, the inhabitants of which, though shunning and shunned by the Jew, "yet clung to the same promises and looked forward to the same hopes[2]." Thither Philip now went down, and entering one of its towns[3], began to proclaim the message of Glad Tidings

[1] Ἀναιρουμένων τε αὐτῶν κατήνεγκα ψῆφον (Acts xxvi. 10), *vote*, not *voice*, as in our Version.

[2] Lightfoot *On the Galatians*, p. 282. For the Jewish feeling respecting the Samaritans, see above, pp. 121, 122.

[3] Κατελθὼν εἰς πόλιν τῆς Σαμαρείας (Acts viii. 5) = *to a city of Samaria*, perhaps Sychar, comp. Jn. iv. 5, and if so, the readiness of the people to receive Philip is easily accounted for.

to its people, and performed many miracles, casting out demons, and healing many that were lame and paralysed. He was received with no less readiness than the Holy One Himself, when sitting on Jacob's well[1], He declared Himself the Messiah to the woman who was a sinner. With one accord the Samaritans *gave heed to his words* (Acts viii. 6).

At this time there was present in the neighbourhood a man, who made no small stir in his day, by name Simon[2]. By his skill as a magician he had succeeded in astounding the people of Samaria to such a degree that he found votaries amongst all ranks and all ages, and was pronounced to be *the Power of God which is called Great*[3] (Acts viii. 10). But in Philip he found a rival whom he could not resist. He might astonish and perplex, but Philip could do more. He could heal, and restore gladness to many a saddened home (Acts viii. 12). The magician, therefore, soon found himself deserted, and many, both men and women, left him, and believing

[1] See above, p. 169.

[2] A native of Gittim (Justin Martyr's *Apol.* I. 26), a village of Samaria. Educated probably at Alexandria, he had there become acquainted with the tenets of the Gnostic school (Clement, *Hom.* II. 22), and had acquired a great reputation as a magician. He was one of those who at this period, according both to Greek and Roman testimonies, travelled about in numbers, and partly as soothsayers, astrologers, and interpreters of dreams, partly as jugglers, excited attention and received general regard. See Dollinger's *Gentile and Jew*, II. 198, 199; C. and H., I. 140.

[3] Our version omits the word καλουμένη, and so renders the verse imperfectly. "The Samaritans describe the angels as δυναμεῖς, *i. e.* uncreated influences proceeding from God. But to distinguish Simon from such an order of beings they added the words *which is called great*, meaning thereby the source of all power, in other words, the Supreme Deity—according to Simon's own expression, quoted by Jerome on Mtt. xxiv. 5, *Ego sum Sermo Dei, Ego sum Speciosus, Ego Paracletus, Ego omnia Dei.*" Smith's *Bibl. Dict.*

the Glad Tidings announced by the Evangelist, were admitted into the Church by baptism (Acts viii. 12). These results made a deep impression on the mind of Simon, and he too professed himself a believer, and received baptism at the hands of Philip (Acts viii. 13).

Meanwhile news that the despised Samaria had received the word of God reached the ears of the Apostles at Jerusalem, and they dispatched Peter and John[1] thither on a special mission of enquiry. They on their arrival prayed that some of those extraordinary gifts, which followed and attested the effusion of the Spirit on the Day of Pentecost, might be bestowed upon the Samaritan believers, and laid their hands upon them (Acts viii. 17), whereupon the endowments, for which they had prayed, were vouchsafed, and attested the planting of a Church in Samaria, standing in an equal rank with the first Church at Jerusalem[2].

Astonished as Simon had been at the miracles of Philip, he was still more astonished at the results of the imposition of the hands of the two Apostles, and he tried to bribe them to bestow upon him the same peculiar power (Acts viii. 18, 19). This mercenary proposal opened their minds to the real character of the man, and with the same just severity with which he had rebuked Ananias, Peter now denounced the wickedness of the pretender, and declaring that his heart was not right in the sight of God, that he had neither part nor lot in the matter, bade him pray that peradventure his evil intentions might be forgiven (Acts viii. 20—22). Struck dumb by the plain-spoken truthfulness of the Galilæan fisherman, and awakened rather to feelings of appre-

[1] The last time this Apostle is mentioned in the Acts; he is only once more mentioned (except in Revelation) as having been present in Jerusalem at St Paul's visit, Gal. ii. 9.

[2] Neander's *Planting*, I. 62.

hension of the Divine vengeance than to repentance[1], Simon implored the Apostles to intreat the Lord for him, that none of the things which they had threatened might come to pass (Acts viii. 24)[2].

After this encounter Peter and John extended their missionary labours to many other villages of the Samaritans[4] (Acts viii. 25), and then returned to Jerusalem. But other work was reserved for Philip, for a Divine intimation bade him go toward the south, along the road leading from Jerusalem to Gaza. Of the roads leading to this well-known city[4], one by Ramleh passed through town and villages; another, better adapted for carriages, through Hebron, and thence through a district comparatively little inhabited[5], and exposed to the incursions of southern marauders, whence it was called *desert*[6] (Acts viii. 26). The latter was the one which the heavenly Voice bade the Evangelist take, and as he tra-

[1] Neander's *Planting*, I. 63.

[2] The subsequent history of Simon Magus is involved in much perplexity. Early ecclesiastical historians represent him as the pertinacious foe of the Apostle Peter, encountering him at Cæsarea on the sea, and subsequently at Rome, which latter place he visited either (i) in the reign of Claudius (Justin Martyr, *Apol.* I. 26. 56), or (ii) in the reign of Nero. His success in the imperial city is said to have been so great that he was deified, and a statue was erected in his honour, with the inscription *Simoni Deo Sancto.* For various accounts of his death, see Burton's *Bampton Lectures*, and Smith's *Bibl. Dict.* Some identify him with a Simon, a native of Cyprus, whom Josephus (*Ant.* XX. 7. 2) mentions as a friend of Felix, the Roman Procurator of Palestine, and as having persuaded Drusilla, sister of Herod Agrippa, to marry him: see Neander's *Planting*, I. 63, and note; Alford on Acts viii.

[3] Contrast this with Lk. ix. 52; see above, p. 229.

[4] See *Class-Book of O. T. History*, pp. 259, 262.

[5] See Robinson's *Bibl. Res.* II. 514.

[6] Some apply this word to the city of Gaza, in the sense that it was destroyed and uninhabited, or that it was unfortified. But this is extremely improbable. Though often destroyed in the wars, the city had been restored.

versed it, probably ignorant of the cause wherefore he was sent, he perceived a chariot, in which one sat reading as he rode. This was a man of Ethiopia[1], a eunuch, the chief officer of Candace, queen of Meröe, and steward of all her treasure, who had come up to worship at one of the Feasts at Jerusalem, and was now returning (Acts viii. 27, 28). Bidden by the heavenly Voice to join the Stranger, Philip quickened his steps, and presently overheard him reading aloud[2], probably in the Septuagint Version[3], the words of the prophet Isaiah (chap. liii. 6, 7):

He was led as a sheep to the slaughter; and like a lamb dumb before his shearer, so opened He not His mouth: in His humiliation His judgment was taken away: and who shall declare His generation? For His life is taken away from the earth.

Understandest thou what thou readest? enquired Philip. *How can I*, answered the other, *unless some man should guide me?* and he besought him to get up and sit down by his side. Then the conversation began. *I pray thee*, said the eunuch, *of whom is the prophet speaking this? of himself, or of some other man?*

Thereupon Philip opened his mouth, and told him who that "Man" was, and preached the glad tidings of HIM, who died, and rose again, and ascended into heaven. As he went on, the eunuch was filled with an

[1] That is from the high land to the south of Egypt, and now comprehending Nubia, Cordofan, and Abyssinia, whose religious and commercial capital was the island of Meröe. Candace was not a personal name, but, like Pharaoh of the older and Ptolemy of the later Egyptian kings, the regular title of the queens of Ethiopia (Meröe). Lechler *in loc.* The eunuch was probably a proselyte of the Gate.

[2] The Easterns usually go on reading aloud, with a kind of singing voice, moving their heads and bodies in tune, and making a monotonous cadence at regular intervals. Kitto's *Bibl. Illust.* VIII. 95.

[3] See above, p. 11.

ardent desire to embrace the faith, and, being probably informed by Philip of the last command of his ascended Lord to the Apostles, on reaching a stream of water, enquired whether aught could hinder his being baptized? Thereupon the chariot was stayed[1], and the two went down to the water[2], and Philip baptized him, and then, either in consequence of some sudden inward summons or by a miraculous withdrawal, was instantly caught away, so that the eunuch saw him no more, and went on his way rejoicing (Acts viii. 39). Meanwhile Philip had passed on to Azotus, the ancient Ashdod[3], and thence evangelizing all the towns[4] in his way, and following the coast-line, proceeded to Cæsarea on the Sea[5] (Acts viii. 40).

CHAPTER II

THE CONVERSION OF ST PAUL.

A. D. 36 or 37—A.D. 40.

IN His parting charge to His Apostles the Saviour had declared that they should be His witnesses *in*

[1] Verse 37 in the received Version is wanting in the Codd. A. B. C. G. H., the Sinaitic MS., more than 60 cursive MSS., and several versions. It is omitted by Lachmann, Tischendorf, Alford, and others.

[2] Robinson would place the scene of the baptism at *Wady-el-Hasy*, between Eleutheropolis and Gaza, not far from the old sites of Lachish and Eglon. *Bibl. Res.* II. 514.

[3] See *Class-Book of O. T. History*, 254, 263, 272. Taken by Judas Maccabæus (1 Macc. v. 68) and destroyed by Jonathan (1 Macc. x. 84), it had been rebuilt by Gabinius (Jos. *Ant.* XIV. 5. 3; *B. J.* I. 7. 7), and bequeathed by Herod to his sister Salome: see above, p. 146.

[4] Ekron, Jamnia, Joppa, Apollonia, perhaps Lydda.

[5] For the foundation of which, see above, pp. 91, 92. On the undesigned coincidence between the mention of Philip here and afterwards in Acts xxi. 8, 9, see Birks' *Horæ Apostolicæ*, pp. 322, 323.

Jerusalem, and in all Judæa, and in Samaria, and unto the uttermost part of the earth (Acts i. 8). In exact accordance with this order the Church, as we have seen, was first founded in Jerusalem (Acts ii. 1), then spread to the cities round about (Acts v. 16), and after the martyrdom of Stephen to Samaria (Acts viii. 5—25). Provision was now to be made for its extension to the Gentiles, and for this purpose a fitting instrument was raised up in the person of no other than the young Cilician Pharisee, whom we have seen consenting to the death of the first Martyr, and *making havoc* of the Church.

At this point, then, it will be well to group together such particulars of his early life as have come down to us.

1. Saul, or as he was afterwards called Paul, was born at Tarsus (Acts ix. 11, xxi. 39, xxii. 3), the capital of Cilicia, situated on the banks of the Cydnus, a river famous for the dangerous fever caught by Alexander while bathing, and for the meeting of Antonius and Cleopatra. Even in early times it was a place of consequence[1], and after belonging to the empire of the Seleucidæ, and for a short time to that of the Ptolemies, espoused the cause of Cæsar during the civil wars, was then named Juliopolis[2] in honour of a visit from him, and made a *free city*[3] by Augustus. Under the early Roman emperors it was famous as a seat of education, and in this respect could vie even with Athens and Alexandria, and could boast of several Stoics, such as Athenodorus, the tutor of Augustus, and Nestor, the tutor of Tiberius. As a place of commerce, it was

[1] See Xen. *Anab.* I. 2. 23.

[2] Cæsar, *Bell. Alex.* Cap. LXVI.

[3] The privileges of an *urbs libera* consisted in (a) being governed by its own magistrates, (b) being exempted from the occupation of a Roman garrison, and from taxes. Its citizens did not necessarily possess the freedom of Rome.

a meeting-point for Syrians, Cilicians, Isaurians, and Cappadocians.

2. The family of Saul were strict Jews, though Hellenists in speech, and of the tribe of Benjamin (Phil. iii. 5). Neither his father's nor his mother's names are mentioned, but we have notices of his sister, and his sister's son (Acts xxiii. 16), and of some more distant relatives (Rom. xvi. 7, 11, 21).

3. Born probably during the later years of the reign of Herod, or the earlier of his son Archelaus[1], as the son of a Pharisee (Acts xxiii. 6), he was *circumcised on the eighth day* (Phil. iii. 5), and received the name of Saul[2]. But from his earliest years he probably had two names, "Saul the name of his Hebrew home, Paul[3] that by which he was known among the Gentiles."

4. From his father he inherited a great privilege, that of Roman citizenship. How his father acquired it is unknown. He may have obtained it for *a large sum* of money (Comp. Acts xxii. 28), or it may have descended to him, or it may have been bestowed upon him in recognition of some service rendered during the civil wars to some influential Roman[4].

[1] C. and H., I. 44. He was a young man at the time of the martyrdom of Stephen.

[2] Either (i) after the name of his father, or (ii) as being a name of traditional celebrity in the tribe of Benjamin, or (iii) "as intended to denote (in conformity with the Hebrew derivation of the word) that he was a son who had long been desired, the firstborn of his parents, the child of prayer." C. and H., I. 41.

[3] Paulus, a diminutive of *Pauxillus*, is a Roman name, so are *Junia* and *Lucius;* those he calls his kinsmen, Rom. xvi. 7, 11, 21; the others are Greek.

[4] "Great numbers of Jews were made slaves during the Civil Wars, and then manumitted. A slave manumitted with due formalities became a Roman citizen. Thus it is natural to suppose that the Apostle, with other Cilician Jews, may have been like Horace (*Sat.* I. vi. 45) *libertino patre natus.*" C. and H., I. 45, n.; Lewin's *Life of St Paul*, I. 4.

5. In conformity with the usual custom of his nation, one of whose proverbs was that *He who taught not his son a trade, taught him to be a thief*, the youthful Saul was instructed in the art of making tents[1], of the hair-cloth known as *Cilicium*, and supplied by the goats of his native province.

6. Carefully nurtured under his father's roof, speaking Greek, and acquainted with the Septuagint version[2] of the Old Testament, he was removed, probably between the age of 10 and 15, to Jerusalem[3], where he was brought up at the feet of Gamaliel[4], and under the superintendence of this wise and candid teacher made progress in his knowledge of Jewish rites above many of his contemporaries in his own nation, and became distinguished for extraordinary zeal for the traditions handed down from his fathers[5] (Gal. i. 14). Under the same teacher he probably added to that knowledge of Greek and of the Septuagint, as also of the elements of Gentile learning, which he had brought with him from Tarsus, a more exact acquaintance with the original Hebrew, as also with the hidden and mystical meaning

[1] For allusions to it, see Acts xviii. 3; xx. 34; 1 Cor. iv. 12; 1 Thess. ii. 9; 2 Thess. iii. 8.

[2] C. and H., I. 38. "It is observed that when St Paul quotes from the Old Testament, his quotations are from the LXX; and that, not only when he cites its very words, but when (as is often the case) he quotes it from memory."

[3] Probably during the supremacy of one of the four governors who preceded Pontius Pilate, i.e. between A. D. 6 and A. D. 25. See above, pp. 149, 150.

[4] For notices of Gamaliel, see above, p. 360, and note.

[5] "St Paul seems to have belonged to the extreme party of the Pharisees (Acts xii. 3, xxiii. 7, xxvi. 5; Phil. iii. 5, 6) whose pride it was to call themselves 'zealots of the law, zealots of God.' To this party also had belonged Simon, one of the Twelve, thence surnamed *the zealot*, ζηλωτής, or Καναναῖος." Lightfoot *On the Galatians*, I. 14. See above, p. 187.

of the Scriptures; a knowledge of aphorisms, allegories[1], and the opinions of the learned; as also the facility of quick and apt quotation; while the study of Greek authors[2] would not be altogether discouraged.

Such was the early life, and such was the training of the champion of the Pharisaic party, who was now to become the great Apostle of the Gentiles.

In his determination to make havoc of the Church, Saul was not content to persecute its members at Jerusalem. *Breathing forth threatenings and slaughter* against them, he determined to seek them out wherever they might be found, and with this intention requested letters of the high-priest[3] empowering him to seize any of "the Way," whom he might find in the city of Damascus, whether men or women, and convey them

[1] Such as that of Hagar and Sarah in Gal. iv. 21, where see Lightfoot's notes.

[2] Hence in his address to the Athenians (Acts xvii. 28) he could quote from the Cilician poet Aratus,

Τοῦ γὰρ καὶ γένος ἐσμέν;

to the refined Corinthians (1 Cor. xv. 33) from the *Thais* of Menander,

Φθείρουσιν ἤθη χρήσθ' ὁμιλίαι κακαί;

he could rebuke the Cretans (Titus i. 12) from the poet Epimenides,

Κρῆτες ἀεὶ ψεῦσται, κακὰ θηρία, γαστέρες ἀργαί.

[3] On the authority of the Sanhedrin over Jews in foreign cities, see above, p. 108, note. Damascus since its capture by Pompeius (see above, p. 67) had been under Roman rule, and belonged to the province of Syria. Many Jews had settled in it since the times of the Seleucidæ (comp. Jos. *B. J.* I. 2. 25; ii. 20. 2), hence there was more than one synagogue there (comp. πρὸς τὰς συναγωγάς, Acts ix. 2). If A. D. 36 was the date of the conversion of St Paul, Caiaphas was the high-priest, and the year would coincide with the deposition of Pilate by Vitellius prefect of Syria (see above, p. 307, note); if, as some think, it took place in A. D. 37, the high-priest was either Jonathan, one of the sons of Annas, and brother-in-law of Caiaphas, whom Vitellius, on the occasion of his visit to Jerusalem at the feast of the Passover in this year.

thence to Jerusalem to be punished (Acts ix. 1, 2, xxvi. 12, xxii. 5).

Armed with these credentials, he set out with a considerable retinue, and having probably passed through Shechem, then called Neapolis, and Samaria, and thence through Galilee towards the sea of Tiberias, crossed the Jordan[1], and made his way along the dreary barren uplands which stretch between the base of Antilibanus and the city of Damascus.

It was on the last, probably the sixth day[2] of this long journey, that about noon (Acts xxii. 6, xxvi. 13), when the sun was burning with the fulness of its noontide heat, that the beautiful city[3] appeared in view. But just as the object of his journey seemed to be attained, suddenly a light, brighter even than that fiery sun, flashed upon the persecutor and his companions (Acts ix. 6, xxvi. 13). Struck dumb with fear he and they fell to the ground (Acts ix. 7, xxvi. 14), and then from the inmost depths of the incomprehensible light there came a Voice, which all heard, but one only was enabled to understand[4] (Acts xxii. 9, ix. 8), and a Form appeared, which none saw save one, the persecutor himself (Acts xxii. 14; 1 Cor. xv. 8). *Saul, Saul*, said the

appointed to the office in place of Caiaphas (Jos. *Ant.* XVIII. 4. 3), or Theophilus his brother, whom he exalted to the pontificate during his second visit at Pentecost (Jos. *Ant.* XVIII. 5. 3). In the same year, A.D. 37, Tiberius died, March 16 (Tac. *Ann.* VI. 50), and was succeeded by Caligula.

[1] Probably near Scythopolis: see C. and H., I. 82: this route would follow the later Roman itinerary.

[2] The distance was about 136 miles, and Saul and his company may have performed the journey, like the modern caravans, in about 6 days, C. and H., I. 81; comp. Lewin, I. 54.

[3] Stanley's *S. and P.*, p. 410.

[4] Compare (i) Jn. xii. 28, and note above, p. 273; (ii) Acts ii. 12, 13; (iii) Dan. x. 7, and see Baumgarten's *Apostolic History*, I. 210. *Audiebant vocem solam, non vocem cum verbis*, Bengel.

Voice in distinct articulate words *in the Hebrew tongue* (Acts xxvi. 14), *why persecutest thou ME? Who art Thou, Lord?* replied the stunned and confused Pharisee. *I am JESUS*, was the answer, *Whom thou persecutest: it is hard for thee to kick against the goad*[1] (Acts xxvi. 14). Trembling and astonished the persecutor went on, *Lord, what wilt Thou have me to do?* and in reply was directed to *arise and go into the city*, and there it should be told him what he was to do (Acts ix. 11).

Thereupon he arose, but when he opened his eyes, all was dark around, for they were blinded by the brightness of the light and the majesty of the Son of God. His companions who had *stood speechless* listening to the *voice*[2], *but seeing no man* (Acts ix. 7), now took him by the hand (Acts ix. 8), and led him into the city, and through the street called "Straight[3]" to the abode of one Júdas (Acts ix. 11).

[1] As the language uttered was the same, the sacred language of Palestine, which the Son of Man had used on earth, so also was the figurative allusion to which it gave expression like the parables He had so often delivered. As the ox rebels in vain against the long sharp-pointed goad (see *Class-Book of O. T. History*, p. 237, note) of its master, and as all its struggles do nought but increase its distress, so did the Apostle vainly struggle against the power of His grace. C. and H., I. 88.

[2] "The present participle marks the continuity of the effort, while the genitive expresses the *mechanical* side of hearing, the impression of sound, and not the apprehension of the meaning as a whole. On the other hand, St Paul says (Acts xxii. 9), *The men who were with me saw the light; but heard not the voice of Him that spake to me* (τὴν δὲ φωνὴν οὐκ ἤκουσαν τοῦ λαλοῦντός μοι): to them the voice was no articulate utterance of that Saviour who was speaking to, or rather talking with, St Paul." Westcott. On the difference between ἀκούω with the *gen.* and *acc.*, see Viner's *Gr. Gram.* XXX. 7, Vol. I. 210, E. T.

[3] Generally identified with the "Street of Bazaars," a long, wide thoroughfare, penetrating from the southern gate into

For three days the blindness continued, and during this period he neither ate nor drank (Acts ix. 9), but remained engaged in solitary prayer (Acts ix. 11) unvisited either by the Christians, who had been alarmed by the intelligence of his approach, or the Jews, who could not sympathise with his present condition. At length one drew near to reveal the Divine will respecting him[1].

There was living at this time in Damascus a disciple named Ananias, held in high estimation amongst all the Jews resident there (Acts xxii. 12). To him the Lord appeared in a vision, and bade him seek out in the house of Judas for one called Saul; for *behold he was praying*, and had seen in a vision a man coming in, and laying his hand upon him that he might recover his sight. At first Ananias would have declined the mission, knowing well the character of him to whom he was to go, and the purpose for which he had visited Damascus. But his objections were overruled; he who had been a persecutor was designed by the Lord to do great things, and to him he must go (Acts ix. 11—16).

the heart of the city which, as in all the Syro-Greek and Syro-Roman towns, it intersects in a straight line. Stanley's *S. and P.*, p. 412.

[1] In reference to the three accounts of the Conversion we notice (i) *the general agreement* with regard to the outward details of the narrative: the occasion, the commission, the place, the time, the light, the company, are the same in all; but (ii) each account contains some peculiar details, and these varieties prove that the descriptions are free and independent, that they are not studied and servile; "they do not echo each other's words, they tell each its own story; there is none of that elaborate guarding and fencing of expressions, none of that careful reconciliation of statement with statement, which every court of justice regards with strong suspicion as a sure indication of design and falsehood." Vaughan, *Church of Jerusalem*, II. 7; Westcott's *Characteristics of the Gospel Miracles*, p. 120; Birks' *Horæ Apostolicæ*, pp. 324—328.

Thereupon Ananias went, entered the house, and beholding the triumphant persecutor lying exhausted and fasting, laid his hands upon him and said, *Brother Saul, the Lord hath sent me, even Jesus who appeared unto thee on the way as thou camest, that thou mayest receive thy sight, and be filled with the Holy Ghost* (Acts ix. 17). He had scarcely spoken when from the eyes of the new disciple of the risen Saviour there fell as it had been scales, and looking up he beheld the face of Ananias (Acts xxii 13), and learned the object of the heavenly vision, and the purpose for which the God of his fathers had chosen him (Acts xxvi. 18). Thereupon he arose and was baptized, and having taken meat was strengthened for the work that lay before him.

The arrival of the delegate of the Sanhedrin was no secret among the Christians at Damascus, and the words of Ananias testify to the fame he had acquired as a persecutor of their body. Great, then, must have been their surprise when they heard of the change which his spirit had undergone, and still more when they saw him entering the synagogues (Acts ix. 20), and fearlessly declaring his conviction that that Jesus, whose followers he had come to imprison, was *the Son of God.* The first effect upon those who heard him was blank amazement, for they were well acquainted with his previous history, and the object of his visit, and they clearly saw that the astounding change which had come over him could not be ascribed to any wayward, irregular impulse, for his energy gathered renewed strength day by day, and the Jews were unable to confute the arguments by which he proved that Jesus was the long-promised Messiah (Acts ix. 21, 22).

After the lapse, however, of some days, it became clear that it would not be safe for him to continue his labours. The fury of the Jews would naturally be roused to the utmost pitch, and it became necessary that he should leave the city. But instead of going up to Jerusalem to consult those who were Apostles before him (Gal. i. 17), he departed to Arabia[1], either the region which bordered on Syria and Mesopotamia and included Damascus itself[2], or the Sinaitic peninsula, the scene of the giving of the law. What was the purpose of this journey we are not told. Perhaps it was to undertake some missionary enterprise, perhaps to engage in solitary communion[3] with Him who had called him to be an Apostle, before he entered upon his active labours.

[1] "A veil of thick darkness hangs over St Paul's visit to Arabia. Of the scenes among which he moved, of the thoughts and occupations which engaged him while there, of all the circumstances of a crisis which must have shaped the whole tenour of his after life, absolutely nothing is known. *Immediately*, says St Paul, *I went away into Arabia*. The historian passes over the incident without a mention. It is a mysterious pause. A moment of suspense in the Apostle's history, a breathless calm which ushers in the tumultuous storm of his active missionary life." Lightfoot on Gal. i. 17.

[2] See the words of Justin, *Dial. c. Tryph.* p. 305 A, quoted by Lightfoot, and C. and H., I. pp. 117, 118. This, however, appears improbable, for (i) it gives to the term *Arabia* an extension which does not seem to have been common; (ii) it distinguishes the Arabia of the first chapters of Galatians from the Arabia of the fourth; (iii) it deprives this visit of a significance which, on a more probable hypothesis, it possesses in relation to this crisis of St Paul's life. But if it was the Sinaitic peninsula then his visit becomes full of meaning; here, "where Moses had received the tables of the Law amid fire and tempest and thick darkness, where Elijah, the typical prophet, listened to the voice of God, and sped forth refreshed on his mission of righteousness, in the fulness of time St Paul, the greatest preacher of Him of whom both the law and the prophets spoke, was strengthened and sanctified for his great work, was taught the breadth as well as the depth of the riches of God's wisdom, and transformed from the champion of a bigoted and narrow tradition into the large-hearted Apostle of the Gentiles." Lightfoot, *in loc.*

[3] Ellicott on Gal. i. 18.

CHAPTER III

ST PAUL'S FIRST VISIT TO JERUSALEM—PETER AT JOPPA.

A. D. 40.

WHATEVER was the precise object of this journey to Arabia, and whatever was its duration, certain it is that the Apostle returned thence to Damascus (Gal. i. 17), and *preached boldly in the name of Jesus* (Acts ix. 27). On this occasion, however, the Jews, unable to confute his arguments, resolved to assassinate him, but their design reached his ears, and every precaution was taken by the Christians that night to secure him from danger.

This, however, was a matter of no little difficulty. In consequence either of hostilities between the Romans and Herod Antipas on the one side and Aretas king of Petra on the other[1], or of the assignment of Damascus by Caligula, the successor of Tiberius, to Aretas, the city was held by the Ethnarch[2] of this monarch (2 Cor. xi.

[1] For the origin of the ill-feeling between Aretas and Herod Antipas, see above, p. 168. In the battle between them the army of Antipas was utterly routed (Jos. *Ant.* XVIII. 5. 3), and Antipas appealed to Tiberius for assistance. On this Vitellius, the prefect of Syria, was commissioned to march against Aretas, and take him dead or alive. But on his march Vitellius heard of the death of Tiberius, March 16, A. D. 37, and abandoned the expedition. The position of affairs was now reversed. Antipas was banished to Lyons; Herod Agrippa received his kingdom from Claudius; and in A.D. 38 it appears probable that Caligula granted Damascus to Aretas. See C. and H., I. 97, 98; Art. in Smith's *Bibl. Dict.;* Milman, I. 372.

[2] This word is used to denote (i) the governor of a dependent district (1 Macc. xiv. 47; Jos. *Ant.* XVII. 11. 4); (ii) a magistrate or consul allowed to Jewish residents living under their own laws in Alexandria and other cities (Jos. *Ant.* XIV. 7. 3).

32), and the Jews having won him and his soldiers over to their side, a strict watch was kept day and night to prevent the Apostle's escape, and deliver him over to execution (Acts ix. 24). In this emergency, therefore, the disciples taking advantage of an unguarded part of the wall and the darkness of the night, let him down in a basket from a window, which opened on the outer country[1] (Acts ix. 25; 2 Cor. xi. 33). Thus delivered from circumstances of great peril, the Apostle turned his steps towards Jerusalem, being desirous, as he informs us, to become acquainted with Peter[2], and in the Holy City he arrived three years[3] after his conversion (Gal. i. 18).

But his escape had been too hurried to allow him to bring with him letters of commendation; when, therefore, he attempted *to join himself to the disciples* (Acts ix. 26), they were all afraid of him, and could not believe that he was united with them in the bonds of a common discipleship. But now it was that Barnabas, who, as we have seen[4], may have become acquainted with him at Tarsus, took him by the hand and brought him to the Apostles, and told them how he had seen the Lord on the road to Damascus, and how in that city he had already spoken boldly in His Name (Acts ix. 27). Thereupon Peter, and James *the Lord's brother*[5] (Gal. i. 18, 19),

[1] C. and H., I. 98.

[2] *To visit Cephas:* ἱστορῆσαι is somewhat emphatic. *A word used,* says Chrysostom, *by those who go to see great and famous cities.* It is generally said of things and places, less commonly, as here, of persons: Lightfoot, *in loc.* and Ellicott on Gal. i. 18.

[3] See Lightfoot's note *in loc.*, and Excursus on *St Paul's first visit to Jerusalem.* In Acts ix. 23 the time is said to have been *many days*, but compare I Kings ii. 38, 39, where *many days* is used to denote a space of *three years:* Paley's *Horæ Paulinæ.*

[4] See above, p. 356, n.

[5] "The Apostle James is named three times in the Epi-

in the absence of the other Apostles, probably on some mission to the churches of Judæa, Galilee, and Samaria (Acts ix. 31), gave him the right hand of fellowship, and for a period of 15 days[1] (Gal. i. 18) he was with them *coming in and going out of Jerusalem* (Acts ix. 28).

As might be expected, the chief sphere of his activity was in the synagogues of the Hellenists, where he had before distinguished himself as a zealous opponent of Stephen. Now, however, he disputed with the same energy and force in support of the very doctrines which he had then persecuted (Acts ix. 29), and brought down upon himself the same furious opposition which had caused the death of the first Martyr. A plot was formed to secure his assassination, and the disciples perceived that he must retire from the work he had commenced in Jerusalem. The Apostle, himself, was unwilling to quit a place, where his former zeal against the faith was so well-known, and his sincerity, as he hoped, would be appreciated (Acts xxii. 19, 20). But as he was one day praying in the temple, he fell into a

stle to the Galatians, but only here with this distinctive title. The history supplies a full key. This visit is evidently the same as in Acts ix. 26—30, while the one in the next chapter was much later, at or near the time of the Council, Acts xv. Hence the first was before the death of James the son of Zebedee, and the other long after it. A distinctive addition to the name was thus as natural in the one case, as it would be superfluous and even suspicious in the other." The same distinction is observed in the book of Acts. In the earlier part the two Apostles of this name are distinguished, *the brother of John*, or *the son of Alphæus*. But after the elder James was martyred, the other is three times called *James* simply, without any addition. This minute propriety is too delicate and refined to be easily accounted for, except by the fact that Luke and Paul were contemporary with the events they record." Birks' *Horæ Apostolicæ*, pp. 197, 198.

[1] On the brevity of this visit, see Paley's *Horæ Paulinæ*.

trance (Acts xxii. 17), and saw his Lord, who said to him, *Make haste, and get thee quickly out of Jerusalem, for they will not receive thy testimony concerning Me;* and when he hesitated to obey the command and pleaded his former zeal in persecuting the faith as a reason why he should stay, the injunction to leave the city was repeated, *Depart, for I will send thee far hence unto the Gentiles* (Acts xxii. 21).

Thus assured that Jerusalem was not to be the field of his labours, he allowed the brethren to convey him to Cæsarea-on-the-sea[1], whence he took ship and sailed to Tarsus, his native city, and there probably devoted himself to preaching in its synagogue, and to missionary activity[2] in the regions of Syria and Cilicia[3] (Gal. i. 21). His brief visit to Jerusalem had not been without some result. He had seen and was recognised by Peter and James, and though he remained for the present personally unknown to the churches of Judæa[4], yet the

[1] Some have thought this was Cæsarea Philippi (see above, p. 218), "but the words κατήγαγον, ἐξαπέστειλαν, imply a sea-port and an embarcation, and Cæsarea, without any addition to distinguish it, is always the principal city of the name." Lightfoot, *in loc.:* see also Birks' *Horæ Apost.* 199.

[2] Probably he now founded those churches greeted in the Apostolic decree, Acts xv. 23, 41. Perhaps "in his own family some of those Christian *kinsmen* (Rom. xvi.) whose names are handed down to us, possibly his *sister* and his *sister's son* (Acts xxiii. 16, 23) were by his exertions gathered into the fold of Christ." C. and H., I. 104.

[3] St Paul's words here, *Syria* and *Cilicia*, are probably not intended to *describe the order* in which he visited the two countries. Cilicia had geographically a greater affinity with Syria than with Asia Minor. The less important country is here named after the more important. Lightfoot on Gal. i. 21; C. and H., I. 103.

[4] As distinguished from that of Jerusalem, whence "he was hurried off to Cæsarea, and there embarking left the shores of Palestine. The other churches of Judæa therefore had no opportunity of knowing him. Judæa is here dis-

intelligence which reached them from time to time[1] that their persecutor of former days was now preaching the Faith, filled them with thankfulness, and they *glorified God in him* (Gal. i. 22—24).

While the Apostle was thus employed amidst the familiar scenes of his childhood, the churches *throughout Judæa and Galilee and Samaria*, lately disturbed by his unceasing animosity, *had peace*, increased in numbers, and walked *in the fear of the Lord* (Acts ix. 31). The rest, however, which they thus enjoyed, may perhaps be ascribed to another cause besides the conversion of their late persecutor[2]. In A.D. 36 Pontius Pilate, as we have already seen[3], was sent to Rome by Vitellius. Thereupon Marcellus was sent out as procurator of Judæa in his place, but on his arrival at Cæsarea was directed to make way for Marullus[4]. In the following year, A.D. 37, Vitellius was recalled from Syria, and was succeeded in that prefecture by Petronius, while Theophilus[5] succeeded his brother Jonathan in the office of high-priest. But a still more important event in the same year was the death of Tiberius[6], and the accession of Caligula. Releasing Herod Agrippa[7], the grandson of Herod

tinguished from Jerusalem, as Italy is frequently distinguished from Rome, *e.g.* probably Hebr. xiii. 24." Lightfoot, *in loc.*

1 Note the force of ἀκούοντες ἦσαν in Gal. i. 23 = *they kept hearing*, just as ἤμην ἀγνοούμενος = *I continued personally unknown*.

2 Milman's *History of Christianity*, I. 373.

3 See above, p. 307, note.

4 Jos. *Ant.* XVIII. 6. 10.

5 See above, p. 383, note.

6 See above, p. 383, note.

7 Jos. *Ant.* XVIII. 6. 10. Herod Agrippa, the son of Aristobulus and Berenice, and grandson of Herod the Great, was born A.U.C. 743, and was brought up at Rome with Claudius and Drusus, and on the death of the latter was banished by Tiberius, A.D. 31, as recalling his memory by his presence. Retiring to Malatha in Idumæa (Jos. *Ant.* XVIII. 6. 2), he was appointed ædile of Tiberias, and five years

the Great, from his prison at Rome, where Tiberius had confined him, he appointed him king of Trachonitis, which had belonged to Herod Philip's tetrarchy, and bestowed upon him also the tetrarchy of Lysanias [1]. But the new emperor was scarcely seated on the throne, before in his insane vanity he ordered divine honours to be paid to himself throughout the empire [2], and directed that a golden colossal statue of himself should be placed in the Holy of Holies at Jerusalem. The execution of this mandate was entrusted to Petronius, and having ordered Sidonian workmen to make the statue, he moved up with his troops to Ptolemais, prepared to set it up by force. But no sooner did intelligence of what was intended reach the Jews than one universal feeling of horror pervaded the nation, and thousands assembled from all quarters without distinction of rank or age or sex, imploring the prefect to desist from carrying out his instructions. Shrinking from the horrible task of commencing a war of massacre and extermination which he saw was inevitable, if the statue was set up, Petronius hesitated, wrote to expostulate with his master, and put off the execution of the order. At the same time

afterwards was readmitted to the court of the Emperor at Capreæ, and became the intimate friend of Caius (Caligula), but for an imprudent speech was thrown into prison. Merivale's *Romans under the Empire*, VI. 11.

[1] Jos. *Ant.* XVIII. 6. 10. His arrival in Palestine with royal pomp excited the bitterest jealousy of Herodias the wife of Herod Antipas, the tetrarch of Galilee. She would not rest till her husband also had obtained a royal title, and in an unlucky hour he repaired with her to Rome to solicit it from Caligula (Jos. *Ant.* XVIII. 7. 2). But Agrippa was beforehand with them, outbid his rival in bribery, and accused him of intrigues with Sejanus, and Caligula banished both the tetrarch and his wife to Lyons in Gaul, A.D. 39.

[2] Merivale, VI. 45. For an account of the indignities endured by the Jews of Alexandria, see Jos. *Ant.* XVIII. 8. 1, 2; Milman, *History of the Jews*, II. 133—139.

Herod Agrippa, then at Rome, implored his patron to pause, and a deputation from Alexandria, headed by the learned and venerable Philo, set forth the stern requirements of the Jewish Law. But Caligula was inexorable, and it is impossible to say what would have been the result[1], had he not been assassinated[2] on the 24th of January, A.D. 41. Thus the Jews were delivered from this terrible indignity.

The rest, then, which the Christians now enjoyed, may not improbably be ascribed to the distractions of Caligula's reign, and to the fact that the Jewish authorities were wholly occupied with frustrating his mad designs. Taking advantage, therefore, of this period of repose the Apostle Peter made a visitation of the different churches founded in Palestine, and amongst other places went down to Lydda, anciently called Lod[3] (1 Ch. viii. 12; Neh. vii. 37), and afterwards Diospolis, situated about 9 miles from the sea-port of Joppa. Here finding a man afflicted with paralysis, who had kept his bed for upwards of 8 years, he addressed him in his Master's name, *Æneas, Jesus Christ healeth thee*, whereupon he rose immediately, restored to perfect soundness. The cure of such a man was quickly noised abroad

[1] "Josephus, *Ant* XVIII. 8. 9, states that Caligula at one moment yielded to Agrippa, and rescinded his orders to Petronius; but on hearing of the resistance the Jews were prepared to make, repeated them more vehemently than ever. The last missive, however, did not reach Petronius till after the news had arrived of the tyrant's death." Merivale, VI. 50, n.

[2] Jos. *Ant.* XIX. 1. 11.

[3] The modern Lidd or Ludd stands in the great maritime plain of Sharon (see *Class-Book of O. T. History*, p. 30), and when covered with its crops of corn, reminds the traveller of the rich wheat-fields of our own Lincolnshire: Robinson, *Bibl. Res.*, III. 145. Thomson, *The Land and the Book*. It received its name Diospolis in the reign of Hadrian, in A.D. 136.

throughout his own town and the neighbouring plain of Sharon, and contributed in no small degree to the spread of the Church in those regions.

While still at Lydda the Apostle received intelligence that the Christian society at Joppa had sustained a grievous loss by the death of a widow of substance, named Tabitha[1] or Dorcas, who had been wont not only to minister with her own hands to the wants of the poor, but in providing clothing for them. The death of such a person caused great regret at Joppa, and the Apostle was no sooner informed of it by messengers, who intreated his presence, than he set out, and on his arrival was conducted to the upper chamber, where the body lay prepared for the burial (Acts ix. 37—39), surrounded by many widows, who stood by weeping, and shewed him the many proofs of the kindness of their benefactress.

Like his Master before him in the chamber of the daughter of Jairus[2], the Apostle thereupon put these mourners forth, and kneeling down[3] engaged in prayer. Then turning to the body he pronounced the words *Tabitha, arise* (Acts ix. 40), whereupon her eyes instantly were opened, and seeing Peter she sat up. Taking her by the hand the Apostle then raised her from the spot where she had lain prepared for burial, and calling in the widows presented her to them alive. The fame of this miracle, confirming as it did the impression already made at Lydda, quickly spread, and caused an accession of many to the Christian Church; and the Apostle perceiving an opportune field of usefulness thus opened

[1] Tabitha is the Aramaic, Dorcas the Greek form, both meaning *a gazelle:* Δορκάς is used in the LXX. as the rendering of צְבִי in Deut. xii. 15, 22; 2 Sam. ii. 18; Prov. vi. 5. We find the name also in Jos. *B. J.* IV. 3. 5.

[2] See above, p. 201.

[3] Like Elisha, 2 Kings iv. 33.

to him, *tarried many days in Joppa with one Simon a tanner* (Acts ix. 43).

CHAPTER IV

THE CONVERSION OF CORNELIUS.

A.D. 41–43.

DURING the Apostle's stay at Joppa an event occurred destined to have no small influence on the spread of the Church.

Cæsarea, as has been already stated, was the head-quarters of the Roman government in Judæa[1]. Among the troops quartered there was a cohort of Italians[2], possibly volunteers, and amongst its officers was a centurion named Cornelius, a devout man, who had learned to worship the one true God[3], and was well known for his almsgiving and uprightness of life (Acts x. 2). One day, about the ninth hour, the hour of prayer, he beheld in a vision an angel who informed him that his prayers and alms were not forgotten before God, and bade him send for the Apostle, now lodging at Joppa,

[1] See above, 147, n.

[2] As distinct from the legionary soldiers, and hence called the *Italian cohort.* "As in the army of modern Austria, the soldiers were drawn from different countries and spoke different languages." C. and H., I. 113.

[3] "There is scarcely any room to doubt that he belonged to the class of *Proselytes of the Gate* (see above, p. 118, n.). Nor can we infer the contrary from the circumstances that Peter and the stricter Jewish Christians looked on Cornelius as an unclean person, and in many respects the same as an heathen. The Proselytes of the Gate were certainly permitted to attend the synagogue worship...yet the Jews who adopted the stricter maxims of the Pharisees, placed all the uncircumcised in the class of the unclean, and avoided living and eating with such persons as defiling." Neander's *Planting*, I. 68.

who would tell him what he should do, and inform him concerning that faith which had already excited much attention in the neighbourhood[1] (Acts ix. 42).

Obedient to the heavenly vision the centurion summoned two of his servants, and a devout soldier attached to his own person, and sent them with the necessary instructions to Joppa. As the three drew near their destination, the Apostle Peter, who had retired for devotion to the flat[2] housetop of his lodging by the seaside[3] at the noontide hour of prayer (Acts x. 9), fell into a trance, and saw the heaven opened, and a great sheet-like vessel[4], let down by its four corners, till it rested upon the earth (Acts x. 11). As he observed it closely, he noticed that it contained *all manner of four-footed beasts of the earth, and wild beasts, and creeping things, and fowls of the air*, and he heard a Voice saying, *Rise, Peter, kill and eat.* But this the Apostle, who from earliest childhood had observed the strict precepts of the Levitical Law[5], stedfastly declined to do: he had *never eaten anything common or unclean.* Then

[1] Neander's *Planting,* I. 69.

[2] Comp. the flat roof of the house of Rahab at Jericho, *Class-Book of O. T. History,* p. 202; of the house of Samuel at Ramah, *ibid.* p. 280.

[3] "Overlooking the waves of the Western Sea, the Sea of Greece and Rome—the sea of the isles of the Gentiles." See Keble's *Christian Year, Monday in Easter Week.* Stanley's *Apost. Age,* p. 93.

[4] It appears doubtful whether δεδεμένον καὶ are genuine in Acts x. 11: they are omitted by Lachmann and Tischendorf, retained but doubtfully by Alford: they are wanting in the Vulgate, which translates *quatuor initiis submitti de cœlo.* At all events these four corners are not unimportant. As they corresponded with the four quarters of the heavens, they conveyed an intimation that men from the north and south, the east and west (comp. Mtt. viii. 11; Lk. xiii. 29), would appear as clean before God, or be called to a participation of His kingdom." Neander's *Planting,* I. 72, n.

[5] See *Class-Book of O. T. History,* p. 156.

the Voice spoke again, saying, *What God hath cleansed, that call not thou common*, and when the strange scene had been repeated three times, probably with the same command, the same remonstrance, and the same reply[1], the vessel *was received up again into heaven* (Acts x. 15, 16).

The Apostle was deeply moved, and while meditating on the possible meaning of what he had beheld and heard, the messengers of Cornelius had arrived, and were making enquiries for him, and at the same moment the Spirit bade him go down and accompany them whithersoever they went, *doubting nothing* (Acts x. 19, 20). Thereupon he descended from the housetop, and having learned from the men the purport of their errand, he brought them in and hospitably entertained them (Acts x. 21—23).

The next day he set out with them towards Cæsarea, attended by certain of the brethren from Joppa, and on entering the house of Cornelius found him in the midst of many of his relatives and intimate friends, whom he had assembled to listen to the Apostle's words. As he crossed the threshold (Acts x. 25), the centurion went forth to meet him, and falling down at his feet would have worshipped him. But Peter raised him up, and reminded him that he also was a man, and then addressed himself to the assembled company. They all knew, he said, that he was a Jew, and how unlawful it was for one of that nation to associate with or enter the house of a foreigner: but God had shewed him that he was not to call any man common or unclean, and therefore he had come without delay, and now desired to know the reason for which he had been sent (Acts x. 28, 29).

Then Cornelius recounted the particulars of his

[1] Vaughan, II. 66.

vision (Acts x. 30—33), and requested the Apostle to announce to him and his assembled friends what he, as a messenger of God, had to say to them. Thus assured that all things had occurred under the Divine guidance, the Apostle opened his mouth, and having acknowledged that God *was indeed no respecter of persons, but accepted out of every nation all that feared Him and worked righteousness*, proceeded to proclaim the glad tidings of his risen Lord. He told them of His life of love; of His victories over disease and the spirit-world (Acts x. 38); of His death by the hands of men (Acts x. 39); of His resurrection, and His appearances afterwards, not to all the people but to chosen witnesses, even the Apostles, who had eaten and drunk with Him (Acts x. 40, 41); of His exaltation to heaven and His future coming to judge the world; of the commission he and the rest of the Twelve had received to proclaim to all that believed in Him the *remission of sins* (Acts x. 42, 43).

While he was still speaking, the events of the day of Pentecost were repeated in the house of the Roman soldier. To the astonishment of the Jewish Christians who had accompanied the Apostle from Joppa, the gift of the Holy Ghost was poured out upon the Gentiles, and they heard them speaking in various dialects and magnifying and praising God (Acts x. 46). Now fully awakened to the meaning of the vision on the housetop, the Apostle enquired whether any could forbid that these, who had already evidently received the gift of the Holy Ghost, should be admitted to the rite of baptism, and then ordered that it should be administered; and thus he who had first preached the resurrection to the Jews, baptized the first converts at Jerusalem, and confirmed the first-fruits of the church in Samaria, now, under direct communication from heaven, first threw down the barrier which separated proselytes of the gate from Israelites, and admitted them on an equal footing into the Christian Church[1].

The news of such an event was not long in reaching Jerusalem, and provoked not only enquiry and comment, but actual complaint, so that when the Apostle returned thither, he found himself warmly censured by not a few of the more exclusive section of the "circumcision," who complained that he had consorted and eaten with men who were uncircumcised[2] (Acts xi. 1—3). Thereupon Peter recounted all the particulars of his visit to Cæsarea from the beginning; how he had seen a vision at Joppa, and how a Divine Voice had accompanied and interpreted it; how the messengers of Cornelius had arrived while he was pondering over the vision, and he had been bidden to accompany them nothing doubting[3]; how taking with him six impartial witnesses (Acts xi. 12), who

[1] Smith's *Bibl. Dict.* Art. *Peter*.

[2] "The more rigid Jews looked with jealousy even on the circumcised proselytes; the terms of admission were made as difficult and repulsive as possible; on the imperfect they looked with still greater suspicion, and were rather jealous of communicating their exclusive privileges than eager to extend the influence of their opinions." Milman, *Hist. Christ.* I. 382, n. "An opprobrious proverb coupled proselytes with the vilest profligates, as hindering the coming of the Messiah (Lightfoot, *Hor. Heb.* in Mtt. xxiii. 15). It became a recognised maxim that no wise man would trust a proselyte even to the twenty-fourth generation." Smith's *Bibl. Dict.* The belief in the necessity of circumcision for the full admission of proselytes is illustrated by the compulsory circumcision of the Idumæans by John Hyrcanus and of the Ituræans by Aristobulus (see above, pp. 59, 61, 146 n.).

[3] "As a loyal and believing Hebrew Peter could not have contemplated the removal of Gentile disqualifications without a distinct assurance that the enactments of the law which concerned them were abrogated by the Divine legislator. The vision could not therefore have been the product of a subjective impression. It was, strictly speaking, objective, presented to his mind by an external influence. Yet the intimation in the state of trance did not at once over-

were then present, he had proceeded to the house of Cornelius, and on his arrival was told of another vision which the good centurion had beheld, the "very counterpart and index of his own;" how when he had only begun to speak and to touch upon the Gospel History, the infallible sign of the Divine Presence had been manifested, and the Holy Ghost had fallen on his Gentile hearers as on the disciples in Jerusalem at the beginning; how this had recalled to his mind his Lord's words, *John indeed baptized with water, but ye shall be baptized with the Holy Ghost*, and he had admitted them to baptism; for who was he, after this visible proof of the Divine Presence, that he could withstand God? (Acts xi. 4—17). The question contained its own answer, and the Christians at Jerusalem not only held their peace, and desisted from further reprehension of the Apostle, but glorified God, saying, *Then hath God also to the Gentiles granted repentance unto life* (Acts xi. 18).

Meanwhile events had occurred at other and more distant places than Cæsarea, shewing that the Christian Church was no longer to be confined to the Jews only or to the sacred land of Palestine. The Christians, whom the persecution that followed after the stoning of Stephen[1] had driven from the Holy City, travelled in different directions, to Phœnicia, the neighbouring island of Cyprus, and to Antioch[2], the metropolis of Syria (Acts xi. 19). For some time they confined their ministrations to the Jews only, but at length some of them, *men of*

come his reluctance. It was not *till his consciousness was fully restored*, and he had well considered the meaning of the vision, that he learned that the distinction between cleanness and uncleanness in outward things belonged to a temporary dispensation." Smith's *Bibl. Dict.*, Art. *Peter*.

[1] See above, p. 373.

[2] For its foundation, see above, p. 10, and notes.

Cyprus[1] *and Cyrene*, on their arrival at Antioch, began to preach the word even to the Gentiles, and with such success that a great number became believers, and turned unto the Lord (Acts xi. 21).

Tidings of these events reaching the Church at Jerusalem, in accordance with the precedent already acted upon in Samaria (Acts viii. 14), it was resolved to send to Antioch one in whom they had entire confidence, and who might report on all that had occurred. The person selected for this important duty was no other than Barnabas, *the son of exhortation*, himself a Hellenist, a native of Cyprus, and in all probability well acquainted with Antioch, one known to be *a good man, full of the Holy Ghost, and of faith* (Acts xi. 24).

Accordingly Barnabas set out, and on his arrival found much to approve in the ministrations of the Hellenistic teachers. They had evidently been blessed with great success, and he laboured earnestly to advance it, *exhorting all to cleave to the Lord with full purpose of heart.* His own endeavours did not lose their reward, for the church at Antioch received many additions to its numbers (Acts xi. 24), but Barnabas saw that *a wise master-builder* (1 Cor. iii. 10) was required for the work, and he therefore set out for Tarsus to fetch Saul. Once more, then, the two met, and Saul proceeded with his friend to the Syrian metropolis, and there side by side they continued to labour for a whole year, and so greatly were their exertions blessed, and so numerous were the additions made to the Church, that it was clear the disciples could no longer be confounded with any sect or party of the Jews. Standing out, then, as a separate community, they acquired a distinctive title, and it was first at Antioch, whose inhabitants were notorious for inventing names of deri-

[1] Perhaps Mnason was one of the number, see Acts xxi. 16.

sion[1], that the honourable appellation of CHRISTIANS was first applied to them (Acts xi. 26). This name they were not likely to assume themselves[2], nor is it probable that it was bestowed upon them by the Jews. They called them in hatred and contempt *the sect of the Nazarenes*[3] (Acts xxiv. 5), and Christ being equivalent to Messiah, they were not likely to apply to them a term they themselves held sacred[4]. The name, therefore, probably originated with the Gentiles, and with the Romans rather than the Greeks. The disciples would often speak of Christ as their leader and chief, and the heathens[5] would naturally call them in mockery and derision *Christians*, or the *Followers of Christ*, just as the partisans of Marius were called Mariani, of Pompeius Pompeiani, of Otho Othoniani, of Vitellius Vitelliani, of Herod Herodiani.

While the two Apostles were thus employed, there arrived at Antioch, A. D. 42, certain prophets[6] from Jerusalem, one of whom named Agabus stood up and

[1] C. and H., I. 118.

[2] "In the Acts, and in their own letters, we find them designating themselves as *brethren, disciples, believers, saints* (Acts xv. 23, ix. 26, v. 14, ix. 32; Rom. xv. 25; Col. i. 2, &c.). Only in two places (Acts xxvi. 28, 1 Pet. iv. 16) do we find the term *Christians;* and in both instances it is implied to be a term used by those who are without." C. and H., I. 117, and notes; Humphry's *Comm. on the Acts.*

[3] Or Galilæans. This last was the contemptuous name by which the Emperor Julian afterwards enacted that they should be called. Humphry's *Comm.*

[4] Neander's *Planting,* I. 99.

[5] Comp. Tac. *Ann.* XV. 44, quos *vulgus* Christianos appellabat: they were sometimes miscalled *Chrestiani;* Tertull. *Apol.* III.

[6] Their office did not always or necessarily include that of predicting future events. Compare the remarks on the O. T. Prophets, *Class-Book of O. T. History,* pp. 276, 277. More generally it indicated extraordinary powers of exposition of the Divine Word.

announced that a great famine was at hand, which in fact came to pass during the reign of Claudius Cæsar (Acts xi. 28), a reign distinguished for earthquakes, bad harvests, and general scarcity[1]. Having full faith in his prophetic words the Christians in the Syrian metropolis[2] determined to send relief, every man according to his ability, to their poorer brethren at Jerusalem, and Saul and Barnabas were selected to convey their contributions to the Holy City (Acts xi. 29, 30)[3].

CHAPTER V

MARTYRDOM OF ST JAMES—DEATH OF HEROD.

A. D. 44

ABOUT the time when these delegates from the church at Antioch arrived on their errand of Christian love at Jerusalem, a severe calamity befell the Church there. On the accession of Claudius, A. D. 41, Herod Agrippa, who had taken an active part in securing his succession[4], was rewarded by the addition of Judæa and Samaria to the tetrarchies of Philip and Antipas which he had already received, and ruled as king over a territory as widely extended as that governed by his grandfather[5].

[1] Tac. *Ann.* XII. 13; Jos. *Ant.* III. 15. 3, XX. 2. 5.

[2] Four local famines are mentioned during the reign of Claudius, (1) in his first and second year, A. D. 41, 42, at Rome; (2) in his fourth year, A. D. 44, in Judæa; (3) in his ninth year, A. D. 49, in Greece; (4) in his eleventh year, A.D. 51, at Rome.

[3] In this verse occurs the first mention of the Christian πρεσβύτεροι, rendered in the Vulgate *seniores*, in the E. V. *elders*. In Acts xx. 28 they are termed ἐπίσκοποι; the last expression pointing to their office, the former to their age and character. For the ancient Jewish Elders, see Numb. xi. 16, and *Class-Book of Old Testament History*, p. 170.

[4] Merivale's *Romans under the Empire*, VI. 102.

[5] Jos. *Ant.* XIX. 5. 1; *B. J.* II. 11. 5. Merivale, VI. 115.

Arriving at Jerusalem, A. D. 42, he dedicated in the Temple, as a memorial of the Divine protection, the golden chain with which he had been presented by Caligula, and which was of equal weight with the iron one he had worn when imprisoned by Tiberius[1], and endeavoured to ingratiate himself with his subjects by the strictest profession of Judaism. He offered sacrifice every day; paid the expenses of certain Nazarites on completing their vows[2]; abstained from every legal impurity; remitted the house-tax of the inhabitants of Jerusalem[3]; encircled the new suburb of Bezetha with a wall; and prepared to strengthen the entire fortifications of the city[4].

Thus determined to ingratiate himself with the Jews, and doubtless at the suggestions of their chiefs, he resolved to take measures for the suppression of Christianity. Accordingly, in A. D. 44, he seized the Apostle James, the brother of St John, and without any apparent process of Jewish law[5] summarily slew him with the sword (Acts xii. 2), thus early admitting him to his Master's baptism[6] (Mtt. xx. 23). Perceiving that this atrocity rendered him exceedingly popular with his subjects[7], he

[1] See above, p. 393, n.; Jos. *Ant.* XIX. 6. I.

[2] Jos. *Ant.* XIX. 6. I; 7. 3. Comp. Acts xxi. 23.

[3] Jos. *Ant.* XIX. 6. 3. He exercised, however, his supreme authority by continually displacing the high-priest. Having deposed Theophilus, son of Annas (see above, p. 382, n.), he substituted Simon son of Boethus (Jos. *Ant.* XIX. 6. 2); he then offered the pontificate to Jonathan son of Annas (Jos. *Ant.* XIX. 6. 4), and on his declining it, bestowed it upon his brother Matthias; in A. D. 43 he deposed Matthias, and appointed Elionæus, son of the Simon mentioned above, to the post (Jos. *Ant.* XIX. 8. I).

[4] Jos. *Ant.* XIX. 7. 2. The prefect of Syria, however, compelled him to desist.

[5] Milman, *Hist. Christ.* I. 374.

[6] See above, p. 257.

[7] "The popular feeling, which from Pentecost till Ste-

arrested Peter also at the feast of the Passover, and committed him to the custody of four quaternions of soldiers[1] (Acts xii. 4), intending at the close of the festival to bring him forth before the people and gratify them with his death.

Great was the sorrow of the Church at the prospect of the Apostle's execution, and unceasing and not ineffectual prayer was made to God in his behalf. For on the night before the day fixed for the spectacle of his martyrdom, while the Apostle was sleeping between two soldiers, bound with two chains, and the sentinels without were carefully guarding the doors, a light suddenly shone into his cell, and an angel touched him on the side, and bade him rise up quickly. Thereupon he arose, and his chains fell from off his hands. *Gird thyself*, resumed the angel, *and bind on thy sandals*. The Apostle did so, and casting his garment about him, and scarcely believing the reality of what was going on, followed his celestial guide through the first and second ward, and thence through the iron gate, which opened of its own accord, into the street of the city (Acts xii. 5—10).

Then the angel departed, and the Apostle realising for the first time the fact of his deliverance, repaired to the house of Mary[2], a sister of Barnabas, where many were gathered together praying. As soon as he had

phen's death was in favour of the Gospel, now set in in the contrary direction. Humphry's *Comm.*

[1] "One quaternion for each watch of the night; of the four men forming the quaternion, two were stationed before the door (Acts xii. 6), and to two the Apostle was chained according to the Roman custom." Veget. *Res Milit.* III. 8, quoted in Humphry's *Comm.*

[2] Comp. Col. iv. 10. Thus while the brother gave up his land and brought its value into the common treasury of the Church, the sister gave up her house for the use of the early Christians. Peter seems to have been on terms of intimacy with her, and this is confirmed by 1 Pet. v. 13.

knocked at the door, a damsel named Rhoda came forth to open it, but recognising his voice was so transported with joy that she ran in and announced that Peter was standing at the door. Those within, however, declared that she was mad, that she had seen his angel or ghost, and refused to believe her words. Meanwhile the Apostle stood without knocking, and at length the door was opened, and the disciples were assured that it was he and no other. They would have expressed their joy with loud thanksgivings, but holding up his hand he beckoned to them to be silent, and then having recounted all that had befallen him, bade them carry the joyful news to James *the Lord's brother* and the rest of the disciples (Acts xii. 11—17). With these words he betook himself to some secure hiding-place.

The morning dawned, and the soldiers rising from their slumbers were overwhelmed with astonishment at finding their prisoner gone, and while with no small stir they were endeavouring to make out what had become of him, Herod sent for them, and when he could not ascertain any tidings respecting their prisoner, ordered them to be put to death, and then left Jerusalem for Cæsarea (Acts xii. 19).

Before the autumn, however, a terrible end had overtaken the tyrant. Tidings reached Judæa of the triumphant return of Claudius from his expedition to Britain[1], and shows similar to those at Rome were commenced at Cæsarea, which was crowded with people from all quarters. On the second day[2] of the festival the king, clothed in magnificent robes, entered the glo-

[1] Ὑπὲρ τῆς ἐκείνου (Claudius) σωτηρίας, Jos. *Ant.* XIX. 8. 2. Compare the language of Philo, *Leg.* 45, alluding to Caligula's safe return from Gaul, quoted in Lewin's *Fasti Sacri*, p. 280. Another opinion is that the festival was held in honour of the birthday of Claudius, August 1.

[2] Jos. *Ant.* XIX. 8. 2.

rious theatre[1] which his grandfather had built, and sitting down on his throne (Acts xii. 21) proceeded to give an audience to certain ambassadors from the inhabitants of Tyre and Sidon. For some reason the people of these Phœnician cities had given him offence, and through the intercession of Blastus, the royal chamberlain, they now sought a reconciliation and a renewal of friendly relations, which was a matter of no small importance, since Phœnicia, as in ancient times[2], depended on Palestine for its supplies of corn and oil (Acts xii. 20). It was early morning[3]. The sun's rays fell upon the apparel of the king glistering with silver tissue, and the excited multitude sitting in a great semicircle, tier above tier, on the stone seats of the theatre, were dazzled with the brightness which flashed forth from the monarch's robes. Presently he spoke, and they shouted, *It is the voice of a god and not of a man.* The king made no attempt to repress their adulation, and in the midst of this idolatrous ostentation an angel of God smote him, and he was carried out of the theatre, smitten with a terrible internal disorder, and eaten of worms[4] (Acts xii. 23). After lingering five days in excruciating agony he died in the fifty-fourth year of his age, having reigned seven years, four over part of his dominions, and three over the whole of Palestine[5], and leaving behind him one son,

[1] See above, p. 92.

[2] See the quotation from Kenrick's *Phœnicia*, in *Class-Book of O. T. History*, p. 355, and comp. Ezek. xxvii. 17; 1 Kings v. 9; Ezra iii. 7.

[3] Jos. *Ant.* XIX. 8. 2. Δευτέρᾳ δὲ τῶν θεωριῶν ἡμέρᾳ στολὴν ἐνδυσάμενος ἐξ ἀργύρου πεποιημένην πᾶσαν...παρῆλθεν εἰς τὸ θέατρον ἀρχομένης ἡμέρας.

[4] Luke *the physician* is more accurate than Josephus in his description of the disease that caused the death of Agrippa. Comp. the deaths of Antiochus Epiphanes, above, p. 38, and of Herod the Great, above, pp. 104, 105.

[5] Jos. *Ant.* XIX. 8. 2, i. e. from A. D. 37 to A. D. 44.

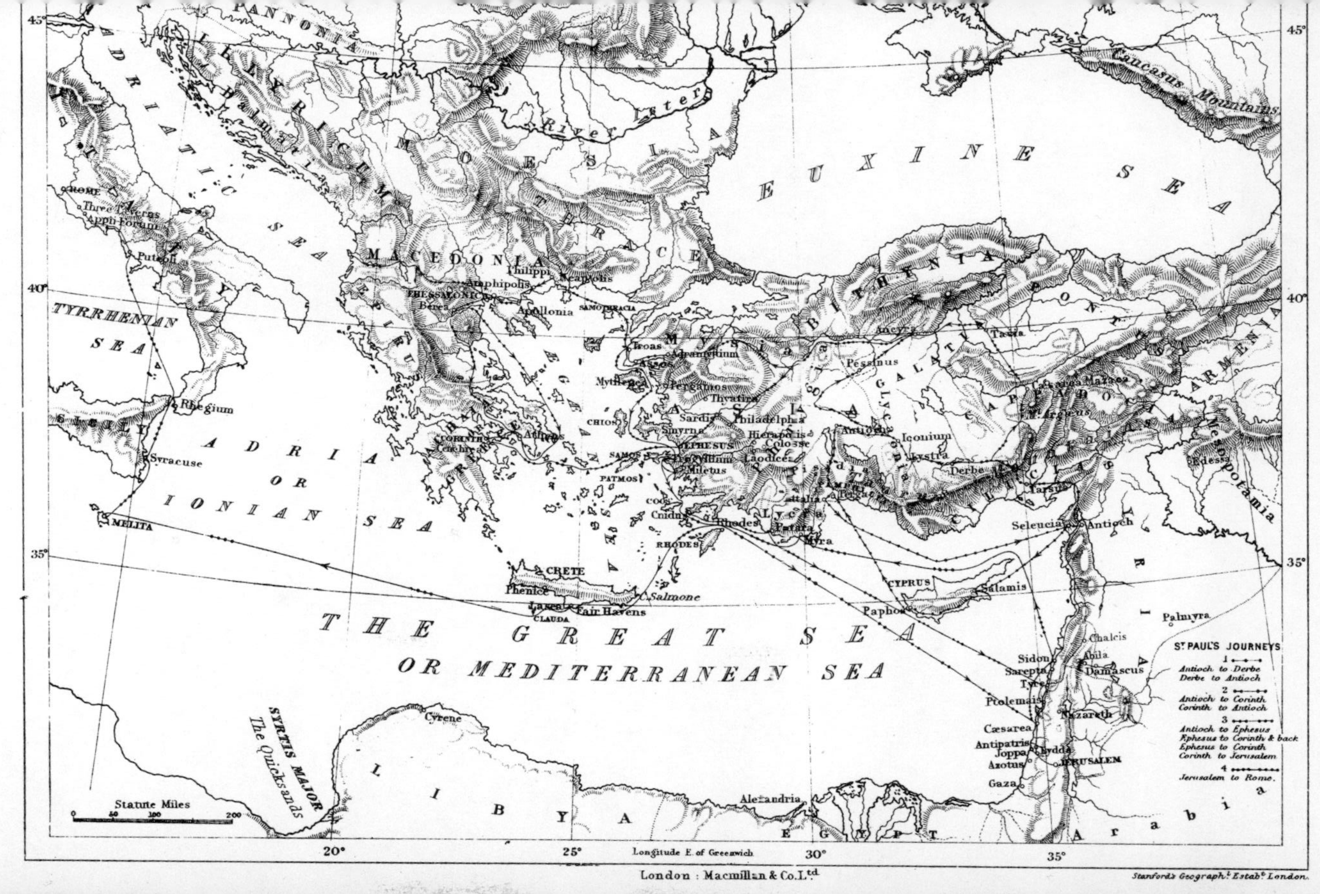
PANNONIA
ILLYRICUM
Dalmatia
ADRIATIC SEA
MOESIA
River Ister
EUXINE SEA
Caucasus Mountains
THRACE
MACEDONIA
EPIRUS
BITHYNIA
PONTUS
ARMENIA
GALATIA
CAPPADOCIA
MYSIA
ASIA
Lycaonia
CILICIA
Mesopotamia
SYRIA
ROME
Three Taverns
Appii Forum
Puteoli
TYRRHENIAN SEA
SICILY
Rhegium
Syracuse
MELITA
ADRIA OR IONIAN SEA
Philippi
Neapolis
Amphipolis
Apollonia
THESSALONICA
Berea
SAMOTHRACIA
Troas
Assos
Adramyttium
Mytilene
Pergamos
Thyatira
Sardis
Philadelphia
Smyrna
CHIOS
SAMOS
EPHESUS
Miletus
Hierapolis
Colosse
Laodicea
PATMOS
COS
Cnidus
Rhodes
RHODES
Patara
Myra
Attalia
Athens
CORINTH
Cenchrea
Ancyra
Tavia
Pessinus
Antioch
Iconium
Lystra
Derbe
Tarsus
Edessa
Seleucia
Antioch
CRETE
Phenice
Lasea
Fair Havens
CLAUDA
Salmone
CYPRUS
Salamis
Paphos
Palmyra
Chalcis
Abila
Damascus
Sidon
Sarepta
Tyre
Ptolemais
Nazareth
Cæsarea
Antipatris
Joppa
Lydda
JERUSALEM
Azotus
Gaza
THE GREAT SEA OR MEDITERRANEAN SEA
Cyrene
SYRTIS MAJOR
The Quicksands
LIBYA
Alexandria
EGYPT
Arabia
Statute Miles
0
50
100
200
ST. PAUL'S JOURNEYS
1
Antioch to Derbe
Derbe to Antioch
2
Antioch to Corinth
Corinth to Antioch
3
Antioch to Ephesus
Ephesus to Corinth & back
Ephesus to Corinth
Corinth to Jerusalem
4
Jerusalem to Rome.
45°
40°
35°
20°
25°
30°
35°
Longitude E. of Greenwich
London : Macmillan & Co. Ltd
Stanford's Geograph.l Estab.t London.

Agrippa, and three daughters, Drusilla, Berenice, and Mariamne[1].

PART III

THE CHURCH OF THE GENTILES.

SECTION I

First Missionary Tour of Paul and Barnabas.

CHAPTER I

CYPRUS, PERGA, THE PISIDIAN ANTIOCH.

A.D. 45, 46.

THE martyrdom of Stephen exercised, as we have seen, an important influence on the development of the Church, scattering the disciples over heathen lands.

[1] Jos. *Ant.* XIX. 9. 1; Milman, *Hist. of the Jews,* II. 161. The unexpected death of Herod Agrippa "seems to have unhinged the plans of the Roman government. So important a charge as the sovereignty of Palestine could be intrusted only to a tried servant of the Emperor; and even Agrippa had given cause of jealousy by the relation he had cultivated with the princes of the frontier. None of his family merited to succeed him. His brother Herod was allowed to continue in the obscure dignity of his petty chiefdom, and his son Agrippa, already resident as a hostage at Rome, was retained there in honourable custody; while the dominions of the great Idumæan reverted once more to the control of the prefect of Syria, and acquiesced, with a few uneasy murmurs, in its full incorporation with the empire." Merivale, VI. 116, 117. Cassius Longinus was now appointed, A. D. 44, to the presidency of Syria, while Cuspius Fadus was sent out as governor of Judæa. Jos. *Ant.* XIX. 9. 2; XX. I. I.

The martyrdom of James the son of Zebedee marks a no less important epoch. It seems to have been the signal for the withdrawal of the Apostles from Jerusalem[1]. The special work assigned there to Peter, the Apostle of the Circumcision, was over. He had founded the Church, opened its gates to Jews and Gentiles, and laid down the conditions of their admission. Consigning, therefore, the direction of the Christian society in Jerusalem to James *the Lord's brother* (Gal. i. 19), the Apostles departed to enter upon wider fields of action.

After completing the object of their journey, and proving the fellowship that existed between the disciples in Syria and Palestine, Saul and Barnabas, accompanied by a kinsman of the latter[2], John surnamed Mark, returned to Antioch. In the Syrian metropolis the three were joined by other teachers, Simeon, surnamed Niger[3], Lucius of Cyrene[4], and Manaen[5] a foster-brother[6] of Herod the tetrarch (Acts xiii. 1), and toge-

[1] Lightfoot *On the Galatians*, p. 285.

[2] He was the son of that Mary, a person of some means and influence, to whose house Peter went after his miraculous release from prison (Acts xii. 12). He was probably, therefore, born at Jerusalem, and is by some identified with the "young man" mentioned in Mk. xiv. 51, 52. Hence he was the nephew of Barnabas (Col. iv. 10), and had possibly been converted by St Peter (1 Peter. v. 13).

[3] Nothing further is known of this Simeon. His first name shews that he was a Jew by birth, his second, that, as in other cases, he took another name as more convenient for intercourse with foreigners.

[4] By some identified with the kinsman or fellow-tribesman of St Paul, mentioned in Rom. xvi. 21.

[5] Manaen = *consoler*, the same name as that of the 16th king of Israel (2 K. xv. 14—22).

[6] Σύντροφος, Vulgate *collactaneus* = ὁμογάλακτος, *foster-brother*, i. e. Manaen's mother (or the woman who reared him) was also Herod's nurse. Others would interpret the word as = *comrade, associate, educated with,* according to a not unusual custom of associating other children with the

ther they continued to instruct and build up the Church. At length while, on one occasion, they were engaged in a solemn service of prayer and fasting, the Holy Ghost intimated, probably through one or more of the prophets then present (Acts xiii. 2), that Barnabas and Saul should be set apart to accomplish a special work, for which they had been called.

In accordance with this intimation, after a solemn religious service (Acts xiii. 3), the hands of the chief members of the church at Antioch were laid upon the two, and accompanied by Mark they repaired to Seleucia[1], and thence sailed to Cyprus, where amongst their connections and friends[2] it might be expected that Barnabas and his kinsman might labour with good results, and where there was already the nucleus of a Christian Church.

After a few hours' sail, therefore, they reached Sala-

sons of persons of rank, to share their amusements and excite them to emulation. Comp. Xen. *Cyrop.* I. 3. 14, and the passages cited in Wetstein on Acts xiii. 1. The Herod alluded to was probably Herod Antipas, who beheaded John the Baptist, and if so, Manaen could hardly have been altogether unacquainted with the circumstances of the Redeemer's life. Josephus (*Ant.* XV. 10. 5) mentions a Manaen, an Essene, who foretold to Herod the Great his future elevation to royal dignity, and who was held by him in high esteem. He may therefore have been the father of the companion of his children, Antipas and Archelaus, who were educated at Rome: Comp. Jos. *Ant.* XVII. 1. 3, Ἀρχέλαος δὲ καὶ Ἀντίπας ἐπὶ Ῥώμης παρά τινι ἰδιώτῃ τροφὰς εἶχον.

[1] The sea-port and fortress of Antioch, and connected with it by the river Orontes. Seleucus had named his metropolis after his father (see above, p. 10), and the maritime fortress after himself. It became a place of great importance, and was made a *free city* by Pompey for its bold resistance to Tigranes. See Smith's *Dict. Geog.*

[2] See above, p. 356, n. Cyprus was (1) near; (2) contained the nucleus of a church; (3) was the birthplace of Barnabas; (4) contained many Jews.

mis[1], the eastern port and ancient capital of the island, and preached the word in its synagogues, of which there appear to have been several. Thence they travelled to Paphos[2], at the south-western extremity of Cyprus, the seat of the Roman government and the residence of the proconsul[3], Sergius Paulus. At his court was one of those Jewish sorcerers, whom we have already seen encountering the Apostle Peter in Samaria[4], named Bar-jesus, or, as he called himself in Arabic, Elymas, *the wise* (Acts xiii. 8). Provoked at the willingness of the proconsul to listen to the preaching of the newly-arrived teachers, he offered a strenuous opposition to his wishes. But Saul, or, as he is now for

[1] A city on the eastern coast of Cyprus, said to have been founded by Teucer (Hor. *Od.* I. 7. 29). The farming of the copper-mines of the island to Herod (Jos. *Ant.* XVI. 4. 5), as also the wine, flax, and honey which it yielded, probably increased the numbers attracted by its harbour and trade. On the revolt of the Jews in the reign of Trajan, when the populous city became a desert, see Milman, *Hist. Jews,* III. 111, 112.

[2] Notorious for the worship of Venus or Aphrodite, fabled here to have risen from the sea (Hom. *Od.* VIII. 362), whose temple was at "Old Paphos," while the harbour and chief town were at "New Paphos," a little distance off. Titus made a pilgrimage to the shrine (Tac. *Hist.* II. 2. 3).

[3] On the provinces and the difference between the proconsul and proprætor, see above, p. 147, n. Cyprus originally was an imperial province, but it was afterwards transferred to the Senate. See Lardner's *Credibility of the Gospel History,* I. 32, &c.: for an engraving of a Cyprian coin of the reign of Claudius, see C. and H., I. 147.

[4] See above, p. 374. On the influx of Eastern sorcerers, astrologers, and soothsayers into Rome, and their influence, see Hor. *Od.* I. 11. 2; Cic. *Div.* II. 42—47; Juv. VI. 562, XIV. 248. Marius always kept in his camp a Syrian prophetess; Pompeius, Crassus, Cæsar, were all addicted to Oriental astrology; the picture of Tiberius surrounded by his "Chaldæan herd" (Juv. *Sat.* X. 93) is well known. See C. and H., I. 141, and notes.

the first time called Paul[1], fixed his eyes upon him, and in the plenitude of that power which he possessed from the Holy Ghost, sternly rebuked him for thus seeking to *pervert the right ways of the Lord*, and denounced an instantaneous judgment: *the hand of the Lord should be upon him, and he should be blind, nor see the sun for a season.* This privation, which the Apostle had himself experienced, was instantly inflicted on the sorcerer, and he had to seek the aid of others in going from place to place (Acts xiii. 11). Such a vivid exhibition of miraculous power produced a deep impression upon the proconsul, and *he believed, being astonished at the doctrine of the Lord* (Acts xiii. 12).

From Paphos the three sailed in a north-westerly direction to the harbour of Attaleia[2] in Pamphylia[3], and thence up the river Cestrus 6 or 7 miles inland to the town of Perga[4] (Acts xiii. 13). Here Mark, either

[1] After this his old name Saul never recurs in the New Testament. "It was an ancient conjecture that the change was made to commemorate the conversion of the Proconsul: this may have been the *occasion;* but the *reason* probably was to make the name more familiar to Roman ears." Humphry's *Comm. on the Acts.* That the Apostle probably had both in his childhood is stated above, p. 380, and possibly "the name Paulus came from some connection of his ancestors (perhaps as manumitted slaves) with some member of the Roman family of the Æmilian Pauli" (C. and H., I. 146). It can hardly be believed to be accidental that the Gentile name rises to the surface at the moment when St Paul visibly enters on his office as the Apostle of the Gentiles.

[2] Founded by *Attalus* Philadelphus, as a port for the trade between Egypt and Syria. It has lasted till the present day, and is now called *Satalia.*

[3] It will be remembered that St Paul had already preached the word in Cilicia (see above, p. 380); he probably now wished to extend it among the contiguous districts.

[4] An important city of Pamphylia, situated on the river Cestrus, as Tarsus on the Cydnus, celebrated for the worship of Artemis (Diana), Cic. *Verr.* I. 20.

yearning after the home he had left at Jerusalem, or affrighted by the perils he was likely to encounter[1], departed from his companions, and returned to Jerusalem, while the others pressed on alone to Antioch in Pisidia, a town of considerable importance, having been built by the founder of the Syrian Antioch[2], and since then advanced by Augustus to the dignity of a Roman *colony*[3].

The population of the Pisidian Antioch was mixed, consisting of Greeks, Romans, and native Pisidians, but the influence of the Jews was considerable, and they had succeeded in making not a few converts. Having waited, therefore, for the ensuing Sabbath, Paul and Barnabas repaired to the synagogue, and after the regular service[4] were bidden by the president of the synagogue, if they had *any word of exhortation*, to address those assembled (Acts xiii. 15).

Thereupon Paul rose up, and *beckoning with his hand* delivered his first address of which we have any record. Like the discourse he had himself heard from the lips of Stephen[5], it was based on the history of the Jewish nation. The call of Abraham, the Wanderings in the wilderness, the occupation of Canaan, the period of the Judges[6], the election of the first King, the accession

[1] On the perils of *robbers* and *rivers* incident to the Pisidian Highlands, see C. and H., I. 154, 155. Some think he wished to join Peter and those Apostles who were preaching in Palestine. We shall find him not unwilling to accompany the Apostles on a second missionary journey (Acts xv. 37).

[2] See above, p. 10, and notes. Its site was discovered by Arundell in 1833, at *Valobatch*, six hours distant from *Akshar*.

[3] The peculiarities of the constitution of a Roman *colonia* will be treated of when we come to Philippi.

[4] For a description of the synagogue service, see above, pp. 111, 112.

[5] Comp. above, p. 368.

[6] On the duration here assigned to this period see Words-

of David; all these important events were touched upon in their order (Acts xiii. 16—22). Of David's seed, he then proceeded, God had promised (2 Sam. vii. 12) to raise up a Saviour, and this promise he had fulfilled. Duly heralded by His predicted Forerunner (Acts xiii. 24, 25), the promised Saviour had appeared in the person of Jesus. The rulers, indeed, of Jerusalem, not knowing Him, or the real meaning of the words of the prophets read in their ears every Sabbath-day, had constrained Pilate to put Him to death, had crucified, and laid Him in a sepulchre; but God had raised him from the dead, and He had been seen after His resurrection[1], not by strangers, but by those familiar with His person, who had been His companions from Galilee to Jerusalem (Acts xiii. 26—31), who were His witnesses to the people of Israel. By His death and resurrection He had truly accomplished the ancient prophecies[2], which could not refer to their forefather David (who was dead, and had long mouldered in the tomb); and now through Him was offered to all the forgiveness of sins, even of those from which they could not have been delivered by the Law of Moses[3].

Such was the purport of the Apostle's first recorded sermon. Its immediate effect was a deep impression upon those who heard it. As they left the synagogue

worth's note *in loc.*; Humphry's *Comm. on the Acts;* Biscoe's *History of the Acts.*

[1] Compare the importance attached to these appearances by the Apostle in 1 Cor. xv. 1—12.

[2] Ps. ii. 7, LXX; Isai. lv. 3, LXX; Ps. xvi. 10, LXX trans.

[3] Compare this address with those of Peter in Acts ii. 27, &c. and x. 30—43, above, pp. 351, 2. In both the chief stress is laid on the Saviour's resurrection (comp. Acts i. 22, iv. 33). We can hardly fail to observe in Acts xiii. 39 the first germ of the deeper teaching of St Paul respecting the insufficiency of the Mosaic Law, developed afterwards in the Epistles to the Romans and Galatians.

many[1] besought the Apostles that these words might be repeated in their hearing on the next Sabbath, and not a few, both Jews and proselytes, accompanied them from the synagogue, and listened to their exhortations that having received the word they would not let it slip, but continue steadfastly in the grace of God (Acts xiii. 43).

Accordingly when the next Sabbath came round *almost the whole city* was assembled to hear the word, multitudes of Gentiles pressing in with the Jews and proselytes. This was more than the stricter section of the Jews could bear, and filled with envy at the assembly of so many strangers, they made an uproar, and opposed the word spoken by Paul with contradictions and even blasphemy (Acts xiii. 45).

Their opposition only nerved the Apostles with still greater boldness, and they openly proclaimed the course they would now adopt. In accordance with their Master's directions, they had addressed themselves first to members of their own nation, but since they despised their message, and deemed themselves *unworthy of eternal life*, they would turn to the Gentiles[2]. This declaration many of the latter then present received with joy, and became believers, so that the word of the Lord was published abroad through the whole region (Acts xiii. 49).

This success provoked still greater opposition. Through the female proselytes in the city the Jews gained the ear of the chief authorities, and succeeded in raising a storm of persecution against the Apostles, and expelling them beyond the limits of the colony (Acts xiii. 50). They did not leave it, however, without a solemn protest against the impiety of its inhabitants.

[1] Lachmann and Tischendorf omit the τὰ ἔθνη inserted in Acts xiii. 42 in the *Textus Receptus*.

[2] Comp. Isai. xlii. 6, xlix. 6; Lk. ii. 32.

In obedience to their Master's directions[1], they shook off the dust of their feet against them, and while, in spite of the persecution that had been raised, the little band of Christians were *filled with joy and the Holy Ghost* (Acts xiii. 52), they proceeded to cross the barren uplands[2] which separate Antioch from the plain of Iconium.

CHAPTER II

VISIT TO LYSTRA, DERBE—DISPUTES AT ANTIOCH.

A. D. 48—50.

ON reaching Iconium[3], as they had done at Antioch, the Apostles repaired to the synagogue, and there proclaimed their message with such success, that a great multitude both of Jews and Gentiles embraced the faith. Thereupon the unbelieving Jews repeated the tactics already found so successful at Antioch. They excited the minds of the Gentile population against the brethren, and stirred up a furious opposition (Acts xiv. 2). On this occasion, however, the Apostles did not feel themselves called to leave the city immediately. They remained at Iconium some considerable time, and spoke boldly in the Name of their Divine Master, who attested the truth of their words by many *miracles and signs.* In the end the population was divided. The one, in-

[1] Mtt. x. 14, 15; Mk. vi. 11; Lk. ix. 5.

[2] C. and H., I. 195.

[3] Now called *Konieh*, situated on the western part of an extensive table-land of Asia Minor, not far north of Mount Taurus. This region was anciently called Lycaonia, and thus Iconium "was on the great line of communication between Ephesus and the western coast of the peninsula on one side, and Tarsus, Antioch, and the Euphrates on the other." See C. and H., I. 174, 175. From its position it was clearly a well chosen spot for missionary operations.

cluding the influential classes, sided with the Jews, the other with the Apostles. At length a conspiracy was formed with the connivance of the magistrates (Acts xiv. 5) to insult and even stone them, and Paul and Barnabas, recognising the signal to leave, betook themselves to the neighbouring Lycaonian towns, Lystra[1] and Derbe[2].

Lystra was the place first visited, and here there was no synagogue, and apparently but few Jews. It was a small town in a wild district and amongst a rude population speaking a dialect of their own, and serving *the gods many and lords many* of primitive heathenism. The Apostles therefore could only make known their message by repairing to places of public resort, and addressing themselves to such groups as curiosity or interest might gather together. On one of these occasions, a man, who had been a cripple from his birth (Acts xiv. 8), and who probably sat for alms in the public thoroughfare, listened to them with deep attention. Thereupon the Apostle Paul, moved with compassion, and probably sensible of the necessity of some miracle to attest his authority, as also perceiving that the man had faith to be healed, fixed his eye upon him and addressing him in a loud voice, said, *Stand upright on thy feet.* In an instant the man sprang up, and leaped, and walked.

[1] Its site is unknown. There are strong reasons, however, for identifying its site with that of *Kir-bir-Kilisseh* at the base of the *Kara-dagh.*

[2] Like Lystra the exact situation of Derbe is unknown. It is certain, however, that it was in the eastern part of the great upland plain of Lycaonia, which stretches from Iconia eastwards along the north sides of the chain of Taurus. For the various conjectures respecting its site, see Smith's *Bibl. Dict.*, and C. and H., I. 178, n. Cicero passed through it on his road from Cilicia to Iconium. Cic. *ad. Fam.* XIII. 73: Cum Antipatro *Derbete* mihi non solum hospitium, verum etiam summa familiaritas intercedit.

Such a cure of such a man in such a manner was speedily noised abroad, and the multitudes gathering together no sooner saw what had been done, than they lifted up their voices, saying in their native Lycaonian dialect[1], *The gods are come down to us in the likeness of men* (Acts xiv. 11). That the gods, in the form of mortal men, did often visit the earth, was a cherished belief amongst many heathen nations, and nowhere more than in the very district now visited by the Apostles[2]. The tutelar deity of Lystra was Zeus, Jupiter, and at the entrance of the town he had a temple, where he was worshipped as its founder and protector. The inhabitants therefore rushed to the conclusion, that in the Apostle Barnabas, probably in consequence of his venerable appearance, they beheld none other than the "father of gods and men," while in his companion, who was *the chief speaker*, they thought they recognised Hermes, or Mercury, the god of eloquence, and the frequent companion of Jupiter on his visits to earth[3].

The news that these deities had honoured Lystra with their presence quickly spread, and reached the ears of the priest of Jupiter. Accordingly he and his assistants soon appeared with oxen and garlands before the residence of the Apostles, prepared to offer sacrifice in their honour. Perceiving for the first time the object of these proceedings, Paul and Barnabas rushed forth from their abode, and meeting the procession approaching the vestibule[4], exclaimed, *Sirs, what*

[1] According to some a Syrian dialect, according to others a corrupt form of Greek. Lycaonia is one of those ethnological rather than political districts of Asia Minor mentioned in the N. T.; politically it was sometimes in Cappadocia, sometimes in Galatia.

[2] Compare the story of Baucis and Philemon in Ovid's *Metam.* VIII. 611, &c.

[3] Comp. Ovid, *Fasti*, v. 495.

[4] Ἐπὶ τοὺς πύλωνας in Acts xiv. 13, does not denote the

do ye? we also are men of like passions with you. And then they went on to declare the real purport of their coming, which was to persuade them to turn from the worship of such false gods, to the living and life-giving God, the Maker of heaven, and earth, and the sea, and all things that are therein, who in the past generations had permitted all nations[1] to walk in their own ways, interposing not by any visible judgment or by any worldwide revelation, but who had not left Himself without witness, doing good to the creatures of His hand, giving *rain from heaven and fruitful seasons, filling their hearts with joy and gladness* (Acts xiv. 15—17).

Even this appeal hardly prevailed upon the people to abandon their intentions. At length they reluctantly retired, and led away the victims without offering them in sacrifice to the Apostles. The impression, however, thus made was on the surface only, and was soon to give place to an entire revulsion of feeling. It had become known at Antioch and Iconium, whither the Apostles had retired. From both places, therefore, certain of the Jews made their way to Lystra, and stirred up the minds of the people against their newly-arrived visitors, representing, it is not improbable, that they were impostors, and practised magical arts[2]. Thereupon, with the fickleness for which they were proverbial, the Lycaonians turned upon the men they had so lately been willing to adore, and actually stoned Paul[3], and

gates of the city, but the vestibule or gate which gave admission from the public street into the court of the house. So it is used Mtt. xxvi. 71 (on which see note above, p. 290); Lk. xvi. 20; Acts x. 17; Acts xii. 13. C. and H., I. 182, n.; Neander's *Planting*, 113, n.

[1] Compare the Apostle's language in Rom. iii. 25.

[2] Comp. Mtt. xii. 24.

[3] This is the occasion alluded to in 2 Cor. xi. 24, 25, "*Once* I was stoned." At Iconium the *design* had been formed of stoning him: "Had the assault been completed,

supposing him to be dead dragged him forth out of their town.

Some disciples[1], however, had been made even in Lystra, and these did not now desert their teacher in the hour of peril. While they were standing around him, and probably using means for his restoration, the Apostle arose, and returned with them to his abode. A longer stay was clearly dangerous, and therefore on the morrow he and his companion left for the neighbouring town of Derbe, and thence, having preached the Word and made several disciples (Acts xiv. 21), they returned through the several towns they had visited, exhorting the disciples to abide constant in the faith, and reminding them that *through much affliction they must enter the kingdom of God*. Moreover in the several churches they had established they now appointed elders[2], and after prayer and fasting, solemnly presented them be-

had the history related that a stone was thrown, as it relates that preparations were made both by Jews and Gentiles to stone Paul and his companions, or even had the account of this transaction stopped, without going on to inform us that St Paul and his companions were *aware of the danger and fled*, a contradiction between the history and the Epistle would have ensued. Truth is necessarily consistent; but it is scarcely possible that independent accounts, not having truth to guide them, should thus advance to the very brink of contradiction without falling into it." Paley's *Horæ Paulinæ*.

[1] One was certainly Timothy, the son of a Jewess named Eunice, his father being a Greek (Acts xvi. 1), whom Paul afterwards found at Lystra, already a disciple, and of good report among the brethren (Acts xvi. 2). In 1 Tim. i. 2, i. 18; 2 Tim. ii. 1, he calls him *his own son in the faith*, and in 2 Tim. iii. 10, 11, reminds him of his intimate and personal knowledge of the sufferings he had endured at Antioch, Iconium, and Lystra (note the accurate order of the places). There is the strongest reason, therefore, for believing that he was now converted to the faith. See Birks' Ed. of Paley's *Horæ Paulinæ*, p. 153, and note on p. 155.

[2] See above, p. 404, n.

fore the Lord (Acts xiv. 23). Thence they proceeded to Perga, and after preaching the Word there, to the sea-port of Attalia. There they took ship, and sailing to Seleucia reached Antioch, and on their arrival summoned the brethren, and announced to them the success of their mission, and the many proofs they had witnessed that *God had opened the door of faith to the Gentiles* (Acts xiv. 27).

Arrived at Antioch, the Apostles continued there for some time, A. D. 47—50, strengthening and confirming the faith of the Church, and during their stay began that contest with the Judaizing Christians with which St Paul was destined to be so largely occupied.

It had by this time become clear that the Christian faith, instead of being the purest and highest form of Judaism, was to prove itself a world-wide universal religion, and that its Jewish elements were to be absorbed and *vanish away.* In every nation and in every place, at Joppa, at Cæsarea, at Antioch, in rude village-towns like Lystra and Derbe, as well as populous cities like Perga and Iconium, it was seen that God accepted without respect of persons those that feared Him and worked righteousness (Acts x. 34, 35).

Such a revolution of feeling towards the Gentile world[1] could not be at once received with entire acquiescence. At Jerusalem, in sight of the Temple, and in the midst of all the associations of his faith and national history, the exclusive feelings, which the Jew carried with him wherever he went, were concentrated and intensified[2]. Hitherto there had been no attempt to define the mutual relations of Jewish and Gentile converts. "All such questions, it would seem, had been tacitly passed over, neither side perhaps being desirous

[1] On the Jewish feeling of jealousy and suspicion even towards proselytes, see above, p. 400, n. 2.

[2] C. and H., I. 197.

of provoking discussion[1]." Events, however, now occurred, which rendered necessary a solution of the question.

Certain *false brethren*[2] (Gal. ii. 12) went down from Judæa to Antioch (Acts xv. 1), and *creeping in unawares*[3], began to observe with no favourable eye the extent to which the Jewish Law was relaxed in favour of the Gentile Christians, and their liberty in Christ Jesus vindicated (Gal. ii. 4). Before long they began to insinuate, not that the observance of certain ceremonies in themselves indifferent was advisable for the sake of expediency, but that the rite of circumcision was essential for salvation; *Except ye be circumcised*, said they to the Gentile Christians, *ye cannot be saved* (Acts xv. 1).

To such a doctrine no one was more opposed than the Apostle Paul. To the subjection which these teachers required, he would not advise his Gentile converts to yield, *no, not for an hour* (Gal. ii. 5). The consequence was, that no small dissension and disputation arose between himself and Barnabas on the one hand, and the false teachers on the other, and no slight anxiety and perplexity harassed the minds of the disciples.

At length it was resolved that he and Barnabas with certain others should go up to Jerusalem, and seek an interview with the Apostles and Elders, with the object of settling the dispute[4]. Any hesitation the Apostle might have felt about the expediency of the course

[1] Lightfoot *On the Galatians*, p. 286.

[2] They were converted Pharisees who had imported their dogmas into the Christian Church.

[3] Compare the words παρεισάκτους, παρεισῆλθον in Gal. ii. 4. "The metaphor is that of spies or traitors introducing themselves by stealth into the enemy's camp." See the passages quoted by Lightfoot.

[4] For an exhaustive note on the identity of the journey mentioned in the Epistle to the Galatians and in Acts xv., see Lightfoot, *Com. on the Gal.* 110—113.

proposed was removed by a special *revelation*[1] (Gal. ii. 2) which conspired with the declared view of the church at Antioch, and intimated to him that the journey found favour with God, and that an authoritative settlement of the question was necessary to the well-being of the Christian churches[2].

Accordingly he himself, accompanied by Barnabas, a Jew and a Levite by birth, and therefore a fair representative of the circumcision, Titus, a living example of the power of God among the heathen[3], and some of the Christian brethren of the towns through which they passed, set out on their memorable journey.

CHAPTER III

THE COUNCIL AT JERUSALEM.

A. D. 50.

FOLLOWING the coast-line of Phœnicia[4], and then traversing the midland districts of Samaria and Judæa, the deputation from the church at Antioch proclaimed in every town they entered the conversion of the Gentiles, and caused *great joy among all the brethren*

[1] The historian St Luke naturally records the external impulse, which led to the mission; the Apostle himself states his inward motive: "What I did," he says, "I did not owing to circumstances, not as yielding to pressure, not in deference to others, but because the Spirit of God told me it was right." The very stress which he lays on this revelation seems to shew that other influences were at work. Lightfoot, *Com.* p. 111.

[2] Compare the combination of the natural and the supernatural in the case of Peter's journey to Cæsarea; see above, pp. 398, 399; and in St Paul's reasons for leaving Jerusalem, above, pp. 391, 392.

[3] Neander's *Planting*, p. 115.

[4] The great Roman road followed the Phœnician coastline. On the previous mention of Phœnicia, see Acts xi. 19, 20; above, p. 373.

(Acts xv. 3). On their arrival at Jerusalem they were welcomed by the Apostles present, as also by the elders, and recounted to them all that God had done by their instrumentality amongst the Gentiles. Very soon, however, the Pharisaic section in the Church which the emissaries at Antioch represented, put forward their objections. They rose up and insisted that the Gentile converts should be circumcised and instructed to conform to the Mosaic Law (Acts xv. 5). Their sentiments, put forward with such determination, revealed the importance of the crisis, and it was resolved that a formal assembly of the church should be convened.

In the interval, knowing how much depended on the decision now invoked, the Apostle Paul held private interviews[1] (Gal. ii. 2) with the more prominent members[2] of the Church, and especially with James, Peter and John, the great Pillars of the new society, and used every effort to remove the prejudices against the reception of heathen converts without conforming to the requirements of the Law, and to avoid misunderstanding as to the great principle he had proclaimed wherever he had preached—the freedom of the Gentile churches.

At length the council met, and consisted of the Apostles, elders, and general body of disciples. The debate was earnest, and led to much disputing (Acts xv. 7), in the midst of which Peter rose up, and reminded his hearers that these recent converts in Syria and Cilicia were not the first Gentile believers[3]. "He himself had

[1] Κατ' ἰδίαν δὲ τοῖς δοκοῦσι, Gal. ii. 2.

[2] See Neander's *Planting*, I. 115, n. "The private consultation was a wise precaution to avoid misunderstanding: the public conference was a matter of necessity to obtain a recognition of the freedom of the Gentile churches." Lightfoot *in loc.*

[3] Neander's *Planting*, I. 117; Baumgarten's *Apostolic History*.

been chosen some years before[1] to preach the word to 'those without' and admit them into the Christian Church, and God *who knoweth the hearts* had shewn that He was no *respecter of persons*, for He had bestowed upon them the same miraculous gifts as upon the Jews, and had purified their hearts by faith. In the face of these facts, then, he for his part could not believe it was right to tempt God by laying upon the necks of the new converts a yoke[2] which neither they themselves nor their fathers had been able to bear, and from which they had only been delivered by the salvation offered through faith in Jesus Christ (Acts xv. 11)."

This address of the Great Apostle of the circumcision was received with attention by the Council, and in the midst of the general silence (Acts xv. 12) Paul and Barnabas rose, and were eagerly listened to while they recounted in a continued narrative what God had wrought by their instrumentality among the Gentiles in Antioch and Cyprus and the cities of Pamphylia and Lycaonia, and declared how He had attested their labours by the signs and wonders which He had enabled them to perform (Acts xv. 12).

When they had concluded, another speaker arose to address the assembly. This was James, *the brother of the Lord*, to whom the direction of the Church at Jerusalem had apparently been committed[3]. No man was more calculated to command the earnest attention and deference of all present. Austere[4] and inflexibly up-

[1] Ἀφ' ἡμερῶν ἀρχαίων, Acts xv. 7, refers to the whole period of the Gospel up to that day, and especially to the conversion of Cornelius about 12 years before.

[2] Compare the Lord's own words, Mtt. xxiii. 4.

[3] See above, p. 410; for indications in the New Testament of his important position comp. (1) Gal. i. 19; (2) Acts xii. 17; (3) Gal. ii. 9; (4) Acts xxi. 18.

[4] From 1 Cor. ix. 5 we gather that, like Samuel, he was married, but in other respects a strict observer of the Nazarite rule; Euseb. *H. E.* II. 23.

right[1], so that both Jews and Christians called him *James the Just*, resembling not only in the earnestness of his exhortations, but even in his outward garb[2], the Baptist or one of the prophets of the older Dispensation, he might be expected to conciliate even the Pharisaic section in the Council.

He began by reminding those present of the reality of the conversion of the household of Cornelius to which Peter[3] had alluded (Acts xv. 14). This taking of a people from amongst the Gentiles was not contrary to, but a direct fulfilment of, the words of ancient prophecy (Amos ix. 11, 12)[4], which foretold that the tabernacle of David should be gloriously revived, and the worship of Jehovah extended to all nations. What, therefore, had occurred in Syria and Cilicia, in Pamphylia and Lycaonia, need not excite any astonishment. God, to whom *all things are known from the beginning*, was but fulfilling His eternal counsels, and the words He had Himself spoken by the mouth of His holy prophets. His judgment, therefore, was that they should not trouble the minds of believers from amongst the Gentiles, or lay upon them any obligations beyond those necessary to ensure peace and goodwill amongst them and their Jewish brethren. The latter from ancient times and from immemorial usage were wont to hear the Law read in their synagogues every Sabbath-day, and any direct violation of its vital principles could not fail to give the deepest offence. He advised, therefore, that the Gentile converts should be required to abstain (1) from that

[1] *Διὰ τὴν ὑπερβολὴν τῆς δικαιοσύνης αὐτοῦ, ἐκαλεῖτο Δίκαιος καὶ Ὠβλίας· ὅ ἐστι Ἑλληνιστὶ περιοχὴ τοῦ λαοῦ καὶ δικαιοσύνη.* Hegesippus quoted in Euseb. *H. E.* II. 23.

[2] See Stanley's *Apostolical Age*, pp. 302, 331; Con. and Howson, I. 205; Smith's *Bibl. Dict.*

[3] He characteristically uses the Jewish form of the Apostle's name, Acts xv. 14, as Peter does himself 2 Pet. i. 1.

[4] The citation is made freely from the LXX version.

which had been polluted by being offered in sacrifice to idols[1]; (2) from the flesh of animals which had been strangled[2]; (3) from the eating of blood[3]; (4) from fornication, and those licentious orgies, which were so closely connected with heathen sacrificial feasts, and nowhere more than in the centres of those very countries about which they had been speaking, the sanctuaries of Antioch[4] and Paphos[5].

These sentiments found acceptance with the majority. Titus[6] was not compelled to submit to circumcision (Gal. ii. 3), and the course adopted by Paul was entirely approved by the other Apostles. James, Peter, and John, who had the reputation of being Pillars[7] of the truth, gave to him and Barnabas *the right hands of fellowship* (Gal. ii. 9), and agreed to

[1] Only a portion of the victims was offered in sacrifice to the heathen gods, the rest was consumed by the offerer with his family and friends, or was sold in the shambles. Hence most public entertainments and many private meals were more or less remotely connected with heathen sacrifices, which, as Thucydides relates (II. 38), became the chief means of social enjoyment. Such meat the more scrupulous Jewish converts would not touch, according to the warning of Malachi (i. 7—12), or the good example of Daniel (i. 8). See Stanley *On the Cor.* I. 150, 151. Hence the doubt and the contention between the Gentile and Jewish converts alluded to in 1 Cor. viii. ix.

[2] See Levit. xvii. 13, 14; Comp. above, p. 118, n.

[3] See *Class-Book of O. T. History*, p. 156.

[4] C. and H., 207; Gibbon, XXIII.

[5] See above, p. 412, n.; Milman, *Hist. of Christianity*, I. 394; Neander's *Planting*, I. p. 121.

[6] Ἀλλ' *οὐδὲ* Τίτος *ὁ σὺν ἐμοὶ* Ἕλλην *ὢν ἠναγκάσθη περιτμηθῆναι*, Gal. ii. 3. *But not even Titus*, though (1) the pressure exerted in his case was so great, though (2) as my fellow-labourer he would be brought constantly in contact with the Jews, see Acts xvi. 3, though (3) *a Gentile, was compelled to be circumcised.* See Lightfoot and Ellicott *in loc.*

[7] Στύλοι, Gal. ii. 9, a title applied by the Jews to the great teachers of the Law, see Wetstein *in loc.*: and, the

recognise unreservedly his independent mission to the heathen as well as their own to the Jews (Gal. ii. 9). One condition only was annexed, that in his journeys among the Gentiles and the dispersed Jews he would not forget the wants and the sufferings of the poorer brethren at Jerusalem[1].

Thus the dispute was settled, and a circular letter (Acts xv. 23) was drawn up embodying the views of the Council. This was entrusted to Paul and Barnabas, and they accompanied by certain *chief men*[2] *among the brethren* (Acts xv. 22), Judas surnamed Barsabas and Silas or Silvanus[3], returned to Antioch, and the whole body of the disciples having been assembled, read it in their ears. Great was the joy manifested at the contents, and no less welcome the consolation after so much discussion and perplexity (Acts xv. 31), which was in no small degree increased by the fact that Judas and Silas, being both "prophets," exhorted and confirmed the brethren in the enjoyment of that free and unfettered liberty now assured to them. After some days they returned to Jerusalem, but Paul and Barnabas prolonged their stay in the Syrian capital, and together with many others proclaimed the message of Redemption, and employed themselves in the general work of Christian instruction (Acts xv. 35).

Church being regarded as the house or temple of God, in the New Testament to Christians; comp. Rev. iii. 12; 1 Tim. iii. 15.

[1] This the Apostle had already done, see Acts xi. 29, 30, above, p. 404; this also he did on the occasion of his last journey to Jerusalem, Rom. xv. 26, 27; Acts xxiv. 17.

[2] John Mark appears to have accompanied them. Comp. Acts xv. 37; Neander's *Planting*, I. p. 125.

[3] Derived from the Latin silva, *a wood:* this seems to hint that he was a Hellenistic Jew, and from Acts xvi. 37 we gather that he was a Roman citizen; by some he is identified with the Silvanus mentioned in 1 Pet. v. 12.

During their stay, for some reason which is not specified, Peter came down to Antioch (Gal. ii. 11). At first he lived in free and social intercourse with the Gentile converts, met them on terms of equality, and ate with them at the Agapæ and on other occasions, in the true spirit of the recent decree, and as he had done in the house of Cornelius (Gal. ii. 12) Before long, however, there arrived from Jerusalem certain brethren, either deputed by James on some special mission, "or invested with some powers from him, which they abused[1]" (Gal. ii. 12). They brought with them their old Pharisaic[2] repugnance against intercourse with uncircumcised heathen, and awed by their presence the Apostle of the Circumcision began timidly to withdraw and separate himself[3] from those whom he had lately met on free and equal terms.

Such conduct roused the deepest indignation in the heart of Paul. Through fear of the converts from Judaism[4] Peter was violating the very principle of the late decree, and by his example causing others to vacillate. Not only the other Jewish converts resident at Antioch[5] (Gal. ii. 13), who had mingled freely with the Gentiles, but even his friend and colleague Barnabas, who had defended their cause at Jerusalem, was carried away with

[1] The refusal to eat meat with the impure was one of their leading principles: comp. Lk. xv. 2, and see above, p. 247.

[2] Lightfoot *in loc.*, who deems this not altogether improbable, and compares Acts xv. 24, xv. 1. See also Ellicott's note.

[3] Ὑπέστελλεν καὶ ἀφώριζεν ἑαυτόν, Gal. ii. 12: "the words describe forcibly the cautious withdrawal of a timid person who shrinks from observation, ὑπέστελλεν denoting the partial, ἀφώριζεν the complete and final separation." Lightfoot *in loc.*

[4] Τοὺς ἐκ περιτομῆς, Gal. ii. 12. Comp. Acts x. 45, xi. 2; Rom. iv. 12; Col. iv. 11; Tit. i. 10.

[5] Οἱ λοιποὶ Ἰουδαῖοι. See Lightfoot's note.

the flood of their dissimulation[1] (Gal. ii. 13). It was clearly necessary to interfere, and accordingly he withstood his fellow Apostle *to the face* (Gal. ii. 11), and rebuked him before all. The dissimulation he had practised carried with it its own condemnation. If he, born and bred a Jew, had made it his principle to discard Jewish customs and to live with the freedom of a Gentile, why did he practically[2] coerce the Gentiles into Judaism. Both of them, though born to all the privileges of the elect nation, not *sinners*[3], as they used proudly to call the Gentiles, convinced that a man could not be justified by the works of the Law but by faith in Jesus Christ, had become believers in Him, that of that justification they might become partakers. How, then, could he seek to impose on others the yoke of conformity to the works of the Law?

What ensued upon this indignant rebuke is not recorded. It is not probable that any actual quarrel took place between the two[4]. Though the character of Peter was impulsive and susceptible of quick and sudden changes, it was loving, generous, and forgiving. Certain it is that afterwards he was not ashamed to allude to the Epistles of his *beloved brother Paul* (2 Pet. iii. 15, 16), albeit that the censure upon himself finds a place in one of them, and though afterwards they seldom met, yet their lives were united in the propagation of one great cause, and in their deaths *they were not divided*[5].

1 Τῇ ὑποκρίσει, their *acting, assuming a part,* which veiled their genuine feelings, and made them appear otherwise than they were.

2 That is, his conduct, if persevered in, would have this effect.

3 Almost a synonym for Gentiles: see 1 Macc. ii. 44; and comp. Lk. vi. 32, 33; Mtt. v. 47; Mtt. xxvi. 45; Lk. xviii. 32.

4 Con. and Howson, I. 215.

5 Ibid. See Smith's *Bibl. Dict.*, Art. *Peter.*

SECTION II

St Paul's Second Missionary Journey.

CHAPTER I

THE SHARP CONTEST—TOUR IN PHRYGIA AND GALATIA.

A. D. 51.

THE sphere of the labours of St Paul, as the Apostle of the Gentiles, having been publickly recognized at Jerusalem, he did not deem it right to linger at Antioch, and therefore proposed to Barnabas that they should revisit the places where they had preached the Word of God, and founded churches. To this his fellow Apostle assented, but was unwilling to undertake the journey unless his relative John Mark accompanied them (Acts xv. 37). St Paul, however, was by no means inclined to suffer one, who had withdrawn from them in Pamphylia, and *had not gone with them to the work*, to become again their companion on a journey requiring resolution and undaunted courage. Barnabas, on his side, was equally earnest in desiring that his kinsman should accompany them, and the consequence was nothing less than a sharp contention between the two, which at last ended in a mutual separation[1]. They agreed to choose each a different path, and to labour independently. Barnabas, therefore, taking with him John Mark[2] sailed to Cyprus, there, doubtless, though

[1] The breach between them, however, appears to have been but temporary. St Paul afterwards mentions his former friend with commendation, see 1 Cor. ix. 6. At Salamis the tomb of Barnabas is shewn.

[2] Mark, too, though now the cause of this sharp conten-

the details of his labours are not recorded, to superintend with advantage the churches already planted there, and to quicken and confirm their spiritual growth.

St Paul, on the other hand, selecting for his companion Silas or Silvanus, who had returned from Jerusalem, and *commended by the brethren to the grace of God* (Acts xv. 40), proceeded to form his own field of labour, instead of trespassing on that of another[1]. As his late colleague, therefore, had selected an insular, so he chose a continental sphere of operations, and traversed Syria and Cilicia confirming the churches[2], and probably exhibiting the circular epistle from the church of Jerusalem.

From Cilicia he and his companion then passed into Lycaonia[3], and once more visited the towns of Derbe and Lystra. In the latter place he found a pleasing proof that his labours during his previous visit had not been in vain. In Timothy, who has been already mentioned[4], who had been carefully nurtured from childhood in the knowledge of the Old Testament Scriptures by his mother Eunice and his grandmother Lois (2 Tim.

tion, afterwards won the Apostle's confidence. He appears to have been with Paul during his first imprisonment at Rome (Philem. 24), and was acknowledged to be *profitable to the ministry* (2 Tim. iv. 11), and a cause of *comfort* (Col. iv. 10, 11).

1 Comp. Rom. xv. 20; 2 Cor. x. 16. Neander's *Planting*, I. 170.

2 For their planting, see above, p. 391.

3 The journey was probably undertaken in the early part of the year A.D. 51.

4 See above, p. 421, n. His father, whose name is unknown, was a Ἕλλην (Acts xvi. 3), a Gentile, and probably died during his son's infancy. If in any sense a proselyte, he could only have been a *Proselyte of the Gate*. Such mixed marriages, though strictly forbidden by the Mosaic Law (Deut. vii. 3), and always condemned by the stricter Jews, were not un-

i. 5), who had witnessed the persecutions which the Apostle had undergone, and now as a Christian enjoyed the confidence of the church at Lystra and Iconium (Acts xvi. 2, 3), he saw one well fitted to do more than supply the place of John Mark, and invited him to become his companion. Timothy, on his part, was ready and willing to join him, and on account of the Jews who were numerous in the town and neighbourhood[1], and probably for the sake of his admission into the synagogue in which the Apostle intended to preach, submitted to the rite of circumcision (Acts xvi. 3). Before

common in the later periods of Jewish history. The children of such marriages were termed Mamzerim (bastards). But even such a child, if a wise student of the Law, "was, in theory, above an ignorant high-priest." Lightfoot, *Hor. Heb.* on Mtt. xxiii. 14, quoted in Smith's *Bibl. Dict.*, Art. *Timothy.* The education, therefore, Timothy received, may possibly "have helped to overcome the prejudice the Jews would have against him on this ground." "It is not improbable that the mother and grandmother of Timothy may have been connected with those Jews from Babylonia whom Antiochus settled in Phrygia three centuries before." C. and H., I. 243, and see above, p. 10.

[1] They knew that his father was a Greek, and that he had been allowed to grow up to the age of manhood without the sign of circumcision—that his "condition was that of a negligent, almost an apostate Israelite." They might "tolerate a heathen, as such, in the synagogue or the church, but an uncircumcised Israelite would be to them a horror and a portent. With a special view, therefore, to their feelings, and making no sacrifice of principle, the Apostle *took and circumcised him*" (Acts xvi. 3). The parents of Titus, on the other hand, *were both Gentiles*, and in his case the Apostle maintained the principle that the Gentiles did not need circumcision (Gal. ii. 3). See Smith's *Bibl. Dict.* "According to the Jewish rules, the child should follow the mother; and the son of a mixed marriage, whose mother was a Jewess, was bound to be circumcised, otherwise the marriage would not have been recognised by the Jewish law." Kitto's *Bibl. Illustr.*

many witnesses (1 Tim. vi. 12) he was then[1] solemnly ordained by the laying on of the hands of the whole assembly of the elders, and of the Apostle himself (2 Tim. i. 6), to do the work of an Evangelist, and proceeded with him and Silas, visiting the churches already founded, and exhibiting the decrees of the Council at Jerusalem (Acts xvi. 4).

The effect of this visitation was speedily felt. Strengthened by the superintendence of three such earnest labourers, the churches were established in the faith, and *increased in number daily* (Acts xvi. 5). The first part of their mission completed, the three advanced in a northerly direction through Phrygia[2] and Galatia[3] (Acts xvi. 6). In the last-named district it does

[1] Probably at Iconium, C. and H., I. 246. From 1 Tim vi. 12 we gather that on this occasion he witnessed *a good confession* before many witnesses; from 1 Tim. i. 18, that *prophecies* sanctioned his dedication to the work; from 1 Tim. iv. 14, that the bestowal of *gifts* accompanied the laying on of hands of the Church and the Apostle himself.

[2] Not at this time the large and populous province of Asia Minor, which it afterwards became in the age of Constantine, but a "geographical expression denoting a debateable country of indeterminate extent, diffused over the frontiers of the provinces of proconsular Asia and Galatia, but belonging chiefly to the former." C. and H., I. 248.

[3] Galatia—the "Gaul of the East"—is a somewhat ambiguous expression, and might denote either (i) the Roman province of that name, or (ii) Galatia proper. The former comprised nearly all the centre of Asia Minor, and was bounded by Bithynia and Pontus on the north, proconsular "Asia" on the west, Pamphylia and Cilicia on the south, and Cappadocia on the east, including south-eastern Phrygia, Lycaonia, Isauria, and part of Pisidia. The latter (and the more probable area of the Galatian churches) was a comparatively small district, having for its three chief towns, Ancyra, Pessinus, and Tavium or Tavia, and occupied by the Gauls, who poured down into Italy and Greece in the third century B.C. Repulsed at Delphi (B.C. 279) a considerable body of these invaders of southern Europe forced their way

not seem to have been the intention of St Paul to have preached the Gospel, being probably anxious at once to bear his message to the more important and promising district of proconsular Asia[1] (Acts xvi. 6). But a sharp and violent attack of a malady, to which he was subject, and which he calls *a thorn in the flesh*[2], *the messenger*

into Thrace, occupied the coast of the Propontis, crossed over into Asia Minor, and before long conquered the whole of the peninsula north of the Taurus. After ravaging the country far and wide they were signally defeated by Attalus king of Pergamus, B.C. 230, and penned up "in a strip of land in the interior of Asia Minor, about 200 miles in length, and stretching from N.E. to S.W.," which was divided among the three invading tribes, the Tectosages, the Trocmi, the Tolistoboii. Hence they increased rapidly in numbers and prosperity, took part as mercenaries in all the wars of the time, and acted as body-guards to the king of Syria and Egypt, and even Herod the Great. After their power had been materially curtailed by neighbouring monarchs, they attracted the notice of the Romans during the campaign against Antiochus the Great, and were subjugated by the consul Manlius; during a century and a half they were then governed by native princes, and finally reduced to a Roman province by Augustus. See C. and H., I. 222—225; and the Introduction to Lightfoot's *Commentary on the Galatians*, pp. 4—7.

[1] Lightfoot, *Galatians*, p. 21.

[2] Comp. 2 Cor. xii. 7 with Gal. iv. 13, 14. Many and various are the opinions respecting the σκόλοψ τῇ σαρκί, the *thorn*, or rather *stake*, here alluded to by the Apostle. The following are the chief: (1) *persecution from his enemies*, the opinion of the Greek fathers; (2) *carnal thoughts*, the opinion of mediæval writers; (3) *spiritual trial*, temptation to despair and doubt, &c., the opinion of the Reformers; (4) *bodily ailment* of some kind, an opinion first expressed by Irenæus, and since adopted by most modern expositors. Combining the two passages cited above we infer (1) that it was marked by extremely acute pain, whence it could be compared to a "stake driven through the flesh;" (2) that it was of a very humiliating nature; (3) that it could not be concealed from others, and exposed him to contempt and even loathing; (4) that it was a grievous hindrance to his constancy and resolution; (5) that it was (possibly) connected

of Satan sent to buffet him (2 Cor. xii. 7), prostrated his physical strength, and he was constrained to linger in Galatia[1] (Gal. iv. 13, 14).

But though the Apostle appeared in the capitals of Galatia—Pessinus, Ancyra and Tavium—bowed down with physical infirmity, he was received with peculiar kindness by the warm-hearted[2] Gauls. They did *not despise nor loath the temptation in his flesh* (Gal. iv. 14). They welcomed him as *an angel of God, even as Christ Jesus*, nay, they *would have plucked out their own eyes*, and *have given them to him*[3] (Gal. iv. 15). His announcement of a crucified Saviour (Gal. iii. 1) they

with that meanness of personal appearance to which he alludes, 2 Cor. x. 10; and (6) that it was recurring (comp. Gal. iv. 13, 14 with 1 Thess. ii. 18; 1 Cor. ii. 3; 2 Cor. i. 8, 9). See the interesting reference to the mysterious malady of Alfred the Great, quoted in Lightfoot's *Galatians*, pp. 173, 174. Amongst bodily afflictions, (a) acute pains in the head, (b) epilepsy, (c) a complaint in the eyes, have found the chief supporters. See Lightfoot's *Excursus*, and Stanley on 2 Cor. xii. 7.

[1] Δι' ἀσθένειαν τῆς σαρκὸς εὐηγγελισάμην ὑμῖν τὸ πρότερον = *On account of an infirmity in my flesh I preached the Gospel amongst you on the former of my two visits.*

[2] It is not improbable that St Paul founded the earliest churches of Galatia (Lightfoot, p. 19). Pessinus was the seat of the primitive worship of Cybele, the "Great Mother," superintended by her fanatical and effeminate priests, the Galli (Cic. *Fam.* II. 12. 2; Pliny, III. 32, 45). Ancyra was the capital of the Roman province, the site of a magnificent temple of marble built by Augustus, the meeting-place of all the great roads in the north of the peninsula, and the resort of many Jews. C. and H., I. 520.

[3] This, however, did not prevent their being afterwards carried away into apostasy. With their wonted fickleness they rapidly changed their sentiments (Gal. i. 6). Compare Cæsar's words concerning the Gauls, *Mobilitate et levitate animi, B. G.* II. 1. *Infirmitatem Gallorum veritus quod sunt in consiliis capiendis mobiles et novis plerumque rebus student, nihil his committendum ratus, B. G.* IV. 5. Comp. Tac. *Germ.* XXIX.

received with eagerness and deep fervour, and many, both Jews and Gentiles, men and women, freemen and slaves[1] (Gal. iii. 27, 28), professed themselves believers, and the churches of Galatia were added to those of Cilicia, Lycaonia and Phrygia.

Considering the circumstances under which this visit was made, it is not probable that it was very protracted, but at first the Apostles were somewhat uncertain in what direction to turn, for new fields of labour opened to them on different sides. At one time they thought of proceeding in a south-westerly direction to the populous cities of proconsular Asia[2], but received a Divine intimation that this was not to be the scene of their labours (Acts xvi. 6). They then turned towards Mysia[3], and were essaying to proceed into Bithynia[4], when a monition from the Divine Spirit, the Spirit of the glorified Redeemer[5], caused them to abandon this route also. Passing, therefore, by the district of Mysia without pausing to evangelise it[6], they proceeded in a north-westerly direction towards the shores of the Ægean, and arrived at Alexandria Troas[7] (Acts xvi. 8).

[1] C. and H., I. 252.

[2] Ἐν τῇ Ἀσίᾳ: see above, p. 344, n. Paley (*Horæ Paulinæ*, 1 Cor. No. 2) well compares the relation of pro-consular Asia to the rest of the peninsula with that of Portugal in relation to Spain.

[3] Ἐλθόντες κατὰ τὴν Μυσίαν = *having come over against Mysia.*

[4] Εἰς τὴν Βιθυνίαν is the reading in the edition of Lachmann and Tischendorf.

[5] Τὸ πνεῦμα Ἰησοῦ is the better reading here.

[6] Vulgate *transeuntes*. This seems to be the force of παρελθόντες here. They *passed along* the frontier of Mysia, as it was popularly understood, and they *passed by* the whole district without staying to evangelise it.

[7] This was its full name (Liv. XXXV. 42); sometimes it was called simply Alexandria, sometimes simply Troas. Its first founder, Antigonus, one of the generals of Alexander, called it *Antigoneia Troas*, and peopled it with the inhabit-

There they stayed for the night, and now, after the Apostle Paul had doubtless been pondering deeply over the nature of the supernatural intimations which had been leading him[1], the mystery was solved. During the night there appeared to him in vision[2], a man from the opposite shores of Macedonia, beseeching him and saying, *Come over and help us* (Acts xvi. 9). The morning dawned, and the purport of the heavenly vision was discussed by the Apostle with his companions Silas and Timothy, and a new colleague, Luke *the beloved physician* (Col. iv. 14), who had now joined him, either by pre-arrangement, or by a providential meeting, or perhaps in consequence of his feeble state of health[3]. They were not long in coming to a conclusion. The vision could have but one meaning. The Lord was assuredly calling them to carry the glad tidings of salvation to the European shores (Acts xvi. 10). Without further delay, therefore, they sought means for crossing over, and having found a vessel on the point of sailing for Europe they embarked and proceeded on their voyage.

ants of some neighbouring cities. Lysimachus, who succeeded to his power on the Dardanelles, increased and adorned it, but altered its name to Alexandria Troas. It was a sea-port town at the north-west corner of Asia Minor, near the site of ancient Troy, and opposite the south-eastern extremity of the island of Tenedos, and its site is now marked by the modern village of *Eski Stamboul*, Old Constantinople. Under the Romans, in consequence partly of the legend of their origin from Troy, partly of its connection by good roads with the interior, and its being the chief point of arrival and departure for those who sailed between western Asia and Macedonia, it became a place of great importance, and Augustus made it a colony, and conferred upon it the *Jus Italicum*, i.e. exempted its land from taxation. Con. and Howson, I. 257, 258; Smith's *Bibl. Dict.*

[1] See Baumgarten's *Apost. History*, II. 107.

[2] Comp. the vision of St Peter at Joppa, above, pp. 397, 398.

[3] C. and H., I. 260.

CHAPTER II

PAUL AND SILAS AT PHILIPPI.

A. D. 52.

THE wind blew fair, when the Apostle and his companions left Troas, and running before it in a straight course they reached, probably the same night[1], the island of Samothrace, and there came to anchor[2]. The next day, passing under the lee of the island of Thasos, they reached the Macedonian harbour of Neapolis, and thence passed inland a distance of about 10 miles to Philippi[3], the first[4] city which the traveller would reach in this part of Macedonia, and a Roman military colony[5] (Acts xvi. 12).

[1] Comp. the return voyage, Acts xx. 6.

[2] "The ancient city, and therefore probably the usual anchorage, was on the N. side, which would be sufficiently sheltered from a S. E. wind." Samothrace is a lofty conspicuous island, visible at Troas towering over Imbros. Smith's *Bibl. Dict.*

[3] The full and proper name was *Colonia Augusta Julia Philippensis.* The father of Alexander built it in a place called Krenides, or *the Place of Fountains*, situated in a plain of extraordinary fertility between the ranges of Pangæus and Hæmus, about nine miles from the sea, and on a spot watered by numerous streams. Augustus made it a *colony*, to be at once a perpetual memorial of his victory over Brutus, and a border-garrison of the province of Macedonia.

[4] The word *first* denotes the *first* city in its geographical relation to St Paul's journey, not the first politically either of Macedonia or a part of it. The chief city of the province was Thessalonica, and that of Macedonia Prima was not Philippi but Amphipolis.

[5] Like Antioch in Pisidia (see above, p. 414), and Alexandria Troas (above, p. 438, n.), Philippi was a Roman colony, a miniature resemblance of imperial Rome. Originally designed as military safeguards of the frontiers, and to check insurgent provincials, the colonies were parts of the fortifications of the empire. The colonists, veteran soldiers, freedmen,

Here the Apostle and his companions stayed *some days* (Acts xvi. 12). Being a military and not a mercantile city, the number of Jews here was small, and consequently there was no synagogue. There was, however, a Proseucha, *a House or Place of Prayer*, a slighter[1] and more temporary structure than the regular places of Jewish worship, outside the gate[2], on the banks of the Gaggitas, the fountains of which gave the ancient name to the city[3]. Those who met here for worship consisted chiefly of women (Acts xvi. 13), and amongst them was one, named Lydia, a proselytess[4] (Acts xvi. 14) of Thyatira[5] (Rev. i. 11), a town in proconsular Asia, famous ever since the days of Homer for its dyed goods, for the reception of which she had an establishment at Philippi.

On the Sabbath the newly-arrived strangers joined the little company by the river-side, and sitting down[6] in the attitude of teachers, spoke to the women there assembled. Lydia was an earnest listener, *and the Lord opened her heart, so that she gave heed to the word spoken by Paul*, and together with her household

or Italians, went thither with all the pomp of a Roman army, and were enrolled in one of the tribes. They were amenable only to their own magistrates, called *duumviri* or, as they delighted to style themselves, *proprætors* (comp. Hor. *Sat.* I. v 34 — 36; Cic. *de Lege Agr.* II. 34), were governed by Roman laws, and had Latin inscriptions stamped upon their coins. See Art. *Colonia* in Smith's *Dict. of Antiquities*.

1 C. and H., p. 270.

2 Ἔξω τῆς πύλης is the better reading in Acts xvi. 13.

3 See above, p. 440, n.

4 Σεβομένη τὸν Θεόν, Acts xvi. 14.

5 A city on the Lycus, founded by Seleucus Nicator, on the confines of Mysia and Ionia, about midway between Pergamus and Sardis; now called *Ak-hissar*. It is mentioned in connection with the dyeing trade in Hom. *Il.* IV. 141, for which it has still a considerable reputation.

6 Comp. Acts xiii. 14; Lk. iv. 20. Comp. above, p. 112.

was admitted into the Church by baptism, probably in the waters of the stream that flowed by the *Proseucha*. Thus the Gospel found a lodgment in Europe, and Lydia, grateful for *the spiritual things*, which the Apostle had ministered unto her, was anxious to minister to him and his companions of her *temporal things*. *Since ye have deemed me a believer in the Lord*, said she, *come into my house, and there abide*. She would take no refusal, and Paul and the rest accepted her offer of hospitality.

At no great distance from Philippi[1] was an oracle of Dionysus, the prophet-god of the Thracians. Thence, or from some similar establishment, there came a damsel *possessed with the spirit of divination*[2], who had been hired by certain Philippian citizens, and brought much gain to her owners by her soothsaying (Acts xvi. 16). Meeting the little company of Christians as they went to and fro from the Proseucha, she followed Paul crying out, *These men are the servants of the most High God, who are come to announce unto you the way of salvation*. This continued many days. At length grieved that this testimony should be borne by one possessed with an evil spirit, Paul turned, and in the name of his Divine Master commanded the evil spirit to leave her, whereupon the word of power was instantly obeyed, and the damsel was restored to her right mind (Acts xvi. 18).

Perceiving that now all hope of any future gain was

[1] High up in Hæmus, among the tribe of the Satræ. Comp Ὁ Θρῃξὶ μάντις, Eurip. *Hecub.* 1267. Smith's *Bibl. Dict.*, Art. *Philippi*.

[2] Acts xvi. 16, Ἔχουσαν πνεῦμα Πύθωνος (the better reading is Πύθωνα). Πύθων = (1) the prophetic serpent at Delphi, (2) the Pythian Phœbus or Apollo, from whom all who claimed the powers of divination received their title, and were called Pythons, exercising their arts by means of internal mutterings and ventriloquism.

gone, the owners of the damsel, filled with anger, seized Paul and Silas, and dragged them into the forum (Acts xvi. 19) before the *duumviri* or authorities of the colony, charging them with creating a disturbance in the place, and introducing innovations in their religion[1]. Such an accusation quickly roused the feelings of the populace, and a furious mob beset the Apostle and his companion as they stood before the magistrates. To retain their popularity the latter saw that they must give in to the popular feeling, and ordered the lictors to strip off the clothes of the accused and scourge them[2] (Acts xvi. 22). The order was forthwith executed, and faint and bleeding from the infliction of *many stripes* (1 Thess. ii. 2), they were thrust into prison, and the jailer was strictly enjoined to keep them safely. Anxious to fulfil his instructions to the letter, he thrust them into *the inner prison*, probably a dark, cold, pestilential cell[3], and made their feet fast in the stocks[4] (Acts xvi. 24).

But though *shamefully intreated* (1 Thess. ii. 2), and thrust under a false charge into a loathsome dun-

[1] *These men,* said they, *are throwing the whole city into confusion, being Jews to begin with; and they are inculcating new customs, which it is not lawful for us to receive or adopt, being Roman citizens* (Acts xvi. 21). The force of the accusation that they were *Jews to begin with* (Ἰουδαῖοι ὑπάρχοντες) will be more fully apprehended by remembering (1) that Judaism was a *religio licita* for Jews, but that they were forbidden to make proselytes among the Romans; (2) that the Jews had lately been driven out of Rome in consequence of an uproar, and that Philippi would naturally imitate the mother-city; *Judæos impulsore Chresto assidue tumultuantes Roma expulit;* Sueton. *Claud.* XXV.

[2] Ῥαβδίζειν = *to beat with rods,* as in 2 Cor. xi. 25.

[3] Probably like the dungeon into which Jeremiah was let down (comp. Acts xvi. 34, ἀναγαγών) with cords (Jer. xxxviii. 6), or the *Tullianum* at Rome. C. and H., I. 280, n.

[4] Τὸ ξύλον, Acts xvi. 24. Comp. Aristoph. *Eq.* 1049, 1376; Herod. VI. 75, IX. 37; and the Latin *nervus,* Plaut. *Capt.* III. 5. 71.

geon, the Apostle and his companion were not in despair. At midnight they were praying and singing hymns to God, while the rest of the prisoners listened with eager attention. But deliverance was near at hand. Suddenly a great earthquake shook the prison to its foundations, every door was opened, every fetter was loosed (Acts xvi. 26). Roused from sleep the jailer instantly concluded that his prisoners had escaped, and drawing his sword was on the point of laying violent hands upon himself, when the voice of the Apostle Paul was heard calling out loudly, *Do thyself no harm, for we are all here* (Acts xvi. 28).

On this the jailer called for lights, and leaped into the inner prison, and trembling with alarm fell down before Paul and Silas, and then leading them forth said, *Sirs, what must I do to be saved? Believe*, was their reply, *in the Lord Jesus, and thou shalt be saved,* and then they proceeded to explain to him and the members of his family, who probably crowded around, what belief in Jesus meant (Acts xvi. 32). The word fell upon good ground, and in the self-same hour, late as it was, the rough Roman officer washed the stripes of his prisoners, and was baptized together with all his house. Then taking them up into his house he set food before them, and as a believer rejoiced in his new-found faith (Acts xvi. 34).

By this time the morning had dawned, and messengers arrived from the magistrates. Either alarmed at the earthquake, or conscience-stricken with having acted with unnecessary harshness, they had come to a different decision respecting the Apostles, and the lictors now bore their orders that they should be released. The jailer received these instructions with the utmost joy, and going with the messengers announced these commands to the Apostles. But St Paul declined to *go in peace*, as he suggested (Acts xvi. 36). He and his companion, uncondemned, and without any form of trial, had been openly scourged, and thrust into prison, in direct violation of their rights as Roman citizens[1]. He refused, therefore, to accept such a secret and ignominious release. *Let them come themselves,* said he, *and lead us forth* (Acts xvi. 37).

Without delay the messengers conveyed the intelligence that the prisoners were Roman citizens to the magistrates, who were in no little alarm, when they discovered what an insult they had unwittingly offered to the Majesty of the imperial city. Hastening, therefore, to the prison, they earnestly besought the Apostles to depart from the colony. Accordingly they came forth, and with quietness and dignity repaired to the house of Lydia, and having seen and bidden farewell to the Christian brethren departed (Acts xvi. 40). Timothy, however, and Luke, appear to have remained for the present behind, to water the seed sown, and to build up the newly-formed Philippian Church.

CHAPTER III

THESSALONICA, BERŒA, ATHENS.

A.D. 52.

LEAVING, then, their first Macedonian converts, Paul and Silas proceeded along the great Roman road, known as the Via Egnatia, to Amphipolis[2], and

[1] "Lex Porcia (A.U.C. 306) virgas ab omnium civium Romanorum corpore amovet." Cic. *pro Rabirio*, Chap. III. "Facinus est vinciri civem Romanum, scelus verberari." Cic. *in Verr.* v. 66.

[2] Amphipolis stood on an eminence on the left bank of the Strymon, about 3 miles from the sea and 33 from Philippi. Originally called "Nine Ways," from the number of Thracian and Macedonian roads meeting here, it was colo-

thence through Apollonia[1] to Thessalonica[2]. In the latter city was the[3] chief synagogue of the Jews in this part of Macedonia (Acts xvii. 2), and hither Paul repaired, and for three consecutive Sabbaths argued with those of his own nation from their own Scriptures, opening them up to them, and shewing that the Messiah there predicted was no temporal Prince or earthly Conqueror, but One who should suffer and rise from the dead, and that

nised by the Athenians, and named Amphipolis from being nearly surrounded by the Strymon. For the battle fought under its walls during the Peloponnesian war, in which Cleon and Brasidas were killed, see Thuc. v. 6—11.

[1] Apollonia is laid down in the Itineraries as being 30 miles from Amphipolis. Its exact position is not known, but "it lay somewhere in the inland part of the journey, where the Via Egnatia crosses from the Gulf of the Strymon to that of Thessalonica." C. and H., I. 295.

[2] Thessalonica, 37 miles distant from Apollonia, is still the most important town of European Turkey, next after Constantinople, and retains to this day the name of *Saloniki*. Originally named Therma (whence the *Thermaic Gulf*), it was rebuilt and enlarged by Cassander, son of Antipater, and named Thessalonica after his first wife, the sister of Alexander the Great. Under the Romans, when Macedonia was divided into four governments by Paulus Æmilius, it was made the capital of the second; when the whole was consolidated into one province, it became practically the metropolis of the whole. During the first civil war it was the head quarters of the Pompeian party and the senate, during the second it took the side of Octavius, by whom it was made a free city (see above, p. 379, n.), a privilege commemorated on some of its coins. Situated on the Thermaic Gulf, and commanding the trade by sea, lying on the Via Egnatia, and connected with other important Roman roads, communicating inland with the wide plains of Macedonia, and possessing all the advantages of a busy commercial town, it formed one of the most appropriate starting points of the Gospel in Europe. Comp. I Thess. i. 8; C. and H., I. 295, 297; Smith's *Bibl. Dict.*

[3] Ἡ συναγωγή, Acts xvii. I, *the synagogue*, not *a* synagogue, as in our E. V.

He had appeared in the person of that Jesus, whom he announced to them (Acts xvii. 3; Comp. 1 Thess. i. 10, iv. 14, v. 9, 10).

His words were variously received. Some, including a considerable number of the Greek proselytes and of the influential women, believed. But the Jews, furious at the spread of such obnoxious tenets, gathered together a mob of idlers from the markets and landing-places, threw the town into an uproar, and falling upon the house of Jason[1], where the Apostle was lodging, sought to drag him and his companion before the *demus*, or assembly of the people[2]. Unsuccessful, however, in finding them, they hurried Jason and certain of the brethren before the magistrates, and charged them with violating the decrees of Cæsar[3] in asserting that there was another King, namely Jesus (Acts xvii. 7). This charge caused the magistrates considerable perplexity. Instead, however, of visiting the Apostle with any punishment, they contented themselves with taking security[4] from Jason and the rest for their future good conduct,

[1] A form which the name Joshua seems sometimes to have taken: see 1 Macc. viii. 17; 2 Macc. ii. 23. He was perhaps a Hellenist, and may possibly be alluded to in Rom. xvi. 21.

[2] The general characteristics of a "free city" have been described above, p. 379, n. Their form of government was very various. In some the old magistracies and customs were maintained without any material alteration. In Thessalonica we find an assembly of the people, *demus*, and supreme magistrates called *politarchs* (Acts xvii. 8), a title still legible on an archway of the town "in an inscription informing us of the number of these magistrates, and mentioning the very names of some who bore that office not long before the day of St Paul." C. and H., I. 308.

[3] On the severity of the laws respecting treason, see above, p. 307, n.

[4] Λαβόντες τὸ ἱκανόν, apparently a translation of the Latin law-phrase *satis accipere*.

and the maintenance of peace, and then set them at liberty.

But though the city was thus quieted, the position of the Apostle was one of great danger. Without delay, therefore, the brethren sent him and Silas under cover of night in a south-westerly direction to Berœa[1]. Here also there was a synagogue, and here Paul found far more candid, generous, and willing hearers than he had met with at Thessalonica. The Berœans not only accepted the message he preached, but searched the Scriptures, and that daily, to see whether his arguments were well founded. The consequences were soon apparent. The promise *seek, and ye shall find* was fulfilled, and many, both Jews and Gentiles, men and women, and amongst the latter sex some of the highest rank, professed themselves Christians (Acts xvii. 12).

But the work thus auspiciously commenced was not destined to go on unimpeded. After no long interval the Jews of Thessalonica, hearing that Paul was preaching with success at Berœa, followed in his track[2], and threw the town into commotion. The danger was imminent, and perceiving that the ceaseless animosity of the Jews rendered any further labours in Macedonia useless for the present, the brethren conveyed the Apostle to the nearest sea-port[3], probably

[1] Berœa, 60 miles distant from Thessalonica, said to have derived its name from the abundance of its waters, now called *Verria*, or *Kara-Verria*, was situated on the eastern slope of the Olympian mountain-range south-west of Pella, and commanded an extensive view of the plain of the Axius and Haliacmon. It still contains 18 or 20,000 inhabitants, and stands second in importance of the cities of European Turkey.

[2] As they had pursued him from Iconium to Lystra; see above, p. 420. See Paley's *Horæ Paulinæ*, 1 Thess. No. 5.

[3] Ὡς ἐπὶ τὴν θάλασσαν, Acts xvii. 14, does not imply that any stratagem was used. The words simply "denote the

Dium[1], and thence by ship to Athens. Silas and Timotheus, who probably had rejoined the Apostle at Berœa, had meanwhile been left there, to strengthen the faith of the new converts, but on the return of those who had conducted Paul to Athens, received his injunctions to join him with all speed (Acts xvii. 15).

Thus the disciple of Gamaliel, once a Pharisee, now a Christian and an Apostle, found himself in the far-famed centre of Grecian culture, the pride of the ancient world, the patroness of Art, Science, and Literature. While awaiting, alone and among strangers, the arrival of his companions, his spirit burned within him, as he beheld on every side proofs of the point to which the inhabitants of the glorious city carried their religious instincts, and the idols and idol-temples with which it was crowded[2]. Even here, however, he commenced in his usual manner. On each Sabbath-day he repaired to the synagogue (Acts xvii. 17), and preached to the Jews and proselytes, and during the week he was to be found in the busy Agora at the foot of the Acropolis and the Areopagus, conversing with any who would listen to his words.

In such a place and among such a people he was not

likelihood that in the first instance they had no fixed plan of going to *Athens*, but merely to the *sea:* their further course was determined by providential circumstances." C. and H., I. 315, n.

[1] Dium, near the foot of mount Olympus, was "the great bulwark of Macedonia on the south," and a Roman colony, like Philippi.

[2] Κατείδωλον (Acts xvii. 16), not *given up to idolatry*, but *full of idols*, like κατάδενδρος, *full of trees*, κατάμπελος, *full of vines*. "Replete as the whole of Greece was with objects of devotion, there were more Gods in Athens than in all the rest of the country, and the Roman satirist hardly exaggerates, when he says that it was easier to find a god there than a man." See Wordsworth's *Athens and Attica*.

likely to lack an audience. *All the Athenians and the strangers that were there,* writes St Luke, *spent their time in nothing else but either to tell or to hear some new thing* (Acts xvii. 21). To them, therefore, the coming of one like the Apostle, burning with zeal, and setting forth with learning and ability new and unheard-of doctrines respecting *Jesus and the Resurrection* (Acts xvii. 18), would be certain to awaken no little interest. Amongst others, who heard him and marvelled at his words, were certain of the world-famous Epicurean and Stoic schools of philosophy. On them his preaching produced a varied effect. Some treated it with scorn, saying, *What doth this babbler*[1] *mean?* Others remarked that he appeared to be setting forth certain new divinities. At length they determined to ascertain the point more closely, and taking him to the Areopagus[2], requested to know[3] the meaning of what he preached (Acts xvii. 19, 20).

So the Apostle took his stand, alone[4] and unaided, "his bodily aspect still showing what he had suffered from weakness, toil, and pain," on the summit of the hill of Areopagus (Acts xvii. 22) in the midst of temples, statues and altars dedicated to the *gods many and lords many* of the heathen world. Horror-struck as he

[1] Σπερμολόγος = (1) a bird that picks up seeds from the ground; (2) a pauper prowling about the market-place; (3) a parasite who lives by his wits, "a contemptible and worthless person." See C. and H., I. 345, n.

[2] For a description of the objects in full view of the Apostle from the summit of Mars' hill, see Con. and Howson, I. 348, &c.; Wordsworth's *Athens and Attica,* ch. XI.

[3] It was no formal trial on a charge of introducing foreign religions. Something might have been founded upon it afterwards; for the present it was a hearing only with a view to information. See Neander's *Planting,* I. 188, n.

[4] On the Apostle's expectation of the arrival of Timothy, see Paley's *Horæ Paulinæ,* 1 Thess. No. 4.

must have been at the spectacle of idolatry which confronted him on every side, he yet with peculiar prudence did not begin by attacking in intemperate language the national worship of his hearers. During his brief sojourn in the city he had observed an altar with the inscription, *To an unknown God*[1] (Acts xvii. 23). "Taking his stone," therefore, to use the expressive language of Chrysostom, "out of their own brook," he determined to make this inscription and the mournful testimony it bore to the vanity of heathenism his text, and from it to speak to them words of eternal life.

This altar, he began, like all things else he had seen in their city, proved their carefulness in religion[2], their earnest desire to worship, and at the same time their ignorance in worshipping. "The unknown God," whose power, by their own confession, they acknowledged, he would declare unto them. The Lord of heaven and earth, who had made the world and all things therein, dwelt not in temples made with hands[3]. He was subject to no exigencies, which made him need anything from his worshippers, seeing that He gave to all life,

[1] Ἀγνώστῳ Θεῷ. To *the* unknown god, however, "would be quite as near the sense of the inscription upon any particular one of such altars," C. and H., I. 350, n. Altars were erected by the Athenians, not only to particular gods, but to Fame, to Modesty, to Energy, to Persuasion, and to Pity; and besides thus deifying abstractions, it was not unusual, on the occurrence of great public calamities, such as the plague at Athens, when they sought aid in vain from their gods of wood and stone, to erect altars to some unknown god, whom they deemed they had offended.

[2] *Δεισιδαιμονεστέρους ὑμᾶς θεωρῶ*, Acts xvii. 22. The word is here used not in any offensive sense. It points to the *extreme carefulness* of the Athenians in matters of religion. See *δεισιδαίμων* in Trench's *Synonyms*, Vol. I. pp. 187—197, and Alford *in loc.*

[3] Comp. the language of Stephen, Acts vii. 48; above, p. 369.

and breath, and all things. For all the nations of mankind, originally made by Him of one blood[1], He had assigned the seasons of their existence and the bounds of their habitation, to the end that they should feel after Him, if haply they might find Him, though in truth He was not far from any of them, as one of their own poets had said,

For we are also His offspring[2].

As the offspring, therefore, of God, and endowed with the faculty of knowing Him, they ought not to have imagined that the Godhead was like unto gold, or silver, or stone, graven by the art and device of man. Such imaginations they might have indulged in times past of ignorance. But these God had overlooked[3], and now commanded all men everywhere to repent, for He had appointed a day, wherein He would judge the world in righteousness by the Man whom He had ordained, and of this He had given to all a pledge and an assurance, in that He had raised Him from the dead (Acts xvii. 30, 31).

At this point the Apostle's address was suddenly interrupted. Some who heard him broke out into laughter, regarding the idea of the resurrection as ridiculous. Others, in the spirit of Felix afterwards (Acts xxiv. 22, 25), said they would hear him again on the subject; and thus amidst mingled indifference and divi-

[1] In opposition to the well-known boast of the Athenians that they were αὐτόχθονες, and of a nobler origin than that of the "barbarians," as they styled the rest of the world.

[2] The words occur (i) in a poem of Aratus, a native of Cilicia, the Apostle's own country; (ii) in a hymn of Cleanthes, a Lycian poet. There is some doubt from which the Apostle quoted. See above, p. 382.

[3] Ὑπεριδών, *i.e.* without inflicting punishment. Comp. Acts xiv. 16; Rom. iii. 25. No such idea as is implied in the words *winked at* of our version belongs to the original word. See Wordsworth *in loc.*

sion, the hearers of the Apostle dispersed, and he *departed from among them.* The word spoken, however, did not fall utterly to the ground. Dionysius, a member of the Court of Areopagus, a woman named Damaris[1], and some others, professed themselves believers in that Redeemer and Judge of all mankind, whom he had preached to them.

CHAPTER IV

ARRIVAL AND STAY OF ST PAUL AT CORINTH.

A.D. 52, 53.

AFTER a stay at Athens, the duration of which is not recorded, the Apostle Paul repaired to Corinth, a place eminently adapted to be the centre of missionary operations, being the capital of the province[2] of Achaia, a large mercantile city, and inhabited by a large number of Jews. At this time the number of the latter was unusually large, owing to a decree issued by the emperor Claudius, in A.D. 50, directing their expulsion from Rome (Acts xviii. 2). The imperial edict here alluded to by St Luke is probably the same as that mentioned by Suetonius[3], who relates that Claudius drove the Jews from the capital, "because they were incessantly raising tumults at the instigation of a certain Chrestus," a name used by mistake, there is little reason to doubt, for Christus, and pointing to mutual hos-

[1] Of Damaris nothing further is known. Dionysius is said by some to have been the first bishop of Athens.

[2] The city had the constitution of a *colony*, and was the metropolis of a *province*. At first it was proconsular, afterwards Tiberius placed it under a procurator of its own, but Claudius restored it to its place among the proconsular provinces. Its full name was *Colonia Laus Julia Corinthus.* C. and H., I. 389; Smith's *Bibl. Dict.*

[3] Suet. *Claud.* XXV. Judæus impulsore Chresto, assiduè tumultuantes, Româ expulit.

tilities between the Jews and Christians respecting the Messiah[1].

Among those thus banished were two natives of Pontus in Asia Minor, named Aquila and Priscilla, who on their way homewards by the ordinary maritime track across the isthmus of Corinth, had settled down there for the present, and engaged in the manufacture of tents, probably of the *Cilicium*[2], or hair-cloth, already mentioned as an important article of trade in the Levant. Whether they were already converted to Christianity or not is doubtful, but as workers at a common trade the Apostle *came and attached himself to them* (Acts xviii. 3), and the intimacy now commenced lasted during the whole of St Paul's life, and his new found friends became not only partakers of a common faith, but rendered him the most important services.

While, however, he laboured working with *his own hands* (1 Cor. iv. 12), he did not neglect his great work as an Apostle. According to his usual practice, he repaired every Sabbath-day to the synagogue, and endeavoured to persuade both the Jews and Gentiles there present (Acts xviii. 4) to believe in Jesus as the promised Messiah and Saviour of the world. Nor were his labours unsuccessful. Many, both Jews and Gentiles, professed themselves believers. Amongst these was the *house of Stephanas*, whom the Apostle calls *the first-fruits of Achaia* (1 Cor. xvi. 15). Another convert, and one of considerable note, was Crispus, a ruler of the synagogue (Acts xviii. 8); a third was Gaius, or Caius,

[1] See Milman's *Hist. Christ.* I. p. 443; Lewin's *Life of St Paul*, I. 294. The return of the Italian Jews from Rome after the day of Pentecost (see above, p. 345) would account for the spread of Christianity to Rome.

[2] See above, p. 381. The name Priscilla appears in 2 Tim. iv. 19 under the form *Prisca*, a well-known Roman name. "Livia and Livilla, Drusa and Drusilla, are used by Latin authors of the same person." C. and H., I. 358, n.

with whom he afterwards lodged. All these he baptized *with his own hand* (1 Cor. i. 14—17).

After he had been thus labouring about two or three months, Silas and Timothy returned from Macedonia (Acts xviii. 5), and relieved the Apostle's intense anxiety respecting the churches he had planted there (1 Thess. i. 2; ii. 13; iii. 6), informing him of the continuance of their faith and love, of their fond remembrance of himself, and their eager desire to see him again (1 Thess. iii. 6). The effect of this welcome news seems to have been an instantaneous increase of the zeal and resolution with which he prosecuted his labours. Already there were signs of opposition to the progress of the truth, and he had begun his work at Corinth *in weakness, and in fear, and in much trembling* (1 Cor. ii. 3). But now a weight was taken off from his mind (1 Thess. iii. 1—6), and *he was pressed in the spirit*, or, according to a preferable reading, he was *pressed by the word*[1] (Acts xviii. 5). His zeal was a positive pain to him. His anxieties removed, he felt he could not restrain the impulse to give utterance to the Word of God, and to apply himself with redoubled energy to his work.

Satisfactory, however, as had been in the main the tidings brought by Silas and Timothy from Thessalonica, some irregularities which had crept in, and some mistaken notions the new converts entertained, required correction. Since the Apostle's visit several of their relatives and friends had died, and they feared that these departed Christians would lose the happiness of

[1] Or *he was* engrossed with *the word;* Instabat verbo. Compare Lk. xii. 50. Hitherto he had been labouring day and night with his own hands, determined to be chargeable to no man. Now the pecuniary supplies brought from Thessalonica (2 Cor. xi. 9; and comp. Phil. iv. 15) enabled him to devote himself still more earnestly to his Apostolic work. See Wordsworth's note *in loc.;* Lewin's *Life of St Paul*, I. 298.

witnessing their Lord's second coming, which they conceived to be close at hand (1 Thess. iv. 13—18). Under the excitement of the same expectation others had abandoned their lawful callings, and fancying that they need not work claimed the support of the richer members of the church (1 Thess. iv. 11, 12). Others, again, had not learned to subdue their carnal appetites (1 Thess. iv. 1—8), and there were symptoms of a lack of order (1 Thess. iv. 9, 10), and a tendency to despise the gift of prophesying, or inspired teaching, in comparison with other and more showy gifts (1 Thess. v. 20; comp. 1 Cor. xiv.).

For these reasons he addressed his first Epistle to the Thessalonians. Meanwhile the progress of the Church at Corinth had awakened the determined opposition of the Jews, who not only obstinately opposed the truth, but poured forth coarse blasphemies on the name of Jesus (Acts xviii. 6). Accordingly the Apostle confronted them sternly, and declaring that their blood must rest upon their own heads, announced his intention of turning to the Gentiles, and made the house of a Gentile convert named Justus, which was contiguous to the synagogue, the place of his public teaching (Acts xviii. 7). The difficulties of his position were thus much increased, and so greatly was he discouraged, that, though Crispus remained faithful, and many of the Corinthians had embraced the faith, he appears to have thought of withdrawing from the city[1]. But while he was thus hesitating, the Lord Jesus appeared in a vision of the night, and bade him be not afraid, but speak forth boldly, for He *was with him, and He had much people in the city* (Acts xviii. 8—10). Thus encouraged the Apostle resumed his labours, and continued them

[1] For illustrations of the Apostle's feelings at this time, see 2 Thess. iii. 2; 1 Cor. ii. 3.

without any apparent interruption for a space of eighteen months.

During this period intelligence received from Thessalonica induced him to address a second Epistle to the Church there. His previous letter had not abated the excitement connected with the expectation of the Saviour's speedy advent. A fanatical section had even laboured to increase it, claiming imaginary revelations from the Spirit (2 Thess. ii. 2), and the authority of a rumoured letter from the Apostle himself in support of their views (2 Thess. ii. 2). To discourage such ideas, and that neglect of daily employments (2 Thess. iii. 6—16) to which they led, the Apostle wrote again, A.D. 53, explaining more fully certain signs he had already told them must precede the Redeemer's second coming (2 Thess. ii. 1—12), and exhorting the Thessalonians to an orderly and diligent life after the example he had himself set when present in their city (2 Thess. iii. 8, 9).

Thus while continuing to labour at Corinth, did he seek to promote the growth of the Churches he had planted in Macedonia. By this time a new pro-consul of Achaia had arrived in the person of Gallio[1], the brother of Seneca the philosopher, and of Mela, whose son Lucan was the author of the Pharsalia. The new governor had the reputation of being a man of remarkable sweetness of disposition and great popularity, whom "every one loved too little, even he who loved him most[2]." Accordingly the Jews thinking they might presume with impunity upon his easy temper, with one

[1] His original name was Annæus Novatus, and he took the name of Gallio from having been adopted into the family of Junius Gallio.

[2] Solebam tibi dicere Gallionem fratrem meum (quem nemo non parum amat etiam qui amare plus non potest) alia vitia non nosse hoc etiam odisse...Nemo mortalium uni tam dulcis est quam hic omnibus. Seneca, *Nat. Quæst.* IV.

accord set upon Paul and dragged him before his judgment-seat[1], alleging the old charge that *he persuaded men to worship contrary to the law* (Acts xviii. 13). When, however, the Apostle was on the point of entering upon his defence, Gallio, probably acquainted with commotions of the same kind at Rome and with the nature of the Jewish opposition to Christianity, refused to listen to it. If the question brought before him had been some act of crime or wickedness, it would have been only reasonable that he should have heard it through. But if, as it appeared to him, it was merely a question of doctrine, of words and names and Jewish law, he would have nothing to do with it, they must see to it themselves; and he drove them from the judgment-seat (Acts xviii. 16).

This decision had a remarkable result. The mob[2], always unfriendly to the Jews, seized Sosthenes, one of the rulers of the Synagogue[3], or perhaps the successor of Crispus, and began to beat him in the very presence of the pro-consular tribunal. But Gallio left him to his fate, and *cared for none of these things* (Acts xviii. 17). Thus the assurance given to the Apostle in the late vision was fulfilled. Though bitter enemies had set upon him, none had "hurt" him, and it had been proved that the Lord *had much people in the city.*

Having tarried, therefore, at Corinth yet a good while, he took his leave of the brethren, and after[4] ter-

[1] On the proconsular power and the tribunal, see above, p. 147, n.

[2] The true reading in Acts xviii. 17 appears to be πάντες, without specifying exactly who they were. It seems, probable, however, that they were Greeks.

[3] See above, p. 111. It is not certain that this is the same Sosthenes mentioned in 1 Cor. i. 1.

[4] Some would understand this to have been done by Aquilla. The form of the sentence is somewhat ambiguous in the original, and the word κειράμενος might be connected

minating a religious vow, taken for some unknown reason, by cutting his hair at Cenchreæ[1], sailed, accompanied by Silas and Timothy, Priscilla and Aquila, in the direction of Syria. A voyage of about 13 or 15 days brought them to the port of Ephesus. There Aquila and Priscilla remained, while the Apostle, after only staying long enough to hold one conference with the Jews in their synagogue, hastened on by sea with his other companions to Cæsarea, and thence by land to Jerusalem, in time to keep the great national festival of Pentecost (Acts xviii. 20—22). His stay was very brief, and after saluting the Church there he returned to Antioch, from which he had been so long absent, and there continued some time (Acts xviii. 23).

SECTION III

St Paul's Third Missionary Journey, and Imprisonment at Cæsarea.

CHAPTER I

VISIT TO EPHESUS.

A.D. 54—57.

AFTER staying some time at Antioch, the Apostle resolved to enter upon his third missionary journey. Accompanied, it is probable, by Timothy[2], he

either with the nearer Ἀκύλας or the more remote Παῦλος. On the Nazarite vow see Num. vi. 3, 5, 13, 14, 18.—*Class-Book of Old Testament History*, p. 158.

[1] Now *Kichries*, about 8 or 9 miles from Corinth across the Isthmian plain.

[2] Silas would seem to have remained behind at Jerusalem. We do not meet with him again in connection with St. Paul. He is next mentioned in 1 Pet. v. 12. It is not improbable that Titus also was now with the Apostle Paul.

began by a systematic visitation of the Churches he had planted in Galatia and Phrygia, establishing all the disciples in the true principles of the Gospel (Acts xviii. 23), and exhorting them to evince their sympathy with their brethren in Judæa, by weekly collections in behalf of the poorer Christians (Comp. 1 Cor. xvi. 1, 2).

While he was thus employed there arrived at Ephesus a certain Jew of Alexandria, named Apollos[1], an eloquent man, and mighty in the Scriptures (Acts xviii. 24). He had been instructed in the way of the Lord, and was acquainted with the main facts of the Saviour's earthly history, but had received no other baptism than that of His forerunner. Aquila and Priscilla listened to his eloquent words in the synagogue of Ephesus, and having sought his acquaintance, did much to correct his imperfect conceptions of Christian doctrine, and to explain to him more accurately the *way of God* (Acts xviii. 26). Though trained in the schools of Alexandria, Apollos was not above receiving instruction from these humble natives of Pontus, and when made fully acquainted with the Christian doctrine was desirous of crossing over into Achaia. On communicating his wishes to the brethren at Ephesus, he received from them much encouragement; and furnished with letters of introduction to the disciples in Achaia, set out for Corinth, where he contributed important aid to the establishment of the Christian Church, employing his extensive acquaintance with Scripture to the confutation of Jewish disputants, and proving incontestably that Jesus was the Messiah (Acts xviii. 28).

Thus where *Paul had planted*, *Apollos watered*, and God *gave* an abundant *increase* (1 Cor. iii. 6). Meanwhile that Apostle's circuit through the Galatian dis-

[1] An abbreviated form of Apollonius. On the Jews of Alexandria and their theological influence, see above, p. 364, n.

trict being ended, in accordance with a promise he had made (Acts xviii. 21) he also came to Ephesus. Here Aquila and Priscilla were awaiting him ready to aid him in his work[1]. They had already dispatched to the Church of Corinth an eloquent teacher, and now there was present a company of about twelve men (Acts xix. 7), who, like Apollos, were acquainted only with John's baptism, and who were probably introduced to the Apostle by his friends from Pontus. Thereupon he enquired of them, *Did ye receive the Holy Ghost when ye became believers*[2]*?* To this they replied that they had not so much as heard of Him and of His great outpouring on the day of Pentecost. This led to further enquiry on the part of the Apostle as to the nature of the baptism they had received, and becoming aware that they had only been made partakers of John's baptism of repentance and preparation, he proceeded to speak of a yet higher baptism to which it was intended to lead up. On this the men were baptized into the Name of the Lord Jesus Christ, and on the imposition of the Apostle's hands were endued with miraculous gifts and enabled to speak with tongues and to prophesy (Acts xix. 4—7).

Ephesus now became the centre of St Paul's missionary labours. Repairing, according to his invariable practice, to the synagogue, he was employed during *three whole months* (Acts xix. 8) in arguing with the Jews from their own Scriptures, and persuading them that the kingdom of God was truly come, and that Jesus was no other than the long promised Messiah. While some

[1] It is not improbable that he again worked with them at the same trade: comp. Acts xx. 34, 1 Cor. iv. 11, 12.

[2] That is, probably, the miraculous gifts of the Holy Ghost, such as were bestowed on Cornelius and his company after their baptism, see above, p. 399. Note the force of the aorist here.

believed and joined themselves to the Christian Church, others were hardened and disobedient, and began openly to calumniate the Apostle's doctrine before the people. Perceiving this, and resolved that their example should not contaminate the rest, he resolved to abandon his attendance at the synagogue, and separating the disciples transferred his instructions to the school of *one Tyrannus*, probably a teacher of rhetoric or philosophy to the young of Ephesus, and who may or may not have been himself a convert (Acts xix. 9).

This continued for two years, A.D. 55—57, and during this period the labours of the Apostle were carried on with unceasing energy. Not only in the school of Tyrannus, but *from house to house* he went about amongst the brethren, instructing them in their most holy faith, and warning them *with tears* (Acts xx. 20—31) to hold fast that which they had been taught, *repentance towards God, and faith towards our Lord Jesus Christ* (Acts xx. 21). The result of such labours, carried on by the Apostle himself, and probably by his immediate[1] converts, was speedily perceptible. An important church was founded at Ephesus itself, over which "presbyters" were appointed to preside (Acts xx. 28), and the Word was made known throughout the Roman province of Asia, and probably contributed to the foundation of the seven famous churches of that region (Acts xix. 10).

Ephesus, it must be borne in mind, was no common city[2]. The capital of the province, the principal empo-

[1] Such as Epaphras, Archippus, and Philemon. See Col. i. 7; iv. 7, 12; Philem. 23. C. and H., II. 13, and note.

[2] It retained even under the Romans its old democratic constitution, and Josephus (*Ant.* XIV. 10. 12; XVI. 6. 4. 7) mentions the βουλή or γερουσία = the *senate*, the ἐκκλησία = *assembly*, the δῆμος = the *people*. As Thessalonica had its *politarchs* (see above, p. 447, n), and Athens its *archons*, so

rium of trade on the nearer side of Mount Taurus, it claimed with Smyrna the honour of being one of the "eyes" of Asia. Though Greek in its origin it was half Oriental in the prevalent worship and the character of its inhabitants, and contained the famous temple of Diana, or Artemis, deemed by the ancients one of the wonders of the world[1]. The original temple, built at the expense of all the Greek cities in Asia, the erection of which was begun before the Persian, and lasted even through the Peloponnesian war, was set on fire by Herostratus on the night that Alexander the Great was born. But in its place there soon arose a still more sumptuous structure, on which all that art and skill could achieve was freely lavished. The Temple-area was 425 ft. long by 220 in breadth, and was surrounded by 127 marble columns, 60 ft. high, each the gift of kings, and 36 of them beautifully ornamented. The roof was supported by columns of green jasper, eight of which may be seen in the mosque of St Sophia at Constantinople, whither they were removed by the emperor Justinian after the temple had been destroyed by the Goths. The altar, richly adorned, was the work of Praxiteles, and here and there were statues from the chisels of the most eminent sculptors. The walls were adorned with the finest paintings in the world, the master-pieces of Apelles and Parrhasius, while the sacred precincts, to the extent of a furlong from the building, offered an inviolable sanctuary to all who sought an asylum there.

The presiding deity of this magnificent pile was an

Ephesus had its own magistrates, amongst whom the γραμματεύς (Acts xix. 35) = *town-clerk* or *recorder*, held a high position.

[1] See generally on Ephesus and its temple, Con. and Howson, I. 73—79; Smith's *Bibl. Dict.*, and *Dict. of Classical Geography*.

ancient, black, wooden idol, said to have fallen down from heaven, representing Artemis, not the huntress-goddess of the Greeks, but an Asiatic divinity[1], the impersonation of nature, the prolific "mother of life," as shown by the many breasts represented on her image.

Round this worship of Artemis there clustered a host of minor superstitions, and Ephesus was at this time the head-quarters of the magical arts. Here were to be bought charms and incantations of all kinds; amulets to preserve men from bodily danger; formulas to ward off the influence of demons; mysterious symbols called "Ephesian letters," copied from the inscriptions on various parts of the idol, deemed a safeguard against all kinds of evil. These arts were not studied merely by strolling vagabonds, for the purpose of imposing on idle women and ignorant men; they were believed by the educated, and studied by men of letters, who wrote many books on the subject, opening up the secrets of the art, which were highly valued and fetched great prices.

Here, then, was a new field for the efforts of the Apostle, and in this stronghold of heathenism it pleased God to work special miracles by his hands (Acts xix. 11), so that napkins[2] and aprons[2] brought from his body

[1] The head was a mural crown, each hand held a bar of metal, and the lower part ended in a rude block covered with figures of animals and mystic inscriptions. Her image resembled an Indian idol rather than the beautiful forms which crowded the Acropolis of Athens. "Like the Palladium of Troy—like the most ancient Minerva at Athens—like the Paphian Venus and the Cybele of Pessinus (see above, p. 437, n.)—like the Ceres in Sicily mentioned by Cicero (*in Verr.* v. 187), it was believed to have fallen down from the sky" (Acts xix. 35). C. and H., I. 78. The ceremonies of her worship were conducted by a troop of virgin priestesses called Melissæ, and a number of priests, eunuchs from the interior of Asia Minor, called Megabizi.

[2] Both the original words used here are Latin. The first,

were enabled to communicate a healing power, to expel disease and deliver the possessed. Such miracles produced a deep impression on those who witnessed them, and before long, as in the case of Moses in Egypt, certain Jewish exorcists, who wandered about the Asiatic cities, strove to effect the same marvellous results by their enchantments. Fancying that the Name of Jesus was used by the Apostle as a kind of spell, and was in fact his secret, they also began to pronounce the same over the possessed saying, *We adjure you in the name of Jesus, whom Paul preacheth* (Acts xix. 13).

One particular family, consisting of seven brothers, sons of one Sceva, a Jewish High-priest[1], were especially addicted to this practice, and on one occasion while thus engaged the evil spirit answered, *Jesus I recognise*[2], *and Paul I know, but who are ye?* and thereupon the possessed flung himself upon them, and with the terrible strength of a madman and a demon drove them forth naked and wounded from the house. This incident was quickly noised abroad throughout all Ephesus, became known both to Jews and Gentiles, and proved that the power of the name of Jesus was one "fatal to counterfeit and impossible to resist." Fear fell upon all. The magicians of Ephesus confessed that this was the finger of God, and many of the con-

σουδάριον, sudarium, occurs in Lk. xix. 20; Jn. xi. 44, xx. 7, and is translated *napkin;* the latter, *σιμικίνθιον, semi-cinctium,* appears to denote a *shawl* or *handkerchief,* or perhaps an apron used by workmen. Baumgarten would connect them with the Apostle's daily labour in his own support. See Wordsworth *in loc.*

[1] Or perhaps the head of one of the 24 courses of Priests.

[2] The Vulgate here has Jesum *novi* et Paulum *scio.* Γινώσκω expresses knowledge of a stronger degree than ἐπίσταμαι (which only occurs elsewhere in Mk. xiv. 68). The former = *I recognise and own His power;* the latter = *I know, am acquainted with.* See Wordsworth's note *in loc.*

verts, who even as Christians had continued the practice of "curious, or magical arts, and had not parted with their books of charms," confessed their errors, and publickly burned the magic scrolls in the presence of the Church. An estimate of the value of these books was made, and was found to amount to upwards of 50,000 pieces of silver[1], *so mightily grew the word of the Lord and prevailed* (Acts xix. 20).

CHAPTER II

LETTER TO THE CORINTHIANS—DISTURBANCE AT EPHESUS.

A. D. 57.

DURING the Apostle's stay at Ephesus disastrous intelligence arrived from Corinth. The Church established there combined two distinct elements, Jews or proselytes and Gentiles, of whom the latter were the most numerous. The natural jealousy between these two bodies repressed during the Apostle's presence, had burst out on his departure, and divided the Church into various parties. Some affected fidelity solely and exclusively to St Paul himself (1 Cor. iii. 4); others, probably the Jewish section, to Peter and *the brethren of the Lord* (1 Cor. i. 12, ix. 5); a third, fascinated by the eloquence and learning of the Alexandrian Apollos (1 Cor. i. 12), had attached themselves to him, and probably "hung halfway between the extreme Jewish and the extreme Gentile party;" while a fourth abjured all devotion to any human teachers, and styled themselves the "Christ" party (1 Cor. i. 12).

In addition to these evils the Gentile faction pushed

[1] About £2000 of our money. The coin called ἀργυρίου in Acts xix. 19, and translated *piece of silver*, was probably the silver *drachma*, of the value of about 10*d*.

their views of Christian freedom beyond all due bounds. The profligacy that disgraced the inhabitants of Corinth and made their name a byword was openly avowed and gloried in (1 Cor. v. 1). To such a pitch, moreover, did they carry their disputes that lawsuits were brought into Roman and Greek courts of Justice (1 Cor. vi. 1—8), and instead of shrinking from the contaminating influence of sensuality at the sacrificial feasts, they freely frequented them even in the colonnades of the temples (1 Cor. viii. 10): the women threw off the head-dress which the customs of Greece and of the East required (1 Cor. xi. 2—16); the most solemn ordinance of the Church was profaned by disorderly and reckless festivity (1 Cor. xi. 17—34); the most showy "gifts" were desired to the disparagement of those which tended only to instruct and improve (1 Cor. xii. 1, xiv. 1—4); mixed marriages were freely contracted (1 Cor. vii. 10—17); and the doctrine of the Resurrection was either denied or emptied of all meaning (1 Cor. xv. 12).

Rumours of these disorders had reached the Apostle from time to time, and he had already sent Timothy[1] and Erastus (Acts xix. 22) from Ephesus to Macedonia, desiring the former if possible to continue his journey to Corinth, and recall to the Church there the image of his own teaching and life. But after their departure members of the household of Chloe arrived informing him that the factions had reached a still more formidable height (1 Cor. i. 11), and that an incestuous marriage, scandalous even to the heathen, of a man with his father's wife, had been allowed to be contracted without rebuke (1 Cor. v. 1). This determined

[1] He does not, however, seem to have reached Corinth on this occasion, and St Paul himself doubted whether he would be able to do so. Erastus is probably the "treasurer" of Corinth alluded to in Rom. xvi. 23; 2 Tim. iv. 20.

the Apostle to write the first of his extant letters[1] to the Corinthians and other Christian communities in the province of Achaia (comp. 1 Cor. i. 2), in which he treated of all these points, directed that the incestuous offender should be expelled from the Christian community, and replied to various questions, which three members of the Corinthian Church, Fortunatus, Stephanas, and Achaicus (1 Cor. xvi. 17), themselves the bearers of the Epistle, had brought for his solution relating to the controversies respecting sacrificial feasts, meat offered to idols, the right of divorce, and the exercise of spiritual gifts in the public ministrations of the Church.

At the time he dispatched this letter, it was the Apostle's intention to proceed through Macedonia to Corinth, and after spending the winter there (1 Cor. xvi. 5, 6; Acts xix. 21) to proceed to Jerusalem, whence he contemplated a journey to Rome itself (Acts xix. 21). Till Pentecost, however, he resolved to stay at Ephesus (1 Cor. xvi. 8), for there *a great door* was opened to him, and there were many *adversaries* against whom he had yet to contend. But these designs were destined to be rudely interrupted.

It was now about the month Artemisius, or the month of Artemis[2], when the annual festival of the goddess was observed throughout Greece and Asia, and a vast concourse of people from all quarters would be brought together. The preaching of the Apostle

[1] From a comparison of 2 Cor. ii. 1, xii. 14, 21, xiii. 1, 2, some would infer that the Apostle paid an unrecorded visit to Corinth during his three years' stay at Ephesus, and on the authority of 1 Cor. v. 9—12 that he afterwards wrote a short letter to the Church there respecting the exclusion of profligates from the Christian body. See C. and H., II. 18—21.

[2] April or May, A.D. 57. See C. and H., II. 84; Lewin's *Life of St Paul*, I. 439; Smith's *Bibl. Dict.*, Art. *Ephesus*.

had by this time produced a great effect both in Ephesus and throughout proconsular Asia, and a great multitude had avowed themselves believers (Acts xix. 26). Consequently the sellers of portable shrines[1] of Diana found their trade sensibly diminished, and *no small tumult arose about the Way.* Prominent among the malcontents was a certain Demetrius, a master-manufacturer of these silver shrines, who found employment for a large body of workmen. These he now called together, and others similarly employed, and set forth the damage which their trade had sustained, and the danger lest the temple of the great goddess Diana, which not only Asia but all the civilized world held sacred, should fall into disrepute. His words found eager listeners, and an excited cry arose, *Great is Diana of the Ephesians* (Acts xix. 28). The commotion thus aroused quickly spread, and the thousands of citizens and strangers, whom the games had attracted to Ephesus, made a general rush towards the theatre. Failing on the way in their attempt to seize St Paul[2], they dragged thither two of his companions, Gaius and Aristarchus of Macedonia. News of the danger of his friends would have urged the Apostle to venture thither himself, but the disciples, aided by the Asiarchs[3], who ex-

[1] It is not certain whether these were models of the whole temple or of the shrine. Such models, however, were eagerly purchased by strangers, and carried by devotees on journeys, or set up in their houses. The material might be wood, or gold, or silver. C. and H., II. 78.

[2] It is not improbable that it was on this occasion he was rescued by Aquila and Priscilla at the risk of their own lives, as mentioned in Rom. xvi. 3, 4.

[3] The Asiarchs, Ἀσιάρχαι (Acts xix. 31), were officers, generally ten in number, appointed like the *ædiles* at Rome, to preside over the games held in different parts of the province of Asia, just as other provinces had their *Galatarchs, Lysiarchs, Bythiniarchs,* &c. "They held for the time a kind of sacerdotal position; and when robed in mantles of purple

ercised high authority during the games, induced him to remain in privacy, and not venture to incur inevitable risk. Meanwhile the crowded seats of the theatre presented a scene of the utmost confusion, some crying one thing and some another, and the majority not knowing *why they were come together* (Acts xix. 29—32). At length the Jews, not unwilling to injure the Apostle's cause, and anxious to clear themselves, put forward one Alexander, who may possibly have been *the coppersmith* mentioned in 2 Tim. iv. 14, and being connected in trade with Demetrius might have been expected to have some influence with the people. So he stood forth and beckoned with his hand for silence. But he was soon recognised as a Jew, and one unanimous cry which lasted upwards of two hours arose from the tumultuous throng, *Great is Diana of the Ephesians* (Acts xix. 34).

When this had partially subsided, another effort was made to calm the storm. The Town-clerk[1] or Recorder, who was the lawful president of the assembly, stood forward and reminded his hearers that the city of Ephesus was beyond all question the devoted "warden[2]"

and crowned with garlands, they assumed the duty of regulating the great gymnastic contests, and controlling the tumultuous crowd in the theatre; they might literally be called the *chiefs of Asia*." C. and H., II. 83; Lewin's *Life of St Paul*, I. 350—353.

[1] This officer "had to do with state-papers; he was keeper of the archives; he read what was of public moment before the senate and assembly; he was present when money was deposited in the temple; and when letters were sent to the people of Ephesus, they were officially addressed to him. Hence we can readily account for his name appearing so often on the coins of Ephesus (see C. and H., II. 89, and p. 79). He seems sometimes to have given the name to the year, like the archons at Athens, or the consuls at Rome." C. and H., II. 81.

[2] Νεωκόρον, Acts xix. 35, literally *Temple-sweeper*, was

of the great goddess Diana and the image that came down from the sky. The statements of a few unknown foreigners could not contradict a fact so patent to all the world. Let them, therefore, avoid doing anything rash or inconsiderate, especially as St Paul and his companions had neither profaned their temple nor uttered calumnious words against the goddess. If Demetrius and his friends had any just cause of complaint, it could be decided in the assize-courts[1], then open, or by an appeal to the proconsul, or, if necessary, in the regular assembly. Above every thing, let the present tumultuous proceedings be discontinued, which could only bring down upon them the displeasure of the Romans, who could not be expected to tolerate such causeless and disorderly doings, however willing to indulge an ancient and loyal city (Acts xix. 35—40).

With these arguments the cautious man of authority tranquillized the assembly, and the crowd dispersed to their own homes. Thus by the intrepidity of his friends[2] Aquila and Priscilla, and the interposition of a Greek magistrate, the Apostle's life was saved; and having assembled the disciples and given them his last farewell, set out towards Macedonia (Acts xx. 1), and accompanied, it is not improbable, by Tychicus and

originally an expression of humility, and applied to the lowest menials engaged in the care of the Temple. Afterwards it became a title of high honour, and was applied not only to persons, but to cities and communities. Thus Ephesus was personified as the "devotee" of Diana, and boastifully stamped the name upon her coins.

[1] Ephesus was an assize-town (*forum* or *conventus*), which the proconsul would visit at stated seasons, attended by his interpreter, for all legal business was conducted in Latin. C. and H., II. 82.

[2] See above, p. 461, n.; for the Apostle's own feelings in respect to the tumult, see 2 Cor. i. 8—11, on which see Paley's *Horæ Paulinæ*. 2 Cor. No. IV.

Trophimus, reached Alexandria Troas[1]. (Acts xx. 4, 5.)

CHAPTER III

TROAS—SECOND JOURNEY TO GREECE.

A. D. 57, 58.

ON the occasion of his former visit to Troas[2] the Apostle had been able to stay but a very short time. Now, however, though disturbed in mind by the late outbreak, he occupied himself for some time in preaching the Word (2 Cor. ii. 12). But a cause of still deeper anxiety harassed him. He had sent Titus to Corinth, either with or soon after the first Epistle, to superintend the great collection now being made for the poorer Christians at Jerusalem, to enforce the instructions contained in his Epistle, and to report the state of the Corinthian church; and he had directed him to return through Macedonia and rejoin him probably at Troas[3], where he hoped to have arrived shortly after Pentecost. But the late tumult had driven him sooner than he had intended from Ephesus, and he waited for Titus at Troas with a heart full of anxiety respecting the Church at Corinth. Day after day passed, and still Titus came not. At length the suspense became unbearable, *his spirit had no rest* (2 Cor. ii. 13) in the prolonged absence of his brother, and though at Troas a door *was opened to him of the Lord*, and he was enabled to lay the foundation of a flourishing church, he resolved to sail to Macedonia, hoping the sooner to meet Titus on his return.

[1] Probably by sea: comp. Acts xx. 13, 14, though it is to be remembered that one of the great roads passed by Smyrna and Pergamus between Ephesus and Troas.

[2] See above, pp. 438, 439.

[3] See Birks' *Horæ Apostolicæ*, p. 237; Neander's *Planting*, I. 247.

Bidding farewell, therefore, to the disciples, he embarked, and probably, as before[1], landing at Neapolis, pressed on to Philippi. There he paused, and for a while was cheered by the zeal and warm affection of his Philippian converts (2 Cor. viii. 1, 2). But still he could think of nothing but Corinth. "Corinth, and Corinth only, was the word which would then have been found written on his heart[2]." Timothy, indeed, appears to have met him at Philippi (comp. 2 Cor. i. 1), but till Titus arrived his flesh could find no rest; he was *troubled on every side, without were fightings, within were fears* (2 Cor. vii. 5).

At last the long-expected messenger reached Philippi, and bore with him tidings sufficiently cheering to relieve the Apostle of the chief load of his anxieties. His first Epistle had not only been received, but bore good fruit. The majority of the Corinthian church had submitted to his injunctions, and were deeply repentant for the sins they had committed (2 Cor. vii. 7—11); the incestuous person had been excommunicated (2 Cor. ii. 6), and afterwards forgiven (2 Cor. ii. 10); and the collection for the poor Christians at Jerusalem had made good progress (2 Cor. viii. 10). All, however, was not as it ought to be. The parties which claimed the authority of Christ, aided by an emissary from Palestine (2 Cor. xi. 4), who had brought letters of commendation from Jerusalem, had grown so powerful as to openly assail both the Apostle's authority and his character, charging him with selfish motives, with fickleness, timidity, and self-distrust, and disparaging his inartificial speech, and the insignificance of his *bodily presence* (2 Cor. x. 10).

The news that the Corinthians had generally submitted to his injunctions, removed a load from the

[1] See above, p. 440. [2] Stanley's *Comm. on 2 Cor.* ii. 13.

Apostle's mind, and filled him with overwhelming thankfulness, but the insinuations of his adversaries roused in him the utmost indignation. Titus was, therefore, immediately directed to return to Corinth with instructions to continue the collection, and bearing a second Epistle, in which the Apostle expressed his heartfelt satisfaction at the tidings brought by Titus (2 Cor. i.—vii.), urged the speedy completion of the contributions (2 Cor. viii. ix.), and vindicated his Apostolical character against the assertions of his Judaizing opponents (2 Cor. x.—xiii.).

With this Epistle, then, Titus accompanied by Luke (2 Cor. viii. 18) and Trophimus, set out for Corinth, while St Paul, as yet unwilling to revisit that city, continued to prosecute his labours in the northern regions of Greece, and to accomplish those plans which he had been unable to complete during his previous visit to Macedonia. But not satisfied with preaching the word in the towns of that province bordering on the Ægean, he appears now to have penetrated into the interior, and even beyond them, to the shores of the Adriatic, *fully preaching the Gospel round about unto Illyricum*[1] (Rom. xv. 19).

This tour probably occupied the summer and autumn of A.D. 57, and then *having no more place in those parts* (Rom. xv. 23), he removed with the approach of winter to Achaia, and took up his abode at Corinth (Acts xx. 2). But while here in the house of Gaius he could enjoy the society of Erastus and Stephanas, of Fortunatus, Achaicus, and others of the brethren, his

[1] See Paley's *Horæ Paulinæ* on this passage. Illyricum was an extensive region lying along the Eastern coast of the Adriatic, and contiguous to Mœsia and Macedonia on the East. It included Dalmatia (2 Tim. iv. 10), which was sometimes used for the whole of the district. Both terms are probably used by the Apostle in their most extended sense.

heart was saddened[1] by painful intelligence concerning the state of the Galatian Churches. The circumstances under which these churches[2] were founded have been already noticed, as also the peculiar affection with which the Apostle had been received there. Now however he learned that his restless enemies the Judaizers, who had been thwarting him at Corinth, were busy also in Galatia, insisting on the necessity of circumcision (Gal. v. 2, 11, vi. 12, 13), inculcating nothing less than submission to the whole ceremonial law (Gal. iii. 2, iv. 21, v. 4, 18), impugning his own credit, representing him as no true Apostle, as having derived his knowledge of the Gospel at second hand, and as nothing in comparison with James, Peter, and John, the Pillars of the Church at Jerusalem (Gal. ii. 2, 9, &c.). Their teaching he heard with the deepest sadness, had completely *fascinated*[3] (Gal. iii. 1) the easily impressible Galatians, and already many had embraced their doctrines with the same alacrity that they had welcomed himself when he proclaimed Christ crucified amongst them. On receiving this intelligence, the Apostle deemed it right to take instant measures for checking the evil before it became incurable, and accordingly addressed them in an Epistle[4], in which he strenuously defended his own independent Apostolic authority (Gal. i. 11, ii. 21), showed that the doctrine of these Judaizers was calculated to destroy

[1] See Con. and Howson, II. pp. 141—143.

[2] See above, pp. 436—438.

[3] Ἐβάσκανεν = *fascinated*, the metaphor being taken from the popular belief in the power of the evil eye. On the fickleness of the Galatian character, see above, p. 437 and note.

[4] Professor Lightfoot, while placing the Epistle to the Galatians between the Second to the Corinthians and that to the Romans, and referring its date to the winter of A.D. 57 or the spring of A.D. 58, seems to think it may have been written during the journey between Macedonia and Achaia. See *Proleg. to the Comm.*, pp. 48—54.

the very essence of Christianity, "to reduce it from an inward and spiritual life to an outward and ceremonial system" (Gal. iii. iv.), and exhorted them once more to walk in a manner worthy of that state of freedom and not of bondage, into which they had been called (Gal. v. vi.).

The Apostle's present stay at Corinth continued upwards of three months (Acts xx. 3), and he probably employed himself not only in convincing and silencing the gainsayers who opposed him, as he had declared he would (2 Cor. xiii. 1—6), and in visiting other churches in the province of Achaia, but also in superintending the great collection for the poorer Christians at Jerusalem, about which he felt so solicitous. This collection was now completed, and certain treasurers were nominated by the whole Church, with whom the Apostle was to carry it on his contemplated journey to Jerusalem (1 Cor. xvi. 3).

Meanwhile a Christian matron, named Phœbe[1], of the port of Cenchreæ, was about to sail in an opposite direction to Rome upon some private business. St Paul therefore availed himself of the opportunity thus afforded of addressing an Epistle to the Church in that city, which he already intended to visit speedily, and with the members of which, though they had not *seen his face in the flesh*, he yet appears, from the numerous salutations at the close of the Epistle, to have been well acquainted. When this Church was founded is uncertain. Christianity may have been planted in Rome by some of the strangers from that city present on the day of Pentecost (Acts ii. 10), or by believing Jews attracted thither in the early days of Christianity, and who had been converted by St Paul's own preaching. Which-

[1] She was probably a widow of consideration and wealth, acting as one of the deaconesses of the Church. See C. and H., II. 166; Smith's *Bibl. Dict.*

ever is the correct opinion, the Church there appears to have been numerous, and though in the first instance its members were probably Jews, who had been converted in the eastern parts of the Empire, they had received large accessions from the Gentiles (Rom. i. 13). Between these two parties disputes had arisen respecting the obligation of the Mosaic law, and while the one could not bring themselves to acknowledge their Gentile brethren as their equals in Christian privileges (Rom. iii. 9—29, xv. 7—11), the other could not make sufficient allowance for Jewish prejudices respecting the observation of days and the eating of meats (Rom. xiv.). Long desirous of visiting the Church at Rome, and probably informed of its condition by Aquila and Priscilla, now resident there[1] (Rom. xvi. 3), he deemed it his duty, as the Apostle of the Gentiles, to compose the differences between the two sections of the Roman Church, to lay down, in opposition to the Judaizers[2], the great doctrine of justification by faith only (Rom. i.—viii.), to explain the mystery of the rejection of the Jews and the admission of the Gentiles into the Christian covenant (Rom. ix.—xi.), and to inculcate on all the duty of mutual forbearance respecting the matters in dispute, and the need of a holy and a Christian life (Rom. xii.—xv. 13).

Anxious to visit Jerusalem before his projected

[1] On the salutation in Rom. xvi. 3, and the return of Aquila and Priscilla since the dispatch of the First Epistle to the Corinthians, see Paley's *Horæ Paulinæ*, No. II.

[2] The Epistles to the Romans and Galatians relate to the same general question. But the Apostle had founded the Church in Galatia, hence he puts the point in a great measure upon personal authority (comp. Gal. i. 6, 11, 12, v. 2); but he had never been at Rome, hence in his Epistle to that Church he puts the same points upon argument. "This distinction between the two Epistles is suited to the relation in which the Apostle stood to his different correspondents." See Paley's *Horæ Paulinæ*.

journey to Rome, the Apostle at the close of his three months' stay in Corinth intended to go by sea to Syria and probably from the port of Cenchreæ (Acts xx. 3). Though, however, his intended visit to the Holy City had for its object the supplying of the wants of the poorer Christians there by the great collection, which had been so long in progress, he could not look forward to it without grave misgiving, knowing as he did the inveterate hostility of the Judaizers towards himself (Rom. xv. 30—32). But even before he could set sail the enmity of the Jews at Corinth ripened into a plot against his life (Acts xx. 3). He resolved, therefore, to make a change in the proposed route, and instead of going to proconsular Asia by sea, he went by land through Macedonia, Berœa, Thessalonica, and Philippi, towards the spot where he had first landed on the shores of Europe. His companions on this occasion were Sopater, a native of Berœa, Aristarchus and Secundus of Thessalonica, Gaius of Derbe, and Timotheus, and two Christians from proconsular Asia, Tychicus and Trophimus (Acts xx. 4). The whole of this company did not at once cross over to Asia with St Paul, but while he and Luke remained at Philippi, preceded the rest to Troas. It was now the season of the Passover, and the Apostle and his companion remained at Philippi till the feast was ended, and then sailed from Neapolis, and after a voyage, which, probably from unfavourable weather, occupied upwards of five days[1] (Acts xx. 6), reached Troas, and there joined the other disciples and abode seven days. We have no details respecting the Apostle's labours during the early part of this week, but on the evening of the Sabbath preceding the day appointed for the ship to sail, the Christians were assembled in an upper-room, lighted up by many lamps, celebrating that

[1] Compare the time spent on the former voyage above, p. 440, and the note.

Breaking of the Bread which now formed so essential a part of their religious services (Acts xx. 7). Impressed with the feeling that the morrow was appointed for his departure, and that the present opportunity might not again recur, St Paul was prolonging his discourse till midnight, when overcome by weariness and the heat of the room, a young listener, named Eutychus, sank into a slumber, and suddenly falling from the balcony where he sat was dashed upon the floor below and taken up dead. Much confusion thereupon ensued and no little lamentation (Acts xx. 10), but St Paul went down and embracing the body said to the bystanders, *Trouble not yourselves, for his life is in him.* Thereupon he was taken up alive, and amidst joy and thankfulness the Eucharistic feast, combined then, as was usual, with a common meal, was resumed, and the Apostle continued his discourse till the dawn of day.

The ship was now ready to sail, and the Apostle's companions went on board. It was arranged, however, that he himself should join the vessel at Assos, a little more than 20 miles distant, and thus secure a few more hours with the disciples at Troas. To Assos, therefore, he proceeded by land, and there embarking, sailed with the rest of his companions to Mitylene, the chief city of Lesbos, and separated from Assos by a narrow channel. Another day's sail brought them to Chios, whence having put in at Samos they lay to for the night at Trogyllium, a cape and town on the Ionian coast. The following morning they got as far as Miletus, the ancient capital of Ionia, about 50 miles south of Ephesus. Here they landed, and St Paul, who was hastening forward to reach Jerusalem, if possible, by Pentecost, sent a messenger to Ephesus to request the elders of the Church to meet him there. They quickly obeyed his summons, and the Apostle took leave of them in an affecting and impressive address, in which he reminded them of his past labours amongst them (Acts xx. 18—21), expressed his conviction that bonds and imprisonment awaited him at Jerusalem (Acts xx. 22—24), and in the most solemn manner warned them to tend the flock over which the Holy Spirit had made them overseers, and to defend the Church of God, which He had purchased with His own blood, against *grievous wolves*, which he too surely foreboded would enter in among them (Acts xx. 25—31).

Having given them these warnings, and finally commended them *to God and the word of His grace*, he knelt down on the shore and prayed with them, and then with an outburst of natural grief they fell upon his neck and kissed him again and again[1], *sorrowing most of all for the words which he spake, that they should see his face no more* (Acts xx. 38).

CHAPTER IV

THE RETURN TO JERUSALEM—THE TUMULT IN THE TEMPLE.

A.D. 58.

DEEP as was the grief of the brethren at the departure of the Apostle, no long time could be devoted to its indulgence. The wind blew fair[2], and the vessel was ready to depart. With sorrowing hearts, therefore, they accompanied him to the water's edge, and there tore[3] themselves away from him and his companions. The voyage was now resumed, and running before the wind the vessel soon reached Cos[4], off the coast of

[1] Note the force of the imperfect κατεφίλουν, Acts xx. 37.

[2] C. and H., II. 239: comp. Acts xxi. 1.

[3] Ἀποσπασθέντας, Acts xxi. 1.

[4] Distant from Miletus about 40 nautical miles, a passage of about 6 hours: C. and H., II. 239.

Caria, and on the following day the island of Rhodes. Thence they proceeded to Patara[1] in Lycia, where the vessel in which St Paul had been hitherto sailing apparently finished its voyage, or was bound for some place further east along the coast of Asia Minor.

In the harbour, however, there lay a vessel just about to sail across the open sea to Phœnicia (Acts xxi. 2), and without a moment's delay they went on board, and made sail. After sighting[2] Cyprus and leaving it on the left hand they made straight for the port of Tyre, and reached it probably in two days. Here their vessel was bound to unlade her cargo, and the anxiety of the Apostle as to reaching Jerusalem in time for the Pentecostal festival being removed, he resolved to remain at Tyre a few days (Acts xxi. 4).

A church had been probably founded at Tyre soon after the death of Stephen[3], and may have been already visited by St Paul during one of his missionary journeys in the region of Syria and Cilicia[4]. However this may have been, the Apostle now enjoyed a week of refreshing intercourse with the Tyrian disciples, and so won their affections that on the day fixed for his departure, they all, with their wives and children, accompanied him outside the city-gate to the sea-shore. There the scene at Miletus was repeated, and after prayer and mutual embraces the travellers proceeded on board, while the brethren of Tyre returned to their homes, their hearts filled with many forebodings, for prophets amongst them had intimated that danger awaited their beloved teacher at Jerusalem (Acts xxi. 4).

[1] The sea-port of the city of Xanthus, 10 miles distant, devoted to the worship of Apollo, and the seat of a famous oracle. Comp. Hor. *Od.* III. iv. 64.

[2] Or *rising* Cyprus, in English nautical phrase. The word, in reference to sea-voyages, means *to see land, to bring land into view, to make* land.

[3] See above, p. 373. [4] See above, p. 391.

Before evening the Apostle and his companions had reached Ptolemais[1]. Here the sea-voyage terminated, and the little company spent a day with the disciples in the place, and then set out on foot for Cæsarea. At Cæsarea Philip[2] the Evangelist had taken up his residence, and in his house St Paul found a welcome shelter. The family of the Evangelist consisted of four virgin daughters, who all possessed the gift of prophecy. Whether they gave the Apostle any intimations of coming danger is not recorded, but he was not destined to remain at Cæsarea long without receiving even more explicit warnings than he had listened to at Tyre. At the time when news reached Jerusalem of the Apostle's arrival at Cæsarea, the prophet Agabus[3], who had predicted the famine during the reign of Claudius, was in the city. Thereupon he straightway hastened to the coast, and entering Philip's house, took St Paul's girdle, and binding[4] with it his own hands and feet, declared in the name of the Holy Spirit that so the Jews at Jerusalem should bind the owner of that girdle, and deliver him into the hands of the Gentiles (Acts xxi. 11).

This explicit intimation of coming trials made a deep impression on all present, and Luke, Trophimus, and Aristarchus, the Apostle's companions, with the Christians of Cæsarea, burst into tears (Acts xxi. 13) and implored him not to go up to Jerusalem. Though deeply affected by their grief on his behalf, the Apostle was not to be moved from his deliberate purpose. He was ready, he declared, not only *to be bound, but to die at Jerusalem for the Name of the Lord Jesus*, and finding his resolution not to be shaken, they desisted

[1] The distance being but 28 miles from Tyre. For a notice of this sea-port, see above, p. 37, n.

[2] See above, p. 378.

[3] See above, p. 403, and note.

[4] Compare for similar symbolic prophetical actions Isai. xx. 2, 3; Jerem. xiii. 1—11.

from all further intreaties, saying, *The will of the Lord be done* (Acts xxi. 14).

The Festival was now close at hand. The Holy City was already crowded[1] with multitudes of pilgrims, and it was an important matter to obtain a lodging. This an early convert, Mnason of Cyprus[2], whose residence was at Jerusalem, undertook to supply; and with him the Apostle, his companions, and certain of the brethren at Cæsarea, having made arrangements respecting their baggage[3], proceeded to Jerusalem.

On their arrival they were gladly welcomed by the brethren, and St Paul could not but have rejoiced in their sympathy. The day following they repaired to the abode of James, *the Lord's brother*[4], and president of the church at Jerusalem, and there found all the Elders assembled to receive them (Acts xxi. 18). Mutual salutation followed, and then the Apostle recounted in a lengthened narrative all *that God had wrought by his ministration among the Gentiles*, and doubtless pointed with pride and joy to the contributions which the delegates from the various churches he had planted had brought for the relief of the poorer Christians at Jerusalem. The narrative made a deep impression, and in united thanksgiving his hearers glorified God (Acts xxi. 20).

In recounting, however, the progress of the churches in Galatia and Achaia it would be scarcely possible for

[1] Comp. above, p. 344, and comp. pp. 162, 163.

[2] See above, p 402, and note.

[3] For the word *carriage* of our Version here used see Judg. xviii. 21; 1 Sam. xvii. 22. Ἐπισκευασάμενοι is the better reading, and denotes *having packed up*, made ready for the journey. The Apostle, it is to be remarked, had with him the proceeds of the great collection.

[4] On his character and influence, see pp. 426, 427, and the notes.

St Paul to fail touching on subjects which would excite painful feelings, and rouse bitter prejudice in many of his hearers[1], and the peculiar dangers he was liable to encounter in the Holy City soon became apparent. The assembly, which had just glorified God for his success in heathen lands, began to call his attention to the strength of the Judaizing faction in the city[2]. They told him it was generally reported and believed in Jerusalem, among the thousands of converted Jews who still remained zealous for the Law, that he forbade their brethren in foreign lands to circumcise their children or observe the Mosaic customs (Acts xxi. 20, 21). This being so, it was advisable to do something that might correct these erroneous ideas. It was impossible that the arrival of one so well known could be concealed, and his public appearance might lead to scenes of violence. They suggested, therefore, that he should adopt the following course.

There were four disciples, who had taken a Nazarite vow, of which seven days remained unexpired, who would at the close of this period present the usual offerings[3] in the Temple. Let the Apostle, then, join himself to them, and defray the necessary expenses of the whole party. This would prove in the most public manner his observance of Mosaic ceremonies, and contradict the calumnies of his enemies (Acts xxi. 21—25). This advice, in which James the Just apparently acquiesced, the Apostle wishing, if possible, to conciliate the church of Palestine, was not unwilling to adopt. Accordingly

[1] C. and H., II. 259.

[2] For notices of the excited and fanatical state of the Jews at this period, see Milman, *Hist. of the Jews*, II. 166, 172.

[3] For these, see *Class-Book of O. T. History*, pp. 158, 159. Agrippa I., it will be remembered, showed his sympathy with Judaism by defraying the expenses of certain Nazarites; see above, p. 405, and the note.

on the following day, after first performing the necessary purifications, he proceeded with the Christian Nazarites to the Temple, and announced to the priests in the name of his friends, their intention of fulfilling their time, and awaiting the moment of the proper offering.

But the Apostle's object was frustrated by circumstances that took place on the very eve of the completion of the period of their vow. Amongst the thousands present in Jerusalem were many Jews from proconsular Asia, who recognised the able disputant, whom they had so often been unable to confute in their synagogues, walking in the streets with Trophimus the Ephesian (Acts xxi. 29). On one occasion they saw him in the Temple-courts, and rushing to the conclusion that he had taken his companion also thither, instantly sprang upon him, shouting, *Men of Israel, help. This is the man that teacheth all men everywhere against the People, the Law, and this place, yea, who hath also brought Gentiles into the Temple, and profaned this Holy Place* (Acts xxi. 28).

Roused to fury a mob quickly rushed towards the spot, and St Paul would probably have been instantly put to death, had it not been for the unwillingness of his foes to pollute the Temple with blood. They therefore dragged him down the steps from the Court of the Women[1] into the Outer Court, and had no sooner passed, than the Levitical guard closed behind them the Corinthian gates[2] (Acts xxi. 30). Once in the Outer Court they began beating the Apostle violently, being

[1] See above, p. 272, and note. It is clear from that passage that this Court contained the Treasure-Chests, but it also appears to have contained chambers, in one of which the Nazarites performed their vows. C. and H., II. 269.

[2] "Made of brass and very strong, shut at midnight with difficulty by twenty men." Jos. *B. J.* VI. 5. 3. Comp. V. 5. 3, cited in C. and H., II. 269, n.

clearly bent on putting him to death, and would have succeeded, had it not been for a providential intervention. The commotion in the Temple-courts had not failed to attract the notice of the Roman sentries in the tower[1] of Antonia, and they instantly informed Claudius Lysias, the commandant of the garrison, that *all Jerusalem was in an uproar* (Acts xxi. 31).

Thereupon, without a moment's delay, Lysias rushed down attended by some centurions and a strong body of troops. The sight of the dreaded arms of the Imperial forces brought the multitude to their senses, and they left off *beating Paul.* The commandant then approached, and apprehending the Apostle, ordered him to be chained by each hand to a soldier[2], suspecting that he was an Egyptian pretender[3], who had lately caused a revolt, and had hitherto baffled the pursuit of the soldiers of Felix the governor (Acts xxi. 38). He then endeavoured to ascertain from the bystanders who his prisoner was and what he had done, but *some cried one thing, and some another;* and finding it impossible to gain any information amidst the tumult, he ordered him to be conveyed into the barracks within the fortress. Accordingly the soldiers proceeded to remove the Apostle, but so furious was the crowd pressing behind them with yells and execrations, that they had to bear him

[1] On this tower, see above, p. 53, n. and p. 91.

[2] Comp. Acts xii. 4, 6; see above, p. 406, n.

[3] He had come from Egypt into Judæa, and giving himself out to be a prophet, collected in the desert upwards of 30,000 men (4000 of whom were Sicarii or "murderers," Acts xxi. 38), whom he persuaded to follow him to the Mount of Olives, promising that the walls of Jerusalem would fall down at his command, and they would be enabled to seize Jerusalem, and assume the government. Felix, however, marched against him, and easily dispersed his force, slaying 4000, and taking 200 prisoners, but the adventurer himself escaped. See Jos. *B. J.* II. 13. 5; Milman's *Hist. of the Jews,* II. 171.

up in their arms up the staircase. Just as they reached the barracks, St Paul, addressing the commandant in Greek, enquired respectfully whether he might speak to him. Startled at being addressed in the Grecian tongue, Lysias in his turn enquired whether he was mistaken in supposing him to be the Egyptian rebel. St Paul replied that he was no Egyptian, but a Jew, a native of Tarsus in Cilicia, *a citizen of no mean city*, and requested permission to address the people. On which the commandant, influenced it may be by the aspect and manner of his prisoner, at once gave his consent (Acts xxi. 40).

CHAPTER V

THE IMPRISONMENT AT CÆSAREA.

A. D. 58.

STANDING then on the stairs, and beckoning to the crowd with his chained hands to invite their attention, the Apostle began to address them in the Hebrew language. Charmed by the accents of their own beloved tongue, the multitude listened with the deepest silence while he tried to dispel their prejudices against himself. Beginning with the well-known circumstances of his birth and education at Tarsus and Jerusalem, he declared that he was a Jew like themselves, that he had been brought up according to the strictest requirements of the Law, and had hated, persecuted, and endeavoured to extinguish the sect of the Christians (Acts xxii. 3—5). He then proceeded to recount the wonderful circumstances of his conversion on the way to Damascus[1], of his blindness, cure, and baptism (Acts xxii. 6—16), and how on his return to Jerusalem, as he was praying in

[1] For a comparison of the Apostle's words on this occasion with the account given in Acts ix., see above, pp. 381, 385, and notes.

the Temple, he fell into a trance[1], saw that Saviour who had appeared to him on his memorable journey, and was commanded by Him to leave Jerusalem, and preach the Gospel to the Gentiles (Acts xxii. 17—21).

Up to this point the multitude listened to the Apostle with the deepest attention, but no sooner had he spoken of his mission to the Gentiles, than they broke out into such furious cries of rage and indignation that the previous clamour appeared as nothing in comparison. The thought of uncircumcised heathen being placed on an equality with the children of Abraham was unbearable. *Away*, they cried, *with such a fellow from the earth, it is not fit that he should live*, and while some flung dust into the air, others cast off their clothes, as if they would stone him on the spot (comp. Acts vii. 58). This fresh outbreak of frantic violence filled the commandant with still greater perplexity. Unable to understand the language in which the Apostle spake, he could only infer from the results it produced that his prisoner had been guilty of some enormous offence. He therefore gave orders that he should be conveyed into the castle, and, since other means had failed, that the secret of his guilt should be ascertained by torture. As in the case of the Saviour's crucifixion[2], a centurion was deputed to superintend the scourging, and like a common malefactor the Apostle was on the point of being stretched or fastened to the post to receive the lashes, when he turned to the centurion and enquired whether it was lawful to scourge one who was a Roman citizen and uncondemned (Acts xxii. 25)? Astonished at such a question, the centurion ordered the scourging to be suspended, and hurrying to the commandant, bade him take heed what he was doing, for the

[1] Compare the account above, pp. 390, 391.
[2] See above, p. 309, and the note.

prisoner was a Roman citizen. Upon this Lysias himself hastened to the spot and enquired whether the news was true, and on his replying in the affirmative, remarked that he had purchased this privilege for a large sum, on which St Paul informed him that he was free-born (Acts xxii. 28). Thus assured of the true position of his prisoner, the commandant ordered the instruments of torture to be instantly removed, and was in no little alarm at the turn affairs had taken.

For the present, indeed, he was obliged to keep him in the Tower, but on the morrow he determined to make a second effort to ascertain the nature of his prisoner's offence, and therefore summoned a meeting of the Sanhedrin, and bringing down the Apostle from the Tower to the hall Gazith[1] placed him before them. Casting a steadfast and scrutinizing glance (Acts xxiii. 1) on the faces of those assembled, many of whom must have been familiar to him, St Paul began by proving that he had lived a conscientious[2] life before God up to that very day. This assertion so offended the high-priest that he commanded those standing near to strike him on the mouth, whereupon the Apostle, filled with indignation at so brutal an insult, replied, *God shall smite thee*[3], *thou whited wall*[4]. *For sittest thou to judge me according to the law, and commandest me*

[1] See above, p. 96. Only a narrow space of the Great Temple-court intervened between the steps of the tower Antonia and this hall. But the Sanhedrin may have met in a place less sacred, into which soldiers might be admitted. C. and H., II. 281.

[2] Compare with this assertion 2 Tim. i. 3.

[3] If this was a prophetic denunciation, it was terribly fulfilled when the hypocritical president of the Sanhedrin was murdered by the Sicarii during the Jewish war. See Jos. *B. J.* II. 17. 9.

[4] Comp. Mtt. xxiii. 27. He compares him to those walls, which composed of mud and other vile materials, made a fair show without, being plastered and whitewashed.

to be smitten contrary to the law? To this the by-standers rejoined, *Revilest thou God's high-priest?* and St Paul, recovering himself, answered that he did not know or consider that Ananias was high-priest, otherwise he would not so have spoken, for it was written in the Law, *Thou shalt not revile the ruler of thy people* (Ex. xxii. 28).

By this time, however, the Apostle had seen only too clearly that there was little prospect of his obtaining an equitable decision from his judges. Knowing, therefore, that there were both Pharisees and Sadducees among them, and that however much they might be united in persecuting him, they were sundered from one another by a deep gulf on one important article of faith, he exclaimed, as indeed he could say with truth, that he was brought to trial, because he had testified of the hope of Israel, and of the resurrection of the dead (Acts xxiii. 6). He had scarcely pronounced these words, when there was an instant division in the Council. The Pharisees present were united in his favour, and a hot debate ensued between them and the Sadducaic faction, who denied any Resurrection and the existence alike of angels and spirits[1]. While the latter party were furious against him, the former declared they could find no fault in him, and if, as he had said in his speech on the stairs, an angel or a spirit had indeed spoken to him[2], they would not criminate him on this account.

A scene of great confusion now ensued (Acts xxiii. 10), in the midst of which Claudius Lysias being afraid lest the Roman citizen should be torn in pieces by them, ordered a detachment to go down instantly, and bring him into the barracks. Thus the Apostle was

[1] See above, p. 115.

[2] The sentence is broken off. The words μὴ θεομαχῶμεν, Acts xxiii. 9, are wanting in the best MSS. See Neander's *Planting*, I. 307, and note.

delivered from the most imminent danger, and in the evening his anxieties were relieved by the appearance of his Divine Master in a vision of the night, bidding him be of good cheer, and declaring that, as he had *testified unto Him in Jerusalem, so he must testify also at Rome* (Acts xxiii. 11).

The following morning however had hardly dawned, before a fresh danger revealed itself. Disappointed on the previous day in their malicious designs, more than forty of the Jews bound themselves by a solemn vow that they would neither eat nor drink till they had put the Apostle to death. Accordingly they went to the chief members of the Sanhedrin, and proposed that they should present themselves before the commandant and request him to allow St Paul to be brought down and placed a second time before them, in order that they might resume the enquiry so tumultuously interrupted, and they, on their part, undertook that he should not reach the council-chamber alive, for they would murder him on his way down from the fortress.

But their design in some way reached the ears of the Apostle's nephew[1], who was now present in Jerusalem, and he no sooner heard of the danger which threatened his uncle, than he obtained admittance into the barracks, and imparted to him the intelligence. Thereupon St Paul called one of the centurions, and requested him to take the young man to Claudius Lysias, for he had something to tell him. The officer complied, and conducting him to the commandant told him of St Paul's message. Claudius Lysias received the young man kindly, and leading him cautiously aside enquired what he wished to say. The other thereupon acquainted him with the plot that had been laid, and was dismissed with strict injunctions not to divulge the fact that he had given this information.

[1] See above, p. 380.

Thus assured of the danger that threatened his prisoner, and knowing that he was responsible for his safety as a Roman citizen, Lysias resolved to send him away that very night under a strong escort to Cæsarea, and there leave him in the hands of the governor Felix. Summoning therefore two of the centurions, he gave orders that 200 of the legionary soldiers, with 70 cavalry and 200 spearmen[1], should be in readiness to proceed thither by nine[2] in the evening. In the meantime he wrote to the governor a dispatch, giving a fair and clear account of the case, save in the statement that he had rescued St Paul in the first instance because he had discovered he was a Roman citizen, and in the suppression of all allusion to his intention to scourge him (Acts xxiii. 26—30).

At the time appointed the escort was ready, and mounted on horseback[3] between the two Roman soldiers, to whom he was chained, the Apostle was conducted from Jerusalem to Antipatris[4]. Here the soldiers halted after their long night-march, and while the cavalry proceeded to Cæsarea, the legionary troops, no longer necessary to the Apostle's safety[5], returned to the fortress of Antonia. It was probably during the

[1] Δεξιολάβους, E. V. *spearmen*, Vulg. *lancearios*. Whatever is the precise meaning of this singular word, it distinguishes here *legionary soldiers* from *cavalry*, and probably means *light-armed troops*. The word implies the use of some weapon simply carried in the right hand.

[2] Ἀπὸ τρίτης ὥρας τῆς νυκτός, Acts xxiii. 23.

[3] With a view to greater expedition Lysias ordered that more than one horse should be provided for the Apostle: comp. Acts xxiii. 24, κτήνη τε παραστῆσαι.

[4] For the building of Antipatris, see above, p. 99, and note.

[5] Lysias had probably sent so large and so mixed a force in view of a possible ambuscade. This was no longer to be feared after leaving Antipatris, but the legionaries might be needed in the fortress of Antonia.

afternoon of the day succeeding[1] their departure that the cavalry reached Cæsarea, and the officer in charge immediately delivered up his prisoner to the governor, with the dispatch from Claudius Lysias. Felix[2] read it, and enquired to what province the prisoner belonged[3], and having ascertained that he was a native of Cilicia, replied that he would hear and decide his case as soon as his accusers had arrived, and ordered that for the present he should be kept in *Herod's prætorium*[4] (Acts xxiii. 35).

[1] C. and H., II. 290; Robinson, *Bib. Res.* III. 46, 60.

[2] As mentioned above, p. 409, n., on the death of Herod Agrippa I., A.D. 44, Cuspius Fadus was appointed procurator of Judæa. He was succeeded in A.D. 48 by Tiberius Alexander, who in his turn, in A.D. 48, made way for Ventidius Cumanus. During his sway a frightful tumult happened at the Passover, caused by the presence of the Roman soldiers in the Antonia, and resulting in the deaths of more than 10,000 persons (Jos. *Ant.* XX. 5. 3; *B. J.* II. 12. 1). Cumanus was recalled in A.D. 52, and succeeded by Felix, a freedman of the Emperor Claudius. From Tacitus (*Ann.* XII. 54) he would seem to have been joint procurator with Cumanus. He was the brother of the Emperor's powerful friend Pallas, and is described by Tacitus as ruling his province with meanness, cruelty, and profligacy, *per omnem sævitiam et libidinem jus regium servili ingenio* exercuit. *Hist.* V. 9: comp. *Ann.* XII. 54, and see Merivale, VII. 195.

[3] Compare Pilate's conduct in reference to the Saviour, above, p. 301.

[4] The word *prætorium* properly denotes the residence of the Roman provincial governors, at which they administered justice. Here it seems to denote some palace built by Herod and now appropriated to public uses. As in our old castles, there were prison-chambers in all such buildings. Kitto's *Bib. Illustrations.*

CHAPTER VI

PAUL BEFORE FELIX AND FESTUS.

A. D. 58—60.

FIVE days after the Apostle's arrival at Cæsarea his accusers made their appearance, headed by the high-priest Ananias, certain of the elders, and an orator named Tertullus[1], whose services had been engaged for this occasion. Accordingly, Felix took his seat on the tribunal[2], and Paul having been sent for, Tertullus formally opened the case. After paying an adroit compliment to the procurator on the comparative quiet which the land enjoyed owing to his vigilance and energy[3], he brought three charges against the prisoner: First, that he was a pestilent mover of sedition among all the Jews throughout the world, which amounted to a charge of treason[4] against the emperor; secondly, that he was a ringleader of the sect of the Nazarenes; and thirdly, that he had made an attempt to profane the Temple at Jerusalem. On these charges he declared the Jews had been about to judge him before their own tribunal, when Lysias forcibly took him away, and referred his accusers to the judgment-seat of Felix.

[1] The name is Roman. He was probably an Italian, and pleaded in Latin. "The accuser and the accused could plead in person, as St Paul did here, but *advocati* (ῥήτορες) were often employed." C. and H., II. 302.

[2] On this, see above, p. 303, n.

[3] Felix during his period of office put down several false Messiahs (Jos. *Ant.* XX. 8; *B. J.* II. 13. 4), the followers of the Egyptian pretender (above, p. 486, and n.), riots between the Jews and Syrians in Cæsarea (*Ant.* XX. 8. 7; *B. J.* II. 13. 7), and cleared various parts of the country of robbers (*B. J.* II. 13. 2), see Merivale, VII. 195.

[4] On the severity of the laws against treason, see above, p. 307, n.

To these allegations the Jews present expressed their consent, hoping doubtless that the procurator would hand over the prisoner to their courts, where his fate would be soon decided. But Felix made a sign to the Apostle to proceed with his defence, and he, after expressing his satisfaction in pleading before one who had been so long familiar with the nation, commenced replying to the charges that had been brought against him. A disturber of the nation, he said, he was not, for on his recent visit to the Holy City but twelve days before, he had neither caused a disturbance, or even disputed in the temple, the synagogue, or the streets. As to his being a ringleader of the sect of the Nazarenes, he had never swerved from his belief in the Law and the Prophets; like his accusers, he believed the doctrine of a resurrection, and strove to keep a conscience void of offence towards God and man. As to profaning the Temple, he had lately visited it as the bearer of offerings for his nation, and to observe some of the strictest ceremonies of the Law, not to gather together a multitude or cause a tumult. Certain Jews of Asia, indeed, had brought an accusation against him, but they ought now to have been present as witnesses, ready to bring forward a specific charge, if they had any (Acts xxiv. 10—21).

Felix, who had listened attentively to the Apostle's address, was well acquainted with the character of the Christian religion, which had not only penetrated into Cæsarea, but also numbered disciples even among the troops[1]. He was, therefore, in a position fully to appreciate the weakness of the allegations against the prisoner, and the misrepresentations of his accusers, and must have felt that the only proper course was to pronounce his acquittal and set him free. But this he could

[1] Acts x. See above, p. 399, and p. 482.

not make up his mind to do, and chose to reserve his final[1] decision till Lysias should arrive, and in the meantime committed the Apostle to the charge of the centurion[2] who had brought him to Cæsarea, with instructions to keep him safely, but at the same time to allow his friends[3] to have free access to his apartments.

A few days afterwards Felix entered the audience chamber with his wife Drusilla[4], daughter of the late king Herod Agrippa. Her beauty is spoken of as something marvellous, and she had been induced by the procurator to leave her first husband, Azizus king of Emessa, to become his paramour. The two now sent for St Paul, and desired to have the Christian doctrines explained to them. Accordingly before the Roman libertine and the profligate Jewish princess, the Apostle preached with his wonted faithfulness, and while he discoursed concerning *righteousness, and temperance, and judgment to come*, Felix trembled. But though he trembled, the profligate governor would not release his

[1] Διαγνώσομαι, Acts xxiv. 22.

[2] There were three kinds of custody recognised by the Roman law: (1) *custodia publica*, or confinement in a public gaol, as at Philippi, see above, p. 443, and n.: this was the worst kind; (2) *custodia libera*, or free custody, usual only in the cases of men of rank who were committed to the charge of some magistrate or senator, who made himself responsible for their appearance on the day of trial; (3) *custodia militaris:* in this species of custody, introduced at the commencement of the Empire, the prisoner's right hand was chained to the left hand of a soldier, who was responsible with his life for his safe detention, and kept him either in barracks or a private house. C. and H., II. 308.

[3] This perhaps included Philip the Evangelist resident there with his family; perhaps Cornelius the centurion; and almost certainly Luke and Aristarchus.

[4] Her brother was Agrippa, the present king of Trachonitis. On the part Simon Magus is said to have played in persuading her to leave her husband, see above, p. 376. n. She was at this time in the 18th year of her age.

prisoner from confinement. *Go thy way,* said he, *for this time; when I have a convenient season I will send for thee.* He knew that the Apostle's relatives moved in a respectable sphere, and he had heard him speak of sums of money[1] intrusted to his care, and he wished it to be understood that his liberation was not hopeless, if bought with a suitable sum[2]. Hence he frequently sent for the Apostle, and conversed with him. But St Paul was not one to stoop to such dishonourable means. He preferred to remain in confinement rather than purchase his freedom with a bribe, and at Cæsarea he continued upwards of two years, or from A. D. 58 to A. D. 60.

During this long period of suspense from active labour, it is not improbable that the Gospel of St Luke was composed under the Apostle's eye, and it is possible that "many messages, and even letters, of which we know nothing, may have been sent from Cæsarea to brethren at a distance[3]." Meanwhile the government of Felix became more and more unpopular, and the disaffection of his subjects was increased by a serious quarrel between the Jewish and heathen population at Cæsarea, in which the troops sided with the latter, and committed gross acts of butchery and plunder[4]. This led to the recall of Felix, A. D. 60; and anxious to conciliate the Jews, who had complained of his administration at Rome, he left Paul in bonds (Acts xxiv. 27).

His successor was Porcius Festus, who like himself had probably been a slave, and was one of the emperor's freedmen. Three days after his landing at Cæsarea he repaired to Jerusalem, and there was introduced to the

[1] Acts xxiv. 17. See Birks' *Horæ Apostolicæ*, p. 344.

[2] Such practices were not unusual with some procurators. See the instance of Albinus mentioned in Jos. *Ant.* XX. 9. 2. The Julian Law strictly forbade taking a bribe from a prisoner.

[3] C. and H., II. 308.

[4] See Milman's *History of the Jews*, Vol. II. p. 173.

high-priest[1] and leading members of the nation. They instantly embraced the opportunity of renewing their machinations against the Apostle, and requested the new governor to allow him to be removed to Jerusalem, intending to assassinate him on the road (Acts xxv. 3). Festus replied that St Paul was in custody at Cæsarea, whither he himself was on the point of returning: the Roman Law did not allow an uncondemned person to be given up as a mere favour: he must have his accusers face to face, and be enabled to make his defence; if therefore they wished to bring any charges against him, they must come down to Cæsarea and there prefer them (Acts xxv. 4, 5, 16).

After a stay, therefore, of 8 or 10 days in Jerusalem, he returned to Cæsarea, and the accusers apparently went down the same day. No time was lost in putting the Apostle on his trial. The very next day Festus took his seat on the tribunal, and ordered St Paul to be put forward. Then the delegates from the Sanhedrin urged their accusations, which appear to have been much the same as those brought forward at the previous trial. But they were utterly unable to support their statements, and the Apostle contented himself with a brief but emphatic denial that he had done anything against the Law, the Temple, or Cæsar (Acts xxv. 8).

The sincerity of his bearing appears to have told favourably with the procurator, and he quickly perceived that he was involved in no political movements (Acts xxv. 18, 19), that he had done nothing worthy of death (Acts xxv. 25), and that the charges against him related only to religious questions between him and his

[1] At this time the high-priest was Ishmael the son of Fabi, Jos. *Ant.* xx. 8. 8. He had been appointed by Agrippa II., to whom the Emperor had entrusted all the ecclesiastical arrangements in the Holy City. Milman, *Hist. Jews*, II. 172.

nation. Unwilling, however, to allow a matter immediately to drop, in which the Jews evidently took so deep an interest, he proposed that he should go up to Jerusalem, and there submit to a formal trial in the presence of himself (Acts xxv. 9). But the Apostle knew full well the danger involved in such a journey. He replied, therefore, that he had done no wrong, as Festus himself knew well, and that if he was guilty he was willing to die, but that since the accusations preferred against him were really groundless, rather than go up to Jerusalem, he would avail himself of his privilege as a Roman citizen; *he appealed unto Cæsar*[1] (Acts xxv. 11). According to the Roman law, it was sufficient that a Roman citizen should merely utter the words *I appeal*, and his case was instantly removed to the supreme tribunal of the Emperor. After a brief conversation, therefore, with his assessors, Festus merely enquired whether he adhered to his determination, and then made answer, *Thou hast appealed unto Cæsar; to Cæsar thou shalt go* (Acts xxv. 12).

Though, however, the appeal had been allowed, Festus was in much perplexity to decide how he might describe the charge against the Apostle to the Emperor. It seemed to him a foolish thing to send a prisoner to Rome, without at the same time specifying the charges against him, but how to do this after the vague and unsatisfactory information elicited at the trial appeared extremely difficult. It happened, however, at this time that Herod Agrippa II.[2], king of Chalcis, with his sister

[1] Under the Republic a Roman citizen could appeal to the tribunes. The power of the latter being absorbed by the Emperors, all appeals were transferred to them, and at this time the Imperial tribunal "was a supreme court of appeal from all inferior courts either in Rome or in the provinces." See Art. *Appellatio* in Smith's *Dict. Antiq.*

[2] Herod Agrippa II., was the son of Agrippa I. and Cypros, a grand-niece of Herod the Great. After he had

Bernice[1], arrived on a complimentary visit[2] to the procurator, and stayed some time at Cæsarea. Agrippa had long been acquainted with all that related to Jewish customs, and had, as we have seen, been invested by the Emperor with the power of nominating the high-priest. Festus, therefore, gladly embraced this opportunity of consulting one so much better informed than himself on the points in dispute, and related all the particulars concerning the Apostle so far as he was acquainted with them (Acts xxv. 14—21), and more especially his reiterated assertion concerning one Jesus *who had died and was alive again.* Agrippa, who could not have heard now for the first time of the great doctrine of the Christian faith expressed a desire to see the prisoner. To this Festus readily assented, and fixed the following day for the interview.

Accordingly at the time appointed Agrippa and Bernice with much pomp entered the audience-chamber, accompanied by their suite and the chief men of Cæsarea, and at the command of Festus, Paul was brought before them. As soon as the Apostle appeared, Festus in a set speech detailed the circumstances under which

been educated at Rome, Claudius, about A.D. 49, appointed him king of Chalcis (Jos. *Ant.* xx. 5. 2; *B. J.* ii. 12. 1), and afterwards, A.D. 53, promoted him to the tetrarchies of Philip and Lysanias (Jos. *Ant.* xx. 7. 1; *B. J.* ii. 12. 8), with the title of *king* (Acts xxv. 13). In A.D. 55 Nero added several cities to his dominions, and he displayed the lavish magnificence of his family. During the Jewish war he sided with the Romans, and at its conclusion retired to Rome, where he died in the third year of the reign of Trajan, A.D. 100. See Lewin's *Fasti Sacri;* Smith's *Bibl. Dict.*

[1] She was the eldest daughter of Herod Agrippa I. Her first husband was her uncle Herod, king of Chalcis, on whose death she lived with her own brother Agrippa II. (Jos. *Ant.* xx. 7. 3). Afterwards she married Polemon, king of Cilicia, and ultimately became the mistress of Vespasian and of Titus. See Tac. *Hist.* ii. 81.

[2] See Blunt's *Scriptural Coincidences,* pp. 358—360.

he had become acquainted with the prisoner, his appeal to Cæsar, and his own anxiety to obtain some definite information which he might lay before his lord[1] the emperor concerning him (Acts xxv. 24—27).

Upon this Agrippa signified to the Apostle that he was permitted to speak for himself, and St Paul stretching forth his manacled hands proceeded to address his numerous and influential hearers. After expressing his satisfaction at the opportunity thus afforded him of speaking before one so well versed as Agrippa *in all customs and questions amongst the Jews*, he went on, much as he had done on the stairs leading up to the Castle of Antonia, to speak of his education according to the strictest requirements of the Jewish law (Acts xxvi. 4—8); of the zeal with which he formerly persecuted the believers in Christ; of the vision vouchsafed to him on the road to Damascus, and the commission he had received to preach the Gospel amongst the Gentiles (Acts xxvi. 9—18); and lastly of his unceasing endeavours to carry out this commission, which had brought upon him the enmity of the Jews, though his teaching was in strict accordance with the Jewish Scriptures, and their predictions of the coming of a Messiah who should suffer and rise from the dead (Acts xxvi. 19—23).

This address made no impression upon Festus. Regarding the idea of a resurrection as foolishness, he ascribed the zeal of the Apostle to an excited imagination, or the effect of over-study[2]. Interrupting him,

[1] Τῷ *κυρίῳ*, Acts xv. 26. Note the title. Augustus and Tiberius had declined it, but their successors had sanctioned its use. See Sueton. *Aug.* LIII; *Tiber.* XXVII.

[2] Τὰ πολλὰ γράμματα, Acts xxvi. 24. The Apostle had alluded to "writings" (vv. 22, 23), "and it is reasonable to suppose that in his imprisonment such *books and parchments* as he wrote for in 2 Tim. iv. 13 were brought to him by his friends." C. and H., II. 318. n.

therefore, he cried out in a loud voice (Acts xxvi. 24), *Paul, thou art mad; much learning doth make thee mad. I am not mad, most noble Festus,* replied the Apostle with dignified courtesy, *but speak forth the words of truth and soberness;* and turning to Agrippa, who had knowledge of these matters, and before whom he could speak freely, he solemnly enquired whether he did not believe the prophets. But the persuasive appeal glanced off from the heart of the profligate prince to whom it was addressed. In playful banter or scornful sarcasm he replied, *Lightly*[1] *thou persuadest me to become a Christian.* On which the Apostle, lifting up his chained hands, made answer, *I would to God that, whether lightly or with difficulty*[2], *not only thou, but also all that hear me this day, might become such as I am, except these bonds* (Acts xxvi. 29). With these words this memorable conference ended. Agrippa had no wish to hear more. He rose up with Festus, Bernice, and their suite, and retired from the audience-chamber. The case of the prisoner was then discussed, and it was agreed that he was guilty of nothing deserving of death or even of imprisonment, and Agrippa remarked that he might have been released had he not appealed to Cæsar. But the appeal had been made, and to the imperial tribunal the Apostle must go.

[1] Ἐν ὀλίγῳ με πείθεις, Acts xxvi. 28. Our version *almost* cannot stand. The expression might mean, (1) *in a little space*, or (2) *in few words*, or (3) *in a small measure*. Perhaps *lightly*="with few words, little pain, as though it were a light thing to take up with so despised a sect," as suggested by Dean Alford *in loc.*, best suits the text: see also C. and H., II. 319, n.; Neander's *Planting*, I, 310, n.

[2] The better reading here is ἐν μεγάλῳ.

SECTION IV

St Paul's Imprisonment at Rome.

CHAPTER I

THE VOYAGE FROM CÆSAREA.

A. D. 60.

As soon, then, as it was actually decided that St Paul should be sent to Rome, he was delivered over with certain other prisoners to a centurion, named Julius, belonging to the "Augustan cohort," or the body-guard of the Emperor, who always treated the Apostle with kindness and consideration.

The ship selected was a vessel of Adramyttium, a sea-port of Mysia, opposite Lesbos, which had probably touched at Cæsarea on a return voyage from Egypt, and was now bound for her own port. In her the Apostle embarked with Aristarchus of Thessalonica, the Evangelist St Luke, the prisoners, and their guard. The wind was fair[1], and on the next day they put into Sidon, probably for the purposes of trade, and here the centurion allowed the Apostle to go on shore and receive the kind attentions of his friends[2].

Loosing from Sidon they were constrained, by reason of adverse winds, to run under the lee of Cyprus, that is, probably, along the north side of the island, and thence, keeping nearer the main-land than the isle, to

[1] "From the distance accomplished, 67 geographical miles, we must infer that they had a fair, or at least a leading wind, probably westerly, which is the wind that prevails in this part of the Mediterranean." Smith's *Voyage and Shipwreck of St Paul*, p. 22.

[2] See above, p. 481.

catch the favouring land-breezes[1], sailed through the open sea of Cilicia and Pamphylia to Myra of Lycia, now a desolate waste, but then a flourishing sea-port. Here the centurion found a ship of Alexandria laden with wheat, which though bound for Italy had been carried to Myra by the same westerly winds which had forced the vessel of Adramyttium to keep to the east of Cyprus. To her, therefore, he transferred his charge, and she set sail, laden with a heavy cargo and upwards of 276 passengers (Acts xxvii. 37).

After loading at Myra, their progress was extremely slow, and in consequence of unfavourable winds it was *many days* (Acts xxvii. 7) before they came over against Cnidus[2], at the extreme S. W. of the peninsula of Asia Minor. From this point their natural course would have been by the north side of Crete and westward through the Archipelago. But with a north-west wind blowing, it was deemed most prudent to run down to the southward, and after rounding Cape Salmone to pursue their voyage under the lee of Crete. Accordingly having worked up with difficulty along the southern coast, they reached the harbour of Fair Havens[3], about 5 miles to the east of which was the town of Lasæa.

Here they were detained a considerable time wait-

[1] "In pursuing this route they acted precisely as the most accomplished seaman in the present day would have done under similar circumstances; by standing to the north till they reached the coast of Cilicia, they might expect when they did so to be favoured by the land-breeze, which prevails here during the summer-months, as well as by the current, which constantly runs to the westward, along the south coast of Asia Minor." Smith, p. 28.

[2] A distance of 130 geographical miles, which with a fair wind might have been accomplished in one day. Ibid. p. 34.

[3] Still retaining the same name. The site of Lasæa, also retaining its old name, was discovered Jan. 18, 1856, about two hours to the eastward of "Fair Havens." Smith's *Voyage, &c.* Ed. 1861; C. and H., II. 341, n.

ing for a favourable change of the wind. But none occurred, and the Fast of the Atonement[1], which took place about the period of the autumnal equinox, having passed, the navigation had become very dangerous. It now became a grave question whether they should remain at Fair Havens for the winter, or seek some other anchorage. St Paul advised that they should remain where they were, and declared his conviction that any attempt to pursue the voyage would be attended with loss, not only of the ship and cargo, but also of the lives of those on board. But the owner and master of the ship were of a different opinion, and the harbour of Fair Havens being incommodious for wintering in[2], the majority decided for leaving at the first opportunity, and, if possible, making for a harbour called Phœnix, on the south coast of the island, and somewhat further to the west[3]. Influenced by the words of the mariners the centurion resolved to adopt this course, and all waited anxiously for a change of the wind (Acts xxvii. 9—12).

At length the long-looked for change took place. A light breeze sprang up from the south, and the mariners thought their purpose was already accomplished. Weighing anchor, therefore, they set sail, hoping to reach

[1] Levit. xvi. 29; xxiii. 27, celebrated on the 10th of Tisri, corresponding to the close of September or beginning of October. See *Class-Book of O. T. History,* p. 155. This was exactly the time when seafaring is pronounced most dangerous by Greek and Roman writers.

[2] It was a good harbour in *some* seasons, but, being an open roadstead, or rather two open roadsteads, was not commodious to winter in. Smith, p. 45.

[3] Literally βλέποντα κατὰ Λίβα καὶ κατὰ χῶρον=*looking toward the S. W. wind, and the N. W. wind.* The harbour was probably the modern *Lutro,* sheltered from the abovementioned winds, and looking *from the water towards the land which encloses it* in the direction of these winds. C. and H., II. pp. 343, 344, and notes.

Phœnix in a few hours. Keeping close to the coast they doubled Cape Matala, and were proceeding "with the boat towing astern (Acts xxvii. 16), forgetful of past difficulties, and blind to impending dangers[1]," when suddenly a violent wind, called Euroclydon[2], came down from the heights of Ida[3] on the Cretan shores, and striking the ship whirled her round with such force that it was impossible for the helmsman to make her keep her course (Acts xxvii. 15). Consequently they were obliged to scud before the wind to the south-west about 28 miles, when they neared the little island of Clauda, and running under the lee of it, with much difficulty succeeded in hoisting the boat on board, which was probably full of water. They then proceeded to undergird[4] the vessel, that is, passed strong cables several times round her hull to prevent the starting of her planks and timbers, and being afraid lest they should drift in to the Syrtis[5] on the African coast, lowered the gear, either reefing the mainsail or lowering the great yard upon deck.

Having taken these precautions they proceeded, steering as close to the wind as the gale would permit, and on the following day lightened the ship by flinging overboard all that could be most easily spared. This, however, relieved but little the strain upon her, and

[1] C. and H., II. 345, and notes.

[2] Rather perhaps Εὐρακύλων = the Latin Euro-Aquilo, an E. N. E. wind.

[3] Κατ' αὐτῆς scil. Κρήτης. Comp. Mtt. viii. 32, κατὰ τοῦ κρημνοῦ, and see above, p. 196 and note.

[4] Βοηθείαις ἐχρῶντο, ὑποζωννύντες τὸ πλοῖον (Acts xxvii. 17) = *they proceeded to use stays or braces undergirding the vessel.* This was lest she should leak and founder. For instances of this procedure, see C. and H., II. 348, n.; Smith's *Voyage and Shipwreck*, p. 106.

[5] A notoriously dangerous bay between Tunis and the Eastern part of Tripoli.

on the third day both passengers and crew assisted in throwing out her tackling, including probably the main-yards. Several days of the utmost anxiety and incessant labour then ensued, during which neither sun nor stars appeared in the sky, and the mariners having lost their reckoning, knew neither where they were nor in what direction to steer, and gave up all hopes of safety. But besides being wearied and dispirited, they were suffering also from hunger, owing to the loss of provisions, and the impossibility of preparing any food. On the 14th day, therefore, of the voyage, the Apostle deemed it right to stand forward in their midst (Acts xxvii. 21) with words of encouragement and hope. After gently reminding them that all this harm and loss might have been avoided had they taken his advice, he bade them be of good cheer, for though the vessel could not be saved, not one of their lives should be lost. Of this he was fully assured, for an Angel of that God, whose he was and whom he served, had appeared to him in the night, and told him that he should appear before Cæsar, and that God had given him the lives of all on board; he, for his part, had no doubt that this would prove true, and added that they must be cast upon a certain island.

What effect these words had upon the hungry and exhausted mariners is not recorded, but we cannot doubt that it contributed not a little to nerve them with fresh courage to meet the difficulties before them. The storm, indeed, still continued with unabated fury, but on the midnight of the fourteenth day as they were drifting through the sea of Adria[1], the sailors suspected

[1] Meaning then not merely that portion of the Mediterranean, to which it is now applied, but all that which lay between Sicily and Malta on the west, and Greece and Crete on the east. See Smith's *Voyage and Shipwreck*.

from the roar of the breakers that they were nearing land. On this they sounded, and found the depth of water to be 20 fathoms. After a brief interval they sounded again, and found it was 15 fathoms. Filled with fear lest the ship should strike and break up, they thereupon let go four anchors[1] by the stern, and waited anxiously for the day (Acts xxvii. 29). During these weary hours, the sailors, aware that the vessel might founder before dawn, lowered the boat under pretence of laying out anchors from the bow for the purpose of steadying the ship, but really to effect their own escape, and leave the passengers to their fate. But the Apostle penetrated their design, and addressing himself to the centurion and the soldiers, declared that unless these remained on board they could not hope to be saved. Thereupon the soldiers, with characteristic decision, cut the ropes, and the boat fell off (Acts xxvii. 32).

Another proof of the ascendency which St Paul had acquired over all on board was soon afforded. But a short space now remained before daylight, and then fresh exertions would be needed. He advised, therefore, that during the interval they should recruit their exhausted energies by partaking of food. Then setting an example himself, he took bread, gave thanks to God before them all, and began to eat. Encouraged by his calmness, the rest did the same, and, strengthened by the meal, made a final effort to lighten the ship by flinging overboard the cargo, which by this time must have been spoilt by the salt water. While they were thus employed, the long-looked for day at length dawned,

[1] "They can now adopt the last resource for a sinking ship, and run her ashore; but to do it before it was day would have been to have rushed on certain destruction: they must bring the ship, if it be possible, to anchor, and hold on till daybreak." Smith's *Shipwreck*, p. 88. For similar instances of anchoring by the stern, see C. and H., II. 357.

and revealed to the sailors a coast, which, however, they did not recognise. But the sight of a small bay, with a sandy or pebbly beach[1], revived their determination, if possible, to run the vessel aground. Every precaution was therefore taken. The cables were cut and the anchors cast adrift; the lashings of the rudders[2] were unloosed; the foresail[3] hoisted (Acts xxvii. 40), and the vessel was run on shore at a spot *between two seas* (Acts xxvii. 41). Here the bow stuck fast on a bank of tenacious clay, while the stern began to break up under the violence of the waves. Certain that the ship must very speedily go to pieces, the soldiers, who were responsible with their lives for the safe custody of their prisoners, afraid that some might swim off and so escape, formed the cruel design of putting them all to death. This, however, the centurion, resolved at all risks to save St Paul, resolutely forbade, and ordered such as were able to swim to cast themselves into the sea first, while the rest, some on spars, and some on broken pieces of the ship, made their way to land; and thus, as the Apostle had said, the whole company escaped safely (Acts xxvii. 44).

CHAPTER II

THE RECEPTION AT MALTA, AND ARRIVAL AT ROME.

A. D. 60, 61.

THUS flung upon the shore, the exhausted voyagers ascertained that the island was none other than

[1] C. and H., II, 362.

[2] Ἀνέντες τὰς ζευκτηρίας τῶν πηδαλίων (Acts xxxvii. 40) = unloosing the lashings of the paddle rudders, which had doubtless been hoisted up and lashed fast when they anchored. C. and H., II. 362, n.

[3] See Smith's *Shipwreck, &c.*, p. 153.

Melita[1], at that time much uncultivated and overrun with wood, and inhabited by a population of Phœnician origin, who not being of Greek or Roman descent were designated *barbarians* (Acts xxviii. 2). But the reception they gave to the shipwrecked crew proved that they were no savages, for hurrying down to the beach, they eagerly afforded all possible relief to their wants. The rain was falling in torrents, and the weather was extremely cold. Lighting a fire therefore on the shore, they welcomed them all to its genial warmth. Foremost amongst those gathering the sticks to increase the much-needed blaze was the Apostle himself, and as he did so, a viper came out of the heat and fastened on his hand. The incident did not escape the notice of the islanders. *This man*, said they, *must be a murderer: he has escaped from the sea, but vengeance suffereth him not to live.* But the Apostle no sooner flung off the creature without suffering any injury, than their feelings underwent an instant change[2], and they said that he was a god. Near the place where the vessel had been lost, Publius, the Roman governor[3] of the island, had some possessions. For three days he entertained the shipwrecked strangers with much hospitality, and the Apostle was enabled to requite his attentions by miraculously healing his father, who lay afflicted with fever and dysentery (Acts xxviii. 8). The fame of this cure soon spread abroad, and others afflicted with disease repaired to the Apostle and experienced similar healing effects.

[1] For a summary of the arguments for Malta, and not Melita in the gulf of Venice, as the scene of St Paul's shipwreck, see Smith's *Voyage and Shipwreck*, and Smith's *Bibl. Dict.*

[2] Compare the conduct of the Lystrians, above, p. 420.

[3] The chief officer of Malta under the governor of Sicily was called πρῶτος Μελιταίων, or *Primus Melitensium*, the very title used by St Luke.

After a stay of three months on the island, the time when the ancients deemed navigation practicable again came round, and Julius secured a passage for himself and his charge in another corn-ship of Alexandria, which had wintered in the island, and was called the Castor and Pollux. Laden with many presents from the grateful islanders the Apostle and his party went on board, and setting sail put into the harbour of Syracuse, where they remained three days. Thence they shaped a course northwards towards the straits of Messina. But the wind was not favourable, and they were constrained, after beating about (Acts xxviii. 13), to put into Rhegium at the entrance of the straits, where they remained one day. On the following morning a south wind sprang up, and they were enabled to reach Puteoli[1], the most sheltered part of the bay of Naples, and the great emporium for the Alexandrian corn-ships[2], and here they were rejoiced to find certain of the brethren, and abode with them seven days (Acts xxviii. 14).

At the end of this period the party commenced their journey towards Rome, distant 150 miles. The first part of their route was probably from Puteoli by a cross-road to Capua, thence along the Via Appia by Sinuessa on the sea, Minturnæ, and Formiæ to Terracina[3]. The

[1] Formerly called *Dicæarchia,* then from its strong mineral springs (*a puteis* or *putendo*) Puteoli, close to Baiæ, and now called *Pozzuoli.* It was the great landing-place for all travellers to Italy from the Levant.

[2] "All ships, on rounding into the bay, were obliged to strike their topsails, with the exception of the Alexandrian corn-vessels, which were thus easily recognised, as soon as they hove in sight." See the quotation from Seneca in C. and H., II. 371. Puteoli from its trade with Alexandria and the East would naturally contain a colony of Jews.

[3] C. and H., II. pp. 376—379. "The foundation of the Via Appia, which was 13 or 14 ft. broad, was of concrete or cemented rubble-work, and the surface was laid with large

next stage brought them to Appii Forum[1], whither the Christians from Rome who had heard of the Apostle's arrival at Puteoli, had come forth a distance of 43 miles to meet him. Deeply moved by this proof of their affectionate zeal, he thanked *God and took courage* (Acts xxviii. 15). Ten miles further on, at a place called the "Three Taverns," a second company was waiting to greet him, and thus in the society of numerous friends whom he had probably known during his labours in the East, the Apostle proceeded through the town of Aricia to the imperial city. There Julius the centurion delivered up his prisoners to the prefect of the prætorian guard[2], an office held at this time by Burrhus, one of the chief advisers of Nero (Acts xxviii. 16). Either influenced by the favourable report of the centurion, or the tone of the letter from Festus, the prefect allowed the Apostle to be kept separate from the rest of the prisoners, and to take up his abode in a hired house

polygonal blocks of the hardest stone, and so nicely fitted to each other that the whole seemed the work rather of nature than of art. The distances were marked by milestones, and at intervals of 20 miles were post-stations, where vehicles, horses, and mules were provided for the convenience of travellers and the transmission of government dispatches." Kitto's *Bibl. Illust.* VIII. 501.

[1] Comp. Hor. *Sat.* I. V. 3, 4:

Inde Forum Appî
Differtum nautis cauponibus atque malignis.

On Anxur or Terracina, see the same Satire, line 26: a few miles beyond it was the fountain of Feronia (Hor. *Sat.* I. V. 24), the termination of the canal which Augustus had formed to drain the Pomptine marshes, and which continued for 20 miles along the side of the road. Over this distance travellers had their choice, whether to proceed in barges dragged by mules, or on the pavement of the way itself." C. and H., II. 379.

[2] Τῷ *στρατοπεδάρχῃ*; Burro, præfecto prætorio, Bp Pearson. Tac. *Ann.* XII. 43; Merivale, VI. 189.

(Acts xxviii. 30), with the soldier to whom he was chained[1].

Three days after his arrival the Apostle sent for the leading men among the Jews, and sought to remove any prejudices they might have formed against him from the circumstances under which he had entered the capital of the West. Though, he said, he had committed no offence against his nation or the customs of his fathers, he had yet been delivered a prisoner into the hands of the Romans. They had examined him, but could discover nothing he had done that was worthy of death, and would have liberated him, had it not been for the opposition of his Jewish enemies. Under these circumstances, not with any intention of accusing his nation before the emperor, he had appealed to Cæsar. His only crime had been his firm conviction of the reality of the promise of the Messiah, and *for the hope of Israel* he was bound with the chains he then wore (Acts xxviii. 17—20).

In reply to this address the Jews assured him that they had received no information[2] to his disadvantage

[1] On the *custodia militaris* see above, p. 496, n.

[2] The ignorance of the influential Jews concerning the Christian Church which existed in the same city as themselves, "is not inconceivable, if we only consider the immense size of the metropolis, and the vast confluence of human beings it contained, and if to this we add that the main body of the Roman Church consisted of Gentiles, and that these wealthy Jews busied themselves far more about other objects than about the concerns of religion." Neander's *Planting*, I. 311. "With regard to Paul himself, it might well be true that they had little information concerning him. Though he had been imprisoned long at Cæsarea, his appeal had only been made a short time before winter. After that time (to use the popular expression) *the sea was shut;* and the winter had been a stormy one; so that it was natural enough that his case should be first made known to the Jews by himself." C. and H., II. 392.

from Judæa, and none of the brethren had arrived alleging anything against him. The Christian sect they knew well was everywhere spoken against, and they would be glad to hear from him any statement concerning its doctrines which he might bo willing to make. A day was accordingly fixed for the desired hearing, and a considerable number repaired to the Apostle's own private lodging (Acts xxviii. 23), and from morning till evening he continued to plead with them, delivering his testimony concerning the kingdom of God, and opening up, both from the Law and the Prophets, the things relating to Jesus Christ. The result was a division amongst his hearers. *Some believed the things which were spoken, and some believed not* (Acts xxviii. 24), and after much discussion the unbelieving portion departed, but not before they had been warned by St Paul that they were incurring the penalty of that judicial blindness of which the prophet Isaiah[1] had spoken (Is. vi. 9, 10), and that the inheritance they renounced would be bestowed upon the Gentiles (Acts xxviii. 28).

After this address the Jews departed. The ways of the great Apostle were not their ways, neither were his thoughts their thoughts. While they retired to dispute concerning the Christian sect, he remained in his own hired house, and there resided upwards of two years, still indeed a prisoner under military custody, but permitted to receive all who came to him, and to preach boldly the kingdom of God, and *those things which concerned the Lord Jesus Christ* (Acts xxviii. 30, 31).

[1] See Mtt. xiii. 15; Jn. xii. 40.

CHAPTER III

THE FIRST IMPRISONMENT AT ROME.

A.D. 61—63.

BEYOND the point where the last Chapter ends, the sacred narrative, contained in the Acts of the Apostles, does not conduct us. The incidents connected with St Paul's imprisonment at Rome, and his subsequent history, must be gathered from various allusions in several letters he wrote during this period.

His trial it would seem, then, was for a considerable time postponed. His accusers, whose arrival was not even expected by the Roman Jews (Acts xxviii. 21), do not appear to have reached Rome before the summer or autumn of the year[1] A.D. 61, and the necessity of obtaining evidence as to the charges against him from Judæa, Syria, Cilicia, Pisidia, and Macedonia, added to the fact that according to the Roman law the witnesses both of the prosecutors and the accused must be examined on each of the charges separately[2], would necessitate an adjournment of the case from time to time to suit the convenience of the Emperor.

During, however, this long period of delay the Apostle was not obliged to remain inactive. Allowed to live in a house by himself, and to receive any who wished to visit him, he had many opportunities of preaching the word, and the glad tidings of the Kingdom (Acts xxviii. 31). Nor were his efforts fruitless. To use his own language, he *begat* many children even *in his bonds* (Philem. 10), and through the numerous and deeply attached friends, by whom he was surrounded, he was enabled to communicate with many of the

[1] C. and H., II. 395.

[2] On the three separate heads of the indictment against the Apostle, see above, p. 494.

Churches which he had planted. Thus there were with him at this time Luke, the beloved physician, and his old companion (Col. iv. 14; Philem. 24); Timothy his favourite disciple (Philem. 1; Col. i. 1; Phil. i. 1); Tychicus[1] (Col. iv. 7; Eph. vi. 21); John Mark, whom he had once[2] been obliged to reject as having abandoned the ministry, but who, he now allowed, was *profitable to him* (comp. Col. iv. 10, 2 Tim. iv. 11); Demas, now, indeed, *a faithful fellow-labourer* (Philem. 24); Col. iv. 14), though soon, alas, to be drawn away by love of *this present world* (2 Tim. iv. 10); Aristarchus of Macedonia (Col. iv. 10); and Epaphras[3] of Colossæ (Col. i. 7).

But amongst these, thus ministering unto him, was one in whom he felt a peculiar interest. This was a slave, named Onesimus, who had run away from his master Philemon[4], a Christian[5] of Colossæ, and had fled to Rome, where, amidst the vast population of the metropolis, he probably hoped to escape the notice of his pursuers. Through circumstances which have not been recorded, the fugitive slave became acquainted with the imprisoned Apostle, and was converted to the faith of Christ. There appears to have been something peculiarly attractive in his character, and so useful did he prove in various private ways, that St Paul would have kept him at Rome and employed him in the service of the

[1] See Acts xx. 4; and above, p. 471.

[2] See above, p. 414, and the note.

[3] Though the name is probably an abbreviation of Epaphroditus, it seems doubtful whether he is to be identified with the Epaphroditus of Philip. ii. 25.

[4] Whether he had also robbed his master or not appears somewhat uncertain, and depends on the meaning of the word ἠδίκησε in Philem. 18.

[5] It is evident from Philem. 19 that he had been converted by the Apostle himself, possibly (i) during his journey through Phrygia (Acts xvi. 6); possibly (ii) during his long stay at Ephesus (Acts xix. 10), when it is recorded that *all they who dwelt in Asia heard the word of the Lord Jesus.*

Gospel (Philem. 13), but, with his habitual regard for the rights of others, he decided that he must first return and be reconciled to his master; and to make this duty less painful, he sent with him a letter[1] to Philemon, in which he requested his master to forgive him, and offered to reimburse any loss he might have sustained by his running away (Philem. 19), and at the same time expressed his thankfulness to God for the account which he had heard of Philemon's faith and love (Philem. 4—7).

But Onesimus was not to return to the East alone. Tychicus was on the point of setting out thither also, and it was the Apostle's wish that he should be the bearer of a letter to the church of Colossæ[2]. Of the condition of this church he had heard through Epaphras, now present in Rome, and who is regarded by some as its probable founder[3] (Col. i. 7), and the news was such as to give him serious concern. Through the coming of some teacher, probably from Alexandria, the Colossians had become imbued with a spirit of a half-Jewish and half-Oriental philosophy, tending to corrupt the simplicity of their faith, and to obscure the dignity of Christ by a spurious union of Jewish observances with a worshipping of angels, and an extravagant asceticism. These growing evils St Paul deemed his duty to counteract, and in the Epistle, of which Epaphras was the bearer, set forth with special prominence the eternal glory and inherent dignity of Christ (Col. i. 15—23), and after

[1] Paley in his *Horæ Paulinæ* notices that St Paul bids Philemon prepare a lodging for him in expectation of his speedy deliverance, which agrees with Phil. ii. 24. The letter itself is often referred to as a model of delicacy and tact.

[2] Or *Colassæ* according to the reading of the best MSS., a city on the Lycus close to Hierapolis and Laodicea. Ethnologically it belonged to Phrygia, but politically was included in the province of Asia.

[3] See Alford's *Prolegom.* to the Greek Test., III. 35.

cautioning the Colossians against false philosophy, legal observances, angel-worship, and asceticism (Col. ii.), exhorted them to various Christian virtues (Col. iii.—iv. 6), referred them to Tychicus and Onesimus for information respecting his condition (Col. iv. 7—9), and requested them to forward the Epistle to Laodicea, and to read that from the same place (Col. iv. 16).

As bearers of these letters Tychicus and Onesimus set out for Asia Minor. But Tychicus was charged with another letter, the Epistle to the Ephesians, either addressed to the Christians in the capital of proconsular Asia, or intended as a circular letter for the use of the various churches in that province[1]. In this Epistle, the thoughts and language of which betray a very considerable resemblance to those employed in that to the Colossians, the Apostle, after a summary (chiefly in the form of thanksgiving) of the Christian doctrines (Eph. i.—iii. 19), exhorted the Ephesians to unity (Eph. iv. 1—16), the abstinence from heathen vices (Eph. iv. 17—v. 21), the faithful discharge of their do-

[1] The doubt about the persons for whom this Epistle was intended arises (i) from the omission of the words ἐν Ἐφέσῳ from the opening verse in the Sinai and Vatican MSS.; (ii) from the fact that, though St Paul spent nearly three years at Ephesus, it does not contain a single personal greeting; (iii) from the apparent intimation in Eph. i. 15 that he knew only by report of the conversion of those he was addressing, and in iii. 2 that they knew only of his Apostleship by hearsay. Hence some (see C. and H., II. 417—420) consider it was addressed to the Church of Laodicea. On the other hand, the testimony of all the versions and "the universal designation of this Epistle by the ancient Church (except in the case of Marcion) as that to the Ephesians, warrants the retention of the words, and the explanation of the peculiarities in Eph. i. 15 and iii. 2, above alluded to, may probably be explained on the supposition mentioned in the text that it was also intended for other Churches dependent on Ephesus in proconsular Asia." See Alford's *Prolegom. in Ep.*, and Ellicott's *Commentary on the Ephesians.*

mestic duties as wives and husbands, children and parents, servants and masters (Eph. v. 22—vi. 9), and urged them, amidst surrounding dangers and temptations, to be vigilant, and to array themselves in the whole panoply[1] of God (Eph. vi. 10—20).

After the dispatch of these three letters in the spring of A.D. 62, the Apostle's heart was cheered by the arrival of a contribution from the Philippians, brought by Epaphroditus, a leading presbyter in that church. Though apparently in ill-health when he set out, he had, in the face of some unusual danger, persevered in his journey (Phil. ii. 30), in order that he might present to the Apostle this fresh proof of the noble liberality of the church over which he presided.

Till the close of the year A.D. 62, or the commencement of A.D. 63, Epaphroditus continued at Rome, and while tendering his services to the Apostle fell dangerously ill. Subsequently, however, he fully recovered, and was filled with anxiety to return to his friends at Philippi, who he learnt were in much distress on receiving intelligence of his sickness (Phil. ii. 26). St Paul was also himself anxious that he should return (Phil. ii. 25, 28), and resolved to make him the bearer of a letter to the Philippian church in acknowledgment of the kindness he had experienced from its members. His own circumstances were somewhat changed since he wrote to the Colossians and Ephesians. Though what had befallen him had tended rather to the furtherance than hindrance of the message he proclaimed, and his chains had become *well-known throughout the whole prætorium*[2] (Phil. i. 12, 13); though also by the energy

[1] The various pieces of the Christian armour here alluded to receive vivid illustration from the circumstances of the Apostle at this time, and the fact that he was chained to a Roman soldier.

[2] By some this has been identified with the palace of

of the Apostle himself and of many of the brethren no little impression had been made on the masses of heathendom in the city (Phil. i. 14—18); yet the course of political events was sufficient to excite considerable apprehension. The virtuous Burrhus was dead[1], and had been succeeded in the command of the prætorian guards by Fenius Rufus and Sofonius Tigellinus, the former a man of no capacity, the latter notorious for determined wickedness. About the same time also Nero contracted an alliance with the infamous Poppæa[2], a Jewish proselytess, whose influence over the emperor was strongly exerted in favour of the Jews, and in furtherance of their cause.

The horizon, therefore, of the Apostle was dark and lowering, and he could not look forward with the same confidence as before to his speedy release (comp. Philem. 22 with Phil. ii. 17, iii. 11), but he could write to the church he had planted at Philippi, and though the time might be at hand for his blood to be poured forth as a libation (Phil. ii. 17) over the sacrifice of his continued zeal in his Master's cause, he could rejoice in their progress and the tidings he had received of their welfare (Phil. i. 3—5). In the Epistle, therefore, of which Epa-

Cæsar on the Palatine Hill (comp. Phil. i. 13 with iv. 22). But though the word *Prœtorium* is applied in the N. T. to the residence of Pilate at Jerusalem (see above, p. 298), and of Herod at Cæsarea (see above, p. 493 n.), it is never applied to the Imperial Palace at Rome. It rather seems to denote the quarters of the Imperial guards, who were in immediate attendance on the Emperor, who was *prœtor* or commander-in-chief of the troops, and whose immediate body-guard would naturally be in a *prœtorium* near at hand. See C. and H., II. pp. 438, 439.

[1] See Tac. *Ann.* XIV. 51. At his death the influence of Seneca was broken, and under the guidance of Tigellinus, Nero's public life rivalled the infamy of his private character. On Fenius Rufus, see Tac. *Ann.* XV. 66, 68; Merivale's *Romans under the Empire*, VI. p. 333.

[2] See Josephus, *Ant.* XX. 8. 11; Tac. *Ann.* XV. 23.

phroditus was the bearer, he expressed his heartfelt thankfulness for all he had heard of their constancy under persecution (Phil. i. 29, 30), and liberality, which distinguished them above all other churches (Phil. iv. 15); exhorted them to continued unity and fortitude, to humility and earnestness (Phil ii. 1—16); expressed his intention of shortly sending Timothy to them (Phil. ii. 17—24); warned them against Judaizing teachers (Phil. iii. 1—8), and urged two female converts of distinction, Euodias and Syntyche, who had been guilty of strife and altercation, to love and reconciliation (Phil. iv. 2, 3), and all to a holy and a Christian life (Phil. iv. 4—9). With this Epistle, which concludes with a significant salutation from the Christians in Cæsar's household (Phil. iv. 22), and points to the progress of the Gospel there, even amidst the scenes of terrible wickedness[1] now enacted in the imperial household, Epaphroditus set out for Macedonia.

CHAPTER IV

ST PAUL'S SECOND IMPRISONMENT AND DEATH.

A.D. 63—68.

THE Apostle's trial, as we have seen in the preceding Chapter, was long delayed. At length, however, a time was fixed for hearing his case, and after a trial in all probability before the Emperor Nero himself, he was, according to the universal testimony[2] of the ancient Church, acquitted of the charges that had been brought

[1] See C. and H., II. 457—459; Merivale's *Romans under the Empire*, Vol. VI. pp. 343, 344.

[2] See the quotations from Clement of Rome, Muratori's Canon, Eusebius, *H. E.* II. 22, Chrysostom, and Jerome, in C. and H., II. 462, 463; Alford's Gk. Test. III. *Prolegom.* pp. 92, 93.

against him. Thus liberated he would be naturally anxious to fulfil the intentions he had expressed in his Epistles to Philemon and the Philippians[1] of revisiting the Churches he had planted in Macedonia and Asia Minor, and others, which had not as yet *seen his face in the flesh.*

Setting out, therefore, from Rome to Brundusium, it is probable that he crossed thence to Dyrrachium or Apollonia, and so travelled by the great Egnatian road to Philippi. We cannot doubt that the joy of the Christians there would be great at being thus able to welcome once more their revered teacher, but his stay there was not likely to have been protracted; and proceeding to Asia, in accordance with his former designs and intentions, he most probably fixed his head-quarters at Ephesus, and thence visited Colossæ, Laodicea, Hierapolis and other Churches[2].

What time he now spent amongst the brethren of proconsular Asia is not known, but it is not altogether improbable that in the year A.D. 64 he carried out his long-intended visit to Spain (Rom. xv. 24, 28), and spent two years in planting churches amongst the numerous Jewish proselytes in all the towns along the Spanish coast from Gades to Tarraco[3]. Thence we may believe

[1] Philem. 22; Phil. ii. 24. It was probably about this time, if he was its author, that St Paul wrote the *Epistle to the Hebrews.* For a synopsis of the various opinions respecting its authorship see Alford's *Prolegom.* Vol. IV. Pt. 1, Westcott's *Bible in the Church.*

[2] See Alford's *Prolegomena* to the Pastoral Epp. Vol. III. p. 93.

[3] See C. and H., II. 471. Clement of Rome (1 *Ep. ad Cor.* c. v.), declares that he went ἐπὶ τὸ τέρμα τῆς δύσεως, which some would extend not only to Spain but even to Britain. Dean Alford expresses an opinion that if not spent in Spain, the interval between A.D. 64 and 66 "may have been spent in Greece and Asia and the interjacent islands:" *Prolegom.* p. 94.

he returned about A.D. 66 to Ephesus, and found to his great sorrow that what he had long ago predicted to the presbyters of that city, when they bade him farewell on the sea-shore of Miletus (Acts xx. 28—31), had been too truly fulfilled. Grievous wolves had indeed entered in amongst them, not sparing the flock; nay, from the very bosom of the Church itself men had arisen, *speaking perverse things, to draw away disciples after them* (Acts xx. 30). Leaders of rival sects, Hymenæus, Philetus, Alexander (1 Tim. i. 20; 2 Tim. ii. 17, iv. 14, 15), had appeared, perverting the minds of the disciples from the simplicity of the faith, and blending with it the subtilties of Greek philosophy, Jewish superstition, and wild Oriental speculation. Other duties, indeed, prevented the continuance of the Apostle's personal supervision of the Asiatic churches, and leaving Timothy at Ephesus, he returned to Macedonia (1 Tim. i. 3). There, however, he appears to have feared he might be detained longer than he had anticipated (1 Tim. iii. 14, 15), and, well acquainted with the peculiar difficulties connected with the position of his beloved disciple, he addressed to him what is known as "the first Epistle to Timothy."

The main objects of this Epistle were two-fold, first, to encourage him in the superintendence of the Ephesian church, and to aid him in his struggle with the heretical teachers spoken of above (1 Tim. i. 3—20). The second was to give him various personal directions respecting the government of the Church itself, such as the manner of conducting public worship (1 Tim. ii. 1—8); the dress and behaviour of women (1 Tim. ii. 9—15); the qualifications of bishops and deacons (1 Tim. iii.); the selection of widows to receive the charity of the Church (1 Tim. v. 3—16); the punishment of offenders (1 Tim. v. 20, 21); and his own life and conversation (1 Tim. vi. 11—19).

In this letter he also expressed his design of shortly returning to Ephesus (1 Tim. iii. 14), and this intention he appears to have carried out. Repairing from Macedonia to the capital of proconsular Asia, he made an expedition thence to the island of Crete, accompanied by Titus (Tit. i. 5). The churches there do not seem to have been now for the first time founded, but to have already been some considerable period in existence. Like those, however, in proconsular Asia, they were "troubled by false teachers, and probably had never yet been properly organised, having originated, perhaps, in the private efforts of individual Christians, who would have been supplied with a centre of operations and nucleus of churches by the numerous colonies of Jews established in the island[1]."

Unable, however, himself to remain long, the Apostle left Titus there, as he had left Timothy at Ephesus, to complete what he had been obliged to leave unfinished, and to organise the Church by the appointment of presbyters in every city (Tit. i. 5). But shortly after his return to Asia Minor, he deemed that a letter from himself might encourage him to confront the opposition he was likely to encounter in carrying out his wishes, and with this he resolved to send general directions respecting the organisation of the Church. From Ephesus, therefore, he dispatched an Epistle to Titus, in which he laid down certain instructions concerning the ordination of elders (Tit. i. 5—9); cautioned him against false teachers (Tit. i. 9—16); described the sound and practical Christianity which he was to inculcate on old

[1] C. and H., II. 487; and see the Articles *Crete* and *Titus* in Smith's *Bibl. Dict.* Jews are mentioned as dispersed in Crete in 1 Macc. xv. 23 (see above p. 54), and in Acts ii. 11 (see above, p. 345, and n.). See also Alford's Gk. Test., Vol. III. *Prolegom.* p. 108. On the quotation respecting the Cretans, see above, p. 382, n.

and young, on masters and slaves, and to exemplify in his own life (Tit. ii. 1—15); and enjoined obedience to rulers, gentleness and forbearance towards all men, and an avoidance of all idle speculations (Tit. iii. 1—11).

At the time of writing this Epistle it was not St Paul's intention that Titus should remain long in Crete. He himself was on the point of leaving Asia for Nicopolis[1], intending to winter there (Tit. iii. 12). On the arrival, therefore of Artemas or Tychicus, whom he intended to send to him, Titus was to endeavour to join him. Accordingly setting out from Ephesus the Apostle repaired to Miletus (2 Tim. iv. 20), and there left his old companion Trophimus[2], who was overtaken with sickness. Thence he sailed to Corinth, and leaving there Erastus, the former chamberlain of that city, passed on to Nicopolis[3], where he would seem to have laboured for a space during the winter.

At this time however the Christians had become distinguished from the Jews, and the objects of suspicion and hostility, and the Apostle's labours at Nicopolis were brought to an abrupt conclusion. Arrested it is not improbable, before the middle of the winter[4], through the restless activity of some of his many enemies, he was sent to Rome to be tried a second time for his life. The terror of his arrest scattered many of his friends. Demas from love of *this present world* forsook him

[1] Most probably the Nicopolis in Macedonia, on a peninsula west of the bay of Actium, erected by Augustus in memory of the battle of Actium, and on the ground which his army occupied before the engagement.

[2] See above, p. 472.

[3] It was conveniently situated for apostolic journeys in the Eastern parts of Achaia and Macedonia, and also to the north where churches perhaps were founded. On St Paul's previous preaching on the confines of Illyricum, see p. 474, and n.; and Birks' *Horæ Apostolicæ*, pp. 296—304.

[4] C. and H., II. p. 494.

and departed to Thessalonica, Crescens to Galatia, and Titus himself, who had joined his master at Nicopolis, possibly by his desire, repaired to the neighbouring Dalmatia (2 Tim. iv. 10). Luke alone remained in constant attendance on the Apostle, and shared with him the perils of his second imprisonment at Rome. This was evidently far more severe than the previous one. Not only was he chained to a soldier, but he was treated as a malefactor (2 Tim. ii. 9), and so perilous was it to visit him that few were willing to seek out his dungeon or to stand by him (2 Tim. i. 16, iv. 16), while he himself could look forward to nothing but certain martyrdom (2 Tim. iv. 6—8).

The course of political events sufficiently accounts for the change in the Apostle's circumstances. Anxious to avert from himself the charge of having set the capital on fire, Nero had let loose the rage of the populace upon the Christians, now very numerous and objects of intense hatred. A familiar passage in the writings of Tacitus[1] tells us how some of them were crucified, some hunted to death with dogs, some wrapped in robes smeared with pitch and set on fire at night before the eyes of the Emperor, who watched their dying agonies arrayed in the costume of a charioteer. Since then the fury of the first excitement had passed away, but so prominent a ringleader of a hated sect as the Apostle would be certain to be treated with much severity.

On the evidence therefore of certain informers, of whom *Alexander the coppersmith* apparently was one (2 Tim. iv. 14), he was put upon his trial, probably before the city prefect[2], in one of the numerous basilicas that stood in the Forum. No friend, no adviser, stood by him (2 Tim. iv. 16), to cheer or to encourage. Alone and

[1] Tac. *Ann.* XV. 44. See Merivale, VI. 351.
[2] C. and H., II. 499.

unaided, save by an Almighty though Invisible Friend (2 Tim. iv. 17), he pleaded the cause of the Gospel before a numerous audience, and *all the Gentiles* heard his testimony, and the result was that of the first of the charges brought against him he was acquitted, and *was delivered out of the mouth of the lion* (2 Tim. iv. 17).

Remanded back to his dungeon to await the second hearing of his case, and not anticipating anything but an ultimate conviction, *ready to be offered* and convinced that *the time of his departure was at hand* (2 Tim. iv. 6), the Apostle, though cheered by the society of Luke and Onesiphorus (2 Tim. i. 16, 17), yearned towards the friend of his earlier days, his own son Timothy. He longed to see him once more, and though he was far away in Ephesus, discharging the duties of his difficult position, he resolved to dictate an Epistle to him, bidding him come with all speed to Rome, and receive his parting injunctions. Accordingly, it was now that the "Second Epistle to Timothy" was written, in which the aged Apostle, with the utmost tenderness and solemnity exhorted his own son to diligence and stedfastness, to patience under persecution (2 Tim. i. 6—15), and a willingness to share in the sufferings of saints (2 Tim. ii. 1—16). In the event moreover of his not arriving in time to receive his last injunction, he charged him, with all the solemnity of one about to appear before the Judge of quick and dead, to be faithful in all the duties of his office (2 Tim. iv. 1—5), and cautioned him against the false teaching which now threatened the very foundation of the Faith (2 Tim. iii.).

Whether Timothy did rejoin the Apostle, as he so earnestly requested, and bring *the cloak* for which with touching simplicity he made request amid the rigours of the winter (2 Tim. iv. 13), is not recorded. Some are willing to hazard the conjecture that he did[1]; but how-

[1] C. and H., II. 514; Smith's *Bibl. Dict.*, Art. *Timothy.*

ever it was, the Apostle's second trial and condemnation were not long delayed. As a Roman citizen, he could not be compelled to endure the lingering tortures, which so many who shared with him the name of "Christians" had lately undergone. But beyond the city-walls, along the road to Ostia, the port of Rome, he was led forth under military escort, to the place of execution; there the sword of the headsman fell flashing down, and he obtained that Crown, which He, whose faithful witness he was, had promised to *all them that love Him* (2 Tim. iv. 8).

Note.

Beside the Apostle, whose glorious career was thus closed by the sword of the executioner, three and three only of the immediate followers of our Lord hold a prominent place in the Apostolic records—James *the Lord's brother*, Peter and John[1].

1. The main facts in the history of James, who was surnamed *the Just*, have been already related, and we have seen how prominent was the part he took at the Council held at Jerusalem[2], A.D. 50. He[3] was the author of the first of the Seven so-called "Catholic or General Epistles," which he addressed, apparently from Jerusalem, to the Jewish Christians residing in Palestine, or scattered among the Gentiles, according to some as early as A.D. 45, according to others as late as A.D. 62.

2. Our last notice of St Peter referred to the time when St Paul *withstood him to the face* at Antioch, because he *was to be blamed*[4]. Subsequently to this date we have no notices in Scripture of his place of abode or of his work. It is probable, however, that after completing the organisation of the Churches in Palestine, and some parts of Asia Minor (1 Pet. i. 1, 2), he resided for some time at Babylon (1 Pet. v. 13), where had been settled from very early times an important

---

[1] See Lightfoot on *St Paul and the Three* in his *Commentary on the Galatians*, p. 276. [2] See above, pp. 425, 426.

[3] It could not have been written by James, the son of Zebedee, for he was beheaded A.D. 44 by Herod Agrippa, and the notes of time in the Epistle itself point to a later date.

[4] See above, p. 431.

community of Jews[1]. Hence, at some period between the years A.D. 63 and 67[2], he addressed his first Epistle to the Jewish converts scattered throughout Asia Minor, for the purpose of confirming them in the Christian faith, encouraging them to endure the persecutions to which they were exposed, and exhorting them to refute the calumnies of their enemies by leading a holy life. The time and place of the composition of his Second Epistle are alike surrounded with difficulties. The most reasonable conjecture appears to be that the Apostle wrote it in his old age, about the year A.D. 68, either from Rome, where he is said to have suffered martyrdom[3], or somewhere on the journey thither from the East.

3. St John, we saw, was at Jerusalem, when St Paul paid his third visit to that city[4], and was then regarded as one of the Chief "Pillars" of the Church. His movements after this date are shrouded in much obscurity. It seems most probable, however, that after remaining for a season in Palestine, he repaired to Ephesus, and laboured amongst the seven Churches of Asia Minor. Thence on the authority of Irenæus and Eusebius we gather that he wrote his three Epistles, according to some as early as A.D. 68, according to others as late as the close of the first century. During the reign of Domitian, A.D. 94 or 95, he was banished to the isle of Patmos, and there wrote his Apocalypse, and afterwards returned to Ephesus, where he died.

4. The writer of one other "Catholic" Epistle remains to be noticed—Jude, called also Lebbæus and Thaddæus[5], the brother of James the Less, and most probably one of the so-called *brethren of our Lord*. We find his name in the lists of the Apostles (Lk. vi. Acts i.), but the only incident relating to him recorded in the Gospel narrative is the question he put to the Saviour on the eve of his crucifixion, *Lord, how is it that thou wilt manifest thyself to us, and not unto the world?* (Jn. xiv. 22). The place where the Epistle was written is not known. Various dates have been assigned to it, some referring it to A.D. 64 or 65, others to A.D. 75 or even later. The readers are nowhere expressly defined; but the reference to Jewish traditions (Jude 9—14) seems to hint that the Christians of Palestine were the objects of his warnings against false teachers, and of his exhortations to steadfastness in the faith.

1 See above, p. 7.

2 See Alford's *Prolegomena*, Greek Test. Vol. IV. Part I.

3 See above, p. 431.

4 See above, p. 425.

5 See above, p. 187.

APPENDIX.

CHRONOLOGICAL TABLES.

I. THE JEWS UNDER THE PERSIANS.

PALESTINE.	B. C.	PERSIA.
Death of Nehemiah	413	
Jaddua, high-priest........	341	
	334	Victory of Alexander on the Granicus.
	333	Battle of Issus.
Alexander visits Jerusalem	332	
	331	Battle of Arbela.
	323	Death of Alexander.

II. THE ERA OF THE PTOLEMIES AND SELEUCIDÆ.

PALESTINE.	B. C.	EGYPT.	B. C.	SYRIA.
Ptolemy Soter captures Je-		Ptolemy Soter	323	
rusalem, plants colonies			312	Seleucus Nicator.
in Alexandria & Cyrene	320	P. Philadelphus	283	
Simon the Just, high-priest	300		280	Antiochus Soter.
Eleazar, high-priest	291		261	Antiochus Theos.
Onias II. high-priest	250	P. Euergetes I.	247	
Ptolemy Philopator, pre-			246	Seleucus Callinicus.
vented from entering the			226	Seleucus Ceraunus.
Holy of Holies, attempts			223	Antiochus Magnus.
to destroy the Jews in		P. Philopator..	222	
Alexandria	216	P. Epiphanes..	205	
Antiochus Magnus ob-			187	Seleucus Philopator.
tains Palestine	203	P. Philometor	181	
Scopas recovers Judæa ..	199		175	Antiochus Epiphanes.
Antiochus regains Judæa	198		164	Antiochus Eupator.
Onias III. high-priest ..	195		162	Demetrius Soter.
AntiochusEpiphanestakes			150	Alexander Balas.
Jerusalem	170	P. Physcon....	146	Demetrius Nicator
Persecution of the Jews..	167			(1st reign).
Rise of the *Maccabees* ..	167		137	Antiochus Sidetes.
Battle of Emmaus, re-de-			128	Demetrius Nicator
dication of the Temple	165			(2nd reign).
Death of Judas Macca-			125	Antiochus Grypus.
bæus	161	P. Lathyrus ..	116	
Jonathan Maccabæus			113	Antiochus Cyzicenus.
murdered by Tryphon,		P. Alexander		
and Accession of Simon	144	and Cleopatra		
First Year of the *Freedom*		joint rulers ..	107	
of Jerusalem	143		95	Antiochus Eusebes
Murder of Simon; John				and Philippus.
Hyrcanus succeeds him	137		83	Tigranes.
		P. Auletes....	80	
			69	Antiochus Asiaticus.
John Hyrcanus throws off			65	Pompeius makes Syria
the Syrian yoke, and				a Roman province.

II.—*continued.*

PALESTINE.	B.C.	EGYPT.	B.C.	SYRIA.
destroys the Temple on Gerizim	130	P. Auletes driven from Egypt	58	
Accession of Aristobulus.	106	Restored by Gabinius....	55	
Accession of Alexander Jannæus	106	Accession of P. Dionysus and Cleopatra	51	
Death of Jannæus; accession of his wife Alexandra	79			
Death of Alexandra, accession of Hyrcanus ..	70			

III. RISE OF THE HERODIAN FAMILY.

JUDÆA.	B.C.	ROME.
Conflict between Hyrcanus and Aristobulus--Pompeius takes Jerusalem	63	Catiline's conspiracy.
	60	First Triumvirate: Pompey, Cæsar, and Crassus.
Gabinius remodels the government	57	
Crassus plunders the Temple . .	54	The Parthian War.
	53	Death of Crassus at the battle of Carrhæ.
	48	Battle of Pharsalia; death of Pompey.
Julius Cæsar appoints Antipater procurator of Judæa	47	Julius Cæsar in Egypt.
	44	Death of Cæsar. March 15.
Death of Antipater	43	Second Triumvirate—Octavius, Antonius, and Lepidus; death of Cicero.
Herod marries Mariamne . . .	42	Battle of Philippi.
The Parthians take Jerusalem: Herod flies to Rome	40	
Herod takes Jerusalem, and becomes king of Judæa	37	Antonius captivated with Cleopatra.
Murder of Aristobulus	35	
Herod summoned before Antonius	34	
	33	War between Antonius and Octavius
	31	Battle of Actium.
His kingdom increased by Octavius	30	Death of Antony and Cleopatra; Egypt becomes a Roman province.
Murder of Mariamne	29	Temple of Janus shut.
Plot to assassinate Herod—He rebuilds Samaria	27 25	Octavius assumes the title of *Augustus;* division of the provinces (see p. 147, n.).
Foundations laid of Cæsarea . .	21	
Herod proposes to rebuild the Temple	20	The standards taken from Crassus restored.
Erection begun	18	
Herod goes to Rome to bring back Alexander and Aristobulus . .	15	
Salome's schemes against them .	14	
Completion of Cæsarea	10	
Execution of Alexander and Aristobulus	6	Tiberius retires to Rhodes.

IV. THE GOSPEL HISTORY.

PALESTINE.	B.C.	ROME.	B.C.	PREFECTS OF SYRIA.
Birth of John the Baptist	5		4	Pub. Sulp. Quirinus 1st time (Lk. ii. 1)
The NATIVITY of CHRIST—Death of Herod	4			
Reign of Archelaus, Herod Antipas, and Herod Philip (see pp. 144-146)	4	Tiberius adopted by Augustus as his son	A.D. 4	
Disturbances at Jerusalem	3			
Archelaus banished to Vienne in Gaul. Judæa becomes a Roman province and is annexed to the prefecture of Syria. *Coponius* the first procurator	A.D. 6		5	Pub. Sulp. Quirinus (2nd time)
		Augustus dies at Nola. Accession of TIBERIUS	14	
		Death of Ovid	17	M. Calpurnius Piso
The Census actually carried out (see above, p. 148). Rising of Judas the Gaulonite. Quirinus appoints Annas high-priest	7	Jews expelled from Italy	19	Cn. Sentius Saturninus
		Influence of Sejanus	22	L. Pomponius Flaccus
		Tiberius retires to Capreæ	26	
Visit of the Saviour to the Temple	8			
Marcus Ambivius, 2nd procurator	10	Herod Antipas in Italy, and there becomes acquainted with Herodias (see p. 168)	27	
Annius Rufus, 3rd procurator	13			
Valerius Gratus, 4th procurator	14			
Joseph Caiaphas appointed high-priest (see above, p. 149)	17			
Pontius Pilate, 5th procurator	26			
Riots at Jerusalem (see pp. 150, 151). The Preaching of John, and Baptism of Christ	27			
Herod Antipas marries Herodias. War breaks out with Aretas. Imprisonment of John the Baptist	28			
Death of the Baptist	29			
The Crucifixion of Christ	30	Era of Seneca		

V. THE APOSTOLIC HISTORY.

PALESTINE.	A. D.	ROME.
The Pentecostal Effusion (May) .	30	Banishment of Agrippina.
	31	Death of Sejanus.
Martyrdom of Stephen, Pilate deposed by Vitellius	36	
Dispersion of the Christians. Conversion of Saul, who spends 3 years in Damascus and Arabia .	37	Death of Tiberius, March 16, accession of CALIGULA.
		Birth of Nero.
Herod Agrippa appointed king of Trachonitis	38	Caligula orders his Statue to be set up at Jerusalem.
Great disturbances at Jerusalem owing to Caligula's order respecting his statue (see p. 393).		
Herod Antipas banished with Herodias to Lyons in Gaul . . .	39	
St Peter's visitation of the Churches (see pp. 395, 396).		
Conversion of Cornelius	41	Death of Caligula, Jan. 24, accession of CLAUDIUS.
Spread of the Gospel to Antioch .	42	
Herod Agrippa I. receives Judæa and Samaria in addition to the tetrarchies of Philip and Antipas, and the title of 'king.'		
Martyrdom of James	44	Return of Claudius from Britain.
Death of Herod Agrippa at Cæsarea	44	
Cuspius Fadus appointed procurator of Judæa.		
Saul and Barnabas sent to Jerusalem with contributions from Antioch	44	
Return to, and sojourn at, Antioch	45—48	
(i) *First Missionary Journey of Saul and Barnabas* to Cyprus, Perga, Antioch in Pisidia, Iconium, Lystra, Derbe	48, 49	
Cumanus procurator of Judæa .	49	
The Council at Jerusalem . . .	50	Birth of Domitian.
(ii) *St Paul's Second Missionary Journey:* he visits		
Lycaonia, Galatia, Troas . .	51	Caractacus brought before Claudius.
Philippi, Thessalonica, Berœa, Athens, Corinth	52	
FIRST EPISTLE TO THE THESSALONIANS.	52	
At Corinth	53	

V.—*continued.*

PALESTINE.	A. D.	ROME.
SECOND EPISTLE TO THE THESSALONIANS	53	
Felix procurator of Judæa.		
St Paul sails from Corinth.		
Fourth visit to Jerusalem. . .	54	Death of Claudius, accession of NERO.
(iii) *St Paul's Third Missionary Journey:*		
Second circuit of Galatia.		
Reaches Ephesus	55	Britannicus poisoned.
At Ephesus	56	
FIRST EPISTLE TO THE CORINTHIANS (Spring)	57	
Leaves Ephesus for Macedonia.		
SECOND EPISTLE TO THE CORINTHIANS (Autumn) . . .	57	
At Corinth.		
EPISTLE TO THE GALATIANS.		
EPISTLE TO THE ROMANS . .	58	
Return to Jerusalem.		
(iv) *St Paul arrested, and sent to Cæsarea*	59	Nero murders Agrippina.
Felix succeeded by *Festus* . . .	60	
St Paul sent to Rome by Festus.	60	Agricola in Britain.
Shipwrecked at Malta (Winter).		
Reaches Rome	61	Tacitus born.
EPISTLE TO PHILEMON (Spring)	62	Death of Burrhus.
EPISTLE TO THE COLOSSIANS.		Nero marries Poppæa.
EPISTLE TO THE EPHESIANS.		
EPISTLE TO THE PHILIPPIANS (Autumn).		
Albinus succeeds Festus	63	Tigellinus, prætorian prefect.
EPISTLE TO THE HEBREWS (?)		
(v) *St Paul's acquittal;* journey to Philippi and Asia Minor .	63	
Journey to Spain (?)	64	Great Fire at Rome. Persecution of the Christians.
Returns to Asia Minor (?) . .	66	Vespasian commands in Judæa.
Journey to Macedonia.		
FIRST EPISTLE TO TIMOTHY.	67	
Voyage to Crete with Titus.		
EPISTLE TO TITUS from Asia Minor (Autumn)		
At Nicopolis (Winter)		
Second Imprisonment at Rome .	68	
SECOND EPISTLE TO TIMOTHY.		
Martyrdom (May or June) . . .	68	Death of Nero, June 9 or 11.

VI. THE HERODIAN FAMILY.

HEROD THE GREAT,

SON OF ANTIPATER, PROCURATOR OF JUDÆA,

married successively ten wives, of whom were

- Doris.
  - Antipater.
- Mariamne I.
  - Alexander.
  - Aristobulus.
    - Herod Agrippa I.—Herod, king of Chalcis.—Herodias. Acts xii. 1. Mark vi. 17.
      - Herod Agrippa II.—Bernice.—Drusilla. Acts xxv. 13. Acts xxv. 13. Acts xxiv. 24.
- Mariamne II.
  - Herod Philip, disinherited by Herod; first husband of Herodias. Mark vi. 17.
- Malthace.
  - Archelaus, Ethnarch of Judæa, Samaria, and Idumæa. Matt. ii. 22.
  - Herod Antipas, Tetrarch of Galilee and Peræa; second husband of Herodias. Luke iii. Mark vi.
- Cleopatra.
  - Philip, Tetrarch of Trachonitis and Ituræa.

INDEX

A.

B.

C.

V.

W.

Z.

THE END.